HANDBOOK OF SOCIAL SCIENCE OF SPORT

(With an international classified bibliography)

Edited by
GÜNTHER R. F. LÜSCHEN
AND
GEORGE H. SAGE
with the assistance of
LEILA SFEIR

Published by
STIPES PUBLISHING COMPANY
10 - 12 Chester Street
Champaign, Illinois 61820

Library of Congress No. 80-54273

ISBN 0-87563-191-6

PREFACE

The social science of sport has experienced remarkable growth and proliferation in the past two decades, but the theoretical and empirical development has not been even. Some topics have surged ahead while others have barely been touched, thus some topics now have a rather extensive literature and others have only a smattering of work. In a situation like this there is a need for a Handbook that can present an overview and appraisal of the state of knowledge, even though it must necessarily be selective and incomplete. Such a volume may also assist scholars to efficiently acquire a foundation for future research and writing. It is our hope that this Handbook will fulfill these needs.

A major goal of the editors has been to solicit articles on some of the most exciting and lively topics in the social science of sport including contributions from anthropological, historical, philosophical, psychological and sociological perspectives.

The introductory paper lays the conceptual and theoretical foundation of sport in sociological perspective. In the following six parts, the design of the volume proceeds from a macro- to a micro-analysis of sport, starting with the analysis of sport in a cross-cultural context, sport in modern society to problems of order and disorder in sport. The Handbook extends to a treatment of the social psychology of play, sport and personality.

Part VII is a classified International Bibliography, which should prove useful for social science of sport scholars throughout the world. It is classified according to major areas of research. Its full use is facilitated by secondary references to be found in the subject index.

An Appendix has been included which lists the major sport and sport science organizations. The editors thought this information might be useful to scholars in several different fields.

Readers who hope to find a final compilation of neatly packaged topics will be disappointed. This is not the present state of knowledge in this field of inquiry. Neither is this Handbook rigidly systematic and all encompassing. It keeps an open perspective and in so doing, the editors hope to stimulate further scientific inquiry from a variety of perspectives.

We are grateful to our contributors for their patience and goodwill. In a way, this is their book, for without their dedication and commitment to a rather long enduring enterprise, it could not have been completed. We thank the Departments of Physical Education, both at the University of Northern Colorado and University of Illinois and the Department of Sociology of the University of Illinois for their support. We acknowledge the support given to us by the Federal Institute for Sport Science in Cologne/Germany. We also appreciate the personal interest of our publisher.

Fall 1980   Günther R.F. Lüschen
                                                 George H. Sage

TABLE OF CONTENTS

INTRODUCTION

SPORT
IN
SOCIOLOGICAL
PERSPECTIVE

Lüschen

Sage

SPORT IN SOCIOLOGICAL PERSPECTIVE

Günther Lüschen and George H. Sage

THE PERVASIVENESS OF SPORT

Sport as a competitive game is found in almost all societies, and despite the claim that a few primitive tribes are supposed to have no competitive games, sport can be counted among the few cultural universals of mankind. If one accounts for rates of involvement in terms of participation in competitive sport, recreational sport, school sport (physical education), sport spectatorship and followership in the mass-media, then sport in industrial societies has become one of the most important institutions of modern life. In quite a few societies the institution of sport, if measured by the overall amount of different forms of participation, has surpassed the institution of religion. In young nations that have won only recently their independence, involvement in international sports is remarkably high and is another indication of the important meaning that this activity has for many people.

No other event could engender such wide interest in the mass media around the world as the Olympic Games and the World Soccer Championship. On a different scale the competitive games of children, often molded after those of the adult world, often created spontaneously on a sand-lot or street, are among the most important activities among boys and increasingly among girls as well.

It should be emphasized, however, that the general interest in this social phenomenon by far exceeds the active personal involvement of the population in the activity itself. Sport is an important leisure activity, and its function extends beyond that of physical and game activity for individuals into aspects of general entertainment and the search for personal as well as local and national identity. This holds for modern as well as for developing societies.

THE SOCIOLOGICAL STUDY OF SPORT AROUND THE WORLD

While a theoretical interest in sport as a social phenomenon can be traced back as far as Plato, while leading sociologists and anthropologists acknowledged the area (H. Spencer 1861; E. Tylor 1896;

M. Weber 1920; F. Znaniecki 1930), and while sport has long been of potential sociological concern to educationalists and philosophers of sport, a strictly disciplinary approach to the sociology of sport has only recently emerged (Lüschen 1959, 1966, 1968, 1970; Erbach 1966; Wohl 1966; Loy and Kenyon 1969; Sage 1970, 1974; Dunning 1971; Ball and Loy 1975; Lüschen and Weis 1976; Bratton *et al.* 1978–79; Eitzen and Sage 1978; Loy, McPherson, and Kenyon 1978; Snyder and Spreitzer 1978). By disciplinary approach we mean the analysis of sport in terms of sociological theory and in terms of the methods of empirical social research.

With regard to sociological theory, quite a few approaches are relevant. By and large they may stress either the societal and system aspect of sport, as in structural theories including Marxist or functionalists theories; or they could stress the aspect of interpersonal relations or symbolic meaning in the study of sport groups or the interaction of individuals. Either way, the sociology of sport may contribute to an advancement of social and sport theory on the one hand and to policymaking and social practice on the other. Presently it is encouraging to see that the sociology of sport is providing theoretical insights that have caught the interest of sociology proper as well as that of a sport science (physical education). Moreover, policymaking agencies as well as sport organizations are beginning to approach sociologists of sport for analysis and advice concerning their practical problems. While it appears to be important for sociology of sport to address itself to issues of social practice, there are many unresolved issues in the theoretical analysis of sport as a system, and primary attention should be directed toward the enlargement of knowledge about the structure and meaning of that system, even if it is only descriptive.

Sociology of Sport: Present Situation and Position

Despite the growing interest in the serious study of sport from a sociological perspective and the involvement of notable scientific organizations, especially the International Sociological Association, the general attention and support for the sociology of sport in colleges and universities, and in institutes and academies of sciences not directly related to sport, still leaves much to be desired. Unlike other subdisciplines of a sport science, sociologists of sport have gained the recognition of professional sociology. But a genuine recognition of its merits and potentials is particularly missing in the science of sport and physical education. While the latter may be due to limited understanding and support in a time of decreasing resources, notably in a field of low progression, sociology of sport itself has also shown limited concern for practical and educational matters. Internationally the situation shows considerable variance with East European sociologists of sport stressing application (Erbach 1966), while Western sociologists focus rather on theoretical analysis (Loy, McPherson, and Kenyon 1978). There is a comparatively strong involvement of sociologists and sport scientists alike in such countries as Canada, England, Finland, Japan, Poland, the U.S.A. and West Germany. And the foundation of the International Committee of Sociology of Sport in 1965 has by now been followed by many national groups of sociologists of sport.

In terms of scientific productivity the sociology of sport belongs to the most productive subdisciplines of a sport science showing a remarkable growth particularly since the 1960s. A recent report based on a selective international bibliography shows up to 1978 a rate of 2,583 scholarly articles and 723 books. While there are problems of a critical mass of scholars with a number of approximately 100 around the world, of inconsistencies in methodology and a missing awareness of paradigmatic approaches, the sociology of sport has made strong contributions to such areas as the comparative analysis of sport and games, social stratification, socialization and the study of groups in sport (Lüschen 1980).

THE STRUCTURE OF SPORT

Having established the pervasiveness of sport and described the growing interest in the study of sport from a sociological perspective, the remainder of this introduction will be devoted to a discussion of the structure of sport. This will help to establish a conceptual and theoretical foundation for the following articles in this volume.

Sport as a Contest

Sport as an activity is playful, competitive, internally and externally rewarding and involves individuals or teams engaged in a contest that is zero-sum in outcome. The outcome is determined by superiority in physical skill, tactics, and strategy. This definition refers to an idealtype of sport that is best represented by such games as soccer or contests like track, boxing, or fencing. Conventionally, however, activities such as chess or mountaineering are included that do not meet the above definition to the fullest. Moreover, not all sport activity is always contestual, but a considerable amount is spent on practice ultimately directed toward the contest.

Sport is primarily an activity based on the physical capacity of the participants, and secondarily a contest where elements of strategy and tactics are introduced. While the controlling patterns are social and cultural, they rely basically on the human body and motoric capabilities. Ultimately, one has to understand this activity as a form in which biological, psychological, social and cultural factors are interdependent. Biological factors are most important as conditions and cultural factors are most important as controls. The different patterns and disciplines in sport can be understood as extensive explorations of the natural capabilities of humans in the context of games. But one has to acknowledge that an activity does occur only if it is culturally and socially meaningful. The dimension of nature is also introduced into sport insofar as an activity may not only be a contest against another person or party, but a contest in which objects of nature have to be mastered. In mountaineering the natural object may completely replace a personal opponent. On the other extreme there are games that are particularly demanding in terms of strategy. In chess physical skill is almost absent and the outcome is based on strategy and tactics alone. In sociological terms, both extremes of the lonely mountaineer and the chess player are engaged in a sport contest, although the one does not fulfill the qualification of an opponent and the other does not fulfill the qualification of physical skill, thus making both, by definition, marginal sport activities (Caillois 1961; Dunning 1971; Ponomarev 1974). An important distinction is also that sport is essentially non-serious, superfluous for human survival and in its activities non-representative, although some of its disciplines represent former war and combat techniques.

Sport as an Institution and Forms of Involvement

Sport as an institution can be understood as that range of activity which is located around sport as a contest described above. As far as active participation is concerned it can be organized explicitly for the purpose of sport competition *(formal sport)*, for spontaneous games and recreation *(informal sport)*, and it can be part of another institution and organization, such as sport in schools, in the military, or at the workplace *(institutional sport)*. With regard to the latter, sport may be determined by the structure of other institutions and show significant modifications from its original structure as an independent contest. In physical education it will be used predominantly for educational purposes and from there may be restricted in its orientation, such as to fitness or movement education. Sport as a communicative activity and for entertainment in the form of spectatorship, fandom, and followership in the mass media or in everyday conversation adds another dimension to this phenomenon *(communicative sport)*. It is a dimension that is rapidly increasing in popularity and results in many unforeseen consequences, from sport as rigid contest to sport experienced as display and drama.

Overlaps with Other Societal Institutions

The *economic* dimension of sport is rather specific insofar as nothing of permanence is being produced through this activity itself.

Yet, the amount of private and public money and economic goods and resources invested in this area are enormous, increasing in industrial societies to a considerable degree of public and private expenditures. With the enlargement of mass media involvement, sport can be used to produce a considerable amount of direct or indirect profit.

The *political* dimension of sport is not acknowledged in all countries, yet there is no question that the achievements of national teams and athletes take on political meaning, and are consequently used for political purposes, e.g., to prove the efficiency of a system or to demonstrate a system's identity on an international level. Even within individual nations such political consequences can be observed in the prestige that sport may bring to a community or region. At one level or the other political institutions do indeed influence the institution of sport indicating the interdependence between politics and sport.

A *religious* dimension of sport is relatively easy to demonstrate. In the ball games of the ancient Maya a religious meaning was very strongly and exclusively attached to games, and sports contests took on ritual functions in Ancient Greece and many other ethnic societies in antiquity. Today sport still performs latent religious functions, and, with its often extensive ritual, contains many quasi-religious and supernatural features. Thus, one should not take lightly such statements as those of Pierre de Coubertin, the founder of the modern Olympic Games, calling the Olympics a modern form of religion.

At times churches consider sport a rival to religion, which in certain places it is. But in this connection it is interesting to note that many modern churches try to incorporate sport within their own organizational range. Not only do religious youth groups take part in sport in modern times, but the foundation of shooting clubs at the end of the Middle Ages was a deliberate attempt by the Catholic church to keep its control over the male sector of its membership.

The *educational* dimension of sport is probably the most obvious, and the formalization of this aspect in school sports and physical education/physical culture is a witness to the centrality assigned to sport in educational terms. In general and on a broader basis sport has a strong impact on education and is an important means of socialization. But it is also important to note that the institution of education may have an impact on sport, and given the rapid expansion of sport in modern life, education needs to be increasingly concerned about it. This responsibility of education is seldom recognized, but in light of a situation where the communicative, entertainment dimension of sport is getting increasing attention, education has to address itself to enlarging the understanding of sport in society as a whole, especially to educating people towards a life-long active involvement in sport as a leisure activity. Education may also have to pay attention to a newly emerging problem, that of proper education and professionalization of top athletes.

Sport and Society
Cultural and economic determinants across countries. Differences in participation rates are fairly widespread across countries. The level of performance and success in international competition is another indicator of an uneven distribution of sport around the world regardless of its basic universal appearance.

Often explanations of high involvement and excellence in performance have been sought on the material level. Historically modern sport seemed to be a subsequent development to industrialization. Thus, claims have been advanced that sport was a "child of technology" or "caused by industrialization." Regardless of the superficiality of such a causal argument, it needs to be emphasized that long before industrialization and modern times there was a heavy involvement in all types of physical activity and games, even to the extent that this became a problem to elite circles in, for example, pre-industrial England and France (Dunning 1973). Furthermore, while both modern sport and industrialization developed parallel to one another, this does not prove the dependence of sport on a material base. Both can well be seen as owing their development and organization to an ideational superstructure, in other words to a culture that fostered both industrialization/technology as well as sport.

There is good evidence for the interdependent relationship between sport and culture from crosscultural studies of different types of games and in the basic principles set forth in the socialization of children. Games of physical skill and those involving skill and strategy, which characterize the system of sport very well, are found in cultures that stress achievement training in childhood, while games of chance are found in those cultures that stress simple responsibility training for their children (Roberts and Sutton-Smith 1962). Moreover, such external conditions as the social and physical environment have a bearing on the type of sport and games a people engage in. For example, people in a hostile environment are less competitive and more cooperative in their games (Glassford 1970).

For modern sports and the Olympic Games such structural relationships have been confirmed by relating belief systems such as types of religion to high achievement in sport (Lüschen, 1967). Seppänen (1980) investigated all Olympic medal winners since 1896 and found that high performance in sport is related to an innerworldly asceticist orientation of countries, such as that found among Protestant societies and in Marxist systems. With regard to the latter, he contends that these systems are particularly well accommodated to the basic values of sport and thus in the future should be relatively more successful than they have been so far. Nowikow and Maksimenko (1972) analyzed economic conditions as determinants of Olympic success in Tokyo, and although they found a high correlation with economic prosperity, they conclude that such conditions are not sufficient to explain the emergence and high achievement of a country in sport.

In factor-analyzing results of the Tokyo Olympics, Ball (1972) concluded that the successful nation-state appears to: be stable and homogeneous in population, have little domestic political competition, be economically prosperous, have a central government staffed by an elite, and have a high probability of being a member of the Communist bloc. From his indicators one can conclude that the above suggested notions of culture, as indicated in his results by the high correlation for "Westernization" and "Religious configuration," explain sport success very well; and the Communist-bloc-factor can, on a different scale, be explained in terms of values and ideology.

The structure of sport within societies. There are a number of descriptive studies of sport in different countries and it would be possible to discuss quite a number of structural correlates of sport in society. For the present purpose only problems of social stratification and political system will be referred to, followed by discussions of major social processes such as socialization, conflict and change.

With respect to social stratification and sport, one of the most notable observations is the overrepresentation of groups in sport that have access to power and enjoy special privileges. Sport was seen by Veblen (1899) as an activity of the elite leisure class, expressing its "robbery instinct." Wohl (1964) historically analyzed the class determination of "bourgeois" sport. In other research in the U.S.A., Sweden, West Germany, as well as in other countries, a close relationship between sport participation in general and that in specific sports in particular was found for members of higher social status and class background (Lüschen 1963; Loy 1969; Stone 1969; Gruneau 1975). The problem is not confined to Western societies, since Ferge's results of the time-budget study for Hungary and other socialist countries reveal a relationship between engagement in sport and social stratum even for countries that are by definition classless (1972). According to Petrovich and Hosek (1974), it takes a special effort to recruit sectors of lower occupational groups into sport.

In sport, just as in the larger society, there is continuous fighting for rank, not on the basis of wealth but on that of performance and achievement. Performance and achievement determine rank in sport;

and this can lead to rather rigid systems of rank order, such as in the differentiated groupings of athletes in socialist societies. This rank order is not to be described in terms of class but in that of status groups. While in principle class and status group are separate dimensions, they show a certain overlap, overlapping also with the dimension of power (Weber 1964). Thus, one should not be surprised if one finds in a system based on an order of ranks by achievement corresponding dimensions of more power and higher class besides the basic status differentiation. Whether sport actually has an effect in reinforcing an existing system of stratification is an important question that awaits an answer. Certainly through socialization as well as through different forms of sponsorship, sport provides avenues for a considerable amount of mobility.

Political system. With respect to political system, not only in young nations of today is sport being used for political purposes and goals of the state, such purpose is also performed in modern societies. Even on the level of communities sport is employed in the service of local politics. Meynaud (1966), with reference to such phenomena, contends that sport is being used more by politics than it influences politics itself. The latter may not necessarily be true on the level of communities, where a number of results from Poland and elsewhere demonstrate for urban and rural communities an effect on social organization and integration (Frankenberg 1957; Pudelkiewicz 1970). On the level of national politics, claims for the political meaning of sport are made particularly by many socialist countries (Riordan 1977). In the perception of the public, sport indeed has a major political significance for political systems of whatever orientation. It is somewhat surprising that the social sciences so far have paid only scant attention to an analysis of sport and politics.

Socialization and sport. Socialization, which is the incorporation of norms and values and the acquisition of socio-cultural skills and techniques, can be discussed in terms of socialization via sport and into sport (McPherson 1980). For the latter an international comparative study is underway in which a team of members of the International Committee for Sociology of Sport are investigating modes of socialization into different sport roles in major countries around the world (Kenyon and McPherson 1978). For the problem of socialization via sport and the development of the individual in society, a number of formidable studies have been completed. As Piaget (1965) has shown in his study of children playing marbles, competitive games provide important insights into such principles of interpersonal behavior as the rule of reciprocity. Helanko (1957) demonstrated from observing adolescent groups engaged in sports the superb role that sport plays for the establishment of group ties. Sutton-Smith (1973), in studying children engaged in games, finds that they are models of conflict, which teach the children to deal with and overcome the detrimental consequences of conflict. Greendorfer (1977), Snyder/Kivlin (1977), and Lever (1976, 1978) have analyzed sex role socialization through sport. Krawczyk (1973) elaborates on the superb role of sport for general acculturation. Oetinger (1953) addresses political socialization. Overall, since sport and games are strongly integrated in and molded by society and its structure, adolescents learn not only basic techniques of interaction, they will also better understand the structure of society.

Conflict and conflict resolution, peace and violence. In interpersonal as well as in international relations sport is often said to contribute to tension release and catharsis of aggression (Lorenz 1965). Several scholars have held to the contrary that sport and competition will build up aggression and conflict (Sherif 1973). One example advanced by believers in sport's function for conflict resolution and peace between nations is the peaceful encounters of teams representing groups and systems hostile to one another. Those denying any such function often will point to the incidents of violence that occur at sports contests. The classic example is the soccer game between Honduras and San Salvador that in 1969 resulted in the so-called soccer-war. More recently attention has been paid to various incidents of violence and hooliganism connected with soccer and other sport events (Gaskell and Pearton 1979; Lang 1980). It is often contended, however, that athletes are not frequently involved and that, therefore, sport is not to blame. However, it cannot be denied that there is violent potential in and around sport. One source may be feelings of alienation and actual deprivation among fans as Taylor interprets for the working class with the "bourgeoisification" and professionalization of soccer clubs in England (1972). And in hockey there is considerable violence among athletes (Smith 1978).

By definition, sports contests are classified as forms of conflict. The subsequent question is only whether such form of conflict means in its consequences destruction and violence. In some cases it does. Overall, however, and in line with the position held by Sutton-Smith (1973), sport contests are rather controlled systems that regulate conflict fairly well in a relationship defined as "association," one outcome of which is, among others, the pattern of fairness which has become a widely accepted form of behavior and in which one cannot materially gain (Lüschen 1970). The principle of fairness which more recently has been considered to be one of the basic features of justice (Rawls 1972) probably denotes best that on a limited scale of interpersonal and intergroup relations a competition without violence and destruction is possible and is the rule rather than the exception. Internal as well as external controls in sport provide such function. However, one should not expect that the consequences of such an encounter can ultimately contribute to a resolution of severe conflicts that have their origin elsewhere. These can indeed be so severe that the *associational* quality of sport is not strong enough to repress them and thus sport may actually be the spark that sets off the fire of violence and destruction. With regard to violence engaged in by spectators and fans, it certainly is the result of inadequate social controls, internally and externally, which lead to destruction. The violent incidents during the Cup Game of Leeds against Munich in 1975 in Paris demonstrate this rather well, since the game was on a neutral field and in a neutral country making the fans void of almost all social control. English reporters deplored the hooliganism (Lang 1980), but it should be mentioned that this form of destruction and violence is not only a British phenomenon but occurs in countries like Germany, Netherland, Turkey, the U.S.A., USSR, Uruguay and others as well. It appears that the extraordinary symbolic meaning that sport contests take on may result in the destructive potential of amorphous groups of fans and even athletes as well. The most important incident of this latter type appears to be the waterpolo contest between Hungary and the USSR in the 1956 Olympic Games in Australia. Sport organizations as well as policymakers dealing directly or indirectly with sport will have to address such problems and will have to look for solutions.

Social change and the socio-cultural system of sport. It has long been maintained that sport is an integrated part of the society and thus reflects societal merits and shortcomings (Plessner 1967). Modern sport in its structure resembles the change toward a more rational scientific orientation of modern society (Wohl 1975). On a different plane it also resembles the problematic structures such as discrimination of minorities (Edwards 1973; Scully 1974) or deprived racial groups (Lapchick 1975). More recently, in line with the critical approach of the New Left, questions have been raised about whether sport is indeed an area of progress. Particularly in the U.S. and West Germany social critics have advanced ideas about the exploitative and suppressive nature of sport (Vinnai 1970; Hoch 1972). Lenk (1972) has been a critic of Marcuse, Ellul, Offe and others concerning their interpretations of the achievement value in modern sport, and he contends that there is an undifferentiated transfer of the critique of achievement in capitalistic society to the system of sport. He holds that there is neither alienation nor manipulation in top sports and that Marcuse's alternative of *libido* for achievement is no alternative for society and sport. This whole area has at this time not led to any conclusive results and resembles in arguments and outcome an earlier period of social criticism towards sport advanced in the 1920's. Buytendijk (1952) earlier held that such criticisms refer more to what endangers sport than what this system actually is; in reality they are rather an outcome of the necessary social controls of this system than an objective analysis of it. At the same time it is true that sport has many ambiguous features and its structure is highly contradictory and ambivalent, which a phenomenological or humanistic sociologist may refer to as basically a dialectical structure. Apologetics and critics obviously refer only to limited aspects of sport and suit their predetermined beliefs with either *thesis* or *antithesis.*

Sport as a Sub-System

A substantial part of research in the sociology of sport deals with an analysis of sport as a closed social system or as interpersonal behavior by itself. Such approaches by design neglect the large, societal context and a paramount task of these approaches seems to be to get a better understanding of the innate structure of the "closed" system of sports teams. This view has as its purpose a better and more unique understanding of the competitive system. Traditional theories of sociology have been strongly bound by societal, notably economic and political considerations. Although sport at one level is influenced by economic conditions, at the same time it is a unique system of interpersonal behavior neither completely work nor completely play, in the closed boundaries of which new experiences and prospects become possible for the individual and society at large. This is not to say that the sociology of sport does indeed provide comprehensive insights about the micro-structure of sport at this time, but the potentialities for new theory developed for sociology from sport are encouraging, and so are the consequences for the individual and society from analysis at this level.

Structure and process in sport groups and organizations. Small groups are the most notable forms of organization in sports, such as in teams and play groups. Thus, there is a wealth of research in which sport groups have been used for field and laboratory experiments in order to learn about rank order in groups, group integration, leadership, and how these are related to team performance and satisfaction. To use one example, the area of leadership theory has learned from sports groups that effective leadership is determined by a whole range of factors among which are power of the leader, leader-member relations, and task complexity (Myers and Fiedler 1966; Martens 1975). Effectiveness of a team is not necessarily dependent on harmony and personal attraction but rivalry and conflict may also be an incentive for better performance (Lenk 1976; Földesi 1978).

The study of sport organizations is of paramount interest for a better understanding of the so-called voluntary organizations (Hoyle 1971). Yet sport organizations and their policies have not received sufficient attention. Exceptions are to be found in the studies of college athletics (Savage 1929, Stern 1979), values of the Olympic movement (Lenk 1964), and the policies of National Olympic Committees (Lüschen 1979).

Sport careers and professionalization. Increasingly there is an awareness that the concept of professionalization goes beyond the material considerations of top athletes; there is a growing awareness that sport resembles a system in which quite a few careers are being pursued, such as sport reporters, sport teachers (Hendry 1975) and coaches (Sage 1975), sport administrators, and sport physicians, to name the most obvious ones (Kenyon 1973). Not all of these careers can be pursued without internal conflict between personal expectation and societal expectation (Heinilä 1964). Moreover, patterns of role progression usually are seen with regard to the successful athlete, while the many cases of failure in sport remain unobserved and little understood (Ball 1976). Besides the fact of high visibility and a growing awareness of this problem (Haerle 1975) there is still little knowledge about the careers and the professionalism of top athletes, whether they are professionals in a private entertainment enterprise or highly successful amateurs of the Olympics. Even less is known about the post-athletic careers of former top athletes (Hill and Lowe 1974).

Sport executives, i.e., team owners, Olympic committee members, belong to a group of decision makers who rely on the support and good will of the members in their sport organizations. At the same time they often belong to a circle of elites that are very independent and seem to be able to hold on to their office for long periods of time. Unlike the career of coaches, who can easily be ousted and who have a clear indicator of their efficiency by winning or losing, executives in sport organizations are not under such pressure and typically hold on to their offices even if they are inefficient. This is, of course, more likely to be found in voluntary sport organizations, but other public and governmental forms may well experience the same problems. Actually, there appear to be few studies that indicate the role of sport executives to be problematic (Grusky 1963; Heinilä 1972). Further research is needed on the topic of sport executives.

Sport and deviance. In line with the above contention of the ambivalent, dialectical structure of sport, it is no surprise that within this system forms of deviant behavior may also develop. Here we refer to the potential for cheating and gambling, of which there are many instances. Athletic groups may at times even become the nucleus of criminal gangs (Thrasher 1936). And, as discussed above, aggressiveness, violence, and dangerous assaults may occur in the sport system. For the most part, however, sport groups and organizations appear to be able to cope with these deviant forms themselves, but there are incidents that ultimately are a violation of public law and thus have to be sanctioned in public courts and not by the quasi-legal bodies of sport organizations. Consequently, there is a recent discussion of legal aspects and sanctions (Warren 1976). The actual deviant potential of sport can be judged only when the behavior of its members is compared with that of members of other institutions. Only recently have questions like the above been addressed by sociologists, and conclusive insights and empirical data are still rare (Landers 1976). A good guess appears to be that the internal and external controls of the sport system develop rather well and forestall an abundance of deviant behavior, but such social controls are not working equally well at all periods in time nor are they easily accepted, particularly when the system of sport is developing more toward display than play.

CONCLUSION

Some Neglected Areas

There are some obvious weaknesses and oversights in sociology of sport. A few like the study of sport organizations and the issue of sport and politics have been mentioned.

An area of suprising neglect is to be found in education and sport. With the exception of educational attainment via sport and the issue of academic achievement of athletes, the structure of sport or physical education and their organization in schools have not received much attention (Snyder and Spreitzer 1980). Even the frequent studies of socialization have not investigated problems like the substantive educational value of sport. This must rank as one of the paradoxes of the field since many of the sociologists of sport are affiliated with physical education/sport science departments.

One may also note that some of the related fields to sociology have addressed social aspects of sport quite differently. Political scientists are hardly involved in making sport better understood. Economists have only recently pursued an analysis of sport (Noll 1980). At the same time anthropologists, historians, philosophers and psychologists have made major contributions to a social science analysis.

In general, sport in its normal form is the center of attention, while the recent interest in problems of sport, violence and aggression is the exception to the rule. This observation pertains also to the population of participants, where marginal groups and their specific problems such as the aged, the handicapped or those who are institutionalized have hardly been addressed in sociology of sport. Yet, marginal groups and deviant forms of behavior may disclose structures that go to the core of a sociological understanding of sport.

Future Prospects

In terms of methodology, behavioral approaches using the responses of individuals in research are most frequent. Action theory and an understanding of systems and social structure are less to be found. While only a minority of studies in the field can be classified as making a strong methodological contribution, the area as such has strong potential for sociology, social science in general and for sport theory alike. Contributions can be expected for a more refined understanding of socially stratified systems, and for sociology of conflict. The non-utilitarian character of sport as an activity may also assist a better understanding of systems that are only insufficiently being described by power or social class. In comparative social research nationally specific games or the way international sports are being structured and pursued may disclose fundamental dispositions of societies. And vice versa, top athletes help us better understand how individuals and groups behave in unique situations.

For sport itself practical payoffs can be expected for such areas as coaching and teaching, as well as for organizational problems. Reference is made here not so much for providing techniques and methods; rather, sociology of sport will make the substance of the field, its organization and the position of those acting as sport practitioners, better understood. Two recent developments in the social sciences may be of interest to the social sciences of sport in general and sociology of sport in particular: Social science research in sport will be able to pursue *evaluation research* in a refined manner. *Policy analysis* is the other area where the study of sport may find practical applications.

In summary, an institution as rapidly expanding in all societies and in the four different forms of *formal, informal, institutional* and *communicative* sport, needs increased attention from the social sciences and from sociology in particular. The contributions in this Handbook will demonstrate and review the existing body of knowledge on a number of major questions from the most general level of sport across societies to the most specific question of individual development in and through sport, games and play. The contributions will address the regular course of events as well as the problematic ones.

REFERENCES

Allardt, E. 1958. On the cumulative nature of leisure activities. *Acta Sociologica* 3,2:165–172.

Ball, D.W. 1972. Olympic Games competition: structural correlates of national success. *Int. J. Comp. Sociology* 15,2:186–200.

Ball, D. and J. Loy, eds. 1975. *Sport and Social Order*. Reading, Mas.: Addison-Wesley.

Ball, D. 1976. Failure in sport. *ASR* 41,4:726–39.

Bratton, R. ed. 1978–79. *CAHPER Monographs 1–12 on Sociology of Sport*. Calgary: University of Calgary.

Buytendijk, I.J.J. 1952. *Het voetballen*. Utrecht: Het Spectrum.

Caillois, R. 1961. *Man, Play and Games*. Glencoe: Free Press.

Cheska, A. 1979. Sport spectacular: a ritual model of power. *IRSS* 14,2:51–72.

Coakley, J. 1978. *Sport in Society*. St. Louis: Mosby.

Dunning, E. 1971. Some conceptual dilemmas in the sociology of sport. Pp. 34–46 in Albonico, R. and K. Pfister-Binz, eds. *The Sociology of Sport*. Basel: Birkhäuser.

Dunning, E. 1971a. *The Sociology of Sport*. London: Cass.

Dunning, E. 1973. The structural-functional properties of folk-games and modern sports. *Sportwissenschaft* 3,3:215–232.

Edwards, H. 1973. *Sociology of Sport*. Homewood, Ill.: Dorsey.

Eitzen, D.S. and G. Sage. 1978 *Sociology of American Sport*. Dubuque, Iowa: Brown.

Erbach, G. 1966. The science of sport and sport sociology. *IRSS* 1,1:59–73.

Ferge, S. 1972. Social differentiation in leisure activity. Pp. 213–227 in Szalai, A. *The Use of Time*. Paris: Mouton.

Földesi, T. 1978. Investigation for the objective measurement of cooperative ability among the members of rowing teams. *IRSS* 13,1:49–70.

Frankenberg, R. 1957. *Village on the Border*. London: Cohen and West.

Gaskell, G. and R. Pearton. 1979. Aggression and sport. Pp. 263–296 in J. Goldstein, ed. J. *Sports, Games and Play*. Hillsdale, N.J.: Erlbaum.

Glassford, G. 1970. Organization of games and adaptive strategies of the Canadian Eskimo. Pp. 70–84 in G. Lüschen, ed. *The Cross-Cultural Analysis of Sport and Games*. Champaign, Ill.: Stipes.

Greendorfer, S. 1977. The role of socialization agents in female sport involvement. *Research Quarterly* 49,2:146–52.

Gruneau, R. 1975. Sport, social differentiation and social inequality. Pp. 121–84 in D. Ball and J. Loy, eds. *Sport and Social Order*. Reading, Mas.: Addison-Wesley.

Grusky, O. 1963. Managerial succession and organizational effectiveness. AJS 69,1:21–31.

Guttmann, A. 1978. *From Ritual to Record*. New York: Columbia University Press.

Haerle, R. 1975. Career patterns and career contingencies of professional baseball players. Pp. 456–519 in D. Ball and J. Loy, eds. *Sport and Social Order*. Reading, Mas.: Addison-Wesley.

Heinilä, K. 1964. The professional dissatisfaction of physical education teachers. *Stadion* 1–2:3–17 (in Finnish).

Heinilä, K. 1966. Notes on the intergroup conflicts in international sports. *IRSS* 1,1:49–69.

Heinilä, K. 1972. Survey of the value orientations of Finnish sport leaders. *IRSS* 7,1:111–17.

Helanko, R. 1957. Sports and socialization. *Acta Sociologica* 2,4:229–240.

Hendry, L. 1975. Survival in a marginal role. The professional identity of the physical education teacher. *Brit. J. Sociology* 26:180-190.

Hill, P. and B. Lowe. 1974. The inevitable metathesis of the retiring athlete. *IRSS* 9,1:5-32.

Hoch, P. 1972. *Rip off the Big Game.* Garden City, N.Y.: Doubleday.

Hoyle, E. 1971. Organization theory and the sociology of sport. Pp. 82-94 in Albonico, R. and K. Pfister-Binz, eds. *The Sociology of Sport.* Basel: Birkhäuser.

Kenyon, G. 1973. Sport and career. Pp. 359-64 in Grupe, O. et al. eds. *Sport in the Modern World.* Berlin: Springer.

Kenyon, G. and B. McPherson. 1978. The sport role socialization process in four industrialized countries. Pp. 5-34 in Landry, F. and W. Orban, eds. *Sociology of Sport.* International Congress Quebec City 1976. Miami: Symposia Specialists.

Krawczyk, Z. 1973. Sport as a factor of acculturation. *IRSS* 8,2:63-75.

Landers, D. 1976. *Social Problems in Athletics.* Champaign, Ill.: University of Illinois Press.

Lang, G. 1980. Riotous outbursts at sport events. Pp. 413-44 in this Handbook.

Lapchick, R. 1975. *Politics of Race and International Sport: The Case of South Africa.* Westport, Conn.: Greenwood Press.

Lenk, H. 1964. *Werte, Ziele, Wirklichkeit der modernen Olympischen Spiele.* Schorndorf: Hofmann.

Lenk, H. 1972. *Leistungssport: Ideologie oder Mythos?* Stuttgart; Kohlhammer.

Lenk, H. and G. Lüschen. 1975. Epistemological problems and the personality and social system in social psychology. *Theory and Decision* 6,3:333-55.

Lenk. H. 1976. *Team Dynamics.* Champaign, Ill.: Stipes.

Lever, J. 1976. Sex differences in the games of children. *Social Problems* 23,4:478-87.

Lever, J. 1978. Sex differences in the complexity of children's play and games. *ASR* 43,4:471-83.

Lorenz, K. 1965. *On Aggression.* New York: Harcourt, Brace and World.

Lowe, B. et al. 1978. *Sport and International Relations.* Champaign, Ill.: Stipes.

Loy, J. 1969. The study of sport and social mobility. Pp. 101-19 in G. Kenyon, ed. *Sociology of Sport.* Chicago: Athletic Institute.

Loy, J. and G. Kenyon, eds. 1969. *Sport, Culture and Society.* New York: Macmillan.

Loy, J. and J. McElvogue. 1970. Racial segregation in American sport. *IRSS* 5,1:5-24.

Loy, J. and J. Segrave. 1975. Research methodology in the sociology of sport. Pp. 289-333 in L. Rarick. *Physical Activity.* New York: Academic Press.

Loy, J.; McPherson, B. and G. Kenyon. 1978. *Sport and Social Systems.* Reading, Mas.: Addison-Wesley.

Loy, J.; McPherson, B. and G. Kenyon. 1979. *The Sociology of Sport as an Academic Speciality.* CAHPER Monograph. Calgary: University of Calgary.

Lüschen, G. 1960. Prolegomena zu einer Soziologie des Sports (Preliminaries to a sociology of sport). *Kölner Zeitschrift Soziologie* 12,3:505-15.

Lüschen, G. 1963. Soziale Schichtung und soziale Mobilität bei jungen Sportlern (Social stratification and social mobility among young sportsmen). *Kölner Zeitschrift Soziologie* 15,1:74-93. Also pp. 258-76 in Loy, J.

and G. Kenyon 1969. *Sport, Culture and Society.* New York: Macmillan.

Lüschen, G. 1967. The interdependence of sport and culture. IRSS 2,1:127–41.

Lüschen, G. 1968. *The Sociology of Sport.* A trend-report and bibliography. Paris and The Hague: Mouton.

Lüschen, G. 1970. Cooperation, association and contest. *J. Confl. Resolution* 14,1:21–34.

Lüschen, G. and K. Weis, eds. 1976. *Die Soziologie des Sports.* Berlin: Luchterhand.

Lüschen, G. 1979. Organization and policymaking in National Olympic Committees. *IRSS* 14,2:5–20.

Lüschen, G. 1980. Sociology of sport: development, present state and prospects. *Annual Review of Sociology* 6, 315–347.

Martens, R. 1975. *Social Psychology of Physical Activity.* New York: Harper and Row.

Meynaud, J. 1966. *Sport et politique.* Paris: Payot.

Myers, A. and F. Fiedler. 1966. Theorie und Probleme der Führung (Theory and problems of leadership). Pp. 92–106 in G. Lüschen, ed. *Kleingruppenforschung und Gruppe im Sport.* Köln: Westdeutscher Verlag.

Nowikow, A. and M. Maksimenko. 1972. Soziale und ökonomische Faktoren und das Niveau sportlicher Leistungen. *Sportwissenschaft* 2,2:156–67.

Oetinger, F. 1953. *Partnerschaft.* Stuttgart: Metzler.

Opie, I. and P. 1969. *Children's Games in Street and Playground.* Oxford: Clarendon Press.

Petrovic, K. and A. Hosek. 1974. The determination of sports activities in the canonical configuration of the latent stratification dimensions. Pp. 135–69 in *Yugoslav Papers.* ISA-Congress Toronto.

Piaget, J. 1965. *The Moral Judgment of the Child.* New York: Free Press (orig. 1932).

Plessner, H. 1967. Spiel und Sport. Pp. 17–27 in Plessner, H. et al. eds. *Sport und Leibeserziehung.* Munich: Piper.

Ponomarev, N. 1974. The social phenomenon of games and sports. *IRSS* 9,1:117–26.

Pudelkiewicz, E. 1970. Sociological problems in housing estates. *IRSS* 5,1: 73–40.

Rawls, J. 1972. *Theory of Justice.* Cambridge. Mas.: Harvard University Press.

Rehberg, R. and W. Schafer. 1968. Participation in interscholastic athletics and college expectations. *AJS* 73,4:732–40.

Riordan, J. 1977. *Sport in Soviet Society.* Cambridge: Cambridge University Press. .

Roberts, J. and B. Sutton-Smith. 1962. Child training and game involvement. *Ethnology* 1,2:166–185.

Sage, G. 1974 (2nd ed.) ed. *Sport and American Society.* Reading, Mas. Addison-Wesley.

Sage, G. 1975. An occupational analysis of the college coach. Pp. 391-455 in D. Ball and J. Loy, eds. *Sport and Social Order.* Reading, Mas.: Addison-Wesley.

Sage, G. and J. Loy. 1978. Geographical mobility patterns of college coaches. *Urban Life* 7,2:253–78.

Savage, H. 1929. *American College Athletics.* New York: Carnegie Foundation.

Scott, M. 1968. *The Racing Game.* Chicago: Aldine.

Scully, G. 1974. Discrimination: the case of baseball. Pp. 221–74 in R. Noll, ed. *Government and the Sports Business.* Washington, D.C.: The Brookings Institution.

Seppänen, P. 1980. Olympic success: a cross-national perspective. Pp. 93–116 in this Handbook.

Sherif, C. 1973. Intergroup conflict and competition. *Sportwissenschaft.* 3,3:138–53.

Smith. M.D. 1975. Sport and collective violence. Pp. 281–300 in D. Ball and J. Loy, eds. *Sport and Social Order.* Reading, Mas.: Addison-Wesley.

Smith, M.D. 1978. Towards an explanation of hockey violence: a referee other approach. *Canad. J. Sociology* 4,1:105–24.

Snyder, E. and J. Kivlin. 1977. Perceptions of the sex role of the female athletes and non-athletes. *Soc. Education* 12,1:23–29.

Snyder, E. and E. Spreitzer. 1978. *Social Aspects of Sport.* Englewood-Cliffs: Prentice-Hall.

Snyder, E. and E. Spreitzer. 1980. Sport, education and schools. Pp. 119–146 in this Handbook.

Spencer, H. 1861. *Education.* New York: Williams and Norgate.

Stebbins, R. 1977. The amateur: two sociological definitions. *Pacific Soc. Rev.* 20,4:582–606.

Stern, R. 1979. The development of interorganizational control network. *Administrative Science Quart.* 24,2:2242–66.

Stone, G. 1969. Some meanings of American sport. Pp. 5–27 in G. Kenyon, ed. *Sociology of Sport.* Chicago: Athletic Institute.

Stone, G. 1972, ed. *Games, Sport and Power.* New Brunswick: Transaction.

Sutton-Smith. 1973. Games, the socialization of conflict. *Sportwissenschaft* 3,1:41–46.

Taylor, I. 1971. Football mad: a speculative sociology of football hooliganism. Pp. 352–377 in E. Dunning, ed. *Sociology of Sport.* London: Cass.

Thrasher, F. 1936. *The Gang.* Chicago: University of Chicago Press.

Tripplett, N. 1898. The dynamogenic factors of pacemaking and competition. *Am. J. Psychology* 9,4:507–33.

Tylor, E.B. 1896. On American lot-games. *Int. Achiv Ethnographie* (Leyden) 9(suppl.):55–67.

Veblen, T. 1899. *The Theory of the Leisure Class.* New York: Macmillan.

Vinnai, G. 1970. *Fussballsport als Ideologie.* Stuttgart: Europäische Verlagsanstalt.

Warren, A. ed. 1976. Athletics. *Law Contemporary Problems* 38,1:1–171.

Watson, G. 1974. Family organization and Little League Baseball. *IRSS* 9,2:5–32.

Weber, M. 1920. *Gesammelte Aufsätze zur Religionssoziologie.* Tübingen; Mohr.

Weber, M. 1956. Class, status and power. Pp. 10–16 in R. Bendix and S. Lipset, eds. *Class, Status and Power.* Glencoe, Ill.: Free Press (orig. 1921).

Wohl, A. 1964. Die gesellschaftlichen Grundlagen des bürgerlichen Sports. *Wissenschaftliche Zeitschrift der DHFK Leipzig* 6,1:1–93.

Wohl., A. 1966. Conception and range of sport sociology. *IRSS* 1,1:5–18.

Wohl, A. 1975. The scientific-technical revolution and the shape of sport. *IRSS* 10,1:10–38.

Znaniecki, F. 1930. *Socjologia wychowania* (Sociology of education). Warsaw. Vol. 2.

Zurcher, L. and A. Meadow. 1967. On bullfights and baseball. An example of interaction of institutions. *Int. J. Comparative Sociology* 8,1:99–117.

PART I

CROSS-CULTURAL

AND CROSS-NATIONAL

ANALYSIS

OF

SPORT AND GAMES

McIntosh

Cheska

Glassford

Seppänen

PART I

CROSS-CULTURAL

AND CROSS-NATIONAL

ANALYSIS

OF

SPORT AND GAMES

McIntosh

Cheska

Glassford

Seppänen

THE SOCIOLOGY OF SPORT
IN THE ANCIENT WORLD

Peter C. McIntosh

INTRODUCTION

The 'Ancient World' is a term which, by common usage in Europe and America, encompasses a considerable period of time from the neolithic agricultural revolution at about 7000 B.C. to the fall of the Roman Empire. The Western Empire collapsed in the sixth century A.D. but the Eastern Empire with its capital city at Constantinople continued to exist for nearly another one thousand years. As a geographical entity the ancient world stretched from the river valleys of Mesopotamia, some would say from the Indus valley on the Indian subcontinent, to the Atlantic coast of Portugal and from the upper Nile to the highlands of Scotland. General statements, therefore, about sport in the ancient world, let alone about the sociology of sport in the the ancient world, are likely to be vague, misleading and inaccurate. It seems best to focus upon a few cultures, recognizing that the features which they displayed may not have been characteristic of other cultures in the ancient world. Four have been chosen, the Minoan culture of Crete in the third and second millenium B.C., the Mycenaean culture of the mainland of Greece in the second millenium B.C., the city state of Greece in the sixth, fifth and fourth centuries B.C. and the urban societies of the Roman Empire from the first century A.D. until the end of the fourth century when the termination of the Olympic Games marked the end of a sporting era.

The sociologist studying these cultures is at once faced with an historical problem. The data available for study are scanty, sometimes unreliable and often difficult to interpret. The earliest extant alphabetical writing is upon an Athenian vase of the early geometric period which has been dated at 735 B.C. Alphabet writing was in use long before, even if we have no surviving examples. Hieroglyphic and linear writing and inscription were far earlier and the recent decipherment of "linear B" from Crete 1450 B.C. has shown that the language being used was Greek. However, the financial accounts and catalogue of contents of the palace of Knossos which comprise the major exemplars of linear B are not the evidence which the sociologist of sport would have chosen for survival from Minoan culture.

The same may be said of other literary and epigraphic remains which we have. We do not know what is missing. Archaelogical discoveries on building sites and sports arenas are a major source of information; so too are inscriptions and artifacts such as pots, paintings, sculpture, coins and medals, but again artists were not historians and the correct interpretation of what is depicted is not always obvious. In this situation, we can hardly do better than follow the precept of Aristotle in his introduction to the study of moral philosophy.

> We must be content, then, in speaking of such subjects and with such premises to indicate the truth roughly and in outline, and in speaking about things which are only true in a general sense and with premises of the same kind, to teach conclusions that are no better. In the same spirit, therefore, should each type of statement be received; for it is the mark of an educated man to look for precision in each class of things just so far as the nature of the subject admits.
>
> (Aristotle, Ethics I. 3. 1094b).

MINOAN AND MYCENAEAN CULTURES

Our major sources of literary evidence on life in Minoan and Mycenaean civilizations are the Iliad and the Odyssey, epic poems of some twenty eight thousand lines of hexameter verse. The age which they portrayed is often referred to as the 'Heroic Age' but they offer a conglomerate account rather than a coherent portrait of a single age. Composition stretched over some two thousand years when the deeds of the heroes and descriptions of their ways of life were handed down by oral tradition. They were finally commited to writing by Homer at about 800 B.C. They thus spanned three arch-aeological eras. At first sight the poems appear to describe life and death in that part of the bronze age when the mainland city of Mycenae was in the ascendant and conducted a long drawn out war against the city of Troy on the mainland of what is now Turkey. The siege of Troy occurred in the thirteenth century B.C. The bronze age collapsed and Mycenae was burnt in 1125 B.C. (Kirk 1964, 25.). It was succeeded by an early iron age in the eleventh and tenth centuries when the Dorians invaded Greece from the North. This was a 'dark age' of which we know little. The epic poems which emerged in written form some time after 800 B.C. described events and objects from several cultures through which they had passed. The beliefs and customs which were observed by the heroes were derived from a similar number of cultures. A single and simple instance of the confusion is the giving of a lump of iron, not bronze, as a prize in two athletic contests organised by Achilles at the funeral of Patroclus.

A general and persistent feature of Homer's poems is emphasis on physical prowess, whether this be manifested in armed combat, in organised athletic contests, in acrobatic dancing, in erotic adventures or in the sheer capacity for survival displayed by Odysseus on his way home to Ithaca from Troy. Before examining this feature more closely it is worth pointing out that the poems were regarded by the later Greeks as an important element in their culture. Just as in Europe after the Napoleonic Wars Scandinavia saw in Gothicism a romantic recreation of an heroic viking past which in turn supported P.H. Ling's development of Swedish gymnastics, and Germany threw up the Turnbewegung which also looked back to mythical and real heroes of great physical and military achievement, so the Greeks from the ninth century onwards sought to recreate their own heroic past of which physical prowess was a prime characteristic. The great athletic and religious festivals at Olympia, Delphi, Isthmia and Nemea were panhellenic festivals uniting those of Greek race throughout the Mediterranean basin. The recital and singing of heroic songs about a greater past and about a physical prowess was a persistent cultural influence in the development of hellenism and panhellenism in the ancient world.

The kind of sport depicted in the Odyssey is somewhat different from that in the Iliad and it is possible that the Odyssey draws upon the Minoan culture of Crete rather than later Mycenaean culture. Odysseus, after many adventures, is shipwrecked and struggles ashore on the coast of Phaeacia. No one has identified the territory nor its people. While Odysseus sleeps, exhausted, in the bushes, the king's daughter Nausicaa comes with her attendant maidens to wash clothes. While they wait for the clothes to dry they play ball. It is clearly a catching and throwing game and after a time there is a misthrow and the ball lands in a pool. The laughter and shrieks awake Odysseus who emerges, modestly concealing his nakedness. In the ball game the use of the preposition μετά—'at' or 'after'—suggests to Harris that it was a misthrow not a miscatch which provided the dramatic incident. The game may thus have been a variant of 'Kingie' or 'Queenie' which, the Opies have shown, has been so ubiquitous in time and place that it is rarely described (Opie in Harris, 1972: 18). The object of this game is for one designated player to hit one of the other players with the ball. He or she then takes over the role of thrower. It is far removed from competitive athletics which were not regarded as the most important physical recreation in Phaeacia; nor were the inhabitants very good at them. When some competitions in boxing, wrestling, running and throwing a weight were arranged Odysseus at first refused to take part but when he was finally goaded into doing so he outthrew and outshone all the local inhabitants. It was in dancing and especially acrobatic dancing that the Phaeacian courtiers excelled. After a demonstration of dancing and leaping combined with throwing a purple ball Odysseus exclaimed, "My Lord Alcinous, ruler of rulers, you told us that your dancers were the best, and now it is proved true. This sight is wonderful." (Homer, Od. VIII: 384).

This is akin to the acrobatic bull dancing which was a prominent feature of the Minoan court in Crete and has been so vividly depicted upon the "Taureador Fresco" (Evans, 1915. III: 144). It was very dangerous and required a high level of skill for proficiency and even for survival. Both in the legendary Phaeacia and in Crete there was a professional corps of acrobatic dancers who were recruited, maintained and patronised by the rulers. We have evidence, then, of simple and traditional child's play which was freely shared by a princess with her servants or friends and also of institutionalised and professionalised acrobatic dancing for entertainment. Patronage of this dancing marked out the aristrocracy, perhaps even the ruling dynasty itself.

The prominence of athletic contests in the life style of the leaders both Greek and Trojan is attested by numerous references in the Iliad. Throwing javelins, throwing discoi, archery and boxing are several times referred to, while athletic similes are used to describe military combat. It is however the funeral games of Patroclus described in Book XXIII which give us the clearest picture of athletics. Achilles organised in honour of his friend a chariot race, a boxing match, a wrestling match, a footrace, a contest in armour, a discus throwing competition, an archery contest, and a spear throwing contest. Both the society and sport within it were hierarchical. Slaves were lowly and were treated as chattels but even others, not of leadership rank, fared little better.

> But whenever he (Achilles) came upon a commoner shouting out,
> He struck him with his scepter and spoke sharply:
> 'Good for nothing! Be still and listen to your betters,
> You are weak and cowardly and unwarlike,
> You count for nothing, neither in battle nor in council.'
>
> (Homer, Iliad in Weil, 1945: 11)

It is not surprising to find that the contests were confined to a few named 'heroes.' The chariot race reveals a pecking order within even that select group. Antilochus overtook Menelaos despite the fact that he had slower horses and defeated him by guile. There was a protest and Antilochus gave way having conceded that Menelaos was older, higher and better, i.e. more heroic than he. A prize was also given to a non competitor, Nestor, in virtue of his venerable age and the achievements of his youth. The organisation of the race was not by any means haphazard. Achilles made the drivers draw lots for starting position and he placed an umpire, 'godlike Phoinix,' at the turning post in this out and back race. The description of the race reads convincingly which is more than can be said for descriptions of the use of chariots in combat. The heroes fought on foot after dismounting from their chariots and Dr. Kirk has concluded that Homer was writing when chariots as luxury items of the very rich had disappeared. He knew that at one time they had denoted noble rank and he knew that they had been used in war but he misunderstood their use and described an almost laughable "equine taxi service" to the front line (Kirk, 1964: 23).

Every contestant received a prize and they were valuable and useful, not merely symbolic. Furthermore the prizes reveal male domination. For the wrestling match the winner was to receive a tripod valued at twelve oxen, and the loser a woman 'skilled in many arts' who was valued at four oxen. In the chariot race the winner received a woman 'skilled in handicraft' as well as a tripod.

Violence has been a feature of sport in a great many societies, but generalizations about violence in sport reflecting violence in society are apt to be misleading. There is evidence that society depicted by Homer was violent. Achilles cut the throats of 12 Trojan captive boys and sacrificed them on the funeral pyre of Patroclus. In his fight with Hector, when he had him at his mercy not only did he show him none but, having killed him, he immolated his corpse by dragging it round the walls of Troy behind his chariot. The athletic contests, by contrast, were constrained not so much by rules as by a code of conduct accepted and well understood by heroes. The boxing match between Epeios and Euryalos ended with a knockout blow to the head of Euryalos but immediately Epeios picked him up and helped him from the ring. The contest in armour between Aias and Diomedes was never completed but was brought to an end by the spectators to avoid bloodshed. The wrestling match between Aias and Odysseus was similarly stopped by Achilles with the words, "No longer press each other, nor wear you out with pain. Victory is with both; take equal prizes and depart " (Homer Iliad XXIII: 735). In the chariot race Menelaos accused Antilochus of driving recklessly on a dangerous part of the course and endangering them both. Antilochus took no notice and after the race a protest was lodged against him for dangerous driving. Weiler has pointed out that 'to be always the best' (αἰὲν ἀριστεύειν) which is the ideal of Achilles, is not to be equated with always winning. The ideal of winning, an agonal ideal, Weiler maintains, came with the Dorian invasion. It is true that Achilles fell short of the heroic ideal and when he refused to go into battle because of a quarrel with King Agamemnon, Patroclus chided him and asked how his descendants would judge such behaviour. This incident, however, underlines the heroic ideal of the Mycenaean culture which was only later transformed into a militaristic and then an agonal ideal (Weiler 1975).

The association of athletic contests with religion in the heroic age has been a subject of some controversy. The anthropomorphism of the gods in Homer is not in dispute. The gods were portrayed as enjoying the same things as the heroes including their sports, to such an extent that they interfered with the course of events. In the footrace it was the goddess Athene who, in answer to a prayer from Odysseus caused Aias, who was winning, to slip on some offal which had been left over from a sacrifice of oxen for the funeral so that Odysseus won. The intervention of the gods in sport and in battle is not uncommon in the Homeric poems but hardly indicates a deep religious significance. Harold Harris is quite scornful of any connection at all between sport and religion. "The descriptions of athletics in Homer show that no such link existed in the age he was depicting. His games in the Iliad are part of a funeral ceremony with the purpose of distributing the belongings of the dead Patroclus to the heroes most worthy of them" (Harris 1972: 16). Had the funeral games for Patroclus been an isolated instance of association between sport and religion, Professor Harris' view might be accepted but the names of thirty three heroes for whom funeral games were held before recorded Greek history are known (Robinson 1955: 30). Such frequent association needs explaining. In 'The Golden Bough' Sir James Frazer suggested that athletic competition was at one time viewed as mimetic magic; that the vigour expended in them was thought to transfer to crops, herds and the race itself. The dead, too, would be assisted in their strenuous journey by the athletic efforts spent by survivors (Frazer 1951: 89ff). This was his explanation of the origin of the Olympic Games in the Mycenaean age long before the first surviving record of a victor in 776 B.C. Certainly there was a persistent tradition in the ancient world that games at Olympia had been celebrated on and off since the fourteenth century and that their origin and periodic revival were associated with religious sanction and religious ritual.

THE GREEK CITY STATES

The city states of the Greek mainland from the seventh century onwards were characterised by a class structure which was reflected in their sport. In Sparta the structure of the state was the result of military conquest and was perpetuated in order to maintain military domination. The citizen body was also a citizen army. Its two kings were leaders in battle as well as in councils of state. In addition to the citizens were resident aliens or perioicoi who engaged in trade and supplied many of the material needs of the citizens. Below them were the Helots, the indigenous and conquered population who were tied to the land in serfdom. It was recorded that the ephors, senior magistrates, declared war upon the helots each year in order to make quite clear their subservient and perilous status. The citizen body, both boys and girls, men and women, underwent a rigorous military and physical training. Military training and physical training for sport were not to be exactly equated. Pausanias and Philostratus indicated a distinction between the pancration, a form of all-in wrestling practised as a sport at the Olympic Games, and pancration as unarmed combat used by the Spartans. In the former certain practices such as gouging the eyes were forbidden but not in the latter. "They fight hand to hand, and with running kicks they bit and gouge, man to man." (Pausanias III. 14. 10). Nevertheless the two forms of training were close enough to have carry over value. Between 776 B.C. and 600 B.C., of sixty six victories recorded for the Olympic Games thirty three were by athletes from the single city of Sparta. According to Aristotle, however, their militarism was their undoing. "While warfare was their means of self preservation, the hegemony which they achieved, occasioned their decline, because they were ignorant of the use of leisure and had mastered no higher form of training than the art of war." (Aristotle, Politics. 127lb.). Between 596 and 300 B.C. the number of victories won by Spartans was exceeded by athletes from three other states and after 300 B.C. their eclipse was even more marked.

In Athens the social stratification was in early years by birth but Solon at the beginning of the sixth century formalised it on a basis of wealth. Citizens with an income of 500 measures of corn 'pentacosiomedimnoi' were the highest class. Below them were the 'hippeis,' horse owners, with an income of 300 measures, then the zeugitae, owners of a yoke of oxen, with an income of 200 measures and at the bottom were thetes with an income of less than 200 measures. By the fifth century the total number of citizens in all classes was about 170,000. Athens also accommodated some 35,000 resident aliens and 120,000 slaves. It seems likely that participation in the Olympic Games and other athletic festivals was restricted to the upper classes of citizens. It was a requirement that competitors must train for 10 months, the last month being spent in the neighbourhood of Olympia, and only richer citizens could afford to be absent from their homes or farms. Obviously chariot racing and equestrian events were confined to those who owned horses. Participation in other events stretched farther down the social scale. Alcibiades junior is recorded by Isocrates as saying that his father disdained gymnastic contests because he knew that some of the contestants were of low birth, inhabitants of petty states and of mean education—

he therefore took up horse breeding which was not possible for one of low estate (Isocrates, 33). Finley and Pleket believe this to have been an instance of personal snobbishness rather than of social distinction within sport (Finley and Pleket 1976: 58). Pleket's view that from the 6th century local contests were opened up to the hoplite middle class cannot be substantiated, as he himself admits, for lack of evidence (Pleket 1975, 73). Even if runners, throwers, pentathletes and fighters were drawn from all social classes of free born Greeks, equestrian events probably remained socially exclusive if only because of the high cost of horses and equipment. After about 400 B.C. it is plausible to suggest that the system of subsidising athletes and rewarding the successful made all events more generally accessible despite the fact that in those records of individual athletes receiving honorary citizenship which have survived, there is little to indicate whether he was 'a product of social mobility or belonged to a municipal elite class' (Pleket 1975. 73). Whatever the social origin of athletes may have been in the classical period, the association of success in sports with political leadership is well attested. Perusal of the list of victors at Olympia from 776 onwards (Moretti 1957) shows a number of men who achieved political power in their own cities. The most specific association of sport with politics is seen in the career of Alcibiades and it is mentioned by both Thucydides and Isocrates writing in 5th and 4th centuries B.C. respectively. In 416 B.C. Alcibiades entered 7 chariots at Olympia and took 1st, 2nd and 4th places according to Thucydides (1st, 2nd and 3rd according to Isocrates). Alcibiades claimed that these victories supported his claim to military leadership in the expedition which the Athenians were contemplating against Syracuse. "For by general custom," he told the assembly at Athens, "such things do indeed mean honour and from what is done men also infer power " (Thucydides VI. 16). Alcibiades was appointed general and the expedition was a disaster. There were a number of writers in the fifth and fourth centuries who expressed a highly critical view of the popular acclaim which athletes enjoyed whether or not this led to political power. Xenophanes in the 6th century inveighed against athletes saying in the course of his diatribe "even if he won a victory with race horses . . . . . yet would he not be as worthy as I. For our wisdom is a better thing than strength of men and horses. But this is a most unreasonable custom, and it is not right to honor strength above excellent wisdom" (Xenophanes, Frag. 2 in Robinson 1955). The playright Euripides and in the fourth century philosophers Plato and Aristotle all decried the popular adulation and the social uselessness of athletes. The criticisms, however, are themselves evidence supporting the claim that Alcibiades made about sport and political power in the fifth century. There was another connection between sport and politics in classical

Greece. The Olympic Games were preceded by the declaration of a truce. This did not stop all wars. What it did was invoke the wrath of Zeus and exclusion from the Games of any athlete from a state which did not afford safe conduct to those travelling to Olympia. In 420 B.C. Sparta was fined for a breach of the truce, refused to pay and was excluded from the religious rites and the athletic contests. Thucydides says that everyone was afraid that the Spartans would force their way in but they did not, whether from religious or political considerations it is impossible to say. The same kind of truce seemed to apply to other panhellenic festivals. Pausanias says that athletes from Elis always refused to take part in the Isthmian Games because two of her citizens had been murdered in Argos on their way to the Games. Elis requested Corinth, the city responsible for the Isthmian Games to exclude Argos. Corinth refused and Elis withdrew her competitors and continued to do so in subsequent celebrations. In 1980 this story had a familiar ring but no one in classical Greece pretended that sport was free of politics.

After the tragic and disastrous war between Athens and Sparta from 431 to 404 B.C. the city states of Greece went into political decline until Philip of Macedon and his son Alexander the Great established their empire over the whole region. There was then an inversion of sport and political power. Alexander was an athlete of ability but gave up competitive events because it was considered inappropriate for a king to be defeated and he disliked being allowed to win. He still encouraged athletics probably for its political pay off as well as for other benefits. Indeed, according to Harris, "when Alexander spread Greek civilization all over the Eastern Mediterranean every city in the newly Hellenized world took steps to provide itself with a stadium to inaugurate athletics meetings" (Harris 1972: 18). Alexander himself took up non-competitive ball play and built a court, sphairisterion, in which to play. Theophrastus writing at the end of the 4th or beginning of the 3rd century says that from then onwards a sphairisterion became one sign of a social climber (Harris 1972: 84). Sport was thus still associated both with social mobility and with the exercise of political power and continued to be so for many centuries and long after the empire of Alexander had given way to the empire of Rome. Although the social and political framework of the Greek city state had gone, Greek athletics persisted and played an important but somewhat different social and political role, as we shall see.

The decision of the upper and middle classes in Britain from about 1860 to deny themselves money or value prizes for successful participation in competitive sport, except in horse racing, and to incorporate this self denial in the definition of an amateur has led to the assumption that remuneration is incompatible with upper class participation. From this a second assumption follows, namely, that those who are remunerated are socially inferior. A social stigma is, then attached to them. These assumptions cannot be made about athletics in the ancient world, certainly not about athletics in the city states of classical Greece.

At the beginning of the 6th century at Athens, Solon, as part of his social and economic reforms, decreed that Athenian citizens who were victorious at Olympia should be paid 500 drachmas and victors at the Isthmian Games 100 drachmas. In the fifth century this smaller amount was somewhere near the annual wage of a working man. A victory at Olympia would certainly enable the athlete to devote himself to training for the next contest in four years' time. There is however no reason to think that 500 drachmas was the equivalent of 500 medimnoi thus putting the victor in the highest socio-economic group for one year (Thompson 1978). As well as cash, remuneration also took other forms. Socrates, on trial for his life, having been found guilty of subversion and having been required to suggest an appropriate penalty said, "Nothing is more becoming, men of Athens, than for a man like me to receive public maintenance in the Guild-hall—a reward he deserves far more than a citizen who has won a victory at Olympia in horse or chariot race—and whereas he needs no maintenance, I do" (Plato, Apology, 26). In other cities, too, rewards for success were considerable. At Acragas in Sicily in 412 B.C. a returning victor was accompanied into his native city by 300 chariots drawn by white horses. This, of course, had no monetary value but free meals seem to have been a common concomitant of public honour. 'Payment by results' was an accepted procedure for Greek athletics. An interesting question is how did an athlete finance his first success? After victory rewards were plentiful but there is little evidence of athletes in the 6th and 5th centuries being paid to train. Gymnasia and palaestrae, facilities for training, were in many cities provided at public expense. Coaching was cheap and coaches were reputedly underpaid, but how did the up and coming athlete support himself? We do not know, but there was certainly no lack of entrants to keep the Olympic Games going for more than 1,000 years, and other panhellenic and local contests, too, for a considerable length of time.

It has been suggested, for instance, by Norbert Elias, that the sport of ancient Greece was based upon an ethos of warrior nobility and upon traditions of 'honour' rather than 'fairness' (Elias 1971: 101). The association of success at Olympia with military prowess has already been stressed. However, there is considerable evidence that the Greeks did indeed value 'fairness.' In the first place they had elaborate rules for ensuring equal chances for competitors and for eliminating factors other than strength and skill. In footraces stone sills, grooved for the athletes' toes still survive in many stadia. As time went on a starting gate, a 'husplex' was devised. The arrangements for starting chariot races were even more elaborate. Because the charioteer nearest the centre turning pole had an advantage the starting stalls were staggered with the inside charioteer furthest forward but not released from his stall until the others were alongside. He therefore had a standing start while they had a flying start. "After this," writes Pausanias, "it is left to the charioteers to display their skill and the horses their speed" (Pausanias VI, 20: 10-13). Other events had their own rules and devices. Enforcement, too, was rigorous. Before the husplex was invented those who started before the signal were flogged. There was an additional sanction. All competitors and their relatives and trainers had to swear an oath to Zeus on slices of boars' flesh to observe the rules. This ritual was based on the recognition that not all offences were detectable but it also evidenced the belief that rule breaking was itself an offence deserving religious sanction. κακούργημα was the offence mentioned by Pausanias, meaning fraud or cheating (Pausanias V. XXIV). The clearest evidence for the value placed upon fairness is the use in sport of the root word δίκη also used for custom, for law and for legal trial. It is also the root word for justice, δικαιοσύνη. The search for justice and its application to life was not only the theme of Plato's dialogues, The Republic and the Laws and of Aristotle's books on ethics, politics and the Athenian Constitution; it was also the concern of the hellan-odikai (δίκη again) and of the state of Elin which administered the Olympic Games. Herodotus writes of a deputation sent from Elis to Egypt in the 6th century B.C. to enquire whether the Egyptians who had a reputation for wisdom, considered the rules for the organisation of the Olympic Games to be as fair as was possible. The word which Herodotus used was δικαιότατα meaning most just. The only modi-fication which the Egyptians suggested was that the Eleans who judged the contests should not themselves compete because they were bound to favour their own countrymen. The advice was not taken.

Love of honour, as well as love of victory φιλοτιμία and φιλονικία were also characteristic of the Greeks. The behaviour and the words of Alcibiades which have already been quoted in another context are evidence of love of honour. Love of victory was not always unbridled but harnessed to social or political purposes. This was succinctly stated by Demosthenes. "The freedom of a democracy is guarded by the rivalry with which good citizens compete for the rewards offered by the people." (Demosthenes XX: 107). Often love of honour and love of victory were displayed together. Heracles, a traditional hero, the "author of many benefits to mankind, devoted his life to a laborious quest of victory and honour" (Lysias ii: 16). Both qualities were praised in the lyrical odes which Pindar wrote in honour of victors at Olympia and other festivals.

> Do thou, of father Zeus, that rulest over the height of Atabyrium, grant honour to the hymn ordained in praise of any Olympic victor and to the hero who hath found fame for his prowess as a boxer; and do thou give him grace and reverence in the eyes of citizens and strangers too. For he goeth in a straight path that hateth insolence.
>
>   (Pindar, O.O. VII: 84-95)

The demeanour of the victor was important as well as the victory itself. The word insolence here is hubris, ὕβρις. In some contexts it could be translated pride, the pride that comes before a fall, νέμεσις. Hubris was abhorred in literature and in legal proceedings as well as in sport. This tempered the value set upon victory which was not overriding. Pleket claimed that '"To participate is more important than to win"—the slogan of the Coubertinians of 1896 and of their successors at the present day—is probably the most unGreek statement that can be made' (Pleket 1975). But how, then, can we explain the advice of Pythagoras which has survived in a literary fragment (Bowra 1953. Chap 11) that men should compete at Olympia but not win. Victory would defile them and make them liable to the envy of others, just as in life itself a love of power and leadership and desire to win were marks of a mania for prestige, δοξομανία—a minority view perhaps but not unGreek. On the other hand there was little praise for the 'good loser.' Pindar certainly rarely mentions a loser and then pictures him slinking home in shame and not even being welcomed back by his mother. Jibes of contempt or obscurity are the lot of the loser (Pindar, Ol. Ode. VIII).

The assessment of violence in Greek athletic contests has been a matter of argument among scholars. There is no doubt that violence was a feature of life and particularly of relations between states. The Spartans declared war annually upon their subservient Helot population. They also gave their young men a public flogging on initiation to manhood and some died from the ritual. Thucydides gives a graphic and dramatic account of events and negotiations which led to a siege of Melos by Athens in 416. The whole of the adult male population was killed and the women and children enslaved. Thucydides did not approve but neither did he suggest that such a practice was unprecedented. Indeed it was not. In such a world the athletic contests were remarkably lacking in violence. Boxing was probably the most violent and bloody. The pancration, too, was violent and occasionally led to accidental deaths but it was nevertheless restricted by some rules. There were accidents, too, in the chariot racing, some of them fatal. The race in armour, which some have claimed gave a military turn to the Games, did nothing of the kind. It was introduced late and came to be regarded as a light hearted event. The sight of naked men running down the stadium wearing nothing but a helmet and greaves and carrying a shield must have delighted the spectators. The ethos of sport tended to discourage violence as did the ethos in drama. No act of violence was done on stage. When Oedipus blinded himself and Medea killed her children, they committed their atrocities off stage. This ethos was in sharp contrast with later practices when Rome had conquered the Mediterranean world and had established a pax Romana. In a world at peace the most violent and bloody affairs were enacted in the theatre and the amphi-theatre. It is to this era that we must now turn our attention.

CITIES OF THE ROMAN EMPIRE

The sack of the city of Corinth by Mummius and his soldiers in 146 B.C. marked the end of the political independence of the Greeks but not the end of their cultural and social institutions. Athletic contests and training for them survived and developed in cities throughout the Eastern Roman Empire. The programme of events in the Olympic Games and other festivals showed little change under the Roman Empire but the substructure of training and organisa-tion took on new forms, and Greek athletics, as an institution, assumed a new social and political importance.

Some of the changes which had taken place by the end of the 1st century A.D. are revealed in two sets of correspondence between Pliny, who was governor of Bithynia, and the emperor Trajan in 111 A.D. In the first set of letters Pliny informs the emperor that the citizens of Nicaea who are rebuilding a gymnasium destroyed by fire have exhausted their funds before completing improvements to the building. The emperor replies:

> The poor Greeks have a weakness for gymnasia so perhaps the citizens of Nicaea have attacked its construction too enthusiastically. But they will have to be satisfied with a gymnasium which is just big enough for their needs.
>
> (Pliny, Epist. IV. 39, 40)

The fact that the governor of Bithynia felt it necessary to refer the matter to Rome indicates that athletics were politically important and that the provision of facilities for training as well as for competi-tion from public funds was accepted as normal. From time to time, then as now, the central government found it necessary to curb public expenditure but Trajan did not deny all financial liability by government.

In the second correspondence Pliny tells the emperor that the athletes thank him for the remuneration which he has fixed for "Iselastic" games,—that is those in which victory is marked by a triumphal entry into the home town by the athlete on his return—but they make two further requests. First, payment should start from the date of the victory not from the date of arrival at home. Second, that back payment of maintenance (obsonia) should be made if a festival has been upgraded to 'Iselastic' after the athlete won his event there. Trajan rejected both demands stating with bureaucratic logic, which is familiar today, that when he downgraded a festival he did not demand a refund of what athletes had previously received (Pliny, Epist. X. 118, 119). Even as early as the 1st century B.C. according to Vitruvius victors in the four panhellenic festivals of Olympia, Delphi, Nemea and Isthmia enjoyed a fixed grant from the public treasury for life (Vitruvius X. 1). These four festivals had come to be known as the περίοδος "the circuit" and at least one of them occurred every year. Under the Roman Empire they were known as crown, sacred, or 'iselastic' games. Other games were added to this category at the Emperor's discretion. This had a higher status than games which were designated merely 'prize games.' At these latter, value prizes were offered and the organisers had to provide the financial incentives to attract competitors. For a long time it was believed that the only reward offered at Crown games was a wreath or garland for the head—στέφανος*—and that it was the home city of the competitor which, for the sake of prestige and by decree of the Emperor provided remuneration. However H.W. Pleket has now produced evidence that a number of crown games did offer value prizes as well as the crown (Pleket 1975: 54-71). In the Fitzwilliam Museum at Cambridge, England in the Leake Collection is a gold medal struck for the crown games instituted in Macedonia by the emperor Gordian in 242 A.D. This medal had intrinsic as well as symbolic value. Similar gold medals were awarded in other sacred crown contests especially those held to mark the emperor's victory over external enemies. At Olympia, however, no value prizes were ever awarded, so great was the continuing prestige and status of that festival.

The correspondence between Pliny and Trajan also reveals that athletes were organized or 'unionized' and this is supported by other

---

*στέφανος is also the word used in the gospels of Mark (XV. 17), Matthew (XXVII. 29) and John (XIX. 2) for the crown of thorns placed by the Roman soldiers in mockery upon the head of Jesus Christ before his crucifixion. It is possible that to contemporaries this symbolised athletic as well as political opprobrium. The normal term for a king's crown was διάδημα, or diadem.

evidence. There were probably local unions or guilds throughout the empire but there were two and later one world wide association. When there were two associations one was open to all who made a living from touring the festivals, the other was restricted to those who had won a victory in one of the crown or sacred Games. They were given a headquarters in Rome by the emperor Hadrian in 134 A.D. and this was confirmed by Antoninus Pius nine years later. To the "xystic guild of athletes"— xystos being the name of a facility for training—"the sacred and garlanded victors who keep the cult of Heracles, greetings. I have ordered a site assigned to you where you will put your cult objects and your records, near the baths erected by my deified grandfather just in the spot where you gather for the Capitoline Games" (IG XIV. 1055b). At about this time both guilds merged into one xystic association. Those who serviced the athletic festivals, the trainers, the veterinarians for equestrian events and others also had their organisations. Athletes then were professionalised to a large extent.

It is necessary to distinguish between professionalism and professionalisation. The former term refers to a state of affairs arbitrarily defined by some authority. If we apply the definition of amateur/professional given by the International Olympic Committee or the International Amateur Athletic Federation from the twentieth century to the ancient world then a very large number of competitors in the Olympic and other Games were professionals during most of the time that those festivals were held. Professionalisation, however, is a process with reference to those possessing a body of knowledge and skill, forming themselves into an organisation requiring entry qualifications and laying down codes of conduct and terms and conditions for the performance of their skills. The correspondence of the Emperors Trajan, Hadrian and Antoninus Pius indicates that the professionalisation of athletes had by then developed a long way from the unorganised individuals who did the circuit of panhellenic and local Games in the fifth century B.C.

In the nineteenth century in Britain the distinction between amateur and professional was at first a social distinction and had nothing to do with making money out of sport by wager or prize. Many upper class competitors did just this. Only late in the century were financial restrictions used to maintain social exclusiveness. In the Roman Empire athletics were not socially exclusive. Furthermore success made for some social mobility. An epigram in honour of T. Domitius Prometheus about 250 A.D. for his victories in the 'circuit' and other Games shows that he was a wealthy man of leisure, deputy director of the Athenian epheboi who was not averse to receiving valued prizes although he did "wrap them up in a sanctifying ideology" (Pleket 1975: 70). At the other end of the social scale, according to

Claudius Galen, were a number of illiterate philistines or 'jocks.' In the middle were those who like the family of Herminus Moros were important in the 'gymnasium' set for several generations. This boxer's membership certificate of the athletic guild was signed by two officers who, like Galen himself, surgeon to the emperor Commodus, were popular in court circles (Robinson 1955: 200-201).

There is some evidence, albeit scanty, that women who were debarred from taking part or being present at the Olympic Games even as late as the 1st century A.D., nevertheless had then their own athletic competitions at Delphi, Isthmia, Nemea, Sicyon and Epidaurus as well as at Olympia itself in honour of the goddess Hera.

In 67 A.D. the Emperor Nero himself, competed in the Olympic Games having had them postponed from 65 A.D. so that he might also take part in the Pythian and Isthmian festivals in the same year. This may have raised the already high social status of the Olympic Games but it reduced competition to absurdity. The emperor had to win. Neither he nor his successors repeated this performance, Nero because he died in 68 A.D. and his successors because they were wiser and were preoccupied with other matters of state.

Greek athletics, then, flourished in the East but in the city of Rome itself, after initial introduction by the first emperor, Augustus, in 30 B.C. they had modest popularity and a doubtful social status. The Actian Games initiated to celebrate the final pacification of the empire and elimination of rivals at the battle of Actium in 31 B.C. were celebrated every 5 years but scarcely survived the Emperor's death. The Augustalia at Naples which included music and dramatic competitions lasted until the 3rd century A.D. Nero founded the Neronia in Rome in 60 A.D. and encouraged knights and senators to compete but the Neronia are not mentioned after 66 A.D. The emperor Domitian established a quinquennial replica of the Olympic Games and built a permanent stadium holding 30,000 spectators, to accommodate them. Augustus had also included a Lusus Troiae in the foundation celebration for the temple and cult of the Divine Julius in 29 B.C. To what extent the competitors were Greek athletes imported for entertainment or were indigenous citizens as Augustus and Nero hoped they would be, must remain in doubt. The Romans tended at first to associate athletics with the pastimes of a conquered race. They also objected to nudity and suspected homosexuality and degeneracy, Cicero quotes Ennius "To strip naked among one's fellow citizens is the beginning of vice" (Cicero iv. 10).

The poet, Horace, too, showed a contempt for Greek athletics (Horace, Epistles II, i. 93) but how else were the sons of Rome to satisfy a desire for physical competition. Some emperors, Nero and Commodus for instance, who wished to degrade the upper classes encouraged senators and knights to fight in the arena as gladiators and the mob would be delighted to see them exbibit themselves 'like slaves or hirelings' (Friedlander 1908-13 in Pearson, 1973: 115) but Augustus Tiberius and Vitellius tried to stop the practice. Games on the Greek model, may therefore have been promoted as an alternative outlet for aspiring young Roman athletes especially among the families of Senators and Knights. Support is given to this view by the account of Games in the 5th book of Virgil's Aeneid (Virgil, Aen. V) which have a remarkable affinity with Augustus' Lusus Troiae. This affinity has been analysed and documented by Ward Briggs who claims that the Lusus Troiae "was Augustus' favorite exercise for the youths of Rome. It was regularly performed only by the very persons to whom Augustus was directing his athletic encouragement, the youths of aristocratic families. Virgil's account is our only source of the details of the maneuvers" (Briggs 1975: 281).

The gladiatorial shows which had been begun during the Republic and were accommodated in the Flavian Amphitheatre, popularly known as the Colosseum, after it was inaugurated by the emperor Titus in 80 A.D. might well fall outside the definition of sport and therefore outside the scope of this chapter. In them commercialised cruelty for public entertainment and political manipulation was carried to the ultimate. However, as they made use of the skills of combat in genuine competition, often to the death, something must be said about their place in the social and political life of Rome.

Rome in the early empire was a city of about 1¼ million inhabitants most of whom lived in appalling conditions in dangerous high rise buildings with no water above ground level. It has been estimated that 170,000 heads of families were supported by a public distribution of food. Thus some 500,000 to 700,000 were state supported. Many were unemployed but even those who were at work, including slaves, had most of each afternoon free from labour. In the reign of Claudius (41-54 A.D.) there were 159 official holidays in the Roman calendar to which were added such special holidays as a capricious emperor might decree. The population under this despotism had no political duties or rights. The combination of poverty, leisure and political inactivity posed serious problems for the government and above all for the emperor. Two of the political instruments used to keep the mass of the people contented and subservient were 'ludi' in the circus and the amphitheatre. The elaborate organisation of mass pursuit and slaughter of wild beasts, the throwing of condemned criminals and others 'ad bestias'—to starved and thirsty beasts of prey —and the multiple combats of gladiators, many of which amounted to the butchery of prisoners, or slaves by experienced and trained killers was deliberately set up by Augustus as an instrument of government and social control to bring to an end a prolonged period of civil strife and urban turbulence in Rome. Under Augustus the system worked and Rome was controlled. Thereafter it continued inexorably under its own momentum and no emperor until Constantine in 326 A.D. felt able to abandon it. Tiberius, who succeeded Augustus, and had no taste for the excesses of the arena tried to dissociate himself from them. He provided no shows and was unpopular and reviled as a result. His successor Caligula learned his lesson and celebrated his accession with a profusion of shows. Thereafter the emperors of Rome felt either constrained or inclined to continue the policy of control by bloody entertainment. It has often been suggested that gladiatorial and other cruel combats were finally swept away by outraged Christian feeling. Certainly Constantine who issued the decree abolishing them had made Christianity the official religion of the empire, but it is probable that economic factors were as powerful as Christian protest (Pearson 1973: 167). The same factors probably led to the decree of Theodosius II who in 393 A.D. put an end to the Olympic Games and other Games on the grounds that they were pagan religious festivals.

Another policy of government, and more beneficient than the provision of 'ludi' was the building of 'thermae' or baths. They not only helped to keep the people contented, they also enabled a minimum level of physical fitness to be maintained by an idle populace. The thermae were far more than bathing establishments. The thermae built by Trajan measured 280 m by 210 m and embraced three main features. The central complex included a cold room, swimming pool, central hall, warm room and hot room, together with dressing rooms and small bathrooms. There were also two open palaistrae surrounded by colonnades. Outside this central complex was open ground laid out as gardens with a running track. Beyond this again was the peribolus containing libraries, reading rooms, gymnasia, ball courts and administrative offices. By the 3rd century A.D. it is probable that 80,000 Romans could be using such facilities at minimal cost or none at any one time. They were available to all and sundry, including slaves, and were used by both sexes. Seneca in his letters vividly described the life of the thermae and the activities of these so concerned to keep fit. He himself merely wanted "short and simple exercises which tire the body rapidly and so save time" (Seneca, Epistles LVI & XV). Juvenal lets us know that fashionable ladies also went to the baths.

> It is at night that she goes to the baths, at night that she gives orders for her oil flasks and other impediments to be taken there; she loves to sweat among the noise and bustle. When her arms fall to her sides, worn out by heavy weights, the skilful masseur presses his fingers into her body, and makes her body resound with his loud smack.
>
> (Juvenal, Satyre VI: 419)

The general need to arrest physical deterioration made the thermae cosmopolitan institutions.

The great authority on keeping fit was Claudius Galen a doctor and prolific writer, many of whose works have fortunately survived. In his monogram entitled 'Exercise with the Small Ball' he writes

> The best gymnastic is that which not only exercises the body but which delights the spirit. This is especially true of small ball gymnastics.
>
> (McIntosh 1957: 56)

The years of the Roman empire may well have been the first time that hedonistic inducements to keep fit had to be devised. In earlier times the exigencies of earning a living, military service or just personal survival in a hard world were sufficient incentives. In his massive work on hygiene, usually known as *De Sanitate Tuenda*, as well as in his minor works, Galen developed physiological theories, classifications of exercises and programmes of work, including routines of weight training, for improving the physical condition of ordinary men and women. He was not interested in athletics. He drew a sharp distinction between normal fitness and athletic fitness and emphasised several times that the latter was dangerous to health and socially useless. Gymnastics devoted to that end was a perversion of true gymnastics and a disreputable occupation (McIntosh 1957: 55).

Galen was not the only writer on physical training. Professionalisation of athletics, whether in the gymnasia, training athletes for the stadium, in the schools of gladiators for the arena or in the army was not confined to performers. It extended to coaches and advisers. There were a host of training manuals in antiquity and one of them written by Philostratus in the 3rd century has survived. He gives us an account of many theories and practices. Some of them now appear absurd; others have provided a basis for subsequent development. Quite laughable are some theories on diet: pigs which have fed on sea garlic or crabs should be avoided and only those fattened on cornel berries or acorns should be eaten while training. He describes in some detail the "tetrad system" of training, or four day cycle only to condemn "for it is because of this that the whole system of gymnastics has gone to rack and ruin" (Robinson 1955: 229). More sensible is a primitive attempt at somatotyping and psychological typing for particular events. With professionalisation came specialisation "If you had been born in Greece" writes Tacitus "where athletics is an honourable profession, and heaven had granted you the sinews of Nicostratus, I should not allow those mighty muscles, simply made for boxing, to be wasted on mere javelin or discus throwing" (Harris 1972: 65).

Military training was another form of specialisation. An account of recruit training by Vegetius written about 390 A.D. describes pace training in marching and weapon training by weight training. The recruit had to learn his art with sword and shield twice the weight of those which he would use on active service and his spear, too, was heavier than his fighting weapon (Gibbon, 1776-88 Vol 1, Chap 1). Professionalisation of physical training whether for sport, entertainment or war and the professonalisation of the performers was a feature of the Roman Empire. It was certainly not confined to physical activities but perhaps was a factor in the persistence and survival of the empire despite the manifest corruption that often occurred in administration and the madness and incompetence of some of its emperors. It is the more flamboyant emperors who have enjoyed the historical limelight but others were activated by a sense of moral purpose. There is a passage in the meditations of Marcus Aurelius advocating a transfer of behaviour from the gymnasium to life outside, a muscular morality, suggesting that the gymnasium was an instrument of socialisation as well as of social control.

> In the field (ἐν τοῖς γυμνασίοις) a player may have scratched us with his nails or give us a blow with his head, in a rage, yet we do not label him for that or hit back or suspect him afterwards of designs against us. Still, we do, in fact, keep away from him, not, however as a foe and not with suspicion but with good natured avoidance. Let us take this as an example in other department of life. Let us overlook much in the case of those who are, so to speak, our opponents in the game (προσγυμναξομένων); for it is possible to avoid them, yet neither to suspect nor to hate them. (ἀπέχθεσθαι)
>
> (Marcus Aurelius VI. 20)

A postscript to this sociological study of sport in the ancient world may be written upon spectators and their role. Not all Greek athletics came to an end with the Olympic Games in 393 A.D. Chariot racing and equestrian events persisted in the Eastern Empire long after Alaric the Goth sacked Rome in 410 A.D. Spectators played a vital part, for chariot racing seemed to be more closely bound up with its spectators than any other sport. In the reign of Justinian in Constantinople they brought it temporarily to an end. This is how Gibbon described the Nika riots which were sparked off by the Emperor Justinian's refusal to release two prisoners who had been condemned to death.

> Constantinople adopted the follies, though not the virtues, of ancient Rome; and the same factions which had agitated the circus raged with redoubled fury in the hippodrome. Under the reign of Anastasius, this popular frenzy was inflamed by religious zeal; and the greens, who had

treacherously concealed stones and daggers under baskets of fruit, massacred, at a solemn festival, three thousand of their blue adversaries. From the capital, this pestilence was diffused into the provinces and cities of the East, and the sportive distinction of two colours produced two strong and irreconcileable factions, which shook the foundations of a feeble government. . . . .

. . . . Insolent with royal favour, the blues affected to stride terror by a peculiar and Barbaric dress, the long hair of the Huns, their close sleeves and ample garments, a lofty step, and a sonorous voice. In the day they concealed their two-edged poniards, but in the night they boldly assembled in arms and in numerous bands, prepared for every act of violence and rapine. Their adversaries of the green faction, or even inoffensive citizens, were stripped and often murdered by these nocturnal robbers, and it became dangerous to wear any gold buttons or girdles, or to appear at a late hour in the streets of a peaceful capital. A daring spirit, rising with impunity, proceeded to violate the safeguard of private houses; and fire was employed to facilitate the attack, or to conceal the crimes, of these factious rioters. No place was safe or sacred from their depredations; to gratify either avarice or revenge, they profusely spilt the blood of the innocent; churches and altars were polluted by atrocious murders; and it was the boast of the assasins that their dexterity could always inflict a mortal wound with a single stroke of their dagger. . . . .

. . . . The hippodrome itself was condemned during several years to a mournful silence; with the restoration of the games, the same disorders revived; and the blue and green factions continued to afflict the reign of Justinan, and to disturb the tranquility of the Eastern empire.

(Gibbon, Vol IV. Ch XL)

These so-called 'factions' existed from the principate of Augustus until the eve of the crusades, about 1200 years. It became a traditional view that they were quasi political parties able even to make or unmake emperors. Marxists claimed that their terrorist activities in the great cities of the Eastern Empire in the 5th and 6th centuries A.D. marked the growth of popular sovereignty. This is too simple to view. It has been my contention in this chapter that the promotion of sport and sporting entertainment was a governmental measure of social control in a system where the exercise of political power by ordinary citizens was prevented. In such circumstances popular emotions found what means of expression they could and circus factions provided one such outlet. It is possible that soccer hooliganism in Britain in the 1970's similarly coincided with a decline of opportunity for popular political expression, but hooliganism does not signify a growth of popular sovereignty nor does it invest the supporters of Manchester United Football Club with the panoply of a political party. Alan Cameron has convincingly shown that the Blues, Greens, and in early days the Whites and Reds too, were fan clubs of supporters and so they remained. "Their sudden leap to prominence in the fifth century is largely illusory, not a new phenomenon at all but the incidental consequence of a reorganisation of public entertainment.

> . . . . Hooliganism at theatre and circus had always been rife in the Roman world. It merely got worse under the Blues and Greens.
>
> (Cameron 1976: 310)

REFERENCES

A. Latin and Greek Authors

The works of all authors are to be found in English translation in the Loeb Classical Library with Latin or Greek and English on opposite pages, published by Heinemann, London. Many portions relevant to sport are included in R.R. Robinson 'Sources for the History of Greek Athletics,' Cincinnati, 1955.

Aristotle	Nichomachean Ethics
Aristotle	Politics
Cicero	Tusculan Disputations
Demosthenes	Orations
Euripides	Plays and Fragment Autolycus
Galen	Exercises with the Small Ball
Galen	Health
Galen	Health, Medicine and Gymnastics
Herodotus	History
Homer	Iliad
Homer	Odyssey
Isocrates	Team of Horses
Juvenal	Satyres
Lucian	Anacharsis
Lysias	Orations
Marcus Aurelius	Meditations
Pausanias	Description of Greece
Philostratus	Gymnastics
Pindar	Olympian Odes
Plato	Apology of Socrates
Pliny	Epistles
Plutarch	Lives
Seneca	Epistles
Strabo	Geography
Suetonius	The twelve Caesars
Tacitus	Annals
Thucydides	History
Vegetius	Military Affairs
Virgil	Aeneid
Xenophanes	Fragments

B. Modern Authors

Balsdon, J.P.V. 1969. *Life and Leisure in Ancient Rome.* New York: McGraw-Hill.

Bowra, C.M. 1964. *Pindar* Oxford:

Bowra, C.M. 1953. *Problems in Greek Poetry.* Oxford

Briggs, W.W. 1975. Augustan athletics and games of Aeneid V. *Stadion* 1,2

Cambridge Ancient History. 1970-75. Cambridge, Eng. University Press

Cameron, A. 1976. *Circus Factions. Blues and Greens at Rome and Byzantium.* Oxford: Clarendon

Daremberg-Saglio, 1877-1919. *Dictionnaire des antiquités grecques et romaines.* Paris: Hachette.

Dover, K.J. 1974. *Greek Popular Morality in the Time of Plato and Aristotle.* Oxford: Blackwell.

Dudley, D.R. 1967. *Urbs Roma.* London: Phaidon.

Elias, N. 1971. The genesis of sport as a sociological problem. In E. Dunning, ed. *The Sociology of Sport.* London: Cass.

Evans, A.J. 1975. *The Palace of Minos at Knossos.* London: MacMillan.

Finley, M.I. and H.W. Pleket. 1976. *The Olympic Games: The First Thousand Years.* New York: Viking.

Frazer, J.G. 1951. *The Golden Bough.* London: MacMillan. Part III 'The Dying God.'

Friedlander, L. 1908-28. *Roman Life and Manners under the Early Empire.* London: G. Routledge. New York: E.P. Dutton.

Gardiner, E.N. 1930. *Athletics of the Ancient World.* Oxford: The Clarendon Press.

Gibbon, E. *Decline and Fall of the Roman Empire.* New York: E.P. Dutton.

Harris, H.A. 1964 *Greek Athletes and Athletics.* London: Hutchinson.

Harris, H.A. 1972. *Sport in Greece and Rome.* London: Thames and Hudson.

Harris, H.A. 1976. *Trivium Greek Athletics and the Jews.* Cardiff: University of Wales Press.

Howell, M.S. and Howell, R. 1979. Physical activities and sport in early societies. In E. Zeigler, ed. *History of Physical Education and Sport.* Englewood Cliffs: Prentice-Hall.

Huizinga, J.H. 1949. *Homo Ludens.* London: Routledge and Kegan Paul.

Inscriptiones Graecae

Jaeger, W. 1934. *Paideia.* Berlin und Leipzig: W. de Gruyter.

Kirk, G.S. 1964. *The Homeric Poems as History.* Cambridge University Press. Reprint of Cambridge Ancient History Vol II, Chap. XXXIX (b)

Lanciani, R.A. 1967. *Ancient Rome in the Light of Recent Discoveries.* New York: Blom.

Liddell, H. and R. Scott. 1878 *Greek-English Lexicon.* Ed. 6. New York.

McIntosh, P.C. 1957. Physical education and recreation in Imperial Rome. In P.C. McIntosh, ed., *Landmarks in the History of Physical Education.* London: Routledge & Kegan Paul.

McIntosh, P.C. 1963. *Sport in Society.* London: Watts.

Moretti, L. 1953. *Inscrizioni Agonistiche Greche.* Roma: A. Signorelli.

Moretti, L. 1957. *Olympionikai, i vincitori negli antichi agoni olimpici.* Roma. Academia nazionale dei lincei. Classe di scienze moral, storiche. Ser. 8.

Myres, J.L. 1930. *Who Were the Greeks?* Berkeley: University of California Press.

Opie, I and P. Opie. 1969. *Children's Games in Street and Playground*. Oxford: Clarendon.

Pearson, J. 1973. *Arena: The Story of the Colosseum*. New York: McGraw-Hill.

Pleket, H.W. 1975. Games, prizes, athletes and ideology. In *Stadion* I, 1:49–89.

Robinson, R. (Sargent) 1955. *Sources for the History of Greek Athletics*. Cincinnati.

Thompson, J.G. 1978. Solon on athletics. *Journal of Sport History* 5, 1:

Weil, S. 1945. *The Iliad the Poem of Force*. Pendle Hill Pamphlet No. 91: Wallingford, Pennsylvania.

Weiler, I. 1975. Αἰὲν ἀριστεύειν In *Stadion* I, 2:195.

Zeigler, E.F. 1973. *A History of Sport and Physical Education to 1900*. Part I. Champaign, Ill.: Stipes.

GAMES OF THE NATIVE NORTH AMERICANS

Alyce Taylor Cheska

An estimated 1,500,000 Indians inhabited the lands now called Canada, United States, and Mexico when the Europeans "discovered" America. The first North Americans were hunters–gatherers who migrated from the Eastern Asiatic lands ten to forty millenia ago.[1] They moved in sequential waves across the Beringian land bridge following the migratory routes of their fauna and flora food supply. In time these people fanned out from the funnel-like northwestern passageway across the northern hemisphere, through the corridor of Mesoamerica, to the southernmost tip of South America. Anthropologists are not agreed concerning the extent of exchange between South America, Mesoamerica, and North America, but there was a cultural contract. The northern Pacific coast Aleut and Inuit peoples who appeared in a later migratory wave were linguistically more recently related to the Kamchadal, Koryak, and Chukchi people of Siberia. Along the 4000 mile east-west continental span the various Inuit groups are linguistically compatable and share many common cultural traits.

CULTURAL CONTEXT

Topographical and hydrographical features divided the land of North America into two zones, Cordillera (with valleys and passages through the highlands) and Plains (with the relative flat lands), making possible criss-cross contact routes for trade, borrowing, war, and conquest. Transactions between tribes provided excellent occasions for the exchange of games. Similar game forms were wide spread even across linguistic barriers; variations developed in adaptation to local ecology, available materials for making gaming implements, and social vehicles for using the game.

The culture areas used to distinguish various regional groupings are not independent or unique, but represent a blending of one area with another. They are: Arctic (including Sub-Arctic), Basin, California, Eastern Woodlands, Mesoamerica, Northwest Coast, Plains,

Plateau, Southwest Desert. Please refer to Figure I for the regions relative geographical location.

FIGURE 1

NORTH AMERICAN CONTINENT
CULTURE AREAS

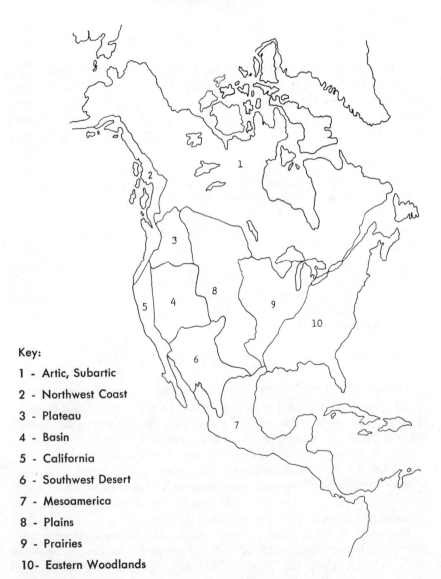

Key:

1 - Artic, Subartic

2 - Northwest Coast

3 - Plateau

4 - Basin

5 - California

6 - Southwest Desert

7 - Mesoamerica

8 - Plains

9 - Prairies

10- Eastern Woodlands

ORIGIN OF GAMES

The playing of games by native Americans was an integral part of their cultures. It has been stated that perhaps one of the most conspicuous similarities within the cultural milieu of the Indian tribes, attracting the attention of early writers, was the devotion to physical diversions, games, and gambling (Eisen 1977: 3).

There were many myths relating to games. Several dealt with the earliest origin of things, of gods playing games, sometimes after resorting to cheating. Within the natives' belief systems, games were officially sanctioned by the gods and culture heroes.

In Mesoamerica the rubber ball games occupied an important role in the daily lives of the Nahuatl and the Mayans. Innumerable references to the game in the codices and depictions of all the major gods as participants gave solid evidence of the ritualistic association that must have been of considerable antiquity (Kemrer 1968).

One myth illustrated the playing and patronage of the Indians' games by the divine Twins, the miraculous offspring of the Sun:

> "They rule night and day, winter and summer. They are the morning and evening stars...The divine Twins were always contending; they are the Indians' original patrons of play and their games are the games now played by men."
>
> (Culin 1970: 32).

Among the Navajo the gambling contest of the Hidden Ball Game (Moccasin Game) was legitimized by the origin myth that this was the manner in which the animals of the night and the animals of the day decided whether the earth would have continuous night or perpetual day. Each group wanted its own way, so a Hidden Ball Game was played. The winning side would have its choice. After two nights of playing the game and much "cheating" by the great destroyer, "Yeitso," who helped the night animals and the cunning Coyote (a culture hero) who helped whichever side was losing, the contest ended with neither side winning:

> So the day dawned on the undecided game. As the animals never met again to play for the same stakes, the original alternation of day and night has never been changed."
>
> (Matthews 1889: 6.)

This gaming technique for deciding major conflicts between the animals provided a symbolic referent for decision-making of man. In like manner, the association of game-playing by the gods might have been the people's rationalization for attributing to their gods what it was they themselves considered meaningful. Hans Damm (1970), German anthropologist, observed that exotic people know and celebrate sportive physical activities in the best meaning of the word, while similar games during cultic events derive from magic motives. It may even be that they demonstrate far distant events in dramatic form in order to radiate godly energies toward the well-being of mankind (Damm 1970: 65). Such energies revolved around the centroid symbol of fertility which provided man means of survival. The ball, as a game implement, frequently carried an iconic meaning of earth, sun or moon. Secondly it inferred fertility in the action of wind, thunder, and lightning, rain in life-sustaining elements in food production.

FUNCTIONS OF GAMES[2]

To better understand the role of games in the American Indian cultures, an examination of their instrumentality is necessary for games are reflective of and contribute toward the continuance of society. Some of these game functions include enculturation, communal cohesion, ritualization and symbolism, prestige, peaceful redistribution of wealth, and acculturation.

Enculturation of the young to the adult skills in culture was accomplished by limitation and directed choices of activities. Sex role differentiation in distinctive behavior society expected of females and males, was present, in child-training practices. Imitative learning was a strong socializing technique. Children were given replicas of objects used by adults, i.e., boys played with miniaturized versions of bows and arrows, sleds, canoes, carved or clay figures of birds, animals and fish, while girls made small models of dwellings, wood, stone, or ivory furnishings, utensils, dolls, and clothing (Flannery 1936; Watkins n.d.; Densmore 1929; Nelson 1897; Hodge 1905). Even gifts given to children assisted in this enculturation, such as the receiving of a Corn Kachina by Hopi boys. The symbolic learning of this "god-doll" was good fortune; therefore, it sometimes was called the Gambler's Kachina. The Hopi female infants were given the "Earth Mother" Kachina, symbolizing fertility, the expected role of women in that society.

Communal cohesion was strengthened through the game phenomenon, for playing in and wagering on games strictly followed kinship loyalties. Games provided rallying mechanisms for strengthening group identity as evidenced often in the literature. Intervillage and intertribal matches were common place. Morgan (1962) noted, "Challenges were often sent from one village to another and were even exchanged between nations to a contest of some of these games (athletic games and games of chance). In such cases the chosen players of each community were called out to contend for the prize of victory" (Morgan 1904: 291). Salter (1971) reported that group cohesiveness reached beyond those directly involved with the game to include the entire tribe. The feeling of unity was further reinforced by the numerous intertribal games and the stakes placed on those games. Stakes, if lost, could precariously tilt the delicate economic balance of the tribes.

Ritualization and Symbolism in games assured satisfying ceremonial experiences by participants and observers. Stewart Culin asserted that back of each game is found a ceremony in which the game was a significant part. He contended that the ceremony had disappeared, and the game survived as an amusement, but often with traditions and observances that serve to connect it with its original purpose of the rituals and symbolism of the various tribes (Culin 1903: 60–61).

The symbolic significance was noted in various ways, i.e., game implement characteristics, apparel worn by players, game procedures, game purposes. The hoop in the game, Hoop and Pole, was sometimes strung in the shape of a spider's web, this magical symbolic spider web spun by the mythical Spider Woman as her protection. A miniature netted shield was frequently employed in Zuni ceremonials (Cushing 1896). Culin (1907) contended that gaming implements were almost exclusively derived from war weapons of the symbolic Twin War Gods; sticks for stick game were arrows, snow snakes were either the club, bows, or arrows. The ball frequently represented the earth, sun or moon. The placing of gaming implements at shrines and altars was found in Western tribes (Culin 1907). Stickball players have been observed wearing attached to their waist bands of tails representing speed, bat wings representing agility or weaving bat whiskers in their rackets' webbing to insure maneuverability. Exemplar of ritualization is the Zuni Kick Ball Race with its elaborate sequence of pre-game activities meticulously supervised by the shaman or priest. Similarly the stickball game ritual is vividly described by Catlin (1973); Mooney (1890); Fogelson (1971).

Prestige as an important aspect of status was achieved in part by participation and winning in many games of physical skill and to a lesser degree in games of chance. Both sexes used the vehicle of physical achievement for recognition; however, seldom did they engage together in the same contest. The increased popularity of the stick ball game in southern Indian towns in the post-contact period is attributed in part to the game's replacement of war as a means of attaining prestige (Fogelson 1971). Blanchard (in press) reported that today in the Mississippi Choctaw individual participation in the team sport process is an important source of social prestige; being athletic is a positive characteristic of both male and female alike, and is often a fundamental element in Choctaw self-concept.

Safety valve for rivalry was provided in game contests. The Gros Ventre had an "enemy friend" relationship in which a man could select a potential rival as helper and companion in war or other great hazards. As the "friends" took liberties with each other through insults, joking, and derision, tension rose. To settle who was better a gambling event was held. The stakes were the property and status of each "enemy friend" (Flannery and Cooper 1946.)

Peaceful redistribution of wealth based on the outcome of games was a common trait of native Americans. Beauchamp (1896) observed that the aborigines had an innate love of gambling, and the idea of gain or loss entered into most of their simple sports. Two ways to gain increased goods, property, or service were based on kinetic competence through merits or the ability to win and on random selection inherent in chance games. Wagering on the outcome of either physical or chance contests was a hallmark of competition. Exchange took place immediately following the event. Great pains were taken to equalize the wagers, but not necessarily in value of items placed in hazard. Mechanism for settling disputes was a common use of dice (gambling) and Lacrosse/Stick ball games. In the 1830's the Cherokee and Choctaw tribes in Georgia played a Stickball game in which the stakes were each tribe's land. Peaceful distribution of a deceased person's possessions was accomplished by the use of a dice game. The Sioux Plum Stone Game (dice) was ceremoniously played by a respected tribal member against each of the deceased kin who always won the game. The wagers were part of the property of the dead (Beauchamp 1896).

Acculturation, the influence of a dominant culture on a less dominant one, is exemplified in the introduction of card playing by the Spanish soldiers in the early 1500s to the court of the Aztec ruler, Montezuma, in Tenochtitlan (site of present Mexico City). There appears to be no record of how or when the Indians adopted card playing, however Virginia Wayland (1961) recorded that the Apache made their own playing cards on rectangular pieces of dried raw hide by hand painting an adaptation of the Spanish suits, using the Spanish symbols of the sword, coin, goblet and club. The Apache cleverly adapted these to meaningful shapes in their own culture, i.e., the club became a saguaro cactus, the European goblet became an arrowhead.

The American team sport games of basketball, football, and softball as well as track events have been traditionally taught in the Bureau of Indian Affairs' Indian Boarding Schools. These, in addition to volleyball, lacrosse, stickball, and rodeo have become an important part of today's Indians' game reportoire (Cheska 1979).

However, according to Blanchard (1975) team games are played with close adherence to the Indian views of moeity cohesion, loyalty and social exchange. Indian youth appear to interpret team sports play more as one of internal socialization than one of "contesting" against others. There appears to be conflicting evidence on this point, Cheska (1979) found that southwest native American youth preferred to win a game and play to their best ability more than to "play for fun." According to Cheska (1979) those youth preferred to participate in team sports, i.e., basketball, baseball, softball, volleyball, football over other recreational choices.

TYPES OF GAMES PLAYED BY NATIVE NORTH AMERICANS

Games Defined: A game is considered to be a pleasurable, free, engrossing, process-oriented activity in which there are agreed-upon procedures, spatial and temporal limits, and uncertain outcomes. Game essentials include: 1) participants, opponents or sides; 2) organized procedures, fixed sequences of action or plot, and 3) uncertain outcome, resolution, or end result (Cheska 1979: 227). One basic component of a game is expressiveness of the participant in action; in other words, it is the enjoyment of the processual involvement. This state or condition of pleasure can frequently be inferred through behavioral cues. This second component of a game is the instrumentality of, by, and through the participant's action directed toward a goal. This game outcome infers accomplishment of a set goal. Physical skill games and strategy skill games ilicit the outcome by relative merit, competency, ability of participant actively contending against opponent(s). In chance games the participants are passive, rather than active, agents, receiving the outcome based on the fall of the dice or guessing the unknown placement of an object. Interestingly, in the Indian view the agent effecting the outcome of chance games is the supernatural being(s). By intervention, favorable or deleterious, the gods affect the conclusion of the game. If wagering or betting on a game's outcome is practiced, the outcome may provide a method of exchange.

Game Classes: The games of the Native North Americans may be divided into three general classes: games of physical skill, i.e., archery; games of chance, i.e., dice; and games of representation, i.e., playing dolls. Games of strategy, i.e., patolli, seldom appear in these cultures; however, European board games were introduced, i.e., capture board game "Fox and Geese". The pre-Columbian Mesoamerican circuit board game, Patolli, may be an important exception.

Within each dominant class, other classes can enter as secondary and tertiary factors. For example, in the boys' game of shooting an arrow into a hillock of sand, attempting to hit an arrow which has

Figure II. Kinds of Native North American Games

Ball Games	Projection Games	Court Games	Dice Game	Guessing Games	Imitation	Re-enactment
Field Games Lacrosse/Stickball Shinny Double Ball Goal Ball Foot Ball	*Accuracy* Archery Arrow and Dart Throwing Hoop and Pole Ring and Pin Shuttlecock Pop-gun	Rubber Ball Game (Tlachtli) Chunkey	Dice Games	Hand Game Hidden Ball Game Stick Game Four-Stick Game	*Boys' replicas:* Bows/Arrows Tops Sleds Snow shoes Canoes Rattles Animal Toys	Cat's Cradle Bull Roarer Buzzer
Foot Games Footcast Ball Hand-and-Foot Ball Kick Ball Race Kick Ball Relay	*Distance* Snow Snake Running				*Girls' replicas:* Dwelling House Furnishings Beddings Utensils Dolls Bull Boat	
Hand Games Juggling Tossed Ball/ Hand Ball	*Speed* Archery Running					

been hidden previously, the physical skill of shooting an arrow accurately was paramount; however, striking the hidden arrow had a decided element of chance which is a secondary factor. The acting out of the game may have represented the bison hunt of the children's fathers which can be considered representation, which is a tertiary factor in this game.

Game Kinds: Within the main classes of games are explicit sections which are further subdivided. *Games of Physical Skill* contain three categories: 1) ball games which can be further differentiated as: a) field games, b) foot games, and c) hand games; 2) projection games for: a) accuracy, b) distance, and c) speed; 3) court games. *Games of Chance* are divided into two categories: 1) dice games, and 2) guessing games. *Games of Representation* consist of activities which are: 1) representative of something, as imitations of process or replicas of objects, and 2) re-enactment of events. Children's and adult games can be included within all of the above categories. Please refer to Figure II–Kinds of Native North American Games which lists games by classes, categories, and specific activities.

GAMES OF PHYSICAL SKILL

1. *Ball Games*

a. *Field Games* were the most popular ball games played by Indians. Of these games of Lacross/Racket were the favorites of men and Shinny and Double Ball of women. Some variations of football games were field games.

There were several common features of the the field ball games which included the following: (1) A smoothed or cleared area of play was made ready with goal post(s) at the mid-point on the end lines. No side lines were designated. (2) Two opposing sides, ranging from six to one thousand players on a team, contended for victory. (3) The games were started by placing the ball in the mid-field spot or dug hole or, at ceremonial and inter-tribal matches, by the tossing in the game ball by a highly esteemed tribe member or visiting dignitary. (4) The ball was advanced toward the opponents' goal by the use of sticks, baskets, or feet. (5) The use of hands on the ball was usually prohibited. (6) A goal was scored by passing the ball through or over the goal or by wrapping a double-ball around the goal post. (7) Crude differentiation of player responsibility was made by assigning persons to the central area of action while others protected the goal. (8) Referees were used in important matches.

(9) The game concluded when one team had scored the agreed-upon number of goals, i.e., four, before the opponents.

William Strachey, first secretary of the Virginia colony, described Indian games of football

> "A kynd of Exercise they have often amongest them much like that which boyes call Bandy in English and may be an auncyent game...they have the exercise of Footeball, in which yet they only forceably encounter with the foote to carry the Ball the one from the other, and spurne yt to the goale with a kynd of dexterity and swift footmanshippe, which is the houour of yt..."
>
> (Strachey 1849: 84).

It should be noted that the players had no restrictions concerning body or stick contact with opponents: therefore, the action was very vigorous. In spite of hard fought games, and often high stakes, players appeared cheerful and did not openly retaliate. Field games were well attended by spectators. One Choctaw stickball game drew a crowd between 5000 to 6000 persons (Catlin 1973).

1) *Lacrosse* (Bagattaway) and *stickball* (sometimes called Rackets) were identical games played with a small wooden or a stuffed buckskin ball which was tossed with a deep pocketed netted racket between teammates or carried toward the opponents' goal. A point was scored by throwing the ball between two poles or striking one of the poles with the ball (Hudson 1976: 409). The playing field length ranged from three hundred feet to over a mile (Baldwin 1969).

Lacrosse, in which each player carried one racket, was more universally played than Racket which the southeast woodland tribes played with two rackets, one in each hand. The buckskin covered ball was firmly stuffed with fur, moss or grass; the wooden ball was rounded by burning and scraping. The wooden ball was considered the original and older form. So that it would hum in flight, right angle holes were sometimes drilled through the ball. In lacrosse and stickball, players usually wore only a waist band and a loin cloth; this was a great contrast to the heavily clothed lacrosse players of today. (N.A.I.T.C. 1978). "Good luck" talismans were presently worn, such as eagle feathers representing keen sight and a deer tail representing speed. According to Davis (1886) bat wings were attached to a player's costume and bat's whiskers woven into racket strings in the belief that this gave him bat-like maneuverability (Davis 1886; Hudson 1978).

Spectators gathered for important games. Heavy wagering was common. The bets were placed on the ground in two separated areas, depending on which team the spectator favored. Referees carefully regulated bets for equivalency. The game commenced by the forerunner of the modern face-off. A man from each team advanced to the center of the field and "with united bats raised it (the ball) from the ground to such an elevation as gave a chance for a fair shake" (N.A.I.T.C. 1978: 12). The game ended when one team scored a pre-set number of goals, ranging from four to twenty.

A few tribes permitted women to play lacrosse or stickball. Among them were the Choctaw, Creek, Ojibway, and Sioux. The Miwok (California) men, using only their feet to kick the ball, played against their women who used two spoon-shaped willow baskets, one in each hand, to scoop, carry, and throw the ball (Kroeber 1920). The North American Indians are credited with introducing Europeans to the game of Battagaway, the Indian name for Lacrosse. This game is still played today by Indians and Anglos alike. Each year the Mississippi Choctaw hold their stick ball championship (National Geographic, 1974) as do the Akwesasne Mohawk (N.A.I.T.C. 1978).

2) *Shinny* a hockey-type field goal game, was played in all seasons throughout most of the continent. A similar game was also played by the Araucanian Indians of Chili as reported by Nordenskiold (1910). It was usually a women's game; however, men of some southwest tribes played it. The playing field length varied from six hundred feet to fifteen hundred feet; the goals were usually two posts or stakes at each end of the field. However, a single post was used by several tribes, namely, the Menominee, Omaha, and Ponca; while the Eskimo, Makah, and Navajo drew lines in the snow or dirt across the end of the field.

The long-handled wooden stick varying from two and a half to three and a half feet, had a curved elongated club-like bottom which formed the striking surface and was similar to a modern field hockey stick. Wooden or buckskin balls were used. Any number might participate on a side, the number of persons on a team ranged from six to fifty. It was difficult to score a goal because each team had goal defenders. Usually the first team to score four goals won the game. Sometimes with each score the losers paid stakes to the winners (Reagan 1919).

3) *Double Ball,* a faster, more difficult variation of shinny, was played by women in the spring and summer. The playing field was shorter than in Shinny. The winning team was the first to pass the double ball through the goals or wrap it around the post (Gilmore 1926). Equipment unique to double ball were two balls or blocks of wood tied together with a six to twenty inch leather thong. The balls were scooped up, carried, thrown, and intercepted by the pointed stick carried by each player. The double ball varied in shape and construction: the Wichita connected two stuffed leather balls by a twenty-five inch leather thong; the northeastern Algonkians used elongated leather bags weighted with sand; southeastern tribes had

braided leather or willow bark strips with heavy knot tied at either end; wooden and bone cylinders were tied together with rawhide cord by the Plains Indians; the Osage women made dried buffalo meat double balls (Cheska 1974). This game has passed into oblivion.

4) *Single Pole Ball or Goal Ball* was played by the Southeastern Indians. "The game was played around a pole from 35 to 50 feet tall set in or near the square ground. Part way up the pole was a mark; a player who succeeded in throwing the ball and hitting the post above this mark scored one point. On top of the pole there was an object— either a square mat, some limbs from a tree, an animal skull, a wooden ball, or the carved image of a fish or eagle. Whoever succeeded in hitting this object scored as many as five points. Among the Creeks twenty points won the game" (Hudson 1978: 421). The small buckskin ball was thrown and caught in the netted pocket of a long stick. Each player was carried two sticks (Lerch and Welch 1978).

Several sixteenth and seventeenth century explorers noted the game. LeMoyne rendered an artistic depiction showing the Timucua Indians playing the game and noted, "They play a game in which they cast ball at a square target placed on the top of a high tree..." (Lorant 1965: 107). Don Tristan de Lune Arellano reported, "All the towns have good-sized plaza outside the town, in which there is a pole like the rollo (stone column in the old Spanish town plaza) of Spain; they are very tall, and they have them for their sports" (Priestly 1928: 239). Adair (1775) reported that the game was played during the summer months between the sexes. The men wagered venison and the women wagered bread.[3] Lerch and Welch (1978) reported that the game is played today very infrequently by the Seminole tribes of Florida and Oklahoma during the annual summer Green Corn Festival (1978: 92–93).

5) *Foot Ball* included a family of games in which a ball was passed, blocked, dribbled and otherwise propelled by the foot. As field games these were similar in dimension, players, and goals to those previously described.

b. *Foot Games* include Footcast Ball, Hand-and-Foot Ball, Kick Ball Race, and Kick Ball Relay.

1) *Footcast Ball* was played by California tribes. A heavy stone ball, weighing up to five pounds was cast or putted from the top of the foot to determine which participant could propel it the farthest. The motion was similar to a stationery place kick in soccer. The non-kicking foot remained stationary (Culin 1907).

2) *Hand-and-Foot Ball,* a women's game, was played by tapping the ball downward with the hand and kicking it up with the foot. In one variation, the thong to which the ball was attached was held

by the hand while the ball was flipped up in the air, then caught by the foot and redirected into the air. The performance was judged on rhythmic repetition and accuracy. The Mandan Sioux women would let the ball fall alternately to the knee and to the foot, tapping it upward in unbroken sequence. In the nineteenth century the Winnebago girls used a ball sewn from a stuffed stocking foot, an ingenious use of Anglo materials. Placing the ball on the toes of one foot the player repeatedly kicked the object upward a few inches without letting it fall to the ground. The first contestant to reach one hundred successive kicks won the game. Wagers were placed on the outcome of most Hand-and-Foot Ball games.

3) *Kick Ball Race* was played in southwestern areas. Two barefooted runners or two opposing teams of four each kicked a two to four inch ball or a small wooden cylinder around a cross-country course of twenty to thirty miles, ending back at the starting point (Underhill 1941). The ball was made of stone or wood (Haury 1945). Intervillage and inter-tribal races were important community events. They often were planned a year in advance. The Tarahumara Indians of Northern Mexico are outstanding long distance runners, proving their prowess even today by mountain "marathon" runs of over forty miles nonstop (Lumholtz 1884; Norman 1976).

The Kick Ball Race had elaborate sequences of pre-game activities, as did the Lacrosse and Stickball games. After the initial challenge issued to another tribe, the shaman (priest) assuming the role not unlike that of a modern coach, supervised many of the necessary preparations, such as the rigorous training of the players including a special diet, sleeping quarters, their purification through fasting and sexual abstinence; the clearing of the course; costuming the players; the pre-game dance; wagering; the starting line up. The declaration of the start of the race was performed by a prominent member of the tribe. With his bare foot the participant would thrust the ball into the air along the course and then speed after it. If the ball fell into the brush, loyal spectators would point to where it fell or, when allowed, replace the ball on the course. After the game came the division of wagered goods and often a feast (Stevenson 1903). The Kick Ball Race acquired ceremonial significance when it was performed for the protection of the crops from destructive wind or for rain in the race area. Stevenson (1903) ably describes the Zuni 25 mile ceremonial race for rain performed for their Gods of War and supervised by the Bow Priests; she also records the details of the betting race.

4) *Kick Ball Relay* was the same as the Kick Ball Race; however, only one-third of a mile was traversed, but covered repeatedly by two opposing teams. Marking sticks were placed at the spot where opposing players passed each other along the course. The winner

was declared when the marker stake finally reached the starting line of the opposing team.

c. *Hand Games* included Juggling and Tossed Ball/Hand Ball.

1) *Juggling* was popular with women of many culture areas. Two to six balls, ranging in diameter from one to five inches, were held in the hands. In rapid succession the juggler tossed two or more balls high in the air while passing others from one hand to the other, without dropping them or stopping. Inuit women were known to juggle four or five round pebbles simultaneously. The Basin Area women used water-worn stones; others used various fruit stones. Contests of skill were occasions for much betting. The woman who could juggle the most balls for the longest time won.

2) *Tossed Ball and Hand Ball* were similar in form and execution; both involved tapping or throwing a ball by the use of hands. The Montagnais of Labrador amused themselves with a game similar to "keep away," by tossing an oblong stuffed seal skin ball from one teammate to another while opponents attempted to intercept it. The Northwest Coast Tlingit and the Teton Sioux tribes threw a thick leather ball back and forth between two lines of players. The Crow women of the Montana area tapped the ball aerially in action similar to today's volleyball set-up. Their ball was a bladder about seven inches in diameter filled with antelope hair and wound together with sinew webbing.

2. *Physical Projection Skill Games* were played for accuracy, distance, or speed. The projective action encompassed: transferring the body force to another object, such as drawing back a bow preparatory to shooting an arrow; using a stick or racket to extend the body's capabilities; or propelling the body forward as in running. *Accuracy* type games included archery, arrow and dart throwing, hoop and pole, ring and pin, shuttlecock, and pop-gun. *Distance* type games included snow snake, canoe sliding. *Speed* type games included repetitive arrow shooting and running. These activities were engaged in by adults and also played with scaled-down implements by children.

a. *Accuracy Skill Games*

1) *Archery* served well to increase and maintain a survival competency. A good archer was held in high esteem, so archery-type games involving hitting stationary, hidden, or moving targets were popular (Morgan 1904).

The common hardwood bow with a recurve design increased the power of the arrow release, maximizing the arrow's velocity. The arrows were rounded from narrow branches or made of cut reeds with hardwood foreshaft insertion. Near the nock two to three feathers were tied to the shaft with thin strands of animal tendons.

The arrows were tipped with flint, chert, or wood, and varied from blunt to sharp edges according to purpose. Leather shoulder quivers held the arrows (Morgan 1904).

Flannery reported the Cree tribe custom:

> "At about six years of age boys were given small bows and arrows, and their greatest ambition is to be able to shoot well enough to kill a bird. Much ado is made over the killing of the first bird. The boy brings it to his grandfather or father who are immensely proud of him. Small though it is, it is duly prepared and then divided among the members of the family. The boy being given none of it, in order to teach him the tribal code of sharing with others."
>
> (Flannery 1946: 50.)

In shooting for accuracy, targets included an arrow standing upright in the ground; arrows arranged upright in a ring; an arrow lodged in a tree; a suspended woven grass bundle; or a roll of green cornhusks. The archer attempted to shoot an arrow which penetrated or dislodged the target(s).

The North Alaskan Inuit in winter moved archery indoors by hanging narrow pieces of wood representing ptarmigan birds from the karigi roof (communal center). Using miniature bows the men vied at shooting small arrows into the target. The man making the first successful hit was expected to bring food for all present. This was consistent with the custom that the skilled, and therefore prestigious, hunter could afford to feed others (Spencer 1959).

2) *Arrow and Dart Throwing* were variations of arrow shooting. In attempting to hit a target, the contestant threw an arrow from his hand. Also popular were darts with feathers inserted at one end, while the other end was pointed (Culin 1907; Howard 1965). A team game of the Shoshone and Arapaho tribes consisted of tossing an arrow in such a fashion that it stuck up right in the ground some two hundred feet away; each contestant then threw his arrow, trying to hit the marker. The side hitting the closest arrow to the marker scored and won the privilege of tossing the "marker" arrow for the next throw. In a more recent Shoshone anglo-ized version, concentric rings, similar to modern target archery face, were drawn on the ground and from the center were given descending numbers. The arrows were thrown for the highest scores (Slaugh 1935). Arrows and darts were also thrown for distance.

3) *Hoop and Pole* and ring and pin as accuracy projection games utilize the same principle, that of driving a straight object through a hole. These games were widespread throughout North America as well as in other areas of the world, such as Africa and Oceania (Raum 1953).

The idea of the dual principles of nature, the masculine and the feminine, were conspicuous in the symbolism of these games. The pole and pin were regarded as masculine; the hoop or ring were symbolic of the feminine principle. Culin remarked:

"The netted wheel (hoop) is copied from the spider-web, the attribute of the Spider-woman, the Earth-goddess, the mother of the Twin-gods."

(Culin 1903: 62)

The Hoop and Pole game was played by men. A wooden hoop, ranging from six to twenty-four inches in diameter was elaborately decorated in various ways by winding dyed sinew, rawhide strips, or by weaving sinew strips to resemble a spider-web. A plain hoop was sometimes divided in half or quarters by differing colors, i.e., red and blue. Sometimes six colored bead columns, projecting into the center, were attached to a small hoop. The throwing poles measured up to fifteen feet in length.

The usual procedure was for two opponents with poles in hand to stand at right-angles to the held hoop. Usually a non-contestant then rolled the hoop past the two opponents. Each player threw his pole, attempting to drive it through the hoop or have the hoop fall on the pole. The player scored who impaled the hoop or had his pole in contact with hoop's higher counting areas which were determined by color and relative position from center (Walker 1909).

4) *Ring and Pin*, sometimes called Ball and Cup, was played universally. Although there were many forms, the procedures can be noted from the deer-foot game. A number of perforated bones from a deer's foot were strung upon a thin leather cord which was attached at the other end to a needle of bone or wood. Holding the pin (needle) by one hand, the player flipped the stringed bones into the air, and caught a particular bone upon the end of the pin (Hodge, 1905). The Southwest Pima and Papago tribes played the game using dried squash rind rings attached on a string that had a small stick fastened at the other end (Underhill 1951). The score was based on placement and size of the rings the player was able to catch with the pin. Vertebrae of fish were frequently used for rings; some Eskimo tribes played with a slender stick and a seal humerus. As a team game each group had up to ten members. Each player had one turn; the game was ten points (Drucker 1951).

5) *Shuttlecock* or Battledore, a batting game localized on the west coastal and southwest regions, was played with a small flat, wooden paddle and a "cock" made from a two to three inch wooden dowel with feathers inserted on one end. Some paddles were wooden

slats lashed to a handle, forming a square hitting surface. The southwestern tribes made their shuttlecocks by plaiting green corn-husks into a two inch flat square, and lashing two bird feathers upright on one side (Stevenson 1903). The game consisted of batting the shuttlecock with the paddle up into the air the greatest number of times without letting it drop to the ground (Drucker 1951).

6) A *Pop-gun* was usually made by boys in the fall season from two round pieces of ash or alder wood or bark. A hole in which a second piece could be inserted was cleared by pushing out the pith in the center of the first piece. A small missile, such as a wad of tree bark, fiber or berries, was shot from the pop-gun at playmates by Eastern Woodland, Southwest, California, and Plains children (Dorsey 1891; Rowell 1943).

b. *Distance Skill Games*

1) *Snow Snake,* a physical projection skill game, was a popular winter sport in northern tribes. In this game participants competed for distance by hurling darts or javelins along snow or ice troughs or through the air. Three kinds of projectiles were used: the snow snake which was a long polished wooden rod, usually with a weighted round knob head; a bone-slider, which was a piece of bone or horn into which two feathers were inserted; and a javelin which was a wooden pole feathered at one end and tipped with horn at the other (Culin 1907; Morgan 1904; Parker 1909). This game was a test of power and skill in sliding the long, slender rod along a channel cut in the snow. The snow was depressed by pulling a heavy log through a cleared space for as long as a half mile and then icing the channel. The "snake" was thrown underhanded by curling the forefinger around the back end and supporting it with the thumb and remaining fingers; however, some players preferred the overhand throwing pattern. The long shaft bent as it slid over the ice or snow, resembling a gliding snake (Beauchamp 1896). Sometimes the snow snake would run over thirteen hundred feet (Reagan 1919).

A *Snow Boat* was a unique Iroquois adaptation which was slid along a trench or path. The boat was a solid fifteen inch long canoe made of hard wood. Participants sometimes poured water on the trench to make it icy, smooth, and fast (Morgan 1904).

2) *Running* was a common method of travel for Indians; however, competitive races were frequently staged during the spring and summer. Most popular was distance running, in which competitors covering as much as thirty miles. Some Ojibway men trained by weighting their ankles with sand-filled leather bags (Hoffman 1980). The Navajo Indians held races frequently. The kick ball racing, previously mentioned, was the most popular Hopi running game. The Tarahumara people of northern Mexico were the best distance runners known; their name literally means running people.

c. *Speed Skill Games*

1) *Archery for speed* was found in some tribes. One archer would stand ready to draw his bow. In releasing the first arrow he attempted to have the arrow in flight as long as possible because the winner was the man who could shoot the most arrows in the air before his first arrow hit the ground (Catlin 1973).

2) *Running for speed* was sometimes coupled with distance running. The first individual or team to return to the starting point or to complete the relay circuit was declared the winner (For further detail refer to section 2.b.2).

3. *Court Games* demanding great physical skill were rubber ball games and chunkey. Of the several rubber ball varieties, only one will be described here.[4]

a. *The Rubber Ball Game* was popular in Mesoamerica, the Caribbean Islands, and in Arizona territory from approximately 100 to 1500 A.D. (deBorhegi 1960). An inventory taken in 1969 of known ball courts identified in Mesoamerica totaled 269, in the Caribbean Islands 24, and in Arizona 87 (Glassford 1969). The two most common shapes of courts were the letter "I" and the "oval" shape. Their dimensions varied from the largest of 482 by 119 feet to the smallest of 65 to 20 feet, both extremes located in Chichen Itza, Yucatan, Mexico. The courts were built of hewn stone and plastered smooth on the inside walls. In the mid-point on each side of the walled enclosure was sometimes mounted a stone or wood vertical ring or goal (Blom 1932). Courts without rings were common in the southern Mesoamerican region excluding the Toltec area, while those with rings have been found in the northern region. The unique ball used was of solid rubber made from the latex of the rubber tree. It should be noted that this was the first known use of a rubber ball in the world. Columbus was so impressed with the rebound qualities of the ball, he carried several samples back to the court of Spain, thus introducing the concept of the rebound ball to Europe. The ball's diameter ranged from five to twelve inches, matching the inside diameter of mounted rings through which the ball could pass. The court marking divided the surface vertically, (lengthwise) rather than horizontally as in basketball. Some I-shaped courts had end zones into which the ball could be hit by agile players.

The two opposing teams lined up with the center player nearest the mid-point of the vertical division line while his teammates, up to four, stood diagonally to the side and behind the center player. The game was commenced by the umpire dropping the ball into center court or by the serving side throwing the ball into their opponent's court. The ball had to be struck with only the thigh, hip and knee; contact with any other part was a body foul. The object of the game was to cause the opposing team to commit an error in play. Ways of scoring included: 1) the ball was sent over the end wall or made contact with it; 2) the ball went dead within the opponent's half of the court; 3) the ball touched a part of an opponent's body other than the thigh, knee or hip. The game could be won outright if a player could hit the ball through the opponent's ring. This was infrequent (Glassford 1969; Clune 1979).

The game was a great spectator sport. There was much wagering on the outcome of the game. The recreational function of the Arizona ball court game can be inferred, for the courts were often constructed at the edge of the villages. In Mesoamerica the rubber ball courts were usually built within the culture's religious complex; and priests were involved in ceremonies surrounding the game. A human sacrifice cult seemed to be connected with the ball game (Kemrer, 1968).

Because the rubber ball varied in weight from five to eight pounds, protective equipment was worn by players: a leather hip apron, gloves, knee pads, face mask, and possibly a head piece. There is disagreement concerning the use of the yoke, a stone collar-like implement which balanced on a player's hip. Yokes are often found in relation with ball court players, being depicted on Mesoamerican figurines, stelae, and wall murals. Whether carved stone yokes were actually worn during play or only for ceremonial purposes has long been a point of controversy among scholars (Ekholm 1946; Kemrer, 1968). The handstones associated with the game are also suspect (De Borhegyi 1961). Other artifacts thought to represent ball player's equipment are palmate stones, hachas, elbow and knee stones.

Probably the peak of the ball court game cult in Mesoamerica was between 450 to 700 A.D. and the height of its popularity in Arizona territory was 900 to 1100 A.D. (Pasztory 1972.) By the time Hernando Cortez, the Spanish adventurer, entered Mexico in 1517, the rubber ball game, Tlachtli, was in decline. In Mesoamerica vestiges of ancient rubber ball games, such as Pelota, were still being played in the 1900's. Kelly (1943), Swezey (1973); and Humphrey (1979) have evidence that such games are played today in remote rural areas of Mexico from Oxaca north.

b. *Chunkey,* a game played by Indian men of the south, was in principle similar to hoop and pole, but chunkey was played in a confined square of hard packed dirt with fine sand strewn over it, making a smooth surface for rolling a small stone disk. The stones were discoidal in shape and varied from two and a half to six inches in diameter and from one to two inches in thickness (Farmer 1953). The disk rolled on its rim over the ground, much like the hoop. The slender poles varying in length from eight to sixteen feet were thrown at the rolling stone (Swanton 1911; Davis 1886). The court's length was approximately two hundred feet. Chunkey play was described by Davis:

> "They play two together having each a straight pole about fifteen feet long; one holds a stone which he throws before him over this alley, and the instant of its departure, they set off and run; in running they cast their poles after the stone; he that did not throw it endeavors to hit it; the other strives to strike the pole of his opponent hitting the stone. If the first should strike the stone he counts one for it, and if the other by the dexterity of his cast should prevent the pole of his opponent hitting the stone, he counts one, but should both miss their aim the throw is renewed."
>
> (Davis 1886: 37–38.)

GAMES OF CHANCE

Games of chance historically have been found in all of the North American culture areas. The two general division games of chance are: 1) Dice games, and 2) Guessing games.

1. *Dice games,* in which a number was determined by throwing an object called a die at random, were played by one hundred and thirty North American Indian tribes belonging to thirty linguistic stocks of an approximate total of three-hundred tribes (Culin 1907). The basic principle of dice games was that each die had two faces or sides distinguished by colors or markings. Depending on the natural resources available, varying materials were used in making dice, such as split canes or reeds, wooden staves or blocks, bone staves, beaver and woodchuck teeth, walnut shells, peach and plum stones, grains of corn, and disks of bone, shell, brass or pottery, and ivory bird shaped dice.

The die was either thrown by hand or tossed within a bowl or basket. Dice cast by hand were tossed in the air against a tautly held animal hide or blanket. They sometimes were struck ends down upon a flat stone or hide disk. Another method was to allow them to fall freely upon the ground, hide or blanket. Dice tossed in a bowl or basket were shaken to upset the dice. A sharp blow on the side of the bowl or basket was also employed as well as striking the container against the ground.

Scoring was based upon the total number of like sides which appeared face up when the dice were tossed. The highest number was assigned when all dice appeared with the same side up; the next highest number was assigned if all but one so appeared, and so forth. Often one side was preferred to another. For example, in the Stick Dice game the flat side was preferred to the rounded side as is evident by the difference in scoring between them. The scoring roughly followed the law of probability, with the highest score given for the least probable fall of the dice.

> 3 round sides up = 10 points
> 3 flat sides up = 10 points
> 2 flat sides up = 3 points
> 2 round sides up = 2 points
> A throw of ten gives another throw

There were several methods of counting or keeping score. In one the score was kept with thin sticks or counters which pass from one opposing side to the other or from a neutral pool to the winner. In another, the score was kept with sticks, each side starting out with the same number of counters. These were forfeited in accordance with the opponent's scoring. The game terminated when one opposing side won all the counters. A third counting system was a circuit, often of small stones, along which a stick was placed progressively in accord with the score of the dice throw. Thus the total of stones could be added from starting point to each side's scoring stick to obtain a cumulative score. The side which completed the circuit first won the game.

Gambling kits, highly treasured by both men and women, contained the individual's gaming pieces held in a parfleche or pouch, usually made of decorated leather or cloth. The Cree Indians believed that a person who sold his gaming set also sold his playing rights to that game for life, because the supernatural powers were included in the sale.

2. *Guessing games* include the Hand game, Hidden Ball Game, Stick Game, and Four-Stick Game.

a. *The Hand Game,* the most common of the guessing games, utilized small short bone or wood cylinders, some solid, others hollow which could be hidden from an observer when held in the hands. These were in matching pairs, one or two sets being used in a game. One piece of each pair was distinguished by having a thong of leather string, strand of cloth, or ring of bark tied about the middle. The unmarked bone was often designated as the "man" and the marked bone was the "woman."

The Hand Game was usually played indoors. On the west coast it was often called the Grass Game because the players customarily hide the two cylinders in bundles of grass (Baldwin 1969). The number of players varied from two to any number; however, there were always only two opposing sides. The opponents seated themselves upon the ground, facing each other, and the stakes were commonly placed between the two lines. The side holding the cylinders, sometimes behind their backs, behind a blanket, or in grass bundles, sang traditional gambling songs, moving their hands and bodies to distract the opposing team's guesser. When the guesser had figured out where the unmarked cylinder was being held, he indicated his choice by swiftly extending his hand and fingers. If he guessed correctly in which opponent's hand or pile the "male" was held, the object went over to his side. If the guesser missed, his side forfeited one stick. The side ending with all the counters, ranging from five to sixteen per game, was declared the victor. This was followed by the exchange of stakes which had been bet. This game has survived and is avidly played at modern Pow Wows (Boyd 1979).

b. *The Hidden Ball Game* or Moccasin Game was played by two sides or teams sitting face to face. One team hid some small object such as a ball, stone, or grain kernel, bean, piece of animal horn or even a bullet in one of several containers, usually numbering four. The receptacles often employed included bamboo cane tubes, wooden cups, or buckskin moccasins. Each container carried distinctive markings for adequate identification. These were frequently covered with sand, bark, or grass.

Following a set procedure or game ritual, the appointed guesser from the opposing team pointed to the container in which he thought the object was concealed, frequently using a decorated pointer. When he guessed correctly his side received a point or counter and the right to guess again. A graduating penalty system was imposed for number of wrong guesses. A game consisted of ten points. Well defined ritual paraphrenalia, appointed guessers, umpires, songs, and rules of betting refined the game. Seldom did women play the Hidden Ball Game in public.

c. *The Stick Game* was played with small wooden, pencil-thin cylinders, painted with bands of bright colors, or with long thin bended or plain splints. In the Northwest Coast area flat yew wood discs were edged with incised markings. Playing pieces varied from eleven to more than one hundred. The game consisted of one team guessing which one of two or more piles contained an odd number of pieces. On the Pacific Coast the sticks or discs were hidden in a mass of shredded cedar bark or dry grass. On the Atlantic Coast the sticks were commonly held free in the hands. Several games were played consecutively and heavy betting usually accompanied each game.

d. *The Four-Stick Game* was played by California, Basin, and Northwest Coast tribes, but was not found in the eastern areas. It was played with four sticks or bones, two larger and two smaller.

The objects were arranged in one of six combinations: 11″; 1″1; 1′1′; ′1′1; ′11′; ″11. Players of one side hid the four pieces under a blanket or large basket tray. The guesser of the opposing side attempted to identify the arrangement of the objects correctly. If he succeeded, he received and thrust into the ground before his team one or two counters, according to the value of his guess. If the guess was wrong, he forfeited one counter and guessed again, but at this stage the hiding team only concealed two of the sticks, one large one and one small. If the guesser was correct on the second try, he received no counter, but the sticks were passed to him, and his team hid them. The counters for a game varied from six to ten. The game ended when one team had all the counters (Cheska 1974).

The North American natives had a great love of gambling. The idea of gain or loss entered into most of their games. Often a player would be willing to stake everything on the turn of a game, the throw of the dice, or accurate guess.

GAMES OF REPRESENTATION

Representation games include two major categories: 1) imitations or replicas of objects, and 2) re-enactment of events.

1. *Imitation or replicas of objects* and the imitations of the actions accompanying the utilization of the objects were largely identified with games of children. In the North American native cultures, representation games were used to teach children through play needed adult skills.

Small versions of bow and arrows, sleds, snow-shoes, canoes, rattle, toys simulating the movements of animals, carved or clay figures of birds, animals and fish were frequently given to boys (Hodge 1905; Walker 1906; Densmore 1929; Flannery 1936; Ewers 1958). The skins of small animals and birds were sometimes stuffed with maple sugar or rice, so young children would become familiar with handling wild life before it became a necessity (Densmore 1929). The girls made small dwelling models in which they placed their wood, stone, or ivory house furnishings, fur bedding, small wood, bone or stone utensils (Flannery 1936; Hodge 1905; Watkins n.d.). Young girls were also given dolls and cradles made from various materials: a wrapped corn husk, pine branch ends trimmed to stimulate appropriate limbs, carved wooden figures, woven reed and moss sewn together in the human shape. (Watkins; Ewer 1958). In northern tribes bull boat replicas were gifts for girls, for when they became adults the flat bottomed, round-walled boat would be used for transporting household wares across water. (Hodge

1905; Densmore 1929). The Inuit parents were particulary apt at providing "play learning" for their children with representative objects for imitation of activities.

Some children's activities were not necessarily representative, but provided unique pleasure. Whip and hand tops for spinning on smooth ice or hardened surfaces were extremely popular. Sleds made by lashing together buffalo ribs were used for sliding down snow covered hills. A buffalo hide which had not been dressed was also used for sledding, thus removing unwanted hair and increasing the skin's pliability (Gilmore 1926). Stilts were used for "high walking" among the Hopi and Shoshone (McCaskill 1936).

2. *Re-enactment of Events* moved closer to Indian mythical tradition.

a. *The String Figures,* often called Cat's Cradle, were common throughout North America and in all other continents. A string loop was manipulated with the hands to form various representations, e.g., a rope, ladder, crow's feet, threading the needle (Haddon 1903). Davidson reported that the Virginia Indians, adults and children, practiced making string figures continuously (Davidson 1929). The Inuits developed elaborate string figures during the long, dark cold winters when much time was spent inside the igloos (Glassford 1976).

b. *The Bull Roarer* and buzz were two forms of noise makers. Both have been associated with ritual ceremonies. Among the Hopi and Apache tribes the bull roarer had a sacred use in assisting the prayers of the Shaman or medicine man to bring on the storm clouds and rain (Mooney 1896). Both are used in many areas of the world under various names, but the concept of loud continuous sound in supplication is general. The Bull Roarer, sometimes referred to as the wind whirler, consisted of a thin blade of wood about a foot long attached to a pliable thong which was fastened to a wooden handle. By holding the handle above the head and swinging in a circular motion, the blade rotated rapidly, making a loud whirling noise. When several persons swung their bull roarers at the same time, the whizzing sound was great. Boys of the Plains made this a contest to see who could keep the bull roarer continually whirling for the longest time.

c. *The Buzzer* or hummer was made from a short bone or a wooden button-like disk which was fastened to the middle of a sinew string about one and a half to three feet long. Sometimes at each end of the sinew string a short stick was fastened to serve as a hand hold. These sticks were taken, one in each hand, and the bone whirled circularly so as to twist the string. When the string became drawn short and taut, it quickly untwisted, rapidly whirling the bone so that its motion would twist the string in the opposite direction. This process was repeated indefinitely, the motion of the bone making a buzzing noise (Mooney 1896).

Sioux boys played a game called "buffaloes fighting" in which several boys spun their buzzers simultaneously to represent the bellowing of the buffalo bulls. They approached each other and struck the bones together. If a player's bone stopped buzzing, he was defeated (Walker 1906).

The string figures, bull roarer, and buzzer were examples of children's toys that earlier were sacred and esoteric, but later survived in play (Flannery 1936).

CONCLUSIONS

The accessibility of most areas of the North American hemisphere made possible extensive borrowing of cultural features, including games, by peoples occupying the continent.

The importance of games in the lives of the North American Indians was reinforced by the belief that their gods played and approved games.

Several functions in the lives of the people were served by games, such as communal cohesion, ritualization and symbolism, prestige, peaceful redistribution of wealth, and acculturation.

Prominent kinds of games played by native North Americans were: A. *games of physical skill* which included 1) field games, i.e. lacrosse/stick ball; foot games, i.e. kick ball race; hand games, i.e. juggling; 2) projection games for accuracy, i.e. archery; distance, i.e. snow snake; speed, i.e. running; 3) court games, i.e. chunkey; B. *games of chance* which included 1) dice games, 2) guessing games, i.e. hand games; and C. *games of representation* which included 1) imitation games, i.e. sleds and 2) re-enactment of events, i.e. cat's cradle.

NOTES

1. The term native American is being used as a synonym for Indian and Eskimo. Both of these terms were early imposed as descriptions of peoples present in North America when "discovered" by Europeans. Indian, which was used to refer to East Indians of south Asia, was mistakenly applied to North American natives whose continent blocked the sought-for western route to the fabulous trade goods of Asia. The term Eskimo (Esquimaux) meaning "eaters of raw meat" was used to describe the Inuit peoples of the areas, Greenland, northern Canada, Alaska and the Arctic Islands.

2. For further in-depth analysis of game functions the reader is referred to an article, "Native American Games as Strategies of Societal Maintenance" by A.T. Cheska, 1979, in which she examines social processes related to games

of sex role differentiation, group identity, decision-making models, and symbolic identification.

3. The author wishes to acknowledge the early single pole ball reference of LeMoyne, (Lorant, Don Tristan, de Lune Arellano, Priestly, and Adair from the reported research of George Eisen's unpublished manuscript "Games and Sporting Diversions of the North American Indians as Reflected in American Historical Writings of the Sixteenth and Seventeenth Centuries," 1977, pp. 5–6.

4. Theodore Stern's book, *The Rubber-Ball Games of the Americas*, Seattle: University of Washington Press, 1949, provides an excellent analysis and geographical distribution of the several game variations using a rubber ball. Ball games of South America, Antille and Central America, Mexico and Southwestern United States are examined from the kind of ball, method of striking the ball and manner of bodily manipulation, as well as competitive ball game and circle games. The rubber ball court game (Tlachtli) and another court game (Pelota Vasca) of Mexico are compared.

REFERENCES

Adair, J. 1775. *The History of the American Indians.* London: Printed for Edward and Charles Dilly.

Baldwin, G. 1969. *Games of the American Indian.* New York: Grosset & Dunlap, Inc.

Beauchamp, W.M. 1896. Iroquois games. *Journal of American Folk-Lore,* 1:32: 269–277, January-March,.

Blanchard, K. 1975. Team sports and social organization among the Mississippi Choctaw." Paper presented at the meeting of the American Anthropological Association, San Francisco, December.

Blanchard, Kendall. *The Serious Side of Leisure: The Mississippi Choctaw at Play.* Manuscript in Press.

Blom, F. 1932. The Maya ball game Pok-ta-Pok (called Tlachtli by the Aztecs). Middle American Research Series, No. 4, New Orleans: Tulane University.

Boyd, Susan. 1979. Stick games/hand games: the great divide. In Farrer, C. and Norbeck, E. (Eds.), *Forms of Play of Native North Americans.* St. Paul: West Publishing Company.

Catlin, G. 1973. *Letters and Notes on the Manner, Customs, and Conditions of North American Indians.* Volume II. New York: Dover Publications, Inc. (Originally published: London: Constable and Company, Ltd., 1884.)

Cheska, A. 1974. Guessing and Gambling Games: Play Patterns of North American Indian Cultures. Paper presented at the meeting of the North American Society for Sport History, London, Ontario, Canada, May, 1974.

Cheska, A. 1974. Guessing and gambling games: Play patterns of North American Indian cultures. Paper presented at the meeting of the North American Society for Sport History, London, Ontario, Canada, May, 1974.

Cheska, A. 1979. Native American games as strategies of societal maintenance. In Farrer, C. and Norbeck, E. eds., *Forms of Play of Native North Americans.* St. Paul: West Publishing Company.

Cheska, A. 1979. Indian youths' sports choices today and some historic notions why. Paper presented at the North American Society for Sport History, University of Texas, Austin, June.

Culin, S. 1903. American Indian games. *American Anthropologist,* New Series, 5: 58–64.

Culin, S. 1907. *Games of the North American Indians.* 24th Annual Report of the Bureau of American Ethnology, Washington: U.S. Government Printing Office.

Cushing, F.H. 1896. *Outlines of Zuni Creation Myths.* Thirteenth Annual Report of the Bureau of American Ethnology. Washington, D.C.: Government Printing Offices.

Damm, Hans. 1970. The so-called sport activities of primitive people: a contribution towards a genesis of sport. In Lüschen, G. *The Cross-Cultural Analysis of Sport and Games.* Champaign, Illinois: Stipes Publishing Company.

Davidson, D.S. 1927. Some string figures of the Virginia Indians. *Indian Notes,* 4:4: 384–395, October.

Davis, A.M. 1886. Indian games. *Bulletin of the Essex Institute,* Salem, Massachusetts: Salem Press.

deBorhegyi, S.F. 1969. America's Ballgame. *National History,* 69:1:48–59, January.

deBorhegyi, S.F. 1961. Ball-game handstones and ball-game gloves. In Lothrop, S. et al. *Essays in Pre-Columbian Art and Archaeology.* Cambridge, Mass.: Harvard University Press.

Densmore, F. 1929. Chippewa customs. Bureau of American Ethnology, *Bulletin 86,* Washington: U.S. Government Printing Office, 65–70, 114–119.

Dorsey, J.O. 1891. Games of Teton Dakota Children. *American Anthropologist,* Old Series, 4:329–345.

Drucker, P. 1951. The Northern and Central Nooktan Tribes. Bureau of American Ethnology, *Bulletin 144,* Washington: U.S. Government Printing Office, 445–452.

Eisen, G. 1977. Games and sporting diversions of the North American Indians as reflected in American historical writings of the sixteenth and seventeenth centuries." Unpublished manuscript, University of Maryland.

Ekholm, C.F. 1946. The probable use of Mexican stone yokes. *American Anthropologist,* 48:593–606.

Ewers, J.C. 1958. *The Blackfeet: Raiders on the Northwestern Plains.* Norman: University of Oklahoma Press.

Farmer, M.F. 1953. Southern California Discoidals. *The Masterkey,* 27:5: 177–183, September-October.

Flannery, R. 1936. Some aspects of James Bay recreative culture. *Primitive Man,* 9:4:49–56, October.

Flannery, R. and J.M. Cooper. 1946. Social mechanism in Gros Ventre gambling. *Southwestern Journal of Anthropology,* 2:391–419.

Fogelson, R.D. 1971. The Cherokee Ballgame Cycle: An Ethnographer's View, *Ethnomusicology,* 15:327–338.

Gilmore, M.R. 1926. The Meso-American rubber ball games. *Indian Notes,* 3:293–295.

Glassford, R.G. 1969. The Meso-American rubber ball games. *Proceedings of the First International Seminar on the History of Physical Education and Sport,* Netanya, Israel: Wingate Institute.

Glassford, R.G. 1976. *Application of a Theory of Games to the Transitional Eskimo Culture.* New York: Arno Press.

Haddon, A.C. A few American string figures and tricks. *American Anthropologist*. New Series. 5:213-223.

Haury, E.W. 1945. Excavation of Los Muertos and neighboring ruins in the Salt River Valley, Southern Arizona. *Peabody Papers*, 24(1)140.

Hodge, F.W. 1905. *Handbook of American Indians North of Mexico*. Bureau of American Ethnology, Bulletin 30, Part I, Washington: U.S. Government Printing Office, 50-51, 127, 483-486.

Hoffman, W.J. 1890. Remarks on Ojibwa ball play. *American Anthropologist*, 3:2:133-135, April.

Howard, J.H. 1965. The Ponca Tribe. Bureau of American Ethnology, *Bulletin, 195,* Washington: U.S. Government Printing Office, 125-130.

Hudson, C. 1978. *The Southwestern Indians*. Knoxville: University of Tennessee Press.

Humphrey, R. 1979. Personal communication. Washington, D.C.: George Washington University.

Kelly, I. 1943. Notes on a West Coast Survival of the Ancient Mexican Ball Game. *Notes on Middle American Archaelogy and Ethnology,* Division of History—Research, Number 26, Washington: Carnegie Institute of Washington, 164-175.

Kemrer, M.F. Jr. 1968. A re-examination of the ball-game in Pre-Columbian Meso-america. *Ceramica de Cultura Maya et al.,* Philadelphia Temple university, 5:1-25, December.

Kroeber, A.W. 1920. Games of California Indians. *American Anthropologist* 22:273-277.

LeMoyne. Engraving of Exercises of the Timucua Indians. In Lorant, *The New World.* New York: Duell, Sloan and Pierre, 1965.

Lerch, H.A., and Welch, P.D. 1978. A ball game played by the Florida Seminoles during the green corn festival. *Research Quarterly,* 49:1:91-94.

Lorant, S. Ed. 1965. *The New World.* New York: Duell, Sloan & Pierre.

Lumhotz, C. 1894. Tarahumari life and customs. *Schribner's Magazine* 3:296-311. 3:296-311.

Matthews, Washington. 1889. Navajo gambling songs. *American Anthropologist.* Old Series, 2:1-19.

McCaskill, J.C. 1936. Indian Sports. *Indians at Work,* 3:2:29-30, July 1.

Mooney, J. 1890. The Cherokee Ball Play. *American Anthropologist* 3:2: 105-132.

Mooney, J. 1896. *The Ghost-Dance Religion.* 14th Annual Report of the Bureau of Ethnology, Part II, Washington: U.S. Government Printing Office.

Morgan, L.H. 1904. *League of the Ho-de-no-sau-nee, or Iroquois.* New York: Dodd, Mead & Company. Originally published in 1851.

National Geographic Society. 1974. *The World of the American Indian.* Washington, D.C.,: National Geographic Society, pp. 142-145.

Norman, J. 1976. The Tarahumaras. Mexico's long distance runners. *National Geographic,* 149:702-18.

North American Indian Travelling College (NAITC) 1978. *Tewaarathon (Lacrosse)—Akewasne's Story of Our National Game.* Cornwall Island, New York: North American Indian Travelling College.

Nordenskiold, E. 1910. Spiele und Spielsachen im Gran Chaco und in Nordamerika. *Zeitschrift für Ethnologie* 42:427-433.

Parker, A.C. 1909. Snow-Snake as played by the Seneca-Iroquois. *American Anthropologist* 11.

Pasztory, E. 1972. The historical and religious significance of the Middle Classic ball game. In J.L. Minh and N.C. Terjero Eds., *Religion en Meso-america.* Mesa Redona, Mexico: Sociedad Mexicana DeAnthropolgia. 441–445.

Priestly, H.I. 1928. *The Luna Papers.* Deland: The Florida State Historical Society, Vol. 1.

Raum, O.F. 1953. The Rolling Target (Hoop-and-Pole) Game in Africa, Part I, *African Studies,* 12:3:104–121.

Reagan, A.B. 1943. Some games of the Bois Fort Ojibwa. *American Anthropoligist,* 21:3:264–278.

Rowell, M.F. 1943. Pamukey Indian games and amusements. *Journal of American Folk-Lore,* 56:221:203–207.

Salter, M. 1972. The effect of acculturation on the game of Lacrosse and on its role as an agent of Indian survival. *Canadian Journal of History of Sport and Physical Education,* 3:1:28–43.

Slaugh, S.F. 1935. The Shoshone love fun. *Indians at Work,* 2:22:28.

Smith, J. 1972. The native American ball games. In Hart, Marie M. *Sport in the Sociocultural Process.* Dubuque, Iowa: Wm. C. Brown, Co.

Spencer, R.F. 1959. *The North Alaskan Eskimo.* Bureau of American Ethnology, Bulletin 171, Washington: U.S. Government Printing Office.

Stern, T. 1949. *The Rubber-Ball Games of the Americas.* Seattle: University of Washington Press.

Stevenson, M.C. 1903. Zuni games. *American Anthropologists,* New Series, 5:468–497.

Strachey, William. 1849. *The Historie of Travaile into Virginia Britannia,* London: Printed for the Hakluyt Society.

Swezey, W.R. 1973. The ballgame La Pelota Mixteca. *Revista.* 1:1:21–24.

Swanton, J.R. 1911. *Indian Tribes of the Lower Mississippi Valley and Adjacent Coast of the Gulf of Mexico.* Bureau of American Ethnology, Bulletin 43, Washington: U.S. Government Printing Office.

Tylor, E.B. 1896. On American lot-games. *Internationales Archiv fur Ethnographie* 9:55–67, Supplement.

Underhill, R. 1941. *The Papago Indians of Arizona and Their Relatives, the Pima.* Washington: U.S. Department of Interior, Bureau of Indian Affairs, Branch of Education.

Underhill, R. 1951. *People of the Crimson Evening.* Riverside: U.S. Indian Service.

von Mathys, F.K. 1976. *Spiel und Sport der Indianer in Nordamerika.* Basel, Switzerland. Schweizerischen Turn–und Sportmuseum.

Walker, J.R. 1906. Sioux games II. *Journal of American Folk-Lore,* 19:72:29–36.

Watkins, F. *Hopi Toys.* Los Angeles: Southwest Museum, Number 19, N.D.

THE LIFE AND THE GAMES
OF THE TRADITIONAL CANADIAN ESKIMO*

R. Gerald Glassford

For thousands of years there have been small groups of people scattered across the frozen top of North America beyond the tree line. They managed to survive by means of a precariously balanced system of hunting and fishing as well as a unique social system that was forged through generations of adaptation. These were the "Inuit," "the People," but better known throughout the world as the "Eskimo." The word "Eskimo" stimulates, for many, an image of a nomadic people whose principle abode was the snow house or igloo, whose primary diet was raw fish and meat, who rubbed noses rather than kissed, who swapped wives, who left elderly people to die sealed in a snow house or out on the wind swept barren land, and who had no formalized system of government. Such a mosaic represents only fragmentarily the traditional heritage of the Inuit.

It is important to realize that the northern part of North America is not a single geographical unit. Several distinct areas exist: the barren lands of northern Alaska sloping down to the continental shelf of the Beaufort Sea; the rugged Richardson and MacKenzie Mountains forging a barrier between Alaska and the Northwest Territories; the Mac-Kenzie River and its valley stretching toward 70° north latitude and bringing with it a strong moderating effect on the land; the open tundra stretching from Tuktoyaktuk to Repulse Bay, the barren and rugged north islands that reach almost to the Pole; and the mineral rich and ancient Canadian or Precambrian Shield. In relation to the rest of North America one simple but important distinction should be made with respect to the Arctic. The "true" Arctic—the land of the Inuit—is considered to be that area north of the tree line and the subarctic that area where trees grow and which was traditionally inhabited by the Indian.

What kind of people were the Inuit? How were they able to exist in a hostile environment where temperatures during the dark winter

*In deference to the people of the North, a few of whom I have been privileged to meet and to know, I would prefer to use the name by which they know themselves—the Inuit—throughout this chapter.

months plummeted to -70° F and where the wind chill (the combined chilling effect of the wind and the temperatures) often exceeded -150°? What physical, physiological, psychological, sociological qualities did these people possess that enabled them to survive? They seem to have a few physical advantages. They have, for instance, limited facial hair which can be a hazard during the cold months since the moisture from exhaled breath catches in facial hair and acts to lower the skin temperature thereby endangering the facial area with respect to frostbite. Their limbs, hands and feet are, in general, shorter or smaller than the white man or black man and the nose cavities through which the Inuit breathes are smaller than those of other races. They do not have the disadvantage of a long thin nose that is so susceptible to frostbite. On the other hand, they have not been blessed with an excessively heavy layer of fat to help shield them from the cold as it does for the walrus, the seal and the polar bear, nor is their metabolic rate significantly different from other groups.

To a great extent the Inuits' existence in a stringent environment seems more dependent upon their responses of a psychological and sociological nature. They are reputed to have a high level of mental "toughness" and are able to continue to respond physically when "the going is rugged." Beyond this they are extremely adaptive, adjusting easily from one situation to another. The Inuit's precarious existence placed certain demands upon his social systems. The primary one was that he had to find a way to survive in small isolated groups yet at the same time to lead a nomadic life. This was due almost exclusively to the Inuits' reliance upon migratory animals and sea-mammals for sustenance rather than upon any form of stationary plant. Food habits alone represent a remarkable example of their adaptation to a harsh world. Before the Euro-North American arrived in the Arctic, the Inuit lived on meat and fish, much of which was eaten raw. This custom was abhorred by many early explorers and missionaries, yet had the Inuit not followed this form of diet he would surely have succumbed to scurvy, a disease which is precipitated by a dietary deficiency of vitamin C and which affected so many southern visitors to the North. If one analyzes Inuit food preferences, it is apparent that what they considered delicacies were rich in vitamins, particularly vitamin C: raw seal liver, raw narwhal or beluga whale skin which they called *muktuk,* and the frozen contents of a seal's stomach. Had Southerners adapted to the Arctic in this fashion many health problems could have been avoided.

Another significant adaptive strategy was the emergence of a nomadic life style. Among the Inuit there was little or no tendency toward any form of a permanent settlement since the land (or small segments of the sea) given the limited weapons and tools of these people, could not support prolonged demands by a group. Also, one of the staple food sources, the Caribou, followed a migratory pattern and a second food source, the seal, was difficult to hunt during the summer months. The consequence of these and other factors was that the Inuit travelled in small groups, not "tribes (Weyer 1931), based extensively on ties of consanguinity (Boas 1964). Many of these groups would form together for periods, particularly during the winter months, as an *ilagiit* (Balikci 1964). These were not political, residential nor ceremonial units but rather an ego-centered kindred, ". . . a category of people in reference to an individual," (Balikci 1964: 29) the purpose of which was to create a larger social sphere than the immediate family group in order to help ensure personal security and to provide a mechanism for marriage regulation. Several significant factors about the Inuit and their life style should be noted with respect to this social system. First, among the traditional Inuit there was a good deal of inter-personal hostility, particularly among unknown groups, although murder in the in-group structure was far from uncommon. Thus a visitation to a distant camp in which no relatives lived was a dangerous undertaking indeed. On this point the Danish explorer and Arctic traveller, Knut Rasmussen noted:

> One would think that in these waste and desolate regions they would feel pleasure when they came across people who could be company for them; far from it. To this day it is customary when a sledge party approaches a settlement that it does not drive right up to the door. An informal arrival like that might give rise to fright and misunderstanding, which would quickly lead to hostilities. And the fact must never be lost sight of that human life was never at any time taken too seriously.
> Rasmussen 1931

Hostile reaction was minimized if a member of the traveller's extended or restricted *ilagiit* was found in the camp. As a consequence, a visitor was generally questioned about his relatives in order to establish the nature of possible consanguinal or social ties (Sovolik, personal communication, 1969). A second example of the operation of this security network was the practice of wife-exchange.

> The custom of interchanging wives . . . leads to a curious extension of the family. . . . The head of a visiting family will often connect himself in this way with the group that he is visiting; he ceases to be a stranger, and therefore a potential enemy, in his new community.
> Jenness 1922: 85–6

Not only would the traveller have companionship on the trail but he would have available a skilled cook and seamstress as well as a person who could help provide him with a degree of security at the camp to be visited.

Among some groups of Inuit, the patterns of marriage were primarily exogamous in order to enhance security: "... the family groupings to which the individual belonged were ideally exogamous. It is evident that a goal in marriage was to extend as far as possible the bonds of mutual aid and cooperation" (Spencer 1959: 75). Thus through exogamous marriage patterns and the *ilagiit,* or extended consanguinal and social unit, the Inuit strove to maximize the security level of the individual. Throughout the Arctic, however, the nuclear family was the basic unit upon which the survival of the Inuit hinged.

The division of labor between the husband and wife was reasonably sharp. Most of the heavy tasks fell into the male domain. They were responsible for hunting, building the lodging, be it snow house or heavy caribou-skin tents, loading and unloading the sleds, and making and repairing tools as well as weapons. To the woman fell the duties of preparing the food, preparing the skins for use and making the leather and fur garments for the family. She was also responsible for gathering together and packing the household goods preparatory for a move. Once on the trail during the winter, the woman, when required to assist, pulled in front of the dogs whereas the man pulled from in front of the sled or pushed from behind. During the summer treks, the man generally carried the tent, his tools, and his weapons. The woman toted the sleeping gear, the seal oil lamp and the cooking pot, while the children were responsible for their sleeping bags and their toys. The family unit worked as a team in skinning animals, in organized caribou drives, fish drives and occasionally in seal hunting (Boas 1964: 63–130).

Cooperative hunting patterns were commonly employed whenever family units joined together as either a restricted or extended *ilagiits* and, understandably, the problem of a fair division of the products was of considerable importance. Similarly, if a hunter working alone had the good fortune to kill some form of game during a time of shortage a system of division was required, for the Inuit recognized that despite his momentary good fortune the time might not be far in the future when he and his family would themselves be in need. The best place to store one's immediate surplus was with others who were in short supply.

There existed among the Inuit a basic dichotomy in the annual cycle of their sharing patterns. Rasmussen has noted the consideration given to "current need" within the *ilagiit* and particularly the tendency for the sharing rules to be relaxed more during the summer months.

> In this hunting the shares are more or less common to all Eskimos. Besides the skin, the hunter's own share is the head, neck and either the whole forequarter or a part of it, whereas the fat hindquarter is gener-

ally shared by the others. . . . Otherwise the sharing of the meat is to
some extent dependent upon whether there is a general shortage or not.
. . . If there is sufficient meat the rules are not always observed to the
letter, but it is always considered to be good form for the one who
brings down a caribou to give his fellow villagers a feast and not cache
all the meat for himself.

Rasmussen 1931: 173

The winter cycle was another matter and it was typified by a more
rigidly controlled sharing mechanism. Van de Velde (1956) has recorded the precise and rather complex rules by which the meat and
blubber obtained by a hunter or group of hunters was shared. As soon
as the seal was brought into the snow house or tent the woman controlling the distribution of the results of the hunt (usually the wife of
the successful hunter or the wife of the head of the *ilagiit*) had the
animal butchered into fourteen main sections each bearing a specific
name. The hunting partners of each man had a specific name based
on one of these sections. So two hunters might call themselves recip-
rocally *aksatkolik* (my shoulder), and whenever one killed a seal he
was obliged to give one shoulder to this man and vice versa. Hence a
fairly rigorous system of food sharing was carried out particularly
during the dark months of winter when starvation was a real possibility and the chances for success at the hunt were reduced. Balikci
(1964: 335) contends that the difference between the rigidity of
sharing patterns during the winter as compared to the summer period
was primarily due to the social organization. The consanguinally related unit was the typical summer unit. In such groups highly formalized sharing rules were generally not required. The extended *ilagiit*
was more frequently found operative in the winter months and therefore rigorous and formal sharing rules were necessary. Through common consent these rules became ritualized and a distribution of
limited goods with a minimum of in-group conflict was assured.

While sharing patterns were fundamental concepts in the life style
of the traditional Inuit, the introduction of modern technology has
been instrumental in significantly changing their way of life. The instrument of greatest significance has been the high powered rifle
which has allowed the hunter to develop a much greater range of
hunting tactics and to reduce his reliance upon his hunting partners.
The caribou drive, the group ambush at the water crossing, the group
patterns of hunting the seal at his breathing holes are gone. The trad-
ing posts, and more recently the money-based exchange systems of
the southern department stores, have produced a decreased interpersonal reliance and an increased reliance of the Inuit on the southern world. Diamond Jenness has poignantly summarized the situation.

> The fur trade thus wrought a revolution in the lives of the Eskimos. In
> Canada it destroyed their economic independence, bound them hand
> and foot to a single commercial company. . . . As far as I can judge from
> my own experience, both the Hudson's Bay Company officially and its
> individual traders genuinely sought the welfare of their Eskimo clients;
> but they were forced to operate in a competitive world, and the Eskimos
> inevitably suffered.
>
> Jenness 1954-55: 29-30

Thus "the old order changeth yielding place to new" and the life style
of the contemporary Inuit is a far cry from the dimension described.
But locked within the former life patterns were elements of fun, a
joie de vivre in which games were an integral part of the life of young
and old alike.

Games were often closely associated with the festive occasions of
the Inuit; their whaling feast, their dark day celebrations, their feasts
in honor of the goddess, Sedna. As an example of the close relationship between the game structure and the festive occasion consider
the *Kaivitjuik,* a winter celebration of the western Arctic (Nuligak
1971: 18-20). The people of this area began to gather together for
their dark days feasts shortly after the sun had disappeared completely
below the horizon and they would jointly share food, stories, and
games, for it was a common practice during these days (or endless
nights) of festivities for the men to challenge one another to tests of
strength, skill or endurance. One of their favorites was the game we
know as "hook and crook" but which they called *akamak.* Two men,
often stripped to the waist despite the low outside temperatures,
would seat themselves upon a hide thrown upon the floor, intertwine
their legs, brace their left hand against their opponent's right knee,
hook their right arms and attempt to straighten the arm of the other
by exerting a steady pull against it. A number of varieties of this
game existed across the North including an arm pull game where a
double-handled implement consisting of two lengths of bone or
wood connected by a thong was used. Another group of games that
were favorites during festive periods were the jumping contests. An
object, often a piece of hide or a leather pouch stuffed with hair and
sand, was suspended from the ceiling of an igloo (frequently an enlarged structure called a *karegi* or *kradjgierk* which was used for such
occasions) or from a pole driven obliquely into the snow when the
contests were held outside. Players sprung into the air using a two
foot take-off and attempted to kick the object before landing again
on both feet. This activity, called *akratcheak,* was continued as the
object was raised high overhead until no one was able to strike the
target with their feet and land correctly. It seemed to be exclusively

a game for the male and several variations were played, the other dominant one being *nikachruk* or one-foot high kick. This game is the same as *akratcheak* except that the player must take off, touch and land on the same foot. These games would continue for hours until the players were fatigued, at which time they might stop to eat or to race their dogs for, at least in the western Arctic after the turn of the twentieth century, the Inuit enjoyed racing their teams.

Above all, however, they loved to drum dance; men, women, children alike loved the rhythm of the *kilaun* or drum and the dances would continue for hours on end. The drum was made of a circular wooden hoop (probably constructed from a precious piece of driftwood in the eastern Arctic) over which had been stretched a membrane of caribou skin. The Inuit did not tune their drum to a particular note, but if a slackness or lack of resonance was detected, they dipped their hand in water and applied it to the membrane which tightened as it dried. The drum stick was simply a rounded splinter of wood fifteen to twenty inches long. In some cases a handle had been attached to the wooden ring in order to give the drummer control while he or she struck the rim or the membrane of the drum on the underside. According to Jenness, drum dance songs which accompanied the dancing could be basically divided into two classes: the *aton* and the *pisik*. In the latter form the drummer wielded the drum while chanting the song and dancing to the beat. In the *aton* the drum was handled by a drummer or a group of drummers who did not participate in the actual song and dance. The songs often told of a chase or a hunt, or a confrontation with an animal spirit, a polar bear, or a long, difficult and dangerous trek. The dancer's actions were quick and jerky with a great deal of emphasis on the use of the arms, the hands and head movements in contrast to the strong emphasis on leg action among the North American Indians. Balancing first on one foot and then the other, the dancer began his song and as the others recognized the words their voices joined the chorus to swell the volume and accentuate the beat. Should the audience lack vigor the dancer might well have exhorted them to greater effort. When one dancer was exhausted or had finished his song another immediately took his place and the dancing continued for days on end (Jenness 1922: 224).

Drum dances were not restricted to the festive periods. Indeed any gathering was viewed as sufficient excuse for a dance and there was never a shortage of participants. Today only a few of the older Inuit recall the old songs, the rhythmic thrumming of the rawhide drum, the chorus of many voices raised to a high pitch telling of their life during and earlier era. As a consequence, a move is underway to try to capture the remnants of this dimension of the more traditional Inuits' life-style on film and tape.

Another major activity of the Inuit which was frequently, although not exclusively, played in conjunction with the *qaqruk* or traditional whaling celebration, was *nalukatuk* (blanket-tossing). The blanket was constructed of several tough walrus hides stitched together to form a base some ten to twelve feet in diameter. Fifteen to twenty-five players gathered around the perimeter of the blanket and one player would stand at the centre of the blanket. The players on the outside edge of the blanket pulled sharply upwards and outwards and the person on the blanket was thrown high into the air. If the thrown player wished to achieve greater height they could spring upwards just as the walrus hides were pulled taut. Due to the unevenness of the pull, players were often thrown clear of the circle of throwers and injuries were not uncommon:

> The woman tossed kept on her feet if she could, and was thrown twelve to fifteen feet in the air. . . . Broken bones and dislocated joints were often the result. I have seen women who have been pointed out as having broken arms, clavicles, etc.
>
> Stefansson 1919: 165

In some parts of the western Arctic the players who pulled the blanket moved under the jumper in order to reduce the chance of their landing off the blanket. In other areas the skin blanket was fastened to stakes thereby reducing the mobility and increasing the danger.

While there are many implied motives as to why the Inuit played *nalukatuk* most informants in the western Arctic indicated that the prime reason they participated was for the thrill which accompanied momentary flight and to demonstrate their courage and ability. Regardless of motivation, the game was widespread in the North and a popular game during the period of whale hunting.

The Inuit game of *nukitautiyuat* (tug-of-war) was frequently played during the ceremonies held during the darkening days of the fall to ensure the banishment of the goddess Sedna to the bottom of the ocean. Sedna was the mistress of the underwater world and of the sea animals upon which the winter phase of the Inuit life depended so heavily. If the Inuit could drive Sedna back to the depths of the sea by wounding her when she attempted to surface through a seal breathing hole they believed that they would not be drawn down through a breathing hole during their winter hunting (Boas 1964: 192–201). In an attempt to gain the favor of the spirit of the weather they also conducted a game of tug-of-war between those members who were born during the summer months (the *aggirn* or the ducks) and those born during the winter months (the *axigirn* or the ptarmigans). A large seal-skin rope was stretched between the two groups and a struggle to pull the opponents off balance followed. If the group whose members were born during the summer months won the contest, it was believed that good weather would prevail (Boas 1964: 196–97).

But *nukitautiyuat* or tug-of-war was not restricted to a ceremonial role. It was a game often played for sheer enjoyment wherein men and women, young and old alike participated:

> Now the rope lay where it had fallen on the ice. A youngster grabbed one end of it, shouting. Someone grabbed the other end, a second, a third, a fourth jumped to one end or other and heaved. There was a mass attack on the rope. . . . Whenever one side gave way, new ones jumped in to help out. Eventually one group, exhausted, was pulled down into a pile, The game broke up in laughter. But a few minutes later, quite unrehearsed and uncoached, the same thing would happen again.
>
> Harrington 1952: 322

Winter or summer tug-of-war was a popular activity and although it was related to festivals it was by no means restricted in any sense.

No description of the festive life and the game structure of the Inuit would be complete without a brief description of their special form of gymnastics. This activity has been witnessed and described by numerous ethnographers and it was apparently pan-Arctic in its appeal (Birket-Smith 1929: 272; 1945: 120; Mathiassen 1928: 221). These gymnastic stunts were performed only by the men and usually in an informal situation. Whether it be during the *kaivitjuik* (winter festival) or during a casual gathering the word would spread quickly that a performance was shortly to occur and adults and children gathered to watch. One feat, called the *aglugiqtatuk* or the *aklunertarneq* according to Birket-Smith (1929: 25) was performed on a single thong fashioned from the hide of a bearded seal or a walrus, immensely strong material. The thong (or thongs if two were used) was passed through holes in the roof of the *karegi* (social house) and anchored in position by means of two strong poles. One of the participants would grasp the thong, pull his knees up to his chest, then extend his legs up through his arms and over the top of the thong. With a strong pull he would draw his body up until he was seated atop the moving thong. While still holding the rawhide line in his hands he then threw himself vigorously backward, caught the thong in the crook of his knee and completed a full circle. The process was continued until the player was exhausted or unable to make a complete circle at which time another was quick to take his place. A similar stunt required that the performer complete giant full body circles around the thong, while a somewhat different stunt (*ujautatuk, itaugaqtok,* or *orsiktartuk* literally translated as "they-make-a-loop") was carried out on double thongs which were looped at one end and fastened through the roof at the other. Diamond Jenness has captured the action of this stunt in the following passage:

> Hanging by his hands the native circles round till his toes are almost touching the rope, then he swings violently back in a half-circle and comes to an upright position, his body balanced against the rope with the weight resting on the hands. From this position, he swings round again in a half-circle, throws his legs violently out and swings back again. The exercise is continued until the performer becomes tired or fails to maintain his balance. Very few of the natives, however, could accomplish the feat at all. The women never attempted it, though they sometimes joined in a simpler exercise in which two small loops were made in the rope about a foot apart. Hanging by these the performer circled round and placed a foot in each loop, then released his hands and hung at full length downwards with his head almost touching the floor. From this position he had to draw himself up again, grasp the loop with hands, release his feet and drop to the floor.
>
> Jenness 1922: 222)

These were difficult stunts requiring strength and flexibility and the Inuit enjoyed demonstrating his abilities to anyone who would care to watch.

Another game that was frequently associated with festivals or special events, but again never restricted to such occasions, was the dart game. Perhaps the following description by Robert Nuligak will serve to illustrate the nature of this activity.

> As the sun reappeared and the gatherings were close to an end, we ended our festivals with dart shooting. The dart, there was only one, was balanced by little wings made from a duck's tail feathers. It flew straight and true. It was carried to each contestant by the one who had made it. The target was a piece of caribou fat *(tunu)* thinned out and formed into the shape of a candle, about four inches long and an inch and a half in diameter. It was set in the middle of the floor. The igloo was large and the onlookers many. Men, women and children were all admitted. Someone would set up a prize and another would aim for the target. The greater the stake, the higher the interest rose. Peals of laughter echoed all around. The winner, the one who hit the target, was in turn expected to put up a prize for the next contestant.
>
> Nuligak 1971: 21

The dart game was generally the last game of the western Arctic's *kaivitjvik* and the groups shortly went their separate ways to their winter camps and their favorite hunting areas. The few games described by no means exhaust the games that were played during the festive periods but they do serve to indicate the range of activities. Another part of their life pattern where games were often played was during the periods of relaxation after the hunt or a day on the trail. These games often involved individual acts of strength, endurance, or the ability to withstand pain, or paired contests involving these physical characteristics.

An example of the former was the game of *iqiruktuk* or mouth-pull. Two players sat side by side, wrapped the arm nearest the other around his neck and inserted the forefinger into the corner of that player's mouth. On a given signal both would pull as hard as possible and the individual who allowed his head to turn in the direction of the pull was declared the loser. A new challenge was quickly issued by another member of the group and the game continued (Zuk 1967: 8). Or the players might engage in a game of *siutigun* or *ayaraq* (to pull or carry by the ear). In one form of this game two players took their weight on their hands and knees or their hands and toes while facing each other but some eighteen to thirty inches apart. A strong raw-hide thong made into a loop was placed over the right ear of each player and then they tried to back away and to draw the opponent with them. If a player could cause enough pain so that the other person would allow his head to turn and thereby release the thong from behind the ear or if he allowed himself to be drawn forward then that player was declared the winner. In an alternative to this game, the rawhide loop was placed over the ear and a heavy weight suspended from it. The player would then attempt to carry that weight as far as he could before the pain caused him to release the weight.

A third game form of this type involved the use of a stick twelve to eighteen inches long and sharpened at both ends. Two players knelt facing each other and the sharpened stick was placed between them so that the point was pressed against the skin just below the nose. The players then tried to force one another backwards.

Tests of strength frequently occurred among the Inuit which included a spread-eagle carry, hand wrestling, head pushing and head pulling. *Kumgisikmiuk* (head pulling) was an activity similar to the southern game of "stubborn calf." The two players face each other supporting their weight on hands and toes. A leather loop was placed around the back of the head of each man and they then tried to pull their opponent across a predesignated mark. Head pushing (*niakomik dinnuroan*) was almost the reverse of *kumgisikmiuk.* The players assumed a position facing each other on hands and knees, forehead to forehead. On a signal they tried to drive each other across the centre dividing line. Arm pull and finger pull games already discussed were frequently practiced in the igloos of the hunters or outside of the skin tents of the summer travellers.

The exhausting activity which the Inuit called *peedletataq* (knee jumping) was also a favorite. The player started from a kneeling position with the toes extended backward and the hands on the hips. By extending the body quickly upward and pressing downward on the front of the feet the player thrust himself up onto his feet then dropped back down to the knees and continued in this manner until he was exhausted (Boas 1964: 164). Men, women and children all participated in this game.

Another group of games which had a somewhat different *modus operandi* to similar Euro-North American counterparts were the games of chance. The game of *nuglutang* was apparently popular among many of the Inuit (Birket-Smith 1929: 271-74; 1945: 118; Boas 1964: 160; Jenness 1924: 221; Low 1903-04: 175; Mathiassen 1928: 219). The implements were simple. A small, flat plate of bone, horn or ivory with a hole drilled in the centre and a series of long, thin rods the tips of which were small enough to enter the aperture in the plate. The plate was hung from the roof of the igloo or tent and anchored to the floor with a stone or some similar heavy object by cords of sinew. Around this bobbing target sat the players each with their rod poised. On the word to begin the players tried to jab the tip of the rod into the target hole and the first person to succeed was declared the winner. The first such "winner" was required to put up a stake (any object that he had that was of value and which he was prepared to gamble away was considered appropriate and these often included knives, cartridges, mukluks, gun powder, and infrequently hunting weapons). The second winner took the prize put up by the first "winner" and replaced it with another. And so the game continued until the players grew weary or stopped to eat. In the long run the only player to lose anything was the first "winner" and the only one to win anything was the last winner (Birket-Smith 1925: 274; Boas 1964: 161; Low 1903-04: 175; Nuligak 1971: 21). A roulette game called *sataktuk* or *saqataq* was played on the same principle during earlier periods in the Arctic region. It should be noted, however, that by the 1900's the gambling patterns typically found in the South had significantly replaced the gambling patterns described above.

Group or team games, while not numerous were, nevertheless, frequently played by the Inuit. *Akraurak* (football) was often observed by ethnographers (Nelson 1899: 335; Birket-Smith 1929: 273; 1945: 117; Low 1903-04: 174; Stefansson 1919: 169) and was played jointly by all, from the toddler to the aged grandmother. The ball was made of hide and stuffed with feathers, hair, moss, grass, or wood shavings. The size of the ball varied as did the shape and the rules of the game, which were minimal at best. The object of the game was to play the ball across the oppositions' goal line. In the eastern Arctic a version of this game was played with a multi-looped whip and the players drove the ball along the ice or through the air with it (Turner 1894: 257). The Inuit also played a game similar in some respects to baseball *(anauligatuk* or *mukpaun)* but perhaps more closely related to German *Schlagball.* Two bases about ten feet long and seventy to a hundred feet apart were established. Teams were not determined but rather a batter hit a ball thrown by a member of the fielding group. He then attempted to run to the opposite base and back before the ball could be fielded and thrown so as to hit him. When this happened the successful fielder replaced the batter and the game continued. The Inuit name for this game was *anauligatuk* or *mukpaun.* It is not known how long this type of game was played by the Inuit but in the 1850's Kane witnessed such a game among a group of children who used the curved rib of some large animal to strike to the ball instead of a stick (Kane 1856: 133). The concept of a compilation of scores or runs was never mentioned in any of the ethnographic reports.

Tag games *(angugaurak)* and games of keepaway *(atariaq* or *ataujartut)* were popular in winter and summer. In some cases the groups for keepaway were divided by sex (Stefansson 1919: 165) whereas in other situations the groups were mixed:

> In this game two played together, tossing the ball between them, and others tried to intercept it. Pregnant women were mixed up in this, mothers and babies on their backs, a very old man, and all the children. I joined them. We slid, we stumbled, we took many spills. The game shifted here and there all over the ice, the ball bouncing in all directions. Sometimes a tiny kid would grab the ball, then patter across the ice hell-bent for the hills, with all of us in pursuit yelling.
>
> Harrington 1952: 34

Such games required a minimum of equipment, were easily organized and involved a maximum of participation, characteristics that were typical across the Arctic.

One further game form which was universally popular among the Inuit was *ayagak* or string figures. Several different forms were played including one wherein the string figure was passed between two players. The playing of *ayagak* was traditionally controlled by taboos which prohibited the Inuit from making the figures outside the snowhouse or the tent. Legend had it that the spirit of the sun was offended by seeing a player making figures and bad weather would subsequently result (Rasmussen 1931: 167). Due to the controlling superstitions and the extensive skills of the Inuit in the making of string figures several major studies have been conducted in the North on this activity alone (Jenness 1942; Paterson 1949).

A group of hand-eye coordination games called *ayagak* or *ajaguktuk* (ring and pin) were extremely popular among the Inuit. The ring or target was made from any of a range of natural materials including vertebra, the skull of a rabbit, horn in which holes had been drilled or stylized objects carved from ivory. The pin was made from a sliver of bone, wood or ivory and was attached to the ring by a sinew string or a soft leather thong. A player would hold the pin in his hand and swing the target upwards so that the pin could be thrust into one of the target holes in the ring. Frequently a story or chant would accompany the playing of the game and as soon as a player missed a target the implement was passed on to the next. Both Rasmussen and Jenness described a game of *ajaguktuk* which involved a chant about the hunting of a polar bear (Jenness 1922: 220; Rasmussen 1931: 358–59). The hole in the ring that represented the head or the nose of the polar bear apparently had major significance. If the player was successful in impaling the target object on the pin by thrusting it into this particular hole he would immediately shout "Piyagla!" ("I've got him!") thereby ending the round. In some areas gambling was occasionally associated with the playing of *ayagak* but it was not a widespread practice.

This overview of Inuit games is not exhaustive but it does serve to indicate something of the range of their game structure, the fact that most of their games required a minimum of equipment, equipment which could quickly be fabricated from materials readily available, and that most required a minimum of space. The majority of their games were of an individual or two-person nature which were based on strength, endurance or agility. Being nomadic people, the Inuit were required to create activities that involved simple rules and simple equipment. If game implements had to be abandoned it was important that they could be replaced at the next camp. Taboos and festivals had a significant impact on the games of these hardy people as did the pragmatic need for preparing the individuals for a harsh, demanding existence in which the Inuit had to know his own physical limitations as well as the limitations of his companions.

The Inuit games fit well into the overall pattern of simplicity and pragmatism, the low division of labor, the characteristic minimal social stratification of their society. Many of the games involved cooperative effort and a lack of emphasis on overt competition as well as a stress upon short-term, few step operators, non-season specific spontaneous, nuclear family-oriented activities. They were, in short, ideally suited to the Arctic environment prior to the intrusion of the southern white culture.

REFERENCES

Balikci, A. 1964. Development of basic socio-economic units in two Eskimo communities. Ottawa: National Museum of Canada, Bulletin No. 202, *Anthropological Series* No. 69.

Birket-Smith, K. 1929. The caribou eskimos. *5th Thule Expedition.* 1921-24, 5. Copenhagen: Gyldeddalske Boghandel, Nordisk Forlag.

Birket-Smith, K. 1945. Ethnographical collections from the Northwest passage. *5th Thule Expedition.* 1921-24, 6. Copenhagen: Gyldeddalske Boghandel, Nordisk Forlag.

Boas, F. 1964. *The Central Eskimo.* Lincoln: University of Nebraska Press.

Harrington, R. 1952. *The Face of the Arctic.* New York: Henry Schuman.

Jenness, D. 1922. The life of the Copper Eskimos. *Canadian Arctic Expedition.* 1913-18, 12. Ottawa: F.A. Acland, King's Printer.

Jenness, D. 1924. Eskimo string figures. *Canadian Arctic Expedition.* 1913-18, 13. Ottawa: F.A. Acland, King's Printer.

Jenness, D. 1954-55. Enter the European...among the Eskimos. *The Beaver* (Winter); 29-30.

Jenness, D. 1966. The Canadian Eskimo. In I.N. Smith, ed. *The Unbelievable Land.* Ottawa: The Queen's Printer.

Kane, E.K. 1856. *Arctic Explorations in the Years 1853, '54, '55.* II. Philadelphia: Childs and Peterson.

Low, A.P. 1903-04. *Dominion Government Expedition to Hudson Bay and the Arctic Islands.* 1903-04. Ottawa: Government Printing Bureau.

Mathiassen, T. 1928. Material culture of the Iglulik Eskimos. *5th Thule Expedition.* 1921-24, 6, 1. Copenhagen: Gyldeddalske Boghandel, Nordisk Forlag.

Nelson, E.W. 1899. The Eskimo about the Bering Strait. *18th Annual Report Bureau of American Ethnology.* Smithsonian Institution, Part I, 1896-1897. Washington: Government Printing Office.

Nuligak, R. 1971. *I, Nuligak.* Toronto: Martin.

Paterson, T.T. 1949. *Eskimo String Figures and Their Origin.* Copenhagen: Ejnar Munksgaard.

Rasmussen, K. 1931. The Netsilik Eskimos. *5th Thule Expedition.* 1921-24, 8: 1-2. Copenhagen: Gyldeddalske Boghandel, Nordisk Forlag.

Spencer, R. 1959. *The North Alaskan Eskimo, a Study in Ecology and Society.* Washington: Bureau of American Ethnology. Bulletin 171.

Stefansson, V. 1919. The Stefansson-Anderson arctic expedition of the American Museum: preliminary ethnological report 1914. *Anthropological Papers.* American Museum of Natural History. 14, 1. New York.

Turner, L.M. 1894. Ethnology of the Ungava District. *11th Annual Report Bureau of American Ethnology.* Smithsonian Institution, 1889-1890. Washington: Government Printing Office.

Van de Velde, F. 1956. Les Regles du Partage des Phoques Pris par la Chasse aux Aglus. *Anthropoligica,* C.S. 3.

Weyer, E. 1931. *The Eskimos.* New Haven: Yale University Press.

Zuk, W. 1967. *Eskimo Games.* Curriculum Section, Education Division Northern Administration Branch, Department of Indian Affairs and Northern Development. Ottawa.

OLYMPIC SUCCESS:
A CROSS-NATIONAL PERSPECTIVE

Paavo Seppänen

Even a rough global review indicates that almost every culture provides activities which can be identified as a kind of sport. The history of the Western world since antiquity tells about the same story. Sport or games have had a function of one kind or another in every phase of human society (McIntosh, 1963). The role that sport has played in different cultures and in different periods of time is not, however, an unchangeable thing but one which greatly varies from time to time and from society to society. This variation also holds true in the case of competitive sport of modern times.

By analyzing the records of the modern Olympic Games it is very easy to see that both participation in the games and success in them have varied greatly. Only a small minority of nations have participated in all the games since 1896 and quite a number of nations participating have never won a medal in them. As a matter of fact, a great majority of less successful nations have together scored considerably less than the United States alone, even less than such small countries as Sweden and Finland alone. Variation due to time has also been obvious. Greece, one of the most successful countries during the first few olympiades, has almost disappeared from the list of medal winners during the last few games. The Scandinavian countries won their greatest number of medals between 1912 and 1948, and the greatest number of Socialist countries' victories have occurred primarily since the beginning of the 50's. Even the achievements of the big powers reveal fluctuations from one period to another.

For a sociologist, the cultural variation and timebound fluctuation in sport and sport achievements are a "why". What enables some countries to win a bulk of medals from one Olympic Games to another, and at the same time prohibits other countries from doing the same? What are the reasons for great periodical fluctuations of the same nations? What, for example, enabled small Finland to challenge the position of such large nations as Great Britain, France, and Germany during the interwar period, yet no longer continue to do so? What made the same country superior to Tzarist Russia in

1912, but a clear loser to the Soviet Union since 1952? Is this variation in sport and sport success just luck, a peculiar stochastic combination of circumstances, or are there some regularities which can be explained through scientific exploration?

This study will attempt to shed some empirical light on the role competitive sport has in different societies and different types of cultures. In doing so, it is assumed that the rise and fall in sport and sport achievement is not an isolated stochastic phenomenon but one which is closely related to social and cultural conditions prevailing in society. Sport and sport achievement is hypothesized as being one type of symptom through which the infrastructure of society becomes salient. The very province of this study does not, however, cover the whole field of competitive sport but concentrates on the analysis of sport success in the modern Olympic Games since the games of Athens in 1896.

Data and Method

The records of medal winners of every Olympic Games from 1896 through 1972 provide the major data for the study. It is assumed that these records give the best available empirical data on the emphasis different societies or different types of societites have given competitive sport. The data represent almost all nations of the world and span a period of more than seventy years. Additionally, the number of events within the games is so high that the risk of stochastic interpretation of records is rather well controlled. In fact, the data provide a relatively good source of information for the comparative analysis of the role of competitive sport in different societies and different cultures. Even though the statistics do not give an overall picture about sport activities within societies, they undoubtedly give information about how effective the emphasis on competitive sport is.

The primary unit of analysis in this study is the nation. Some groupings of nations serve as secondary units of analysis. Despite the heavy emphasis on individualism in the official ideology of the modern Olympic Games, the principal unit of participation has always been the political entity of the nation. Opening ceremonies where national anthems and flags symbolize nationalities are all expressions of the principal role of nationality in the games. Additionally, "unofficial" point totals for nations are reported in newspapers and sports statistics all over the world glorifying the achievements of political units as much as those of individual sportsmen.

In measuring the success of different nations and different groups of nations, a rather simple method was used. For each gold medal a nation or group of nations was credited 3 points, for silver 2 points, and for bronze 1 point. Total scores for each nation and group of nations were derived by adding up the points. Statistics were based on the statistics of the games. Statistics indicate that 76 nations in all have won medals and additionally have scored points from Athens in 1896 to 1972 in Munich. 24 of these nations have also won medals in the Winter Olympic Games since Chamonix in 1924.

Total point raw scores do not, however, provide the best index for measuring the success of different societies. The method of adding up points does not take the size of the competing unit into consideration and consequently neglects one of the most important requirements of fair sportmanship: competition under equal terms. The unweighted scores are as unsatisfactory indices of sport success of a nation as would be comparisons of GNP as index of the standard of living. For example, although the standard of living is not higher in India than in Norway, the gross national product of India is greater. In the same light, nations scoring more than others need not necessarily be better in sport. Thus the raw scores of sport success are not good indicators of the role competitive sport has in society.

In this study the raw total point scores were weighted by the population of the nation. It is true that even this alternative is open to criticism and needs qualification. Because the number of entries in each olympic event is limited, a nation with a greater population will not have a direct advantage. In fact, the ratio of the number of entries per event to a countries population will always be greater for the less populated countries. There is, however, no reasonable way to construct an index in which both the size of the population and the relatively unequal possibility of participation could be taken into consideration at the same time. Instead, a categorization of nations where both large and small countries were represented in different groups was used. Although this alternative meant rejection of the general index of success, it did provide possibilities for valid comparisons between groups of nations and at the same time between societies representing various types of cultures and social conditions in general.

The final index of sport success used in analysis is a coefficient (C_s) which indicates the ratio between actual and expected success for a nation or

$$C_s = \frac{\text{per mille proportion of total points}}{\text{per mille proportion of the world population}}$$

The index is applicable in the case of any type or unit either national or multinational. Caution for too liberal a use of the index in comparisons between large and small nations is, however, given because of the relative inequality of possibility of participation.

General Conditions of Sport and Sport Success

Any human activity can be considered as based upon at least three conditions: (1) genetic qualities of a human being, (2) physical circumstances around him, and (3) social and cultural conditions under which he lives. There is no doubt that any sport activity is a function of one or another combination of these conditions. Genetic capacity is a necessary condition of sports activity, for without it sport would not exist. Although genetic qualities are a necessary condition of sports activity they are not a sufficient condition of high sports performances.

Genetic qualities do not explain the total variation occurring in sport activity and sport success. Consequently, at least a part and very often a considerable part of sport activity and sport success can be thought of as a function of either the physical and/or social conditions under which people live. The genetic qualities of human beings may well explain differences in performance between man and woman, between old and young, between tall and short and even between different races. They do not, however, explain why Nordic societies are more actively engaged in skiing or Alpine countries in down-hill events, nor do they explain why black people of the United States have been much more successful than those of Nigeria or Mosambique, or why whites of Portugal and Spain have been much less successful than those of Scandinavian countries. The success of the Scandinavian countries in skiing and the success of Austria, France, and Switzerland in the Alpine events at least partly depends on their favorable combinations of natural conditions for winter sports. Yet not even natural conditions can explain the variation in track and field, football, swimming, boxing, wrestling etc. As a matter of fact the correlation between swimming success and the natural swimming conditions of a country is a negative rather than positive one. The only explanation for the remaining variation seems to be in social and cultural conditions of societies. This, of course, is the main focus of sociological interest.

On Sociological Interpretations of Sport Success

It is very difficult to carry out research projects which give real empirical evidence of causal relationships between characteristics of society and such a behavior as competitive sport. It is even more difficult when the unit of analysis is a whole society. The conditions prevailing in society are never exclusively directed toward a single manifestation of behavior such as sport. Nor are the effects of society's characteristics on man's behavior directly observable. The interpretation of the relation between sport and society or culture will necessarily remain at level of ideal type in the sense of Max Weber. For a meaningful analysis, sport should be considered a symptomatic activity in which some characteristics of society are manifested or if we want to put it otherwise, variation in emphasis on sport can be interpreted as a function of variation in the type of society.

What then are the characteristics of society which should be taken into consideration in the analysis of competitive sport and sport success? If sport is a symptom of some essential factor in society, then it is obvious that the most basic characteristics of the society are of great importance in the analysis. The most general qualities of any society are those which refer to *ideational conditions* or superstructure on the one hand and those which are *structural conditions* or infrastructures of society on the other. The line between these two characteristics of society is not very clear. The former refers to things which are variously called social expectations, values, norms, beliefs, ideology etc, whereas the latter covers such things as division of labor, power relations, productive forces, production relations, economic system. When both of these groups of social conditions seem to be closely related to each other, the type of society or the *type of culture* prevailing in society can be considered to be one or another combination of these groups.

The analysis of achievement and sport brings up a crucial question. What combination of ideational and structural conditions or what type of culture best explains sport achievement and the role of sport in society? Karl Marx suggested that the basic cause of any social phenomenon is to be found in the infrastructure of society, in productive forces and production relations. Undoubtedly economic elements of society play a central role in the behavior of the members of any society. In a statistical analysis of participation and success of different nations in the Olympic Games of Helsinki 1952, a very high correlation between the economic conditions of a country and its sport achievement was shown (Jokl 1956). Even though economic conditions of society are one of the basic conditions for sport achievement and effective sport activity in general, they are hardly sufficient conditions to explain the great variety in sport activity and sport achievement. An analysis of the European Athletic Championship in Budapest 1966, determined a negative correlation between the standard of living of a country and its athletic achievement (Seppänen 1967). Economic conditions merely provide a necessary basis for sport activity and do not give any guarantee for how these conditions are used for advancing sport. On an individual level this becomes even more obvious. The richest man is hardly the best in sport, even when only the richest man has sufficient conditions for effective physical activity.

The discussion about the rich and the poor leads to another important structural dimension of society—to social class. The relationship between class structure and achievements is a rather poorly explained area, although numerous opinions have been presented. There is no doubt that class structure and social stratification have some effect on the achievements of members of society, even in sport. Various kinds of sport can be characteristic of different classes or strata of a society (McIntosh, 1963 and Johansson, 1953). Additionally, it is obvious that there are underprivileged classes in some societies that do not have access to any kind of sport, at least in the meaning of modern competitive sport. In a society with very great class differences and at the same time with very great differences in social expectations, both participation in competitive sport and sport success will supposedly be relatively low. Sport will be a privilege of a thin elite and a negligible activity of underprivileged classes.

The ideational structure of society is the type of precondition that Max Weber (1930) interpreted the rise of modern Capitalism with. Many others beside him have successfully used the same approach. Particularly interesting from the point of view of the analysis of competitive sport and sport success are those efforts in which achievements, in general, have been the focus of study (Tawney 1958). The authors of these analyses unanimously suggest that the ideational—primary religious—ethos of culture, plays the decisive role in economic growth and in economic achievements in general.

Weber's analysis of the rise of Capitalism rests on the theory that Puritan believers differed from Catholics by their different internalizations of religious precepts, their anxious concern with the uncertainty of salvation. In the Puritan world, each man had to face the stern and inscrutable majesty of God alone and unaided. In his responses to his critics, Weber, declared that this intensified motivation had been a causal factor of great, but uncertain magnitude. Like Weber, David McClelland also suggests that a particular type of ideational atmosphere is a precondition to internalization of achievement motivation and at the same time economic prosperity (1961). If these interpretations are valid, then social expectations, as they appear in internalized religious dogma or in other type of ideational structure, can be important preconditions for achievement and obviously for sport achievement too. The role of the ideational structure or superstructure of society as a condition of achievement is greatly variable. Regardless of the quality of the ideational structure, at least a certain degree of social or cultural integration of national unity is needed before the effects of ideas can occur in the achievements of the unit. Without such integration the ideational structure of society is too heterogeneous to persuade a national society to any remarkable common activity. Most of the African countries seem to be in this position. In these societies, the nation-building process has not yet reached the phase in which a common ideology, either sacred or secular, penetrates into the core of major institutions and into all areas and all classes of society. This process in the form of rising nationalism, is only in its beginning in the majority of African societies. The traditional ideology of most African societies is hardly more than an intermixture of conflicting tribalism and a variety of local religions. Under these conditions, any pursuit of high national achievement—sport achievement included—is not expected. The sport success of African societies can be hypothesized as a strong probability rather than an actual fact. Under the conditions of rising nationalism, the role of sport will, however, rapidly change.

The actual success of African nations in the Olympic Games is greatly below the level which could be expected on the basis of the population of these countries. The only exception is the success of Kenya in Mexico City in 1968, and in Munich in 1972, which could be considered the first symptoms of the effects of rising nationalism on sport success.

As to the role of different ideational structures, Weber's analysis of world religions seems to render a reasonable starting point. In his wide-ranging studies, Weber (1963), noticed that religious ethics or cultural ethos, in general, appears in social institutions in very different ways. The decisive aspect of religious ethics is not the intensity of its attachment of magic and ritual or the distinctive character of the religion in general, but rather its theoretical attitude toward the world. Weber particularly emphasizes two dimensions of religious orientation to the world. The first one distinguishes between resignedness and mastery as alternative paths to salvation and the second makes the distinction between positions of orientation towards the existing social order. The path of mastery over the world Weber calls *ascetism* and that of resignedness or adjustment he calls *mysticism,* whereas the positions of orientation towards the existing social order are expressed in his terminology by dichotomy: *innerwordly* and *otherworldly* orientation. The innerworldly position avoids a radical break with the institutional order of society. Otherworldly position tries to minimize contacts with the established societal order. By cross-tabulating the distinction between otherworldly and innerworldly positions with ascetism and mysticism Weber derives a typology of four different religious solutions or orientations to salvation: innerworldly ascetism, innerworldly mysticism, otherworldly ascetism, and otherworldly mysticism.

Weber's typology may also serve as a starting point for classification of ideational structures of different societies. As Weber himself hypothesized, religious values or religious models of orientation toward the world belong to the basic elements of the ideational structure of almost any society. If this holds true, then the spirit of achievement, even in the form of sport achievement, may also be partially understood as a function of the religious ethos or religious deep-structure of society.

Sport Success as a Function of Ideational Superstructure

There are four great groups of religious tradition in the world, Buddhism, Confucianism, Hinduism, and Judaism-Christianity-Islam. In their position toward the world order, Buddhism and Hinduism represent the otherworldly orientation in Weber's terminology and the two other groups—Confucianism and Judaism-Christianity-Islam represent the innerworldly orientation. The distinction between innerworldy and otherworldly oriented ideational deep-structures appears to be of great importance in the analysis of achievement. The escapism element of otherworldly oriented religions hardly increases the likelihood of any type of wordly achievement, even though this is, at least in some way, possible. By comparing the actual success of countries reflecting innerwordly and otherwordly religious orientation, it is easy to verify the hypothesis of innerworldly oriented superiority (Table 1).

Table 1. Coefficients of Success in Olympic Games 1896–1968

Otherworldly oriented countries		Innerworldly oriented countries	
Hindu	0.0	Confucian[2]	0.0
Buddhist[1]	0.0	Islam[3]	0.1
		Jewish[4]	0.0
		Christian[5]	3.0

1) Japan with considerable Buddhist population not included, because of national primacy of Tokugawa and Shinto traditions in Japaneses culture. As Socialist countries Mongolia, North Korea and North Vietnam excluded.

2) China before the revolution, and Taiwan.

3) Albania since 1948 excluded as a Socialist country.

4) Israel

5) U.S.S.R. since 1920; Bulgaria, CSSR, Hungary, Poland, Romania, and Yugoslavia since 1948; Cuba since 1960 and GDR since 1968 excluded as Socialist countries.

Although the success of Hindu and Buddhist nations on the one hand and Confucian and Jewish on the other is not observable, the success of Islam and particularly that of Christian countries gives evidence to the hypothesis. The success of the Jews represented only by small Israel since the Second World War hardly shows the real emphasis on sport in Jewish culture. If the success of Jewish sportsmen representing different countries were taken into account the figures would show approximately the same achievement level as those of Christian countries. The variation of success within the group of innerworldly oriented countries is also very great. On the one hand, these are Confucians with very low emphasis on sport success and on the other, certain Christian countries with very high scores of achievement. According to Weber, variation in economic achievement can be explained by taking into account the typical paths of salvation in each religion. The orientation toward the mastery of the world or innerworldly ascetism, represented primarily by the Protestants, would lead to a high level of economic activity, whereas resignedness or high adaptation to the world—innerworldly mysticism—presented primarily by the Confucian ideational deep-structure, would lead to low level achievement. This general hypothesis could be applied to include sport achievement. Because of the variety of churches and denominations within the Christian—as well as Islam-tradition, a further qualification of the typology is needed.

Weber, (1963, 166) considers Protestantism, particularly its Puritan tradition, to be the extreme form of innerworldly ascetism. Protestants strongly emphasize the importance of mastery over the world order or participating in the institutions of the world, but in opposition to them. As a matter of fact, the world is presented to the religious virtuoso as his responsibility. He has the obligation to transform the world in accordance with his ascetic ideals. In a way it provides an ideational atmosphere within which the pursuit of achievement of various kinds—economic, intellectual, scientific, and even athletic supposedly thrives. Additionally, Protestantism seems to extend its high requirements not only to the elite of society but also to the masses by emphasizing the central position of individual responsibilities in religious decision.

Catholicism, on the other hand, does not so systematically accentuate the rational mastery over the world as Protestantism does, nor does it set the individual's requirements so high by standing between the spiritual and the worldly involvements of man in such a way that man's moral obligations before the divine are atomized. As Weber repeatedly says, it was possible for a Catholic to gain absolution for particular sins, one by one. There was hence no basic focusing of responsibilities for the total pattern of life as in Protestantism. In accordance with Weber, it can be hypothesized that the achievement level of Catholic countries will be relatively lower than that of Protestant countries.

The Orthodox, the third major branch of Christianity does not differ greatly from the other Christian religions in its position on the world. St. Paul's well-known phrase "in the world but not of it" can be considered a common ideal of the Orthodox. On the other hand, the Orthodox way to salvation seems to be greatly different from Protestantism, showing a slight tendency to adaptation to the world order and not to changing it. This was especially true in the case of the Russian Orthodox Church with its slight tendency to inner-worldly mysticism. The tendency toward adaptation and resigned-ness as a general social expectation to the social order has hardly encouraged large masses in terms of personal achievement. The level of achievement in sport may be hypothesized to be considerably lower than that of Protestants and lower rather than higher than that of Catholics.

Judaism also seems to belong to those religions which do not reject the world. According to Weber, Judaism differs from Puritanism pri-marily in the relative absence of a *systematic* mastery over the world. Representing a kind of moderate innerworldly asceticism, its achieve-ment level can be expected to be lower than that of Catholicism. As to sport achievement, the verification of the hypothesis is very dif-ficult because of the relatively short existence of the very small country of Israel. In fact, the achievements of Israel are more a probability than an already apparent fact.

Islam, like any other great religion, exhibits various forms and ele-ments. These are not, however, reviewed here in detail. In the same way the innerworldly position is characteristic of Christianity and Judaism, it is also characteristic of Islam. Although it includes ele-ments of "inhibited" stages of ascetism (Parsons), it does not basic-ally aim at the systematic change of the world order. Its activating effect extends primarily to some kinds of elites, to religious warriors and conquerors, but not to the large masses of people. From Protes-tantism, it differs almost diametrically because of its lack of rational effort at mastering the social order. The mystical, rather than ascetic quest for salvation, can be regarded as typical of average Muslims. The level of achievement can be hypothesized to be approximately as high as that of the Orthodox Christians.

Among the great religions of the East only Confucianism is re-garded by Weber as innerworldly oriented. In this religion Weber, however, observes the extreme example of adaptation to the world order and at the same time an ideational structure almost diametrical to Protestantism in its position of mastery over the world. The achieve-ment level—sport achievement included—can be hypothesized as being relatively low within this culture.

The results of the Olympic Games in 1896–1968 clearly verify the hypotheses presented above. Protestant nations have been about 3–4 times more successful than Catholic ones, whereas the success of Catholic nations has been considerably higher than that of Orthodox and Islam nations. The success of Confucians has been even lower than that of Muslims. With a few exceptions, they have stood almost entirely outside great international sport events.

Table 2. **Coefficient of success of countries with innerworldly oriented religion versus asceticism and mysticism in the Summer Olympic Games 1896-1968 and in the Winter Games 1948-68.**

	Primarily	1896-1968	1948-68
High level of innerworldly ascetism	Protestant[1]	4.4	3.8
	Jewish	0.0	0.0
	Catholic[2]	1.4	0.9
	Orthodox[3]	0.5	0.2
	Islam[4]	0.1	0.2
High level of innerworldly mysticism	Confucian[5]	0.0	—

1) East Germany excluded in 1968 as a Socialist country.
2) Czechoslovakia, Hungary and Poland excluded since 1948 and Cuba since 1956 as Socialist countries.
3) Russia included 1896-1912, excluded since 1920 and Bulgaria, Rumania and Yugoslavia excluded since 1948 as Socialist countries.
4) Albania excluded since 1948 as a Socialist country.
5) China excluded since 1948 as a Socialist country.

Weber's brilliant analysis of the role of the ideational structure of society lacks, however, at least one important aspect. He limits his analysis of the superstructure based only upon religion. It is possible that this approach was adequate in Weber's time. But, in modern society, an innerworldly orientation towards the basic elements within the ideational structure of society can be even more intensified than it has ever been in Protestantism. This does not mean that man is more eager to seek salvation through innerworldly asceticism today than he was in the Puritan age, but it does suggest that the pursuit of mastery over the world can, in modern society, be a goal in itself, not only a by-product in the path to salvation as it was assumed to be in society with a primarily religious ideational structure. In other words, the basic element of the ideational structure of at least some societies can be entirely secular. If this holds true, it should also have some consequences in the analysis of achievement.

The ideational structure of the Socialist societies is one which is not based on religion, in its traditional meaning, but on a secular type of social philosophy. It may vary slightly in different Socialist societies, but its basic elements are with in the Marxian tradition. The Marxian interpretation of the world, contrary to St. Paul's ideals, does not only act in this world but also is of it, a fact entirely opposite of any religion based upon supernatural authority.

If the basic elements of the ideational superstructure of society can be interpreted either in sacred or secular terms, as it is assumed here, then Weber's typology based solely on sacred elements needs qualification. Particularly of concern, is the role of Socialist ideology in the analysis of any type of achievement and especially in the case of sport achievement. In the ideological structure of Socialist society, sport has not only a latent but also a manifest function in the building of Socialist society. There is little doubt that one of the core tendencies of Socialist idology is mastery over the world order including achievement in fields of social activity. In as much as the cultural ethos of Socialist society can be considered even more innerworldly oriented than the position of Protestant societies, sport achievement may also be hypothesized as being higher.

Comparison between four types of societies: Socialist, Protestant, mixed Protestant-Catholic, and Catholic countries proves the validity of the hypothesis. The more innerworldly oriented the ideational structure of society is, the higher the level of sport achievement. Catholic countries are less successful than mixed Protestant-Catholic countries. Protestant-Catholic countries are less successful than Protestant countries, even though the difference between them is rather small. Lüschen's survey of young athletes in West Germany offers additional support as to the validity of the hypothesis at the individual level. Over-representation of Protestants is very obvious in German sport in general, and especially prevalent among high achievers both in swimming and track and field (Lüschen 1967). Comparison between Socialist and Christian countries is of particular interest. Protestant societies have traditionally played the leading role in international competition. Their success in all the Olympic Games since 1896 has been more than 7 times better than expected in accordance with the population of these societies. This success continued until the Munich Games where the success of these countries was still more than 3 times the expected value. More interesting however, is the trend since 1948. At the same time the success of Protestant countries has been decreasing, the success of Socialist countries has shown an increase. In the games since 1960 the Socialist countries collectively have been even more successful than the Protestant countries. This trend clearly indicates a great emphasis on sport and especially on sport achievement in the Socialist countries. It is not necessary in this article to describe further the special conditions within Socialist societies, (which promote high sport achievement). It is sufficient to show the clear interrelationship which exists

Table 3. Sport success of Socialist, Protestant, mixed Protestant-
Catholic countries in the Summer Olympic Games 1896–
1968 and 1948 to 1972

Success coefficient in

Type of Society	1896-1968	1948	1952	1956	1960	1964	1968	1972
Socialist[1]	–	0.8	2.0	3.3	3.7	3.7	3.5	3.0
Protestant[2]	7.4	6.0	4.2	4.8	3.5	3.7	3.3	3.0
Protestant-Catholic[3]	3.6	4.4	2.9	2.5	2.9	3.2	3.3	2.3
Catholic[4]	1.6	1.7	1.1	0.9	0.8	0.8	0.7	0.3

1) Albania, Bulgaria, Czechoslovakia, Hungary, Mongolia, Poland, Rumania, U.S.S.R., Cuba since 1960, North Korea since 1956, and G.D.R. since 1963. China and North Vietnam excluded.

2) Australia, Denmark, Estonia (1920–36), Finland, Great Britain, Iceland, Latvia (1920–36), New Zealand, Norway, Sweden, and South Africa (excluding the games 1964–68). Minorities less than 10 per cent not taken into account.

3) Bahama-Islands, Bohemia (1896–1912), Canada, Czechoslovakia (1920–36), Germany excluding the games 1920, 1924, and 1948 when it was not allowed to participate and 1968–72 when West Germany and East Germany participated as separate nationalities, West Germany 1968, Hungary (1896–1936), Jamaica, Netherlands, Switzerland, Trinidad, U.S.A., and West Indies 1960.

4) All Central and South American countries (excluded Cuba since 1969 and Jamica, Trinidad and West Indies 1960), Austria, Belgium, France, Ireland, Italy, Lithuania (1920–36), Lichtenstein, Luxembourg, Monaco, Philippines, Poland (1896–1936), Portugal, San Marino, Spain.

between the highly innerworldly oriented cultural ethos or the ideational superstructure and achievement as it appears in international sport success.

Another interesting characteristic in the achievement of Socialist countries is the fact that they have very different pre-Socialist backgrounds. The Soviet Union, Bulgaria, and Rumania were primarily Orthodox, Yugoslavia an intermixture of Catholic, Orthodox, and Islam, Hungary and Czechoslovakia intermixtures of Catholic and Protestant, Poland and Cuba Catholic, GDR Protestant, Mongolia Lama Buddhist, and China primarily Confucian. What the change in the type of society and in the ideational superstructure caused in the sport achievement of these countries appears in the table below.

Omitting China and Albania, which have stood outside the great international sports events and also represent another type of Social-

Table 4. Success coefficient of Socialist countries in the Summer Olympic Games before and after the revolution according to the type of religion during the pre-revolution period (1896–1972)

Type of society before revolution	Before the Socialist period	During the Socialist period
Buddhist (Mongolia)	—	3.3
Confucian (China)[1]	—	—
Islam (Albania)	0.0	0.0
Orthodox-Islam-Catholic (Yugoslavia)	0.7	1.5
Orthodox (Bulgaria, Rumania, U.S.S.R.)	0.0	2.9
Catholic (Cuba, Poland)	0.7	2.3
Catholic-Protestant (Czechoslovakia, Hungary)	5.0	10.2
Protestant (East Germany)[2]	3.1	14.3 (only 1968 and 1972)

1. The achievements are not calculated because of the lack of information. Some occasional successes such as several World championships in table tennis and Chinese records in track and field refer, however, to the same tendency observed in the other Socialist countries.

2. Because of the joint team with West Germany only the games of Mexico and Munich are taken into account. Coefficient for "before Socialist period" is that of undivided Germany.

ist society, the change towards greater success has been quite remarkable. This is especially true when the rising level of achievement in general is taken into consideration. The high achievement level in Protestant societies is considered a function of the ideational ethos in Protestant culture. The same assumption seems to hold true even more strongly in the case of the Soviet type of Socialist culture. The elements of high personal responsibility, as well as a kind of competitive ethos, are characteristic of both of them. Additionally the expectations supposedly extend not only to the thin elite of society but also to the masses. A kind of equalitarianism is prevalent at least in the social expectations of these societies. If this assumption holds true, then the higher achievement in sport should be apparent also in the case of women. One of the most important expressions of equalitarianism is the equality of sexes. In other words, the basic hypothesis

Table 5. Success coefficient of societies with various ideational structures in the womens events in the Summer Olympic Games 1900–1972

Type of Society	Success coefficient in		
	1900-1936	1948-1968	1960-1972
Socialist	1.0[1]	4.1	4.3
Protestant	8.3	5.4	3.8
Mixed Protestant-Catholic	6.1	3.8	3.7
Catholic	0.6	0.3	0.2
Hindu	—	—	—
Buddhist	—	—	—
Confucian[2]	—	0.3	0.4
Islam	—	—	—
Orthodox	0.2	0.0	0.0
Shinto-Buddhist[3]	2.5	0.2	0.4

1) Pre-Socialist Albania, Bulgaria, Czechoslovakia, Cuba, Hungary, Poland, Rumania, Russia 1896–1912, Yugoslavia.
2) Taiwan
3) Japan

regarding the position of the ideational structure of the world should also apply to the achievements of women.

The results indicate approximately the same tendency as in general achievement. The Socialist countries have surpassed others in the 60's, even though the difference between them and Protestant countries is not great.

When the success of women is compared with that of men the results suggest that the success of women in Socialist countries has been even better than that of men. It appears that the achievement expectation of the two sexes is more equal in Socialist societies than in societies with an ideational structure based upon religion. This kind of role equivalence is apparently not only limited to sport but also extends to many other fields of social life. The high percentage of women in the labor force, the high proportion of them in professional occupations, and the relatively active participation in almost all societal affairs tell the same story, as is observed in the case of sport achievement.

Without any detailed comparison, it is also possible to see a regularity in the relative success of women and men in general. The more innerworldly oriented a society is, the more equal the success of women and men in sport achievement. It is obvious that the ideational structure, with tendency toward mastery over the world, decreases role unequality, perhaps unequality in general.

The declining trend in the success of the Protestant nations is an additional focus of interest. The trend can partially be explained by a continual increase in the level of competition, but further explanation is needed. If the possibility of mere stochastic variation were omitted, as seems reasonable, there should be something in the very conditions of Protestant societies that has changed. A promising alternative is to compare the conditions of Protestant societies before and after World War II. Even though the basic ethos of society may be the same in both periods of time, it is possible that some sub-element in the societal structure or social situation has changed.

A careful analysis of the achievements of Protestant countries shows that there are rather great variations in the trends of success of different nations. The success of Great Britain, the only large Protestant nation, if intermixtures of Protestant and Catholic are excluded, shows no great fluctuation. British success was very high only during the period prior to World War I, when the British pattern of sport was first introduced and accepted into the basic structure of the modern Olympic Games. On the other hand, the success of small Protestant nations, represented primarily by Scandinavian or Nordic countries, gives a greatly different picture. As a whole, the success of these countries has been far greater than any other country or group of countries. The figures for overall success are very startling.

Table 6. The 10 most successful single countries in the Summer Olympic Games 1896-1972

Country	Resp. period	Total score of points	Success coefficient (C_S)
1. Finland	(1896-1972)	497.5	27.1
2. Sweden	(1896-1972)	768.3	24.4
3. Estonia	(1920-1936)	39	20.6
4. Hungary	(1896-1936)	189.5	9.6
Hungary	(1948-1972)	389.3	18.4
5. G.D.R.	(1968-1972)	181.5	14.2
6. Norway	(1896-1972)	211	13.4
7. Denmark	(1896-1972)	235	12.0
8. Switzerland	(1896-1972)	272	11.5
9. Australia	(1896-1972)	349	7.5
10. Bahamas		14	6.0

The success coefficient for Finland in all the Summer Games is a high of 27.1, for Sweden 24.4, for Norway 13.4 and for Denmark 12.0.

When both the Summer and the Winter Games are taken into account the corresponding coefficients are 32.4 for Finland, 29.7 for Norway, 26.8 for Sweden and 11.4 for Denmark. Only Estonia (1920–1936), East Germany (1968–1972), Hungary and Switzerland have had success comparable with the Scandinavian countries. Additionally interesting is the fact that East Germany the most successful nation among Socialist countries is not only Socialist but Protestant as well. In fact, the G.D.R. is the only nation in the world where Protestant tradition and Socialism are combined. The rise of the Scandinavian countries extends from the Games of Stockholm in 1912, to the Games of Helsinki 1952. The real boom, however, is limited to the interwar period in the 20's and the period immediately before World War I, or in other words, to the period when participation in the Olympic Games was still rather negligible and systematic training of sportsmen hardly more than in its beginning.

Table 7. The most successful countries in the Summer Games in Munich 1972

Country	Type	Total score of points	Success coefficient
1. G.D.R.	(Soc.)	128.5	19.4
2. Hungary	(Soc.)	49.5	11.8
3. Bulgaria	(Soc.)	43	10.5
4. Sweden	(Prot.)	30	9.7
5. Australia	(Prot.)	40	8.4
6. Finland	(Prot.)	15	8.3
7. Norway	(Prot.)	9	6.0
8. New Zealand	(Prot.)	6	5.6
9. Cuba	(Soc.)	14.5	4.4
10. Mongolia	(Soc.)	2	4.2
11. Kenya	(Developing)	15	3.7
12. Rumania	(Soc.)	28	3.6
13. F.R.G.	(Mixed Prot.-Cath.)	76.5	3.3
14. Poland	(Soc.)	39	3.1
15. Czechoslovakia	(Soc.)	16	2.9
16. Uganda	(Developing)	5	2.6
17. Switzerland	(Mixed Prot.-Cath.)	6	2.5
18. U.S.S.R.	(Soc.)	226	2.4
19. U.S.A.	(Mixed Prot.-Cath.)	189.5	2.4
20. The Netherlands	(Mixed Prot.-Cath.)	12	2.4

Even if there has not occurred any greater fall since World War II, the most successful nations have, however, been Socialist countries like East Germany, Hungary, Bulgaria and recently Cuba, and Mongolia.

Table 8. The most successful countries in the Summer Games in
          Montreal 1976

Country	Type	Total Points	Success Coefficient
1. G.D.R.	(Soc.)	195	38.3
2. Bulgaria	(Soc.)	46	17.3
3. Finland	(Prot.)	17	11.4
4. Cuba	(Soc.)	29	10.9
5. Hungary	(Soc.)	34	10.3
6. Trinidad	(Cath.)	3	8.0
7. Jamaica	(Cath.)	5	7.4
8. Rumania	(Soc.)	44	6.9
9. Mongolia	(Soc.)	2	6.9
10. Sweden	(Prot.)	14	6.0
11. Poland	(Soc.)	47	4.5
12. Norway	(Prot.)	5	4.1
13. Switzerland	(Mixed Prot. Cath.)	7	4.1
14. F.R.G.	(Mixed Prot. Cath.)	71	3.8
15. U.S.S.R.	(Soc.)	262	3.4
16. Denmark	(Prot.)	5	3.3
17. C.S.R.R.	(Soc.)	14	3.2
18. U.S.A.	(Mixed Prot. Cath.)	195	3.1
19. Belgium	(Cath.)	9	2.8
20. Yugoslavia	(Soc.)	15	2.2

An analysis of the success coefficients of countries participating in
the 1976 Summer Olympic Games indicated a continuance of the
trend of Socialist countries to surpass others in achievement. East
Germany ranked with an even higher margin as the most successful
nation in the world followed by Bulgaria, Finland, Cuba and
Hungary. The analysis also indicated a continued declining trend in
the success of Protestant nations.

The absence of Kenya and Uganda from the twenty most successful nations list in the 1976 Summer Games should be noted. Several
African nations, including both Kenya and Uganda, boycotted the
1976 Games.

Also of importance to note is the fact that the success coefficient
moves up in general because of a lower share of the world population
among successful countries in the Olympics. Mongolia, which scored
2 points in both the 1972 and 1976 Olympics, moved up because of
such a population decline.

There is no doubt that the greatness of the Scandinavian and small
Protestant nations was, in general, at least partially based upon the
relative weakness of the others. The Scandinavian countries, more
than any other countries, made use of the favorable conjunctures that

the world of international sport offered before World War I, during the interwar period, and partially after World War II. As a matter of fact, just this early emphasis on sport achievement is a good manifestation of the role of competition and relatively high achievement level in general in the ideational ethos of Protestant Scandinavia.

The Protestant ethos is not, however, the only possible condition for high sport achievement in the Scandinavian societies. Especially interesting is the success of Finland during the interwar period and prior to it. Finland is a country which eagerly pursued national independence and received it after World War I. As a nation, she was almost unknown outside of her borders. She had also experienced a Civil War in 1918. Establishing a new political order in a country which had recently experienced an internal war apparently created a very great integration problem. Additionally, the international political situation was rather unstable from the point of view of Finland. Under these circumstances, Finland was probably the first country in the world in which international success in competitive sport was systematically organized to serve purposes of national integration of society. There is little doubt that sport and sport success in international events served as an important instrument, not only in the nation building process of Finland, but also in the establishment of Finnish nationalism.

This also holds true in the case of some other nationalities of Europe, especially new independent nations. It is worth while to note that only the success of new Protestant nations was very high in the interwar period. In societies with Catholic or some other type of ideational superstructure, no high sport success was apparent. Of special interest is a comparison between the new Baltic countries. The Protestant Estonia and Latvia were very successful but Catholic Lithuania was not. The success of Albania, Bulgaria and even Poland was also considerably below what could be expected according to population.

Table 9. The success of new independent nations of Europe during the interwar period in the Summer Olympic Games 1920–1936

Type of Society	Coefficient of success
Protestant (Estonia, Finland, Latvia)	45.0
Catholic (Lithuania, Poland)	0.8
Mixture of Catholic, Orthodox and Islam (Yugoslavia)	0.7
Orthodox (Bulgaria)	0.0
Islam (Albania)	0.0

Even though nationalism may have been an additional condition of high sport success in small European nations, it appeared only in connection with the ideational structure of the Protestant background. Additionally, it is important to remember that the high success of the other Scandinavian countries, except Finland and partially Norway, was not preconditioned by newly won independence. This does not, however, necessarily deny the presence of nationalistic elements in the sport success of Scandinavian countries.

The role that nationalism has played in international sport success received its first manifestation of great magnitude in the 30's when the nationalistic big powers, such as Mussolini's Italy, Hitler's Germany and also Japan, discovered its importance as an instrument of nationalistic integration. The sport success of all these countries was considerably higher during the Nazi and Fascist period than earlier. The success of Japan has not decreased since World War II, whereas that of West Germany and Italy has. The relatively high success of Italy and of France are representative of high success among Catholic countries. Besides Italian Fascism during the interwar period, it is possible that the rather long traditions of secular—innerworldly—philosophies of France and Italy have had their influence on the overall ideational structures of these countries.

Table 10. The success of Germany, Italy, and Japan in the Olympic
Games in different periods of time

	Coefficient of success			
	1896-1928	1932-1936	1952-1968	1972
Germany[1]	2.9	5.9	2.8	3.3
Japan	0.4	1.7	2.1	1.6
	1896-1920	1924-1936	1948-1968	1972
Italy	2.0	4.2	3.4	1.5

1) Includes East Germany for 1952-1964.

From Sport Success to the Function of Competitive Sport

The sport success of different societies has been reviewed and interpreted as a function of the ideational structure of society. Christ's words: "Let your light so shine before men, that they may see your good works. . ." is manifested especially within the achievements of Protestantism; even more so in the high achievements of Socialist nations with the demanding requirements of Marxist theory: "From everybody according to the capacity." The interpretation of sport success does not, however, explain why the role of competitive sport is high in one type of society and low in another. A question of great importance arises: Does sport serve a certain political function important to Socialist and some Christian societies or is it only that achievement is a byproduct of ideology without any particular function?

There is no simple answer to this question even though some assumptions may be made. According to the traditional ideals of the Olympic Games and other international competition, great sport events should serve as an institution for international friendship and mutual understanding between nations, races, religions, and types of different social and economic systems in general. It is possible that national sport may also have this kind of function. But are the countries pursuing friendship and mutual understanding just Socialist, or Protestant, or intermixtures of Protestant and Catholic, or even Nationalistic? *Hitler's* Germany, *Mussolini's* Italy, Japan in the 30's, and the super powers of today are hardly the best examples of pursuit of peaceful cooperation in international affairs, even though they are examples of countries with high sport success.

Instead of advancing peaceful co-existence and understanding between nations, competitive sport may also have a political function of an entirely different nature. Intensified international competition can also lead to an overintegration within national or other armed units and intensified hostility toward other nations or group of nations. Although there is no reason to exaggerate the role of sport in international conflict, it would not be reasonable to omit this possibility from the analysis. The soccer war between Honduras and El Salvador in 1969 is a fresh example of minor magnitude, whereas the simultaneous intensification of sport achievement and war preparations in Germany, Italy and Japan in the 30's is a manifestation of activity with terrible consequences. By intensifying national pride and by producing overintegration, competitive sport may be an important instrument in the hands of those in power.

The systematic pursuit of high success in the Olympic Games and in other great international sport events has continuously grown in importance since World War II. The role of international competitive sport as an integrative institution of society has obviously been realized more clearly than ever before. Whether international sport helps to promote peace between nations or is a manifestation of the power struggle in cold war between super powers or power blocks is hard to say. At any rate, the Olympic Games and other great international sport events seem to become a stage of international politics rather than a meeting ground for the individual sportsmen. Competition under equal terms, one of the leading ideas of the modern Olympic Games, is little more than an ideal without any real essence. The increasing emphasis on the national role of sport and how it conflicts with the old-fashioned official ideals of international sport is a worthwhile topic for further study.

Table 10. The absolute success and the population weighted success (C_S) of different nations in the modern Olympic Games 1896–1972.

		Summer points	Games C_S	Winter points	Games C_S	Total points
Argentina		92.5	1.0	–	–	92.5
Australia		349	7.5	–	–	349
Austria		115	3.5	143	37.5	258
Bahama-Islands		14	6.0	–	–	14
Belgium		289.5	5.5	7	1.6	216.5
Bohemia	1896–1936	6	0.4	–	–	6
Brazil		23	0.1	–	–	23
Bulgaria	1896–1936	–	–	–	–	–
	1948–1972	102.5	5.4	–	–	102.5
Cameroon	1948–1972	2	0.5	–	–	2
Canada		181.8	2.4	64.5	7.0	246.3
Ceylon		2	0.1	–	–	2
Chile		11	0.4	–	–	11
Columbia		3	0.0	–	–	3
Cuba	1895–1956	27.7	1.3	–	–	27.7
	1960–1972	24.5	2.3	–	–	24.5
Czechoslovakia						
	1920–1936	62.5	3.8	3	0.6	65.5
	1948–1972	156.3	5.4	15	3.2	171.3
Denmark		235	12.0	–	–	235
Egypt[1]		31	0.3	–	–	31
Estonia	1920–1936	39	20.6	–	–	39
Ethiopia		13	0.1	–	–	13
Finland		497.5	27.1	143.3	66.5	640.8
France		763.3	3.7	65.5	2.7	828.8
Germany[2]		707.7	3.3	74	2.8	781.7
East Germany						
	1968–1972	181.5	14.2	34	16.6	215.5
West Germany						
	1968–1972	129.5	3.1	25	3.4	154.5
Ghana	1948–1972	3	0.4	–	–	3
Great Britain		963.5	4.4	22	0.9	985.5
Greece		160.5	4.2	–	–	160.5
Haiti		3	0.2	–	–	3
Hungary	1896–1936	189.5	9.6	3	1.8	192.5
	1948–1972	389.3	18.4	3	1.1	392.3
Iceland		2	3.0	–	–	2
India		30	0.0	–	–	30
Iran		44	0.5	–	–	44
Iraq		1	0.0	–	–	1
Ireland		18	1.5	–	–	18
Italy		47	3.0	43	1.7	690
Jamaica	1960 excl.	22	3.8	–	–	22
Japan		355.5	1.0	8	0.2	363.5
Kenya	1948–1972	35	3.0	–	–	35
Latvia	1920–1936	5	1.4	–	–	5
Lebanon	1948–1972	5	2.6	–	–	5
Luxembourg		5	3	–	–	5
Mexico		44.5	0.3	–	–	44.5
Mongolia	1948–1972	7	3.0	–	–	7
Morocco		2	0.1	–	–	2
Netherlands		233.5	4.7	52	8.9	285.5
New Zealand		50	4.7	–	–	50
Niger	1960–1972	0.5	0.1	–	–	0.5
Nigeria	1948–1972	1	0.0	–	–	1
North Korea						
	1946–1972	6	0.4	1.5	0.7	8.5
Norway		211	13.4	274.3	141.6	485.3
Pakistan	1948–1972	13	0.1	–	–	13
Panama		2	0.6	–	–	2

Peru		3	0.1	–	–	3
Phillippines		7	0.1	–	–	7
Poland	1896–1936	22	0.5	–	–	22
	1948–1972	165.5	2.5	7	0.6	172.5
Portugal		9	0.3	–	–	9
Puerto Rico		1	0.1	–	–	1
Rumania	1920–1936	3	0.2	–	–	3
	1948–1972	125.5	3.0	1	0.1	126.5
Russia	1896–1912	13.5	0.1	–	–	13.5
Singapore		2	0.2	–	–	2
South Africa[1]		95	1.8	–	–	95
South Korea						
	1948–1972	10	0.3	–	–	16
Spain		14.5	0.1	3	0.2	17.5
Sweden		766.3	24.4	133	35.6	901.3
Switzerland		272	11.5	85	29.7	357
Taiwan	1948–1972	7	0.4	–	–	7
Trinidad[2] and Tebacco		8	2.3	–	–	8
Tunisia		6.5	0.5	–	–	8.5
Turkey		100	0.8	–	–	100
Uganda	1948–1972	6	0.7	–	–	8
United Arabic Republic						
	1960	2	0.1	–	–	2
Uruguay		13.5	1.3	–	–	13.5
U.S.A.		279.8	3.4	166.8	1.7	2957.6
U.S.S.R.[3]	1952–1972	1141	2.6	189	2.8	1330
Venezuela		4	0.1	–	–	4
West Indies 1960		2	2.2	–	–	2
Yugoslavia 1920–1936		1	0.6	–	–	16

1) 1960 excluded
2) Games 1920, 1924, and 1948 excluded

REFERENCES

Ball, D. 1972. Olympic Games competition: structural correlates of national success. *Int. J. Comp. Soc.* 15, 2:186–200.

Graham, P. and H. Überhorst. 1976. *The Modern Olympics.* Cornwall, N.Y.: Leisure Press.

Sveriges Rijksidrottsförbund. 1953. *Svensk Idrott.* Malmö: Allhem.

Jokl, E. 1956. *Sports in the Cultural Pattern of the World.* Helsinki: Institute of Occupational Health.

Levine, N. 1974. Why do countries win Olympic medals? Some structural correlates of Olympic Success. *Soc.Social Res.* 28, 3:353–360.

Lüschen, G. 1967. The interdependence of sport and culture. *IRSS* 2, 1:127–142.

Lüschen, G. 1969. Social stratification and social mobility among young sportsmen. Pp. 258–76 in Loy, J. and G. Kenyon. *Sport, Culture and Society.* New York: Macmillan.

McClelland, D. 1961. *The Achieving Society.* Princeton: VanNostrand.

McIntosh, P. 1963. *Sport in Society.* London: Watts.

Nowikow, A. and M. Maksimenko. 1973. Soziale und ökonomische Faktoren und das Niveau sportlicher Leistungen in verschiedenen Ländern. *Sportwissenschaft* 2,2:156–167.

Pfetsch, F. 1975. *Leistungssport und Gesellschaftssystem.* Schorndorf: Hofmann.

Seppänen, P. 1967. Huippu-urheilun sosiaalista edellytyksistä ja funktioista. *Stadion I.*

Seppänen, P. 1972. Die Rolle des Leistungssports in den Gesellschaften der Welt. *Sportwissenschaft* 2,2:133–155.

Tawney, R.H. 1958. *Religion and the Rise of Capitalism.* New York.

U.S. President's Committee. 1976 *Report on Olympic Sport.* Washington, D.C.: Government Printing Office.

Weber, M. 1930. *The Protestant Ethic and the Spirit of Capitalism.* New York: Scribner.

Weber, M. 1963. *The Sociology of Religion.* Boston: Beacon.

PART II

SOCIAL INSTITUTIONS

AND SPORT

IN MODERN SOCIETY

Snyder/Spreitzer

Sage

Greendorfer

Kelly

SPORT, EDUCATION, AND SCHOOLS

Eldon E. Snyder and Elmer Spreitzer et al.

The purpose of this article is to review the social scientific litera-ture on sport and education with the purpose of highlighting certain aspects which are amenable to the scientific method. The data gathered by social scientists still require, however, interpretation within a broader value context. The fact that we must continually reformulate our position concerning sport and education is not therefore a source of distress but rather delight, since it is a means of self-actualization for the fortunate few of us who are blessed with having our vocation and avocation as one.

When conceptualized broadly, education coincides with the term socialization which refers to the assimilation of social norms, values, and skills that enable one to function effectively as a member of society. This process by which persons internalize the culture around them results in the maintenance of social continuity, pre-dictability, and patterning from a societal perspective. Socialization is also a type of constraint in the sense that it leaves a social imprint, limits the range of acceptable behavior, and thus induces conformity.

Within the context of sport, social scientists have analyzed sociali-zation from two basic perspectives. One focus has been on the process of *socialization into sport*—that is, assimilation of the mental and physical characteristics requisite for participation in sport. The second focus revolves around *socialization via sport;* here the interest is in the consequences and concomitants of sports parti-cipation for both the individual and society (Sage 1974). These separate aspects of sport socialization are illustrated in the diagram below:

Socialization into the sport role $\longrightarrow$ participation $\longrightarrow$ Consequences and concomitants of sport involvement

In our analysis of the twofold process of sport socialization, we focus on these processes as they occur in the context of school systems. In this respect we emphasize the role of sport within educational institutions; it should be noted, however, that socialization is a lifelong process, and sport is no doubt intertwined with individual development across all stages of the life cycle. In fact, we recommend that future research could well be directed at determining the functions of sport for *adults* on a lifelong recreational basis.

SOCIALIZATION INTO SPORT

When sport is analyzed as a dependent variable, we are interested in the social learning that results in the acquisition of the sport role(s.). These roles may be either actual participation (primary involvement) or as a spectator (secondary involvement). For example, Kenyon (1970) investigated the social and psychological correlates of "consumption" of major league baseball games and the Olympic Games in Mexico City. Using a sample of college students, Kenyon identified the following school-related variables as being associated with these two forms of sport involvement: encouragement by physical education teachers, general interest in sport during high school, secondary involvement in sport during high school, and secondary involvement in sport during college. Additionally, Kenyon noted the importance of familial, peer influences, as well as perceived athletic ability as correlates of sport involvement. Following Kenyon's lead, McPherson (1972) surveyed high school students from three metropolitan schools to determine the process by which they were socialized into the role of sport consumer. Involvement in sport for both males and females was promoted by the social influence of the family, peers, school, and community organizations.

Recent research (Snyder and Spreitzer 1976a) shows that the patterns observed by Kenyon and McPherson with respect to males are also replicated in surveys of female sport participation. Comparisons of adolescent female athletes and nonathletes indicate that the athletes tend to come from home backgrounds where their parents were interested in sports and provided encouragement for them; additionally, siblings and relatives were more likely to encourage the athletes to participate in high school sports. The findings also confirmed that female athletes receive positive reinforcement for their athletic role from peers, teachers, and particularly coaches.

The studies cited above have focused on the variables associated with the participation of high school and college youth in sport. Another method of studying this process is to take a retrospective view from the vantage point of adult involvement in sport roles. Survey research indicates that adult sports involvement for both males and females can be traced back to childhood and reinforcement as a youth. Findings from a community sample (mean age of 42) revealed that the following factors were associated with adult involvement in sport: parental interest in sport, parental encouragement to participate in sport, participation in formally organized (e.g., school) athletic programs as a youth, self-perception of athletic ability, and involvement in sport by one's spouse (Spreitzer and Snyder 1976).

Kenyon and McPherson (1973: 307–308) utilized a systems model in their analysis of socialization into sport:

> Given a degree of role aptitude (cognitive and motoric) the role aspirant is variously influenced within each of the social situations in which he inevitably finds himself, with the net effect being the acquisition of a propensity for learning the [sport] role in question. Furthermore, this motivates him to rehearse the role, which in turn leads to the learning of the role. In propositional form:
>
> 1. The greater the role aptitude, the greater the system-inducing propensity for role learning.
> 2. The greater the system-induced propensity for role learning, the greater the role rehearsal, and vice versa.
> 3. The greater the propensity for role learning, the greater the role learning, i.e., degree of socialization.

Kenyon and McPherson (1973: 308) illustrate these propositions in the following diagram:

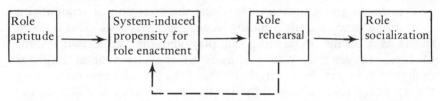

They further expand this model into the following two-stage social systems model (Kenyon and McPherson 1973: 309):

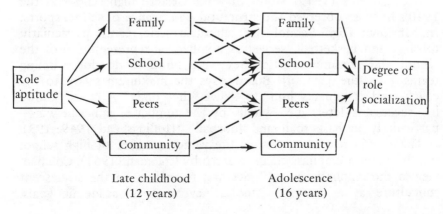

Within each of these social systems, role learning (such as involvement in the sport) is governed by the values, norms, sanctions, and situational facilities that are present within the social systems.

SPORT WITHIN SCHOOLS

While induction into sport roles takes place within the family, through peers, neighborhood and community influences, a central agency of socialization into sports is clearly the school. For most youth the school athletic program provides the primary institutional arrangement for formalized sport involvement. In this section we consider the schools and the correlates of formal athletic participation by adolescents.

The importance and pervasiveness of school sports in the 1920's were emphasized by the Lynds when they described "school life" in Middletown High School. They pointed out that athletics have a position of obeisance in the high school yearbook with the largest number of pages, and "the highest honor a senior boy can have is captaincy of the football or basketball team..." (Lynd and Lynd, 1929: 214). The predominance of sports among high school youth was also noted in the classic study by Waller (1932). With reference to the subculture of the school, he indicated that athletics are primary and the most revered school activities (Waller, 1932: 112–113). Waller cited the advantages of school sports in serving as a catharsis and a means of focusing the attention of students on a unifying and morale-building school activity. He also viewed sports as a means of learning fair play and the "important lessons of life." In general, Waller considered the effect of athletics as desirable; however, he pointed out that "the preachments concerning the sporting code which drop so frequently from the lips of the coaches are more than neutralized in practice by the pressure which these men put upon their players to win games" (Waller 1932: 114).

Hollinghead's (1949) study of a midwestern high school in the 1940's likewise observed the structural significance of school sports. In Elmtown High School the school athletic teams, particularly football and basketball, served as a collective representation of the school and community. Coaches were hired to develop winning teams and "the [school] Board pays the maximum salary to the coach, and it expects him 'to deliver the goods.' A coach knows his 'success' is determined wholly by the number of games he wins— particularly in basketball and football" (Hollingshead 1949: 193).

The dominance of sports in the value structure of high school youth was also emphasized in research by Coleman (1961). Coleman viewed the emphasis on athletics and popularity in the adolescent subculture as a threat to the achievement of academic goals.

Interestingly, some of the data presented by Coleman do not support this presupposition, and a follow-up study of high school youth by Snyder (1969) showed that boys who said they would like to be remembered as "star athletes" were more likely to complete college than the students who said they would like to be remembered in high school as the "most popular" or as "brilliant students."

Significant social changes have occurred in the American society since the publication of Coleman's *Adolescent Society.* Is sport still as important in the status of adolescents? A study by Eitzen (1976) suggests that it is. To assess the contemporary importance of sport for high school males as compared to findings from the Coleman study, Eitzen included many of the questionnaire items originally used by Coleman. On one of the items ("If you could be remembered here at school for one of the three things below, which would you want it to be?") the results show interesting similarities: "Athletic star"—Coleman 44 percent, Eitzen 45 percent; "brilliant student"—Coleman 31 percent, Eitzen 25 percent; "most popular"—Coleman 25 percent, Eitzen 30 percent (Eitzen, 1976: 142). Although Eitzen found important variations in the status-granting function of athletics according to the size of high schools and type of community, he concluded that sport participation continues to be a dominant criterion for status among adolescent males.

SOCIALIZATION VIA SPORT

Academic Orientation

One of the frequent stereotypes of the male athlete is that of the "dumb jock." It is not surprising then that some of the earliest correlational studies of athletic participation dealt with aspects of academic achievement. Contrary to the stereotype, the findings generally indicate a moderate positive correlation between athletic participation and an academic orientation. For example, Schafer and Armer (1968) studied a sample of 585 high school boys and found a mean grade point average of 2.35 for the athletes and 1.83 for the nonathletes. When the control variables of father's occupation, intelligence, type of curriculum, and grade point average were applied, the average grade point difference between the subsamples was reduced but still favored the athletes (2.35 compared with 2.24). Schafer and Armer (1968) likewise found that the athletes had higher educational expectations. Thus, 82 percent of the athletes planned to complete two years of college, while 75 percent of the nonathletes planned for two years of college. Furthermore, 62 percent of the athletes versus 45 percent of the nonathletes planned to complete four years of college.

What are likely explanations for the positive relationship between involvement in sport and an academic orientation? Schafer and Armer (1968: 25) offer the following possibilities:

1. Perhaps athletes are graded more leniently because teachers see them as special or more deserving.
2. Perhaps exposure in the sports subculture to effort, hard work, persistence, and winning spills over into nonathletic activities such as school work.
3. Perhaps the superior physical condition of athletes improves their mental performance.
4. Perhaps some athletes strive to get good grades to be eligible for certain sports.
5. Perhaps athletes make more efficient and effective use of their limited study time.
6. Perhaps the lure of a college career in sports motivates some athletes to strive for good grades.
7. Perhaps the higher prestige that students obtain from sports gives them a better self-concept and higher aspirations in other activities such as school work.
8. Perhaps athletes benefit from more help in school work from friends, teachers, and parents.

Other studies focusing on academic orientation and athletic participation have produced additional findings. For example, Rehberg and Schafer (1968: 734) hypothesized that the strength of the positive relationship between athletic participation and educational expectations is stronger for the boys who are *less* disposed toward education beyond high school than for boys who are *more* disposed toward attending college. The dispositional variables in their analysis included social status, academic performance, and parental encouragement to attend college. The following summary table indicates that there is an interaction effect between athletes' participation and educational expectations with respect to the dispositional variables.

The data in the Rehberg-Schafer (1968) study indicate that the positive relationship between athletics and educational expectations must be qualified. The relationship is evident only for boys who are otherwise not disposed toward attending college. To some extent these findings may reflect a "ceiling" effect; Rehberg and Schafer (1968: 739) suggest that the low endowment boys stand to gain the most from their participation in athletics and the concomitant heightened peer status. In short, they seem to develop an orientation toward educational achievement because of the

Table 1. Interaction Effects of Educational Expectations and Athletic Participation: Percentage of Respondents Reporting Educational Expectations to Four or More Years of College (Third-Order Relationships)*

Disposition Variables			Athletic Participation				
			Yes		No		Y**
Social Status	Parental Encouragement	Academic Performance	%	N	%	N	
High.....	High	High	95	40	96	57	-.18
		Low	68	31	49	45	.37
	Low	High	75	8	75	16	.00
		Low	67	6	11	18	.88
Low.....	High	High	85	52	84	73	.04
		Low	45	82	25	121	.44
	Low	High	69	13	50	46	.38
		Low	26	38	7	82	.64

*Adapted from *Rehberg* and *Schafer,* 1968:738.

**Computed with 2x2 cross-classification, i.e., four years of college-less than four years of college, athletic participation-non-athletic participation, to enhance statistical reliability.

influences of their peers—members of the leading crowd in high school which is college oriented.

Findings from a study of Picou and Curry (1974) provides further elaboration of the relationship between athletic participation and educational aspiration among high school boys. Following the lead of Rehberg and Schafer (1968) they studied athletes and nonathletes who were predisposed and non-disposed toward college attendance from rural and urban backgrounds. Dispositional backgrounds were determined by socioeconomic origins, parental encouragement, and grade point average of the respondents. The results of this study indicate that athletes from low socioeconomic backgrounds, with little parental encouragement to attend college and lower academic records, have higher scholastic aspirations than the nonathletes. These findings are supportive of the Rehberg and Schafer conclusions. Additionally, the Picou and Curry (1974) data show that this trend is particularly evident among rural athletes in contrast to urban athletes.

Additional explorations of the relationship between athletic achievement and educational aspiration were carried out by Picou (1978) for black and white males. Data from this study support the notion that athletic participation results in youths internalizing values, norms, and behavior via sports that spillover and enhance academic perfomance in the student role. Furthermore, athletic participation may increase contact with achievement-oriented peers, teachers, coaches, and family members who have a positive influence on adolescents' educational ambition. These explanations assume an indirect effect of athletic behavior on the academic role, mediated through these intervening variables. However, the most interesting conclusion reached by Picou is that while this model was applicable to the white students, it was not supported by his analysis of the black students. Thus, control of the intervening variables discussed above did not significantly reduce the effect of athletic achievement on the educational ambitions for blacks. Picou suggests that other intervening variables operate among blacks, perhaps psychological processes that should be considered in future research. Black youth may be more likely to experience an overemphasis on sports and concomitant unrealistic educational aspirations. Thus these latter two studies focusing on athletic participation and academic orientation suggest that the explanatory model of the sport-academic nexus may also vary by race and degree of urbanism.

Spady (1970) suggests that the recognition athletes receive in high school may stimulate their desire to attend college in order to enhance further their status. His study cites longitudinal research on high school graduates which indicates some dysfunctions of athletic particiption. Spady notes that when peer-based recognition associated with athletic participation are the exclusive source of educational aspirations, these aspirations are likely to be unrealistic and "inflated," in which case future educational success is improbable.

Research by Spreitzer and Pugh (1973) sheds further light on the correlation between athletic participation and educational aspirations while controlling for possible variations in student value climates between high schools. Thus, the unrealistic and "inflated" educational expectations of athletes described by Spady may be limited to high schools where athletics rather than scholarship is the source of peer status and heightened educational aspirations. Data shown in Table 2 support the hypothesis that the positive relationship between participation and expectations is highest in those high schools where the athletic specialist is accorded a great deal of prestige. The relationship is washed out in schools where the primary means of status is based on scholarship.

Table 2. Educational Expectations by Athletic Participation, Controlling for School Value Climate*

Athletic Specialist Value Climate

Education Expectations	Athletes (%)	Non-Athletes (%)
16 or more years	80	57
13–15 years	7	13
12 years	13	30
	(N=85)	(N=107)
(3 schools)	Gamma=.47	

All-Around Boy Value Climate

Educational Expectations	Athletes (%)	Non-Athletes (%)
16 or more years	59	43
13–15 years	23	20
12 years	18	37
	(N=24)	(N=60)
(2 schools)	Gamma=.33	

Scholar Specialist Value Climate

Educational Expectations	Athletes (%)	Non-Athletes (%)
16 or more years	52	53
13–15 years	23	23
12 years	25	24
	(N=31)	(N=53)
(2 schools)	Gamma=.02	

Mixed-Type, Indeterminate Climate

Educational Expectations	Athletes (%)	Non-Athletes (%)
16 or more years	58	49
13–15 years	19	17
12 years	23	34
	(N=130)	(N=214)
(6 schools)	Gamma=.19	

*Adapted from *Spreitzer* and *Pugh,* 1973:179.

Hanks and Eckland (1976) conducted a follow-up analysis of a national probability sample of high school sophomores initially surveyed in 1955. Their research design included males and females at the high school and college levels and focused on completed years of education as an adult. They concluded that there is no evidence to support the notion that either high school or college athletics are detrimental to educational attainment and, at least for males, they appear to be mildly salutary. Moreover, extra-curricular participation in general was a good predictor of ultimate educational achievement; furthermore, they believe that "the institution of sports has been largely *compartmentalized* in America. While perhaps a source of community or campus solidarity and even of alumni support, for the vast majority it has little relevance to the primary functions of the educational institutions which support it" (1976: 292).

Further elaboration of the relationship between formal participation in school sports academic variables is provided by Otto and Alwin (1977). They gathered data on high school males in 1957 and conducted a follow-up study fifteen years later in 1972. They hypothesized that the indirect effect on sport participation on aspirations and attainment would be mediated by two intervening mechanisms—perceived peer status and significant others' influence. Data from their study support earlier research indicating that participation in athletics has a positive effect on educational and occupational aspirations while controlling for socioeconomic status, mental ability, and academic performance. Participation not only had a positive effect on aspirations but also on eventual educational and occupational attainment and income. Their findings showed no support for the hypothesis that perceived peer status mediates or independently accounts for variance in attainment. Rather, the data show that the effect of athletics is largely mediated by the influence of significant others. They suggested three additional probable socialization effects from athletics:

> First, participation in athletics may teach interpersonal skills that are readily transferable and marketable outside of athletics. Second, athletics may serve an allocation function by raising the visibility of participants and providing them with an early success definition or label. Third, athletics may introduce participants to interpersonal networks, contacts, and information channels that are beneficial in establishing careers (1977: 112).

In the consideration of these correlational data gathered on high school males we note two important points. First, the relationship between involvement in sport and academic pursuits may not be uniform for all participants. The relationship may be most evident among boys otherwise not disposed to academic endeavors, the best athletes, and at schools that place an emphasis on athletics. Secondly, the correlations are not necessarily indicative of a causal relationship between participation and academic pursuit. For example, students with a low academic orientation may not enter, or they may be selected out of the athletic stream. Additionally, studies by Lueptow and Kayser (1973–1974) and Hauser and Lueptow (1978) indicate that while high school male athletes had higher grade averages than nonathletes, the athletes in their samples did not show relative improvement in grades during their high school years. These latter findings are consistent with Stevenson's (1975) conclusion that differences between athletes and nonathletes reported in most of the literature are primarily due to antecedent dissimilarities rather than to the socialization effects of sport participation (selectivity). Furthermore, Rehberg and Cohen (1975) studied 936 high school seniors using a design that compared youth whose only extracurricular involvement was athletics with youth who had pluralistic involvements. They found that the unidimensional "pure" athletes compared unfavorably academically with the class as a whole and with their fellow athletes who are also in other school organizations. Thus, while 25 percent of the class and 48 percent of the multidimensional athletes wanted to be among the "best" students, only 16 percent of the pure athletes expressed this desire.

With the recent growth of distaff sports it is desirable to expand our knowledge of this aspect of athletic participation. Snyder and Spreitzer (1977) studied a sample of high school female athletes and nonathletes to determine the relationship between athletic participation and academic orientation. The findings from their research show that the female athletes tend to have higher grade averages and educational goals than their nonathletic counterparts. Their data also permitted a comparison between girls who were involved in athletics and those who were seriously involved in music. Athletics and music are parallel socialization experiences in the sense that they both require self-discipline, commitment, coaching, and performance. The findings show that the girls who were involved in both sport and music had higher grade averages and educational goals than the girls who were involved only in athletics or music. When comparing those girls who were involved solely in music with those involved solely in athletics, the athletes tended to report slightly higher educational goals but had slightly lower grade averages

When we look at athletic participation and academic pursuit at the postsecondary level there are few studies available. Relatively few high school athletes participate on intercollegiate teams, and the high degree of selectivity that is present for college participation make causal inferences even more problematic. Valid comparisons between collegiate athletes and nonathletes are also difficult because of variations in institutional quality, degree programs, type of sport, and other potentially contaminating factors. Exploratory research conducted at the University of Minnesota for the graduating classes of 1966 and 1967 found that the academic grade point average for

Table 3. Selected Educationally Related Variables According to Participation in Sport and Music*

	Sport & Music (N=193)		Sport Only (N=523)		Music Only (N=75)		Neither (N=252)		P
	X̄	S.D.	X̄	S.D.	X̄	S.D.	X̄	S.D.	
Educational Expectations	15.3	1.5	15.0	1.9	14.9	1.9	14.5	1.9	.000
Grade Average	6.2	1.2	6.0	1.2	6.2	1.3	5.9	1.3	.047
Mother's Educational Encouragement	3.9	1.1	3.8	1.2	3.9	1.1	3.7	1.2	.452
Father's Educational Encouragement	3.6	1.3	3.6	1.3	3.6	1.2	3.5	1.4	.654
Teacher's Educational Encouragement	3.4	1.2	3.3	1.3	3.0	1.4	3.2	1.3	.085
Mother's Education	12.8	1.8	12.9	2.2	12.8	2.0	12.2	2.0	.000
Father's Education	13.0	2.6	13.5	2.8	13.7	3.2	12.5	2.8	.000
Peer Plans for College	3.4	0.7	3.4	0.8	3.3	0.8	3.2	0.8	.018

*Adapted from *Snyder* and *Spreitzer*, 1977:51.

athletes was 2.42 as compared to 2.40 for nonathletes (Pilapil, *et al.*, 1970: 29). Additional comparisons between the athletes and nonathletes indicate that 50 percent of the athletes as compared with 41 percent of the nonathletes earned a four-year degree within five years after entering college. Data from the Minnesota study also show that athletes in the classes of 1966 and 1967 had a higher percentage of the original group in attendance quarter by quarter than the nonathletes. For example, at the end of the 12th quarter, the percentage of athletes remaining was 75 as compared with 47 of the nonathletes (Pilapil, *et al.*, 1970: 27). In summary, the University of Minnesota study does not show that athletic participation is negatively correlated with academic pursuits. However, research conducted at North Texas State University among football players shows less satisfactory results. Harrison (1976) reported that the mean GPA of the players was below 2.0 (on a 4.0 scale) for the 234 players in his sample at all academic levels except for the second semester seniors. Autobiographical accounts of former collegiate athletes have also noted that the athletic role at major universities may conflict with academic pursuits (Meggyesy, 1971; Shaw, 1972).

Conventionality

One commonly held assumption regarding athletic participation is that it serves to "keep kids out of trouble," presumably because they are taught conventionality (via sport). One major piece of research on this topic does, indeed, lend support for this presupposition (Schafer, 1968). However, when social class and grade point average were used as control variables, the relationship appears only for disadvantaged boys. Examination of the findings in Table 4 reveals small differences in the percentages except for boys in the subpopulation where delinquency rates are the highest. Delinquency was sharply reduced among the athletes in this subgroup.

Additional research by Landers and Landers (1978) compared the court records of delinquency among high school students who were involved in several forms of extracurricular activity: athletics only, service and leadership, athletics and service-leadership, or no form of extracurricular participation. Rates of delinquency were highest for those students who were not involved in any form of extra-curricular activity. The rates were lower, and approximately the same, for students participating in athletics or some other form of extracurricular activity. Students with the lowest rates of delin-quency were those who were in *both* athletics and service-leadership type of extracurricular activities. The relationship between athletics and several aspects of deviance was further investigated by Buhrman (1977). He studied high school girls in Iowa and found that athletic participation was negatively related to smoking, drinking alcoholic

**Table 4. Delinquency Rates for Athletes and Nonathletes Controlling
For Father's Occupation and Grade Point Average***

	Delinquent	Non-Delinquent	Total	N
White Collar				
High GPA				
Athlete	4%	96%	100%	(74)
Non-athlete	8%	92%	100%	(113)
Low GPA				
Athlete	11%	89%	100%	(27)
Non-athlete	5%	95%	100%	(94)
Blue Collar				
High GPA				
Athlete	8%	92%	100%	(36)
Non-athlete	11%	89%	100%	(57)
Low GPA				
Athlete	10%	90%	100%	(20)
Non-athlete	23%	77%	100%	(126)

*Adapted from Schafer, 1968:41.

beverages, cheating on tests, and getting into trouble with the police. Furthermore, he found that the quality of athletic performance was positively related to conventional behavior.

One explanation for these findings is that participation in sports and extracurricular activities provide rewarding experiences to students and they do not want to jeopardize their continued participation by violating the official school or community norms. Additionally, the commitment of time to extracurricular activities may preclude time spent in deviant behavior, and students may fear the loss of peer status that results from deviance. However, a causal relationship between athletic participation and conventionality remains problematic. It is possible that boys and girls who are the most conventional are initially attracted to sports. Additionally, coaches are not likely to allow "trouble makers" to remain on the team, and perhaps athletes who are involved in "delinquent" behavior are less likely to be officially "booked" in the police records than the nonathletes.

Personality Characteristics

The consideration of numerous studies focusing on the personality traits of athletes and nonathletes are beyond the scope of the present paper. Brief mention is appropriate, however, of several studies that are germane to the topic of sport and education. One of the frequent educational justifications of school athletic programs is that they teach "good sportsmanship." Comparative studies of athletes and nonparticipants do not support the notion of a causal relationship between participation and learning the principles of fair play (Kistler, 1957; Richardson, 1962; Singer, 1969). The conclusions of these reports indicate that the athletes exhibited responses that were less sportsmanlike than the nonathletes. We would speculate that the emphasis on competition and winning in athletic contests may at times conflict with the teaching of sportsmanship.

The sound mind in a sound body principle has had considerable medical and psychological support, and numerous studies have sought to demonstrate the value of a healthy body for a healthy mind. Unfortunately, difficulties in measurement and perhaps an overzealous attempt to "prove" the worth of exercise and sport to mental health have confounded the issue. Layman (1974: 404) has published an extensive survey of the literature on this topic; several conclusions from her review are worthy of enumeration:

1. Under certain conditions, competitive athletics may enhance learning, social development, and the acquisition of desirable personality traits.
2. From a mental health standpoint, 'varsity' type athletics for boys appear to have no particularly harmful effects at the high school and college levels. However, at the elementary school and junior high school levels, 'high pressure' competition seems to benefit some but to have harmful effects on others.
3. Physical education activities and sports provide a setting which is favorable to the development of discriminating values and socially acceptable character traits.
4. In sports it is customary to stress the desirability of sportsmanship, fair play, honesty, cooperation, teamwork, tolerance, and other so-called character traits, and to encourage their development. However, it has been found that habit patterns developed and expressed in athletic activities do not automatically transfer to other situations.
5. Motor skill ranging from school boy to the highest competitive levels has not been shown to correlate appreciably with personality variables.

Research concerning the social psychological correlates of athletic participation of females is sparse; this state of affairs is partially the result of the retarded development of sport for girls and women.

Indeed, to be feminine and an athlete have been traditionally viewed as contradictory roles that can lead to undesirable psychological consequences. A recent study of women who were competing in national intercollegiate championships (gymnastics, swimming, and track) and a control group of college women nonparticipants on three dimensions of psychological well-being does not support the assumption of negative affective consequences (see Table 5). Although the female athletes in this study were deeply involved in their athletic role, the findings presented in Table 5 indicate no undesirable consequences for the identities of the participants. Additional research reporting data on high school girls does not suggest that athletic participation has deleterious effects (Snyder and Spreitzer 1978b). Once again we emphasize that the causal relationship between athletic participation and psychological well-being is not clear. Perhaps the most psychologically secure females are able to handle the potential role conflict that goes with being a female athlete, and perhaps the rewards that flow from being a competent athlete counterbalance the negativism associated with the potential role conflict.

The school sports environment cannot be categorically defined as functional or dysfunctional. Research suggests that involvement in sports begins at an early age with parental expectations, role models,

Table 5. Comparison of Women Athletes and Nonathletes on Psychological Well-Being*

	Athletes	Nonathletes
"Generally feel in good spirits	%	%
Most of the time	71	51
Much of the time	26	42
Some/seldom	3	7
	P = .001	
"Very satisfied with life"		
Most of the time	64	48
Much of the time	31	41
Some/seldom	5	11
	P = .001	
"Find much happiness in life"		
Most of the time	74	59
Much of the time	22	33
Some/seldom	4	8
	P = .001	

Significance determined by Chi-square test.
*Adapted from Snyder and Kivlin, 1975.

and reinforcement, and continues into the school environment. As student cohorts pass through the school system, sports become one of the school activities that contributes to the socialization process. By the junior high and high school years the selective process results in a "weeding out" of many students from the athletic stream. The consequences of this "screening process" brings together coaches and players who have both selected each other (a "goodness of fit"), and thus the setting is conducive for continued socialization. Sport socialization may "build character," or on the contrary as some researchers have suggested, "if you want to build character try something else" (Ogilivie and Tutko 1971). In this context Orlick (1974:2) notes:

> For every positive psychological or social outcome in sports, there are possible negative outcomes. For example, sports can offer a child group membership or group exclusion, acceptance or rejection, positive feedback or negative feedback, a sense of accomplishment or a sense of failure, evidence of self-worth or a lack of evidence of self-worth. Likewise, sports can develop cooperation and a concern for others, but they can also develop intense rivalry and a complete lack of concern for others.

In the same vein Schafer (1971) has argued that our educational institutions are primarily concerned with the teaching of "correct attitudes" and transmitting the existing, and basically conservative, values that are functional in our society. Such educational goals result in inordinate conformity and teach the blind following of orders rather than a critical and questioning citizenry (Schafer, 1971: 5). Schafer feels that organized school sports contribute to this conservatizing influence and serve to transmit *status quo* values by emphasizing the importance of external rewards, teaching the passive acceptance of orders, and generally developing bureaucratic personalities. At the university level the big time sports establishments are not primarily concerned with building character. Rather they are highly bureaucratized business establishments that sometimes resort to unethical practices to achieve the goals of winning and the resultant gate receipts.

An extension of research concerning the correlates of athletic participation is the analysis of the *degree of involvement* within the athletic subculture. The selection and/or the socialization processes are also likely to be operative in explaining the gradient effects between journeyman and superstar performers. Players who are substitutes are not likely to be as deeply involved in the athletic subculture and its norms, values, rewards and sanctions as highly visible athletes. During practice sessions and game situations, the role of substitute is different from the regular performers. This role differentiation and the concomitant social expectations carry over into relationships with peers, teachers, coaches, and other adults. The explanations offered for differences found in previous studies between involvement and noninvolvement in athletics can logically be extended to the differences in degrees of involvement between athletes. Table 6 crosstabulates team involvement of high school basketball players with college plans, coach's advice, and the perception of their coach's influence.

Table 6. College Plans, Coaches Advice, and Perceived Influence According to Degree of Athletic Success Among High School Seniors*

	Substitutes (N=69) %	Starters (N=89) %	Stars (N=41) %
Probably Will Attend College and Will Attend College	80	91	95
Coaches Often Gave Advice: Whether to Attend College	26	48	75
Players Perceive Their Coaches to be a Great Influence	31	51	79

*Adapted from Snyder, 1975:197.

Within schools sport is institutionalized as physical education, where skills and games of the sports world and rationally created exercises (calisthenics) are used for general educational purposes. In most school systems around the world this subject is an integral part of the curriculum and it is usually compulsory for all students. Beyond the mere organizational arrangement very little is known about the social impact of these programs. They are said to have an influence on social behavior in the broadest sense, in addition to the skills being taught which can potentially be used through the whole course of life. Social scientists have so far paid little attention to physical education and its social significance. Their emphasis, as indicated in the reported research, has rather been on athletic programs in school and on the consequence of athletic participation for educational and social attainment.

SCHOOLS AND SPORT:
SOME ORGANIZATIONAL CONSIDERATIONS

Schools, like business concerns, prisons, military units, political parties and other large social groupings, represent complex organizations. A complex organization consists of (1) stable patterns of interaction, (2) coalitions of groups having a collective identity (e.g., a name and location(s), (3) interests in accomplishing given tasks, and (4) power and authority structures (Corwin, 1967: 161). Large school systems and universities meet these generic criteria. Our organizational analysis concentrates on the policies and objectives of educational systems as well as the structural determinants of these policies. The policies and objectives of school systems vary from elementary to the university levels. A central concern at all levels is to bring about some desired changes (learning) in the pupils; however, with the higher levels of education the organizations and policies become more complex. Thus, universities are not only institutions of teaching and learning, but they also provide research and public service—medical services, child care, food service, housing, psychological and professional counseling, plant management, investment activity, recreation, employment, research marketing, publishing house, newspaper, fund raising, alumni affairs, etc. Frequently these disparate functions have conflicting objectives.

Sports within schools, at least in the United States, emerge out of the physical education curriculum; in the upper elementary or junior high school level they become a semiautonomous subsystem that parallels the formal curriculum. This is also true of some other extracurricular activities. In the high school, as we noted earlier in this paper, sport represents a major means of achieving status and prestige; the structure and administration of the program begins to require considerable attention in terms of time, money personnel, space, and other resources. At the university level the largest athletic departments resemble business corporations with a considerable functional autonomy from other aspects of the university organization (see Snyder and Spreitzer, 1978b for further elaboration of the organization of sport in higher education.)

The nature of sport at each of the educational levels has different characteristics. In the elementary and early junior high school levels sport tends to be playful, less serious, with little emphasis on the outcome (e.g., winning and losing), unstructured, available to the less skilled, and is typically engaged in for the pure enjoyment (intrinsic satisfaction), and for the initial learning of sport skills. In each of the successive educational levels the nature of sport changes and the above characteristics diminish. At the major university level sport becomes almost worklike (grants in aid); it is serious, highly bureaucratized, restrictive, and subject to external utilitarian pressures—winning and losing, gate receipts, TV contracts, and national prestige. These contrasting characteristics of sport vary according to the educational level, intramural or varsity sport, type of sport (team or individual, revenue or nonrevenue producing), size of the institution, and male or female athletic competition. Elsewhere we have labeled these gradations as informal, semiformal, and formal sport (Snyder and Spreitzer 1978b: 20-21). Figure 1 summarizes these attributes that characterize sport at the different educational levels.

Figure 1. Attributes of Sports at Different Educational Levels

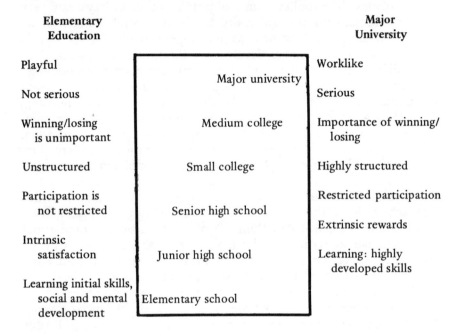

Elementary Education		Major University
Playful	Major university	Worklike
Not serious		Serious
Winning/losing is unimportant	Medium college	Importance of winning/ losing
Unstructured	Small college	Highly structured
Participation is not restricted	Senior high school	Restricted participation
		Extrinsic rewards
Intrinsic satisfaction	Junior high school	Learning: highly developed skills
Learning initial skills, social and mental development	Elementary school	

The characteristics of sport at the respective educational levels dovetail with the overall structure and policy-making process. At the university level, sport can become a bureaucratized and semi-autonomous subsystem such as in the athletic department of a university in a major athletic conference. The paradigm shown in Figure 2 summarizes the structural arrangements present in most major university athletic departments (see Lüschen, 1974, for a similar paradigm applicable to general sport organizations).

Inputs to the Organizational Structure
The manifest policies and goals of the athletic departments of major universities are determined by the organizational structure as well as by external inputs to the athletic subsystem. There are many agencies that impinge on the sport subsystem that provide an external base of support. In many respects our social values are oriented toward the world of sport. Sport pervades many segments

Figure 2. Summary Paradigm of the Organizational Characteristics of Sport within a Major University

System Inputs	Organizational Structure	Output: Manifest Policies and Goals
Favorable social values	High integration	
Considerable university input	High coordination	Financial solvency is primary
	Relative autonomy	
Alumni support		Winning is primary
	Specialized and	
Community support	committed personnel	Individual develop-
		ment is secondary
Athletic conference regulations	Considerable power/ influence	
	Bureaucratization	

of our society; it is production and goal-oriented. Many people believe in the value of sport to mold good citizens and to teach the values of hard work, discipline, and achievement. The university as a social institution and a reflection of some segments of society is under considerable pressure to provide resources to maintain a competitive athletic program. In many respects the prestige of a university's athletic teams is equated with the university's prestige. Thus, it is understandable that alumni, community groups, and booster clubs are desirous of being affiliated with athletic excellence. The influence of athletic external regulatory structures—National Collegiate Athletic Association conference—must also be considered in the overall policy making process of a university's athletic department. These organizations establish policies designed to insure a competitive parity, but a consequence is that their definitions of the maximum becomes the minimum (e.g., grants-in-aid and scholarship requirements) because of the fear of a school becoming noncompetitive.

Organizational Structure

Administrative arrangements within large athletic departments reveal a high degree of integration, coordination, specialization, hierarchial chain of command and bureaucratization. Gate receipts, external funding, and separate university budgeting procedures make the athletic department relatively autonomous and impervious to interference from other agencies within the university; in fact, some are incorporated and financially independent of the university.

Faculty representatives to universitywide athletic committees are frequently "friends of athletics" and do not provide an adequate check and balance system. Evidence also suggests that athletic administrators and coaches generally have a strong commitment to the world of sport and its value system. In short, the organizational structure of most large athletic departments provides considerable power/influence within the university community for pursuit of their goals and policies which may or may not be educational in nature.

RECENT CONTROVERSIES

In the last decade a number of controversies have emerged that involve sport within educational institutions. In 1968 Olsen *(The Black Athlete: A Shameful Story)* argued that there was blatant discrimination against the black athlete in the collegiate ranks. Yetman and Eitzen (1972) studied the participation of blacks on collegiate basketball teams during the years of 1954–1970. Their findings indicated that since 1958 blacks have been disproportionately overrepresented in the top five positions and underrepresented in the second five positions on collegiate basketball teams. They interpreted these findings to indicate that discrimination operated such that black players must be better than white players to succeed in sport. Thus, if they are selected for the team they must be excellent players and the journeyman blacks are discriminated against by not being selected for the team. Follow-up data since 1970 reports that although blacks continue to be overrepresented in starting positions, the percent of blacks who are starters has declined from 76 percent in 1962 to 61 percent in 1975 (Eitzen and Yetman, 1977: 12).

Paralleling and related to the controversy surrounding the possible discrimination against blacks are a number of accounts of injustices in the treatment which athletes receive from coaches and athletic administrators. These writings generally depict the coach as ultraconservative, authoritarian, and exploitive of athletes for the ultimate goal of winning contests (Scott, 1971; Hoch, 1972; Edwards, 1973). Sage (1975) found that the attitudes and values of most coaches, specifically collegiate coaches, are not much different from the norm of "middle-class, middle America." In short, the characteristics of coaches and the sport programs they support are a microcosm of the norms in the American industrial society (Sage, 1975: 422). This conclusion of course does not refute the charge that injustices exist in the treatment and use of athletes.

More recently, women's liberation has appeared in the world of sport to seek a more equitable distribution of resources and rewards as well as to emancipate girls and women from restrictive sex roles.

Federal guidelines for Title IX of the Education Amendments Act of 1972 have had serious ramifications for the majority of the public schools and colleges in the United States. Title IX has provided the impetus for the upgrading of girls' and women's sports. Consequently high schools and colleges are expanding the number of sports open to females, purchasing equipment, hiring coaches, and providing financial grants-in-aid for female athletes at larger institutions.

This legal mandate to establish equality of athletic opportunity for both sexes has hit the universities at the same time that most of them are faced with severe financial cutbacks. Major athletic programs have been forced with rising costs to market their "product" in the most economical manner. With financial survival at stake, athletics at the major universities have adopted even more of the techniques of big business. To be economically sound requires winning teams, prestigious coaches, and a heavy recruiting budget. Revenues are increased through concessions, selling programs, parking, renting athletic facilities and competing for the entertainment dollars of the public. To achieve these policies requires that sport assume policies and goals that in many respects are contrary to the educational goals of physical education and preparation of students for a worthy use of leisure time. The economic crisis has resulted in a greater involvement by university administrators in the deliberations of the NCAA and the considerations of the basis by which grants-in-aid are awarded. In general the role of intercollegiate athletics is being more closely scrutinized at all levels within the college and university.

SUMMARY AND CONCLUSION

In our consideration of sport and education we have outlined the social scientific literature dealing with sport and education. Since a major emphasis on sport takes place within educational institutions, we have focused our attention on this aspect of socialization. Numerous studies have analyzed the correlates of sport involvement among high school and college students. More of these investigations demonstrate differences between the participants and nonparticipants. Unfortunately, in the absence of longitudinal studies, the causes and effects of these differences are difficult to untangle. It is likely that some of the differences are a function of the selectivity that operates at the initial stages of athletic involvement. Moreover, because of the differential experience of athletes and nonathletes, we have reason to believe that some observed variance is a function of the socialization that takes place as a consequence of one's participation. We have also outlined some aspects of the function of sport as a subsystem within the larger educational system, with a focus on higher education.

Sport is one of the most pervasive institutions in our society. It interfaces with many other institutional spheres, including education. A great deal of progress has been made in the early years of sociology of sport in outlining relevant variables for investigation. Investigations in the realm of sport and education may be viewed as the building blocks for further theoretical and methodological development. Additional research concerning the interactive process between sport and educational institutions will continue to elicit the interest of the educational practitioner as well as amplifying the body of social scientific literature.

With respect to future research, we suggest that scientific research should take sport seriously in the sense of conceptualizing sport as an immanent, autonomous sphere of human experience. That is, sport should be conceived as a form of human endeavor that begins and ends within the individual and which has its own reason for existence. In other words, the intrinsic aspects of sport should be brought to the foreground. Csikszentmihalyi (1975) has formulated a conceptual framework for the analysis of autotelic activities in his challenging book entitled *Beyond Boredom and Anxiety: The Experience of Play in Work and Games.* He suggests that we need to study activities such as sport from an "autotelic" perspective (from the Greek *auto* = self and *telos* = goal, purpose). In this context, sport is not viewed as some form of external compensation or as preparation for future needs, but rather as an intrinsically satisfying activity whose reward is coterminous with the behavior itself.

We are arguing for a phenomenological perspective in research on sport. We need, in particular, to investigate the enduring consequences of sport within educational systems as well as among the general adult population. This perspective requires that we shift our attention from the mass participation spectator sports to the learning of physical activities and sports that will be autotelic in the later stages of the life cycle. This approach suggests that we need to investigate the role of sport within the adult's overall life style and life space. Rather than focusing on extrinsic payoffs from sport participation, we recommend a refocusing of future research to incorporate what Csikszentmihalyi (1975: 36) terms the *flow* experience:

> From here on, we shall refer to this peculiar dynamic state—the whol-istic sensation that people feel when they act with total involvement—as *flow*. In the flow state, action follows upon action according to an internal logic that seems to need no conscious intervention by the

actor. He experiences it as a unified flowing from one moment to the next, in which he is in control of his actions, and in which there is little distinction between self and environment, between stimulus and response, or between past, present, and future experience. Flow is what we have been calling "the autotelic experience."

The conceptualization of *flow* is reminiscent of Maslow's peak experiences, and social scientists have analyzed sport in terms of such high points. We emphasize, however, that a focus on flow or peak experiences needs to be applied outside the context of elite performers. It is quite likely that persons can experience sport in an autotelic sense even at lower levels of the ability spectrum. In fact, an interesting study could be designed to investigate possible threshold levels of ability at which point autotelic experience can emerge in such sports as cross-country skiing, handball, racquetball, tennis, and marathon runs.

From a pedagogic perspective, the concern with autotelic experience raises the question of how to structure physical education instruction and sport involvement in a way that will maximize the probability of autotelic involvement and which will encourage lifelong participation because of the pattern of self-reinforcement. In this context, then, the instructional focus should not be on an absolute level of skill acquisition, but rather on self-perceived progress and internalization of an autotelic posture toward sport.

In conclusion, we argue for a broadened conception of the role of sport in the socialization process and education. In particular, we stress the need to study the trajectory of sport involvement over the entire life cycle. In addition, we suggest that the intrinsic dimension needs to be given greater attention in our research on sport as well as in our sport instruction. Any attempt to make sport intrinsically rewarding to a larger proportion of our population will require that our curriculum and instruction include a broad range of graduated physical activities that cover the waterfront of innate and learned skills. "To provide intrinsic rewards, an activity must be finely calibrated to a person's skills—including his physical, intellectual, emotional, and social abilities. Such a personalized concern for each individual is antithetical to the structure of mass society with its rigidly bureaucratic forms of production, education, and administration" (Csikszentimihalyi, 1975: 100). Sport programs in schools whether they are of the competitive type or physical education classes, can provide an entry into physical activity. These activities should be a source of intrinsic enjoyment while at the same time there may be transfer effects to other areas of life. The transfer of such behavior patterns is of course a basic goal of education. To what degree this process actually occurs in schools will have to be answered by future studies of sport and education.

REFERENCES

Buhrman, H. 1977. Athletics and deviancy: an examination of the relationship between athletic participation and deviant behavior of high school girls *Review of Sports and Leisure* 2 (June): 17–35.

Coleman, J.S. 1961. *The Adolescent Society.* New York: The Free Press.

Corwin, R.G. 1967. Education and the sociology of complex organizations. 156–223 in D.A. Hansen and J.E. Gerstl. *On Education. Sociological Perspectives.* New York: John Wiley and Sons.

Csikszentmihalyi, M. 1975. *Beyond Boredom and Anxiety.* San Francisco: Jossey-Bass.

Edwards, H. 1973. *The Sociology of Sport.* Homewood, Illinois: The Dorsey Press.

Eitzen, D.S. 1976. Sport and social status in American public secondary education. *Review of Sport and Leisure* 1 (Fall): 139–155.

Eitzen, D.S. and N.R. Yetman. 1977. Immune from racism? *Civil Rights Digest,* 9 (Winter): 3–13.

Hanks, M. and B. Eckland. 1976. Athletics and social participation in the educational process. *Sociology of Education* 49 (October): 271–294.

Hauser, W. and L. Lueptow. 1978. Participation in athletics and academic achievement: A replication and extension. *Sociological Quarterly* 19 (Spring): 304–309.

Hoch, P. 1972. *Rip Off the Big Game.* Garden City, New York: Doubleday and Company.

Hollingshead, A.B. 1949. *Elmtown's Youth.* New York: John Wiley and Sons.

Kenyon, G.S. 1970. The use of path analysis in sport sociology with special reference to involvement socialization. *IRSS* 5,1:191–203.

Kenyon, G.S. and B.D. McPherson. 1973. Becoming involved in physical activity and sport: a process of socialization. Pp. 303–332 in G.L. Rarick ed., *Physical Activity: Human Growth and Development.* New York: Academic Press.

Kistler, J.W. 1957. Attitudes expressed about behavior demonstrated in specific situations occurring in sports. National College Physical Education Association for Men. *Annual Proceedings* 60:55–58.

Landers, D. and D.M. Landers. 1978. Socialization via interscholastic athletics: its effects on delinquency. *Sociology of Education* 51 (October): 299–303.

Layman, E.M. 1974. Contributions of exercise and sports to mental health and social adjustment. Pp. 403–428 in W.R. Johnson and E.R. Buskirk (eds.), *Science and Medicine of Exercise and Sport.* New York: Harper, Row Publishers.

Linde, H. and K. Heinemann. 1968. *Leistungsengagement und Sportinteresse.* Schorndorf: Hofmann.

Loy, J.W. and A.G. Ingham. 1973. Play, games, and sport in the psychosocial development of children and youth. Pp. 257–332 in G.L. Rarick eds., *Physical Activity: Human Growth and Development.* New York: Academic Press.

Lueptow, L.B. and B.D. Kayser. 1973–74. Athletic involvement: academic achievement and aspiration. *Sociological Focus* 7 (Winter): 24–36.

Lüschen, G. 1974. Policy making in sport organizations and their executive personnel: a proposal for a cross-national project. Pp. 367–382 in M. Archer ed., *Current Research in Sociology*. Paris: Mouton.

Lynd, R.S. and H.M. Lynd. 1929. *Middletown*. New York: Harcourt, Brace and Company.

Meggyesy, D. 1971. *Out of Their League*. Berkeley: Ramparts Press.

Ogilvie, B.C. and T.A. Tutko. 1971. Sport: if you want to build character, try something else. *Psychology Today* 5 (October): 61–63.

Olsen, J. 1968. *The Black Athlete: A Shameful Story*. New York: Time-Life, Incorporated.

Orlick, T.D. 1974. The sports environment. *Paper Canadian Symposium Sports Psychology*.

Otto, L. and D. Alwin. 1977. Athletics, aspirations, and attainments. *Sociology of Education* 42 (April): 102–113.

Picou, J.S. 1978. Race, athletic achievement, and educational aspiration. *Sociological Quarterly* 19 (Summer): 428–438).

Picou, J.S. and E.W. Curry. 1974. Residence and the athletic participation-educational aspiration hypothesis. *Social Science Quarterly* 55 (December): 768–776.

Pilapil, B.E., J.E. Stecklein, and H.C. Liu. 1970. *Intercollegiate Athletics and Academic Progress: A Comparison of Athletes and Nonathletes at the University of Minnesota*. Minneapolis: University of Minnesota.

Rehberg, R.A. and M. Cohen. 1975. Athletes and scholars: an analysis of the compositional characteristics and image of two youth culture categories. *IRSS* 10,1:91–107.

Rehberg, R.A. and W.E. Schafer. 1968. Participation in interscholastic athletics and college expectations. *AJS* 73 (May): 732–740.

Richardson, D.E. 1962. Ethical conduct in sport situations. National College Physical Education Association for Men. *Annual Proceedings* 66:98–104.

Sage, G.H. 1975. An occupational analysis of the college coach. Pp. 395–455 in D.W. Ball and J.W. Loy eds. *Sport and the Social Order*. Addison-Wesley.

Sage, G.H. 1974. Socialization and sport. Pp. 162–172 in G.H. Sage ed., *Sport and American Society*. Reading, Mas.: Addison-Wesley.

Savage, H.J. 1929. *American College Athletics*. New York: Carnegie Foundation, Bulletin 23.

Schafer, W.E. 1968. Some social sources and consequences of interscholastic athletics: the case of participation and delinquency. Pp. 29–44 in G.S. Kenyon (ed.), *Aspects of Contemporary Sport Sociology*. Chicago: Athletic Institute.

Schafer, W.E. and J.M. Armer. 1968. Athletes are not inferior students. *Transaction* 5 (November): 21–26, 61–62.

Schafer, W.E. 1971. Sport, socialization and the school.*Paper Symposium Sociology of Sport*. Waterloo, Ont.

Scott, J. 1971. *The Athletic Revolution*. New York: The Free Press.

Shaw, G. 1972. *Meat on the Hoof*. New York: St. Martin's Press.

Singer, R.N. 1969. Reaction to sport and personality dynamics. National College Physical Education Association for Men. *Annual Proceedings* 72: 76–80.

Snyder, E.E. 1969. A longitudinal analysis of the participation between high school student values, social participation, and educational–occupational achievement. *Sociology of Education* 42 (Summer): 191–200.

Snyder, E.E. 1975. Athletic team involvement, educational plans, and the coach-player relationship. *Adolescence 10* (Summer): 191–200.

Snyder, E.E. and J.E. Kivlin. 1975. Women athletes and aspects of psychological well-being and body image. *Research Quarterly* 46 (May): 191–199.

Snyder, E.E. and J.E. Kivlin. 1976. Correlates of sport participation among adolescent girls. *Research Quarterly* 47 (December): 804–809.

Snyder, E.E. and E.A. Spreitzer. 1977. Participation in sport as related to educational expectations among high school girls. *Sociology of Education* 50 (January): 47–55.

Snyder, E.E. and E.A. Spreitzer. 1978a. Socialization comparisons of adolescent female athletes and musicians. *Research Quarterly* 49 (October): 342–350.

Snyder, E.E. and E.A. Spreitzer. 1978b. *Social Aspects of Sport.* Englewood Cliffs: Prentice-Hall.

Spady, W.G. 1970. Lament for the letterman: effects of peer status and extra-curricular activities on goals and achievement. *AJS* 75 (January): 680–702.

Spreitzer, E.A. and M.D. Pugh. 1973. Interscholastic athletics and educational expectations. *Sociology of Education* 46 (Spring): 171–182.

Spreitzer, E.A. and E.E. Snyder. 1976. Socialization into sport: an exploratory path analysis." *Research Quarterly* 47 (May): 238–245.

Stevenson, C. 1975. Socialization effects of participation in sport: a critical review of the literature. *Research Quarterly* 46 (October): 287–301.

Waller, W. 1932. *The Sociology of Teaching.* New York: John Wiley and Sons.

Yetman, N.R. and D.S. Eitzen. 1972. Black Americans in sports: unequal opportunity for equal ability. *Civil Rights Digest* 5 (August): 20–34.

SPORT AND RELIGION

George H. Sage

There may seem to be little in common between religion and sport, but it has been contended that contemporary sport has all the characteristics of formal religion. In the past two decades the power and influence of sport has increased enormously while at the same time formalized religion and the church have suffered a decline of interest and commitment (Stark and Glock 1968). Sport has taken on many of the characteristics of religion, and indeed it has been argued that sport has emerged as a new religion, supplementing, and in some cases even supplanting, the traditional religious expressions (Rudin 1972). Rogers (1972: 392) contends that "sports are rapidly becoming the dominant ritualistic expression of the reification of established religion in America." Similarly Harry Edwards (1972: 392) noted: ". . . if there is a universal popular religion in America it is to be found within the institution of sports."

A few examples will illustrate how organized sport has taken on the forms of religion. Every religion has its idols (saints and high priests) who are venerated by its members; likewise sports fans have persons whom they worship: the saints who are now dead, such as Knute Rockne, Babe Ruth, and, of course, Vince Lombardi, who earned a place among the saints for his articulation of the basic commandment of contemporary sport: "Winning is the only thing." The high priests of contemporary sports, i.e. college and professional coaches, direct the destinies of large masses of followers.

In addition to the fundamental commandment of sport, according to Lombardi, numerous proverbs fill the world of sport: "Nice guys finish last," "When the going gets tough, the tough get going," "Lose is a four-letter word," etc. These proverbs are frequently written on posters and hung in locker rooms for athletes to memorize.

The achievement of athletes and teams are manifested in numerous shrines which have been built throughout the country to commemorate and glorify sporting figures. These "halls of fame" have been built for virtually every sport played in America, and some sports have several halls of fame devoted to them.

Symbols of fidelity abound in sports. The athletes are expected to give total commitment to the cause, including abstinence from smoking, alcohol, and, in some cases, even sex. The devout followers who witness and invoke traditional and hallowed chants show their devotion to the team and add "spirit" to its cause. It is not unusual for sports fans to travel hundreds of miles, sometimes braving terrible weather conditions, to witness a game, as a display of their fidelity.

Similar to religious institutions, sport has become a function of communal involvement. One cheers for the Green Bay Packers, the New York Knicks, or the Los Angeles Dodgers. The emotional attachment which some fans have for their teams verges on the religious fanaticism previously seen in holy wars against heretics and pagans. Opposing teams and their fans, as well as officials, are occasionally attacked and brutally beaten.

THE CHANGING ASSOCIATION OF SPORT AND RELIGION

According to Rudolph Brasch (1970: 1) athletic activities began as religious rites: "Its roots were in man's desire to gain victory over foes seen and unseen, to influence the forces of nature, and promote fertility among his crops and cattle." Playing games was a way for primitive peoples to assure revival of nature and the victory of vegetation.

The ancient Greeks worshipped beauty and entwined religious observance with their athletic demonstrations in such a way that it was difficult to define where one left off and the other began. The most important athletic meetings of the Greeks were part of religious festivals; the Olympic games were held in honor of Zeus, king of the Greek gods, while the other Panhellenic games honored other gods. Victorious athletes presented their gifts of thanks upon the altar of the god or gods whom they thought to be responsible for their victory.

Religious support for sport found no counterpart to the ancient Greeks in Western societies until the beginning of the 20th century. The traditions of Western Christianity, in alliance with Plato's philosophic dualism, have posed body and spirit dualistically to each other and have elevated the spirit above the body. In traditional Christian religious doctrine of salvation, salvation was declared to be primarily of the soul, thus religious scholarship and church liturgy clearly gave priority to the soul, while the body received scant attention.

In America, economic pressures, political tendencies, and social conditions have been the chief forces responsible for a drastically changed relationship between religion and sport in the 20th century. Increased industrialization has turned the population into a nation of urban dwellers, while higher wages have been responsible for an unprecedented affluence. The Protestant Work Ethic has lost its potency, and increased leisure has enhanced the popularity of sports. According to Hogan (1967: 133–134), the story of changes in the attitudes of religionists in the 20th century "is largely one of accelerating accommodation." Much of Protestant America has come "to view sport as a positive force for good and even as an effective tool to promote the Lord's work." Sports and leisure activities have become an increasingly conspicuous part of the recreation program of thousands of churches. Swanson (1968: 58) summarized the new role of the church:

> Throughout the twentieth century, the church has moved steadily further into recreation. Camping programs, athletic leagues, organized game periods at various group meetings, and even full-time recreation directors are all evidences of a positive relationship between religion and play.

Perhaps the change in church attitude toward sport is best described by Cozens and Stumpf (1953: 104): "If you can't lick 'em, join 'em!"

RELIGIOUS AGENTS AND AGENCIES
USE SPORT TO PROMOTE RELIGION

From a position of strong opposition to recreation and sport activities, the church has made a complete reversal within the past century, and now heartily supports these activities as effective tools to promote "the Lord's work." Church-sponsored recreation and sport programs provide a service to its members, and sometimes the entire community, that is often unavailable in an accepted form anywhere else. Church playgrounds and recreation centers in urban areas provide facilities, equipment, and instruction that municipal governments have often not been able to provide. YMCA, YWCA, CYO and other church-related organizations perform a variety of social services, one of which is the sponsorship of sports leagues.

Another objective the church has in promoting sport is to strengthen and increase membership among the congregation. At a time when churches were just beginning their extensive support for recreational and sports programs, one clergyman said: ". . . there is a selfish reason why the church should offer recreation of some sort—because it aids the church and enlivens the people" (Eastman 1912: 234). In a time of increasing secularization, such as the United States has witnessed in the past 50 years, it is understandable why churches accommodate activities that solidify and integrate membership.

Some religious leaders outwardly avow the association between religion and sport in their preaching. One of the most popular contemporary evangelists, Billy Graham, is an enthusiastic supporter of the virtues of sports competition and the sanctity of Christian coaches and athletes. He has made sports a basic metaphor in his ministry. According to Graham (Are sports good for the soul? 1976), the basic source of Christianity, the Bible, legitimates sport involvement. He has said: "The Bible says leisure and lying around are morally dangerous for us. . . . Sports keep us busy."

Church-supported colleges and universities—both Catholic and Protestant—use their athletic teams to attract students, funds, and public attention to institutions that are often lacking funds and are frequently academically inferior as well. The most recent example of a religious university deliberately using intercollegiate athletics for its promotion is Oral Roberts University in Tulsa, Oklahoma. When evangelist Oral Roberts founded this university in 1965, one of his first actions was the establishment of an athletic program to bring recognition and prestige to the university. According to Oral Roberts, athletics is part of his Christian witness, and since nearly everyone in America reads the sports pages, a Christian school cannot ignore these people. Thus, since sports are the No. 1 interest of people in America, for the university to be relevant, he had to gain the attention of millions of people in a way that they could understand (Boyle 1970).

The most salient outgrowths of religion's use of the sport has been the formation of organizations composed of coaches and athletes which provide a variety of programs designed to recruit new members to religion. The first of these groups, the Fellowship of Christian Athletes (FCA), which was founded in 1954, has as its avowed purpose "to confront athletes and coaches and through them the youth of the nation, with the challenge and adventure of following Christ and serving them through the fellowship of the church. . . ." It attempts "to combat juvenile delinquency, to elevate the moral and spiritual standards of sports in an unprincipled secular culture; to challenge Americans to stand up and be counted for or against God and to appeal to sports enthusiasts and American youth through hero worship harnessed."

The FCA uses older athletes and coaches to recruit younger ones; it has a mailing list of over 55,000 and a staff of over 75. Its most important single activity is the annual week-long summer conferences where coaches and athletes mix religious and inspirational sessions with sports instruction and competition. The executive director of the FCA said: "It's 50 percent inspirational and 50 percent perspirational" (McGuff 1970). Another important facet of the FCA is the high school and college group session programs known as the "huddle-fellowship program" in which high school and college athletes in a community or campus get together to talk about their faith, engage in Bible study, and pray. They also engage in projects such as serving as "big brothers" for delinquent or needy children, visiting nursing homes, helping the handicapped, and serving as playground instructors. There are now some 1,600 high school huddles in the U.S. and over 200 college fellowships, the bulk of which are found in the

South, Southwest, and Midwest. In recent years female athletes have been admitted to the FCA and their membership in the organization is growing rapidly. FCA also sponsors state and regional retreats, provides various informational materials such as films, records, tapes, and it publishes a periodical *The Christian Athlete.*

Another religious group formed mostly by former athletes is a division of the Campus Crusade of Christ and is called Athletes in Action (AIA). With special dispensation from the NCAA, the AIA fields several athletic teams made up of former college athletes. These teams compete against amateur teams throughout the country each year, and as part of each appearance the AIA athletes make brief evangelical speeches and testimonials to the crowds and distribute free religious materials (Jares 1977).

Other organizations also enlist the assistance of athletes in spreading the gospel. The Pro Athletes Outreach (PAO) sends professional athletes on "speaking blitzes" of the country. The athletes deliver witness and testimonial speeches to groups of largely young people.

Of all of the purposes and/or consequences of religion's association with sport, certainly one of the most important is the use of athletes, coaches and the play environment to recruit new members to the church. In a series for *Sports Illustrated,* Frank Deford (1976, April 19) reported that the use of athletes as amateur evangelists is so widespread that a new denomination has been created: Sportianity. *The Wittenberg Door* (1975), a contemporary religious journal, has derisively labeled this movement "Jocks for Jesus."

The practice of using "jock evangelists" is explained by one of the directors of FCA in this way: "Athletes and coaches . . . have a platform in this country. Athletes have power, a voice" (Deford 1976, April 26: 69). One of the Sportianity's leading evangelists, has argued that people view athletes as stars, and they will therefore listen to what they have to say. Another advantage to using athletes to reach other athletes is access. As one former AAU wrestling champion and AIA assistant athletic director noted: ". . . I can get into a fraternity, a locker room, where nobody else would be permitted" (Deford 1976, April 19: 92).

Athletes and coaches, then are commonly used to sell religion. The technique is simple: Those who are already committed to religion convert the athletes. Since athletes are among the most visible and prestigeful persons in our society, they are used in spreading the gospel to their teammates and others with whom they interact. Combining the popular appeal they have as celebrities with the metaphors of the sports world, athletes are able to catch and hold the attention of large groups of people. Roger Staubach (The Christian Woodstock 1972: 52), former Dallas Cowboy quarterback, told a group of people at the International Student Congress on Evangelism, in a pep talk on "The game of Life," "the goal we must get across is our salvation...and God has given us a good field position."

There is little inclination on the part of religious leaders and the various organizations that make up Sportianity to confront the pressing social issues of sport or the larger society. There is a general reluctance to take a stand on moral issues within sports or the wider society. The various Sportianity organizations and their members have not spoken out against racism, sexism, cheating in sport, the evils of recruiting, or any of the other unethical practices, excesses, and abuses that are well known in the sports world. In the final analysis, sports morality does not appear to have been improved by the Sportianity movement. Instead, Sportianity seems willing to accept sports as is, more devoted to maintaining the status quo than resolving the many problems which exist in sport today.

The value orientations underlying competitive sports in America are more or less secularized versions of the core values of Protestantism. If we place the values inherent in the Protestant Ethic and American sports values side by side, it immediately becomes apparent that the two are congruent, that is, there is a significant equivalence between them. The Protestant stress on successful individual achievement is in keeping with the values of sport. The notion that one's achievement stamps the "chosen" from the "doomed" is evident in sport in the form of the "winning is everything" ideology. Winners are the good people and personal worth is equated with winning. Success-striving, self-discipline, hard work, and work as a calling, the original tenets of the Protestant Ethic, are the most valued qualities of an athlete. The characteristics that the good Christian should possess are also those needed by the successful athlete, and the temper of organized sports is competitive, with an overriding sense of wins and losses. In describing the intercollegiate athletic program at Oral Roberts University, its founder Oral Roberts, said: "Just playing the game is not enough. It's all right to lose some but I'm not much for losing. We're geared up for winning here" (Deford 1976, April 19).

The notion that God is glorified best when athletes have dedication, self-discipline, and give totally of themselves in striving for success and victory is central to the theology of Sportianity. As one spokesman for Sportianity put it, no athlete "can afford to discredit Jesus by giving anything less than total involvement with those talents that he has been given in this training and competition" (Dirkson 1975: 54). If God has granted one athletic ability, then one is obligated to use these abilities to glorify and honor God; anything less than total dedication to the task is not enough. Discipline, sacrifice, training, and unremitting work by athletes not only leads to success (Workers are Winners), but they are seen as ways of using ability that was given by God; this is seen as glorifying God, an important Protestant requirement. Success can be considered as the justly deserved reward of a person's purposeful, self-denying, God guided activity.

It is perhaps no coincidence that the belief systems of Protestantism and modern sports are so congruent. The two institutions use similar means to respond to their members' needs. They try to enforce and maintain through a strict code of behavior and ritual a strict belief system that is typically adopted and internalized by all who are involved in that particular institution. They serve cohesive, integrative, and social control functions for their members, giving them meaningful ways to organize their world.

USES OF RELIGION BY ATHLETES AND COACHES

Religious observance and competitive sports constantly impinge upon each other, and magicoreligious practices of various kinds are found wherever one finds athletics. Coaches and athletes have great respect for the physical skill and technical knowledge required for successful performance, but they are also aware of their limitations. As a supplement for skill and practical techniques, sports participants often employ religious practices in conjunction with sports competition. The coaches and athletes do not believe that these practices make up for their failure to acquire necessary skills or employ appropriate stragety, but these practices do help them to adjust to stress by providing opportunities to dramatize their psychological anxieties, thus reinforcing self-confidence. Religion invokes a sense of "doing something about it" in undertakings of uncertainty in which practical techniques alone cannot guarantee success. The noted anthropologist, Bronislaw Malinowski (1948), on the basis of this research came to the conclusion that when great uncertainty about the outcome is associated with vital activities, the use of magicoreligious or other comparable techniques as a means of allaying tension and promoting adjustment is inevitable.

Perhaps the most frequently employed use of religion by athletes is prayer—prayer for protection in competition, prayer for good performance, and prayer for victory are three examples. Sometimes the act of prayer is observed by a Catholic crossing himself before shooting a free throw in basketball or a team at prayer in the huddle before a football game.

Very little is known about the actual extent to which individual athletes use prayer in conjunction with sports participation, but it seems evident that if some athletes are actually seen praying others may be doing so without outward, observable signs. In some cases, coaches arrange to have religious services on the Sabbath or on game days. At present, almost every major league baseball and football team holds Sunday chapel services, and Sunday services are also held in sports as varied as stock-car racing and golf (Deford 1976, April 19). One of the claims for this type of service is that the sharing of rituals and beliefs strengthens a group's sense of its own identity and accentuates its "we feeling." There are probably other reasons why coaches sanction religious observances. Larry Merchant (1971: 26) suggests that prayer may be used simply because it cannot do any harm: "It might not help, but how much can it hurt? The other coach does it and you can't let him get the edge."

Although there is little empirical work on the use of prayer by athletes and coaches, Marbeto (1967) collected data on male baseball, basketball, football, and tennis athletes and coaches from 23 colleges and universities in California. Fifty-five percent of the coaches and athletes indicated that they pray at least sometimes in connection with athletic contests. They pray for a variety of specific reasons, but to do their best and to win are the most frequently expressed reasons. Most who prayed did so before the contest, fewer did so during the contest, and fewer did so after the contest.

Marbeto (1967) reported that those who pray in athletics are likely to be regular church-goers. They have usually had a strong religious upbringing. His data on church attendance and the use of prayer suggested that the prayers for assistance in the game are said primarily out of habit. According to Marbeto:

> Quite often the person who goes to church regularly prays in numerous phases of his daily living. Thus, the athlete who prays at game time probably does it because of his past conditioning, not because the contest illicits such prayers more than other stressful episodes in his life (p. 68).

When his respondents were divided into those at church affiliated colleges and those at public institutions, Marbeto found that athletes and coaches at church affiliated schools indicated that they feel more dependent upon a spiritual power or ultimate being than their counterparts at public colleges. There was also considerable difference in the two types of institutions with respect to team prayers. Eighty-two percent of the coaches at church colleges have team prayers in connection with the contest, while only 10 percent of the coaches from the public schools encouraged or set aside time for team prayer.

Marbeto (1967: 87–88) reported that 51 percent of the respondents who prayed believe that the use of prayer may indirectly affect the outcome of the game. One athlete responded: "I never play my best if I haven't recited the Lord's prayer first." Another said: "My experiences tell me that sincere prayer can be the winning factor."

MAGIC AND SUPERSTITION IN SPORT

Magic flourishes in situations of uncertainty and threat; it is most commonly invoked in situations of high anxiety about accomplishing desired ends. The origin of most magical rites can be traced to fears experienced individually or collectively. They are associated with human helplessness in face of dangers and unpredictability, which gives rise to superstitious beliefs and overt practices to ward off impending danger or failure and bring good luck. According to Malinowski (1948: 116):

> We find magic wherever the elements of chance and accident, and the emotional play between hope and fear have a wide and extensive range. We do not find magic wherever the pursuit is certain, reliable, and well under control of rational methods. . . .

Malinowski's thesis about the conditions under which magic appears is applicable to the world of sport. Athletes and coaches are engaged in an activity of uncertain outcome and in which they have a great deal of emotional investment. Even dedicated conditioning and practice, and the acquisition of high level skill do not guarantee victory because opponents are often evenly matched, and player injury and other dangers are often present; thus, "getting the breaks" or "lucking out" may be the determining factor in the outcome of the contest. Having a weakly hit baseball fall in for a base hit or a deflected football pass caught by an intended receiver are examples of luck or "getting the breaks" in sports. Although the cliché "the best team always wins" is part of the folk wisdom of sports, athletes and coaches commonly believe that this is not always so, and indeed believe that factors leading to a win or a loss are somewhat out of their control.

Drawing on Malinowski's theory, it appears that athletes and coaches would use magic to bring them luck and to assure that they "get the breaks," thus supplying them with beliefs which serve to bridge over the uncertainty and threat in their pursuit of victory. It would also enable them to carry out their actions with a sense of assurance and confidence and to maintain poise and mental integrity in the face of opponents. In Malinowski's (1948: 70) words:

> The function of magic is to ritualize man's optimism, to enhance his faith in the victory of hope over fear. Magic expresses the greater value for man of confidence over doubt, of steadfastness over vaciliation, of optimism over pessimism.

It is difficult to assess just how extensive the uses of magic are in sport, since there is very little empirical study of the use of magic in sport. Stories about athletes and coaches in newspapers and magazines leave little doubt, though, that magical beliefs and practices play a prominent role in the life of athletes and coaches. They tend to employ almost anything imaginable that might ensure "getting the breaks," and this often involves some form of ritualistic superstitious behavior. Indeed, stories about the magical rites that pervade sports make a witch doctor look like a super sophisticate.

Applying the Malinowski thesis to baseball players, Gmelch (1971) hypothesized that magical practices should be associated more with hitting and pitching than with fielding, since the first two involve a high degree of chance and unpredictability whereas average fielding percentages or success rate is about 97%, reflecting almost complete control over the outcome. From his observations as a participant in professional baseball, Gmelch reported a greater incidence and variety of rituals, taboos and use of fetishes related to hitting and pitching than to fielding. He concluded:

> . . . nearly all of the magical practices that I participated in, observed or elicited, support Malinowski's hypothesis that magic appears in situations of chance and uncertainty. The large amount of uncertainty in pitching and hitting best explains the elaborate magical practices used for these activities. Conversely, the high success rate of fielding, . . . involving much less uncertainty, offers the best explanation for the absence of magic in this realm (p. 40).

Gregory and Petrie (1975) investigated magical practices among members of six intercollegiate athletic teams at a Canadian university and found that the ranking for sport superstitions were similar between teams and individual sport athletes. They also reported that team athletes indicated greater support for superstitions related to equipment and its use, order of entering the arena of their playing position, dressing room rituals, repetitive rituals, and sports personalities, while individual sport athletes evidence greater support for superstitions related to wearing charms, lucky lane numbers, team cheers, and crossing oneself before participation (Table 1). They conclude that magical practices were prevalent among athletes of their sample, and "that 137 respondents endorsed 904 superstitions (with repetition) which could be grouped into 40 categories clearly indicating the strength of superstition in sport" (p. 59).

Judy Becker (1975) recently described the numerous rituals, taboos, and fetishes employed by athletes at Yale University. For example, in hockey the use of the word "shut-out" was taboo—such as "let's protect the shut-out." Once in a game in which Yale went into the locker room with a 4–0 lead and someone violated this rule

Table 1. Frequency of Endorsements of Sport Superstitions Among Athletes by Sex

Athletes (N = 137)

Sport Superstition Category	Male (N=66)	Female (N=71)	Overall f
Uniform	77	117	194
Equipment	81	25	106
Clothes	52	32	84
Routines	46	27	73
Charms	14	23	37
Food	19	14	33
Numbers	8	17	25
Order or Playing Position	20	12	32
Balls	12	11	23
Coaches' Beliefs	11	8	19
Religion	14	5	19
Repetitive Actions	14	5	19
Spectators' Beliefs	14	3	17
Sports Persons	9	3	12
Speaking	2	10	12
Hair	1	19	20
Dressing Room	15	4	19
Team Cheers	2	11	13
Crossing Self	7	3	10
Personal Beliefs	6	4	10
Jewelry	9	4	13
Coins	10	3	13
Colors	3	3	6
Facilities	4	4	8
Travel	7	0	7
Hands	2	4	6
Date Toss of Coin	5	3	8
Pre-game Night	1	6	7
Scoring	0	5	5
Whites	6	1	7
Time	5	1	6
Good Samaritan	5	0	5
Rabbit's Feet	2	0	2
Shaving	2	3	5
Rules	1	2	3
Sex	1	0	1
Weather	2	1	3
Injury	2	0	2
Concentration	0	1	1
Horseshoes	0	1	1
Touching Wood	0	1	1

ADAPTED FROM: Gregory and Petrie (1975:63).

it disturbed the entire team. Within 10 minutes after the teams returned to the ice, the opponents had tied the score. One of the most common magical practices involved clothes fetishes, such as wearing a particular article of clothing. One track athlete believed that "new shoes go fast," so he got new spikes before each meet. Becker reported that uniform numbers had magical connotations for many athletes, and they would go to great lengths to obtain their lucky number.

Religious practices exist because they perform important functions for a group and the individual. At the personal level psychic needs are met by religious experience. At the group level, religion is an important integrative force because it organizes the individual's experience in terms of ultimate meanings that include but also transcend the individual; ceremonies and rituals promote integration, since they reaffirm some of the basic customs and values of society. Human social relationships are dependent upon symbols of one kind or another, religion supplies the ultimate symbols, the comprehensive ones, the ones on which all other ones make sense. It should not be surprising that magicoreligious practices are employed in sports. After all the sports participants are part of a larger social system in which religiousity abounds.

REFERENCES

Are sports good for the soul? 1976. *Newsweek.* (January 11): 51–52.

Becker, J. 1975. Superstition in sport. *Intern. Journal Sport Psychology* 6: 148–152.

Boyle, R.H. 1970. Oral Roberts Small BUT OH, MY. *Sports Illustrated* 33, (November, 30): 64–65.

Brasch, R. 1970. *How Did Sports Begin?* New York: David McKay.

Cozens, F.W. and F.S. Stumpf. 1953. *Sports and American Life.* Chicago: University of Chicago Press.

Deford, F. 1976. Religion in sport. *Sports Illustrated* 44, (April 19): 88–102.

Deford, F. 1976. The word according to Tom. *Sports Illustrated* 44, (April 26): 65–69.

Dirkson, J. 1975. The place of athletics in the life of the Christian. *Sport Sociology Bulletin* 4, Spring: 48–55.

Eastman F. 1912. Rural recreation through the church. *The Playground* 6, (October).

Edwards, H. (1972). Desegregating sexist sport. *Intellectual Digest* 3, (November): 82–83.

Eitzen, D.S. and G.H. Sage. 1978. *Sociology of Sport in America.* Dubuque, Iowa: D.C. Brown.

Gmelch, G. 1971. Baseball magic. *Trans-Action* 8, June: 39–41, 54.

Gregory, C.J. and B.M. Petrie. 1975. Superstitions of Canadian intercollegiate athletes: An inter-sport comparison. *IRSS* 10, 2: 59–68.

Guttmann, A. 1978. *From Ritual to Record.* New York: Columbia University Press.

Herrigel, E. 1961. *Zen and the Art of Archery.* New York:

Hogan, W.R. 1967. Sin and sports. In R. Slovenko and J.A. Knight eds., *Motivations in Play, Games, and Sport.* Springfield, Ill.: Charles C. Thomas.

Krickeberg, W. 1948. Das mittelamerikanische Ballspiel und seine religiöse Bedeutung. *Paideuma* 3: 118-90.

Jares, J. 1977. Hallelujah, what a team! *Sports Illustrated* 46, (February, 7): 41-42.

McGuff, J. 1970. Quoted in Sporting comments. *The Kansas City Star* (May 24): 25.

Malinowski, B. 1948. *Magic, Science, and Religion and Other Essays.* Glencoe, Ill.: Free Press.

Merchant, L. 1971. *And Every Day You Take Another Bite.* New York: Doubleday.

Marbeto, J.A. Jr. 1967. *The Incidence of Prayer in Athletics as Indicated by Selected California Collegiate Athletes and Coaches.* Master's thesis. University of California, Santa Barbara.

Merchant, L. 1971. *And Every Day You Take Another Bite.* New York: Doubleday. *Century* 89, (April 5): 392-394.

Rudin, A.J. 1972. America's new religion. *Christian Century* 89, (April 5): 384.

Schloz, R. et al. 1973. Sport and religions of the world. Pp. 595-606 in O. Grupe et al. eds. *Sport in the Modern World.* Berlin and New York: Springer.

Schloz, R. and H. Wissmann. 1972. Sport from theological and science of religion aspects. Pp. 40-100 in H. Baitsch et al. (eds.). *The Scientific View of Sport.* Berlin and New York: Springer.

Stark, R. and C.Y. Glock. 1968. *American Piety: The Nature of Religious Commitment.* Berkeley: University of California Press.

Swanson, R.A. 1968. The acceptance and influence of play in American Protestantism. *Quest.* 11, (December): 58-70.

The Christian Woodstock. 1972. *Newsweek.* (June 26): 52.

The Wittenberg Door. 1975. No. 24 (April-May, June-July).

Previously published in major parts in Eitzen and Sage *op. cit.*

SPORT AND THE MASS MEDIA

Susan L. Greendorfer

Sport has been an enormous social and cultural enterprise during the twentieth century. It has diffused to every aspect of social life, and its impact has been extensive. For instance, there were over 45 million paid admissions to professional football and baseball in 1975. Similarly, more than 80,000 spectators attended the Superbowl, while an additional 64 million watched the game on television. More recently, an estimated average of 15.9 million households viewed the 1976 Winter Olympics each night of the first week of competition. Yet, spectatorship has not been the only sphere in which Americans have been involved in sport. Expenditures for all sporting goods have increased steadily since 1948 (Snyder 1965).

This emergence of sport parallels the rise of technology and development of advanced communications systems. Similar to the pervasive influence of sport, the mass media have also had a profound effect on human life by creating change and restructuring social patterns. Today both institutions play a substantial role in popular or mass culture. Moreover, both represent lucrative leisure time industries.

Although the connection between the mass media and sport has been recognized for several decades, attention has been focused on one-way relationships—namely, the impact that technology has had on sport (Betts 1953). The influence of sport on the media has rarely been considered. Therefore, an understanding of the interdependence as well as the mutual development of both institutions is necessary. If over forty hours of prime time television coverage is devoted to the Winter Olympics, and if 1,100 hours of television time is allotted to sports in a given year, there is certainly a complex relationship worthy of investigation.

Therefore, this chapter focuses on events and factors which have contributed to the present symbiotic relationship between the mass media and sport. In addition the following premises are emphasized: 1) despite the particularly strong influence from television, sport has been involved with *all* the media; 2) sport has been *enveloped* by the various media—technological development of each medium has only intensified this degree of involvement; 3) the entanglement between sport and the media has been *economically motivated*; and 4) several educational institutions supportive of sport have become promoters; this shift in roles has resulted in a gradual shift of goals, to the extent that present goals are more in concert with the objectives of the mass media than with the objectives of sport.

Since this topic encompasses broad considerations, the present discussion has been limited to four general topics. The first includes a brief description of the general effects of the mass media. The second section traces the historical relationship between sport and the various media from the time of their technological inception. In the third and fourth sections attention is focused on a specific medium, television, because it has produced the greatest impact on social life as well as on sport. Extremely important in these sections is the consideration of economics, the specific factor which cements the sport-media relationship. Hence, section three considers the influence of television on sport, while the following section considers the flip side of the coin—the influence of sport on television. The chapter concludes with a discussion of some implications of this examination, with particular attention given to intercollegiate sport.

EFFECTS OF THE MASS MEDIA

The term *mass media* includes all the organized means of communication by which an individual can reach large numbers of diverse people quickly and efficiently (Larson 1964). Generally, this system of communications falls into two categories: *printed media* such as newspapers, magazines and books, and *broadcast media* which include radio, television, and movies.

The mass media as a social institution have produced some overall consequences or effects on society and social life which bear mentioning. First of all, the media have narrowed physical, temporal and social distances (Larson 1964). As a consequence the media must cater to a wide spectrum of a public which possesses diverse interests. Thus, the media must identify content with common appeal. Secondly, the mass media have the potential to initiate organized social action through exposure. Similarly, a major effect of the media is to reinforce existing norms and to maintain the status quo. Although the media have potential to serve as a change agent, rarely do they so serve. While the mass media have been effectively used to channel basic attitudes, there is little evidence of their having served to change these attitudes (Lazarsfeld and Merton 1949). Still another aspect of the mass media is their ability to confer and legitimize social status. The media bestow prestige and enhance the authority of individuals and groups. Visibility and exposure are essential features for status achievement, and the media serve as primary agents for both. In addition to the status effect, the media are a major source for identifying and evaluating heroes and villains. Thus, an emphasis is given to personality; regardless of social sphere such figures can be identified in business, politics, education, or sport. Finally, the mass media represent an institution strongly dominated by the economy. Since the media are supported by business concerns geared to the economy and social system, they contribute to the maintenance of such systems (Lazarsfeld and Merton 1949).

These general factors, then, serve as a theoretical framework for the historical analysis which follows. The time line in Table 1 presents a broad overview, while at the same time denotes specific events at particular points in time.

Table 1. Time Line—Mass Media and Sport

Year	Event
1440	Johann Gutenberg invents movable type printing press.
1486	Dame Juliana Berners, Prioress of Spowell Nunnery writes treatise on hawking, fishing and other field sports.
1733	(May 5) First sports story in an American newspaper. *The Boston Gazette* carries the prizefight between John Faulconer and Bob Russel on the "Bowling Green at Harrow on the Hill." It was copied directly from a London daily.
1750	The *New York Postboy* referred to horse racing.
1796	The *Charleston City Gazette* carries notices for Charleston Golf Club.
1801	The first sports publication in England: "The Sports and Pastimes of People of England."
1811	The *New York Post* describes a boat race.
1819	Colonel John Stuart Skinner, postmaster of Baltimore, publishes the first American periodical on sports, *The American Farmer*. Published the results of hunting, fishing, shooting, and bicycling matches as well as essays on the philosophy of sports.
1823	The *New York Evening Post* carries the first full-scale account of a boxing match.
1827	The *American Farmer* expands to become *The Farmer's Mechanic's, Manufacturer's and Sportsman's Magazine.*

1828   *The American Turf Register* is published.

1831   *The Spirit of the Times,* the first weekly on sports, is started. Most successful of all early sporting periodicals.

1842   First reported baseball.

1848   The Associated Press began.

1850's   The only member of newspaper staff who in any way resembled the modern sports editor was the turf man. Horse racing and cricket were the most popular sports of the day, and only the *New York Anglo-American* and the *Albion* covered cricket. Henry Chadwick began to cover cricket matches between the United States and Canadian teams for the *New York Times.* He received no pay. The visit of a British cricket team in 1859 caused so much interest that the *Herald* finally hired Chadwick. He later reported baseball.

1862   Chadwick becomes the first sports reporter, baseball.

1866   Opening of the Atlantic cable.

1870   Middie Morgan becomes the first female sportswriter. She covered races and cattle shows for the *New York Times.*

1883   Joseph Pulitzer bought the *World* and set up the first sports department. By 1892, all great papers had them. Reports of baseball, horse racing, pedestrian tournaments and other events were combined into a single article. They were less concerned with personalities than with final score.

1886   The *Sporting News,* a St. Louis weekly began. It was and is devoted to baseball. It has become the bible of the diamond.

1889   Thomas Edison invents the kinetoscope, forerunner of motion pictures.
         Joe Villa, sports editor of the *New York Sun,* uses the play-by-play technique for the first time in covering the Harvard-Princeton football game. The *Sun* devoted three columns to the game.

1890   The modern news summary appeared. Before that time, sports coverage was given big build-ups. Headlines contained definite statements of partisanship, stores were highly opinionated.

1895   Hearst begins the first sports section in a newspaper.

1890's   Era of the yellow press known for its slangy and facetious style. This exploitation did much to promote national interest in league baseball and in prize fighting.

1897   First fight news, covering the Corbett-Fitzsimmon fight.

1899   The wireless was used for news reporting in connection with the international yacht races.

1907   The United Press began.

1916   The first radio broadcast, DeForest reports the presidential election results. He reports them incorrectly.

1921   Baseball games and fights are on KDKA. Florent Gibson becomes the first sports broadcaster.
            The Dempsey-Carpentier fight becomes the first million dollar gate.

1922   Congress authorizes the Department of Commerce to issue licenses on wave lengths. Herbert Hoover was then Secretary of Commerce.
            The Chicago-Princeton football game is on radio.

1923   The first televised broadcast between New York and Philadelphia.

1925   The first play-by-play broadcast of major league baseball and football.

1926   The Birth of a Nation is shown, the first sound picture. The first national broadcast, the World Series.

1927   Congress passes the Radio Act, setting up a five-man commission, the Federal Radio Commission.
            NBC is established.

1928   General Electric starts televising regularly.
            CBS is established.

1934   Communications Act. Radio Act and FRC of 1927 are made more comprehensive. All communications regulated by one agency.
            The Federal Communications Commission is established, a 7 man group with 7 year terms. It has control of radio, telephone, telegraph, and television.

1935   Technicolor is developed.
            The AP wirephoto is developed. This has implications for sport since many of the pictures that appear on the sports page are AP wirephotos.

1937   The Executive Sports Editor is established.

1940   Emergence of sports cartoons.

1945   ABC is established.
           The AP sports wire is established for the opening day of major league baseball.

1949   The FCC editorializes on fairness, The Fairness Doctrine. All sides must be heard, equal time, equal opportunity.

1951   NCAA votes to restrict telecasting of its member's games.

1953   Color is authorized by the FCC using the RCA compatible system for television.
           The federal district court rules that the broadcasting and televising of professional football is interstate commerce. They rule that the exclusive jurisdiction over radio and television within a 75 mile radius comprises a geographic monopoly.

1958   The merger of the UP and INS into the UPI.

1960   Telstar goes up.

1961   Legislation passed by Congress to exempt the NFL from Antitrust law. (NFL as a league granted the right to negotiate for television coverage.)

1963   The first instant replay on television.

1973   Congress enacts Public Law 93–107, which amends Communications Act of 1934. (This is the Anti-blackout ruling; if home game is sold out 72 hours prior to the game, the game cannot be blacked out in home area.)

1974   Congress evaluates effect of PL 93–107 and concludes "no-shows" are not the result of legislation PL 93–107 stands as enacted. Ticket sales in NFL reach all time high.

THE MEDIA AND SPORT—HISTORICAL RELATIONSHIP

Newspapers

In order to support some of the underlying premises a logical starting point would be with the printed word—specifically, the sport story and the sport page. Although the first sports story in an American newspaper appeared in 1733 (see Table 1), attention to printed sport items did not actually begin until the 1850s. By 1890 the first recognized sport section appeared. The ultimate objective of the sports pages was to indicate wins and losses. Thus, sports pages have evolved from box score announcements to descriptions. Evidence of this trend can be found as early as 1889 when the first play-by-play reporting occurred. By the turn of the century several athletes were portrayed as heroes, and sportswriters had created cliches and sport terms which are still published in the sports pages.

Thus, the Period of Acceptance (1835-1860) evolved to the Period of Consolidation (1860-1890), which marked the beginning of *yellow journalism* (Heath and Gelfand 1951). Of particular importance during this latter period is the fact that newspaper publishers competed with one another for features which would increase sales. Although it was not until the Period of Growth (1890-1914) that the full impact of yellow journalism reached the sporting world, there was a growing belief that the sports page sells the paper. This belief is still evident (Woodward 1949). In fact, surveys have indicated that the most widely read section of American newspapers is the sports section, since sport encompasses the type of news which interests the greatest number of people across all socio-economic levels. Furthermore, the number of inches (space) allotted to sports coverage has increased steadily through the years.

While sportswriting flourished between 1914 and 1930 (The Golden Age), the economic collapse of the 1930s prompted many papers to decrease the size of their sports sections. However, by this period the educational level of reporters was higher than during previous periods, and the quality of sportswriting had significantly improved. The initiation of the Associated Press sports wire in 1945 nationalized and formularized sports coverage (Poe, 1974); moreover, sports cartoons became an integral part of the sports page. By the 1950s sports had become so popular that the results of athletic contests began to appear on the front page with a reminder that details could be found on the sports page. From this period to the present any substantial changes in sportswriting can be explained by personality or attitude changes of sports reporters, not technological developments.

Radio

The next significant media development specifically related to sport was that of radio broadcasting. Between 1922 and 1925 radios permeated American society. Since sport appealed to all, it was viewed as a common denominator, and, hence, was an *expected* part of radio programming. Despite such expectations, during the late 1920s sport owners paid radio networks and stations to broadcast games. One of the first sport broadcasts involved baseball, which was followed by broadcasts of the Davis Cup matches and the Dempsey-Carpentier heavyweight championship fight. This latter event demonstrated the entertainment value of sports broadcasts, which, in turn, incorporated sport into broadcasting economics (Parente, 1974). Moreover, public preference for exceptional rather than regular events further augmented the sport-economic-broadcasting relationship. Of particular importance is that by the 1930s networks and stations were paying for sports broadcast rights. Large sums of money were involved; moreover, profits from radio rights were evident by 1938. This development marked a reversal of roles between the networks (from benefactor to client) and sport owners (from client to supplier or benefactor).

There were two consequences which were attributed to the popularity of sports broadcasts. The first involved sports reporting, whereby a practice of re-creating games and events was initiated. Re-creation involved either delayed transmission of games (e.g., the broadcast occurred after the game had been played) or fictitious play-by-play reports made by announcers who were not at the game themselves but who received general boxscore results and some information pertaining to highlights of each inning. This practice was finally outlawed in 1955. The second consequence resulted in a shift of announcers' employers. Originally sports announcers were hired by the networks or radio stations and paid by sponsors; eventually ball clubs paid them directly. By the 1940s most sports announcers no longer worked exclusively for radio stations but for teams; their jobs included announcing games, entertaining fans, and *promoting* teams. This shift of employers proved to be a permanent alteration to radio broadcasting; today most announcers are associated with teams rather than with stations or networks.

Television

The medium creating the most notable effect on sport has been television, mainly through the realization of profit and the increased visibility given to sport. These effects have been profound. However, it must be remembered that television was also a product of technological change and development. Hence, television represents a consequence of as well as a catalyst for social change. Furthermore, the fact that sport was firmly entrenched in other media before the advent of television cannot be ignored. While these other media had a significant influence on sport, a reciprocal relationship also existed. Sport enhanced the economic situation of these same media. Therefore, the events cited in this section should be placed in the perspective of social change which involved *both institutions* rather than focusing attention on a one-way influence which maintains that change in sport was initiated by television.

Television, in some form, has been a reality since the early days of radio. However, the years between 1946 and 1950 represent a significant period in the development of television. During this time the number of television sets sold increased from 5,000 (in 1946) to over 7,000,000 (in 1950). This profusion continued through the 1960s. Moreover, 95% of the population owned at least one set in 1960

(Durso 1971). In 1971, 99.7% owned a black and white set, while 42.5% had a color set—thus indicating dual ownership (Parente 1974). According to McLuhan (1967) television involves participation and involvement in depth of man's whole being. Consequently, the medium's major changes have been to create a total participation among viewers (McLuhan 1967). Perhaps this interpretation best explains how television has established itself as the outstanding mass communications medium of our time less than a decade after its inception. In addition television has become the foremost advertising medium in America and the main source of popular entertainment (Chester et al. 1963).

Despite television's early presence in this century's technological developments, it was not until 1939 that the first sports telecast took place (a baseball game between Princeton and Columbia). However, a trend of sports telecasting became evident by 1941, aided by the subsequent development of the telephoto lens, additional cameras at sport sites, and improved skills or techniques of sports broadcasting. Furthermore, the new medium required substantial changes in sports announcing, since visual images decreased the necessity for constant sport "chatter." Subsequent developments led to an emphasis on accuracy and knowledge of the sport, a consequence created by increased public demand for better sportscasting. Moreover, errors, myths, inaccuracies—which were often undetected on radio—were not tolerated on television.

During the early years of commercial television America was just learning to spend its leisure time watching variety shows. However, sport represented a major portion of the screen offerings. With improved technological equipment as many as five boxing matches, eight football games, eight to ten hours of wrestling, plus several nights of roller derby could be viewed during a single week of programming (Johnson 1970). Thus, the original impact of television was to promote sport; this relationship was ideal for the first few years of televised sport. (Specific developments are discussed in the next section.)

Since money as well as publicity and prestige was available through the medium of television, college football became a regular viewing pastime; during the early fifties college football had no restrictions on telecasts. Also profiting from television revenue was professional boxing, which appeared almost every night of the week. During the 1950's boxing flourished. Similarly, commercial television also brought major league baseball to the entire population. Major league stars could be seen and imitated, while batting and pitching styles could be analyzed. The fans clamored for major league performance which they believed to be of better quality. Despite this demand for quality performance, major league baseball as well as the minor leagues suffered a decline in interest in the late fifties. (Contributing factors and consequences are discussed in the next section.)

Moreover, it did not take long before sport entrepreneurs became aware of the profit in selling broadcast rights to television. For example, as early as 1946 the New York Yankees sold television rights directly to stations. This practice eventually was adopted by the entire baseball league which began to negotiate for the sale of telecast rights. By 1972, 24% of professional baseball revenue was due to television income (Horowitz 1974). Similar patterns were evident in professional football. In 1952, 36% of NFL revenue was acquired through the sale of telecast rights, with $50,000 distributed to each NFL team. By 1960 this figure had escalated to $200,000 per team. In 1972 each of the twenty-six teams received $1.6 million from television (Parente 1974). Finally, in 1978 a $700 million contract with the NFL was signed giving each NFL team an estimated $6 million over the next four years. Professional basketball has also increased its revenue through the sale of telecast rights (Horowitz 1974).

Although it has been argued that the sport structure—particularly professional football—would collapse without television (Johnson 1969, 1971), there are some significant considerations about football which may offer a different perspective. While television was constantly improving technologically and growing in acceptance as a leisure time activity, the game of football was increasing in complexity, incorporating different strategies, and attracting larger crowds. The sudden-death championship game of 1958 between Baltimore and New York marked the beginning of an era for professional football. For example, the two-platoon system was introduced; passing, running, kicking, and defense specialists evolved as separate roles; the college draft became truly effective; significant administrative decisions regarding telecasts were made (e.g., home game blackouts). In 1960 several policies were instituted beginning with the negotiation of television contracts and the sharing of revenue among all the teams in the league. To insure survival of newer clubs as well as improvement in weaker clubs, *the league contracted with the networks for all the clubs.* This economically motivated policy had legal implications which resulted in a special Congressional Act in 1961 exempting the NFL from certain antitrust laws (see Table 1). These monumental decisions had specific consequences for the renewal of contracts in 1964. By then football and television had become mutually dependent upon each other. Television was a source of revenue while football was a source of high ratings.

Professional sport has not been the only sphere touched by the sale of broadcast rights as a source of revenue. Nor has televised sport been limited to the professional ranks. Intercollegiate football, through NCAA negotiations, first sold telecast rights in 1952 for

$1.1 million. The broadcast package rose to $16 million in 1975, with an estimated $18 million projected for the 1976–1977 season (Van Dyne 1975). The most recent amateur sport complex involved in television coverage has been the Olympic Games. The 1972 Olympics involved approximately $13 million (Johnson 1970), the 1976 Winter Games alone involved $22 million (Leggett 1976), and the 1980 Summer Olympics $85 million.

Despite the economic significance, another trend has also been evident. There has been a continuous increase of television time devoted to sport. For instance, ABC devoted 43 hours to the 1976 Winter Olympics at Innsbruck and 75 hours to the Summer Games in Montreal, most of which took place during evening prime time. An estimated 150 hours were planned for the 1980 Summer Olympics. Furthermore, 1,100 hours of major network time in 1975 was devoted to sports, with indications that more time would be allotted for sports in 1976—an estimated 500 hours by ABC alone (Leggett 1976). Relative to overall television time, sports programming in the United States amounts to 6%, while Western Europe, Eastern Europe, and Asia devote 16%, 4–13%, and less than 10%, respectively (Parente 1974). Also worthy of comment, the largest television audience ever (800 million people) was attracted by a sport event, the final ceremonies of the 1972 Olympics (Lüschen 1975), while in the United States, the ten most popular telecasts of 1975 were *all* sports events (Leggett 1976).

One difficulty inherent in interpreting historical and social change is the problem of verification. Another lies in what is called fallacy of the single cause, whereby one particular relationship between phenomena is appealing or so striking that it is accepted as *the* specific explanation for the present situation. Therefore, this section is concluded with a few conservative observations and suggestions. Sport is a highly salient feature of American life. According to Lüschen (1975) sport attracts more interest than any other institution except the family. Perhaps its saliency has made it profitable rather than its profitability making it salient. Logically, then, although sport has received extensive exposure through the media, particularly television, it cannot be concluded *ipso facto* that sport's popularity depends on television. Although television has brought profit to sport, sport has exerted reciprocal influence on television, thereby creating an interdependence between the two institutions.

IMPACT OF TELEVISION ON SPORT

One of the first observations that occurred with the advent of television was an alteration in the mode of fan consumption of sport. Essentially, there was a shift in the relationship between the fan and sports events. Interest was mediated through television rather than through newspaper reports or actual attendance at the game. With this shift the question arises whether one medium affects another; more specifically, whether or not television injured the other media. Initial reports indicate that radio induced advertisers to divert money from newspapers after 1929; however, recovery was evident by 1945. Hence, there is little evidence that radio's growth was at the expense of newspapers (Levin 1960). In fact interest from one medium can be transferred to another. Moreover, it has been hypothesized that the increase in number of sports magazines as well as listening to radio reports about sports events is attributed to the interest in sport initially generated by television.

In contrast there are conflicting reports relative to television's impact on ticket sales and actual game attendance. The most recent Congressional Reports pertaining to professional football indicate that gate receipts and ticket sales reached an all time high *after the ban of home game blackouts,* thereby demonstrating little or no impact due to television exposure. On the other hand, there is evidence that attendance at college football and at minor league baseball games suffered because of television. In the early 1950s the NCAA was the first to notice that massive television exposure could create a drop in game attendance. Decreased attendance created a financial crisis; as a result the NCAA enlisted the services of National Opinion Research Center (NORC) to extensively study the problem of non-attendance. The ultimate outcome resulted in a policy limiting the amount of televised college football games. However, it took ten years for attendance at college games to reach levels achieved in 1948. A second sport affected by constant television exposure was professional boxing. Recently the National Football League used boxing as an example to support its arguments for the reinstatement of home game blackouts. However, the Congressional rebuttal maintained the main reason for the decline of boxing was not lack of blackouts. Rather, non-selectivity in television matches, premature matching of undeveloped boxers, and poor administrative decisions were cited as reasons for loss of interest in boxing.

Although these examples represent instances in which television exposure could affect attendance and interest, decline of attendance was not the only impact television exerted on professional baseball. As of 1950 telecasts of major league games were readily available to the public, which created a decreased interest in minor league teams—until only 155 such teams remained in 1969—a drop from 488 in 1949 (Johnson 1969). Despite the profit from television revenue, by 1953 actual attendance at major league games was decreasing. The nature of the new medium, television, seemed to have dislodged baseball from the social center of American life (McLuhan 1964).

According to McLuhan (1964) baseball is a game of fixed positions, isolated action, and task specialties—all of which represent staff and line in management organization. Moreover, when culture changes, so do games in that culture. Baseball is a lineal expansive game in which timing and waiting are the essence, with the entire field in suspense waiting upon the performance of a single player (McLuhan 1964: 212). In contrast football, basketball, and ice hockey are games in which many elements occur simultaneously with the entire team involved at the same time. While a sport of many actions with synchronized timing of players, action strategies and game plans corresponds well to television, isolated individual performance does not transfer well to the television screen. A recent examination of baseball telecasts revealed that only seven minutes of action take place during the course of a baseball game. Consequently, we must remember that football by its very nature represented a "sellable" product that adapts more easily to the medium of television.

IMPACT OF ADVERTISING ON SPORT

Television is an important aspect of the advertising industry; therefore, its first priority is to advertising. In order to make a profit networks not only desire a large audience (quantity) but the right kind (quality). Since television networks do not profit *directly* from sport, they must negotiate for telecast rights with a league or governing body of sport; then they must sell commercial time to interested sponsors.

Even in the earliest days of telecasting advertising attention was drawn to sport, since sports programming provided the proper composition as well as size of audience which sponsors wish to reach. Advertisers appeal to middle-class, family oriented, young-minded men who have or seek influence. Characteristically, the sports fan is predominantly male, young (ranging in age from eighteen to forty-nine), affluent, and middle class (with a higher socio-economic and educational status than most television audiences). These factors, then, might explain why or how television has affected sports.

During the 1960s sports programs were relegated to afternoon time periods. Only on occasion were sports programs televised during prime time directly opposite expensive programming. By the late 1960s the three major networks increased prime time sports telecasts—perhaps due to rising interest in sports programming, perhaps due to advertising economics, perhaps both. Consequently, several changes or modifications occurred in order to *adapt sports more suitably to advertising needs and requirements.*

Prior to 1960 the majority of rules, strategy, or structural changes in sports were implemented with the notion of improving the game or creating greater interest for live spectators. In contrast it has been argued that during the last fifteen years many of the changes within sports were implemented not for the purpose of improvement but for the purpose of restructuring sport to be a more marketable commodity (Johnson 1971; Parente 1974). Thus advertising needs dictated structural changes. More specifically, to hold the viewer's attention changes which insured continuity of suspense were introduced. For example, golf shifted from medal play to stroke play; tennis instituted a tie-breaker; NFL halftimes were reduced from 20 to 15 minutes.

The influence of television created the most radical types of change in professional football. One innovation was Monday night games; a second involved the NFL–AFL merger which ultimately resulted in conference realignments. Both decisions were motivated by the desire to strengthen professional football by increasing profits from television revenue. Furthermore, merger and realignment produced several consequences: 1) a balanced number of teams in each division; 2) balanced television market areas; 3) creation of the Superbowl; 4) a play-off system between the divisions; 5) more games—and ultimately more television revenue. In addition specific rule changes were introduced in order to permit more commercial interruptions; namely, the two-minute warning, official time outs at the end of each quarter, and various official time outs during the course of a game, which are determined by certain rules of thumb. Interruptions follow a general rule of thumb—never within the 20 yard line, but all right if seven minutes elapse without a touchdown.

The influence of television and profit from telecast revenue have not been limited to professional sports. Intercollegiate football has also realized substantial revenue through the sale of broadcast rights. For example, through NCAA negotiations individual colleges receive approximately $243,928 for a national telecast and $177,500 for a regional appearance (Van Dyne 1975). Since college football competes with the NFL for telecast money, several recent decisions have influenced the degree of intercollegiate football's commitment to television.

In previous years a maximum appearance rule which limited television appearances of Division I teams and provided for some regional small college appearances from teams in Division II and III was operative. However, the most recent NCAA negotiations (1976–77) involved an $18 million contract for telecasts of 30 national and regional games as well as allowing *a new flexibility for networks.* More specifically, the network will select the teams that will appear. Most likely this decision favors big-name, winning teams from strong conferences.

Other effects have also been evident. College football ratings dropped between 1971 and 1974 (from 14% to 12%); furthermore two major sponsors were lost in the process. In order to increase the ratings in 1975 several decisions regarding game times were made. First of all, night games were scheduled so as not to compete with other sports events. Secondly, such scheduling was determined by the television network. Not only have starting times for intercollegiate football and basketball games been set to conform to audience and advertising interests, but such arbitrary scheduling has had ramifications on other aspects of the intercollegiate sports program. For example, a varsity girls' basketball game which was played prior to the men's game in the same arena was halted before completion in order to allow the men adequate warm-up time. This decision was not a reflection of the priority of men's over women's basketball. Rather, it was an *expedient media decision* making the sport's schedule conform to a telecasting schedule. An additional consequence has resulted in the gerrymandering of regional games. These decisions have had the effects of nationalizing regional games, of focusing on powerhouse teams, and allowing the network to avoid the previous limitations of national appearances by one team. As a result, television exposure has focused on winners.

According to Van Dyne (1975) only a fraction of the NCAA's 700 member institutions are involved with television revenue; thus, sharing has been limited to major conferences. Moreover, some powerful teams are not aligned with a conference and do not have to share television money (e.g., Notre Dame, Penn State). Therefore, any proposal to distribute revenue among the three divisions would significantly decrease present proportions. Furthermore, adoption of such a proposal could have serious consequences for the NCAA. Specifically, big-time powerhouse schools could form their own league and negotiate for television rights, and thus, sever connections with the NCAA. Although such a situation is hypothetical at the present time, this consideration alone reflects the complexities involved in the sport-television relationship.

IMPACT OF SPORT ON TELEVISION

Although the mass media have been considered a major influence on sport, particularly in spheres of entertainment, business, and organizational structure, the significant effects sport has exerted on the media—especially television—cannot be ignored. For instance, there would be a void in programming without sports events. Moreover, sport, as well as television, has altered patterns of social life. What would Sunday afternoon be without professional football, basketball, and baseball? What would Saturday or New Year's Day be without intercollegiate football? Which programs would replace these events, earn as much television revenue, and attract the size and type of audience that sport does? According to a Roper survey the largest radio and television audiences are reached when sport and similar special events are broadcast (Chester et al. 1963).

Of particular importance is the dependence of television on dollars of commerce, earned primarily through advertising. Two factors contribute to sport's influence in this realm. First of all, sport programming affords prestigious identification for an advertiser; thus, extensive network advertising may result from sponsors who wish to increase their success originally achieved through sport sponsorship. Secondly, sports events have provided networks with substantial revenue from advertisers, since sport attracts large amounts of advertising money. For example, a minute of commercial time for intercollegiate football costs $100,000, whereas other sports events attract rates between $69,000 and $239,000 a commercial minute. As has been suggested previously, television revenue is just as likely to be a consequence of sport's saliency as well as a cause of sport's popularity. The relationship at the present time is symbiotic and cannot be reduced to a single factor.

With respect to the "sellability" as well as the popularity of sport, major networks are forced to compete with one another for broadcast rights. Not only is competition keen among the major networks, but private networks have also indicated a willingness to negotiate for sports telecasts. For example, the NFL has previously considered contracts with the Hughes network. Thus, the success and/or demand for sport has created television competition. Moreover, such competition between networks has been extended beyond broadcast rights. The networks need the best programming in order to compete for ratings, to gain prestige, and to project a strong image. Consequently, a mutual dependency has been created. On the one hand sport (particularly professional football) has received massive television exposure. On the other hand there has been increased public demand for sports telecasts. Thus, the quality coverage by a network initially helps promote sport; then, in turn, sport helps to promote the network. The more a network broadcasts sport events, the higher its ratings and stronger its image.

The quality of administration in sports organizations has also had an impact on television, albeit in a rather circuitous fashion. The most appropriate example is professional football; however, men's intercollegiate sports (specifically the NCAA) and perhaps the merger of the professional basketball leagues also exemplify such examples. Specific to professional football, in order that the sport survive television revenue was distributed fairly and equally among all the teams. An alternative decision would have resulted in financial inequalities among teams, with perhaps the weakest and poorest teams eventually dissolving. This decision led to a merger between conferences and a centralization of authority through a commissioner who was given power. Such restructuring had legal as well as economic ramifications, since the NFL had to receive exemptions from anti-trust and anti-monopoly laws (see Table 1). The effect of restructuring resulted in the NFL's bargaining as a cartel for television rights for all of professional football. These specific developments significantly affected the bargaining power of football, since all the entrepreneurs consolidated into a central administrative structure. As a result, the networks were forced to compete with each other for telecast rights, if they wished to televise football. This competition led to broadcast "packages" which included doubleheaders, increased television exposure, and immense amounts of money. Thus, a balance of bargaining power had shifted in the direction of sport. Moreover, the impact of such a shift resulted in television's dependence on professional football.

Despite the financial web linking television and sport, another type of interrelationship exists—the role of technology in the telecasting of sport. Again, the relationship is reciprocal; it cannot be determined whether technological developments initially influenced sports or whether sports first influenced technological changes. Nevertheless, sports fans are aware of the many developments in the telecasting of sport, particularly of those technological products specific to sport. For example, the use of cranes, blimps, and helicopters has been introduced into sports telecasts. Similarly, color, slow motion, instant replay, the split screen, and the zoom lens have all been utilized to refine and improve the quality of sports telecasts. Since these technological developments are specific to sports and have been used predominantly in a sport context, they shall be considered as consequences of the impact of sport on the medium. Another development reflecting sport's influence on television has been the introduction of a magazine approach to sports broadcasting, evidenced by such programs as "The Wide World of Sports" and others.

As can be observed, then, although television has had a tremendous impact on sport, the relationship certainly has not been one way. Indeed, the present stage of mutual interdependence connotes reciprocity of influence, mutual benefit, and hence, symbiosis. Furthermore, the relationship between these two institutions is complex and has been couched in the context of social change—social change as it affects sport as well as social change as it affects television.

While the major attention in mass media research is directed toward technological change and toward television, issues like the structure of television programs and the other media need continued attention as well (Smith and Blackman 1978).

The sports page (Woodward 1949; Pearman 1978) is still an important source of information, receives high attention by newspaper readers and may well fulfill differential functions that the drama of sports television does not provide. Newspaper reporting has been the subject of a content analysis dealing with the emergence of stereotypes over time (Tannenbaum and Noah 1959). National tendencies in television reports (Schmidt 1965) have also been addressed in one of the few program analyses of the mass media. With regard to the latter it is surprising that differential informations about the magnitude of television programs in sport are hardly available at this time (University of Tampere 1973).

Occupational careers in the mass media as they relate to sport have been addressed only in a qualitative analysis of the sports journalist (Smith 1976).

POLICY IMPLICATIONS FOR INTERCOLLEGIATE SPORT

Since this chapter has been primarily concerned with the relationship between the mass media and professional sport—intercollegiate sport served as a peripheral consideration—it could be argued that there are no policy implications for sport in general. However, such a perspective would be short sighted, especially when current trends in intercollegiate sports are examined. College basketball has served as an important source of programming; college football has had a connection with television for twenty years, with recent negotiations demonstrating a significant shift in decision making; furthermore, some women's sports programs have attempted to negotiate for broadcast rights. Thus, recent trends indicate a tendency toward greater involvement between intercollegiate sport and the media, particularly television. Furthermore, motivations similar to those of professional sports have prompted this relationship; namely, economics and the desire for broad exposure.

When intercollegiate schedules are disrupted and starting times can be changed at the last minute, when intercollegiate schedules are structured around television and media needs, and when intercollegiate sports programs become dependent on television revenue for survival—then, implications are great. The most fundamental issue concerns the decision making process, which has revolved around expediency rather than philosophical positions. An unconscious shift of goals and objectives has occurred through the years. Priorities have been given to economic survival, school reputations, and the role of winning as a function of the two previous factors. The first policy implication, then, would necessitate a clarification of goals, a restatement of purpose, or an admission that decisions are economically motivated for system maintenance as well as nurture of elite performance by a select few. As such, the educational values of such programs as well as college or university context for these programs becomes questionable.

Furthermore administrative decisions overly influenced by economic needs have placed intercollegiate sport programs into the role of promoter or entrepreneur. This role caters more to the demands of the media and the needs to insure economic success than it does to the needs of the participants and to the purposes of sport. Hence, intercollegiate sport, like professional sport is in the process of selling itself beyond the capacity to control its own destiny. The loss of autonomy often results in a gradual shift of goals, shift of philosophical basis, and shift in concerns that receive primary attention. The second policy implication, then, involves a philosophical examination—which by rights should accompany any re-examination of goals and structure. As a result, philosophical principles of intercollegiate sport should be written, should be operationalized, and should be followed—not ignored once they are written.

As a final consideration, let us recall some historical facts. Students will wish to play, to compete, and to participate—regardless of budget size and, oddly enough, regardless of broadcast rights. Participation in sport is significant in most cultures; thus, the question is whether students will participate under the auspices of programs dedicated to their needs and espoused educational values—which created sports programs in a collegiate setting to begin with—or whether fewer and fewer will participate each year in programs whose priorities are dedicated to financial strength which will in turn ensure consistent winning.

REFERENCES

Betts, J.R. 1953. The technological revolution and the rise of sport, 1850–1900. *Mississippi Valley Historical Review*, 40, 2: 231–256.

Birrell, S. and J. Loy. 1979. Media sport: Hot and cool. *IRSS.* 14, 1: 5–19.

Chester, G., et al. 1963. *Television and Radio.* 3rd ed. New York: Appleton-Century-Crofts.

Dumazedier, J. 1935. *Television et éducation populaire.* Paris: UNESCO.

Durso, J. 1971. *The All-American Dollar: The Big Business of Sports.* Boston: Houghton-Mifflin Company.

Famey-Lamon, A. and F. Van Loon. 1978. Mass media and sports practice. *IRSS.* 13, 4: 37–45.

Fasting, K. 1976. *Sports and TV.* Oslo: Norwegian Confederation of Sports.

Givant, M. 1979. Pro football and the mass media: Some themes in the televising of a product. *Review of Sport and Leisure.* 3, 2: 69–32.

Heath, H. and L. Gelfand. 1951. *How to Cover, Write and Edit Sports.* Ames, Iowa: The Iowa State College Press.

Horowitz, I. 1974. Sports broadcasting. Pp. 275–324 in R. Noll, ed. *Government and the Sports Business.* Washington, D.C.: The Brookings Institution.

Johnson, W. 1969. TV made it all a new game. *Sports Illustrated,* 31, 26 (December 22): 86–102.

Johnson, W. 1970. TV accepted the call. *Sports Illustrated,* 32, 1 (January 5): 22–29.

Johnson, W. 1970. Adventures of super spy. *Sports Illustrated.* 32, 2 (January 12): 44–52.

Johnson, W. 1971. *Super spectator and the electric lilliputions.* Boston: Little, Brown and Company.

Larson, O. 1964. Social effects of mass communication. Pp. 353–54 in R.E. Faris, ed. *Handbook of Modern Sociology.* Chicago: Rand-McNally.

Lazarsfeld, P. and R. Merton. 1949. Mass communications: popular taste and organized social action. Pp. 453–80 in W. Schramm, ed. *Mass Communications.* Urbana: University of Illinois Press.

Leggett, W. 1976. He was right on the button. *Sports Illustrated,* XXXXIV, 8 (February 23): 48.

Levin, H. 1960. *Broadcast Regulation and Joint Ownership of Media.* New York: New York University Press.

Lüschen, G. 1975. The institution of sport in sociological perspective. *Position Paper to UNESCO,* on behalf of International Committee for Sociology of Sport (ICSPE/ISA).

McLuhan, M. 1964. *Understanding Media.* New York: Signet.

McLuhan, M. and Q. Fiore. 1967. *The Medium is the Message.* New York: Bantam Books.

McPherson, B. 1975. Sport consumption and the economics of consumerism. Pp. 239–75 in D. Ball and J. Loy, eds. *Sport and Social Order.* Reading, Mass.: Addison-Wesley.

Parente, D. 1974. *A History of Television and Sports.* Unpublished Doctor's Dissertation, University of Illinois, Urbana.

Pearman, W.A. 1978. Race on the sports page. *Review of Sport and Leisure.* 3, 2: 54–68.

Poe, R. 1974. The writing of sports. *Esquire,* 82, 4: 173–175; 373–380.

Report of the Federal Communications Commission. 1974. On the Effect of Public Law 93–107: The Sports Anti-Blackout Law. On the Broadcasting of Sold-Out Home Games of Professional Football, Baseball, Basketball, and Hockey. Committee on Commerce, April, 1974. Washington, D.C.: U.S. Government Printing Office.

Schmidt, H.D. 1965. Versuch einer Inhaltsanalyse nationaler Tendenzen in Sportreportagen (attempt towards a content analysis of national tendencies in sport reports). *Psychologische Rundschau.* 16, 1:43–51.

Smith, G.L. and C. Blackman. 1978. *Sport in the Mass Media.* CAHPER Sociology of Sport Monograph. Calgary: University of Calgary.

Snyder, R. 1965. *Trends in the Sporting Goods Market: 1947–1965.* Chicago: National Sporting Goods Association.

Tannenbaum, P.H. and J.E. Noah. 1959. Sportugese: a study of sports page communication. *Journalism Quarterly.* 36, 2:163–170.

Toyama, J. and S. Greendorfer. 1970. Mass Media and Sport. Unpublished Annotated Bibliography, University of Wisconsin.

U.S. Congress, House. Committee on Interstate and Foreign Commerce. 1973. Evaluation of the Necessity for TV Blackouts of Professional Sporting Events. 93rd Congress, 1st Session, July 1973. Washington, D.C.: U.S. Government Printing Office.

University of Tampere. Institute of Communications. 1973. *A Comparative Analysis of International Television Programs.* Tampere/Finland: University of Tampere (mimeographed).

Van Dyne, L. 1975. NCAA and ABC Sports. *Chronicle of Higher Education.*
    11, 6 (October 20): 3.
Woodward, S. 1949. *Sports Page.* New York: Simon & Schuster.

LEISURE AND SPORT:
A SOCIOLOGICAL APPROACH

John R. Kelly

The denotation of the term "sport" seems relatively clear. Lists of organized activities such as football and tennis spring to mind. The central meaning of "leisure" is less exact. Leisure may be defined broadly to include most nonwork or narrowly and qualitatively to designate rare and treasured experiences. This lack of definitional consensus has deterred many social scientists from dealing with leisure. Although definitional discussions can be tedious, relating sport and leisure will require some such analysis.

Further, the place of sport in adult leisure will be examined. Sports as leisure, the meaning of leisure sports, and sports as a value conditioner in leisure socialization will be briefly explored. The aim is to sketch an outline of the relationship of leisure and sport from the perspective of social contexts and meanings.

DEFINITIONS AND RELATIONSHIPS

Definitions of sport, leisure, and play have considerable overlap. However, within the most common definitions there are central themes that provide a basis for distinguishing sport and leisure and defining the element of play.

Definitions

Sport. Listing sports is easy. Classifying sports as indoor and outdoor, professional and amateur, and formal and informal is only slightly more difficult. However, a definition that draws parameters around sport including and excluding clearly and cleanly agreed-on kinds of activity is more difficult to formulate.

Standard dictionary definitions may be very general such as "an active pastime or diversion" with athletics or hunting mentioned as examples (*American Heritage Dictionary,* 1969) or more limiting such as "an athletic activity requiring skill or physical prowess and often of a competitive nature" (*Random House Dictionary of the English Language,* 1972). The more limited approach is supported by

Edwards (1973: 55f) who excludes many diversions and games and much play by stressing physical effort and competition. Sport involves "activities having formally recorded histories and traditions, stressing physical exertion through competition within limits set in explicit and formal rules governing role and position relationships, and carried out by actors who represent or who are part of formally organized associations having the goal of achieving valued tangibles or intangibles through defeating opposing groups" (57-58). Edwards refers primarily to competitive, institutionalized team sports.

Most scholars would be more inclusive. Lüschen (1968, 1970) stresses institutionalization and physical activity with competition as a common goal, but would include more individual and informal activity than Edwards. Loy is perhaps most comprehensive in his definitional effort (Loy and Kenyon 1969: 56-71) when he delineates game, institutional, social organization, and social situation dimensions of sport. Sport as game may be playful in the sense of being free, unproductive, uncertain, and even make-believe. The game aspect also includes rules, competition, physical and mental skills, and physical mastery. This game approach to defining sport is probably most common. However, it demonstrates the polarities of an inclusive definition by including freedom and rules, intrinsic motivation and competition, skill and uncertainty.

The dimension of institutionalization in Loy's approach points to organized teams and sponsors, developed equipment and skill, symbolic display and ritual, and learning contexts. Further dimensions less explicitly analysed are those of social organization with authority, roles, and structures and the social situation with levels and modes of involvement and interaction. Few games or organized leisure activities are excluded by Loy's effort which is more of an analytical framework than a definition.

What are the persistent themes of these definitions? Physical activity and effort and a degree of regularity in form are central to every definition. The regularity may be expressed in rules, forms, development of skills, and social organization. Further, the dimension of relative measurement by competition, performance standards, outcomes, or judgment is included in every definition. Usually present is the element of play in the sense of some uncertainty of outcome and freedom of participation. On the other hand, many of the aspects of sport mentioned by Loy are seen as present in some but not all sports. They are common characteristics, but not definitional parameters. Physical effort, regularity, and measurement seem to be the three definitional dimensions. An inclusive definition would be: Sport is organized activity with accepted regularities and forms in which physical effort is related to that of others in some relative measurement of outcomes.

Leisure. The central dimension of all definitions of leisure is freedom. Leisure is chosen, not required; discretionary, not obligatory. The second universal dimension is derived from the first. Since work must be done and leisure cannot be "necessary", then leisure is "not-work" (Kelly, 1972). However, a number of additional themes run through the most common definitions of leisure.

Joffre Dumazedier's definition is probably the most used by sociologists. "Leisure is activity—apart from the obligations of work, family, and society—to which the individual turns at will, for either relaxation, diversion, or broadening his knowledge and spontaneous social participation, the free exercise of his creative capacity" (1968: 16–17). In a social science encyclopedia, he stresses freedom from obligation, disinterestedness in relation to economic gain, satisfaction that is an end in itself, and a meeting of individual needs (1969: 251). Personal satisfaction intrinsic to the activity, freedom of choice, and detachment from extrinsic ends, especially those related to employment, are the three basic dimensions.

Other definitions may accentuate one or more of the dimensions. A psychologist holds perceived freedom as primary with motivation intrinsic to the choice and the activity as an end in itself defining the freedom (Neulinger 1974: 16). Leisure, then, is defined by the state of mind of the participant. Two models include both differentiation from work and relative freedom from constraint as central, but suggest that these are social as well as psychological conditions (Parker 1971; Kelly 1972).

Like sport, leisure may be defined narrowly or inclusively. In a model proposed by the author, the most restricted definition is labelled "unconditional leisure." Unconditional leisure is relatively free from social constraints related to work, family, or community roles. It is chosen for its own sake, with motivations and ends intrinsic to the activity. "Complementary leisure," on the other hand, includes the element of role expectations, especially those of family and social position, in the decision process. Complementary leisure is not required or necessary, but is role-related and mixes intrinsic satisfactions with social constraints and extrinsic goals. Leisure has an essential social dimension in the building and maintaining of social bonds (Cheek and Burch 1968).

In a recent revision of the typology, Kelly (1978) reports that research in three American communities has extended the kinds of leisure to include compensatory and relational motivations. About 20 percent of the significant leisure activities of adults has a measurable element of compensation for work constraints in their selection. Also, most of the activities containing role expectations among the motives actually were complementary in a positive sense. "Relational" activities were chosen primarily because of satisfactions in the building and maintaining of the relationships rather than because of role constraints. Leisure, then, may be (1) unconditional with intrinsic satisfactions and goals or complementary in being (2) recuperative or compensatory as a contrast to work conditions, (3) relational with the associations rather than the activity primary in the satisfaction, and (4) role-determined with social expectations being salient to the decision. Leisure in general may be defined simply as "activity that is chosen primarily for its own sake" (Kelly 1978).

In no case is leisure defined by the form or the content of the activity. Almost anything can be leisure in some context and nothing is always leisure in any context. Unlike sport, leisure is defined by its meaning to the actor rather than by what people do. Leisure, then, is both inclusive in encompassing all kinds of activity and exclusive in potentially ruling out any list of activities for some participants. In fact, choices of "favorite leisure activities" may differ widely depending on whether or not lists are presented, what is on the lists, the context of the inquiry, and, of course, who is asked. For example, "daydreaming" ranks high when very comprehensive lists are given students for ranking, lower for adults, and is not available for selection on most "recreation surveys." On the other hand, in a planned community built around two golf courses, golf did not make the top thirty when adults chose their six "most important" leisure activities (Kelly 1978).

A related concept, that of "play," is like leisure in being defined by dimensions other than the form of the activity. The most common defining elements have been that play is voluntary activity and has motivations intrinsic to the activity (Ellis 1974: 16). However, the similarity with definitions of leisure and especially unconditional leisure is not complete. Play is usually defined more by freedom in the doing of the activity with leisure defined more by freedom in the choice and social context. In play, the freedom is expressed in the activity itself. Nevertheless, play would seem to be a persistent element in leisure. Leisure is to a large extent playful and play generally leisurely in the centrality of freedom for both. Sport, on the other hand, is frequently neither leisurely nor playful.

How Are Leisure and Sport Related?

In this discussion, the more inclusive definitions of both leisure and sport will be assumed. "Leisure" will include activity with some measurable relational and role elements and with the possibility of being negatively conditioned by work constraints. "Sport" will include not only the competitive and institutionalized team sports, but also other activity that includes physical effort, regularity in form, and some measurement of performance. Sport, then, can include fishing as well as baseball and tag as well as track.

Leisure has been categorized according to meaning to the participant and social context. Sport may best be categorized socially by participation forms rather than motivations and goals. Figure 1 presents one way of classifying sports.

Figure 1: A Sports Classification Scheme

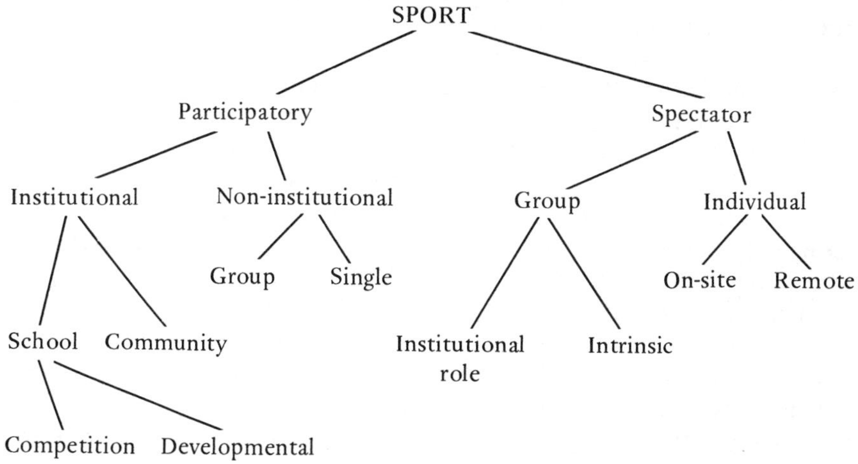

SPORT

Participatory

Spectator

Institutional

Non-institutional

Group

Individual

Group   Single

On-site   Remote

School   Community

Institutional
role

Intrinsic

Competition   Developmental

It is not possible to take any kind of activity and say that it is always or never leisure. However, some kinds of sports have social contexts so constrained by institutional requirements or decisions so shaped by extrinsic goals as to seldom qualify as leisure. Among participatory kinds of sport, two would generally be excluded from leisure. The first is professional sport activity that is the primary employment of the participant. Although the athlete may or may not enjoy participation, it is not leisure in that the sport is required by a primary social role. In much the same way competitive sport in college may be so clearly preparation for later professional engagement that its goal is extrinsic. A sport is hardly done for its own sake when the athlete has hired a manager and a lawyer to represent his professional interests.

A second type of sport participation that is seldom leisure would be developmental school programs. When a student is required to take a number of PE courses designed for the physical development of the student rather than for intrinsic satisfaction, then institutional role requirements exclude leisure. No choice is open to the student. However, under some conditions, participation in a required game may be in a playful or leisurely style. Playful participation may take place in a non-leisure setting.

The only kind of spectator sport that would be generally excluded from leisure would be one in which being at the contest is required by some institutional role or employment. Professional cheerleaders at a National Football League game are not only working, but frequently appear anything but playful in their gyrations. Some schools may offer no acceptable alternative to appearing at the "big game" to support the team. Parents with children on athletic teams may have little choice about being spectators unless they radically redefine their roles as parents.

However, for the most part spectator sports are viewed as leisure by the spectators. They go to contests because of previous satisfactions and attachments or they view sports from the remote locale of the television screen as at least the preferred alternative for that period of time. Such watching is usually leisure, but is it sport? The sociology of sport has included the spectator as an integral part of the organization of sports even though watching may not involve two of the central dimensions of sport: physical effort and measurement of performance. Sport provides a focus for passive leisure as a spectator and the spectator provides a context of meaning and sponsorship for the contest. The degree of engagement in the contest varies so widely among spectators that an excited on-site spectator may be said to be doing the sport in a way that the casual and distracted TV watcher is not.

In much the same way, the motivations and goals of some sport participation may raise doubt as to whether or not it is leisure. Not only the professional but frequently the amateur, especially in the school context, engages in the sport with institutional expectations and extrinsic rewards very much in mind. Participating in a sport that the student does not like when peer or parental expectations are overpowering is hardly leisure. On the other hand, probably few kinds of activity are less constrained than non-institutional sports for adults. Even the common health and fitness reasons given for such participation take second place to satisfactions with the activity and with the interpersonal relationships associated with the sport (Kelly 1978).

Of course, although play is central to much sport participation, the elements of freedom and spontaneity may be considerably reduced by the rules and the performance measurement. Participation that is only satisfying when a standard is met or the contest is won is something less than intrinsic in meaning. Any group activity is somewhat constrained by role expectations and regularities of interaction. Some sport situations may be so rigidly constrained by competition expectations that the participant does not seem to "play" the sport at all. The format of a sport, both in regulations and social expectations, may allow for little or no "play" in the sense of free, unproductive, and intrinsically-satisfying activity. Leisure is defined by the quality of the experience for the actor and play by the quality of doing the activity. Sport is defined by its form and therefore may or may not be either leisure or play.

ADULT LEISURE AND SPORT

Sport participation may be leisure when either engaging in sport or watching others do it. The place of sport in the whole spectrum of leisure activity is the first issue to be addressed here. The other issues revolve around the meaning of such participation for leisure. First, do the reasons for sport participation present a special case in leisure? Second, how does sport participation effect the meaning and values of leisure socialization? In general, what is the relation of sport to adult leisure activity and orientations?

Sport as Adult Leisure

Two approaches to adult sport participation may yield somewhat different impressions. The first looks at the aggregate figures of those who do or watch the most popular sports. The impression given is of enormous numbers and considerable significance in the society. The second approach examines the value placed on a wide range of kinds of leisure activities by the adults who do them and at participation rates by time invested. The second impression is of the relative lack of importance of sport to most adults.

First, aggregate figures for sport participation are generally available and are given elsewhere in this volume. Some of the more common and striking totals would include the following:

On-site spectator sports have gross paid admissions in the United States of over $500 million a year. In 1976, over 50 million admissions were paid to horseracing, 50 million to auto racing, 32 million to professional baseball and the same to college football, 19 million to greyhound racing and 15 million to professional football (Statistical Abstract of the United States 1977). Peaks were dampened somewhat by recession and auto fuel limitations, but have shown overall increases since 1965. These figures are dwarfed by the proportions of the television audience watching sports. The average professional football game draws over 10 percent of the audience with over 40 percent watching the Super Bowl and special local audiences exceeding 50 percent. Over 20 percent watch the "World Series" of American professional baseball and 8 percent an average game (Bogart 1972). On a national scale, professional spectator sports are a major enterprise with a significant impact on social schedules, habits, and interactions.

Especially for some smaller communities, high school football and basketball are central symbols of community identity. Not only on Friday night or Saturday but during the week, adult identification with the local "Spartans" or "Buffalos" commands attention. Attendance is more than entertainment; it is a ritual of community solidarity. On-site watching of many levels of school and amateur sports is a major leisure activity for many, especially the parents of participants.

Participation figures are also impressive. In 1976 in the United States, estimates are that over 100 million persons swam, 10 million played golf at least fifteen times, 15 million tried water skiing and 11 million snow skiing, 29 million played tennis, and bowlers far outnumbered all but swimmers (Kelly 1980). The 40 million who played volleyball, 23 million who tried billiards, 10 million shuffleboarders, and 9 million horseshoe tossers should not be overlooked (Kando 1975). Even though the number engaging in recreation such as walking for pleasure (54 million), picnicking (74 million), and sightseeing (60 million) far exceeds those engaged in sport, the total of sport participants is impressive. Further, the estimates may not include all who try a sport once or twice. Even allowing considerable margins of error, sport watching and participation involve a lot of people.

On the other hand, in the leisure hierarchies of American adults, sports appear much less formidable. Inclusive studies of the relative importance of leisure activities have been few. The vast range of activities that can be leisure has limited most research to preselected lists of outdoor recreation, sports, or cultural activities. A 1957 report on leisure in the United States found "participating in sports" ranked eleventh in frequency of participation with eight percent of the population over fifteen having engaged in such activity "yesterday." Sport participation was found to decrease with age and to increase with more years of education (de Grazia 1964: Table 8).

An international study using the time-diary method of gathering data indicates differences from country to country in the average amounts of time devoted to sports and physical culture (Szalai 1973). For employed adults, sport participation ranges from 50 minutes a day for males and 27 for females in the Federal Republic of Germany to 12 minutes for males and 5 for females in the United States. In general, males tend to give about twice as much time to sports and physical culture as females. However, sports are given on the average about one-tenth the time as the mass media except in the FRG where the media command less than twice the time of sports. The national differences appear to reflect both variations in leisure opportunities and programs and in the cultural emphasis on sport in the country.

In the Kansas City studies of adults (1957), Robert Havighurst and his associates found that participating in and watching sports first-hand ranked behind formal and informal groups and travel in frequency of being selected as favorite activities. More recently, in three American communities pair and individual outdoor sports, spectator sports, and pair and individual indoor sports ranked between fifteenth and twenty-fifth in frequency of being selected among the five or ten "most important" kinds of leisure activities (Kelly 1978). Far ahead were family activities such as marital affection and intimacy, conversation, outings, visiting family and friends, play with children, and eating out and cultural activities such as reading for pleasure, listening to music, and watching television.

The difference in perspective is crucial. The Kansas City research included only those over 40 and the three-community sample was 80 percent over 30. Sports would have been found higher on the lists of both men and women in their late teens and early twenties. For some in the adult samples sports were quite significant. Further, inclusive definitions of leisure take in those complementary activities that constitute the interaction regularities of our most salient relationships. Sport participation may be quite important occasions to an adult and still rank well below interaction with spouse, children, and close friends or regular at-home activities like reading. When asked which activities he or she would be least willing to give up, sport participation seems to be less central than daily relationships and activities to most adults, especially those who are married and are parents.

The Meaning of Leisure Sports

Several proposals concerning the meaning of sport participation for adults have been advanced. Elias and Dunning (1970) suggest that the meaning of sport may be in a "quest for excitement in unexciting societies." Sport participation may not be a release of tension as much as a restoration of tension and excitement. Ellis further proposes that play may be understood as "arousal-seeking" (1972). The uncertainty of sport, the measurement, and the contest are chosen to arouse and carry out dynamics of decision and action. A second evident meaning of sport for adults relates to physical benefits for health and fitness presumed to accompany such activity.

The third meaning is found in the associations of participation. Attendance at spectator events tends to be in groups, usually family and friends for adults. As indicated, some is related to the participation of kin, usually children, or colleagues. Some expresses institutional relationships of the school or community. To what extent the relationships are central rather than the activity would have to be examined event by event. In any case, participation on teams or with regular partners and opponents in a sport has a significant social element.

Sport may also function in society in ways related to its self-contained nature as a dramatic but "non-serious" event. In a life with little drama and considerable routinization, sport provides a fresh beginning for each event, an outcome, and an engaging process (Lasch 1977). Even the spectator participates in this drama of a contest. A collectivity of spectators may have a temporary feeling of community and solidarity as a counter to estrangement and alienation. Sport is an event with self-contained meaning that may yield a sense of significance without results that have serious consequences for primary social roles.

Probing perceived reasons for participation in the study of leisure in a planned community near Washington D.C. provides some preliminary analysis of the reasons selected as a salient by adult sport participants.

All three of the kinds of reasons for engaging in sport—excitement, health, and associations—are reflected in ranking of the first three reasons selected by participants in the New Town. In all, 255 adults selected 75 participant sport activities among the 1171 leisure activities most important to them. The intrinsic liking of the activity is reflected in the general "I like it" being chosen as the first reason for 90 percent of the sport activities and two-thirds of all the leisure activities. However, reasons ranked second and third point to why the activity is seen as providing satisfaction and pleasure.

Enjoying companions, health, excitement, mastery, rest, and relaxation appear on both lists, but in different order. Sport motivations and satisfactions are, quite predictably, more associated with the physical exertion and perceived benefits. Leisure in general tends to be more related to associations and personal expression and development. Activity, mastery, and health benefits rank higher than associations or

Table 1. Ranking of Reasons for Participation by New Town Adults in Sports and Leisure Activities

Rank	For Sports (N)	For All Leisure (N)
1	"I like it" (67)	"I like it" (912)
2	"It's active exercise" (30)	"I enjoy the companions" (337)
3	"It's healthful" (9)	"It strengthens relationships" (282)
4	"I like developing a skill" (17)	"It's restful" (261)
5	"I like doing it well" (15)	"I feel relaxed" (228)
6	"I enjoy the companions" (14)	"I grow as a person" (214)
7	"It's restful" (13)	"It's my self-expression" (142)
8	"It's exciting" (12)	"It's exciting" (133)
9	"I feel relaxed" (10)	"I like doing it well" (108)
10	"It's my self-expression" (9)	"It's healthful" (88)

rest for sports. However, the small number of sports selected allows only for tentative interpretations.

Also, different kinds of sport were associated with different dominant reasons. Tennis participants disproportionately chose reasons of active exercise and skill mastery; golfers mentioned skill mastery; indoor sports players stressed active exercise, companions and excitement; team sport exercise and companions; motorized sport participants emphasized excitement; and swimmers exercise, health, and rest and relaxation. There is at least the possibility that different kinds of sport not only attract different kinds of people but provide somewhat different perceived satisfactions.

The definitions of sport that include physical exertion and some measurement of mastery or skill are reflected in the reasons given for participation by adults. The regularity of rules and contexts provides the form for exercising the action and degree of mastery. Health is presumed to be related to the physical exertion and relaxation to the contrast of exercise to sedentary work conditions. The form of regularity and content of physical efforts are the context for mastery of skills and their measurement and for the regular associations of participation. For sport more than for leisure in general, satisfactions are related to doing the activity and are intrinsic to that activity rather than associated with family and peer roles and relationships.

Sport and Leisure Socialization

Introduction into sport activity and socialization into the skills and attitudes appropriate to the activity has received some attention from social scientists. Several methods have been proposed for such research (Kenyon 1970; McPherson 1972). Research in the United States has documented the influence of the family (Snyder and Spreitzer, 1974; 1976). Both the family of orientation and the family of procreation are common contexts of beginning and learning sports. Parents interested in sport encourage their children to participate and adults encourage their spouses. Further, self-images of athletic ability foster or discourage participation.

In the same American New Town, a similar pattern was found. Of the 75 sports activities chosen as important, the centrality of the family and a lifelong career of beginning new activities were found. Seven percent of the sport activities were begun alone. Twenty-six percent were begun in childhood with the family of orientation, 24 percent as a child with peers, 11 percent at school, 15 percent as an adult with the family of procreation, and 17 percent as an adult with friends. A sport like tennis was divided almost evenly between the childhood and adult contexts while swimming was begun in the family of orientation for almost 70 percent of the adults who found swimming important in their leisure participation pattern. Sports important to adults are like the rest of leisure in having been begun in childhood for about two-thirds of the activities.

The possible transition from required sports participation in school classes to later leisure in the context of life-cycle role changes suggests that a sport begun in school may take on fuller meaning. One of their case studies examines the centrality of sport and competitive excellence for an eighteen-year-old youth. The participation begun in school had become an integral part of the personal and social identity of this young man whose self-esteem rose and fell as his athletic fortunes waxed and waned (Rapoport and Rapoport 1975). The importance of sport to social development may not be reflected by its low carryover to adult leisure partly because of the common drop in team sport participation after leaving school.

Not only the context but the meaning of sport socialization has been recommended for examination. Any activity and any set of associations has the potential of conditioning the values and orientations of those who have regular participation schedules, especially in childhood. Insofar as sport stresses the measurement of skill and mastery through standards and competition, it may be said to be "unleisurely." Definitions of leisure that stress its intrinsic values and freedom would tend to exclude activity that is highly role-determined such as school sport or that emphasizes success in competition as a primary goal. The goal would then be extrinsic to the activity.

The measurement aspect of sport and the intrinsic meaning element of leisure would appear to be in conflict. Research that relates the degree of childhood socialization into competitive sports to adult leisure choices and orientations would provide empirical evidence on the possibility of this conflict in personal development. Sport participants may have a less leisurely orientation to nonwork activity than those without such prior socialization. On the other hand, adult sport participation may be both a carry-over from childhood experience and only one kind of leisure in the entire spectrum of an adult's activity. Further, participation in sport may have different personal functions from being a regular spectator. The structure and measurement of participation may be related to motivations of exertion, health, and mastery while being a spectator is related to social identity, companionship, and relaxation.

SUMMARY

In general, the differentiation between sport sociology and leisure sociology has blocked research into the relationship of sport and leisure. Sport may be viewed as one kind of adult leisure with meaning related to its definitional dimensions of physical effort and measurement of mastery. Leisure in general seems to be chosen by adults for reasons giving greater weight to satisfactions intrinsic to the activity and related to self-expression for unconditional leisure and to building and enriching relationships for complementary leisure. As orientations of leisure change during the life cycle (Kelly 1974) so orientations toward leisure sports may change during the leisure career of adults. Sport would seem to be a particular kind of leisure with its own forms and functions as well as its special context and orientations.

REFERENCES

Bogart, L. 1972. *The Age of Television*. 3rd edition. New York: Ungar.

Cheek, N.H. and W.R. Burch. 1976. *The Social Organization of Leisure in Human Society*. New York: Harper and Row.

deGrazia, S. 1964. *Of Time, Work, and Leisure*. Garden City, NY: Doubleday.

Dumazedier, J. 1968. *Toward a Society of Leisure*. New York: Free Press.

————. 1969. Leisure. *International Encyclopedia of the Social Sciences*. Vol.16. New York: MacMillan.

————. 1974. *Sociology of Leisure*. Amsterdam: Elsevier.

Edwards, H. 1973. *Sociology of Sport*. Homewood, IL: Dorsey.

Elias, N. and E. Dunning. 1970. The quest for excitement in unexciting societies. Pp. 31–51 in G. Lüschen ed., *The Cross-cultural Analysis of Sport and Games*. Champaign, IL: Stipes.

Ellis, M. 1972. *Why People Play*. Englewood Cliffs, NJ: Prentice-Hall.

Hammerich, K. 1971. *Kritische Untersuchung zur Freizeitpädagogik*. Ratingen: Henn.

Havighurst, R. 1957. The leisure activities of the middle-aged. *AJS* 63, 1: 152–62.

Kando, T. 1975. *Leisure and Popular Culture in Transition*. St. Louis: Mosby.

Kaplan, M. 1960. *Leisure in America*. New York: Wiley.

Kelly, J. 1972. Work and leisure: a simplified paradigm. *Journal of Leisure Research*. 4: 50–62.

————. 1974. Socialization toward leisure: a developmental approach. *Journal of Leisure Research*. 6: 181–193.

————. 1978a. A revised paradigm of leisure choices. *Leisure Sciences*. 1: 345–363.

————. 1978b. Leisure styles and choices in three environments. *Pacific Sociological Review*. 21: 187–207.

————. 1980. *Leisure*. Englewood Cliff, NJ: Prentice-Hall.

Kenyon, G. 1970. The use of path analysis in sport sociology with special reference to involvement socialization. *IRSS*. 5, 1: 191–203.

Lasch, C. 1977. The corruption of sport. *The New York Review*. April 28.

Loy, J. 1969. The nature of sport: a definitional effort. Pp. 56–71 in Loy, J. and G. Kenyon eds., *Sport, Culture, and Society*. New York: MacMillan.

Lüschen, G. 1978. *The Sociology of Sport*. Paris: Mouton. 1968.

————. 1970. Sociology of sport and the cross-cultural analysis of sport and games. Pp. 6–13 in G. Lüschen ed., *The Cross Cultural Analysis of Sport and Games*. Champaign, IL: Stipes.

————. 1973. Some critical remarks concerning the sociology of leisure. *Leisure and Society*. (Prague) 3, 1: 165–75.

McPherson, B. 1972. The influence of four social systems on the process of sport consumer role socialization. Paper at the Scientific Congress of the XXth Olympiad, Munich.

Outdoor Resources Review Commission. 1961–62. Report 1-32. Washington: Government Printing Office.

Parker, S. 1971. *The Future of Work and Leisure.* New York: Praeger.

Rapoport, R. and R.N. Rapoport. 1975. *Leisure and the Family Life Cycle.* London: Routledge.

Scheuch, E. and R. Meyersohn eds. 1972. *Soziologie der Freizeit.* Köln: Kiepenheuer und Witsch.

Snyder, E. and E. Spreitzer. 1974. Socialization into sport: an exploratory path analysis. *Research Quarterly.* 47: 238–245.

———. 1974. Sociology of sport: an overview. *Sociological Quarterly.* 15: 467–487.

Szalai, A. et al. 1973. *The Use of Time — Daily Activities of Urban and Suburban Populations in Twelve Countries.* The Hague, Netherlands: Mouton.

PART III

SOCIAL STRUCTURE,

SOCIAL PROCESSES

AND SPORT

Lüschen

Stone

McPherson

Harris

THE SYSTEM OF SPORT—
PROBLEMS OF METHODOLOGY,
CONFLICT AND SOCIAL STRATIFICATION

Günther Lüschen

Besides the behavioristic approach in sociological analysis, which for the sociology of sport ultimately raises questions about sport as an activity and an individualistic point of view, there is the systems or structural approach in sociology. This approach considers any social element to be part of an organized whole in which individual parts are interdependent and explanations are ultimately derived from system qualities not from individual features. One of the analytic distinctions that can be made is that of internal and external system (Homans, 1950). For the sport system the internal system would incorporate all those elements that are strictly sport determined, while the external system of sport would refer to those features of sport that are shaped by society and its institutions as well as by individual or personality features brought into the system of sport.

Sport contests are marked by a considerable amount of ritual and rites of passage. These indicate the general relevance of the internal and external system in a sport contest. The ritual line-up before and after a game of soccer or basketball may at first sight be considered just ceremony, but it also has meaning for delimiting the world of sport from society at large. And the uniforms of players signal that they leave their external personal identity behind and take on a new one as part of the internal system of sport. At the occasion of rule infractions or fouls there appears, what one may call rites of passage. The player committing a foul breaks up the internal system of sport; in a way he/she steps out of the internal system by violating a rule or common understanding. The referee will then penalize the player in order to reestablish the internal system. It is also quite common that the player will engage in a typical rite of passage by offering his/her hand or act in some other symbolic way to show that he/she is sorry and wants reconciliation. In system terms, this act is a move to enter the internal system again after one has put oneself out of it or a referee has done so by penalization.

The interpretation of ritual and rites of passage, cited above, imply a type of analysis that, in the interpretation of observable facts, goes beyond what can be verified by immediate tests. Such is the approach known as structural analysis. Not only does structural analysis imply the interdependence of single parts, it also advances from a level of observable facts to a higher level of abstraction, sometimes referred to by Lévi-Strauss as "deep structure" or as "form" by Simmel.

Georg Simmel has referred implicitly to both the internal system and to *form* or *deep structure* when for the social contest he demands that one look at "nothing but the contest itself" (1917). A notion of structural analysis of sport is also evident when Wittgenstein refers to games of language and holds that one should look at the *grammar* of language (1960).

Previous sociological studies of sport have stressed a strictly behavioral approach and, in systems analysis, have not been too concerned with the deep structure or grammar of sport. One should add that such a structural approach is definitely empirical; however, it advances in its comprehension to a higher, secondary level. Analytical suggestion and inductive reasoning are blended into one another (Schmalenbach 1977). Examples that come close to such a concept in the sociological study of sport are the dynamics of soccer teams (Elias and Dunning 1966), motivational factors among sport participants (Kenyon, 1969), the conceptual discussion as to whether sport is ludic action (Ingham and Loy, 1973), the dialectic of children's games (Sutton-Smith 1978), the incorporation of research results into a systems analysis (Loy, McPherson and Kenyon (1978), figurational dynamics (Dunning 1979) or the study of sport and community (Stone 1980). For the following discussion three major problems of social structure in the system of sport will be pursued: (1) The definition and *game—theoretical* character of sport, (2) the problem of conflict and integration in the sport contest based on "dual organization" or "association," and (3) the issue of rank differentiation or social stratification and sport.

DEFINITION AND COMPLEXITY OF SPORT

Although Wittgenstein observes that it is difficult to find what in the *"family"* of games are the same structures, there are a number of valuable approaches to such analysis as in Johan Huizinga *"Homo Ludens,"* (1938). It was Caillois who extended Huizinga's analysis, and on this basis sport belongs to the category of games of agon (1961). Yet, sport also contains elements of mimicry and vertigo, while the fourth category of chance is supposedly absent. In a football game, after the coin has been tossed, chance is by definition ruled out as a decisive element in the outcome of the contest.

In the central event of the institution of sport there is the contest, which is a system delimited by time and space. The contest symbolizes a certain negation of the outside world and is not defined by utilitarian interests. As part of the external system there are of course economic interests, yet they do not constitute a crucial element of the internal system. There are similar structural characteristics in art, which represent non-utilitarian structures as well and transform human activity onto a level where art has value in itself *(l'art pour l'art)* or in the mere aesthetic. The sport contest is actually much less real and does not leave observable products and material and symbolic determinants or impacts. Like art, sport is not necessary for survival; and after Durkheim's concept it can be classified as "non-representative" of other social action. The training with the javelin among the Mandans for the purpose of war is thus not to be included in this definition nor is the swimming of the natives in Northwest-Australia for the purpose of providing food. In modern society sport takes on representative meaning only in its external system as part of a community or school or other social group. On the basis of all of this, sociological explanations that start from theories of reinforcement or utility are thus inappropriate; they actually measure a different structure than sport. Homans seemingly is aware of such problems when he mentions that many competitive games are interesting in themselves providing an intrinsic reward. What kind such rewards are, what the consequences for such relations are, remains unfortunately unresolved by Homans when he discusses the elementary forms of social behavior (1961: 131). Csikszentmihalyi (1975) describes such experience with a newly coined term, *"flow."* Flow refers to simple enjoyment and release, as found among mountineers, for example, but describes the athlete's experience within the internal system of sport as well.

The philosopher Anderson and the psychologist Moore referred to similar qualities when they called social games *"autotelic"* and behavior engaged in for the fun of it *"autotelic action."* They contend that this quality is not only an element of the individual, psychological level but of the social and cultural level as well. In terms of rules this results in rules of irrelevance. At the same time they hold that because of the socio-cultural immersion of this system games are important for socialization because they provide insight into culture and society (1965).

Dunning (1971) has argued against a position that identifies sport only as play and an end in itself. Sport as an activity has indeed to be seen on a continuum between play and work. It may be performed almost exclusively for utilitarian reasons and profit, as in professional sport. The distinction of internal and external system would allow analyses of professional sport as a mattter of the external system. Yet, even the system of professional sport will still show non-utilitarian elements and a structure that are an outcome of the internal sport-specific system.

Beyond problems of classification by Caillois and others there is a necessity for analytic tools to understand the suggested social structure of decision-making and strategy. Dealing with such approach is the so-called game-theory which is a mathematically based theory developed by von Neumann and Morgenstern. Despite the fact that it is based on the assumption of rationality and deals basically with economic decisions, game theory contains a number of theoretical insights and concepts which appear useful for a structural analysis of sport (Schlenker and Boroma 1978).

One may point to the fact that sport contests are so much more complex than the games of the mathematical game-theory that its results are often not valid. Yet, concepts and hypotheses developed in this area are eminently useful to raise questions and pose hypotheses for the reality of sport contests.

If one were to consider games like soccer or football one would soon become aware of the complexities of such games and the difficulty of forecasting game outcomes, with soccer having an even higher level of uncertainty than football. At the same time predictions of a move or play will often go as predicted even at times with extraordinarily complex moves. Here lies the fascination of such games, where the element of surprise is at times very strong. On this basis, Buytendijk explains the high popularity of soccer (1953). Sport contests of individual athletes are of course much less complex, and tactics as well as strategies are not as relevant as in team sports or in games like chess designed as strategic games.

The sport contest contains two fundamental processes to be discussed that show the internal system of sport in relative clarity: The interdependence between conflict and integration and the differences of rank emerging as a result of a contest.

CONFLICT AND INTEGRATION IN THE SPORT CONTEST

When sport is referred to in terms of conflict it is often held that the sport contest as competition does not fit a narrow definition, or that it is only a quasi-conflict, mainly because it is not directed toward the destruction of the opponent. Of course, the amount of consideration of the opponent (fairness in sport) is quite obvious. However, parties at war are oriented toward the dominance over an opponent rather than his destruction. Immanuel Kant refers to such structures implicitly in his essay on *Eternal Peace.* In a conflict like war, as in that of the sport contest, there appears thus a dimension of inter-dependence or sociability that is according to Goffman found also in general *"social encounters"* (1961). In a casual meeting, in a conversation there is the necessity for both parties involved to be considered for the upkeep of such a simple social system. For sport Lüschen referred to this pattern as *"association"* (1970). In *association* both sides respond to a system level or to their mutual interests without the expectation of a reward. Thus, this mode of behavior, also referred to as *antagonistic cooperation* (Sumner), should be distinguished from cooperation which is defined by a share in rewards. *Association* finds one of its most obvious expressions in the pattern of fairness which is an integrative act, seemingly cooperative, without the expectation of a reward.

Max Weber implies this pattern of *association* when for a card game he mentions that the parties involved succumb to the rules of the game, and that only thereafter could one assume the rule to be a cause of conformity (1922). Wittgenstein observes the same phenomenon, when he mentions that a competitive game is not ruled and regulated to begin with, and thus rules are not constitutive for a game (1960). Simmel talks about the unifying power of the contest. "One unites in order to fight, and one fights under the mutually recognized governance of norms and rules" (1923, 200). And Elias and Dunning recognize the system dimension, when they hold that a contest must have a *"tonus"* (1966).

There are a number of factors in sport contests which determine the degree of *association.* For different types of sport disciplines *association* appears to be relatively weaker in boxing than in rugby. This is at least in part an outcome of the social context in which these sports occur. As part of the external system, factors like social class seem to have an impact. And on the societal level it appears that different societies and cultures place different emphasis on *association.* In the martial arts of Asia, conflict appears to be very rigid, yet consideration of the opponent is very high. In certain arts of China fought with sticks the opponent is never actually hit. And in the art of Aikido there is continuous reassurance of the opponent. It is a contest with but not against the opponent. And it is typical for Aikido as for other sports that the rank order so vital for this sport subculture is not only determined by the number of wins but by the skill one possesses. Also Firth (1930) reports for the dart players in Tikopia that the winners of a contest will try to accommodate the losers by providing food immediately after the game. *Association* is also to be found in the games of children. Piaget

(1932) observes that it is expected of a total winner to distribute his marbles after he has won them all; otherwise he will be beaten up.

Beyond the associative conditions in sport contests there are, as part of the external system, related structural elements in culture and society which indicate that the associative element in a sport contest is related to fundamental conditions of human and societal existence. Konrad Lorenz in interpreting aggression sees sport as having a function for catharsis of aggressive potential in society (1963). Here the problem is only stated as a psycho-physical one and Eibl-Eibesfeldt mentions an aggressive drive which is displayed *(ausgelebt)* in sport (1970). While he mentions controlling forms of aggression in single combats and duels, the social and cultural level to which *association* refers gets very little attention. An approach dealing predominantly with the individual and physical level, as in Lorenz or Eibl-Eibesfeldt, runs ultimately into considerable difficulty. With quite a similar methodological approach, the Sherifs (1961 and 1973) account for an increase of conflict and aggression in a contest. In both approaches the sociocultural level remains a residual category. But only on this level is the puzzle of *association* in a contest, the interdependence of conflict and integration finally to be explained and understood. Because conflict is inter-related with *association* the sport contest is obviously less problematic than one would expect after reading the Sherifs' work, and it is less positive than one would believe after reading Lorenz.

Seemingly we have here structural contradictions which fit the label *dialectic.* Sartre in his dialectical critique mentions the game of soccer when he wants to exemplify the dialectic of personal and social structure (1960: 471). Also von Krockow implies a similar analysis for sport (1972). Actually, one should not be opposed to refer to this structural pattern of sport as *dialectic.* Rather, one should reject a notion that a dialectical structure is not open to a rational and logical analysis in this context. Quite a bit can be gained from such structural complexities of association and contest by taking a look at other societies and cultures in order to get an understanding of the general meaning of such pattern and the degree to which sport is enmashed with society at large.

In anthropology the problem we are dealing with, the duality of the sport contest, is referred and akin to what is understood as *dual organization.* While structural units and elements in certain ethnic societies are in opposition to one another, they are nevertheless part of an organized whole. Kinship groups *(moieties),* dual parts of a village, or age-groups are in contest with one another, also in sport-like games, yet they display their conflict with a high amount of mutual consideration and as part of an often elaborate ritual which works as a control toward disruptive consequences. While Lévi-Strauss has argued that dual organizations may soon disappear (1967), our analysis seems to imply that there are forms of dual organization even in modern societies in such an event as a sport contest. Jensen in dealing with the same problem of what he calls *"two-class-systems"* mentions sport in this context and finds that dual organizations and the contests attached to them have and have had a fundamental function in the history of mankind (1947).

One of the best examples is the log-race of the Timbira Indians in Brazil which was thoroughly analyzed in the context of the overall social structure of Timbira tribal societies by Curt Nimuendaju (1946). The log-race is an important event in the life of these tribes and is engaged in by all types of dual groups on many occasions. It is a team sport in which a heavy wooden log of up to 200 pounds is alternatively carried by each individual member of the team to the goal, most times located in the center of the village. While the winners and good racers enjoy some recognition, there are no rewards after the race. Yet the contest is performed with much vigor. Besides quite a few informal casual engagements in the log-race, Nimuendaju mentions seven specific ceremonial races among the East-Timbira whereby the opposing groups may represent family systems, age groups, geographical groups or the two sexes. While in the latter form the outcome is clearly pre-determined, despite the fact that the women get a handicap, it is customary for the men to help the women carry the log. Obviously *association* is rather strong in this type of contest. Jensen considers these contests of a different quality than modern sport contests, which he sees as *l'art pour l'art*, while, many times, the contests of the ethnic societies have strong religious functions. Of course, he overlooks the fact that modern sports also fulfill certain quasi-religious functions. And vice versa, Nimuendaju considers the ritual and religious meaning of the log-race less important than is generally believed. He explicitly refers to the log-race as the national sport of the Timbira.

What is very obvious from the above example as well as from others (Firth 1930) is the strong associational element that is paramount in these contests based on and actually displaying *dual organization.* The question that arises is of course how strong this structural control in the sport contest is. There is no question that modern sport has definite limits in the amount of aggressiveness and conflict that can be controlled by *association.* If conflicts between two systems at large are too strong, if a conflict potential between parties has gradually been built up, then the *association* of the sport contest is often too weak for an efficient control of such conflict. The soccer war between Honduras and San Salvador in 1969, the bloody encounter between Hungary and the USSR in waterpolo in the 1956 Olympics, the yearly fights between the Glasgow Celtics and Rangers in and around soccer are such notable examples. A problem also exists in so far as the *association* engaged in by the opponents on the field may not be transferred to the fans and spectator ranks, a fact that should be of increasing concern to the sport federations and the public. Associational structures are not sufficiently developed in many instances, although there are elaborate rituals at the Olympic Games or in American university sport events. Overall, sport contests represent a pattern in which rather fierce competition and conflict can be engaged without any detrimental and disruptive effects for the participants or the system at large. It remains a matter of the internal system; to what degree sport contests do have a function of catharsis is not totally clear. A symbolic meaning may be all on which one can definitely agree at this time of limited insight. However, Sutton-Smith also recognizes certain socializing effects of competitive games in so far as they lead to a better understanding and coping with conflict situations (1973).

SOCIAL STRATIFICATION
AND THE DIFFERENTIATION OF RANKS

In sport itself as an outcome of individual contests and a whole series of events there exists a rank order of teams and of individual athletes. Society at large is stratified along lines of class, prestige or individual status and status groups. These are seemingly equivalent structures found in both stratified sport and society. Thus, it is no surprise that questions of the relationship of sport to social stratification in society or within sport have generated considerable interest. Together with the issue of social mobility in and through sport, social stratification is one of the better researched areas in sociology of sport.

The *Outdoor Recreation Resources Review Commission* (1961) found in its studies a direct relationship between the amount of income and degree of participation in outdoor and sport activities. The relationship is not perfectly linear because the factor of age accounts for part of amount of income and thus explains why the highest income groups are slightly less engaged in sport.

Thorstein Veblen (1896) saw sport as a typical activity of the upper classes. While sport has, since his time, increasingly become a leisure activity of the "middle mass" in terms of participation and spectatorship, one still notices a higher engagement among people of middle and upper class. And within sport, on the basis of members' class background, there is a distinct hierarchy with sport disciplines such as sailing, riding, tennis and golf attracting upper-middle and upper class members, while such sports as boxing, cycling are mainly activities of lower class members (v. Euler 1953; Lüschen 1969; Gruneau 1975). There are certain disciplines that seem to cut across social classes, and on an international scale these are typically the popular big sports like soccer. Attitudinal data by Stone (1969), measuring sport interest and identification, show football, basketball and hockey to be identified by Minneapolis residents regardless of class, while golf, skiing, swimming and tennis are more often referred to by higher strata and baseball, boxing, wrestling and bowling by lower socio-economic strata.

Gruneau (1975) in a structural analysis deals with both the social class and status dimension and basically holds that "social inequalities (in sport) are rooted in the material order" and consequently would be a matter of the external system. He cautions that institutional and political arrangements underlying sport and controlling participation should be analyzed as well. He also hints that the status dimension needs close consideration.

While it cannot be argued that material conditions and institutionalized controls based on social class determine participation and structure within sport overall and in specific disciplines even more, one should be careful to not argue in terms of class and a Marxian conception of stratification alone (Hoch, 1972). For a more differentiated argument and analysis one can refer to Max Weber's stratification theory, where he distinguishes social class (determined by market conditions), status group (determined by honor and prestige) and the dimension of party/power (1953, orig. 1921). If one deals with the rank hierarchy within sport, it appears that the dimension of status group is the most essential, while class is of lesser importance and power of least importance. Problems of class and power in society are mainly relevant for the external system. They can be accounted for in terms of access and participation in sport. The dimension of status group is of importance to the external system insofar as sport in general and specific sport disciplines are an expression of status group culture. But the internal system of sport can also be described as a matter of status group culture itself. And it is unique insofar as it introduces a rank order that is rigidly achievement-determined and individualistic. With regard to the latter orientation it allows the individual to overcome the predicaments and obstacles in terms of class and power. The implied process will be one of the most important topics for future analysis.

The outcome of a sport contest determines a rank order, which to a certain degree is influenced by ascribed criteria displaying Darwin's principle of the survival of the fittest. Such biological condititions may be controlled to a degree by means of training and by differential organization within sports such as the weight classes in boxing. However, there is no question that the rank order in sport is strongly determined by inherited physical conditions—a fact almost totally overlooked in discussions of sport and social stratification. It is an interesting feature in this context that in the change and evolution of individual sport disciplines those based mainly on physical strength become less and less important in modern sports, a number of Olympic contests and American football notwithstanding. Also tactical and strategic considerations are increasing to the point where a top performance is at times the result of the work of a whole staff (Krawcyzck *et al.* 1973).

The winner in a sport contest does not produce anything in material terms, yet he earns prestige, a championship and sometimes material gain. Because the latter in the system of sport, particularly the internal one, is rather the exception than the rule, the analysis of ranks in sport should first of all be a matter of status rather than of social class. The strong commercialization in many sports is rather a phenomenon of the external system. It is quite interesting to observe the fragile economic base of many professional sport organizations. Investments in sport are quite hazardous because the investments normally are not turned around often enough. European soccer clubs are notoriously underfinanced and American sports are often engaged in not for profit but in order to run losses for tax write-offs (Okner 1974). Individual athletes are controlled by structures of class as well, but not to the same degree as they differentiate themselves along the dimension of status and status groups. Moreover, Western societies' professional sport is universally not very important.

In the internal system of sport the matter is prestige and honor, and even in the external system rank is enjoyed foremost in terms of status not of economically determined class. Professionals never fail to say that they are engaged in sport not only for the money. Also the strong individualistic determination of an athlete's fate runs counter to an interpretation on the dimension of social class. Despite all of this, most of the analyses concerning social stratification in sport have used an economic determinism and concept of class; the attempt, to press for whatever Marxian conception in the analysis, has even lead to talk about the athlete as a small businessman (Krüger, 1972). Here are structures of rank which are highly incompatible. On this basis a system like the USSR can, without any problem concerning the dimension of social class, introduce a new order of ranks within athletics which in its differentiation and rigor has no parallel in Western societies (Shneidman 1979). Because the *merited masters* of sport, the *masters* of sport, the athletes of the *first* to *third category,* to name the five upper strata, refer to the dimension of status; the class dimension is not at all involved.

At this time it is difficult to fully understand the structural relationship of sport to the status group dimension, which is based on life-style, honor and prestige. The individual dimension in sport is probably stronger than in the concept of status group as it was originally conceived and defined by Max Weber. The third category of rank differentiation in Weber is the dimension of power. There appear few overlaps although one may interpret that the sport contest itself very much resembles a struggle for power. Power is by and large relinquished after an opponent has been defeated. A winner has very little claim over the loser. Yet, a star athlete may indeed get considerable leverage with regard to his club or officials. Again this question needs further study. And what is referred to is of course the dimension of power as it relates to the sport contest and the outcome of an encounter between two parties or individuals. Problems of power in sport organizations are a different matter. The dimension of power as it controls sport is a matter of the external system.

Power and control of sport by economic and political interests or vice versa, the deprivation and exclusion of the powerless in sport, has been a major topic in sport and stratification analysis. Reference is made to gender and racial factors (Loy; McPherson and Kenyon 1979). On a different scale Vinnai argues that the existing structure of capitalist society and interest groups use sport to retain power and control, contending that *"the goals on the soccer field are the self-inflicted goals of the deprived"* (1970). Empirical results disclose that participation in sport whether actively or passively in spectatorship are a matter of advanced location of individuals in the stratification system reinforcing the existing order, particularly for the broad middle mass. However, contentions by Vinnai and others (Hoch 1972) may have some merit for sport as entertainment and the ultimately limited mobility chances in professional sport that have become the concern of minority leaders.

The change of position in the system of social stratification, the process of social mobility, can mean a collective mobility of whole groups or individuals. The strongly individualized rank system of sport is indicated by the fact that the issue of collective mobility is of little relevance for the analysis. That minority groups may use sport as an avenue toward success and status recognition is one of the few exceptions. Mobility of individuals through sport is so far the most frequently analyzed topic. Starting with observations that the rate of upwardly mobile is substantially higher than the downwardly mobile among athletes, it is concluded that sports support upward mobility by such processes as:

1. Socialization to middle class norms, values and behavior patterns
2. Motivating individuals to achieve and disclosing the structure and essentials of hierarchial systems in society
3. Providing sponsored mobility through educational or occupational incentives
4. Providing direct mobility within sport through such careers as athlete, sports teacher, coach
5. Allowing the transfer of rank and prestige obtained in sport to other dimensions of the stratification system (Lüschen, 1969; Loy 1969)

Particularly in the U.S., educational attainment and sport is a frequent topic of analysis indicating a positive correlation between sport and educational mobility; it discloses in the end a structure where sport is part of the educational system with a considerable amount of autonomy (Otto and Alwin 1977; Phillips 1979).

Mobility in the system of sport itself is a comparatively less attended topic. It would be a matter of the internal system and would analyze the sport careers of individuals from one sport of different rank to the other or the career from an ordinary participant to the status of champion. The high attention paid to the latter has resulted in little awareness of the fact that unfulfilled mobility aspirations are frequent in this competitive system. In a way, sport is rather a system of failure than success for the individual athlete (Ball 1976, Bend and Petrie 1977). The structural meaning and behavioral consequences of this feature need further study and exploration. It may be a consequence of the non-essential character of sport for survival, its basis in play, its determination by the status group dimension, that even in an economically determined system like professional boxing, very few of a broad base of aspirants reach the top and of these even fewer are able to retain and transfer a position of high status (Weinberg and Arond 1952).

An interesting feature of the rather differentiated order of ranks that emerges from sport is to be seen in the fact that it runs counter to tendencies to give more recognition to the principle of equality in modern societies. The latter is to a high degree determined by social class considerations, and thus does not immediately concern the status-bound system of sport; it may disclose that the principle of equality does not mean an even allocation of status and resources but an equality of chance to move freely according to one's individual achievements. Indeed the openness of the system of sport in terms of ranking, where only achievement counts, is highly in line with the values of modern societies.

With regard to the latter it needs careful observation whether an emerging conflict over limitations of material resources in modern society may curtail mobility via sport even further. Declining resources may also create a conflict of values over a system that seemingly lives from the illusion of unlimited resources and expansion, particularly in the institution of the sport record. Yet with regard to stratification in general, sport may also provide a system of rank differentiation that allows a differentiation in the status dimension and that is only partially dependent on material resources. Consequently, the future of society, given less material resources, could shift toward non-material differentiation and favor a stratified system and activity like sport. It would be the opposite to what many social critics, stressing the expressive dimension of movement and sport, expect for the future.

CONCLUSION

The discrepancies between internal and external system, between individual and social structure, between conflict and integration, between winning, defeat and social rank, between utilitarian and non-utilitarian behavior, all of which have run through the preceeding discussion, assign a structural quality of high ambiguity to sport that one would like to call dialectic. The universal dual-organizational structure obviously describes a dialectical structure as well. It is important in this regard that for the sport contest, with the observability of the above phenomena, the reference to dialectics as a matter of substance does not lead to the rejection of empirical research and formal logic. And it does not suggest dialectics in terms of method at all. What has been tried here is the transformation of empirical observations and its integration in a systems analysis. This is exactly how the procedure of structural analysis of sport should proceed. It may have been noticed that a comparative analysis provides much of the insight that in an experimental lab-situation will get lost all too often (Lenk and Lüschen, 1975).

Finally, it should be stated that the structural analysis conceptualizes the system of sport (notably in the sport contest and its system of rank) as a fundamental structural pattern of human and social existence. This provides as much for sociology and sport science in terms of scientific insight as for the individual athlete, who experiences in and through sport borderline situations of human existence. He/she learns about dimensions of social discrepancies, which as conflicts are contained by such patterns as *association* that foremost guarantee human life. At this point questions arise which go beyond a sociological analysis because they no longer have an empirical reference. The structural analysis faces its limits at this point and philosophy has to take over.

REFERENCES

Anderson, A. and O. Moore. 1965. Puzzles, games and social interaction. Pp. 68–79 in D. Braybrooks, ed. *Philosophical Problems in the Social Sciences.* New York: Macmillan.

Ball, D. 1973. Ascription and position: a comparative analysis of 'stacking' in professional football. *Canad. R. Sociology Anthropology.* 10,1:97–113.

Ball, D. 1974. Control versus complexity. *Pacific Soc. Review* 17:167–184.

Ball, D. 1976. Failure in sport. *ASR* 41,5:726–39.

Bartos, O. 1968. *Simple Models of Group Behavior.* New York: Columbia University Press.

Beals, A. and B. Siegel. 1966. *Divisiveness and Social Conflict.* Stanford: Stanford University Press.

Bend, E. and B. Petrie. 1977. Sport participation, scholastic success and social mobility. Pp. 1–44 in Hutton, *Exercises and Sport Sciences Reviews.* Vol. 5. Santa Barbara: Journal Publishing Affiliates.

Berryman, J. and J. Loy. 1976. Secondary schools and Ivy League letters. *Brit. J. Sociology* 27,1:61–77.

Buytendijk, F.J.J. 1953. *Het Voetballen* (Soccer). Utrecht: Het Spectrum.

Caillois, R. 1961. *Men, Play and Games.* Glencoe, Ill.: Free Press.

Csikszentmihalyi, M. 1975. *Beyond Boredom and Anxiety.* San Francisco: Jossey-Bass.

Davis, J. 1970. *Game Theory.* New York: Basic Books.

Dunning, E. 1971. Some conceptual dilemmas in the sociology of sport. Pp. 34–47 in R. Albonico and K. Pfister-Binz, eds. *The Sociology of Sport.* Basel: Birkhäuser.

Dunning, E. and K. Sheard. 1979. *Barbarians, Gentlemen and Players.* New York: New York University Press.

Dunning, E. 1979. The figurational dynamics of modern sport. *Sportwissenschaft,* 9,4:341–359.

Eggleston, J. 1965. Secondary schools and Oxbridge Blues. *Brit. J. Sociology* 16,2:232–42.

Eibl-Eibesfeldt. 1970. *Liebe und Hass.* Munich: Piper.

Elias, N. and E. Dunning. 1966. Dynamics of sport groups with special reference to football. *Brit. J. Sociology* 17,3:388–402.

von Euler, R. 1953. Idrottsörelsen av i Dag (Sport of Today). Pp. 147–278 in Sveriges Idrottsförbund. *Svensk Idrott.* Malmö: Allhem.

Firth, R. 1930. A dart match in Tikopia. The sociology of primitive sport. *Oceania* 1,1:64–96.

Fox, J.R. 1961. Pueblo baseball: a new use for old witchcraft. *J. Am. Folklore* 74,1:9–16.

Gaskell, G. and R. Pearton. 1979. Aggression and sport. PP. 263–96 in J. Goldstein, ed. *Sports, Games, and Play*. Hilsdale, N.J.: Erlbaum.

Goffman, E. 1961. Encounters. Indianapolis: Bobbs-Merrill.

Gruneau, R.S. 1975. Sport, social differentiation and social inequality. Pp. 121–184 in D. Ball and J. Loy, ed. *Sport and Social Order*. Reading, Mas.: Addison-Wesley.

Hammerich, K. 1972. Berufskarrieren von Spitzensportlern. *Sportwissenschaft* 2,2:168–81.

Heinilä, K. 1966. Notes on the intergroup conflicts in international sport. IRSS 1,1:49–69. Also in Lüschen, ed. 1970. *The Cross-Cultural Analysis of Sport and Games*. Champaign: Stipes.

Hoch, P. 1972. *Rip off the Big Game*. Garden City, N.Y.: Doubleday.

Homans, G. 1950. *The Human Group*. New York: Harcourt, Brace and World.

Homans, G. 1961. *Social Behavior: Its Elementary Forms*. New York: Harvourt, Brace and World.

Huizinga, J. 1961. *Homo Ludens*. Boston: Beacon (orig. 1938).

Ingham, A. and J. Loy. 1973. The social system of sport: a humanistic perspective. *Quest* 19, Jan.: 3–23.

Jensen, A.E. 1947. Wettkampfparteien, Zwei-Klassen-Systeme und geographische Orientierung. *Studium Generale* 1,1:38–48.

Jeu, B. 1972. Definition du sport. *Diogene* 80,1:153–167.

Kant, I. 1949. *Zum ewigen Frieden*. Frankfurt: Siegel.

Kenyon, G.S. 1969. A conceptual model for characterizing physical activity. Pp. 71–81 in J. Loy and G. Kenyon, eds. *Sport, Culture and Society*. New York: Macmillan.

Kiviaho, P. 1974. The regional distribution of sport organizations as a question of political cleavage. *Sportwissenschaft* 4,1:72–81.

Krawczyck, Z. et al. 1973. The dialectics of transformation in modern sport. Pp. 55–60 in O. Grupe et al. eds., *Sport in the Modern World*. New York: Springer.

von Krockow, C. 1972. *Sport in der Industriegesellschaft*. Munich: Piper.

Krüger, A. 1972. Der Leistungssportler als Kleinunternehmer (The top athlete as small businessman). Leistungssport 2,3:211–16.

Lenk, H. et al. 1972. Perspectives of the philosophy of sport. Pp. 31–58 in O. Grupe et al. eds. 1975. *The Scientific View of Sport*. New York: Springer.

Lenk, H. and G. Lüschen. 1975. Epistemological problems and the personality and social system in social psychology. *Theory and Decision* 6,3:333–355.

Lévi-Strauss, C. 1967. *Structural Anthropology*. Garden City: Doubleday.

Lorenz, K. 1965. *On Agression*. New York: Harcourt, Brace and World.

Loy, J. 1969. Game forms, social structure and anomie. Pp. 181–99 in R. Brown and B. Cratty, eds. *New Perspectives of Man in Action*. Englewood-Cliffs: Prentice-Hall.

Loy, J. 1969. The study of sport and social mobility. Pp. 101–119 in G. Kenyon, ed. *Sociology of Sport*. Chicago: Athletic Institute.

Loy, J.; McPherson, B. and G. Kenyon. 1978. *Sport and Social System*. Reading, Mas.: Addison-Wesley.

Lüschen, G. 1969. Social stratification and social mobility among young sportsmen. Pp. 258–76 in J. Loy and G. Kenyon. *Sport, Culture and Society*. New York: Macmillan.

Lüschen, G. 1970. Cooperation, association and contest. *J. Confl. Resolution* 14,1:21–34.

Lüschen, G. and K. Weis, eds. 1976. *Die Soziologie des Sports.* Berlin: Luchterhand.

Lüschen, G. 1976. Toward a structural analysis of sport. *Am. Phys. Educat. Academy* Papers 2:71–80.

Matejko, A. 1975. The diagnosis of conflict in sport. *Rev. int. de sociologie* (Madrid) 33,1:63–87.

Nimuendaju, C. 1946. *The Eastern Timbira.* Berkeley: University of California Press.

Noll, R. ed. 1974. *Government and the Sports Business.* Washington, D.C.: The Brookings Institution.

Oetinger, F. 1956. *Partnerschaft.* Sttgart: Metzler.

Okner, B. 1974. Taxation and sports enterprises. Pp. 159–84 in R. Noll, *Government and the Sports Business.* Washington, D.C.: The Brookings Institution.

Otto, L. and D. Alwin. 1977. Athletics, aspirations and attainments. *Soc. Education* 50,1:102–13.

Outdoor Recreation Resources Review Commission (ORRRC). 1961–62. *Report # 1–32.* Washington, D.C.: Government Printing Office.

Phillips, J. 1979. Sport and educational attainment. *Paper ASA-Meetings;* Boston.

Piaget, J. 1965. *The Moral Judgment of the Child.* Glencoe, Ill.: Free Press (orig. 1932).

Sartre, J.P. 1960. *Critique de la raison dialectique.* Paris: Gallimard.

Schlenker, B. and T. Boroma. 1978. Fun and games: the validity of games for the study of conflict. *J. Confl. Resolution* 22,1:7–38.

Schmalenbach, H. 1977. *On Society and Experience.* Edited and introduced by Lüschen, G. and G. Stone. Chicago: University of Chicago Press.

Sherif, M. and C. 1961. *The Robber's Cave Experiment.* Norman: Oklahoma University Press.

Sherif, C. 1973. Intergroup conflict and competition. *Sportwissenschaft.* 3,2:138–153.

Shneidman, N. 1978. *The Soviet Road to Success.* Toronto: Ontario Institute for Studies in Education.

Simmel, G. 1923. *Soziologie.* Berlin: Duncker und Humblot (orig. 1908).

Simmel, G. 1950. *The Sociology of Georg Simmel.* Edited by K. Wolff. Glencoe, Ill.: Free Press.

Snyder, E. and E. Spreitzer. 1978. *Social Aspects of Sport.* Englewood-Cliffs, N.J.: Prentice-Hall.

Stone, G. 1969. Some meanings of American sport. Pp. 5–27 in G. Kenyon, ed. *Sociology of Sport.* Chicago: Athletic Institute.

Stone, G. 1980. Sport as community representation. Pp. 214–245 in this *Handbook.*

Sumner, W. 1908. *Folkways.* Boston: Ginn.

Sutton-Smith, B. 1973. Games, the socialization of conflict. *Sportwissenschaft* 3,1:41–46.

Taylor, I. 1971. Football mad: a speculative sociology of football hooliganism. Pp. 352–77 in E. Dunning, ed. *Sociology of Sport.* London: Cass.

Veblen, T. 1934. *Theory of the Leisure Class.* New York: Macmillan (orig. 1896).

Vinnai, G. 1970. *Fussballsport als Ideologie.* Frankfurt: Europäische Verlagsanstalt.

Vinnai, G. 1972. *Sport in der Klassengesellschaft* Frankfurt: Fischer.

Weber, E. 1971. Gymnastics and sports in fin-de-siecle France: opium of the classes? *American Hist. Rev.* 76,1:70-98.

Weber, M. 1953. Class, status and party. Pp. 63–75 in R. Bendix and S.M. Lipset eds. *Class, Status and Power.* Glencoe: Free Press (orig. 1921).

Weinberg, S. and H. Arond. 1952. The occupational culture of the boxer. *AJS* 57,3:460–69.

Wittgenstein, L. 1960. *Philosophische Untersuchungen.* Frankfurt: Suhrkamp.

Wohl, A. 1964. Die gesellschaftlich-historischen Grundlagen des bürgerlichen Sports. *Wissenschaftliche Zeitschrift der DHFK Leipzig* 6,1:1-93.

SPORT AS A COMMUNITY REPRESENTATION

Gregory P. Stone

Among western sociologists, sport has been generally neglected in the study of community life. Often identified with leisure—filling in waking time left over from work—and perhaps because of Veblen's sardonic view of the conspicuous play displayed by the late nineteenth century leisure class (Veblen 1934) of the industrial nations, sport has been implicitly considered a superfluous activity, a "side involvement" (Goffman 1963: 43) of community life. This was quite probably the case for communities caught up in the sweeping changes of emergent industrial capitalism, metaphorically facilitated by the Protestant ethic (Weber 1930), and aptly called "the bleak age" (Hammond and Hammond 1947). Such a state of affairs undoubtedly persisted in the industrial cities of the early twentieth century up to the early thirties or even to the end of World War II when we might well say most of the problems of mass production had been solved. Moreover, the superficial view of sport as irrelevant has been consolidated by the relegation of play to childhood in the later industrializing phases of western civilization. Like all other sciences, sociology, then, has been affected by its socio-historical milieu. By and large, sport has been ignored because of its seemingly reprehensible and conspicuous display by the arrogant idle rich or by its presumably childish nature. Paradoxically, the snobbish attitude of the idle rich has also been un-wittingly adopted in the stand-offish attitude sociologists have taken toward those professional sports that recruit their performers from the working masses.

Such a perspective, fortunately, has not been adopted by all western sociologists, although we must at least grant the vast bulk of soci-ologists a point. There have been communities in particular social, economic, and historical circumstances where sport did not have a central place in their social organization. It may be, for example, that sport is of relative unimportance in some small, isolated tribal com-munities such as the Sanema Indians in south central Venezuela (Stone and Stone 1976). In contrast we immediately think of the extensive Lacrosse matches among the six Nations of the Iriquois in upper eastern North America. Little, if any, cross-cultural analysis has been made of those socio-economic conditions that may account for the differences, and it is not enough to explain them presumptuously in terms of "culture." That is reasoning in too tight a circle. Moreover, most residents in the towns of seventeenth century England did not exactly lead the "sporting life." Sport was also a holiday or holy day (in the face of much resistance) affair in the towns and cities of the late nineteenth and early twentieth century United States. We note that much of what has been termed "grand theory" was developed in sociology at that time, both in the United States and Europe.

Even among such original thinkers, there have been exceptions, and recent research is compatible with the central place they assigned to sport. Two dimensions of these exceptions are worth mentioning. The first is methodological. Sports, particularly team games, have been employed as homologues for the analysis of community organization. Thus, George Herbert Mead emphasized the importance of "taking the role of the generalized other" as a phase in the formulation of one's conception of self. One plays out positions so arranged that they constitute the organization of the community in which he lives, and one develops a reflected conception of self as he generalizes the organization of others in the community, addressing his own acts to their organized expectations of his performance. Mead makes the specific analogy to the team player in a game (Mead 1934: 152-164). To play the game he must address his performance to the expectations of the generalized team. On the one hand, there simply is no time in the contest for the player to assess and summate the expectations of his performance held by each separate member of the team. On the other, too great a preoccupation with the expectations of one or two other teammates would distort his own team play and contributes to team (or community) disorganization. The team, for Mead, is a metaphor useful for the interpretation of the place community organization has in the development of the self.

Seeley et al., in their benchmark study of a Canadian suburb (1956), hit upon the metaphorical value of sport in community analysis inductively. By noting the importance of hockey and Canadian football in the daily lives of dwellers in Crestwood Heights, they observed that those

...typically male, typically North American games, seem to represent symbolically the structure of competition.... By analogy, the structure of the relationships within which the person bent on a career plays out his roles may be illuminated by looking at the game.

(Seeley et al. 1976: 357)

The writers proceed to enumerate several characteristics of team games: dual competition, league organization, combative styles of play, a framework of rules administered by neutral officials, public involvement in spectatorship, the prominence of "star" performers, and team cooperation. They conclude, perhaps somewhat overwhelmed by the expanse of their metaphor, by specifying the pertinence of the model for community analysis:

> A more detailed analysis of the game cannot be pursued, though a study of changes in it, of field rules, the foul, the fumble, and the stratagems of secrecy, suspense, and surprise are all relevant...and would illuminate more fully the basic competitive structure within which careers in Crestwood Heights are made and validated. The points of analogy are many.
>
> (Seeley et al. 1976: 358)

The discussion continues with examples of the "sporting character" of daily life in Crestwood Heights, a discussion more suggestive than definitive.

A second dimension of the exceptional implementation of sport, play, or games in community analysis demands their direct comprehension, conceptualization, and utilization for interpreting social organization. Sport is not viewed here as an enlightening metaphor or model, abstractly applied to the analysis of some other social form. A classical example is provided by Max Weber's study of the city. In considering the sociologically definitive characteristics of cities— size and the sustained economic activities of commerce and trade— Weber viewed cities as essentially (in a social *and* historical sense) "market settlements." However, the perpetuation of such settlements in time required the development of both political and military structures. Urban economies must be administered and urban boundaries must be fortified, garrisoned, and patrolled. This is especially the case in the early stage of urban development (Weber 1962: 71-87). Given the frequent linkage of sport and military training, it is easy to see how Weber—that ascetic Protestant—was led to consider sport in his historical studies. But, in seeking to explain the diversity of cities within the general character limited by his attempts at definition, Weber was quite impressed with the cities of classic and heroic Greece:

> In addition to the market and urban residence of the nobility...other important phenomena were...found. The *agones* (contests) which later dominated the whole range of life arose from the knightly concept of honor and military teaching of the young on the drill ground.
>
> (Weber 1962: 152)

We are all aware of the interpretative significance Johan Huizinga assigned to the agonistic component in his study of man, the player (Huizinga, 1955). Indeed, no definition of sport can fail to include it! Yet, Weber was more concrete and attributed causal significance to the contest and to sports in the development of the Hellenic world, especially in contrast to that of Rome. "The *agones...* were the source of the decisive course of Greek development" (Weber 1962: 244). We might add that sport provided a basic unit of time for that civilization. The "olympiad" was a measure of four years (*Encyclopedia Britannica,* 1976, vol. 2: 274).

Weber remarked in detail on the extension of the contest:

> All events of the gymnasium assumed this form and were thereby made "socially acceptable": spear fighting, wrestling, fist fighting, above all prize races.... The *agones* were organized with prizes, umpires, contest rules and interpenetrated the whole of life. Alongside the Epics it became the single most important bond of Hellenic world in contrast to all barbarians.
>
> (Weber 1962: 244)

While the contribution of horses and wagons to contests was a source of status for more eminent Greeks, "...in the nature of the form, the plebeian *agones* had to be recognized as equals." (Weber 1962: 244). With incomparable insight, Weber perceived the origins of democracy in the nakedness of contestants. He began by observing the total nudity of Hellenic sculpture, except for weapons, and the hold it took on all art forms and daily conversation.

> From Sparta, the place of the highest military training, an influence diffused over the Hellenic world and even the loincloth fell away. No community on earth has ever brought an institution such as this to the center of all interest such that all artistic practice and conversation were dominated by it, even the Platonic dialogues.
>
> (Weber 1962: 255)

In the contests, particularly racing and wrestling, where all citizens participated, nudity was a fundamental social leveller, since clothing, above all, represents the wearer's social or community position. "Never have prestige feelings suffered such a loss of distance as in these naked tournaments of the Greeks" (Weber 1962: 245). Weber's discussion of the city ends on this note where, in our view, a beginning or a reconsideration is called for.

Admittedly, a giant leap from classical Greece to contemporary Bermuda levies a severe tax on the imagination. However, in Frank Manning's study of black clubs in Bermuda (Manning 1973) we find another example of a community study that demonstrates the central significance of sport for social organization and daily life. Bermuda is defined as a community, despite the fact that it includes three urban settlements—Hamilton, St. George, and Somerset—because it is the most densely populated island in the Western Hemisphere, though one of the smallest, and a motorist can travel its entire length in an hour without having to exceed the 20-mile-per-hour speed limit (Manning 1973: 40). Moreover, insularity endows territories with a kind of geographical completeness difficult to establish in the networks of cities, suburbs, and towns that comprise continental metropolitan regions, especially since they cease to persist as walled fortresses.

In contrast to the tendency for Western sociologists to regard sport as an element of leisure and, consequently, filling in time left over from work, Manning specifically notes that

> This ongoing schedule of sports, celebrations, and entertainment lends substance to the club members view of his life as a continuing cycle of play in which work and other non-play activities are literally an "interlude."
>
> (Manning 1973: 71)

Since this mode of symbolization and stylization is relatively recent, reaching its current peak after World War II and during the mid-sixties, it is tempting to interpret the central importance of sport, play, and entertainment as unusual for communities, in this case a mere reflection of tourism which has become the dominant industry of the island. As a matter of fact, Manning began his study with that view as a guiding hypothesis, but was forced to discard it.

Bermuda's black population is organized by clubs which include about half the adult male black population in their membership (Manning 1973: 30). The fourteen black clubs on the island have recently formed auxiliaries for women and youth and continue to increase their membership and their number. Black Christian denominations are also an important organizing force in the social organization of the island community. They outnumber the clubs in nominal membership and are still growing. This is especially the case for the pentecostal sects, as the blacks sever their ties with Anglican denominations to consolidate their rising "black consciousness." However, their most loyal members are married women who demand attendance by their young children. Males drop out in late adolescence and join clubs which become the focal point of their daily round of life. This is seen by some as "back-sliding," but little guilt is expressed, and a majority of Manning's informants expressed a belief that they would ultimately be "born again" or "converted" at some later stage in life when, as one put it, they "slowed down." *The action is in the clubs—in sports, entertainment, and at the bar* (Manning 1973: 60-83).

Black organization began in 1838 with lodges organized for mutual assistance, a similar form found in many ethnic groups in the cities of the United States. Clubs were first organized at the end of the nineteenth century (about 1888) with similar purposes, but with different emphasis. "Two of the earliest clubs, in fact, were formed when a cricket rivalry between two lodges became too big for the lodges to promote" (Manning 1973: 33). Thus, the emphasis given to sport and play in Bermuda emerged indigenously and generically. It was not an outgrowth of a tourism economy. Historical analysis confirms this assertion (Manning 1973). The initial impetus was segregation in sports. Specifically cricket was played on the fields of the white clubs to which blacks were not permitted access. They consequently formed their own teams. Although some clubs acquired liquor licenses, sports have persisted as a prime focus of activity. This sport function increased in importance after World War II with the introduction of soccer. In the '60s integrated leagues were formed.

> By then, however, most white clubs had discontinued or de-emphasized cricket and soccer, and were concentrating instead on sports not generally popular among blacks, such as yachting, rugby, field hockey, and squash. Blacks were left with virtually unchallenged dominance in cricket and soccer, the major team sports.
>
> (Manning 1973: 36).

Black clubs also provided other programs in response to the earlier pattern of segregation. They facilitated the development of a black "social" calendar, provided other recreational activities, such as gambling, and became general "all purpose" centers. Of particular note is the establishment of such entertainment events as dances, shows, fairs, and cruises. Black clubs, then, stand at the center of social organization, for in 1970 they represented 59 per cent of the entire Bermuda community. Their basic activities are sports, entertainment, and bar behavior (not at all exclusively drinking, see Manning 1973: 187-209). As such, they organize the activities and world view of most black Bermudans. In all this, sports and "the game" are of overriding significance.

In this introductory statement, it has been asserted that most sociologists in their studies of communities have either ignored sports or relegated their examination to at least a secondary position, preferring to focus on work and its social context or consequences. Over and against this, it has been demonstrated that some sociologists have employed team games as abstract models facilitating the study of community organization. Most rare are those social scientists who place sports, games, and contests squarely in the center of community organization and history. In the accounts of these social scientists, specifically Weber and Manning, the discerning reader will already have noted that an important feature of sport is its emergence as a representation of society, community, or subcommunities such as ethnic groups and status circles. In Durkheim's terms it is a collective representation (Durkheim 1947b: 432-39) or a social fact (Durkheim 1938: 1-13). As such, it is a source of social solidarity. Communities here are understood to be named places where a number of people can live out their lives, have children, and engage in different activities. It is often the case, especially in cities, that ethnic concentrations qualify as communities by our definition. When they are legally part of a larger town or city political unit, however, we have not considered such concentrations separately. Likewise, in our analysis, we have excluded ecological—symbiotic and spacial—dimensions as a focal point. Those interested in such dimensions of the problem may consult the excellent recent work of John F. Rooney, Jr. for the United States (Rooney 1974). Our primary interest is in sport as a collective representation of the communities in which it occurs, the persistence of such representations, and the consequences for social organization and social psychology.

COMMUNITY AND SPORT

A community's name is the most complete representation of its totality, and it encompasses all its diversity at the same time. At times community nick-names—"The Windy City," "Mo City," "The Apple," "Bean Town," and the like—more adequately and poignantly summarize the city than the proper names—Chicago, Detroit, New York, or Boston—but nick-names are more ephemeral. They fade, pass on, and are replaced, while the proper names endure. As collective representations, they are, in Durkheim's sense, social facts (Durkheim 1938: 1-13) or objects of their own kind. They are external to those they represent: no present-day Chicagoan, Detroiter, New Yorker, or Bostonian (proper or not) is responsible for the name that represents his community. And they are constraining: down the hills of centuries past rolls the admonition that is still in use today—"When in Rome, do as the Romans do." We might add, "whether you like it or not." It is the name, the objectification and representation of the community, sustained in communication to which communities owe their persistence beyond the lifetime of their members.

Names are not the only collective representations of communities. Other more concrete symbols—places and structure—come to represent the communities in which they are found. Chicago has its Tribune Tower, Wrigley Building, lake front, and Outer Drive; Boston, Beacon Hill and the Commons; New York, the Statue of Liberty, the Empire State Building, the Great White Way, and Times Square; San Francisco, Nob Hill and Fisherman's Wharf. Considerable sentiment is mobilized by such objects and places among community residents. The Commons in Boston has long resisted proposed changes in land use, and an uncompleted freeway juts out starkly short of Fisherman's Wharf, blunt testimony to the affection with which San Franciscans attach themselves to that representation. Needless to say the cable cars still run there long after they have served the function they were built to perform. Collective representations persist for reasons other than those that brought them into existence. Sport teams, bearing the community name (or totem), have become this kind of collective representation, as have players and sports, themselves.

SPORT AS A COLLECTIVE REPRESENTATION

It is clear that different sports came to represent different nations—hockey, Canada; baseball or basketball, the United States; cricket and rugby, England; hurling, Ireland; curling, Scotland; bullfighting, Spain; bocce, Italy; judo, Japan; ping-pong, China; and on and on. Some sports, like soccer or, as we say, "European" football, have become so international in popularity that they have lost their national identities. If sports represent nations, team and athletes represent communities.

This seems to have its beginnings in inter-community rivalry, as true today as it was amongst those representing the Greek city-states at the Olympic games almost 2500 years ago. Water transportation made this kind of assembly by athletes from different cities possible. In the United States, it was not until the late 1860's that the railroads facilitated the development of such sport contests (Somers 1972: 126). Prior to that time, beginning in 1842, baseball, the "pioneer mass sport" of the United States, was organized on a local metropolitan basis with the formation of the Knickerbocker Club by New York businessmen under Alexander J. Cartwright (Martindale 1960: 465). Local amateur leagues were common around large cities. Although the military occupation of New Orleans during most of the Civil War retarded the development of baseball there, the Louisiana State Baseball Association was established in 1868, followed by two additional city leagues in the early 1880's. Such urban leagues, frequently involving cities in relatively close proximity, were considered "amateur," though winning players were paid. The community followings rallied by these teams did much to wrest the sport from the control of high status groups and establish baseball as a full blown professional sport in the last quarter of 19th century United States, "hastening acceptance of...the democraticization and commercialization of the national game" (Somers 1972: 123–124). The point is that inter-urban rivalry destroyed the exclusiveness of baseball, was extended by the proliferation of rail transportation, stimulated professionalization, and established true *collective* representations of the urban masses as teams bearing city names—Chicago, Louisville, Buffalo, Cincinnati, St. Louis, Philadelphia, and New York, to name only a few. Rivalries involving the masses, heightened urban solidarity, giving some credence to Sumner's "in-group—out-group" principle.

Prior to the rise of urban sports, on the frontier and in the more remote small towns, more violent sports pitting individual combatants against one another exerted a solidifying influence by mobilizing the anticipations, moods, and conversations of locals more thinly scattered over territories. The closer to the frontier, the more colorful and violent the entertainment (Martindale 1960: 459–60). Boxing had all the elements of the spectacle, earlier seen in the Roman *ludi*. Nor was human combat the only spectacle. At the edges of early 19th century American society, cock-fighting, dog-fighting, and bear-baiting were also to be found. In the mining country of Montana, for example,

> Occasionally, a fight to the death between a bull and a grizzly could be witnessed. The promoters of those contests would dig a large pit to trap the bear, then—using a long pole—would poke rags soaked in chloroform at the animal. The grizzly was taken to town and chained to a post. Still chained, he would be pitted against one or more bulls in a rickety arena.
>
> (Brier 1969: 4)

Spectacles, however, are conversation-pieces, and conversations about them, before, during, and after the event bring people together in an emotional rapport. Combatants become sources of identification for the fans. In Montana, the boxing frenzy reached its zenith in the mid-sixties with "the great glove fights" of the Montana hero, Con Orem. On January 7, 1865, The Montana *Post* reported the situation in Virginia City:

> The spirit of the P.R. [prize ring] seems to have entered everyone in town. Since the...Orem-O'Neill fight, whereever we went in the past

> week the respective merits of one or the other of the combatants was
> the topic of conversation—sometimes in language more strong than
> poetical. The friends of both parties claim their man to be the best.
>
> (Brier 1969: 48, fn 8)

The fight, held on January 2, 1865, lasted 185 rounds and, taking
three hours and five minutes, culminated in a draw! It was refought
in conversation and in the press for months and years afterward.
Eventually, Orem published challenges in the Montana *Post* which
was sent on an exchange basis to several big eastern newspapers.
(Brier 1969: 1 and 61.)

By 1867 or 1868, interest in prize-fighting declined. "Other
sports such as baseball, horse-racing, and dog-fighting were gaining
in popularity." (Brier 1969: 108). Montana had a government and a
promising economy.

> The prize ring...appeared to capture better than most sports the spirit
> of the age...by reducing the values of American society to a pair of
> gladiators meeting in the ring for a fight to the finish....Professional
> boxing also...restored a sense of individualism to national life. As
> the tempo of industrialization and urbanization accelerated, America
> became a mass society composed of people whose lives were governed
> increasingly by the machine and the time clock, and whose individual
> accomplishments were dwarfed by the collective efforts of all. The
> prize ring seemed to reverse this process by glorifying champion fist-
> fighters who had risen far above the ranks.
>
> (Somers 1972: 160)

Again, once it had entered domains of governmental and status
jurisdiction, it faced a half-century struggle for full legitimation.

Yet even this kind of conflict has a solidarity-building consequence. Hunting and fishing had evolved from a means of securing
food (West 1945) to a sport provoking invidious comparisons
(Gallaher 1961) in a small Missouri community (population, 1500;
central village, 300) over a period of 15 years (1939–1954). Hunting
and fishing have become "...mostly sport and recreation...the sum
spent in pursuing them far exceeds any monetary value...assigned
to the game taken." (Gallaher 1961: 104) For some men this
amounts to several hundred dollars. Many own more than one
outboard motor, and some own two boats;

> ...all sportsmen own multiple pieces of equipment...and the well-
> outfitted owns many items of special clothing. Some men derive great
> satisfaction merely from the ownership and care of their equipment.
> ...[C]onspicuous consumption...[marks] the economic behavior of
> many...sportsmen.
>
> (Gallaher 1961: 104-105)

Attempts to enforce fish and game laws were viewed as machinations of city people. "People should regulate themselves" was the dominant belief, and this was

> ...particularly true of people who still hunt and fish for part of their subsistence...[S]tate game laws are a violation of...the "God-given right to hunt and fish."
>
> (Gallaher 1961: 150)

Gallaher footnoted the observation:

> ...most of these people...are convinced that state game and fish laws are engineered by city people to protect the game for [their own] enjoyment.
>
> (Gallaher 1961: 275, fn 56)

The meaning of such sports afield has changed over time, but the conflict remains:

> ...hunting and fishing now function primarily in the assignment of male prestige....For some men prestige depends on excellence in these activities, and the major criterion of excellence depends...on the quantity of game secured....[O]thers, for the sake of prestige, recreation, or subsistence, hunt and fish on days declared out-of-season by the state game commission....[The] major complaint of conservation agents...[is that]...it is next to impossible to obtain convictions of known violators in the county courts.
>
> (Gallaher 1961: 150)

Such self-protection by residents of the county, extending into the court house, almost smacks of conspiracy, and perhaps nothing builds solidarity more than the sharing of secrets in the presence of outsiders. It is, of course, impossible in the metropolis for *all* the residents to share a secret and collectively conceal it from those who live elsewhere.

Sport as a source of solidarity can be found wherever it is a representation of the collective community. In a Welsh village, for example, football became a symbol of unity and cohesion against the outside world. Not only was the honor of the village conceived to be at stake in each game, but daily contact with the club was thought socially important to the village. After the end of the 1955 season, however, when the club moved the playing field outside the village, the football club was isolated to some extent from the social life of the village (Frankenberg 1957: 110-16).

High school sports have accomplished for the smaller cities and towns what professional sports have done for the metropolis. As an example:

> For Plainville adults the high school represents a new focus of com-
> munity life and ritual. Those who sanction and attend the basketball
> games, plays, debates, and musical contests think of them as symbols
> of community "modernity"—as events which prove that Plainville
> either is, or is trying to be, especially in educational matters, "just as
> up-to-date as other communities."
>
> (West 1945: 80)

The basketball team of "Elmtown" has emerged as "a collective
representation of the high school to a large segment of the community" (Hollingshead 1949: 193). "Community pride is the issue
in basketball games" (Hollingshead 1949: 194). In "Middletown,"
the Lynds ascribe the promotion of civic loyalty to two activities:
first, the Chamber of Commerce and, second, "An even more widespread agency of group cohesion is the high school basketball team.
...Today more civic loyalty centers around basketball than around
any other thing" (Lynd and Lynd 1929: 485). Apparently the
emerging importance of high school sport (particularly basketball)
as a collective representation was realized in the early twentieth
century, probably after World War I. The Lynds compared the
1894 high school yearbook with that of 1924.

> Next in importance to the senior class...in the earlier book...were
> ...the faculty and the courses taught by them, while in the current
> book, athletics shares the position of honor with the class data, and a
> faculty twelve times as large occupies relatively only half as much
> space....as foreign to the present high school as...the early class motto
> "Deo Duce"...is the present dedication, "To the Bearcats."
> This whole spontaneous life of the intermediate generation that clusters
> about the formal nucleus of school studies becomes focussed, arti-
> culated, and even rendered important in the eyes of adults through
> the medium of the schools athletic teams—"The Bearcats."
>
> (Lynd and Lynd 1929: 212)

While sport may be viewed as a collective representation of
communities in which it is performed, a documented assertion of
the fact is inadequate without further documentation of its pervasive
saliency in community life. In the rustic gold-rush days of Montana
in the 1860's, sport vied with the mourning of the dead for an
audience. Larry Barsness' study of Alder Gulch and Virginia City
has been cited:

> A good fight could even draw mourners away from the *rara avis* of
> the town's diversions, a first-class funeral. So the sheriff discovered
> when the male portion of the crowd dwindling and followed the
> defalcators over Boot Hill to the coulee beyond, where, sure enough,
> two Negroes were sparring.
>
> (Brier 1969: 66, fn 11)

James West has reported the interest given to sports in 1939 by high school students, using the words of the vocational agriculture teacher: "People remember all the ball players from the 1931 winning team, but they don't even know about the prizes my boys take every year" (West 1945: 80). Visiting Plainsville fifteen years later in 1954, Gallaher paid less attention to student involvement in games and focussed on adult outdoor recreation and sponsorship of sport. Of the people living in Plainsville, he writes:

> Most…definitely believe that work hours should be shortened, that people should have more time to enjoy life.…leisure time is more important than ever…as evidenced by…vacations and, among men… money spent for sporting equipment, as well as…time and money spent on hunting and fishing expeditions within and without the state.
> (Gallaher 1961: 214)

And Plainvillers pay to cultivate sports in the school system. The coach-social science teacher received a salary of $3100 a year, topped only by the vocational-agriculture teacher ($3600) and the superintendent of schools ($4000) (Gallaher 1961: 87). In 1955, the coach received a $500 raise to prevent his leaving; elementary teachers' pay was raised $80 (Gallaher 1961: 166). Similarly, in Elmtown, businessmen, professionals, and workers demanded that the Board of Education and the superintendent hire a winning coach, and he was paid a maximum salary (Hollingshead 1949:193).

To be a winning coach in Elmtown means, especially, to defeat "Diamond City." Elmtown is two and a half times as large as Diamond City, and, in the view of the residents, "bigger is better." Elmtown is also considered "cleaner." Teams carry this pride to the contests. The basketball season culminates in a three game series with Diamond City. In 1941–42, Elmtown lost all three games in addition to the football game. After the second loss, in basketball, the citizens offered theatre tickets, merchandise, and in some cases, money to the players if they won the remaining game. One wealthy man offered a dollar a point to each scorer. Two fathers of players matched the offer for their sons. In the closing minutes of the game, fouls were called on the superintendent, the coach, and the Elmtown rooters, and two players were ejected from the game. One of those knocked a Diamond City player to the floor before he was ejected. A fan gave him five dollars after the game as a reward for his "good work" (Hollingshead 1949: 191–94). As Durkheim observed in his *Division of Labor* (Durkheim 1947a), the collective representation is passionately embraced, and violations of it, however construed, evoke an immediate, direct, and violent response.

We can observe the same emphasis, though violence and deviousness are not reported, in Middletown.

> The athletic activity of today culminates in basketball in the high school...during which the city's civic pride is deeply involved: leading citizens give "Bearcat parties" prior to...the final games, hundreds of people unable to secure tickets stand in the street cheering a scoreboard, classes are virtually suspended in the high school, and the children who are unable to go to the state capitol to see the game meet in a chapel service of cheers and songs and sometimes prayers for victory. In the series of games leading up to "the finals" the city turns out week after week to fill to the doors the largest auditorium available.
>
> (Lynd and Lynd 1929: 284)

The observation was footnoted:

> Basketball sweeps all before it. The city council voted to spend $100,000 for a new gymnasium...when the cry on all sides was for retrenchment in city expenditures....The bond issue was finally overruled through appeal...to the state authorities. It is widely reported that "the chief thing that got [the new superintendent of schools] elected...was that he put Middletown on the map as a basketball town."
>
> (Lynd and Lynd 1929: 284-285, fn 16)

That study was carried on in 1925. Ten years later, the Lynds revisited Middletown and reported that $347,000 had been obligated for a new gymnasium seating 9,000 in the late '20's (Lynd and Lynd 1937: 221). They also reflected on the passing of the old "days when being a successful basketball coach had made a Middletown teacher successively high school principal and then school superintendent."

Such collective representations are passionately husbanded not only by school and municipal officials in small towns and cities, but also in the metropolis. On March 18, 1977, the press reported that Mayor Abraham Beame of New York threatened to go to court to prevent the New York Jets from playing their first two "home" games of the season in New Jersey. Beame said the legal move was "a sad day for major sports that we must resort to the courts to force the parties to fulfill their obligations to the city and its people." The next day a tentative agreement was announced to keep the Jets in Shea Stadium. Thus, the New York *Times* Service continued, a measure of prestige was regained for New York City, which would have been left without a major professional football team (Minneapolis *Tribune,* March 18, 1977: 7-C; March 19, 1977: 4-B). Similar conflicts persist in 1980 as the Los Angeles *Rams* open their season in Anaheim and the Oakland A's continue to threaten deserting that city for an as yet unnamed site.

Exposure in the community press is another way of testing the saliency of sport in the community mind. Unless the reception of sport on television and radio is observed, figures only reveal the saliency of sport for the mass *society*. Gallaher did make pertinent inquiries of the use of television by Plainvillers and found that

> Television fans favor hillbilly music, news, weather,...sports (particularly wrestling) and variety and adventure programs. Special events, such as the baseball world series, championship boxing matches, and major political speeches, find non-owners visiting friends who own sets....Interest in sports, incidentally, as in past years, is heightened by friendly betting pools.
>
> (Gallaher 1961: 27)

In Elmtown, the newspaper consistently apologizes for team losses. The sports "dope" column is widely read, and the paper features at least two sport stories each week, sometimes recounting for the third or fourth time the past or expected play of the "stars" (Hollingshead 1949: 193). The sports pages in the United States press do tend toward redundancy. The leading paper of Middletown devoted four per cent of its news coverage during the first week of March, 1890 to organized sports. By 1923, the coverage had increased fourfold to sixteen per cent in that same week (Lynd and Lynd, 1929: 284). The increase occurred in participant sports; spectator sports, except for the few who might assemble to watch a shooting match, were not included in the 1890 issues. In 1890, three competitive shoots with clubs from other towns, two fishing trips, and two hunting trips were reported. The first week in March, 1923 reported three baseball games, seventy-three bowling matches, three basketball games, three weekly shoots by gun clubs, four golf tournaments, nine football games, one bicycling party, one prize fight, and one YMCA track meet.

As far as the metropolitan press is concerned, this author has kept a haphazard running account for twenty-five years.

> In 1955, my morning paper at the time, the Detroit *Free Press*, devoted five pages to sporting news (roughly 400 column inches excluding advertising) and two and one half pages to news of business and industry (roughly 240 column inches). Available back issues acknowledge that that issue was not at all unrepresentative. Twelve years later, in a different place, I found four pages devoted to sporting news and four pages to news of business and industry in the Minneapolis *Tribune*. Column inches, excluding advertising were about equal (355 and 346, respectively). However, that was Thursday, May 11, 1967. The Min-

nesota Twins had not played on the preceding day, nor was there much else, except for the routine, to report in the world of sport....258 column inches of the business pages were *solely* devoted to listings on the American Stock Exchange, the New York Stock Exchange, listings of Toronto stocks, grain futures, U.S. Treasury Notes, etc. Thus 88 column inches were devoted to substantive accounts of news in the business world. Obviously nowhere near as great a proportion of the sports pages was devoted *solely* to reporting of scores.

(Stone 1973: 72)

Almost ten years later, May 2, 1977, the morning *Tribune,* a suburban edition with less coverage than the city edition, contained eight pages devoted to sport and one page to business (291 column inches compared to 45 column inches, excluding advertising). But that was Monday, and there were no stock market, grain future, treasury note, or foreign exchange rate reports. If we eliminate the 39 column inches given over to the reports of league standings and final scores of various matches (not baseball box scores), the ratio is still 252:45. If we grant an additional page (120 column inches) to the business section for various market reports and retain the 39 inches for the sports pages, the ratio comes more into balance (291:165). In other words for the last twenty-two years, undisciplined observations of the metropolitan press consistently demonstrate that sports receive more coverage than any other single institution in the United States. A scrutiny of the *Tribune* on May 31, 1980 shows no departure from the trend.

As for politics, this may well extend further back in time. The scheduling of a triple event in boxing for September 5, 6, and 7, 1892 in New Orleans, the match in which Corbett defeated John L. Sullivan for the championship,

...released a wave of boxing enthusiasm throughout the country.... Local papers carried lengthy accounts of the fighters' training activities; ...Many out-of-town newspapers sent reporters to the city; a writer for the *National Police Gazette* contended that "the whole civilized world" was anxiously awaiting the results of "the greatest pugilistic carnival in the history of the world." The amount of space devoted to the contests moved a correspondent for Frank Leslie's *Illustrated* to complain that the leading dailies had "scant space to give to the movements and utterances of the presidential nominees," Benjamin Harrison and Grover Cleveland.

(Somers 1972: 179)

So did sports push presidential politics off the columns of the major dailies, not only in New Orleans, but also New York, Chicago, and Cincinnati, to name but a few. Moreover, attendance at the event provided another occasion for the reaffirmation of community solidarity.

> As people of all classes sat cheek by jowl, party differences and sectional lines were obliterated, presidential candidates were forgotten, businesses were neglected, and the police of other cities lost their best customers and felt relieved.
>
> (Somers 1972: 183, quoting the New Orleans *Daily Picayune*)

Therefore, community studies at various magnitudes of population size and over a vast reach of history and space confirm the assertion that sport is a collective representation passionately (if at times irrationally and irresponsibly) embraced by community members. Moreover, it is a salient part of their awareness, quite probably due to the fact that it is a focus of conversation, publicity, and, in more recent times, the mass media. Finally, it is a unifying force for those communities it represents, and this is at once a consequence of the inter-community conflict it engenders and the intra-community communication network it establishes.

There are many other ways that sport exerts an influence on community life, and this article cannot begin to enumerate them all. However, the importance of the bicycle and the bicycling craze which crested in the 1890's cannot be neglected here.

> After the 1890's bicycling rapidly evolved into a major interest. In 1890 a million bicycles were in use, and annual production soon amounted to more than this number. Every young man—and many women—had a bicycle, and every city had its bicycle club.
>
> (Martindale 1960: 463–464).

In 1895, the New Orleans *Daily Picayune* is reported to have "estimated...that Americans spent fifty million dollars each year for bicycles and related equipment," a sum that supported "an industry which gives employment to thousands of bread winners" (Somers 1972: 231). Of even greater importance is the impact that the organization of cyclists at that time had on the future of personal transportation in the United States. This is discussed in great detail as it is traced in the community of New Orleans and up through the levels of state government. We can provide one example:

> As scores of riders pedaled city streets and country roads, complaints about the condition of public thoroughfares inevitably developed. Local cyclists had displayed some interest in the national movement to improve the country's highways in the 1880's...The Louisiana Road Club was formed in June 1896, expressly "for the purpose of improving the roads of this state."...Although it would be a gross exaggeration

to maintain that cyclists single handedly brought about macadamized streets and highways, they nevertheless launched a campaign that quite literally paved the way for the automobile.

(Somers 1972: 230–231)

Far to the north, the same impact of bicycling on the quality of roads has also been documented for cities and towns of Canada (Jobling 1976: 68–69). Both studies also note the importance of the bicycle in the general emancipation of women for participation in sports. Still we maintain that the overall significance of sport was manifested in its emergence as a collective community representation:

> At a time when some features of urban life, such as rapid, poorly planned growth, an increase in specialization, the division of labor, and the infusion of heterogeneous elements into the city, tended to isolate people and to destroy all sense of community, sports acted as a countervailing force. The athletic arena was a great mixing bowl that brought together people of different classes and ethnic backgrounds and gave them common interests.
>
> (Somers 1972: 285).

Some would take exception to this line of argument. Examining the behavior in the middle and lower "class" bars of Hamilton, Ontario during Grey Cup Week when the Hamilton Tiger-Cats met the Saskatchewan Roughriders for the 1972 Canadian Football League. Listiak leaped rather rapidly to conclusions about society from observations in eleven beer parlors and lounges in the center of a city, to be sure a city one would expect to be involved in the match:

> It is hard to imagine how such behavior functions to restore community integration and solidarity. Social distance cannot be said to have decreased significantly...except within the middle class. If anything was solidified, it was the existing social distance between the classes. The classes remained pretty endogamous *(sic)* in their behavior, the middle class engaging in celebrations..., developing feelings of solidarity among themselves as well as feelings of civic pride; the lower class simply going about its normal routine. Moreover, it was only middle-class business establishments in the downtown business core which involved themselves in "putting on a show" by dressing up windows in Grey Cup themes, putting up signs such as "Welcome Visitors," "Go Tigers Go," etc., and by selling Grey Cup souvenirs and paraphernalia.
> In reality, Grey Cup Week 1972 was found to be basically a middle-class "binge" sponsored, promoted, and profited from mostly by businessmen and politicians.
>
> (Listiak 1976: 421)

This demurral is quoted at some length because, in some twenty-five years of exploring the general problem of community identification, this author has become convinced that there is more to the observation of the alienation of "the other America" then sheer ideological assertion. Yet, there are questions to be raised. First, there is considerable literature on taverns and bars as "class" and other socially differentiated *territories.* Such territories, on a much smaller scale, are as walled, garrisoned, and patrolled as were ancient fortress cities and towns. In other words, the settings in which Listiak conducted his inquiry were established, staffed, and patronized to maintain distances. It does not come as a complete surprise to learn that such territories retained their "class" integrity under the impact of Grey Cup Week, but this, in itself, is theoretically important. Had Listiak gone to a setting or settings designed for mingling across "class" distances, such as the stadium parking lot on the day of the game or the game itself, his results might have been different. Dean Anderson, of Iowa State University, has made such observations of the "tailgate parties" in the stadium parking lot on the mornings of Minnesota Viking football games and in the evenings following the games. Second, some sports themselves appeal to different socio-economic strata. Football was predominantly a middle stratum sport in Minneapolis in 1961, a finding quite commensurate with Listiak's findings. However, in a restudy done in 1976 by Anderson and Stone 1979), it seems as though the introduction of professional football to the Minneapolis metropolitan area has "massified"—broken down socio-economic differences in—the football audience. If further analysis bears this out, Listiak has a point, although some differences in sports involvement among Canadiens compared with people in the United States may exist. Notwithstanding, Listiak's critique is one to be taken seriously and, as we shall see, for somewhat different reasons than he has in mind.

THE DIFFUSION OF SPORT AND ITS WEAKENING AS A COLLECTIVE COMMUNITY REPRESENTATION

Durkheim (1947a) attributed the proliferation of the division of labor and the weakening (not the disappearance) of the collective *conscience* to the concurrent increase of population size, physical density, and moral or dynamic density. The latter variable was never specified, though Durkheim, in *The Rules of Sociological Method* (Durkheim 1938: 113-116), did acknowledge that he had neglected its importance. At times he speaks of moral or dynamic density as the rate of communication, and no technological invention has increased that rate more than television. Its impact on sport as a community representation is clear. The importance of market areas—statistical constructs—has obliterated the importance of named places of residence in the consideration of team locations. Yet, at least the Lynds ascribed the decline of sport interest in some part to the forerunner of television—the radio. They write, "The depression years have apparently pulled some of the Bearcats' teeth, and there is some question...whether basketball will ever regain its former frenzied preeminence" (Lynd and Lynd 1937: 291). Aside from the loss of ticket sales forced by the severe depression of the '30's, the Lynds list four "factors" involved in the decline of basketball. First, note is made of the $347,000 "white elephant" the citizens of Middletown were left with when, in the late '20's, a fourteen year obligation was incurred to build a new gymnasium. Second, they assert that radio broadcasting seriously cut into attendance. Third, teams had proliferated. Teams representing the new college, the college laboratory school, and the junior high schools had been added. Fourth, intramural sports programs were developed in the schools, and new sports were added. Teams, themselves, also grew in size. In 1931, there were 150–200 boys on all the athletic squads at Central High School: in 1935, 400–500. In 1925, there were four high school sports (basketball, football, track, and baseball). By 1935, seven other sports had been added (tennis, golf, wrestling, cross-country, volleyball, softball, and horseshoe teams). Various intramural leagues were established in the several junior high schools and at the two high schools in the city (Lynd and Lynd 1937:291–92). "This broadening of the participation base has meant less symbolic participation as spectators by 'drugstore' athletes lounging about the downtown soft drink hang-outs" (Lynd and Lynd 1937: 292).

Certainly we can see analogies on a national scale, as sports have proliferated in the United States. We now find hockey and soccer in Texas! Leagues and teams have burgeoned. Johnson, writing in 1970, notes, "Today major league franchises for baseball, hockey, basketball, and football total eighty-seven. Ten years ago there were but forty-two" (Johnson 1971: 57). In 1977, there were one hundred and three, including eleven teams in the World Hockey Association. This national proliferation, with its detrimental effect on sport as a collective representation in many communities, as well as its positive effect on those recently granted franchises, is due almost exclusively to television. Obviously the number of players in major leagues has increased sharply over the last twenty years, and, at this writing, the full impact of women's sport cannot be apprehended in even a rudimentary way.

Sports in the United States is, *first of all,* a business! Walter O'Malley explains:

> ...we were making the same money we had been making ten years before....We were standing still, even though we had won five pennants in those years....we'd have been positively bankrupt in five more years if we had stayed in Brooklyn.
>
> Johnson 1971: 28–29).

So, in the beginning of what may come to be called "the great diaspora" of American sport, it was a quest for a market *location* that led community based teams to pull up roots in what still seems to be blatant and cruel disregard of fan loyalty. Now, however, it is the quest for markets in which the commodity of athletic skill can be distributed over the invisible channels of television frequencies:

> Television brought the big leagues to the hinterlands, first by remote transmission of flickering pictures, then by causing real-life franchises to spring up everywhere. It is true that the jet airliner must be credited in part for coast-to-coast expansion since it made it feasible to play a game one day in Los Angeles and the next in Boston.... [T] he nation's ...affluence...put the money for high-priced tickets into the pockets of most of the citizenry. But the power of television has caused it more than anything. The medium has a unique if perhaps involuntary capacity for homogenizing all things, for minimizing cultural differences between regions.... [O] nly after the wizards of television have judged a town to be a sound market...can it become a viable candidate to be a big league city....It is almost only because of the promise of television wealth that the Boston-Milwaukee Braves are now in Atlanta, that the former Minneapolis Lakers have flown off to Los Angeles, that the Chicago Cardinals of the NFL are in St. Louis, that the Philadelphia-Kansas City A's are in Oakland, that Brooklyn lies fallow, and that there is no trace of the Polo Grounds any longer along the Harlem River. It is essentially the promise of television money that has brought us a whole magnificent list of new nick-names to cheer and boo and teach grandchildren to revere.
>
> (Johnson 1971: 55–57)

And unlikely names—why did the NFL grant a franchise to Tampa, Florida? Again television played a major role:

> At present two major measurements are used to determine the television potential of a city. Area of Dominant Influence (ADI) allocates every county in the United States to that metropolitan area which dominates its viewing habits....Designated Market Area (DMA) assigns districts according to their viewing habits during prime time and is

therefore a more sophisticated measure of the advertising potential than the cruder geographical allocations of ADI....Tampa may rate only twenty-seventh in population, but rates 20-18 ADI-DMA in television potential, ahead of such established markets as Cincinnati, Buffalo, Denver, New Orleans and San Diego.

(Michener 1976: 305-307)

There is another dimension of the business world that contributes to the weakening of sport as a community representation—the *law of depreciation.* James Michener has made a searching analysis of this phase of sport (Michener 1976: 357-363). He traces the natural history of ownership in the major leagues: first "men of great dedication and expertise," then the "business tycoons" who used sports essentially to advertise their products, like beer and chewing gum, and, finally, the corporate manager. It is this last type who perceived sport not only as advertising, but—more crucial— a tax write-off. Players may be depreciated over time, like the equipment of any business, for the amount that is paid for them. Toward the end of this period the owner may wish to sell and there may be many buyers available. But the owner wants to sell the "intangibles" of his business—the good will and name of the club—for these may be allocated to capital gains, another favorable tax break. The buyer, on the other hand, wants to purchase "tangibles"—the property—so he can reinstitute the depreciation tactic anew. This seeming irreconcilability between buyer and seller was incredibly disregarded by the government which used to allow each party to allocate the purchase price in whichever way was most profitable. As soon as the sale was consummated the buyer could depreciate each player, as Michener says, "from scratch," whether or not the seller had almost totally depreciated them. Of course, the precedent is established in the sale and purchase of any business property. In the case of professional basketball, the government, quite reasonably set the period of depreciation for players between three and five years.

But this had a crucial bearing on the conduct of sports, because it was no longer profitable to retain ownership of a team after the five-year depreciation period had elapsed.... [I] t became more profitable...to buy a team than to keep one.... This explains the wild shifting of franchises over the past fifteen years.

(Michener 1976: 360)

If we couple this with the fact of increasing absentee ownership, the weakening influence on sports as collective community representations is clear.

In far too many cases teams have been owned not by local people interested in the welfare of both the team and the community, but by outsiders, sometimes from the opposite end of the nation, who happened to be in a financial position in which ownership was a practical rather than an athletic consideration.

(Michener 1976: 363)

The effect has not been unnoticed by fans, as the following embittered letter-to-the-editor shows:

It would appear that Minnesota and the Twin Cities should give up in their attempts to retain and satisfy major-league teams. We have to recognize the Los Angeles "Lakers," possibly the Florida "Fighting Saints." But now must we be embarrassed with the Seattle "Twins" and the New York "Vikings"?

(Minneapolis *Tribune*, March 18, 1976: 6-A)

As it turned out, the St. Paul Saints merely faded away as the WHA struggled for survival, and in 1977 Seattle received an expansion franchise in the American League. However, the "Twins" and the "Vikings" still awaken considerable anxiety among those in the metropolitan area who have conceived an enlarged domed stadium as a major and necessary investment to retain those teams.

The weakening of sport as a collective community representation in the United States is further demonstrated by the replacement of city names with state names for teams, in an effort to extend the peripheries of the market. Consider the California Angels, the Minnesota Vikings, the Golden State Warriors, or the Minnesota Twins and North Stars, and examples in the ABA. This diffusion of representation is not received blandly by fans:

We are at the beginning of another baseball season, but once again Minneapolis and St. Paul are without major-league representation. The Minnesota Twins play in this area, but there is no team which bears the label Twin Cities.

I am sure that people in other parts of the country do not immediately think of Minneapolis and St. Paul when reference is made to the Minnesota baseball team. I have been unable to develop any real interest in the Twins because I don't feel they represent my city in the way the Red Sox and the Cubs represent Boston and Chicago, respectively. And when one considers that a team often draws fans from a large region, including other states, one sees that the name "Minnesota" is not really appropriate, anyway.

So let's give our metropolitan area the big-league status which it's entitled to by renaming the local team the Twin Cities Twins or the Minneapolis-St. Paul Twins.

(Minneapolis *Tribune,* April 16, 1976: 7-A)

On the other hand, fans may identify with the *team* name. In the summer of 1966, this author conducted an informal survey of men-on-the-street in New York. It was assumed that the meteoric rise of enthusiasm for the Mets was due, in part, to the fact that the departure of the Giants for San Francisco had left a void which the Mets had filled by rallying the loyalties of abandoned Giants fans. This was an incorrect assumption. Not a single Giants fan encountered on the street had transferred his loyalty to the Mets. Each fan was following the San Francisco Giants in the press or on TV whenever they appeared. Even so, the move had pulled their identifications with New York out of the city and to the West Coast. The effect might well have been one of cosmopolitanization rather than a weakening of identification. Their identities followed the team and were, apparently, not grounded in a spatially demarcated community. Manning provides a parallel in his analysis of Bermuda clubs which invited the audiences of the spectacles they staged to think of themselves as "black":

> These symbols encourage the audience to put aside their particularistic identity as "coloured Bermudans" and to adopt a more universal identification that relates them to other peoples of African ancestry on the basis of common ethnicity, common experiences stemming from colonialism and slavery, and a common cultural heritage.... To phrase it differently, the identity conveyed through entertainment moves the club audience from an insular society, where they are known and socially valued in terms of their relation to a white ideal, toward a cosmopolitan black world where shared symbols and sensitivities form the basis of a cultural order independent of white standards.
> (Manning 1973: 169)

Whether or not cosmopolitanization is valued, it does have the consequence of weakening local community ties and identifications.

We are left, then, with the question of ascertaining whether and to what extent sport can be thought of as a community representation, making for the solidarity of its members, or a social fact which has become diffused throughout the society, the nation, and even the world on the frequencies allocated to radio and, especially, to television. In confronting the question, two dimensions of inquiry must be emphasized: first the size of the community population; second, historical time. In very small towns, like Plainville, what are conventionally regarded as oudoor sports or sports afield were, early in the socio-economic time of the town, a way of life and not separate activities carried on in time left over from work that could symbolically represent community unity. Here we find work, later to become imbued with play, as work *per se,* somewhat reminiscent of work in such tribal communities as the Sanema

Indians. The study of Plainville is picked up again after a lapse of fifteen years. Sport has emerged—a playing at hunting and fishing—but is part of the conspicuous display of the economically advantaged.

Team sports were established as community representations in Elmtown, Middletown, and in late nineteenth century New Orleans after those communities had already undergone industrialization and had entered a "later" socio-economic epoch. Note well that all those studies were carried on or concerned with communities that had not yet entered the age of television. Curiously, radio provided a rallying point for the people in Middletown concerned with sport in 1925, but, *for reasons not convincingly set forth,* by 1935, the radio was seen as a major factor in decreasing the interest of the people living in that small city. Television did bring people together in Plainville 1955, when television sets were not so widely distributed as they are today. In contrast, those studies made most recently point more precisely to the diffusion of professional sports and their waning importance as collective community representations. Indeed, perhaps the high school (Coleman 1961) has replaced professional sport as a community totem in some cities and towns, or, in some cases, perhaps the development of sport stopped at "adolescence" and never left high school.

> In the past Springdale had had an athletic association whose purpose was to provide public support for sporting activities. It concerned itself with backing town athletic teams, giving athletic banquets and cooperating with the state conservation department....With more recent changes in sports habits, local sporting activities do not hold the interest they once did and the athletic association has ceased to exist.
>
> Sports have become more individual in character and are pursued in more expensive ways. Community baseball teams are no longer able to recruit players in a systematic way. Fishermen who once fished local streams now make long trips to fishing resort regions. Springdalers have now organized their own bowling and rifle teams which compete in regional circuits; golf and tennis enthusiasts drive thirty miles to play.
>
> Organized sports are now limited to the high school athletic program and to youth recreation. High school teams, American Legion Little League Baseball, Youth Recreation handicraft programs and swimming instruction—these are the major areas of organized sporting and athletic activities and they provide the basis for spectatorship in the community.
>
> (Vidich and Bensman 1960: 28)

Of the few community studies focussing on sport in smaller towns and cities, this, in fact, seems to be the case. Middletown in 1935 presents a glaring exception. Only two pages are devoted to sport in that volume (Lynd and Lynd 1937: 291-292) except for very occasional scattered references. Thinking of my own adolescence in 1935, when high school sport was very much a community affair, I tend to be sceptical of their analytic focus in the revisit. Even one of their own observations belies the insignificance they attached to sport during the depression. They write "...in 1931, despite the depression, the citizens gave gold watches to the basketball team when it exalted the city by winning the state championship " (Lynd and Lynd 1937: 291).

Since high school championships are won in state capitols, usually cities, the unifying effects, surely evident in the small towns of the United States, may well find their way periodically into the city Larry Batson has written sensitively on the point:

> In our part of the world, at least, no other event is as broadly appealing, as unreservedly satisfying, as a state high school sports tournament. It is a diversion, of course, but also an affirmation of much that is worthwhile.
>
> They are clean and uncomplicated, these tournaments. For older people, they are a reminder of a time when our lives were less complex, when we were better people than we are now. Or so we tend to believe, blessedly having forgotten much....
>
> People who haven't seen a game in years, who have no link to any of the teams, who had no idea yesterday morning who was playing, had favorites by nightfall....
>
> Some will say they have no team, no favorite, but merely enjoy the enthusiasm and drama. For this lie, these people will be forgiven. It is enough that they abandon dignity for a few days. They need not confess it.
>
> For the players and the schools these tournaments are a joyous explosion of pride. For the rest of us, a reminder of innocence. And if our memory is flawed, what harm?
>
> "Amateur athletics at its purest," said Bud Grant, coach of the Vikings. "Something we don't have any more at any other level."
>
> It was there in amateur baseball when Grant was a youth, "small-town pride and competitiveness that has been lost," he said. "And at the university, too, in those days...the university brought everyone together, all the way from Montana. Now with the recruiting and cajoling, something has gone.
>
> "Now, the state tournaments, all the sports, are the unifying force. There is nothing like them—the atmosphere, the raw enthusiasm of an arena packed with kids."
>
> (Minneapolis *Tribune*, March 10, 1977: 1-B and 3-B)

Further light on the general problem of the relationship between sport and community solidarity is shed by those rare studies that have inquired into the translation of personal involvement with sport and personal identification with the larger community the sport represents, however directly or remotely.

SPORT AND COMMUNITY IDENTIFICATION

In his excellent study of spectatorship, Johnson has mobilized some pertinent observations on this problem. He selected Morristown, Minnesota, a rural hamlet of 670 people sixty-five miles south of Minneapolis. Here, where the corn-fields reach into the village limits, he claims to have found "Super Spectator in the flesh" (Johnson 1971: 219). Stanley Peroutka, forty-six years old and manager of the Land O' Lakes Creamery, tells why:

> It used to be... [f] armers didn't give a damn about sports then. They wouldn't go to no high school games and they wouldn't let their sons go out for sports either because it took them away from the farm. Hell, my farmers didn't know a touchback from a touchdown then. ... [N] ow... [t] hey're talking zigouts and flare passes and blitzes just like they're Bud Wilkinson. A lot of them like baseball best though because they understand it a little better. Most of 'em... have played kitten ball at a Sunday School picnic and they understand the game. Now that *we* got the Twins, there's a real strong baseball following here. I think there's even more people going to our Sunday town team games because of it too. I know that a lot of my farmers at the creamery go up to five, six Twins games a year. Hell, ten years ago these guys never even seen the town team play and here they're up at the big leagues all the time now.
>
> (Johnson 1971: 221–222)

After reporting other similar observations, the conclusion is inescapable. "It is quite a wedding of the worlds, is it not? The major leagues and Morristown, Minnesota, living happily ever after" (Johnson 1971: 222). At least they were living *happily* in 1970! Eternity will have to wait.

In his interesting account of patients variously involved with a sport who have come to his office seeking psychiatric help, Arnold Beisser has observed:

> It is not surprising that in this fluid, centerless mass the citizens seek, sometimes desperately, groups with which they can identify, so to feel they belong... [S] ports appear to have something of the same social function.... The fan in relationship to his team is like the member of a family or tribe. He can show intense feelings.... he partakes of the secrets of the tribe.... he exhibits tangible evidence of belonging.
>
> (Beisser 1967: 173)

He goes on to discuss the case of a St. Louis Cardinal fan who moved to Los Angeles. Apparently, the move was not only one of relocation but intense dislocation, for the displaced fan appeared to Beisser as an extremely disoriented and bewildered person who could not find his way around the city to perform the elementary activities of quotidian life. The case presents almost a fairy-tale dénouement. Beisser facilitated the reidentification of this "tribal person" with the relevant recently established "totem" of Los Angeles—the Dodgers—and the rootless fan was recostumed with a Dodgers' cap. All this entered into and was an important part of the patient's reorientation and successful therapy. Even one case, however, exemplifies how deeply community identifications can penetrate the self via the route of sports involvement.

This author's study of sport fandom and urban identification seems to be the only study on a large scale that has directly attacked the problem (Stone 1968). What has come to be called "classic" urban sociology emphasizes the individuation, depersonalizing, segmentalizing, and alienating social psychological consequences of urban living in its preoccupation with the trend away from the presumably warm and intimate primary relations of the rural countryside to the cold and calculating secondary relations neces- sarily engaging people caught up in the urbanization process. After World War II, empirical studies began to multiply documenting the existence of primary or quasi-primary relations in unlikely metro- politan settings, such as stores, taverns, orchestra halls, ghettoes, and slums, as well as among readers of the local community newspapers and those who periodically reclined on couches as they recited their troubles to the willing ears of psychiatrists and psychoanalysts (for a price, of course).

In 1960, this author researched sport involvement as a source of subjective identification among the residents of Minneapolis and its suburbs. Intentionally the cards were stacked against the likelihood of verifying the general hypothesis. The hypothesis was, therefore, specified to read: Under objectively improbable conditions, sport fans will more frequently develop subjective identifications with their larger community of residence than will residents less involved or uninvolved with sports. A systematic analytic sample of 566 was drawn and the hypothesis was tested on 515 adult men and women from high, middle, and low socio- economic strata, living in the central city or suburbs of metropolitan Minneapolis, and providing adequate responses for the test. Two measures of community identification were employed: 1) a measure of objective integration with the community, and 2) a measure of subjective identification or "felt belongingness." Sport involvement was indicated by self reference as a fan of a sport designated as the respondent's favorite spectator sport. Fandom was independently verified. Fans whose favorite sport was a spectator sport were termed "spectator fans;" those whose favorite sport was a participant sport, but who saw themselves as fans of some spectator sport, were called "participant fans." All others were designated "non-fans." From this group, one hundred respondents with low objective integration scores were selected, and differences in subjective identification with the larger community were analyzed for fans and non-fans. After a finer analysis, it was found that subjective identification with the community under objectively improbable conditions (low integration scores) was most frequent among participant fans (67%); next highest among non-fans whose favorite sport was a participant sport (44%); and lowest among spectator fans and non-fans (28% and 25%). Thus, in the Minneapolis metropolitan area in 1960, sport participation buttressed by involved spectatorship contributed to community identification under objectively improbable conditions. Sheer involved spectatorship did not, and non-fans showed even less subjective identification, although the difference was not statistically significant, under such conditions. These *directions* held when socio-economic stratum was held constant (frequencies were insufficient for more precise statistical tests).

CONCLUSION

We can now assess how these diverse studies bear on the problem of whether and to what extent sport as a collective representation of community life has become diffused and weakened in the larger society. Our data have been taken, for the most part, from studies conducted in the United States. First, there is no question about the diffusion of sport—its diffusion has been massive. In the 1960 Minneapolis study, only six of five hundred and sixty-two persons responding to the question: "What activities do you think of, when you hear the word, 'sport'?" mentioned no activities (Stone 1976b: 145–146). Five hundred and forty (95%) named one or more favorite sports (Stone 1976b). Anderson and Stone's recent retest of that study (1979) shows that even that proportion has increased. As a matter of fact, with the increase of leisure time in the United States, both spectatorship of and participation in sports have undergone dramatic increases. Data supporting this assertion are almost everywhere at hand and too extensive to enumerate here. They are to be found in market studies, Nielsen ratings, and special researches such as those carried out by the National Outdoor Recreation Resources Review Commission in the early 'sixties. A recent imposing survey of such materials and their analysis has been provided by Barry McPherson (1975: 243–75).

It is far more difficult to assess whether or not the force of sport as a unifying representation has been weakened due to the lack of any early benchmark studies specifically devoted to the question. On balance, however, this does seem to be the case, particularly for spectator sports. Our guess, for example, is that high school sports cannot compete with professional sports for the attention of spectators, though the attention to them may well be more intense. This may, in fact, be true of the players themselves who may be observed dramatizing professional players rather than "playing their own game" as they compete on high school fields or in gymnasiums (Johnson 1971: 200-221). Nevertheless, spectatorship does seem to have the consequence of heightening community involvement derived through sport participation, and sport participation is increasing in the larger United States population as it is facilitated by increasing leisure time. Furthermore, note should be made of the ways in which the spectator, at least symbolically, has been brought into the game itself. In basketball this can be observed in the evolution of the backboard. Originally constructed of chicken wire to prevent spectators from interfering with the play, the backboard became a board. As a wooden rectangle, it became incorporated into the play. Then it was transformed into a semi-circular board to provide the spectator with a less restricted view. Now it is glass and permits a full view of the game by the spectator, despite his seating location (Stone 1976a: 137-38). It is certainly pertinent that the "player of the game," in whose name and to whose university a one thousand dollar scholarship is awarded, was designated by NBC as the Notre Dame student body whose relentless cheering presumably inspired the Notre Dame victory over Marquette University (1977 NCAA Champions) at the end of the regular 1976-77 season.

REFERENCES

Anderson, D. and G. Stone. 1979. A fifteen year analysis of socio-economic strata differences in the meaning given to sport by metropolitans. Pp. 167-184 in M. Krotee, ed. *The Dimensions of Sport Sociology*. West Point: Leisure Press.

Beisser, A. 1967. *The Madness in Sports*. New York: Appleton-Century-Crofts.

Brier, W.J. 1969. *The Frightful Punishment: Con Orem and Montana's Great Glove Fights of the 1860's*. Missoula: University of Montana Press.

Coleman, J.S. 1961. *The Adolescent Society*. Glencoe, Illinois: The Free Press.

Durkheim, E. 1938. *The Rules of Sociological Method*. Chicago: University of Chicago Press.

Durkheim, E. 1947a. *The Division of Labor in Society*. Glencoe, Ill.: Free Press.

Durkheim, E. 1947b. *The Elementary Forms of the Religious Life*. Glencoe, Illinois: The Free Press.

Encyclopedia Brittannica. 1976. 15th edition.

Frankenberg, R. 1957. *Village on the Border: A Study of Religion, Politics and Football in a North Wales Community.* London: Cohen and West.

Gallaher, A., Jr. 1961. *Plainville Fifteen Years Later.* New York: Columbia University Press.

Goffman, E. 1963. *Behavior in Public Places.* Glencoe, Illinois: The Free Press.

Hammond, J.L. and Barbara Hammond. 1947. *The Bleak Age.* London: Penguin Books, Ltd.

Hollingshead, August B. 1949. *Elmtown's Youth.* New York: John Wiley and Son, Inc.

Huizinga, J. 1955. *Homo Ludens: A Study of the Play Element in Culture.* Boston: The Beacon Press.

Jobling, I.F. 1976. Urbanization and sport in Canada. Pp. 64–77 in R.S. Gruneau and J.G. Albinson, eds. *Canadian Sport: Sociological Perspectives.* Don Mills, Ontario: Addison-Wesley.

Johnson, W. 1971. *Super Spectator and the Electric Lilliputians.* Boston: Little, Brown and Company.

Listiak, Alan. 1976. Legitimate deviance and social class: bar behavior during Grey Cup Week. Pp. 403–433 in R.S. Gruneau and J.G. Albinson, eds. *Canadian Sport: Sociological Perspectives.* Don Mills, Ontario: Addison-Wesley.

Lynd, R.S. and H.M. Lynd. 1929. *Middletown.* New York: Harcourt, Brace and Company.

Lynd, R.S. and H.M. Lynd. 1937. *Middletown in Transition.* New York: Harcourt, Brace and Company.

Manning, F.E. 1973. *Black Clubs in Bermuda.* Ithaca: Cornell University Press.

Martindale, D. 1960. *American Society.* Princeton: D. Van Nostrand Company.

McPherson, B.D. 1975. Sport consumption and the economics of consumerism. Pp. 243–75 in D.W. Ball and J.W. Loy, eds. *Sport and Social Order.* Reading, Mass.: Addison-Wesley.

Mead, G.H. 1934. *Mind, Self, and Society.* Chicago: University of Chicago Press.

Michener, J.A. 1976. *Sports in America.* New York: Random House, Inc.

Minneapolis *Tribune.* March 18, 1976; April 16, 1976; March 10 1977; March 18, 1977; March 19, 1977; May 2, 1977; May 31, 1980.

Rooney, J.F. 1974. *A Geography of American Sport: From Cabin Creek to Anaheim.* Reading, Mass.: Addison-Wesley.

Seeley, J.R. et. al. 1976. Sports and career in Crestwood Heights. Pp. 354–61 in R.S. Gruneau and J.G. Albinson, eds. *Canadian Sport: Sociological Perspectives.* Don Mills, Ontario: Addison-Wesley.

Somers, D.A. 1972. *The Rise of Sports in New Orleans.* Baton Rouge: Louisiana State University Press.

Stone, G.P. 1968. Sport fandom and urban identification. Paper. *AAS-Meetings.* Dallas.

Stone, G.P. 1973. American sports: play and display. Revised version. Pp. 65–85 in J.T. Talamini and C.H. Page, eds. *Sport and Society.* Boston: Little, Brown and Company.

Stone, G.P. 1976a. Soziale Sinnbezüge des Sports in der Massengesellschaft.

Pp. 132-45 in G. Lüschen and K. Weis, eds. *Die Soziologie des Sports.* Darmstadt: Luchterhand.

Stone, G.P. 1976b. Some meanings of American sport: an extended view. Pp. 143-55 in M. Hart, ed. *Sport in the Socio-Cultural Process.* 2nd edition. Dubuque, Iowa: William C. Brown.

Stone, G.P. and G.I. Stone. 1976. Ritual as game: playing at becoming a Sanema. *Quest,* 26, summer: 28-47.

Veblen, T. 1934. *The Theory of the Leisure Class.* New York: Modern Library.

Vidich, A.J. and J. Bensman. 1960. *Small Town in Mass Society.* Garden City, N.Y.: Doubleday.

Weber, M. 1930. *The Protestant Ethic and the Spirit of Capitalism.* London: Allen and Unwin.

Weber, M. 1962. *The City.* New York: Collier Books.

West, J. 1945. *Plainville, U.S.A.* New York: Columbia University Press.

SOCIALIZATION INTO AND THROUGH SPORT INVOLVEMENT

Barry D. McPherson

INTRODUCTION

Socialization is a complex social process designed to produce as an end product an individual who is prepared (i.e., socialized) for the requirements of participation in society in general, and for the performance of a variety of social roles in specific sub-groups within that society.

While the socialization process has functioned in both primitive and modern societies, it is only since the early 1900s that the phenomenon has been the subject of scholarly investigation. Initially, the findings and explanations were based on the insights and observations of philosophers and psychologists who were intrigued with the problem of how the human animal became a human social being. With the advent of experimental psychology, interest in child development was initiated, including the study of child rearing-techniques. More recently, a third stage has suggested that individuals are involved in the socialization process throughout the life-cycle, and hence, studies related to adolescent and adult socialization have appeared in the literature (Brim and Wheeler 1966; Goslin 1969: 821–1002; Mortimer and Simmons 1978).

This article describes conceptual frames of reference and outlines the process of socialization in general; reviews recent findings which seek to describe socialization "into" a variety of sport roles; and, reviews the general socialization effects resulting from participation in sport.

THE SOCIALIZATION PROCESS

Theories and Conceptual Approaches

In recent years a vast amount of literature pertaining to the process of socialization has appeared, including four major publications (Clausen 1968; Goslin 1969; Sewell 1963; Zigler and Child 1969). A review of this literature indicates that several conceptual and theoretical approaches have been utilized, including psychoanalysis, psychoanalytically-oriented social anthropology, a normative-maturational approach, a developmental-cognitive approach, a genetic and constitutional approach, and various learning theory approaches. To date, the social learning orientations have been the most productive in terms of both theoretical development and empirical findings (Bandura and Walters 1963; Brim and Wheeler 1966; Clausen 1968). Furthermore, an understanding of the process has been facilitated by the contributions of role theory (Sarbin and Allen 1968) and reference group theory (Kemper 1968).

Social learning theory is based on the concepts of "modeling," "imitation," and "vicarious learning." Bandura and Walters (1963) and Bandura (1969) argued that most social behavior, including the learning of specific social roles, is acquired by observing the behavior of significant others (role models or reference groups), without the observer reproducing the observed behavior at that point in time. That is, unlike traditional stimulus-response learning, the novice does not immediately practice the behavior and receive feedback or direct reinforcement. Rather, the behaviors are observed, assimilated and subsequently exhibited in appropriate situations. The models for this imitation process can be real (e.g., adults, peers) or symbolic (e.g., observing television characters whereby the individual does not have direct face-to-face interaction with the role model).

Role theory recognizes that a child is born into an ongoing society with common symbols, established patterns of behavior in recognized social positions, and, it is through others that the child learns these elements of the social world. This theory seeks to explain the process by which an individual becomes a functioning member of the group, and does not seek to account for the unique expression in interpersonal relationships of particular attitudes, opinions and traits. According to role theory the learning process consists of the role of socializer, occupied by established members of the system (i.e., significant others), and the role of socializee, occupied by the newcomers (Jones 1965).

Reference group theory is a third paradigm which has some utility in helping us to understand the socialization process. According to this model "a person orients himself to groups and other individuals and uses them as significant means of reference for his own behavior, attitudes or feelings" (Deutsch and Kraus 1965: 193). The importance of reference groups in the socialization process was first noted by Kemper (1968) who suggested that reference groups have different functions as socializing agents in that they can serve as normative groups, role models, or audience groups. Thus, the normative group (e.g., the family) interacts with the individual and provides guides to action by establishing norms and espousing values; the role model demonstrates how something is done in a technical sense; and, the audience group, which does not take notice of the individual, is recognized by the individual who attributes certain values and attitudes to this group and attempts to behave in accordance with these values.

In summary, a great deal of social learning occurs through observation, imitation, role-playing, interaction with significant others and identification. However, it must be remembered that individual patterns of learning may vary because of sex, social class, community or ethnic differences within the same society; or, because of individual differences in life-style or exposure to social learning agents.

The Process of Socialization

Although an extensive review of the parameters influencing the process of socialization (cf. McPherson 1972) is not possible here the following is a synopsis of the "social role-social system approach" advocated by Sewell (1963). The three main elements of the socialization process include: *Significant others* (Woelfel and Haller 1971) or socializing agents who serve as role models; *social situations* (e.g., the home, school, gymnasium, neighborhood) and, *role learners* who are characterized by a wide variety of relevant ascribed and achieved personal attributes (e.g., personality traits, attitudes, motivations, values, attitudes, motor ability, race, ethnicity, gender). More specifically, the learning of a social role takes place when a role aspirant is exposed to a variety of stimuli and reinforcements provided by significant others (e.g., parents, peers, coaches, teachers, professional athletes, etc.) who are within one or more norm-encumbered social systems such as the family, school, church, peer group, sport group, or the mass media. Furthermore, within each social system these significant others have the potential to facilitate or inhibit role learning depending on the unique values, norms, sanctions and opportunity sets (Smelser 1962) they provide at any given point in time.

It must be recognized that a given social system (e.g., the school) may be supportive, indifferent or in direct opposition to the learning of a role, and that the influence of a given system may vary over time depending on the role aspirant's stage in the life-cycle. For example, while parents and siblings may be important, if not essential, in the socialization process during childhood, they become of less importance, or of no importance, when considering the learning of specific roles during young adulthood.

To illustrate the foregoing, the following digression provides an example of how and to what extent an individual is socialized into the role of elite hockey player (Clark 1977; McPherson 1977). Although a certain amount of trial-and-error learning occurs, especially with respect to the learning of sport skills, much of the learning occurs through imitation and modeling of significant others including: parents and siblings within the family system; coaches, peers and other players in the hockey milieu; teachers and peers within the schools; and, those who appear in the mass media, including reporters, telecasters, and professional athletes (Goldstein and Bredemeier 1977; Smith and Blackman 1978). Each significant other has the potential to facilitate or inhibit a child's development depending on the values, norms, sanctions and opportunity set provided at a given point in time. For example, if hockey, and especially the attainment of a high level of success, does not rank high in the leisure or career hierarchy of values held by parents, peers and teachers; if positive reinforcement for achieving in hockey is not received from these significant others; and, if an opportunity set is not provided so that equipment, ice-time and coaching are available, then it is highly unlikely that an individual exposed to this type of socialization setting would ever become involved in hockey, or become an elite hockey player, regardless of how much natural ability they may have.

On the other hand, an individual with parents, friends, coaches and teachers who encourage and reinforce their interest and success in hockey; who learns that professional or Olympic hockey is a legitimate career path; and, who receives good equipment and coaching; is likely to continue in the game and establish aspirations to attain the highest level of success that his physical skills permit. In fact, this latter social milieu often permits an individual with marginal physical skills to attain high levels of success, whereas in the former environment he may drop out of competitive hockey because he does not receive sufficient social support from his significant others.

Factors Influencing Role Acquisition

The nature of the role dictates to some extent the socialization process, and therefore an understanding of the characteristics of a particular role is an essential prerequisite to the study of the process whereby that role is learned. Thus, the first problem for an investigator involves identifying and classifying the many roles within a given social system. Kenyon (1969) presented a conceptual framework outlining a number of primary and secondary roles, such as participant, consumer and producer which are found within a sport system. These three categories can be further delineated to include specific participant (e.g., hockey, football, tennis players), consumer (direct or indirect), or producer (e.g., team, owner, manufacturer, official) roles. Moreover, each of the specific roles includes a behavioral, cognitive and affective component which may vary in importance depending on the role. For example, whereas the role of sport consumer may demand higher levels of involvement in the cognitive and affective dimensions, the role of official would require more skill in the behavioral and cognitive dimensions (McPherson 1976b).

Although it is not possible in this paper to delineate the role expectancies associated with a variety of sport roles, as an example, those who play the role of sport consumer may be expected to: (1) invest varying amounts of time and money in numerous forms of direct and indirect secondary sport involvement; (2) have varying degrees of knowledge concerning sport performers, sport statistics, and sport strategies; (3) have an affective (emotive) involvement with one or more individuals or groups in the sport system; (4) experience, and either internalize or verbalize feelings and mood states while consuming a sport event; (5) employ sport as a major topic of conversation with peers and strangers; and, (6) arrange their leisure-time lifestyle around professional and amateur sport events.

Regardless of the role, there appear to be four stages which a role incumbent must pass through in order to be socialized into that role (Thornton and Nardi 1975). Each stage is characterized by an increasing awareness of implicit or explicit expectations encompassing: how they should behave in that social position; the appropriate attitudes and values they should hold; and, the specific knowledges or skills they should acquire. Thus, each stage involves interaction between individuals and externally induced expectations.

The first stage is anticipatory wherein the role aspirant, not yet in the position, holds a number of stereotyped expectations. These are often incomplete representations of reality in that only the overt, positive facets of the role are known and recognized. For example, for the role of professional athlete, the job insecurity, the fatigue of travelling, and the possibility of a short career with an involuntary retirement are seldom recognized by children or adolescents.

Thornton and Nardi (1975: 876) describe the second stage as the "formal" period wherein the individual enters the social position and encounters official and formal expectations concerning behavior and abilities. This stage is characterized by a high degree of consensus between the significant others and the role aspirant which results in conformity. This would be characteristic of a first year professional or college athlete (i.e., a rookie).

The "informal" third stage involves the learning of unofficial and informal expectations pertaining to the attitudinal and cognitive features of the role which are transmitted through interaction with individuals. Much of this learning for the professional athlete takes place in the "backstage" area (Goffman 1959) such as, restaurants, locker rooms and hotel rooms. It is in this stage that the individual begins to shape the role to "fit" himself, his past experiences and future objectives, and to work out an individual style of role performance (Thornton and Nardi 1975: 879).

The "personal" stage occurs last and is an extension of the previous stage. Individuals now are able to impose their own expectations and conceptions on roles and thereby modify role expectations according to their own personalities. By this stage in the process they are able to influence the expectations others hold for them and thereby merge the "self" with the "role." Thus, we see similar roles played with different "style," both on and off the field.

The process is also influenced by a number of macro and microsystem factors and by ascribed social categories. At the macro level, within a given society, there is often a dominant ideology which reflects the social values and norms and which influences the behavioral patterns in that country or community, including those related to sport. Thus, there tend to be both intra-societal regional differences and cross-national differences in the socialization process.

Within both macro and micro social systems, readily identifiable social categories influence the socialization process. These categories, most of which are ascribed rather than achieved, include: social class background, ethnicity, religion, gender, place and type of residence, ordinal position and age. Since it is possible to group people into social categories, rights, expectations and opportunities in a variety of domains are allocated according to prevailing values or beliefs. These ascribed attributes often dictate an individual's life chances. For example, these categories may influence whether the individual has access to certain sport opportunities or sport organizations. Interestingly, most of these attributes derive from the family system but remain as influential factors throughout the life-cycle and operate in most social systems. If an individual is situated in two or more of these categories (e.g., a lower class black female) they may experience discrimination and therefore the possibility of their becoming involved in certain leisure phenomena may be highly restricted. Other categories such as social class background, ethnicity, and religion influence the socialization process by virtue of both the opportunity set that members of certain groups can provide, and by the prevailing values, attitudes and norms which derive from these specific sub-cultures.

Further, although changes are occurring, there are unique sex differences in the socialization process (Hall 1978; Greendorfer 1978b; Loy, McPherson and Kenyon 1978: 224–225; Lever 1978). This occurs because there are different expectations for the "female" and the "male" role in most societies as a result of differing values, norms and sanctions which are considered appropriate with respect to involvement in sport and physical activity (Lever 1976).

An individual's ordinal position also influences the socialization process in that a first born does not have the same opportunity to imitate siblings as does the later born. For example, Nisbett (1968) suggested that first borns, compared to later borns, are more psychologically dependent upon adults, have less freedom selecting activities, are more vulnerable to stress, and are less capable of enduring pain. Furthermore, both Nisbett (1968) and Gould and Landers (1972) found that the first born child is much less likely than later borns to participate in more dangerous sports such as hockey, football, and wrestling. Similar findings have been reported by Yiannakis (1976) and Casher (1977). More specifically, Casher studied individual sports of a low-harm and high-harm nature and found that the proportion of athletes in the more dangerous sports increased directly with birth order from first born (41%) to second born (45%) to third born (75%).

Age is another social category which influences the process. That is, there are age-related norms which are unique to particular cultures or sub-cultures and which determine appropriate or inappropriate behavior at particular points in the life-cycle. Thus, whereas a female may be permitted to participate in sport and physical activity during childhood, she may receive negative sanctions for continuing this type of behavior as she approaches early adolescence. Age, alone and in conjunction with gender can greatly influence the process of socialization into sport roles (McPherson 1978b).

The geographical area where an individual spends the first ten or fifteen years of life also influences the process. It is this location within the country and within a community (whether one lives in a rural or urban environment, in an apartment or a house, or in the suburbs versus the urban core) which determines the opportunity set that is provided to become involved in specific leisure activities (Rooney 1974).

To summarize, the socialization process is a complex phenomenon which is highly dependent upon formal and informal learning, imitation of significant others, and the influence of a variety of system-induced factors and ascribed social categories. The remaining sections discuss these parameters as they pertain to socialization and sport.

SOCIALIZATION INTO SPORT ROLES

Introduction

Despite the importance of understanding how and why some people become involved in sport while others do not, relatively little research has been undertaken in this area. However, some recent efforts have been directed toward this problem and findings are presented for two major modes of sport involvement: primary involvement, including the role of elite (Olympic calibre) athlete and college athlete; and, secondary involvement, including the role of sport consumer, coach and sport executive. In addition, related information is presented to indicate the impact of macro and micro systems and social categories on the process of becoming socialized into sport roles. Throughout, the reader should note that the social systems exert varying degrees of influence according to the sport, the stage in the life-cycle, the gender of the role aspirant, and, the particular component of the role being considered (i.e., the behavioral, affective or cognitive domain).

Socialization Into Primary Sport Roles

Kenyon and McPherson (1973) and Kenyon (1977) considered the factors which influence an individual to achieve the role of Olympic track and field athlete. For most, involvement in sport began early in life with 96 percent indicating that they participated in football, basketball or baseball in elementary school. Moreover, over 65 percent indicated that they participated in football, basketball or baseball in elementary school. Furthermore, over 65 percent reported that they were "winners" the first time they competed in a sport event, thereby suggesting that a high degree of sport aptitude was present at an early age. However, ability alone does not totally account for their involvement and later success in the role of track and field athlete since 50 percent of the subjects did not participate or compete in track and field until after they entered high school. That is, the learning of the role was situationally influenced by significant others who either competed themselves and served as role models or taught and reinforced the role behavior within a specific social setting, namely, the school. For example, over 75 percent of the respondents indicated that their interest in the activity was first aroused in school. In addition, over 80 percent of the athletes reported that they attended a school where the students and teachers valued track and field and considered it to be an important extra-curricular activity. Thus, a social situation which values certain patterns of behavior and provides opportunities for the learning of that behavior influences which roles will be learned.

In addition to the social situation, significant others with whom the respondents interacted also contributed to the socialization process. This influence appeared to be sport specific. For example, a peer group (e.g., track athletes) and school personnel (teachers and coaches) were reported as the agents who were most responsible for arousing an initial interest in track and field. This contrasts with the response to a similar question concerning involvement in the traditional team sports of baseball, basketball and football where the parents were found to be considerably more important than school personnel. In general, it appears that the elite track and field athlete receives encouragement and reinforcement from many sources, several of which act simultaneously.

McPherson (in Kenyon and McPherson 1973) examined the psychosocial factors influencing college tennis and ice hockey players to become involved in sport. He found that interest in sport was initially aroused within the family, mainly by the father. In many cases the parents were still actively involved in sport as a participant, and thus served as role models. However, during the high school years family influence decreased and any new interest in physical activity was aroused mainly by peers, coaches and physical education teachers. Thus the source of influence changes at different periods in the life-cycle. It was interesting to note that approximately 75 percent of the respondents reported that they were secondarily involved via the mass media (e.g., television, radio and newspapers) prior to their participation in sport. In summary, it appears that college athletes receive a stimulus to compete from involved peers and from a home environment which considers sport to be an important facet of life. This latter finding is supported by Pudelkiewicz (1970: 93) who found that a positive evaluation of sport by Polish parents gives rise to sport interests among the children. Similarly, Snyder and Spreitzer (1973) found a positive relationship between parent's interest in sport and the respondent's sport involvement. This held for both sexes and all three dimensions of sport involvement (i.e., the behavioral, affective and cognitive domains).

Family support may be even more essential for female athletes as noted by Malumphy (1970) who found that the family was a major factor in college women continuing to compete. Furthermore, the influence of the mother may be more important for some sports than for others. For example, the study reported by McPherson (in Kenyon and McPherson 1973) indicated that mothers were more influential in arousing interest and providing reinforcement for the tennis players than for the hockey players.

A final significant other for college athletes is the professional athlete. Almost all respondents reported they had an "idol" and, since a Canadian sample was utilized, it is not surprising that most of the idols listed by both hockey and tennis players were outstanding professional hockey players. However, as the tennis respondents reached college age, a highly ranked tennis player often replaced the hockey idol. It was interesting to note that for the hockey players there was a positive relationship, which increased with age, between the position played by the respondent and that played by the idol.

In a related study by Kenyon and Grogg (in Kenyon and McPherson 1973) eighty-seven intercollegiate athletes in a variety of sports at the University of Wisconsin were interviewed. The social situation in which interest in a specific sport was first generated varied by sport. For example, interest in baseball was initiated about equally in the home and the school; for fencing and crew the school was most important; for football and hockey the home and neighbourhood; for swimming, the home and club or recreation agency; and, for track the home and the school. Finally, the data suggested "opportunity set" differences. For example, the athlete's place of residence during high school varied among sports in that none of the hockey players, swimmers, or tennis players grew up in the open country or on a farm, indicating, as one might expect, that specific facilities and a motivational climate necessary for learning and perfecting certain sport roles are not readily available in rural areas.

Vaz (1972), in a study of the culture of young hockey players, found that certain criteria were essential for initiation into the role of professional hockey player. He reported that aggressive fighting behavior is normative, institutionalized conduct and as such is an essential facet in socializing future professional hockey players. This behavior, because it is institutionalized, becomes an integral part of the role obligation of young hockey players and is learned by subsequent novices via formal and informal socialization. A similar but more detailed analysis of professional hockey players was provided by Faulkner (1975).

More recently, Clark (1977) sampled 116 Junior A and 133 College hockey players in Ontario to determine whether patterns of early socialization vary for those who were about the same age (e.g., 18–20) but who competed at different levels of competition. To illustrate, most professional hockey players are drafted from Junior A teams and hence this level of competition represents pre-professional training. This was clearly illustrated by the motives reported for being still involved in hockey at this age. Whereas the college players reported pursuing hockey mainly for fun and enjoyment, the Junior A players reported that they were training for a career in professional hockey. While the early socialization experiences were relatively similar, the Junior A players appeared to receive significantly more encouragement, both material and non-material, to pursue a hockey career as they grew older. Not surprisingly, the college players were superior students at all stages in the life-cycle. Thus, inherent in the socialization process may be unique values and inherent skills which channel those who have similar life-chances in childhood into different career paths in the later adolescent years.

Similarly, McPherson (1977) administered a questionnaire to 109 players in the National Hockey League. Again, the players recalled that most social reinforcement was received from the family, especially the father during early childhood and adolescence. Not surprisingly, during the high school years, 21% indicated that teachers discouraged their participation, most likely because of inferior academic performance. The mean age at which the players report that they first realized that they had the ability, interest and motivation to attempt a professional hockey career was 17.3 years. A firm decision was made for most 1 year later and hockey became a full-time occupation for most at a mean age of 19.7 years.

In one of the first attempts to utilize path analysis in the study of sport phenomena, Kenyon (1970) examined the factors influencing college students to become involved in sport at two stages in the life-cycle, namely, high school and college. An examination of the path coefficients indicated that a male who has a high level of sport aptitude, who lives in a large community which has adequate facilities and instructors (i.e., a good opportunity set), and who receives encouragement from significant others from within and outside the school will have a greater chance of being socialized into a primary sport role.

While most of the early studies of sport role socialization concentrated exclusively on male athletes, more recent studies have demonstrated that while the general model holds (Greendorfer 1978a; Hall 1976, 1978) for females, there are sex differences in the process which appear to focus on opportunity set and significant others. For example, Theberge (1977), in a study of 82 women professional golfers, found that the most significant others in their career socialization were parents, peers and a teaching professional. Moreover a form of social differentiation was present in their occupational socialization process in that 66% became increasingly dependent with age on access to private golf clubs for playing privileges and lessons. In fact, by 13 years of age most were receiving private lessons from teaching professionals at private clubs. Again, this indicates the extent to which the sport role socialization process is somewhat sport specific.

A number of studies in recent years have examined the influence of a variety of significant others on the sport role socialization process for females (Bohren 1977; Greendorfer 1977, 1978b; Greendorfer and Lewko 1978; Smith 1978; Snyder and Spreitzer 1976). Generally, these studies have found that a high value climate which encourages sport involvement must be present in the family, often in the form of actual participation by both parents (especially the mother) and overt encouragement for their daughter's involvement. Moreover, while the family and peer group, especially male athletes, appear to be the most influential significant others for women, regardless of sport, there appears to be a need for a greater number and variety of significant others for females as opposed to males, if they are to continue being involved into the high school and college years.

Finally, since involvement in sport during adulthood is of recent concern, some mention should be made of the importance of childhood socialization for later participation during the adult years of the life-cycle. Studies by Spreitzer and Snyder (1976), Kelly (1977), Laakso (1978) and McPherson (1978b) have all found that involvement as an adult is greatly influenced by whether sport became part of one's life-style during childhood. This is consistent with the continuity theory of aging (Atchley, 1977) which suggests that behaviors, attitudes and values acquired at one stage in the life-cycle predispose an individual to similar patterns of social participation at later stages. Thus, although longitudinal studies are not present, it might be predicted that a favourable sport role socialization process initiated within a nuclear family will have pronounced cumulative effects upon subsequent generations, assuming opportunity sets are reasonably comparable.

In summary, it appears that college athletes and Olympic aspirants become interested and involved in sport by age 8 or 9; that they participate, usually with a great deal of success, in a number of sports before they begin to specialize in one sport; that they receive positive sanctions to become involved and to compete from a number of significant others, of which the family, peer group and coaches appear to be the most influential. Although the general socialization process has a number of common elements, there are differences in the process between sports, for each sex and at different stages in the life-cycle.

Socialization Into Secondary Sport Roles

In comparison to the study of primary sport roles, relatively few studies have been concerned with socialization into such secondary roles as sport consumer, coach and sport leader. In one of the earliest studies of the sport consumer, Stone (1957) found that the formation of loyalty to a team occurred prior to formation of loyalty to a specific player. He also noted that men form these loyalties at an earlier age than women, and that there are class differences as to when these loyalties are initiated.

In a paper primarily designed to test the utility of path analysis for sport sociology, Kenyon (1970) investigated the causal factors influencing college students to consume major league baseball and the 1964 Summer Olympic Games. Although most of the variance in the two models remained unexplained, this initial attempt indicated that the most influential factors leading to baseball consumption were, in order of importance: sport aptitude, general sport interest in high school, involvement by same-sex peers in sport consumption, and secondary involvement in baseball during high school. The most important factors accounting for the consumption of the Mexico Olympic Games included: secondary involvement in the previous Olympic Games, and knowledge about the athletes who participated in the Tokyo Olympics.

In a secondary analysis of factors hypothesized to be important in the sport socialization of male adolescents in Canada, the United States and England, Kelly (1970) found that frequency of attendance at sport events was directly related to family size and indirectly related to age. He also noted that the frequency of attendance at winter sport events was positively associated with social class background in Canada and the United States, but negatively associated in England.

McPherson (1976b) constructed and tested an axiomatic theory to explain the process whereby urban-dwelling adolescents were socialized into the role of sport consumer. It was hypothesized that the degree of consumer role socialization is a function of the collective influence of significant others and the opportunity set found in the family, peer group, school, and community social systems. This study employed multiple regression analyses to test an additive and a multiplicative model for both a male and a female cohort. The results indicated, that for the male cohort, the peer group, the family, and the school were the most influential social systems in order of importance. For the female cohort, the family, the peer group and the community were most important. This study suggested that social systems vary in their degree of influence in the process of learning a specific leisure role and that the process varies by sex. Furthermore, it appears that adolescents are socialized into a specific role by being exposed to significant others who engage in consummatory behavior, and thereby serve as role models and reinforcing agents for role aspirants who subsequently imitate and interact with them.

In a more detailed analysis (McPherson 1976a) the specific factors operating within each system were analyzed. It was found that, for males, if there is a high frequency of interaction concerning sport phenomena with significant others in the family and peer group, and if there is a high degree of sport consumption by the peer group, then socialization into the role of sport consumer is facilitated. Similarly, for females, if there is a high frequency of sport-oriented interaction with significant others in the family and in the community, if the family and peer groups have a high degree of sport consumption, and if the family places a high value on sport participation and sport consumption, then socialization into the role of sport consumer is likely to occur more readily.

Although many leadership roles are found within sport, few have been the subject of empirical inquiry. Bratton (1971) investigated the demographic characteristics of executive (e.g., president, vice-president, treasurer, regional representatives, etc.) members of two Canadian amateur sport associations and found sport differences. For example, the volleyball executives were ten years younger than the swimming executives, and a majority played the role of player as well as that of executive. Furthermore, Catholics were under-represented and people of British origin held a large proportion of the executive positions.

In a more comprehensive study of sport executives, Beamish (1978) compiled a socio-economic and demographic profile of 146 volunteer executives in 22 national amateur sport associations in Canada. He found that 68 percent were drawn from high status white collar occupations, 66 percent had a university degree and most were in the highest quintile in terms of annual income. Furthermore, most were involved in sport themselves, with 50 percent having competed at the provincial level at least, and 25 percent having been a competitor at the international level. Other background factors indicated that most were from large urban centres and most of their fathers were located in high status white collar occupations. Thus, a selected sample of elites within Canada are responsible for developing and administering amateur sport policies. In terms of socialization into this position of influence it would appear that an upper-middle class background, a university education and participation as an elite athlete are important opportunity factors in the process. Similar findings have been reported by Kiviaho (1973) for Finnish sport executives. In fact, he found that as executives move up the organizational hierarchy from the local to the district to the national level, a higher occupational position and greater success in sport as an athlete become increasingly important criteria for advancement.

Finally, two other studies have provided descriptive information about the background characteristics of college and youth league coaches. Loy and Sage (1972) analyzed the social background of college football and basketball coaches and found that they came from lower socioeconomic backgrounds. Similarly, McPherson (1974) found that most of the volunteer Canadian (N=852) and American (N=88) minor hockey coaches were originally from blue-collar backgrounds. However, the present occupational prestige of the coaches was found to be equally distributed across the Blishen (1967) Socioeconomic Index, thereby suggesting that volunteer leaders from all socioeconomic strata are involved in minor hockey today.

Societal Factors and Social Attributes
Influencing Socialization Into Sport Roles

As noted earlier, within a given society there is usually a dominant ideology which reflects the social values and norms of that society, including those related to sport.

Recent studies have provided some empirical support that there is a relationship between both ideology (values, norms, beliefs, social expectations) and social structure (division of labor, power structure, class differences) and degree of sport involvement and level of sport performance. Seppänen (1972) examined the relationship between ideology and Olympic success and found that where either Protestant or socialist values predominate a high level of success (i.e., medals) has been attained. In both types of societies achievement via hard work and mastery over others is highly valued. However, he further noted that in recent years the socialist countries have made the greatest improvement because they promote these values more and promote them in all facets of life, not just in the sport milieu. Thus, sport success seems to be a reflection of dominant societal values. In a similar study, Ball (1972) found that Olympic success was related to the possession of human and economic resources, along with a centralized form of political decision-making and authority which maximizes the allocation of these resources.

Similar findings were reported by Novikov and Maksimenko (1972) and Grimes, Kelly and Rubin (1974). They noted that a nation's social structure is related to successful performance, and that in recent years the socialist countries have shown a more consistant increase in performance than the capitalist countries. Levine (1975), based on an examination of the 1972 Summer Olympic Games, found that the following four factors correlated highly with the number of Olympic medals won: gross domestic product, area of the country, having a socialist economy, and newspaper circulation.

Most recently, Kiviaho and Makela (1978) compared the influence of non-material (social and cultural) and material (economic) factors on both absolute success (total number of medals won or points received) and relative success (number of victories in proportion to the population). They found that the non-material factors were less useful in explaining Olympic success. Moreover, more of the variance in absolute success was explained, particularly by per capita income, population size and socialism. Thus, absolute success may reflect the amount of resources which are utilized, whereas relative success may reflect the effectiveness with which resources (even if limited) are used.

Within both the macro and micro social systems a number of ascribed social categories dictate an individual's life chances in sport and determine whether they have access to sport opportunities or sport organizations. For example, the importance of class background as it relates to opportunity set has been noted by a number of investigators (Eggleston 1965; Lüschen 1969; Gruneau 1971; Loy 1972; Crawford 1977). In many countries the lower classes are less involved than the middle or upper classes in most sports, and are virtually excluded from many elite sport roles. For example Gruneau (1972), in an analysis of the athletes of the 1971 Canada Winter games, found that most came from the upper-middle or upper socioeconomic groups.

Other social categories influencing involvement in sport are ethnicity and race. For example, studies by Landry *et al.* (1971), Gruneau (1972) and Marple (1974) have shown that Francophones in Canada are under-represented on Provincial, National and International teams, despite out-performing Anglophones in certain skills (Marple 1974). Similarly, Roy (1974) found that Francophones do not have equal access to the positions of coach and general manager within professional hockey after their playing career is terminated, while McPherson (1978c) found that the process of sport role socialization for both primary and secondary involvement varies for Anglophone and Francophone adults.

In the United States, studies by Loy and McElvogue (1970), Yetman and Eitzen (1972), Pascal and Rapping (1972), Scully (1974), and Eitzen and Sanford (1975) have reported that blacks are under-represented at certain playing positions, thereby indicating that through the socialization process they do not receive the opportunity or encouragement to occupy certain sport roles. More specifically, McPherson (1975) has suggested that blacks may be differentially socialized into specific sport roles.

In addition to class background, race, and ethnicity, religion may also influence the process. Again, this variable is linked to the family of origin. The evidence suggests that Catholics are under-represented while Protestants are over-represented among elite athletes and executives (Seppänen 1972). However, to date no definitive explanation for this finding has been presented although it has been suggested that it is related to the "Protestant Work Ethic."

Another social category which influences the degree of involvement in specific sport roles is the geographical area where an aspirant spends the first ten to fifteen years of life. As noted by Rooney (1974) and Sage and Loy (1978) certain countries and regions of a country produce significantly higher proportions of athletes and coaches, respectively.

Gender is also an important variable in socialization into sport roles. As noted earlier, role learning is facilitated when significant others within each social system provide and reinforce common values and norms. Unfortunately, this is not always the situation experienced by young women during childhood and adolescence.

For example, within a given community a female may see her mother and older female siblings participating and competing in a sport and thus desire to imitate this behavioral pattern. However, she may receive negative sanctions from the school or the peer group (who do not receive this reinforcement in their home). Even within the school system there may be conflicts. For example, whereas a physical education teacher may provide support and encouragement for involvement in sport, a teacher of another subject may provide discouragement. Similarly, there are wide between-community (rural vs. urban) and between-nation differences in values and norms concerning female involvement in sport. For example, in the socialist countries of Eastern Europe boys and girls have equal rights and access to sport activities; sport is a way of life for both males and females; and, equality of rights for women is a norm which has been attained in almost all facets of life.

Because of social system differences it is difficult to establish common values and norms concerning the role of women in sport. This makes social change that much more difficult to attain and may create role conflict for females who get interested in physical activity. Thus women are faced with the dilemma as to whether they should behave according to what is expected of them in their ascribed role as female (whatever that may be in the local community) or whether they should follow their interests and strive to achieve and learn new roles such as that of athlete, business person, politician, etc. For example, in a recent study by Sage and Loudermilk (1979) 26% of the 268 collegiate female athletes reported perceiving role conflict to a great or very great extent. Moreover, athletes who participated in sports which were not traditionally socially approved for women experienced significantly greater role conflict. In this situation they are in a double-bind; they have to worry not only about failure, but also about the reaction of others if they are successful.

This role conflict for females could be resolved in a number of ways. First, they might engage in instrumental acts to modify the external ecology such as attempting to prove their femininity in dress or action (e.g., verbal reactions to the "sex" test at the Olympic Games); by separating the conflicting roles in time and space so that they do not compete in school sport, but only in the community so that they are known as a "female" at school; or, by playing the two roles in a Jekyl and Hyde routine whereby they are highly competitive while playing the sport role and then refuse to discuss or acknowledge their sport roles while playing other social roles. A second way to resolve the conflict might be to attempt to change the beliefs of others and convince them that the "athlete" role is compatible with the "female" role; or they might try to change their own beliefs by arguing that others don't have the right to accept the traditional female stereotype and follow an alternative life-style. The third way to resolve the role conflict could be the most serious and yet the most common as females reach the adolescent years. That is, they drop-out of sport as a participant.

A final category influencing the socialization process is the subculture in which some individuals have been socialized. For example, if one is a member of a particular ethnic, religious or racial group they are often faced with norms and values which differ from those of mainstream society. These differences may have an impact on the socialization process, including the learning of sport roles. For example, McPherson (1975) argued that involvement in specific sport roles by blacks is self-induced rather than due to overt or subtle discrimination by white leaders within the sport system. Based on a descriptive analysis of 96 white athletes and 17 black athletes who competed in the Olympic track and field trials in 1968, it was noted that the opportunity set, the value orientations, and the type of role models present early in life may account for involvement in a particular sport by members of a minority group. More specifically, it was hypothesized that members of a minority group may segregate themselves into specific sport positions due to imitation of members of the minority group who have previously been highly successful in a specific sport role. Some support for this modeling hypothesis was presented by Castine and Roberts (1974). Based on a questionnaire administered to 129 black college athletes attending both predominantly black and predominantly white universities, they reported that 57 percent of the sample who admitted to having a sport idol before high school played the same position as their idol while at high school. Similarly, 48 percent played the same playing position as their sport idol while they were in college.

In summary, the process whereby primary and secondary sport roles are learned seems to vary by sport, by specific roles within a sport, by nation, by sex, and by stage in the life-cycle. Moreover, the process is influenced by both macro and micro system parameters, including ascribed attributes of the socializee. In short, the learning of specific sport roles is a complex phenomenon which is not adequately understood at this point in time.

SOCIALIZATION VIA SPORT

Since sport involves role-playing it is frequently considered to be a basic contributor to the socialization process. For example, since the attitudes and beliefs of individuals have their origins in primary social interaction, it is argued that games and sport provide a milieu for this interaction so that the child can internalize the complexities of the adult world.

Turning to an analysis of the socialization effects which result from playing sport roles, it must be noted that little empirical evidence exists to substantiate the many claims that have been made for the contribution of sport, physical education and physical activity to the general socialization process (Stevenson 1975). As Loy and Ingham (1973: 298) conclude in their review of the relationship between play, games and sport and the psychosocial development of children and youth:

> Socialization via play, games and sport is a complex process having both manifest and latent functions, and involving functional and dysfunctional, intended and unintended consequences. Since research on the topic is limited, one must regard with caution many present empirical findings and most tentative theoretical interpretations of these findings.

The variety of socialization outcomes that have been predicted to result from participation in sport and physical activity can be classified into three types: the development of individual traits and skills;

behavioral and attitudinal learning about the environment; and, learning to interact with the environment. Although it is beyond the scope of this paper to extensively review the literature in each of these areas, a brief overview follows. Groos (1898) noted the saliency of play and games during infancy and childhood in both lower vertebrate and superior primates. The work of Harlow (1964) with young monkeys further demonstrated that the playpen is as important as natural mothering for some facets of the socializing process. This suggests that the dimension of playing games versus non-playing has far reaching consequences for socialization.

Anthropologists have frequently suggested that play and game experiences are structurally isomorphic to experiences in a larger society. For example, in many societies it is largely through imitative play that the individual is patterned for the culture he lives in. As children develop, play behavior becomes more highly structured and may take the form of more complex games. For example, Roberts and Sutton-Smith (1962) in a cross-cultural study of 56 societies related prevalent game forms to cultural configurations. They reported that games of strategy are more likely to be found in structurally-complex societies and are linked directly with obedience training; that games of chance are found where a culture's religious beliefs emphasize the benevolence or coerciveness of supernatural beings and are linked with training for responsibility; and that games of physical skill are salient whenever the culture places a high value on the mastery of the environment and on personal achievement. In their development of the conflict-enculturation hypothesis of game involvement, Roberts and Sutton-Smith suggested that conflicts induced by child-training processes and subsequent learning lead to involvement in games, which in turn provide buffered learning or enculturation important both to the player and to their societies. Such observations certainly emphasize the inter-relatedness of game behavior, variations in child-training practices, and general cultural demands.

Sociologists and psychologists have also examined the importance of play and games in the socialization process. Levy (1952) stated that childhood participation in competitive sports is one of the most important educational elements in society, and although they may not be of the real world, they have essential functions for socialization, integration, and as a general reinforcement of the social structure. To illustrate, although causality can not be established, Landers and Landers (1978) reported that among high school males, lower rates of delinquency were found for those involved in extra-curricular activities. More specifically, those who were involved in both sport and non-sport activities had the lowest rates, while those not involved in any extra-curricular activities had the highest rates.

Ritchie and Koller (1964) reported that sport is functional in the socialization process in that the play orientation and play experience gained in childhood is carried over into adulthood. Specifically they noted that play and games involve attitudes, values, norms, roles and skills that are similar to those found in adult work activities (Bailey 1977). Similarly, Lindesmith and Strauss (1964: 206–209) noted that participation in play and game activities enable a child to gain a repertoire of social skills necessary for participation in the adult world. More recently, Larson *et al.* (1975) considered the short-term and long-term consequences of participation in youth sport. They concluded that participation has a socialization effect which continues into adulthood. Helanko (1960) stated that sport is a significant factor in socialization to the basic rules of social behavior in a group; while Webb (1969) reported that sport and games provide the medium for socializing individuals into the values of society.

Kenyon (1968) challenged this belief when he suggested that there was little, if any, evidence to indicate that experiences in such diffuse roles as "democratic citizen" or "responsible individual" are provided through sport or physical education programs. He suggested that through physical education an individual may be socialized into specific roles such as that of athlete, spectator, or official. Snyder (1970) concluded, without presenting data, that some physical activity results in the development of role-specific characteristics, while other activity contributes to the learning of diffuse roles.

If socialization via sport occurs, the nuclear family appears to play a prominent role and the influence varies by social class (Watson 1977). Moreover, very clear sex differences in the process emerge during the early childhood years. For example, Lever (1976, 1978) and Duquin (1977) report sex differences in the early sporting experiences of children. More specifically, Duquin (1977) found that young girls are seldom exposed in children's literature to female role models who are involved in sport or physical activity. Similarly, Lever (1976, 1978) found that boys play different types of games and more complex games during early childhood. She suggests that girls may therefore learn fewer skills which are essential for success in occupations based on organizational skills such as, interpersonal competition, leadership, interacting in large groups and strategic thinking.

While many have considered participation in sport and physical activity to be functional for socialization, others have considered it to be dysfunctional. Spencer (1896) believed that games and sport were essentially useless for society. Soule (1955) noted that many considered the frivolity of games to be damaging since adult life requires the performance of many serious and unpleasant duties, whereas play and games over-emphasize pleasure-seeking pursuits.

Similarly, Aries (1962) stated that tennis, bowling and the like are essentially quasi-criminal activities, no less serious in their deleterious social effects than drunkeness or prostitution. More specifically, Bend (1971) reported that participation in sport can be dysfunctional from at least two perspectives. First, it may lead to personality problems in that individuals develop unrealistic perceptions of the self, they become extremely narrow individuals in terms of interest, and they may become over-aggressive in their pursuit of excellence (Bailey 1977; Tyler and Duthie 1979). Secondly, he suggested that participation in organized sport may lead to the learning of deviant norms such as, cheating, violence, and a win at all costs philosophy. In fact, Goldstein and Bredemeier (1977) conclude that the media, and particularly television, has led to an increase in the professionalization and formalization of sport at all age levels. They argue that television has influenced children to learn that the outcome is more important than the process. Hence, the effects of televised sport are dysfunctional in that children learn that violence, illegal strategies and extrinsic motivation are highly valued and essential to success. Thus, if socially acceptable norms and values can be generalized from sport experiences, it can similarly be argued that deviant values and norms may also be generalized to other situations.

In summary, there are many beliefs and hypotheses concerning the role of play and physical activity in the general socialization process. However, to date, there is little empirical data to support the beliefs and hence little is really known about the relationship between sport participation and general social learning. Thus, parents, coaches, physical educators and administrators should moderate their attempts to proselytize the value of sport as a socializing medium until more evidence is available.

SUMMARY

Socialization is a learning process wherein a novice, through observation, imitation and interaction with significant others (role models) within social systems such as the family, school, peer group, mass media and sport team, acquires the affective, cognitive and behavioral components of a social role. This process applies to the learning of specific roles within sport. Moreover, the role acquisition appears to occur in four stages and is influenced by ascribed personal attributes which an individual brings to a learning situation, and by the dominant values and ideology present in the community or society where they reside.

An analysis of the learning of sport roles indicated that the process varies by sport, by stage in the life-cycle, and by sex. More specifically, social systems exert varying degrees of influence depending on the sport role and the particular component of the role being considered (i.e., the behavioral, cognitive or affective domain), and that the process varies cross-nationally and intra-nationally where unique sub-cultures exist. As with other social roles, such factors as the dominant societal ideology and such ascribed attributes as social class, ethnicity, race, religion, sex and ordinal position influences who does or does not learn a specific sport role, and who is not given the opportunity to attain elite levels of performance.

The final section of this paper indicated that while many have claimed that participation in play, games and sport enhances the socialization process for children and adolescents, there is little empirical evidence to substantiate the beliefs or hypotheses. Furthermore, statements concerning the dysfunctional outcomes of involvement in sport have recently been made, but similarly lack empirical support at this time. In short, role-specific expectations are situationally determined and may not carry over to other social roles unless the situational and role expectations are similar.

Based on the limited knowledge concerning socialization and sport to date, educators and administrators must realize that they do not operate in a vacuum as they initiate and operate programs to get people involved in sport and physical activity. Rather each social system has the capacity to support or hinder the efforts of other systems. Thus, to encourage the development of physical activity as an integral facet of life-styles, social systems must reinforce each other. For example, the school, the family, the peer group, community recreation agencies, amateur sport organizations within community and federal or state agencies must support each other. Of all these systems, the school probably has the greatest potential to provide leadership in efforts to change the socialization process concerning sport roles since it already interacts in a variety of ways with such systems as, the family, the peer group, government agencies and community agencies.

Based on the findings to date, it appears that there are sex differences in the process of learning sport roles and that the process varies depending on the sport and the specific role within that sport. Furthermore, since socialization occurs throughout the life-cycle it must be recognized that individuals can be socialized into sport roles beyond the adolescent years and therefore greater efforts should be directed to socializing or re-socializing adults into sport roles. While elite status may never be attained, participation in a wide variety of sport roles is possible until late in life. Thus, different socialization practices must be utilized depending on the sport role, the sex of the socializee and the stage in the life-cycle. Furthermore, programing should also consider class, racial, ethnic and religious differences since it will be of little long term use to introduce individuals to a sport role if their sub-cultural heritage, life-chances or opportunity set mitigates against them ever being involved or playing the role later in life. Finally, those involved in sport and physical activity must show restraint as they attempt to justify or legitimate new or existing programs, since, to date, there is little empirical evidence to support the belief that what is learned on the playing field is transfered to other social contexts.

REFERENCES

Ariés, P. 1962. *Centuries of Childhood.* New York: Vintage Books.

Atchley, R.C. 1977. *The Social Forces in Later Life.* 2nd edition. Belmont, Cal.

Bailey, I.C. 1977. Socialization in play, games and sport. *Physical Educator.* 34, 4: 183-187.

Ball, D.W. 1972. Olympic games competition: structural correlates of national success. *Intern. Journal Comp. Sociology.* 15, 2: 186-200.

Bandura, A. 1969. Social-learning theory of identificatory process. Pp. 213-262 in D.A. Goslin, ed. *Handbook of Socialization Theory and Research.* Chicago: Rand McNally.

Bandura, A. and R.H. Walters. 1963. *Social Learning and Personality Development.* New York: Holt, Rinehart and Winston.

Beamish, R. 1978. Socioeconomic and demographic characteristics of the national executives of selected amateur sports in Canada (1975). *Working Papers in the Sociological Study of Sport and Leisure.* (Kingston, Ont.), 1. Queen's University.

Becker, H.S. et al. 1961. *Boys in White: Student Culture in Medical School.* Chicago: University of Chicago Press.

Becker, H.A. and B. Geer. 1967. The Fates of Idealism in Medical School. Pp. 163-173 in P.I. Rose, ed. *The Study of Society.* New York: Random House.

Bend, E. 1971. Some Potential Dysfunctional Effects of Sport Upon Socialization. Paper. *Third International Symposium on the Sociology of Sport.* Waterloo, Ont.

Blishen, B.K. 1967. A socioeconomic index for occupations in Canada. *Canadian Review of Sociology and Anthropology.* 4 February: 41-53.

Bohren, J. 1977. *The Role of the Family in the Socialization of Female Intercollegiate Athletes.* Ph.D. Thesis. University of Maryland.

Bratton, R. 1970. Demographic characteristics of executive members of two Canadian sport associations. *Journal Canadian Association of Health, Physical Education and Recreation.* 37, Jan.–Feb.: 20-28.

Brim, O.G. and S. Wheeler, eds. 1966. *Socialization After Childhood.* New York: Wiley.

Casher, B. 1977. Relationship between birth order and participation in dangerous sports. *Research Quarterly.* 48, March: 33-40.

Castine, S.C. and G.C. Roberts, 1974. Modelling in the socialization process of the black athlete. *IRSS.* 9, 3-4: 58-73,

Clark, W. 1977. *Socialization into the Role of College and Junior a Hockey Player.* Masters Thesis. University of Waterloo.

Clausen, J.W., ed. 1968. *Socialization and Society.* Boston: Little, Brown and Company.

Crawford, S. 1977. Occupational prestige rankings and the New Zealand Olympic athlete. *IRSS.* 12: 5–15.

Deutsch, M. and R.M. Kraus. 1965. *Theories in Social Psychology.* New York: Basic Books.

Duquin, M. 1977. Differential sex role socialization toward amplitude appropriation. *Research Quarterly.* 48, May: 288–292.

Eggleston, J. Secondary schools and Oxbridge blues. *Brit. J. Sociology.* 16, 21: 232–242.

Eitzen, D.S. and D.C. Sanford. 1975. The segregation of blacks by playing position in football: accident or design? *Social Science Quarterly.* 55, March: 849–959.

Faulkner, R.R. 1975. Coming of age in organizations: a comparative study of career contingencies of musicians and hockey players. Pp. 525–558 in D.W. Ball and J.W. Loy, eds. *Sport and Social Order.* Reading, Mass.: Addison-Wesley.

Goffman, E. 1959. *The Presentation of Self in Everyday Life.* Garden City, N.Y.: Anchor Doubleday.

Goldstein, J. and B. Bredemeier. 1977. Socialization: some basic issues. *Journal of Communication.* 27: 154–159.

Goslin, D., ed. 1969. *Handbook of Socialization Theory and Research.* Chicago: Rand McNally.

Gould, D. and D. Landers, 1972. Dangerous sport participation: a replication of Nisbetts' birth order findings. Paper. *North American Society for the Psychology of Sport.* Houston.

Greendorfer, S. 1977. Role of socializing agents in female sport involvement. *Research Quarterly.* 48, May: 304–310.

Greendorfer, S. 1978a. Socialization into sport. Pp. 115–140 in C.A. Oglesby, ed. *Women and Sport: From Myth to Reality.* Philadelphia: Lea and Febiger.

Greendorfer, S. 1978b. Differences in childhood socialization influences of women involved in sport and women not involved in sport. Pp. 59–72 in M. Krotee, ed. *Dimensions of Sport Sociology.* West Point: Leisure Press.

Greendorfer, S. and J. Lewko. 1978c. Children's socialization into sport: a conceptual and empirical analysis. Paper. *World Congress of Sociology.* Uppsala.

Greendorfer, S. 1979. Childhood sport socialization influences of male and female track athletes. *Arena Review.* 3: 39–53.

Grimes, A., W. Kelly and P. Rubin. 1974. A socioeconomic model of national Olympic performance. *Social Science Quarterly.* 55, Dec.: 777–783.

Groos, K. 1898. *The Play of Animals.* New York: Appleton.

Gruneau, R. 1972. *A Socioeconomic Analysis of the Competitors of the 1971 Canada Winter Games.* Masters Thesis. University of Calgary.

Hall, A. 1976. Sport and physical activity in the lives of Canadian women. Pp. 170–199. in R. Gruneau and J. Albinson, eds. *Canadian Sport: Sociological Perspectives.* Don Mills, Ont.: Addison-Wesley.

Hall, A. 1978. *Sport and Gender: A Feminist Perspective on the Sociology of Sport.* CAHPER Sociology of Sport Monograph Series. Calgary: University of Calgary.

Harlow, H.F. 1964. The heterosexual affectional system in monkeys. In W.G. Bennis et al., eds. *Interpersonal Dynamics.* Homewood, Ill.: Dorsey.

Helanko, R. 1960. Sports and socialization. *Acta Sociologica.* 8, April: 229–241.

Jones, F.E. 1965. The socialization of the infantry recruit. Pp. 258–279. in B.R.

Blishen et al., eds. *Canadian Society: Sociological Perspectives.* Toronto: Mac-Millan.

Kelly, J.R. 1977. Leisure socialization: replication and extension. *Journal of Leisure Research.* 9, 1: 121–132.

Kemper, T.D. 1968. Reference groups, socialization, and achievement. *ASR.* 33, Feb.: 31–45.

Kenyon, G.S. 1968. Sociological considerations. *Journal American Association of Health, Physical Education and Recreation.* 39, Nov.–Dec.: 31–33.

Kenyon, G.S. 1969. Sport involvement: a conceptual go and some consequences thereof. Pp. 77–84 in G.S. Kenyon, ed. *Sociology of Sport.* Chicago: Athletic Institute.

Kenyon, G.S. 1970. The use of path analysis in sport sociology. *IRSS.* 5, 1: 191–203.

Kenyon, G.S. 1977. The process of becoming an elite track and field athlete in Canada. Pp. 163–169 in J.Taylor, ed. *Post-Olympic Games Symposium.* Ottawa: Coaching Association.

Kenyon, G.S. and B.D. McPherson. 1973. Becoming involved in physical activity and sport: a process of socialization. Pp. 303–332 in G.L. Rarick, ed. *Physical Activity: Human Growth and Development.* New York: Academic Press.

Kiviaho, P. 1973. The recruitment of sport leaders at different organizational levels in Finland. Pp. 368 in O. Grupe et al., eds. *Sport in the Modern World.* New York: Springer.

Kiviaho, P. and P. Makela, 1978. Olympic success: a sum of non-material and material factors. *IRSS.* 13, 2: 5–17.

Laakso, L. 1973. Characteristics of the socialization environment as the determinant of adult sport interests in Finland. Pp. 103–112 in F. Landry and W. Orban, eds. *Sociology of Sport.* Miami: Symposia Specialists.

Landers, D. and D. Landers. 1978. Socialization via interscholastic athletics: its effects on delinquency. *Soc. Education.* 51, Oct.: 299–303.

Landry, F. et al. 1971. Les Canadiens-Francais et Les Grands Jeux Internationaux. Paper. *International Symposium Sociology of Sport.* Waterloo.

Larson, D. et al. 1975. Youth sport programs. *Sport Sociology Bulletin* 4,2:55–63.

Lever, J. 1976. Sex differences in the games children play. *Social Problems.* 23, April: 478–487.

Lever, J. 1978. Sex differences in the complexity of children's play and games. *ASR.* 43, 3: 471–483.

Levine, N. 1975. Why do countries win Olympic medals? Some structural correlates of Olympic games success: 1972. *Sociology Social Research.* 59, 2: 353–360.

Levy, M.J. 1952. *The Structure of Society.* Princeton: Princeton University Press.

Lindesmith, A.R. and A.L. Strauss. 1964. The social self. Pp. 206–209 in R.W. O'Brian et al., eds. *Readings in General Sociology.* Boston: Houghton-Mifflin.

Loy, J.W. 1969. The study of sport and social mobility. Pp. 101–110 in G.S. Kenyon, ed. *Sociology of Sport.* Chicago: Athletic Institute.

Loy, J.W. 1972. Social origins and occupational mobility patterns of a selected sample of American athletes. *IRSS.* 7, 1: 5–23.

Loy, J.W. and J.F. McElvogue. 1970. Racial segregation in American sport. *IRSS.* 5,1: 5–23.

Loy, J.W. and G. Sage. 1972. Social origins, academic achievement, athletic achievement, and career mobility patterns of college coaches. Paper. *American Sociological Association Meetings.* New Orleans.

Loy, J.W. and A. Ingham. 1973. Play, games, and sport in the psychosocial development of children and youth. Pp. 257–302 in G.L. Rarick, ed. *Physical Activity: Human Growth and Development.* New York: Academic Press.

Loy, J.W. B.D. McPherson and G.S. Kenyon. 1978. *Sport and Social Systems.* Reading, Mass.: Addison-Wesley.

Lüschen, G. 1969. Social stratification and social mobility among young sportsmen. Pp. 258–276 in J.W. Loy and G.S. Kenyon, eds. *Sport, Culture and Society.* New York: MacMillan.

Malumphy, T.M. 1970. The college women athlete – questions and tentative answers. *Quest.* 14, June: 18–27.

Marple, D.P. 1974. An analysis of the discrimination against the French Canadians in ice hockey. Paper. *Canadian Sociology Anthropology Meetings.* Toronto.

Maukson, H.O. 1963. Becoming a nurse: a selective view. *Annuals* AAPSS 346, March: 88–94.

McPherson, B.D. 1972. Socialization into the role of sport consumer: the construction and testing of a theory and causal model. Ph.D. Dissertation. University of Wisconsin.

McPherson, B.D. 1974. Career patterns of a voluntary role: the minor hockey coach. Paper. *Canadian Sociology and Anthropology Meetings.* Toronto.

McPherson, B.D. 1975. The segregation by playing position hypothesis in sport: an alternative explanation. *Social Science Quarterly.* 55, March: 960–966.

McPherson, B.D. 1976a. Consumer role socialization: a within-system model. *Sportwissenschaft.* 6, 2: 144–154.

McPherson, B.D. 1976b. Socialization into the role of sport consumer: a theory and causal model. *Canadian Review Sociology Anthropology.* May: 165–177.

McPherson, B.D. 1977. The process of becoming an elite hockey player in Canada. Pp. 170–179 in J. Taylor, ed. *Post-Olympic Games Symposium.* Ottawa: Coaching Association.

McPherson, B.D. 1978a. Success in sport: the influence of sociological parameters. *Canadian Journal Applied Sport Sciences.* 3, March: 51–59.

McPherson, B.D. 1978b. Aging and involvement in physical activity: a sociological perspective. Pp. 111–125 in F. Landry and W. Orban, eds. *Physical Activity and Human Well-Being.* Vol. 1. Miami: Symposia Specialists.

McPherson, B.D. 1978c. The sport role socialization process for Anglophone and Francophone adults in Canada: accounting for present patterns of involvement. Pp. 41–52 in F. Landry and W. Orban, eds. *Sociology of Sport.* Miami: Symposia Specialists.

McPherson, B.D., L.W. Guppy and J.P. McKay. 1976. The social world of children's games and sport: a review in J. Albinson and G. Andrews, eds. *The Child in Sport and Physical Activity.* Baltimore: University Park Press.

Mortimer, J.T. and R.G. Simmons. 1978. Adult socialization. In A. Inkeles, J. Coleman and N. Smelser, eds. *Annual Review of Sociology.* Volume 4. Palo Alto, Cal.: Annual Reviews.

Nash, D.J. 1968. The socialization of an artist: the American composer. *Journal of Personality and Social Psychology.* 8, 2: 351–353.

Niemi, R. and B. Sobieszek. 1977. Political socialization. In A. Inkeles, J. Coleman and N. Smelser, eds. *Annual Review of Sociology.* Volume 3. Palo Alto, Cal.: Annual Reviews.

Nisbett, R.F. Birth order and participation in dangerous sports. *Journal of Personality and Social Psychology.* 8, 2: 351–353.

Nixon, H. 1976. Sport socialization and youth: some proposed research directions. *Review Sport Leisure.* 1, 1: 45–61.

Novikov, A.D. and M. Maksimenko. 1972. Sociale und ökonomische Faktoren und das Niveau sportlicher Leistungen. *Sportwissenschaft.* 2: 156–167.

Pascal, A.H. and L.A. Rapping. 1972. The economics of racial discrimination in organized baseball. Pp. 119–156 in A.H. Pascal, ed. *Racial Discrimination in Economic Life.* Lexington, Mass.: Heath.

Pooley, J.C. 1971. *The Professional Socialization of Physical Education Students in the United States and England.* Ph.D. Thesis. University of Wisconsin, Madison.

Pudelkiewicz, E. 1970. Sociological problems of sports in housing estates. *IRSS.* 5: 73–103.

Redmond, G. 1978. *Sport and Ethnic Groups in Canada.* CAHPER Sociology of Sport Monograph Series. Calgary: University of Calgary.

Ritchie, O.W. and M. Koller. 1964. *Sociology of Childhood.* New York: Appleton-Century-Crofts.

Roberts, J. and B. Sutton-Smith. 1962. Child training and game involvement. *Ethnology.* 1, 1: 166–185.

Rooney, J.F. 1974. *A Geography of American Sport: From Cabin Creek to Anaheim.* Reading, Mass.: Addison-Wesley.

Rostow, W.W. 1971. *The Stages of Economic Growth.* Cambridge: Cambridge University Press.

Roy, G. 1974. The Relationship Between Centrality and Mobility: The Case of the National Hockey League. Masters Thesis. University of Waterloo.

Sage, G.H. and S. Loudermilk. 1979. The female athlete and role conflict. *Research Quarterly.* 50, 1: 88–96.

Sage, G.H. and J.W. Loy. 1978. Geographical mobility patterns of college coaches. *Urban Life.* 7, July: 253–274.

Sarbin, T. and V. Allen. 1968. Role theory. *Handbook of Social Psychology.* Volume One. Pp. 488–567 in G. Lindzey and E. Aronson, eds. Reading, Mass.: Addison-Wesley.

Scully, G.W. 1974. Discrimination: the case of baseball. *Government and the Sports Business.* Pp. 221–273 in R.G. Noll, ed. Washington, D.C.: The Brookings Institute.

Seppänen, P. 1972. Die Rolle des Leistungssports in den Gesellschaften des Welt. *Sportwissenschaft.* 2: 133–155.

Sewell, W.H. 1963. Some recent developments in socialization theory and research. *Annals AAPSS.* 349, September: 163–181.

Smelser, M.J. 1962. *Theory of Collective Behavior.* New York: The Free Press.

Smith, G. and C. Blackman. 1978. *Sport in the Mass Media.* CAHPER Sociology of Sport Monograph Series. Calgary: University of Calgary.

Smith, M.D. 1978. Getting involved in sport: sex differences. *Sociology of Sport.* Pp. 113–120 in F. Landry and W. Orban, eds. Miami: Symposia Specialists.

Snyder, E. 1970. Aspects of socialization in sports and physical education. *Quest.* 14, June: 1–7.

Snyder, E.F. and E. Spreitzer. 1976. Family influence and involvement in sports. *Research Quarterly.* 44, Oct.: 249–255.

Snyder E. and E. Spreitzer. 1973. Correlates of sport participation among adolescent girls. *Research Quarterly.* 47, Dec.: 804–809.

Soule, G.H. 1955. *Time for Living.* New York: Viking press.

Spencer, H. 1896. *The Principles of Psychology.* New York: Appleton.

Spreitzer, E. and E. Snyder. 1976. Socialization into sport: an exploratory path analysis. *Research Quarterly.* 47, 2: 238–245.

Staniford, D.J. 1978. *Play and Physical Activity in Early Childhood Socialization.* CAHPER Sociology of Sport Monograph Series. Calgary: University of Calgary.

Stevenson, C.L. 1975. Socialization effects of participation in sport: a critical review of the research. *Research Quarterly.* 46, Oct.: 287–301.

Stone, G.P. 1957. Some meanings of American sport. *Proceedings National College of Physical Education Association for Men.* 60: 6–29.

Sutton-Smith, B. 1972. *The Folk Games of Children.* Austin: University of Texas Press.

Theberge, N. 1977. Some Factors Associated With Socialization Into the Role of Professional Women Golfers. Paper. *Canadian Psycho-Motor Performance Symposium.* Banff, Alberta.

Thornton, R. and P.M. Nardi. 1975. The dynamics of role acquisition. *AJS* 80, Jan.: 870–885.

Tyler, J.K. and J.H. Duthie. 1979. The effect of ice hockey on social development. *Journal of Sport Behavior.* 2, Feb.: 49–59.

Vaz, E. 1972. The culture of young hockey players: some initial observations. *Training: Scientific Basis and Application.* Pp. 222–234 in A. Taylor, ed. Springfield, Ill.: Thomas.

Watson, G. 1977. Games, socialization and parental values: social class differences in parental evaluation of Little League Baseball. *IRSS.* 12, 1: 17–48.

Webb, H. 1969. Professionalization of attitudes toward play among adolescents. *Sociology of Sport.* Pp. 161–179 in G.S. Kenyon, ed. Chicago: Athletic Institute.

Westby, D.L. 1960. The career experience of the Symphony musician. *Social Forces.* 38, March: 223–224.

Woelfel, J. and A.O. Haller. 1971. Significant others, the self-reflexive act and the attitude formation process. *ASR.* 26, Feb.: 74–87.

Yetman, N.R. and D.S. Eitzen. 1972. Black Americans in sports: unequal opportunity for equal ability. *Civil Rights Digest.* 5, Aug.: 21–34.

Yiannakis, A. 1976. Birth order and preference for dangerous sports among males. *Research Quarterly.* 47, March: 62–67.

Zigler, E. and I.L. Child. 1969. Socialization. *A Handbook of Social Psychology.* Volume 3, G. Lindzey and E. Aronson, eds. Reading, Mass.: Addison-Wesley.

FEMININITY AND ATHLETICISM

Dorothy V. Harris

What are big boys made of? Independence, aggression, competitiveness, leadership, assertiveness, task orientation, outward orientation...And what are big girls made of? Dependence, passivity, fragility, low pain tolerance, nonagression, noncompetitiveness, inner orientation, interpersonal orientation, empathy, sensitivity, nurturance..." (Bardwick 1971). If one were to ask what the psychological demands of competitive sport or vigorous physical activity were, the response would most probably be more compatible with "what little boys are made of," as opposed to "what little girls are made of."

Traditionally, sports involvement has been the prerogative of the male in most societies. It has been assumed that the psychological and physical demands of competitive sports provide a laboratory for training and instilling masculine characteristics in the participants. The behavioral demands of sport reinforce what is typically masculine and what the male is supposed to emulate. Society continues to applaud the positive physical, psychological, and social benefits *he* gains from participation. On the other side of the picture, the psychological and physical demands of strenuous competitive sport are not generally considered compatible with society's stereotyped image of what the ideal female should be. Many believe that the experience brings out undesirable behaviors in the female; indeed, it appears to her detriment to pursue such involvement.

Masculinity and femininity, as culturally defined, have been extremely resistant to change. This has been especially true where sport and athletic competition have been concerned. The traditional role of the male has allowed him to determine the range of behavior he will condone as being feminine. That is, behaviors that females engage in that are not reinforced in a positive manner by males, become "unfeminine" and undesirable. In short, those behaviors that are admired in the female do not include those that appear necessary for success in competitive sport.

Women in sport are both a social reality and a social anomaly. This results in confusion with regard to roles and perceptions of women in sport. If masculinity and femininity serve as appropriate social conceptions of the polar differences in the behaviors of males and females, and if sport is largely assumed to be the prerogative of the male, hence masculine, then the role of the female in sport is a social anomaly. Thus, the female's intrusion into sport makes mockery of the masculine domain. Throughout history, females have been apologetic for their intrusion and they have compensated for their "assumed" lack of femininity by participating in only certain types of sports and by not making such serious commitments to sport involvement. Traditionally, sport involvement has been more acceptable and reinforced to a much greater extent for the male in society. As a result, females have appeared to "sense their place" in sport and in general, have promoted an ideology that has justified and perpetuated it.

Role Conflict

Role conflict for the female athlete would appear to have its basis in the cognitive dissonance or disparity inherent in traditional conceptions of femininity and athleticism. Serious commitment to sports involvement is the antithesis of what the female is "supposed" to emulate in society. Athletics are culturally masculine. The role conflict, that is the incompatibility of athletics and femininity, has been longstanding. Rogers (1929) suggested that females should spend their time developing traits necessary to attract males who would become worthy fathers for their children by building material and social behaviors and attractive physiques. He suggested that intense forms of physical and psychic conflicts, such as those observed in athletics, with the Olympics providing the extreme, tend to destroy the female's physical and psychic charm and adaptability for motherhood.

In American culture, the female is neither expected nor required to develop athletic ability, only physical attractiveness; the possession of strength and skills beyond a variable minimum is relatively unimportant for girls. Bowen (1967) stated that the male athlete discovers early that his athletic accomplishments serve to open doors to almost universal social acceptance while the female athlete will find certain groups consider her socially undesirable.

The etiology of this negative sanctioning of the female athlete appears to be grounded in the notion that serious participation in athletics, by virtue of its physical and psychological demands, is incongruous with what is considered "appropriate" feminine behavior. The primary concerns stem from two major fears, the fear that somehow the female will become masculinized in her appearance, and the fear that she will become masculinized in her behavior.

The differences in attitudes and acceptance towards males and females in sport originate in the differences in traits that society ascribes to each sex. Kagan and Moss (1962), basing their definitions on observations and research during a longitudinal study of children, described the traditional masculine model as athletic, active sexually, independent, dominant, courageous, and competitive while the female was described as passive and dependent, socially anxious, sexually timid, fearful of problem situations, and ambitious about home-making activities rather than career ones. Others (Douvan and Adelson, 1966), in looking at female development, resorted to classifying girls into three groups: feminine, nonfeminine, and antifeminine girls. "Feminine" girls were those who were other-directed, whose self-esteem was gained through helping others. They displayed little motivation for personal achievement and preferred security to success. "Nonfeminine" girls were described as the slow developing group who said they felt more important and useful when they were participating in competitive sports and games. "Antifeminine" girls were those who stated that they did not intend to marry. These girls were perceived as psychologically deviant. In short, only those girls who followed the traditional roles of expectations were considered "normal" while all the others were labeled as either slow developers or psychologically deviant.

Cheska (1970) presented a paradox when she pointed out that the traits that are considered undesirable in the female include aggressiveness, independence, ambition, and having goals other than being a wife or mother, and that these are the specific traits needed by young women if they are to succeed in attaining a different role.

Bardwick (1971: 143) made some pertinent comments about this identity crisis that the young female athlete may experience. She said, "If a girl has had many years in which she has been permitted to participate in what will be perceived as masculine activities, and to the extent that success in these activities, especially individual competitive ones, form a core part of her self-esteem, it will be difficult for her to assume a clearly feminine sex-role identity and preference for the feminine role." Bardwick said further, "...the motorically active, preadolescent girl will achieve status through competitive sports. Later, in adolescence, especially when teenagers are cruel in their demands, she will undergo a deep crisis..." This crisis that Bardwick makes reference to occurs when the young female athlete perceives dissonance between what she thinks herself to be and what society expects her to be. There is dissonance between assertiveness and submissiveness, between smelling sweet and being sweaty, between being tough and being gentle, between being vigorous and being inactive, between being athletic and being feminine. One cannot tolerate this dissonance too long; it must be resolved.

Traditionally, the female athlete has resolved her conflict between what she perceives herself to be as an athlete and what society expects her to be by withdrawing from sport involvement. This withdrawal generally occurs during adolescence when the female body begins to mature and she has her "femaleness" reinforced constantly. And, because society determines that her status becomes increasingly linked to her femininity as traditionally defined, she withdraws from sport involvement.

Some females continue their competitive sport involvement but focus upon "feminine appropriate" sports such as swimming, tennis, golf, gymnastics and so on. Somehow, these sports are not considered masculine as team sports and track and field, so participation in them does not create the same degree of conflict. Still other females compensate their perceived threat to femininity by attaching feminine artifacts to their attire for their sports performance. Ruffles, pastel colors, lace, design and style are ultra-feminine by society's standards. It is as though one is saying, "In spite of the fact that I am a well skilled athlete, I am still feminine, see?".

The athletes that cause the most concern are those who withdraw from any social situation which requires them to participate in a traditional manner. They too, experience conflict between what the stereotyped role of the female is supposed to be and what they perceive themselves to be as an athlete. They resolve their conflict by withdrawing from the traditional role of the female. The penalty for this resolution of conflict is greatest because the behavior is farthest from what the traditional female is supposed to emulate.

Fortunately, increasing numbers of females are discovering that they can cope with any dissonance perceived by adapting to the demands of the situation in which they find themselves. They are secure enough in their own selfhood to the point that they are able to function confidently in both athletic and traditionally feminine social situations without feeling that they have to trade-off any sense of their feminine selfhood. They feel equally adequate and secure dressed in the most traditional feminine attire and assuming the "expected role" as they do looking like the sweaty, weary athlete they enjoy being. Ideally, females (and males) should be socialized so they are confident enough in their selfhood to cope with all sorts of situations without having their selfhood threatened. As society begins to allow greater latitude in behaviors, more females will discover that they can continue their involvement and serious commitment to competitive sports without perceiving conflict.

Etiology of Role Orientations

As research begins to examine the female and her role and to sort out what is the product of one's socialization from the product of one's biological sex, it becomes more and more evident that characteristics previously considered sex related are culturally determined.

The behavior of females, as well as males, is minimally dependent on biological differences and much more dependent upon the restricted position of both males and females in our society. Socialization is essentially concerned with rearing children so they will become adequate adult members of the society to which they belong. In so long as males and females are socialized effectively to accept stereotyped roles for their sexual identity, they can be expected to accept and demonstrate the "appropriate" role behavior in fulfilling them. Parents and society teach children to be boys and girls by rewarding appropriate sex-role behavior and punishing cross-gender behavior. Gender role and orientation appear to depend on learned experience as well as somatic variables. Marmor (1973) said that gender role and gender identity, although generally related to the biological sex of a child, actually are not shared by biological factors but by cultural ones. According to Marmor, once a child's biological ascription is settled, a myriad of culturally defined cues begins to be presented to the developing infant which are designed to shape its gender identity to its assigned sex. Others like Tiger (1969) have attributed the differentiation of sex roles to cultural evolution.

From birth, infants begin to interact with adults. From the very first experience with adults, male and female infants are treated differently. Little girls are handled more gently than little boys, are spoken to in different tones, and addressed in different terms. By 13 months, male infants have already learned to be more curious, more independent and more self reliant than females of the same age even though females are physically more mature. The motive appears to be cultural; most mothers believe that boys should be encouraged to explore and master their world. Society tends to see infantile behavior as feminine and there is less parental-cultural stress on girls to give up such behavior and dependency on adults and others. While her male counterpart is building a concept of self-esteem based on accomplishments which are tangible and objective, the female learns not to gratify impulses that adults find offensive and to rely on others to determine whether she has done well or poorly in any given situation. She learns to please, to defer, to wait for reinforcement; this becomes a big part of the "feminine" role. Typically, a young child can exhibit behavior that is either masculine or feminine appropriate. The adults to whom the child is exposed will reinforce that behavior which they deem appropriate to the child's sex. The child presumably begins to form attitudes about behaviors which are acceptable or not acceptable. Hampson and Hampson (1961), pointed out that the impact of this acculturation is so powerful that, in certain cases of pseudo-hermaphroditism in which the child's biological sex is mistaken for that of the opposite sex, the incorrect gender identity becomes so powerfully established by the age of two or three that it becomes psychologically destructive to the child to try to change it. They concluded, on the basis of their findings, that psychological sex or gender role appears to be learned, that is, that it is differentiated through learning during the course of many experiences of growing up. Salzman (1973) supported this notion when he wrote that the attitudes, characterological traits, and behavior characteristics of the female may not be due to her biological sex, but rather to a multitude of demands, restraints, expectations, and controls which any given culture places on her.

Many theorists working with the psychology of women feel that the real explanation of the status of the female is not something implicit in the nature of the female, but rather a manifestation of the male ego. As indicated earlier, men have traditionally defined the concept of femininity and have emphasized the importance of the feminine image. In many situations, the natural desire and motivation for competitive experiences in the female may be totally stifled by male disapproval, either directly or indirectly. Girls are taught from the very beginning that their relationship to the male is a position of obsequiousness. They are taught to direct their behavior toward "pleasing" the male and the only attitude of competitiveness that they are permitted is toward other females for the position of favor from the male's perspective. In short, her identity as an individual is related to her role and relationship to the male.

Much of the research indicated that the cultural attitude toward the female is significantly different from that towards the male. These differences in cultural attitudes are the result of male-female orientations rather than resulting as a direct function of some innate, biologically-based predictions.

Research Evaluations of the Female Role

Traditionally, men and women have regarded men more highly in terms of the social desirability of the traits attributed to males and females (McKee and Sheriffs 1959; Rosenkrantz et al. 1968). A more recent study in 1970 by Broverman and colleagues indicated that male and female clinical psychologists agreed as to the attributes characterizing healthy behavior for men and women in today's society. They also concurred that these behaviors were different for men and women; these differences closely paralleled the dominant sex role stereotypes of society. When characterizing the healthy behavior of the adult male, of the adult female, and of an adult with sex unspecified, the clinical psychologists described the behavior of the adjusted male and the adjusted adult as being quite similar. However, when describing the healthy behavior of the adult female, it differed significantly from that of the healthy adult in today's society. The behavior of an adjusted adult was described as independent, logical, and self-confident; whereas, the adjusted female was described as being emotional, dependent, and passive. The authors concluded that for the female to be adjusted, she must accept and adjust to behavioral norms for her sex even though these behaviors are considered to be less healthy than those expected to be demonstrated in the average adjusted, competent, mature adults.

Further evidence of the expected behavioral traits of the female in society was disclosed by Weisstein (1969) when he said that the American culture characterized women as emotionally unstable, inconsistent, weaker, nurturant rather than productive, and lacking in a strong super ego. They are more intuitive than intelligent and, if they are at all normal, they associate their goals with home and family.

Studies during the late sixties and early seventies which have examined attitudes about the female's participation in sport have produced a fairly generalized pattern of results. Most studies support the notion that serious commitment to competitive sport is incompatible with society's view of apporpriate feminine behavior. Layman (1968) reported that college students viewed terms such as athlete, football, coach, basketball, baseball and shotput as masculine. Folk dancing was seen as either neuter or feminine. Males saw gymnastics, archery, physical education major, and teacher as less sex-role typed but more masculine than did females. Female physical education majors viewed physical education major, shotput, and gymnastics as more feminine than other females' ratings. In general, competitive team games and activities involving strength had higher masculine ratings than did individual activities requiring skill but less strength. Laymen concluded that females learn early that rough play is inappropriate and football and boxing are definitely not considered feminine.

Harres (1966) surveyed individuals to determine the general attitude toward women's athletic competition and found that swimming and tennis were considered to be the most highly desirable sports for females. Volleyball was ranked third, followed by track and field, softball and basketball. Harres concluded that while general responses were favorable toward athletic competition, they were not highly favorable for women. In another study completed in California in 1968, DeBacy (1970) was interested in what males thought of women's competition. She found that they preferred the females to participate in individual sports.

In a series of studies completed at The Pennsylvania State University, the self-perceptions of female athletes have been examined under several different conditions such as general social versus athletic situation, or creative versus structured sport disciplines.

In a study conducted in England, Hall (1972) compared the image of a "feminine" woman and an "athletic" woman as viewed by female participants and nonparticipants in competitive sport. The female participants' concepts of the feminine and athletic woman were significantly less dissonant and more congruent than they were for the nonparticipants. The latter perceived the feminine woman more favorably than the athletic woman.

Less Dissonance Indicates Better Adjustment

In 1976 Monk compared the self- and ideal self-profiles of female field hockey players. She also compared the amount of dissonance perceived between the two selves to determine if there were differences in the level of personal adjustment among groups. Monk observed that since the women's movement in the 1960's, trends have developed that serve to relax male-female role differentiations. Social pressures against the female participating in athletics are beginning to diminish; one can be athletically skilled without feeling one's femininity is relinquished. A wider latitude of acceptable feminine behavior is more prevalent and females can feel free to learn to move skillfully and to engage in competitive sports with little if any threat to their feminine image. Monk's premise was that the female athlete may be constantly struggling with negative feedback relative to her athletic behavior because it is in violation of role expectations. According to Monk, if this were the case, the female athlete would have a more negative self-image than her nonathletic counterpart. She based her supposition on the statement made in preface of a book by Klafs and Lyon (1973) which suggested that the American society has imposed a stereotyped model of femininity which has generally excluded the well-skilled athletic girl with a competitive personality. As a result, the female who is able to move skillfully and who has a desire to win in competitive athletics perceives an immediate threat to her self-concept as a female. Or, according to Monk, through her skill acquisition and through other positive feedback that she has gained from her participation, she may have a more positive self-image than someone who is not active in athletics and has not had this feedback from her experiences.

According to Monk, application of this type of model to the female participating in athletics is vital to the understanding of the effects of sport participation. The female who elects to pursue competitive athletics receives both positive and negative feedback. The specific nature of operant feedback components and the influence these have on the self-image is a dimension of behavior overlooked in most research.

The basis of Monk's study was founded on certain suppositions that are found in the literature. In general, the traditional female role is incongruous with athleticism. Behavioral traits traditionally associated with femininity are in direct contradiction to those necessary for competitive sports; this produces a source of conflict for the female athlete. The role orientation of the female in society is largely culturally determined, not physiologically based. However, females are not bound to any specific role orientation; if they perceive other roles as more desirable, they may elect to pursue them. Lastly, the literature indicates unequivocally that the female role is less desirable than the male role in society; this holds true for views of both males and females.

According to Monk, a role conflict is experienced by the female who chooses to be athletically active and this perception adversely affects the self-concept. However, since the behavior, that is, the involvement in athletics, persists in some in spite of this negative feedback, there must be sources of positive feedback which serve to nullify the perceived conflict. In investigating some of these components among different levels of field hockey players and among nonplayers, Monk reported that the degree of dissonance between the self and ideal-self was similar across all groups, however, the most experienced and committed players making the varsity team were most self-confident, dominant and spontaneous than nonplayers. The level of personal adjustment was not significantly different among the groups. Apparently, in spite of the notion that athletic participation is not compatible with expected role orientation, the negative feedback that a female athlete received as a result of violating this role did not adversely influence the athlete as she did not differ from her non-participating peers. This suggested that her persistence of involvement in athletics must have provided sources of positive feedback to counter the prevailing negative social feedback.

Other investigators have also tested this assumption and reported similar findings. Snyder et al. (1975) reported that their findings did not reveal negative associations between being a female athlete and two measures of self-identity. On the contrary, positive relationships emerged in the opposite direction. Snyder et al. concluded that these findings raised serious doubts about the assumptions of the conflict being inherent in female athletes which might produce a negative self-perception.

A More Contemporary Perspective

The position that has dominated the writings of social and behavioral scientists is that masculine and feminine attributes are essentially bipolar opposites. The presence of feminine characteristics tends to preclude the appearance of masculine ones. Indeed, the absence of a feminine attribute is by definition, equivalent to masculinity. Conversely, masculine characteristics are assumed to preclude feminine ones and their absence is to define femininity. In most societies, the appropriate goal of socialization is to inculcate sex-appropriate attributes in members of each sex so that they may be capable of executing successfully the sex-roles that society has asigned them by virtue of their biological role. In fact, the link between masculine and feminine characteristics and sex-roles has been assumed to be so strong that these psychological dimensions are frequently discussed under the general sex-role rubric.

Distinction between the sex-roles is universal among human societies; males are assigned different tasks, rights, and privileges, and are generally subject to different rules of conduct than females. Males and females are typically assumed to possess different temperamental characteristics and abilities whose existence is used to justify the perpetuation of double standards of behavior. Definitive data are lacking about whether there are genetically determined differences in the tempermental make-up of males and females. However, there is abundant evidence to support the fact that human personality is highly malleable. Observed differences in the behaviors of the two sexes in a given society can be shown to be strongly influenced by the sex-specific child-rearing practices and by the nature and severity of the sex-role differentiation promoted by that society.

Psychologists have tended to accept as given the complex set of sex-related phenomena and to focus attention on the processes by which individuals come to correspond in their behaviors and attributes to the expected norm for their sex within their culture. Psychologists have also been interested in the variability among individuals and have attempted to identify the factors that promote or interfere with the development of expected and appropriate patterns of behavior. Psychological inquiries have been based on the notion that the categorical variable of biological gender is intimately associated with masculine and feminine role behaviors and presumed psychological differences between males and females. This bipolar conception of masculinity and femininity has historically been the one that has guided the research efforts of psychologists. The major psychometric instruments designed to measure masculinity and femininity have been set up as unidimensional scales.

While the bipolar approach to the psychological aspects of masculinity and femininity has been the major one, dualistic approaches have also been proposed. In the psychoanalytic tradition, Jung distinguished between masculine *animus* and feminine *anima* and proposed that both were significant aspects of the psychological makeup. More recently Bakan (1966) has offered *agency* and *communion* as coexisting male and female principles. *Agency* demonstrates self-awareness and is manifested in self-assertion, self-expansion, and self-protection. *Communion* implies selflessness and concern for others. Both modalities are essential if society or the individual is to survive. Bakan further associated agency with masculinity and communion with femininity. Thus, according to Bakan, masculinity and femininity, in the sense of *agency* and *communion* are two separate dimensions, however, the manifestation of one neither logically or psychologically precludes the possession of the other.

Helmreich and Spence (1976) contend that the relationship among the various components of masculinity and femininity such as biological gender, sex-roles, sexual orientation and especially psychological attributes of masculinity and femininity and the adoption of conventional sex-roles is not as strong as has been traditionally assumed. Their position reflects the more contemporary concept that masculinity and femininity represent two separate dimensions which vary independently. Helmreich and Spence have developed a new instrument, the Personal Attributes Questionnaire (PAQ), to assess masculine-feminine components of behavior. While they have maintained the psychological aspects of masculinity and femininity, they have discarded a strictly bipolar model and structured an essentially dualistic concept.

The PAQ is composed of a masculinity and a femininity scale. The items which comprise the masculinity scale refer to those attributes which are considered to be socially desirable in both sexes but were found to a greater degree among males during preliminary investigations. Conversely, those attributes considered to be socially desirable for both sexes but observed to a greater extent among females created the femininity scale. Two scores are generated, one for each scale and an individual is classified according to his or her position relative to the scale medians. Helmreich and Spence have devised a simple classification scheme as shown in Table 1. At the lower right quadrant are those individuals who have scored above the median on both masculinity and femininity; these are labeled *androgynous.* In the upper right quadrant are those individuals who scored high in masculinity and low in femininity. Males who corresponded to the typical male stereotype and females judged as cross-sex fell in this group and were labeled *masculine.* The lower left quadrant included those individuals who displayed the typical feminine attributes or those males who displayed cross-sex behaviors; these were labeled *feminine.* Those who did not fall in any of the previous three categories, that is, they fell below the median on both masculinity and femininity were placed in the upper left quadrant and categorized as *undifferentiated.*

Using several hundred subjects, Helmreich and Spence have studied the relationship between the two scales. They have found a tendency for high masculine scores to be associated with low scores on the other scale. A bipolar conception would suggest that the sets of scores should be negatively related. If one has a high masculine score the feminine score would be low. As indicated, this was not the case with those individuals sampled by Helmreich and Spence.

Table 1. Sex-role Classification: Personal Attributes Questionnaire

MASCULINITY

F E M I N I N I T Y	Below Median	Above Median
Below Median	Undifferentiated	Masculine
Above Median	Feminine	Androgynous

Source: Helmreich, R. and J.T. Spence, 1976.

In order to examine the relationship between sex-role identity and self-esteem, Spence, Helmreich, and Stapp (1975) have correlated the PAQ data with Scores on the Texas Social Behavior Inventory, a measure of self-esteem. They found that the self-esteem of the undifferentiated was lowest, that of the feminine category next lowest, followed by masculine. The highest self-esteem was observed in the androgynous group. The differences between the means were significantly large and the relationship of sex-role classification and self-esteem held true for both males and females. The college population had the same percentage of males and females classified as androgynous, more males as masculine and more females as feminine and approximately the same percent as undifferentiated.

In summary, the Helmreich and Spence data suggested that masculinity and androgyny were related to desirable behaviors and to positive self-esteem in both males and females. These desirable attributes provided the androgynous individual, either male or female, with behavioral advantages over those falling in other categories. In an attempt to validate their findings, Helmreich and Spence studied unique populations of females where the existence or nonexistence of differences in the distribution of masculinity and femininity might support their theoretical proposition. A group of female athletes was included. The data from these women suggested that high-achieving women are more likely to possess both masculine and feminine attributes than their male counterparts without suffering any deficit in their femininity. On the contrary, they displayed significantly higher self-esteem than those females who were classified as feminine.

Application of the Androgynous Concept to Athletic Groups

In a series of studies which began in 1976, Harris and Jennings (1977) have found no evidence to support the supposed, inevitable trade-off of the female athlete's self-esteem and femininity for making a serious commitment to sport participation. The data generally support those of Helmreich and Spence in suggesting that those females who succeed in areas of endeavor considered stereotypically masculine do not do this at the expense of their femininity. As a matter of fact, the data suggest that high-achieving women are more likely to possess both masculine and feminine attributes than their male counterparts without suffering any deficit in their femininity. Androgynous individuals, male or female, appear to have behavioral advantages over others.

In the first study of 68 female distance runners (Harris and Jennings 1977) 33.8% were androgynous, 27.9% masculine, 17.6% feminine and 20.6% undifferentiated. Helmreich and Spence (1976) had reported 39% were androgynous, 31% masculine, 10% feminine, and 20% undifferentiated.

A second study involved 96 female athletes participating in a wide variety of sports, Harris and Jennings (1978) reported 54% were androgynous, 21% masculine, 14% feminine, and 11% undifferentiated. Among the 72 nonathletic women 38% were androgynous, 24% masculine, 28% feminine, and 10% undifferentiated.

In a study of 125 males and 150 females 22% of the males were androgynous, 31% masculine, 12% feminine and 35% undifferentiated. Forty-five percent of the females were androgynous, 23% masculine, 21% feminine and 11% undifferentiated. Yet another study looking at 64 male and 92 female athletes found 51% of the female athletes androgynous, 23% masculine, 15% feminine and 11% undifferentiated while 25% of the male athletes were androgynous, 34% masculine, 11% feminine and 30% undifferentiated. It should be noted that both of these studies used college-age subjects. The high percentage of undifferentiated males may reflect the slower maturation rate of the male, indicating that he has not established an identifiable behavioral frame of reference as yet.

Throughout all of the studies reported here individuals who were classified as androgynous also had significantly higher self-esteem. Masculine individuals, both male and female, had the next highest self-esteems while those classified as feminine and/or undifferentiated had significantly lower self-esteems. These studies indicated that it is not being male or female per se or being an athlete, but the psychological attributes that provide the behavioral frame of reference which was related to self-esteem.

Exploring the Relationship of Androgyny and
Achievement Motivation

Paradoxically the one consistency in the achievement motivation literature, has been the *inconsistency* of results when females have been studied (Karabenick and Marshall 1974; Weiner et al. 1971). Possibly because it is easier to ignore than to explain, and since the female data were not conducive to consistent or clear results, many of the major investigators (Atkinson 1958; Heckhausen 1967) have concentrated their efforts on studies which have included only males. This exclusion of females reached rather extreme levels—out of a whole book related to achievement motivation theory Atkinson confined his references to women to a single footnote. The trend appeared to be getting worse, for in an earlier book, Heckhausen (1967) allotted 9 of 215 pages to female achievement motivation.

Among those researchers who chose not to ignore women, such as Mehrabian (1969), the inconsistent results were attributed to the possibility that different measures of achievement motivation are required for females and males.

For a time, Horner's (1968, 1970, 1972) fear-of-success hypothesis appeared to be a viable solution to the methodological and substantive problems plaguing the achievement motivation area. The fear-of-success hypothesis suggested that differences in the achievement behavior between the sexes might be attributable to stable, and gender related, dispositions—with females being motivated by fear-of-success and males by success. However, the research designed to test Horner's hypothesis has in turn been characterized by methodological problems and inconsistencies.

Despite an obvious lack of conclusive research substantiating a female achievement deficit, a cultural stereotype characterizing males as being more intelligent, more achieving, and more competitive than women has existed (Broverman et al. 1972). However, a renewed interest in examining the reality of these supposed achievement motivation sex differences has concomitantly occurred with the women's movement of the past decade (Mednick et al. 1975).

As the achievement motivation literature is too vast to even partially review within this paper, only the background necessary to evaluate the new approaches will be provided.

The unitary, fantasy-based concept developed in early 50's by McClelland and his colleagues (McClelland et al. 1953) had great influence on the achievement motivation literature, and their assessment technique dominated the research during the 1950's and 1960's. Though their method provides global achievement scores, no attempt is made to investigate potential interrelationships of the components of achievement.

Other researchers, for example, Mehrabian (1969) and Jackson, Ahmed and Heapy (1976) have questioned this unitary conception of achievement motivation. These investigators posit that a unitary concept is too simplistic, and as a result, fails to have predictive validity in real life settings.

Agreeing with this latter premise and further hypothesizing that some of the inconsistencies in the achievement motivation literature could be attributed to its unitary conceptualization, Spence and Heimreich (1978) have developed an objective instrument designed to assess several components of achievement motivation. Their instrument, the Work and Family Orientation (WOFO) scale, has four component scales. They are: 1) work—the desire to work hard and keep busy; 2) mastery—the desire to cope with challenging tasks, and to meet inner standards of excellence; 3) competitiveness—reflecting a desire to win over other people; and 4) personal unconcern—being unconcerned with others' negative reaction to one's achievement.

The WOFO was designed on the premise that the nature of achievement motivation is essentially the same in both females and males, therefore, a single set of scales could be applicable to both sexes. This perspective allows for the possibility that though the achievement motivation construct does not differ fundamentally between the sexes, males and females might differ in types of situations in which they choose to express their achievement needs. Stein and Bailey (1973) have suggested that women experience desires to succeed (in contrast with Horner's fear-of-success theory mentioned earlier), but that these strivings are directed toward typically feminine tasks. This differential-aspiration hypothesis would predict that observed sex differences have occurred more as a function of focus of aspiration than of fundamental psychological differences between the sexes.

In the series of studies to follow, the subjects were college students who completed both the Personal Attributes Questionnaire and the Work and Family Orientation Scale developed by Helmreich and Spence. In all of the analyses, the classifications of androgynous, masculine, feminine and undifferentiated were used as levels of one factor to examine the independent variables of mastery, work, competitiveness, and personal unconcern.

The subjects involved in our first study were female athletes (n=96) and nonathletes (n=72). A 2 x 4 (student category x PAQ) analysis of variance was computed on each scale of the WOFO. A main effect for PAQ category was significant for the mastery, work, and competitiveness scales, indicating that the mean scores for the four sex-role classifications differed.

The general pattern on all three scales was that the androgynous subjects had higher scores than the feminine and undifferentiated subjects, with the addition that on the mastery scale the masculine subjects classified as feminine or undifferentiated. These results suggested that those females who had both instrumental and expressive attributes also had higher levels of the achievement-associated characteristics of mastery, work, and competitiveness.

On the fourth scale, personal unconcern, the results were more complex as a significant interaction was observed between the PAQ and student category factors. While the nonathletes' scores were relatively stable across PAQ categories, this was not the case for the athletes. Those athletes classified as feminine scored significantly lower on personal unconcern than the androgynous and masculine athletes and significantly lower than the feminine nonathletes, suggesting that the evaluation of others was important to those female athletes whose psychological attributes were stereotypically female. This finding differed from Spence and Helmreich's results since they reported that female athletes in general indicated higher levels of concern than did the female students. While a similar main effect was found it must be considered as spurious because of the significant interaction. It would be inaccurate to state on the basis of these data that *all* female athletes showed more concern, since subsequent tests on the interaction effects revealed that the effect was attributable primarily to the feminine-typed athletes.

After finding support for Spence and Helmreich's concepts in this all-female sample, attention was turned specifically to the question of sex differences in achievement motivation. In the second study both female (n=150) and male (n=125) college students were tested. The data were analyzed similarly to the preceding study except that the first factor was sex (as opposed to student category).

Mirroring the first study, there was a PAQ main effect on the mastery, work and competitiveness scales, with the general pattern that those subjects who were classified as androgynous or masculine had the higher scores. There was also a main effect for sex on the work scale, indicating that one sex had higher scores. Contrary to stereotypic predictions, however, this one sex difference finding was in favor of the women as they had the higher scores.

The final investigation of the relationship of androgyny and motivation proceeded one step beyond Spence and Helmreich's work by studying a sample of female (n=92) and male (n=64) athletes. The by now familiar main effect for PAQ was once more observed on the mastery, work and competitiveness components. Again, the significant differences occurred between those athletes categorized as androgynous or masculine and those classified as feminine or undifferentiated. Thus, these results supported the conviction that it was one's psychological attributes and not one's gender that affected an individual's achievement motivation levels.

As in the preceding study a sex main effect occurred on the work scale, indicating that the sexes differed. Again the women had the higher scores.

What can one conclude from this mass of data? First of all, the results from the studies presented are, in general, similar to Spence and Helmreich's, especially in regard to the findings pertaining to an individual's sex-role classification. All of the results indicated that androgynous and masculine subjects, regardless of gender, revealed higher levels of mastery, work, and competitiveness.

These results lend credence to the assumption that deficits in achievement motivation are at least partially explained by differences in the stereotypic characteristics associated with masculinity and femininity rather than gender. Thus, evidence tracing the origin of achievement motivation differences to varying distributions of instrumentality and expressivity is accumulating. Those individuals, regardless of gender, who have incorporated an instrumental orientation are more achievement oriented. Bedeian and Zarra (1977) have reported similar results. In their study, those females classified as having a non-traditional sex-role orientation scored significantly higher on an achievement motivation scale than did their traditional counterparts.

There were some differences between the results presented here and Spence and Helmreich's. In their college study analagous to the second investigation reported here, the one observed sex difference occurred on the competitiveness scale with the males having the higher scores. In contrast, only on the work scale did Harris and Jennings find a sex difference. It indicated that the females had higher levels of this component; providing a refreshing contrast to all the data indicative of female achievement deficiencies. Explaining this reversal, however, is more difficult than describing it. Hazarding a guess, one could postulate that the differences between the results of Spence and Helmreich and Harris and Jennings are attributable to differences between the samples and to differing amounts of change in society's attitudes and individuals' assimilations of those attitudes.

Another disparity between Spence and Helmreich's investigations and those of Harris and Jennings involved the interaction effects on the personal unconcern scale in the first study. The significantly higher levels of personal concern evidenced within the feminine category of female athletes indicated that the behavioral demands of highly competitive athletics were incongruous with the traditional feminine sex-role orientation. This may provide a partial explanation for why many highly-skilled female athletes drop out of sports. Simultaneously, this implies that coaches and educators should be directing more attention to this group of female athletes.

In a comprehensive study dealing with various aspects of sex-roles Jones and associates (Jones et al. 1978) asked their subjects to indicate if they desired to alter aspects of their psychological attributes relevant to the instrumental and expressive domains. Interestingly, it was the feminine females who expressed the greatest desire for increases on the instrumental related attributes. As the authors caution, this should not be interpreted as a desire to behave in an instrumental fashion. The studies conducted by both Jones et al. (1978) and Harris and Jennings imply that the feminine group expressed both a desire to act instrumentally and a concern with the ramifications of doing so. The instrumental demands inherent in sport indicate that it can provide an excellent opportunity for women to learn to develop their instrumental capacities. Coaches and educators should assume the responsibility of being aware of potential conflicts and to help alleviate them.

Alper (1977), in a review of the achievement motivation literature, suggested that it was time to redirect the focus of the achievement motivation literature from Horner's fear-of-success concept to investigations dealing with women who tell success stories. An abundance of women who fulfill Alper's criterion of success can readily be found within athletic environments. The use of such populations and the continued investigation of achievement motivation from the perspective of assimilated attributes rather than gender, will perhaps lead to a clearer understanding of motivation. Certainly the results of the present series of studies indicate that pursuing this path can be enlightening.

SUMMARY

Increasing levels of understanding and changing attitudes about human behavior have indicated that the stereotyped masculine and feminine roles for males and females respectively are no longer appropriate for socializing human beings to function effectively in today's society. As a result, many of the personality instruments which perpetuate these stereotyped expectancies for male and female behavior are no longer appropriate.

Males and females are very much alike psychologically in many respects. Some of the ways that they differ can be explained by how they have been socialized to meet the stereotyped expectancies rather than being explained by a biological basis. Athletes, some of whom are male and some who are female, appear to be more alike than different behaviorally. This suggests that one's behavioral frame of reference must be compatible with the behavioral demands of the environments that the individual seeks.

The behavioral demands of competitive sport are more dissonant with the stereotyped expectancies of feminine behavior. This explains why there has been more concern about the conflict that the female athlete may experience than that of the male athlete. With new ways of conceiving behavior, that is, a dualistic as opposed to a bipolar perspective, male and female athletes have been demonstrated to be more similar than different in their behaviors. Further, other behaviors are better explained when examined within this perspective. Behaviors such as self-esteem and components of achievement motivation appear to be more related to one's behavioral frame of reference than one's gender.

There is an obvious need for more research regarding the possible side effects of changing the definitions of "masculine" and "feminine" that are traditionally used as the standard for rearing boys and girls. The evidence available in no way supports the notion that attempts to foster sex-typed behavior as traditionally defined will produce more effectively functioning men and women.

Based on what has been learned about behavior to date, it appears that societies have the option of minimizing, rather than maximizing, sex differences through socialization practices. This is especially pertinent to the kinds of opportunities that are presented to males and females for sport competition as well as the reinforcements and rewards that are inherent in these competitive situations. Social institutions and social practices are not merely reflections of the biologically inevitable, according to Maccoby and Jacklin (1974). The social institution of sport needs to change many of its practices to insure that all who seek competitive sport experiences to maximize their potential have the same rewards and reinforcements, regardless of sex. For much too long the female has had her "femininity" questioned when she makes a serious commitment to competitive sport; conversely, the male has had his "masculinity" questioned when he chooses not to pursue such efforts.

It is up to human beings to determine what behaviors are needed to be learned by all human beings to foster the life styles they most value. Educators and coaches, likewise, must decide the attributes that are needed for the athlete to be effective behaviorally in competitive sport situations. One's biological sex does not appear to have very much to do with these behavioral dispositions.

REFERENCES

Alper, T. Where are we now? Discussion of papers 1975 AERA Symposium on sex differences and achievement. *Psychology of Women.* 1:294–303.

Atkinson, J.W., ed. 1958. *Motives in Fantasy, Action, and Society: A Method of Assessment and Study.* Princeton, N.J.: Van Nostrand.

Bakan, D. 1966. *The Duality of Human Existence.* Chicago: Rand McNally.

Bardick, J. 1971. *Psychology of Women: A Study of Bio-Cultural Conflicts.* New York: Harper and Row.

Beach, B. 1974. Males' perceptions of highly-skilled female participants. Masters Thesis. The Pennsylvania State University.

Bedeian, A.G. and M.J. Zarra. 1977. Sex-role orientation: effect on self-esteem, need achievement and internality in college females. *Perceptual and Motor Skills.* 45:712–714.

Bowen, R.T. 1967. A man looks at girls sports. *JOHPER*. 38:42–44.

Broverman, I.; Broverman, D.; Clarkson, F.; Rosenkrantz, P. and S. Vogel. 1970. Sex-role stereotyping and clinical judgments of mental health. *Journal Consult. Clin. Psychology*. 34:1–7.

Broverman, J.K.; Vogel, S.R.; Broverman, D.M.; Clarkson, F.E. and P.S. Rosenkrantz. 1972. Sex-role stereotypes: A current appraisal. *Journal Social Issues*. 7:146–152.

Cheska, A. 1970. Current developments in competitive sports for girls and women. *JOHPER*. 41:86–91.

DeBacy, D.; Spaith, L. and R. Rusch. 1970. What do men really think about athletic competition for women? *JOHPER*. 41:28–29.

Douvan, E. and J. Adelson. 1966. *The Adolescent Experience*. New York: Wiley.

Hall, M. 1972. A "feminine" woman and an "athletic" woman as viewed by female participants and non-participants in sport. *Brit. Journal Physical Education*. 43–46.

Hampson, J.L. and J.G. Hampson. The ontogenesis of sexual behavior in man. Pp. 1401–32 in W.C. Young, ed. *Sex and Internal Secretions*. Baltimore: Williams and Wilkins. Volume 1.

Harres, B. 1966. Attitudes of students toward women's athletic competition. *Research Quarterly*. 39:227–84.

Harris, D.V. 1975. Research studies on the female athlete; Psychological considerations. *JOHPER*. 46:32–36.

Harris, D.V. 1973. *Involvement in Sport: A Somatopsychic Rationale for Physical Activity*. Philadelphia: Lea and Febiger.

Harris, D.V. and S.E. Jennings. 1977. Self-perception of female distance runners. In P. Milvy, ed. *The Marathon*. New York: New York Academic of Sciences.

Heckhausen, H. 1967. *The Anatomy of Achievement Motivation*. New York: Academic Press.

Helmreich, R. and J.T. Spence. Sex-roles and achievement. Pp. 33–46 in R.W. Christina and D.M. Landers, eds. *Psychology of Motor Behavior and Sport*. Volume 2. Champaign, Ill.: Human Kinetics.

Horner, M.S. 1972. Femininity and successful achievement: A basic inconsistency. In J.M. Bardwick, et al., eds. *Feminine Personality and Conflict*. Belmont, Cal.: Brooks/Cole.

Horner, M.S. 1968. *Sex Differences in Achievement Motivation and Performance in Competitive and Noncompetitive Situations*. Ph.D. Thesis. University of Michigan. Diss. Abstracts. 1969, 30, 407B.

Jackson, D.N.; Ahmed, S.A. and N.A. Heapy. 1976. Is achievement a unitary construct? *Journal of Research in Personality*. 10:1–21.

Jones, W.H.; Chernovetz, M.E. and R.O. Hansson. 1978. The enigma of androgyny: Differential implications for males and females? *Journal Consult. Clin. Psychology*. 46:298–313.

Kagan, J. and H.P. Moss. 1962. *Birth to Maturity*. New York: Wiley.

Karabenick, S.A. and J.M. Marshall. 1974. Performance of females as a function of fear of success, fear of failure, type of opponent, and performance-contingent feedback. *Journal of Personality*. 42:220–237.

Klafs, C.E. and M.J. Lyon. 1973. *The Female Athlete: A Coach's Guide to Conditioning and Training*. St. Louis: Mosby.

Layman, E. 1968. Attitudes toward sports for girls and women in relation to masculinity-femininity stereotypes of women. Paper. *AAAS Meetings.* Dallas, Texas.

Maccoby, E.E. and C.N. Jacklin. 1974. *The Psychology of Sex Differences.* Stanford: Stanford University Press.

Marmor, Jr. 1973. Changing patterns of femininity: psychoanalytic implications. Pp. 221–238. In J.B. Miller, ed. *Psychoanalysis and Women.* New York: Brunner/Mazel.

McClelland, D.C.; Atkinson, J.W.; Clark, R.A. and E.L. Lowell. 1953. *The Achievement Motive.* New York: Appleton-Century-Crofts.

McKee, J. and A. Sheriffs. 1959. The differential evaluation of males and females. *Journal of Personality.* 25:356–371.

Mednick, M.T.S.; Tangri, S.S. and L.W. Hoffman. 1975. *Women and Achievement: Social and Motivational Analyses.* New York: Halsted.

Mehrabian, A. 1969. Measures of achieving tendency. *Educational and Psychological Measurement.* 29:493–502.

Monk, S.V. 1976. *An Investigation of the Self and Ideal-Self Profiles and the Dissonance Between Them Among Field Hockey Players.* Masters Thesis. Pennsylvania State University, State College, Pa.

Rogers, F.R. 1929. Olympics for girls. *School and Society. xxx.*

Rosenkrantz, P.; Bee, H.; Vogel, S.; Broverman, I. and D. Broverman, 1968. Sex-role stereotypes and self-concepts in college students. *Journal Consult. Clin. Psychology.* 32:287–295.

Salzman, L. 1973. Psychology of the female: a new look. *Psychoanalysis and Women.* Pp. 201–220 in J.B. Miller, ed. New York:Brunner/Mazel.

Sheard, K.G. and E.G. Dunning. 1973. The rugby football club as a type of 'male preserve': Some sociological notes. *IRSS.* 8:5–24.

Snyder, E.E.; Kivlin, J. and E.E. Spreitzer. 1975. Female athletes: an analysis of subjective and objective role conflict. Pp. 165–180 in D.M. Landers et al., eds. *Proceedings North American Society Psychology of Sport.* University Park: Pennsylvania State University.

Spence, J.T. and R.L. Helmreich. *Masculinity and Femininity: Their Psychological Dimensions, Correlates, and Antecedents.* Austin: University of Texas Press.

Spence, J.T.; Helmreich, R. and J. Stapp. Ratings of self and peers on sex-role attributes and their relation to self-esteem and conceptions of masculinity and femininity. *Journal Personality Social Psychology.* 32:29–39.

Stein, A.H. and M.M. Bailey. The socialization of achievement orientation in females. *Psychological Bulletin.* 80:345–356.

Sutton-Smith, B.; Rosenberg, G. and E.F. Morgan. Development of sex differences in play choices during preadolescence. *Child Development.* 34:119–126.

Tiger, L. 1969. *Men in Groups.* New York: Random House.

Weiner, B.; Frieze, I.; Kukla, A.; Reed, L.; Rest, S. and R.M. Rosenbaum. 1971. *Perceiving the Causes of Success and Failure.* New York: General Learning Press Module.

Weisstein, N. 1969. Woman as a nigger. *Psychology Today.* 3:20, 22, 58.

PART IV

SPORT GROUPS,

ORGANIZATIONS

AND

SPECTATORSHIP

Landers/Brawley/Landers

Lüschen

Noll

Spinrad

GROUP PERFORMANCE, INTERACTION AND LEADERSHIP

Daniel M. Landers,

Lawrence R. Brawley and Donna M. Landers

Competitive goal-oriented sport exists within a social context. Focusing only on the individual dimension ignores that athletic competition takes place within, between, or in relation to groups. The members of sport groups like any other task or socially oriented group relate to each other in regularized, patterned ways. These regularized aspects of groups, often referred to as group dynamics, may not affect each group member in the same way. The team leader, for instance, may disproportionately influence interaction processes in the group and thereby play a crucial role in the team's performance outcome. The purpose of this review is to summarize some of the pertinent findings and scientific principles derived from research on group dynamics theory and illustrate how these principles relate to sport-group performance, group functioning and leadership. Before proceeding with such a review, a definition of groups is necessary.

Definition and Conceptual Classification of Sport Groups

Sport Groups Defined

There are many types of groups. Some groups are composed of persons who seek membership for the social functions of the group (e.g., fraternal societies and clubs). Other groups come together to complete a well-defined task. These latter groups are generally small, being composed of more than one but less than 20 members. Task-oriented groups are of primary concern here since they typify sport groups. Group size and task-orientation restrictions are often imposed by the rules of the game. Therefore, a *sport group* can be defined as a task-oriented group, consisting of 2–20 people who are motivated and dependent on each other to complete their specific sports assignments. The "dependency" of group members is important for it is qualitatively different than those research areas concerned with nondependent, noninteractional performance (e.g., coaction paradigm of social facilitation).

A well-developed group would contain many additional properties beyond the aforementioned minimal requirements. The properties of well-developed groups include: (a) collective action to complete their task; (b) self definition as members of the group ("we-feeling"); (c) external acknowledgement of the group's existence; (d) shared rules, norms, and values that have consequences for group members; (e) a system of interlocking role and status positions; (f) desire to maintain the group (cohesion); and (g) unified identity among members. In addition, these properties are more evident when groups act together over time. It should be noted that laboratory groups brought together for a special purpose (ad hoc groups) are likely to be different from well-developed groups typically examined in field studies. In support of this, Cartwright and Zander (1968) note that well-developed groups possess more of these properties than ad hoc groups.

Group-Task Classification

Of the many conceptual analyses of the requirements of group tasks, Steiner's (1972) classification is the most appropriate for explaining task problems posed in team-sport activities. This classification takes into account the three task determinants of group performance: task demands, member resources, and group processes. Task demands are the actual prescriptions (i.e., game rules) as to how the task is to be performed. Member resources constitute all of the skills, abilities and knowledges that individuals bring to the group situation. Unlike task demands and member resources, how efficient a team might be cannot be measured or evaluated until play begins. The determination of the actual steps taken by individual group members in completing a task is what is referred to as group process. These three determinants must be analyzed and considered together with other task factors that affect group performance.

In terms of group members completing the task, most team sports can be categorized as either simultaneous or sequential. For simultaneous team sports, the group member's efforts occur at the same time (e.g., crew or team pursuit in bicycle racing) and the combined efforts of the group contribute to the score or goal. For sequential team sports, individual group members perform one at a time and individual scores are summed to arrive at a group score. In both instances, simultaneous and sequential, the task is considered additive. Some sports may possess both simultaneous and sequential features, particularly those that have each of their members performing a number of different subtasks that contribute to the group goal (e.g., football, soccer). The distinction between simultaneous and sequential tasks may be of importance in the degree of coordination or process which group members must employ. Generally, the more group tasks involve simultaneous action among members, the greater will be group-process problems of coordination and motivation.

A second task categorization is the distinction between unitary and divisible tasks. Sport-group members performing unitary tasks are required to perform exactly the same type of skill as all other members, as in the case of teammates in a 400-m relay. Divisable tasks involve a division of labor with each team's players performing different subtasks, such as passing, kicking, catching and running skills in football. Some sports, for example baseball, involve both divisible (fielding-position responsibilities) and unitary tasks (batting). This task distinction is also important for team-member selection and group-process considerations. It can be stated that as the number of subtasks increases for divisible tasks, the job of coordinating team process and member resources becomes much more difficult.

INDIVIDUALS AND GROUPS

Many investigators have been interested in the optimal combination of individuals for maximal group performance. This is undoubtedly a complex problem for it depends upon the individual's past experience, the type of task performed, and the measure of effective performance. Many of these elements have been integrated into Steiner's theory of group performance. Research support for this theory has come from comparisons of individual versus group performance, and the investgation of factors associated with the physical environment of the group.

A Theory of Group Performance

Through a careful analysis of task demands and each individual's skills and abilities, it is possible to get an estimate of the group's potential performance. An example of the measurement of potential performance are Ringelmann's data for rope pulling (Steiner 1972: 31–32, 80–81). If each of two men can raise 63 kg from the floor by individually pulling on a rope, then the potential for their joint effort should be 126 kg. Ringelmann's results, however, showed a 7% loss in efficiency as two men simultaneously pulled on the rope. Instead of pulling 126 kg, as theoretically expected, they could pull no more than 118. Note that if only actual-performance outcome were considered as a measure, then the groups would obviously perform better than individuals (118 vs. 63). However, when a less obvious measure of performance efficiency or force exerted per person is employed, groups are less efficient than individuals.

The discrepancies between actual- and potential-performance constitute loss due to what Steiner calls *faulty social process.* In the case of rope pulling, these losses largely accrue from motivation and/or coordination problems. The motivation problems are attributed to the individual's feeling "hidden" in the group, consequently the individual is less inclined to exert maximum effort. Coordination in this situation can be due to the individuals pulling at different times or slippage of the feet and hands.

Ringelmann's rope-pulling finding led to the following theoretical statement relating individuals to groups: actual performance equals potential performance minus loss due to faulty social process (Steiner 1972). Note that in this theory actual-performance outcome can never exceed potential performance. If it does, the problem may be attributed to an inaccurate determination of each member's potential performance. This formulation can explain the success of a group (or individual) over another either by their having a better supply of relevant resources (i.e., potential performance is higher), or because their processes more fully meet the demands of the task, or both. Therefore, in all questions asked concerning group performance or comparisons of individual performance with group performance, the answers will always depend upon (a) the nature of the task, (b) the individual's skills and abilities that are brought to bear upon it, and (c) the efficiency with which they can employ process to convert their individual resources into a group performance of high quality.

Individual Versus Group Performance

If one considers a member's actual-performance outcome and ignores individual efficiency (potential performance), research suggests that groups are more effective than individuals on additive tasks which require a variety of information and a number of steps that must be completed in a definite order. Gurnee's study (cited in Steiner 1972) on working alone or in groups is illustrative of this point. A subject's goal was to learn through repeated trials the correct option at each two-option decision point in the maze task, and to traverse the maze without making any errors. At each decision point group members voted on which path to follow. This procedure permitted the 10 members to match themselves to specific subtasks (i.e., a point on the maze), whereas individuals who worked alone were compelled to assume total responsibility at every step in the maze. Gurnee's findings clearly showed that groups made fewer errors than did individuals.

Although the task demands did not explicitly assign individual responsibility for specific subtasks, Gurnee noted that this strategy was apparent. Subjects in groups made the task divisible and lessened their work demands compared to individuals working alone on a unitary task. The advantage of divisible tasks in some group situations is exemplified in a field study comparison of two forms of gymnastic judging (Landers 1969). The gymnastic performances were filmed and judges scored the identical performance according to one of two methods. In this study, the unitary task for each judge was the assignment of numerical ratings to all areas considered for evaluation: difficulty, composition, and execution. Then the judge's scores were averaged to arrive at a single score. The above arrangement was compared to a divisible-judging method in which each judge only performed one subtask (i.e., rated either difficulty, composition or execution). Then each judge's rating was added to form the group score. It was found that divisible-task performance was more effective, resulting in less process loss for divisible judging than unitary judging.

The advantages of unitary- or divisible-task performance has been a major concern among small-group researchers examining industrial productivity. Lorenz (1933), for instance, studied assembly-line workers in a shoe factory. Their divisible work was done in six stages passing from person to person, each of whom contributed her particular operation. This arrangement averaged over 60 pairs of shoes each day while individuals working alone (unitary) on all six operations could complete only 43 pairs. Through subsequent field-experimental studies, Lorenz was able to isolate the relative contribution of several factors which provided an overall 39.9% advantage for divisible- over unitary-task performance. Of this percentage, 16.8% was due to a reduction in coordination losses, 13.5% was a result of individual specialization, and 9.6% was a consequence of increased motivation due to the presence of coactors. Studies such as this concerning sequential-additive tasks support the conclusion that divisible-task structures enable members to have a higher (or more accurate) performance outcome than unitary-task structures.

Several studies have been conducted to determine how individuals can best be combined to predict team-performance outcome. In these laboratory studies, subjects performed cognitive and motor tasks individually or in teams of two persons. It was found that team performance was, on the average, less productive than the sum of the individual performances previously determined from a pretest. This decline in efficiency in the group situation is consistent with Ringelmann's study and with Steiner's theory. Here group interaction may inhibit the maximal-potential contributions by its members. This was particularly evident for motor-task performance, where a knowledge of individual performance was a poor indicant of group performance (Comrey 1953). The motor-performance testing procedure employed by Comrey forced each group member to proceed alternately. In this situation, the faster, more competent member of each group could only use his speed on 50% of the task. Under these conditions, therefore, the high-ability member was handicapped and group-performance outcome was more highly correlated with the ability of the less competent member than that of the more competent.

When the task demands were changed to allow the more competent group member to contribute more than 50% to the task, the more competent member's performance was a better predictor of group-performance outcome than the slower member's individual scores (Comrey 1953; Wiest et al. 1961). Furthermore, the more similar the two members of a team were in individual proficiency, the more likely they were to form a proficient and effective team. Overall, however, measures of individual performance were a poor predictor of the extent to which the two members of a team facilitated or interferred with each other when working together.

The previous findings suggest that the enhanced or impaired performance of groups over individuals is dependent on many task factors. These factors affect the extent of interaction among members and as a result influence which member resources prevail. Individuals are better on tasks that require centralized organization of parts, whereas groups are better on sequential-additive tasks. But, when the measure of effectiveness on additive tasks is the amount of each individual's potential contribution, individuals are generally shown to be more efficient.

Physical Environment of the Group

Often in sport, task demands specify the size of the group and the position responsibilities of members. As will be seen, these task variations influence both the nature and degree of interaction.

Group size. According to Steiner's theory, the size of the group is directly related to process loss. That is, larger groups have a greater discrepancy between their actual- and potential-group performance. Using Ringelmann's rope-pulling data, Steiner (1972) found the relative coordination/motivation losses to be approximately equal to the number of coordination links in the group. For example, in a two-person team there is one coordination link, with a three-person team there are three coordination links, and in an eight-person team there are 28 coordination links. Thus, the discrepancy between actual and potential performance is directly proportional to the number of links needed to coordinate the task.

A clarification of Ringelmann's findings was later made by Ingham et al. (1974). The 7% process loss reported earlier was only found by Ingham et al. in increases up to Group Size 3. After Group Size 3 process loss asymptoted and remained relatively stable to Group Size 6. This discrepancy with Ringelmann's findings may have been a result of the extra precautions taken in the Ingham et al. study to minimize some forms of coordination loss.

The most important aspect of the Ingham et al. study was their controlling coordination loss while varying process loss due to motivation. Motivation losses, of course, can occur as members transfer responsibility for pulling to other teammates. To investigate this, subjects first pulled alone, then were blind-folded and led to believe that they were to perform again, but this time in a group of a given size. In reality, the blind-folded subjects again pulled alone so comparisons could be made between their pulling force when they were actually alone and when they perceived that they were pulling in a group. The results showed that the motivation loss was approximately 7% to Group Size 3 and then stabilized, remaining constant through Group Sizes 4-6. Therefore, it can be concluded that group size is a factor affecting the amount of motivation and coordination loss. The research in this area has not shown groups (of any size) to achieve their potential performance, but thus far only ad-hoc groups have been investigated.

When compared to the previously summarized results, the results obtained for nonadditive tasks are quite different. With some tasks, as in some forms of PGA golf, only the best performer's score is taken as the team score. In such situations, increases in group size enhance the probability of including more-competent people in the group. Increases in group size result in better performance, as Frank and Anderson (1971) have shown for production tasks (generation of images and ideas). By the same reasoning, on tasks where group performance is determined by the least-competent member, increases in group size result in progressively poorer performance. In Frank and Anderson's study, it is interesting to note that as group size increased, and when performance was based on the most-competent member, subjects perceived the group as pleasant. But, as group size increased, and performance was determined by the least-competent member, the pleasantness ratings decreased.

The four group sizes (2, 3, 5 & 8) used by Frank and Anderson also permitted the examination of other cognitive effects. Members of task-oriented groups generally prefer a given group size for maximal group functioning. For example, laboratory discussion groups preferred a size of approximately five members. Frank and Anderson (1971) found that larger groups (5 & 8 members) rated the task as easier, more beneficial and less effortful than smaller groups composed of two or three members.

In addition to these cognitive effects the groups atmosphere is rated differently dependent on whether the group size is odd or even. For example, odd-size groups (3 or 5 members) were rated as more pleasant, warm, cooperative and less serious than even-sized groups (Frank and Anderson 1971). This seemingly bizarre finding has been frequently found in discussion-type groups. Apparently, it is due to the greater probability of "stand-offs" occurring in even-sized groups.

In summary, the size of a group affects (a) the amount and distribution of group participation, (b) the member's reactions to the group, and (c) the probability of the group achieving consensus. As a partial consequence of these effects, group-performance outcome varies with group size. Moreover, group-performance outcome increases with group size when the group's task is either additive or solely dependent on the most competent member's score. On the other hand, performance outcome of the group usually decreases with increases in group size when the group's task is dependent entirely on the contribution of the least able group member.

Spatial positioning. Group structure has traditionally been examined in terms of positions and roles assigned to those positions. Role-positions frequently have varying amounts of status or prestige afforded them by group members. For example, in American society leaders tend to occupy head positions at a table while their lieutenants occupy side positions. In addition, laboratory groups having to compete with one another prefer to sit opposite and near where they can monitor the performance of the competitor (Sommer 1965). It is obvious from these examples that arrangements of people in groups are not a chance occurence. The position a person may choose (or be awarded) is often determined by (a) task demands, (b) the nature of the task, (c) the necessity for efficiently functioning communication and/or feedback networks, and (d) the necessity of coordinating the processing of task-relevant information (as with group leader). These four dimensions are next considered in laboratory settings before turning to research on sport groups.

Laboratory investigations of group structure frequently focus on the paths of communication and resultant interpersonal relations in various communication networks. Leavitt (1951) for example, investigated the *Wheel, Y, Chain,* and *Circle* structures in five-member laboratory groups. In order to successfully complete the experimental task, information from all positions had to be filtered to one position where its occupant had to select the common-task solution and channel it to other group members. Results of the Leavitt study showed that the Wheel, Y, Chain, and Circle evidenced an increasing order of performance time, number of errors, and number of messages to achieve the correct solution. The operating structure that finally developed for the Wheel, Y, and Chain was stable once achieved. The Circle structure, on the other hand, had the greatest amount of instability in operating structure. Members of Circle group structures sent more messages than other group structures, some of which were suggestions for improving the organization and functioning of their work group.

An additional finding of this study was that the occupant of the centermost position (in Wheel, Y, and Chain structures) most often selected the common solution and sent this information back to positions on the periphery. This positional advantage resulted in individuals in "central" positions evolving as decision makers more often than "peripheral" members. These centrally located individuals were better satisfied with the group and their own personal efforts, and were generally perceived as leaders by other group members. In this and other laboratory studies, the central-position member whose acts are a prerequisite for locomotion by fellow members, is viewed as having a stronger desire for his group to achieve success and is most apt to emerge as the group's leader.

Some of the research on group structures and leadership in sport groups has stemmed from the theoretical model on organizational structure proposed by Grusky (1963). Based on previous laboratory and field findings in small groups, Grusky formulated a model to explain the behavioral patterning of member-occupants of constituent positions along the following three interdependent dimensions: (1) spatial location; (2) nature of the task; and (3) frequency of interaction. Grusky theorized that all else being equal, the more central one's spatial location the greater the likelihood dependent or coordinative tasks will be performed by the occupant of the central position, and the greater the rate of interaction with occupants of other positions. In addition, performance of dependent tasks (e.g., throwing someone out in baseball) is hypothesized to be positively related to frequency of interaction. These predictions were supported by Grusky's finding that professional baseball managers were more likely to be recruited from high interaction (i.e., infielders and catchers) than low-interaction positions (i.e., outfielders and pitchers). Other investigators (cf. Loy 1970) have also supported Grusky's predictions by finding that high interactors were overrepresented among team captains, most valuable players, and were more likely to become college coaches than low interactors. Contrary to the results found by Grusky, however, pitchers in these studies tended to be selected for leadership positions more often than would be expected to occur by chance.

The relationship between centrality in the group structure and positive interpersonal relations has been alluded to in the discussion of Leavitt's results. Subjects occupying central positions, whether it be a housing residence near a central courtyard or the centermost position in a B–29 bomber crew, are more popular than individuals occupying peripheral positions. Similarly, when interscholastic baseball players have been divided according to Grusky's classification of high interactors and low interactors, the highest ratings for popularity were received by high interactors (Loy 1970).

GROUP COMPOSITION AND STRUCTURE

The spatial positioning of group members is only one of many structural factors affecting interaction within groups. Additional structural factors, such as member statuses and roles, group norms and leadership, also affect interaction and performance. Before examining these aspects of group structure a review of some of the research on group composition will first be presented.

Group Composition

Social scientists have often noted that the individual characteristics of group members will affect how the group performs. Research on group composition has focused primarily on three areas: assigned-member characteristics (e.g., personality, demographic-background variables, and race), interpersonal attraction, and group cohesiveness. cohesiveness.

Assigned-member characteristics. Teams having players of homogeneous-social composition are generally more successful (in winning games) than teams of heterogeneous composition. Eitzen (1973) obtained these results with 288 high school basketball teams. In his study, each coach responded to a questionnaire by giving the number of cliques present on his team as well as information on father's occupation, family prestige in the community, race, religion, and place of residence. Teams were then classified as being homogeneous or heterogeneous on the five demographic variables. Not only did homogeneously composed teams have better win-loss records than heterogeneous teams, they also had fewer cliques. It appears that social differentiation enhances clique formation which in turn can produce disruptive effects on athletic teams and reduce their chances of winning.

A homogeneously composed team is generally an asset, but there are exceptions. For example, both laboratory and field studies, have consistently shown performance outcome to be curtailed in groups homogeneously composed of individuals with similar achievement motivation (Klein and Christiansen 1969). This finding may best be explained by the old adage of there being too many Indians and not enough chiefs (or vice versa). If there is not some differentiation on member personality factors related to achievement motivation, there may be a built-in strain that hampers the emergence of group leaders. Ineffective leader-follower relations impair the effective interaction necessary for proper group functioning.

Oftentimes in group composition studies, performance has not been the outcome variable of major research interest. Interest in biracial or coeducational groups has obvious social import in terms of attitude change. A study by McIntyre (1970) compared prejudicial attitudes of 46 black and white boys who had participated in biracial flag football teams to a control group of boys with restricted biracial participation. By the end of the five-week period involving 20 contact sessions, there was trend for the white experimental subjects to have more favorable attitudes toward blacks than the white-control group. This attitudinal trend, however, was not evident among blacks. This latter finding may be a function of a lack of differentiation between the black-experimental and black-control groups, since the school from which both black groups were selected contained a 25% white population.

The relatively small sample (four groups) did not allow McIntyre to investigate the role of team-performance outcome on subjects' attitudes and perceptions of the other race. Recent laboratory evidence, however, suggests that the team-performance outcome affects interpersonal attraction and perceptions of competence of white subjects toward both white and black teammates (Blanchard et al. 1975). In this study, white subjects exhibited less attraction for a black teammate (but not for a white teammate) when he performed less competently. The combination of low competence and a low-performance outcome on the cooperative game employed in this study produced the least liking and least respect for blacks. The negative-affective states for black teammates disappeared following group success. It appears that without some degree of perceived-team success subjects resort to scapegoating and project blame toward those for whom they have socially-learned performance stereotypes.

Interpersonal attraction. Affective feeling toward other group members has been examined in relation to interaction among group members and group performances. In these studies, investigators have examined interaction by recording verbal communication or by recording more specific forms of interaction, such as passing or throwing a ball from one player to another. This latter, more direct form of interaction was employed by Klein and Christiansen (1969) to study three-man basketball teams. These investigators varied the composition of each team so that there were always two players who liked one another, with a third teammate who was sociometrically rejected or not even rated (i.e., sociometrically isolated). They observed that during a competitive game the frequency of passes was greatest for the sociometrically chosen teammates, least for the isolated members, with the rejected members falling in the middle range. This relative-interaction ranking disappeared when the game score became close.

In this situation, individual ability and potential for scoring overrode sociometric biases.

Other investigators (Cratty and Sage, 1964) have allowed group interaction (discussion of a maze-task solution) between trials in order to compare fraternity pledges who had close-friendship bonds (primary groups) to those that did not know one another (secondary groups). The members of the primary group who were allowed to interact between each trial were much faster in traversing the maze than secondary groups. One consistent observation was that secondary-groups selected leaders have the fastest individual-performance times more often than primary groups where leadership was retained by the presidents of their respective pledge classes. This differentiation in leadership affected the nature of interaction to the extent that primary groups discussed a broader range of task-irrelevant topics than secondary groups.

Group cohesiveness. Cohesiveness is the resultant of all forces that maintain a member's desire to remain in the group and his desire to resist forces that would disrupt or destroy the group. This group property has often been referred to as group solidarity or the "togetherness-teamwork" which a team displays. It has generally been inferred through measures of interpersonal attraction, although sole reliance on this measure ignores the multidimensionality of this concept. Gross and Martin (1952) stress that to determine the sum of forces acting to maintain group membership, the interdependence of factors such as task, motivation, and structural characteristics of a group must be considered.

The research relating cohesiveness to performance has shown mixed results. Landers and Lüschen (1974) suggest that these results are explainable in terms of divisible- or unitary-task performance. Where sports were primarily divisible, high cohesiveness was associated with high performance. Unitary sports, however, were associated with studies finding either no relationship, or in some cases a negative relationship.

When cohesiveness and performance are considered, Landers and Lüschen (1974) proposed that on a unitary-task (e.g., bowling) the lack of dependence between members for task completion promoted competition within the team rather than developing cohesion. This suggestion is consistent with the bulk of research evidence indicating that high-cohesive groups exert a greater influence over their members and are more effective in achieving their goals than low-cohesive groups.

Past research has focused on either (a) cohesion causing successful group-performance outcome, or (b) successful performance outcome causing cohesion. This cause-effect relationship between cohesion and performance outcome (teams win-loss record) has recently been clarified by studying groups over time (i.e., over a playing season). Studies examining the direction of this relationship in ice hockey teams and teams of scientists in an underwater habitat have convincingly demonstrated that performance is the causative factor. Carron and Ball (1976), for example, obtained team-cohesiveness ratings from members of 12 ice hockey teams in early-, mid- and post-season competition. Comparing the correlations between team cohesiveness and performance outcome across the season, Carron and Ball found high positive correlations only when the performance-outcome measure from a previous time period (mid- or post-season) was correlated with cohesiveness at the same or later time in the season. This finding supports the conclusion that performance causes cohesiveness and not the converse.

Group Structure

The differentiation of group members from one another with respect to any particular dimension (i.e., affect, influence, communication) under consideration is determined by a person's position in the group. For instance, a given group member may simultaneously be the person who communicates the most to other group members, but has the least influence in the group. Within the group, every member occupies a position and it is this pattern of positional relationships that constitutes group structure. The position one occupies in the group has a certain degree of prestige or value associated with it. This aspect of group structure is referred to as social status, or simply, status. The status within groups generally tends to be hierarchical. This hierarchical arrangement has been related to the frequency and duration of member interaction and performance of group members. A well developed status hierarchy is a property of a stable group.

Hierarchial status. The relationship between status hierarchy and sport performance was first observed by Whyte (1955) in his observations of an adult gang living in an Italian-slum area in Boston in the late 1930s. The bowling performance of gang members was positively correlated to their respective hierarchical position in the group. Through bowling a group member could maintain, gain or lose prestige. This relationship may have come about because of the group leaders who were primarily responsible for selecting group activities. It was natural for them to encourage an activity in which they were proficient. Once initiated, this social-status differentiation was perpetuated through subtle and overt forms of communication (e.g., praise and razzing). Individual performance that was incongruous with this group's expectations tended to be disruptive to the stability of the group. As a result, psychological pressures were employed by the group until the individual's performance was in accord with his group status.

Through a series of imaginative laboratory- and field-experimental studies, Sherif and his associates (Sherif and Sherif 1969) have greatly clarified the performance expectancies observed by Whyte. They examined well formed, stable groups by comparing the group's estimates of actual- and/or future-motor performance for members of varying status. The tasks employed were dart throwing and throwing softballs at a target. Once groups were shown the target area, the target was covered so as to reduce objective-performance determination, thus permitting groups to make subjective-performance judgments based on the individual member's status. After each individual threw, his teammates would estimate his actual performance. These studies support the conclusion that the higher the individual's status, the greater the overestimation of his performance by group members; the lower his status, the greater the tendency to underestimate. In short, expectancies of other members function like attitudes which may be particularly important in affecting estimates of performance measures that are inherently subjective. Scheer and Ansorge (1975), for example, have demonstrated that highly experienced gymnastic judges award scores according to their predetermined expectancy that gymnasts who appear last in their team-performance order will be better performers than their teammates who preceded them. Judges scoring videotaped performances awarded higher scores to identical performances viewed last as opposed to early in the competitive order.

Group norms. In addition to the status afforded each position, the group establishes rules which specify acceptable behavior in the group. These informal rules of conduct are called social norms. They differ from the formal task-rules that have been referred to as task demands. The social norms sometimes apply to all members of the group, but in other instances may only apply to certain positions in the group. Continued deviation from group norms often elicits sanctioning behavior or rejection by other group members. Likewise group norms, once established, can effectively influence individual-member attitudes and behaviors. Small-discussion groups have been used by group-dynamics investigators to foster group norms that members are privately willing to abide by, but are deterred from because of a conflicting norm or insufficient motivation to change. Group discussion forces members to vocalize their problems, interests and personal relations in achieving the group norm. The discussion technique has been effectively employed in promoting long-range behavioral change to refrain from consumption of alcoholic beverages, and to achieve substantial fitness changes and reduction in weight (Warren 1969). This research has demonstrated that it is far easier to sway a whole group of people by the creation of a group norm than to change a single individual's attitudes and behaviors by exposure of the individual to educational materials or propaganda.

The long range influence of group norms on behavior change is also evident for individuals trained as a part of workshops or special training sessions. Too often individuals trained in this manner have difficulty applying what was learned. Lippitt (1949) has shown that when group members have commonly shared norms and values, the individual increases his motivation to achieve the specific aims of the training session. After a workshop, in groups previously equated for performance, he found that individuals trained in isolation were only slightly more active than before, whereas those who had been members of strong training teams were much more active.

Group goals. A group goal, or an end state desired by a majority of group members, can be identified by observing groups. The goals of sport groups are readily identifiable (i.e., winning or breaking a record). The investigation of group goals has usually been accomplished by employing a level-of-aspiration paradigm. In this paradigm, individuals or groups are asked what score is expected for future performance after having experienced previous success or failure on the task. These level-of-aspiration studies reveal that individuals establish goals for the group and respond to goal achievement in the same way that they respond to personal goal achievement; that is, individuals and groups raise their level of aspiration following success and lower it following failure. Emerson (1966) employed this level-of-aspiration principle to investigate mountain climbers whose goal was to climb Mt. Everest. The success-failure manipulation was the naturally occurring weather conditions that either favored or hampered the group's goal striving. Under these conditions optimal-group motivation in achieving their goal was found when neither success nor failure were assured and there was a 50-50 chance of each occurring. It is under these uncertain conditions that goals are redefined upward or downward by group members seeking goal-relevant information through perception and communication. When the environment provided predominantly optimistic information (relative certainty of success), communication was predominantly pessimistic. Pessimistic environmental information produced the opposite effect. This patterned interaction within the group's communication structure acted to maintain uncertainty as well as clarify and sustain group-goal striving.

Oftentimes, successful accomplishment of the group goal cannot be achieved without causing another group to fail in accomplishing its goal at the same time. This dilemma is characteristic of zero-sum competition. Given the right conditions, intergroup hostility and tension are sometimes associated with competition. The series of experimental studies of young boys in summer camp situations illustrate how intergroup hostility develops and how it can be controlled by reforming the goals of the group (Sherif and Sherif 1969). Through the frustrations associated with winning and losing athletic contests and by some additional manipulations by the investigators, each group of boys perceived its opponent group to be antagonistic and untrustworthy. Intergroup hostility resulted. This produced a situation characterized by heightened cohesiveness among the members of each group. Each group's goals were refocused to retaliate against and ward off the threat imposed by the other group. After approximately five days of this frustration and tension, an attempt was made to reduce the intense intergroup conflict that had developed. To do this, Sherif and Sherif arranged situations which were realistically perceived by the boys (called superordinate goals) and necessitated joint efforts of both groups to accomplish mutually desirable goals. The use of a series of superordinate goals reduced between-group hostilities, and significantly lowered the amount of intergroup tension. In addition, a noticeable realignment of group boundaries occurred. Members of each group began forming friendships with boys outside their group. As new cooperative-group goals began to form, leaders emerged who were better equipped to facilitate the newly developing-interpersonal relations.

Leadership. From the work by Sherif and Sherif (1969), and other investigators as well, it is evident that the leader may be one of many group members depending on the goals and process demands that exist at any point in time. Research designed to identify leaders on the basis of a single personality type has been unproductive. Instead, leadership is dependent on the social atmosphere prevalent at the time. Lippitt and White (cf. Lippitt 1949) for instance, have shown in hobby-club groups that young boys responded differently to democratic-, authoritarian- and laissez-faire-leadership styles. The laissez-faire style was less efficient (poor quality work), less organized and less satisfying to group members than the democratic style. In the democratic-leadership styles, worker motivation and originality were greater than that found in other styles. Although the authoritarian style evoked greater discontent and aggressiveness than the other styles, the amount of work done was greater than found with democratic leaders. Recent evidence, however, suggests that this latter finding should be regarded with caution since neither authoritarian- nor democratic-leadership styles have been consistently related to higher group productivity.

Most researchers (cf. Fiedler 1968) now consider leadership to be more complex than previously conceived, often depending on: (a) the social power of the leader in controlling and enforcing member behavior as regards group norms and goals; (b) the structure of the group task; (c) the relations between the leader and followers in the group; and (d) the leader's task ability and his leadership style. Fiedler assessed leadership style by obtaining evaluative ratings from leaders of their most- and least-preferred coworker. It is assumed that the greater degree of differentiation between these ratings, the less concerned the leader is in maintaining interpersonal relations in the group. By employing a three-factor model (factors a, b, and c above) of leadership effectiveness, Fiedler could predict the relation between group performance and leadership when group performance was high. Thus, more considerate, person-oriented leaders were associated with higher group performance when "(a) the task is structured but the leader is disliked and must, presumably, be diplomatic and concerned with the feeling of his men and (b) the liked leader has an unstructured task and must, therefore, depend upon the...cooperation of his members" (Fiedler 1968: 371–372). Task oriented and less considerate leaders were associated with optimal-group performance when leader-follower relations were good, the task was structured, and social power played a minor role. Research on various types of groups (Fiedler 1968; Hardy 1971) has supported most of Fiedler's predictions, except when the task was structured and leader power was weak. In this instance, no difference was found between the leadership styles. This research underscores the inherent interrelatedness of group structure, leadership and group performance.

Examination of leadership in sport has proceeded in much the same manner as it has in the field of social psychology. Although earlier research indicated that team leaders were often the more skilled or popular players, the majority of this research has not been theoretically inspired. A notable exception is Bird's (1976) examination of women volleyball coaches and players. Based on Fiedler's model, Bird hypothesized that coaches and players of winning teams would perceive the leadership style of the coach to be more task-oriented than socio-emotional. This hypothesis was only partially confirmed in that coaches viewed themselves as task-oriented, but players perceived the same coaches as socio-emotional. In addition, perceived-leadership styles for winning teams differed according to the level of competition. Winning coaches in the more highly competitive division were seen as socio-emotional while losing volleyball teams saw their coaches style as task-oriented. The opposite was evident in the less competitive-volleyball division. Bird noted that players on the more competitive teams may not have needed a task-oriented leader as they were sufficiently task directed. In other words, the leaders may have had to modify their style according to situational and group factors unique to the particular form of competition.

REFERENCES

Bird, A.M. 1976. Leadership and cohesion within successful and unsuccessful teams: Perceptions of coaches and players. Pp. 176–182 in D. Landers, ed.

Psychology of Motor Behavior and Sport. Volume 2. Urbana, Ill.: Human Kinetics.

Blanchard, F.A.; R.H. Weigel and S.W. Cook. 1975. The effect of relative competence of group members upon interpersonal attraction in cooperating interracial groups. *Journal Personality Social Psychology.* 32, Sept.: 519–30.

Carron, A.V. and J.R. Ball. 1976. Cause-Effect Characteristics of Cohesiveness and Participation Motivation in Intercollegiate Hockey. Unpublished manuscript. University of Western Ontario.

Cartwright, D. and A. Zander, eds. 1968. *Group Dynamics: Research and Theory.* New York: Harper.

Comrey, A.L. 1953. Group performance in a manual dexterity task. *Journal Applied Psychology* 37, June: 207–10.

Cratty, B.J. and J.N. Sage. 1964. Effect of primary and secondary group interaction upon improvement in a complex movement task. *Research Quarterly.* 35, Oct.: 65–74.

Eitzen, D.S. 1973. The effect of group structure on the success of athletic teams. *IRSS* 8: 7–16.

Emerson, R.M. 1966. Mount Everest: A case study of communication feedback and sustained group goal-striving. *Sociometry* 29, Sept.: 213–227.

Fiedler, F.E. 1968. Personality and situational determinants of leadership effectiveness. Pp. 362–380 in Cartwright, D. and A. Zander, eds. *Group Dynamics.* New York: Harper and Row.

Földesi, T. 1978. Investigation for the objective measurement of cooperative ability among the members of rowing teams. *IRSS* 13,1:49–70.

Frank, F. and L.R. Anderson. 1971. Effects of task and group size upon group productivity and member satisfaction. *Sociometry* 34, March: 135–149.

Gross, N. and W.E. Martin. 1952. On group cohesiveness. *AJS* 57, May: 546–54.

Grusky, O. 1963. The effect of formal structure on managerial recruitment: a study of baseball organization. *Sociometry* 26,2:345–352.

Hardy, R.C. 1971. Effect of leadership style on the performance of small classroom groups. *Journal Personality Social Psychology* 19, Sept.: 367–374.

Ingham, A.G.; Levinger, G.; Graves, T. and V. Peckham. 1974. The Ringelmann effect: Studies of group size and group performance. *Journal Experimental Social Psychology* 10, July: 371–84.

Klein, M. and G. Christiansen. 1969. Group composition, group structure, and group effectiveness of basketball teams. Pp. 397–407 in J.W. Loy and G.S. Kenyon, eds. *Sport, Culture, and Society.* New York: Macmillan.

Landers, D.M. 1969. Effect of the number of categories systematically observed on individual and group performance ratings. *Perceptual and Motor Skills.* 29, Dec.: 731–35.

Landers, D.M. and G. Lüschen. 1974. Team performance outcome and the cohesiveness of competitive coacting groups. *IRSS* 9,2: 57–71.

Leavitt, H.T. 1951. Some effects of certain communication patterns on group performance. *Journal Abnormal Social Psychology* 46, Jan.: 38–50.

Lenk, H. 1976. *Team Dynamics.* Champaign, Ill.: Stipes.

Lippitt, R. 1979. *Training in Community Relations.* New York: Harper.

Lorenz, E. 1933. Zur Psychologie der industriellen Gruppernarbeit. *Zeitschrift Experimentelle und Angewandte Psychologie* 45: 1–45.

Loy, J.W. 1970. Where the action is: A consideration of centrality in sport situations. Paper. *2nd Canadian Psychomotor Learning and Sports Psychology Symposium.* Windsor, Ont.

Lüschen, G., ed. 1966. *Kleingruppenforschung and Gruppe im Sport.* Opladen: Westdeutscher Verlag.

McIntyre, T.D. 1971. A field experimental study of cohesiveness, status, and attitude change in four biracial small sport groups. *Dissertation Abstracts International.* 32: 1A-1114A.

Moede, W. 1920. *Experimentelle Massenpsychologie.* Leipzig: Hirtzel.

Moede, W. 1927. Die Richtlinien der Leistungspsychologie. *Industrielle Psychotechnik* 4:193-209.

Scheer, J.K. and C.T. Ansorge. 1975. Effect of naturally induced judges expectations on the ratings of physical performance. *Research Quarterly* 46, Dec.: 463-70.

Sherif, M. and C. Sherif. 1969. *Social Psychology.* New York: Harper.

Sommer, R. 1965. Further studies of small groups ecology. *Sociometry* 28, Dec.: 337-48.

Steiner, I.D. 1972. *Group Process and Productivity.* New York: Academic Press.

Tripplett, N. 1898. The dynamogenic factors in pacemaking and competition. *American J. Psychology* 9,4: 507-533.

Warren, C.L. 1969. An investigation of the group approach to weight reduction and improvement of physical fitness in college women. Paper. *Meeting of AAHPER.* Boston.

Weist, W.M.; Porter, L.W. and E.E. Ghiselli. 1961. Relationship between individual proficiency and team performance and efficiency. *Journal Applied Psychology* 45, Dec.: 435-40.

Whyte, W.F. 1955. *Street Corner Society.* University of Chicago Press.

THE ANALYSIS OF SPORT ORGANIZATIONS

Günther Lüschen

Sport organizations incorporate a wide variety of social con-glomerates from physical education classes and a professional sport club, the National Collegiate Athletic Association (NCAA) to a national federation for hockey, the International Olympic Commit-tee (IOC) or the International Sport Union of Railroad Workers. Some of these organizations fall under the category of voluntary organizations; some of them are outright compulsory. All fulfill the definition of formal or complex organizations in varying de-grees of formalization and in the pursuit of specific goals.

The Definition and Study of Organizations

Organizations are social units which delimit membership and have an internal differentiation of roles. Organizations are oriented toward the fulfillment of specific goals and purposes. Organizations incorporate bureaucratization and rational procedures to realize their goals and purposes. This definitional approach applies to all types of organizations and could include the organization of a school and an afternoon *Kaffeeklatsch* held once every week between ladies. Also it covers all forms of sport organizations mentioned above. In the end such definitions leave more questions open than they resolve. One may observe that a universal definition and theory of organizations have been particularly cumbersome for sociology and other social sciences such as administration, political science, psy-chology, and social planning.

In the past organizations have been analyzed by sociologists in terms of specific typologies. Conventional approaches addressed sport organizations as voluntary, while such organizations as hospitals and prisons were called compulsory. In a different approach, asking the question *"cui bono?"* (who benefits?), Blau and Scott (1963) distinguish a four-fold typology: (1) *mutual benefit associations,* where the prime beneficiary is the membership, (2) *business concerns,* where the owners are the prime beneficiaries, (3) *service organiza-*

tions, where a group of clients is the prime beneficiary, and (4) *commonweal organizations,* where the public at large is the prime beneficiary. When applying this typology to sport organizations one recognizes that sport clubs are mutual benefit associations, while the professional baseball club in the United States is a business concern. Service organizations in sport can be observed in such establishments as a communal recreation department or some large sport clubs in Europe which increasingly provide a service by offering sport to a public buying such a product. And, such organizations as the United States Olympic Committee (USOC) or the Federation of Sport and Technique in East Germany can be viewed as commonweal organizations since they field an Olympic team for the benefit of the country in the one case and train for national defense purposes in the other.

Very prominent in the earlier study of organizations was the analysis of executive roles and behavior. Max Weber's three types of legitimate authority (governance) have been the starting point of many theoretical discussions and empirical studies of executives. Similarly, Max Weber's idealtype treatment of the bureaucracy was the basis for arguments delineating structure and process in organizations assuming impartiality and rationality.

Recently typologies of organizations and typologies of executive behavior have attracted less interest in the study of organizations. And while the analysis of communication patterns, rank hierarchies, and role requirements are still very much in the forefront of analyses, there has been an increased interest in organizational process, policy, and output. Rationality is not always a feature of organizational action. Wilensky finds "Organizational Intelligence" (1967) seemingly low in political organizations and administrations. And, according to Crozier, the executive in an attempt to secure position and enlarge power typically creates "zones of uncertainty" (1964). While the breakdown of organizational procedure caused by interpersonal rivalry, problems of incompetence or misplaced motivation leads to irrationality among executives and organizational staff, there is the necessity to analyze the degree of rationality and effectiveness in organizational design (Simon, 1962).

The sociology of organization faces not only problems with regard to an integrated theory for a variety of organizational forms and the interchanges between personal and social structures. There is an additional problem because the study of organizations requires carefully devised strategies that extend beyond the standard methods of social science research (Price, 1972). Survey sampling of individuals is certainly applicable to the study of organizations. Yet, this standard method will be helpful predominantly for the analysis of membership structures and individual attitudes only. An investigation of organizational structure, where the bureaucracy as a formal element is the focus of analysis, will often be better served by a careful content analysis of documents, statutes and proceedings. Budgets, statistical and aggregate data in an organization will also be useful. An investigation of organizational policies directed toward the executive level of an organization will find neither sampling nor the employment of a standardized questionnaire particularly helpful. Rather an in-depth, open-ended interview of all executives should be used and constitute what is referred to as elite interviewing (Dexter, 1970). Objectivity under such circumstances is of course a problem. Yet, one can gain in terms of validity because the executives of an organization, intimately involved in everyday procedures and often displaying a high degree of identity, notably with voluntary organizations, will have most valuable insights. The problem is rather one of reliability. In elite interviewing, cross-checks between different interviews as well as with outsiders to an organization are necessary. Moreover, a multiplicity in method of analysis is often advisable under such circumstances. Multiple method will combine interviews and analyses of written documents, budgets, and aggregate data of the organization for proper reliability checks.

A Descriptive Overview of Sport Organizations

The formal organization of sport shows a multiplicity that cannot be subsumed easily under one label. In terms of voluntarism, physical education classes in school, sport programs in the military, or the sport groups in prison are not voluntary, and they also pose problems with regard to delimitation from the organizations at large of which they are a part. As distinguished from these, such organizations set up exclusively for sport as tennis clubs or a national federation of badminton can be called voluntary, and the membership of individuals, of clubs or of regional and state organizations is also clearly identifiable.

In international perspective, sport organizations are a reflection of national interest structures, historical constellations, and international, cosmopolitan developments. With regard to the latter, the Olympic movement has in its organization experienced a remarkable growth and continuity with the IOC as an organizational body that developed above national and individual sport interests. Moreover, this organization initiated the establishment of some 140 National Olympic Committees. The latter vary in their structure to a considerable degree across individual countries, yet they perform similar functions.

In a different dimension the international federations in individual sport disciplines such as FIBA (Federation Internationale de Basketbal Amateur), FIFA (Federation International de Fotbal Amateur), FIG (Federation Internationale de Gymnastique) are the highest organizational authorities controlling the observation of standardized rules, international competitions and the Olympic contests in their respective discipline. While these federations are, for all practical purposes, organized for the technical execution of a sport, they exert political influence in international sport and reflect in their executive body the realities of international sport politics.

As for the organization of sport on the national level, the structure in the United States is primarily determined by educational and economic interests and is highly decentralized. In amateur sport there are three major organizations (AAU, NCAA, USOC) that are relatively independent of one another and claim jurisdiction over major parts but not over all individual sport disciplines. The major professional sports such as baseball, basketball, football, and ice-hockey have their national, independent organizations as well. There are few countries with an equal variety of sport organizations on the national level. Finland has four separate national organizations determined by social class and political interests; Austria on the same basis has three national organizations. The best known examples of centralized sport organizations are the Deutscher Sportbund (German Sports Federation) and the Swedish Rijksidrottsförbund (Swedish National Federation) both of which are joint organizations of individual sport federations such as soccer and track, and of state sport organizations and local clubs with an individual membership in both countries that surpasses the labor union membership. While the above organizations are independent (although they receive some government subsidies), governmental or institutional controls are a typical feature of sport in the USSR where a State Committee for Physical Culture oversees all sport affairs (Riordan. 1976). Controlled by the government but less centralized is the sport movement in China (Kolatsch, 1972). Based on

Table 1. The Organization of Sport on the National Level in Terms of Control and Centralization.

Control	Centralized	Decentralized
Political	USSR	China
Institutional, semi-political, social class	France Italy	Austria* Finland*
Independent	Bulgaria West Germany Sweden	USA

*One of the organizations in each Austria and Finland on the national level to be classified as independent.

the principle of centrality versus type of control or independence, Table 1 gives an overview for the organization of sport at the national level.

Recently political influences and controls have become apparent in national and international sport organizations. There are ministries of sport not only in governments of East Europe but in France, England and many developing countries as well. Initiated by UNESCO, there is now an intergovernmental committee that addresses issues of international sport. While this committee and other political organizations are often without a clear mandate and have only limited control, international and national sport organizations have become increasingly interdependent with political structures.

The organization of sport at the local level shows an equal variety between and within different countries. The typical organization in West Germany is the independent sport club. In the USA, it is the department or association at a high school, college, or university. In the USSR it is the military, industrial or youth organization.

The concept of voluntarism in sport organizations related to the membership in different forms of clubs and groups can refer to the executive and supervisory level in sport organizations as well. Sport organizations are led and are being run in their daily affairs to a high degree by volunteers and by executives providing services without pay. The personal members of the IOC, coopted rather than elected into their ranks, are the most visible, typical example. One should note that the voluntarism among executives and staff members is, at present, in a considerable change with increased professionalization emerging among occupants of such positions and a definite tendency to provide more payment for services rendered to a sport organization.

The notion of voluntarism and informality on the one hand and the basic concern in sport for high achievement on the other, imply a form of conflict in sport organizations that is one of the most interesting aspects of organizational research in sport. This problem is indicated in a situation where high performance and success is a consistent concern for sport itself, while the performance of the organizations is rarely questioned. Consequently, executives in sport organizations have a long period of office, and, typically, the organizational effectiveness in sport is rarely studied. It is perhaps no accident that even in professional sport clubs the efficiency of the club organization is rarely questioned. Failures are personalized, resulting in the dismissal of coaches and not in attempts to reorganize a club.

THE SOCIOLOGICAL STUDY OF SPORT ORGANIZATIONS

There have been a number of forerunners to the study of sport organizations. Savage et al. (1929) provided an elaborate analysis of American college and university athletics dealing with the development of major and minor sports, administrative control, the position of coaches, recruitment, financial support of athletes, and press relations. The study, supported by the Carnegie Foundation, ultimately raised questions of basic values and value conflicts between education and athletics. The study, based on an investigation of 25 colleges and universities in Canada and the U.S., a sample of 1292 athletes, and site visits of more than 130 schools, used documents, aggregate data and attitudinal accounts. The same authors addressed the problem of current developments under the auspices of the Carnegie Foundation in 1931. While they recognized severe economic problems and value conflicts, they expected at that time "the return to a more sincere appreciation of the values of sport and sportsmanship" (p. 53).

Dealing with problems of organization and administration of sport, the qualitative and descriptive insights of Hughes and Williams (1944) provide an analysis that is of interest not only for practitioners but for organizational analysis of American school sport as well. Diem (1953) published an extensive account of international and German national sport organizations. The study contains historical and statistical data. A study of the folklore of clublife describes the subculture of Viennese sport clubs (Hrandek, 1958).

The most extensive and sociologically strong analysis of this earlier period in the study of sport organizations is represented by the festive account of the Swedish Sport Federation published on the occasion of it's 50th anniversary (1953). Detailed and representative data give valuable insights with regard to social stratification of the membership and executives in the Swedish Sport Federation overall and in individual sport disciplines. The study extends into ecological considerations of facilities and communities. It also analyzes public subsidies and forms of government and political control.

Programmatic Considerations for the Study of Sport Organizations

Eric Hoyle (1971), in a major article "Organization theory and the sociology of sport," addresses problems of boundary definitions and explores the fruitfulness of the typological approach. Problems with inconsistencies of typologies lead him to suggest use of a formal analysis with only a limited number of variables or to address problems that are specific to sport organizations. For the latter the variable approach is being replaced by an extensive and often qualitative analysis of such a problem as the poor relationship between British athletes and sport administrators. Organizational theory as such, despite many shortcomings, is being advocated as a guideline for analysis as well as for the solution of practical problems in sport organizations.

Loy et al. (1978) address theoretical insights of the middle range. In their review of existing material, on the basis of a social relations approach, they suggest a focus on leadership, personnel turnover, recruitment, interpersonal relations, and organizational (team) performance. They argue from previous research as well as sport experiences and focus on small-scale organizational aspects.

Lüschen (1975) proposed treating single National Olympic Committees as units of analysis and held that a cross-national study of the then total number of 136 committees would provide quantifiable data of structurally different but functionally similar organizations. Multivariate analysis could in such a project provide insights into the differential importance of organizational, personnel, and societal factors for organizational output in the form of specific policies as well as of success in the organization of Olympic teams.

A general outline for social research of sport organizations needs to address a variety of questions acknowledging the multiplicity of organizational types as well as internal structures and external contexts. Furthermore, issues of organizational policy from questions of identification of organizational goals, planning, implementation of organizational policy to policy realization and evaluation would have to be pursued. The existing research in the area of sport organizations and a modest methodological approach suggest that the study of sport organizations centers around four major areas:

1. **The structure and development of membership in sport organizations.**
   Implicit in this area are concerns for planning and policy of sport organizations. This area is strongly influenced by the survey research method with an emphasis on either demographic characteristics or attitudes of individual members. In the strict sense, the analysis of the organization is secondary and often accidental. The typical research question here is: How can the membership be enlarged or the existing membership be more satisfied with the organizational program?
2. **The structure and conduct of executives and staff members.**
   Here the concern for the actions of executives and the reflection of organizational structure is equally strong. The typical research question is: How do executives build and enlarge their basis of power, and what personal and organizational interests are reflected in their conduct?
3. **The structure and type of sport organizations.**
   This would appear to be the core of organizational research with concerns for external context of an organization, degree of bureaucratization, communication and influence patterns, goals and normative structure, organizational subculture. Here one of the typical questions is: How is integration and effective-

ness of a sport organization secured, and how are patterns of inter-personal relations and system commodities linked up with such a process?

4. **Policy, planning and organizational performance.**
   This newly emerging subfield, stimulated by complex method-ological concerns and necessities for better planning alike, is concerned with principles of policy, planning and policy evalua-tion. A typical question would be: In what way does the struc-ture of sport organizations and of different sub-types follow a consecutive pattern of steps in policy identification and imple-mentation; what is the level of rational in the typical informal structure of a sport organization and what influences the pro-cess?

In a broad sense, the more recent research projects on sport organizations can be subsumed under these four divisions. The following review will acknowledge the most typical material.

Recent Research of Sport Organizations
Membership structure. Studies of membership in sport organiza-tions are first facilitated by relatively easy accessibility through surveys. They are secondly an easily definable object of study, since sport organizations and clubs have relatively clear member-ship criteria. Thirdly, they are of considerable practical value for membership policies in sport organizations resulting in the execu-tion of such projects in many countries and with the financial back-ing and general support of sport organizations and public sport administrations. In line with practical concerns, variables in these studies include demographic variables as well as criteria of social and regional stratification. Examples are studies of sport in Den-mark (Andersen, 1957), Sweden (Sveriges Rijskidrottsförbund, 1953, Halldén 1966), Belgium (Claeys et al., 1974), West Germany (Lenk, 1972), Japan (Takenoshita, 1965; Niwa, 1966), Bulgaria (Genov 1958), Netherlands (Vlot, 1964), and Poland (Wohl, 1969).

In the most recent study of this type Schlagenhauf (1978) in-vestigated West German sport clubs organized within the ranks of the 16 Mill. member Deutscher Sportbund. The study, beyond great detail on a number of issues, provided some surprising results. While soccer claims the highest nominal membership, sport club members themselves report that they participate primarily in swim-ming as an activity overall, and, that, within the confines of their clubs, they participate mainly in field handball and gymnastics in that order. The author notes that the most recent surge of new members toward sportclubs in West Germany has resulted in a major change of participation patterns: Schlagenhauf found the sport club movement widely unprepared for a new membership that no longer seeks sport clubs as a place of social identification but prefers them as agencies to provide a service. Nevertheless, for the membership as a whole, sport clubs still provide functions for status and community identification. Traditionally sport clubs were a domain of the middle class and of men, the membership now extends increasingly into the lower class and into the female population.

Structure and Conduct of Executives and Staff Members. Despite the prominence of some executive bodies in sport organizations, there are not many investigations dealing with executive behavior and even fewer that approach systematic study. Espy (1979) deals with the political influence structure and organizational developments in the more recent history of the Olympic movement. Executive behavior figures as a key variable, yet it is not systematically treated in terms of decision-making or policymaking. Von Euler (1953) finds that executives in Sweden are recruited from a higher position in the system of stratification than the membership overall in the Sport Federation and in individual sport disciplines.

Other studies dealing with coaches in sport organizations address career patterns (Sage, 1975). Such studies reflect only indirectly upon the organizational context and the strict performance demands under which such careers proceed. The major exception to this observation is the study by Grusky (1963; a, b) linking managerial recruitment to formal organization and managerial succession to organizational success of a baseball club.

For the study of executive conduct, Heinilä (1972) provides one of the most ambitious analyses in the investigation of the value orientations of Finnish sport executives. Applying the organizational typology of Blau and Scott and concepts from Parsonian action theory, Heinilä finds executives displaying "pluralistic ignorance" about the organizational goals and the values of fellow executives. At the same time, these sport executives, as elected representatives, are strongly membership oriented and display features of a democratic leadership style. In so doing they seem to secure their own position and reflect that their organization is primarily a mutual benefit association.

The Structure of Sport Organizations. This general topic can incorporate a wide variety of questions from typologies, normative structure, communication structures to labor relations and formal structure on the team level. In the end, such analyses may extend into economics (Noll, 1974) and legal aspects of sport organizations (Warren, 1973). A more refined approach in terms of organization theory will obviously stress aspects of social systems and external as well as internal controls.

Loy and McElvogue (1970) have identified the preponderance of discrimination in American baseball and football organizations and have initiated a number of follow-up studies of the same problem. Analyses of individual renumerations in professional team sports (Scully, 1974) were less conclusive showing that black superstars with high seniority commanded the highest salaries, while, for average players discrimination in salaries by race was apparent. Scovill (1974) has specifically addressed the question of labor relations in professional sport clubs; this is an issue that is particularly significant for professional sport organizations in industrialized countries.

Goals and values of the Olympic organization and movement has been the focus of an elaborate study by means of content analysis, historical and aggregate data as well as participant observation (Lenk, 1964). Lenk identifies six goals dealing with human perfection, interdependence with antiquity, religious affiliation, social involvement and understanding, organizational independence of the movement, and national education. According to the analysis, only goals of organizational independence have been fully realized; other goals have been realized only partially, and the analysis finds religious affiliation not realized at all. Lenk finds a high number of contradictions in the culture of the international Olympic organization, yet the analysis clearly recognizes the Olympic movement as an effective organizational implementation.

The network analysis of the NCAA by Stern (1979) is qualitative and historical in nature. The analysis proceeds on the basis of four structural determinants of organizational control: administrative structure, system coupling, multiplicity of ties, and new network resources. The study in its historical account interprets a number of key enforcement decisions that established the present tightness of organizational control in the NCAA in between 1948 and 1952. American university and college sport has also been the focus of analysis in a number of trade books providing valuable detail and insight (Michener 1976).

Dynamics of conflict and change in two rivalling sport federations of the game of rugby in England are the focus of a case study by Dunning and Sheard (1976). Issues of politics in sport administration are analyzed for France (Amiot, 1969). And the political and organizational processes of Soviet sport have been the center of three qualitative accounts of formal structure and socio-political interdependence (Morton, 1963; Riordan, 1977; Shneidman, 1978). The problem of political and social cleavages is the topic of a multivariate analysis of national sport organization in Finland (Kiviaho, 1974).

Organizational Policy, Planning and Performance. Some of the most crucial questions of policy analysis are hidden in organizational planning, policy, and performance. At the lower level of sport organizations, Grusky's investigation of organizational effectiveness as linked to managerial succession (1963b) can be cited as an example. A replication of his study by Allen, Panian and Lotz (1979) finds managerial succession explaining little variance of a team's success but being rather a negative predictor. They find, however, that a managerial change in between seasons has some positive effect. At the higher level of complexity in sport organizations, questions of organizational performance are seldom raised. Frey's (1978) discussion of effectiveness of American amateur sport is one of the few exceptions.

In a pilot study to a cross-national project of National Olympic Committees and their policies, Lüschen (1979) uses the subjective evaluation of policy goals versus policy realization in order to understand conflicts and the differential execution of policies. He finds that among 21 National Olympic Committees their own executives consider their organizations to do well with regard to fostering international understanding and policing the amateur principle. They are less positive for the promotion of sport in general within their respective countries. In evaluating organizational policies on the basis of four theoretical goals (fidelity, responsiveness, effectiveness, and efficiency), the executives give their committees high marks for efficiency, while they indicate that their committees have problems with regard to fidelity, i.e., the pursuit of committee policies such as fostering a good Olympic team in line with the long-range interests of their own society. According to the pilot project, such problems appear more prevalent in National Olympic Committees of developing countries, which executives also complain that they find only limited understanding for their specific problems among committees in modern societies and in the Olympic movement overall.

CONCLUSION

The study of sport organizations is at this time in the stage of early development. A number of the existing studies demonstrate the methodological fruitfulness and practical applicability of studying sport organizations. The rapid increase of the institution of sport with a consecutive high number and multiplicity of organizations will be a continuous challenge to provide more and better insights for clubs, federations, and the national and international bodies of sport. Such research will contribute to the practical problems of sport, it will provide better knowledge about the structure and process in sport organizations, and it will enhance the understanding of complex, formal organizations as well.

REFERENCES

Allen, M.P.; Panian, S.K. and R.E. Lotz. 1979. Managerial succession and organizational performance: a recalcitrant problem revisited. *Adm. Scie. Quarterly* 24, 2:167–180.

Amiot, M. 1969. Politique et administrations. *Sociologie du Travail* 11,2:113–144.

Andersen, H. et al. 1957. Sport and games in Denmark in the light of sociology. *Acta Sociologica* 2,1:1–28.

Ball, D. 1974. Replacement processes in work organizations: task evaluation and the case of professional football. *Sociol. Work Occupation* 1,1:197–217.

Blau, P. and W.R. Scott. 1963. *Formal Organizations.* London: Routledge and Kegan Paul.

Bratton, R. 1970. *Consensus on Association Goals Among Executives of Two Canadian Sports Associations.* PhD-Thesis. Urbana: University of Illinois.

Cap, A. 1969. Importance des "Universiades"; leur action sur le développement des relations dans le sport universitaire international. *Televichovny Sbornik* (Prague) 11:145–183.

Claeys, U. et al. 1974. *Organisatie en financiering van de sport voor Allen* (Organization and financing of sport for all). Leuven: University. Part I and II.

Crozier, M. 1964. *The Bureaucratic Phenomenon.* Chicago: University of Chicago Press.

Dexter, L.A. 1970. *Elite and Specialized Interviewing.* Evanston, Ill.: Northwestern University Press.

Diem, C. 1953. *Deutsche and internationale Turn-und Sportverwaltung.* Köln: Sporthochschule.

Dunning, E. and K. Sheard. 1976. The bifurcation of Rugby Union and Rugby League. *IRSS* 11,2:31–71.

Eitzen, S. and N. Yetman. 1972. Managerial change, longevity and organizational effectiveness. *Adm. Scie. Quarterly* 17,1:110–116.

Espy, R. 1979. *The Politics of the Olympic Games.* Berkeley: University of California Press.

Euler, R. von 1953. Idrottsörelsen av i Dag (Sport of today). Pp. 147–278 in Sveriges Rijksidrottsförbund. *Svensk Idrott.* Malmö: Allhem.

Frey, J.H. 1978. Organization of American amateur sport: efficiency to entropy. *Am. Behav. Scientist* 21, Jan.:361–378.

Genov, F. et al. 1955. *Organizacija na fiziceskata kultura i sporta NR Balgarija* (Organization of physical culture and sport in Peoples Republic of Bulgaria). Sofia: Profizdat.

Grusky, O. 1963a. The effects of formal structure on managerial recruitment. Sociometry 26,2:345–353.

Grusky, O. 1963b. Managerial succession and organizational effectiveness. AJS 69,1:21–31.

Halldén, O. 1966. *Ungdomens förenings-och fritidsliv* (Youth organizations and leisure behavior). Stockholm: Statens offentliga Utredningar. 47.

Harf, J.E.; Coate R.A. and H.S. Marsh. 1974. Trans-societal sport associations; a descriptive analysis of structures and linkages. *Quest* 22:52–62.

Heinilä, K. 1979. The value orientations of Finnish sport leaders. *IRSS* 14,3–4: 59–74.

Hoyle, E. 1971. Organization theory and the sociology of sport. Pp. 82–93 in R. Albonico and K. Pfister-Binz, eds. *Sociology of Sport*. Basel: Birkhäuser.

Hrandek, R.A. 1958. Beiträge zur Kenntnis des Wiener Vereinslebens. *Österreichische Zeitschrift für Volkskunde* 61,3:205–219.

Hughes, W.C. and J.F. Williams. 1944. *Sports, Their Organization and Administration*. New York: Barnes and Noble.

Johnson, A.T. 1978. Public sports policy. *Am. Behav. Scientist* 21,3:319–344.

Kiviaho, P. 1974. The regional distribution of sport organizations as a function of political cleavages. *Sportwissenschaft* 4:72–81.

Kiviaho, P. 1976. Contextual analytical study about environmental effect on organization membership and the choice of organization. *IRSS* 11,1:17–35.

Kolatsch, J. 1972. *Sports, Politics and Ideology in China*. New York: David.

Latten. W. 1933/34. Bürokratisierung im Sport. *Kölner Vierteljahrshefte für Soziologie* 12,3:297–304.

Lenk, H. 1964. *Werte, Ziele, Wirklichkeit der modernen Olympischen Spiele*. Schorndorf/Stuttgart: Hofmann.

Lenk, H. 1972. *Materialien zur Soziologie des Sportvereins*. Ahrensburg: Czwalina.

Loy, J.W. and J. McElvogue. 1970. Racial segregation in American sport. *IRSS* 5,1:5–24.

Loy, J.W.: McPherson, B. and G.S. Kenyon. 1978. *Sport and Social Systems*. Reading: Addison-Wesley.

Lüschen, G. 1974. Policymaking in sport organizations and their executive personnel: a proposal for a cross-national project. Pp. 367–382 in M. Archer, ed. *Current Research in Sociology*. Current Sociology. The Hague: Mouton.

Lüschen, G. 1979. Organization and policymaking in National Olympic Committees. *IRSS* 14,2:5–20.

Manders, W.M. and J.A. Kropman. 1977. *Kaderbehoefte bij Sportverenigingen* (Personnel needs of sport clubs). Nijmegen: Instituut Toegepaste Sociologie.

March, J.G. ed. 1965. *Handbook of Organizations*. Chicago; Rand McNally.

Marsh, A.W. 1930. Athletics. Pp. 296–300 in Vol. 2 *Encyclopedia of the Social Sciences*. London: Macmillan.

Matejko, A. 1975. The diagnosis of conflict in sport. *Rev. Intern. Sociol.* 33, 1:63–87.

Michener, J. 1976. *Sports in America*. New York: Random House.

Miermans, C.G.M. 1966. Het verschijnsel sport in organisatorisch perspektief (Sport under organizational aspects). *Sportcahiers* 1:52–66.

Morton, H. 1963. *Soviet Sport*. New York: Macmillan.

McPherson, B. 1976. Involuntary turnover: a characteristic process of sport organizations. *IRSS* 11,3–4:5–15.

Niwa, T. 1966. Kleingruppenforschung in Anwendung auf Sportgruppen und Sportvereine. Pp. 259–267 in G. *Lüschen*, ed. *Kleingruppenforschung und Gruppe im Sport*. Opladen: Westdeutscher Verlag.

Noll, R. ed. 1974. *Government and the Sports Business*. Washington, D.C.: Brookings.

Price, J. 1972. *Handbook of Organizational Measurement*. Lexington, Mas.: Heath.

Riordan, J. 1977. *Sport in Soviet Society*. Cambridge: Cambridge University Press.

Sage, G.H. 1975. An occupational analysis of the college coach. Pp. 391–455 in D. Ball and J. Loy, eds. *Sport and Social Order*. Reading: Addison-Wesley.

Savage, H. et al. 1929. *American College Athletics*. New York: Carnegie Foundation.

Savage, H. et al. 1931. *Current Development in American College Athletics*. New York: Carnegie Foundation.

Schlagenhauf, K. 1977. *Sportvereine in der Bundesrepublik Deutschland*. Schorndorf/Stuttgart: Hofmann.

Scovill, J. 1974. Labor relations in sports. Pp. 185–220 in R. Noll *op. cit.*

Scully. G. 1974. Discrimination: the case of baseball. Pp. 211–274 in R. Noll *op. cit.*

Shneidman, N.N. 1978. *The Soviet Road to Olympus*. Toronto: Ontario Institute for Studies in Education.

Sills, D.L. 1968. Voluntary associations. Vol. 16 of *Int. Encyclopedia Soc. Sciences*. New York: Macmillan.

Simon, H. 1962. The architecture of complexity. *Proceedings Am. Philos. Soc.* 106:467–482.

Stern, R.N. 1979./The development of an interorganizational control network: the case of intercollegiate athletics. *Adm. Scie. Quart.* 24,2:242–266.

Sveriges Rijksidrottsförbund. 1953. *Svensk Idrott* (Swedish sport). Malmö: Allhem.

Takenoshita, K. 1964. Social factors affecting sports participation. *Research J. Phys. Ed.* (Tokyo) 7,4:10–20.

Theberge, N. and J. Loy. 1976. Replacement processes in sport organizations: the case of professional baseball. *IRSS* 11,2:73–93.

United States Senate. 1978. Amateur sports act. *Hearings Committee Commerce, Science, Transportation*. Washington, D.C.: Govt. Print. Office.

Vlot, N.C. 1964. A sociological analysis of sport in the Netherlands. Pp. 198–212 in E. Jokl and E. Simon. *Int. Research in Sports*. Springfield, Ill. Thomas.

Warren, A. ed. 1973. Athletics. *Law Contemp. Probl.* 38,1:1–171.

Wheeler, R.F. 1978. Organized sport and organized labor: the workers' sport movement. *J. Contemp. History* 13, Apr.:191–210.

Wilensky, H. 1967. *Organizational Intelligence*. New York: Basic Books.

Wohl, A. 1969. Engagement in sports activity on the part of workers of large industrial establishments. *IRSS* 4,1:83–127.

Yerles, M. 1980. *Similarities and Differences in Modes of Integration and Strategies among French and Quebec Sports Executives*. PhD-Thesis. Urbana: University of Illinois.

ALTERNATIVES IN SPORTS POLICY

Roger G. Noll

The decade of the 1970s has been particularly rich in episodes within the sports business that raise important issues of public policy. Curt Flood launched and lost an antitrust suit against organized baseball, but some of the aims he sought were obtained by Andy Messersmith and Dave McNally through arbitration of a labor dispute. Two baseball umpires entered and lost a labor relations complaint that they had been discharged for attempting to form an umpires' union. Both football and baseball experienced their first league-wide player strikes, and baseball an umpire's strike. The two major professional football leagues completed a merger, then saw their revenues from the sale of television rights increase while their player costs, in the absence of interleague competion, declined. The two major professional basketball leagues, after several years of competition for players, petitioned Congress for an antitrust exemption to permit them to merge, then eventually merged without receiving legislative approval. The nation's capital found itself without a baseball team as the Senators' Minnesota-based owner shifted the franchise to Texas and both leagues, at least temporarily, turned down an appeal from local citizens and even from a committee of congressmen to let the city buy a replacement. In a repetition of the scenario enacted by the three other major professional sports in the past fifteen years, the fledgling World Hockey Association (WHA) was organized to compete—and, as things developed, eventually merge—with the highly successful National Hockey League (NHL). And in almost every major city in the country, lavish facilities costing tens of millions of dollars were being opened, constructed, or planned, more often than not at taxpayers' expense.

The principal concern of the sports fan is about matters that affect him clearly and directly: the availability of contests (live and broadcast) and the quality and evenness of athletic competition. The effects on these matters of the operating rules of professional sports are not easily perceived, even by those most intimately connected with the game. But at least some aspects of these effects emerge from the analysis of various aspects of the industry developed by economists. This chapter brings these strands together in a discussion of the policy alternatives available in dealing with the concerns of the fan. The first section deals with the operating rules of sports leagues. The second section examines how the performance of the industry would be altered by changes in its operating procedures. The third section discusses the institutional means—such as the proposed federal sports commission—for making the operating rules of sports more consistent with the public interest.

THE STRUCTURE OF SPORTS

A professional sports league is essentially a cartel, with the purpose of restricting competition and dividing markets among firms in the industry.* Each league has three types of restriction: one dealing with interteam competition for players, another with the location of league franchises, and a third with the sale of broadcasting rights.

The Player Reservation System

The target of nearly all the antitrust cases in professional team sports has been the player reservation system, which limits competition among teams for players. This system includes rules governing the signing of new players, the promotion of players from minor to major leagues (of primary importance only in hockey and baseball), and the transfer of players from one major-league roster to another. These rules differ in detail from sport to sport, but their intention is everywhere the same—to limit, if not prevent, the competitive bidding among teams for the services of players.

The reserve clause. The component of the player reservation system that receives the most public attention is the so-called reserve clause—that is, a clause in the contract of each player that assigns to a specific team the exclusive right to deal with him for his entire playing life. Technically, only baseball and hockey actually have a reserve clause. In these sports a player normally can change teams only if his current team grants another team the right to deal with him or releases him from the obligations of his contract. The exception is that in baseball veterans with six years experience can enter a "free agent" draft in which a limited number of teams will bid for their services. Football and basketball have rules that appear

---

*The fact that leagues are cartels has no policy significance by itself. As sports entrepreneurs have long contended, restrictions on competition in business practices may be necessary in order to promote competition on the playing field. The validity of this contention is at the heart of the policy debate over the social justification for restrictive business practices in professional sports.

less restrictive than the reserve clause. In both sports a player may "play out his option" according to the provisions of the "option clause" in his contract, much as a six year veteran can do in baseball.* The option clause states that a team has the exclusive right to retain a player's services, without his consent, for one year after the term of the contract has expired. If the player does not sign a new contract after his old one expires, his salary is set at some fixed proportion, determined through collective bargaining, of what it was the previous year, and at the end of the year he is free to negotiate with other teams. Thus, under an option system the team has exclusive rights to deal with a player for only one year beyond the term of the contract, whereas under a reserve system the right is perpetual.

While in theory the option system gives the player more opportunity to decide for himself where he will play, in practice it is almost as restrictive as the reserve system. The most important reason for this is the "Rozelle rule," which provides that a team signing a player who has played out his option must indemnify the player's former team. Subject to constraints imposed through negotiations with the players' union, a designated arbitration authority decides the amount of compensation, which is some combination of rights to future draft choices, veteran players and cash payment.** A player who plays out his option thus sacrifices a substantial amount of current income for the risky proposition that he will get through the year uninjured and without loss of skill, and will then find another team willing to pay him a significantly higher salary—enough to compensate him for the loss of income and assumption of risk—despite the threat of a substantial indemnity payment if they sign him. It is not surprising that few players have played out their options and signed with new teams.

The agreement not to compete. While reserve and option clauses receive the most public attention, they are not the most important component of the player reservation system. Clauses of personal service contracts that require an individual to work for a single enterprise for a long period of time have limited legal validity, as is demonstrated during periods of interleague competition, when a team that loses a player rarely succeeds in obtaining a judgment from the courts requiring him to fulfill his contract. For example, star players like Spencer Haywood in basketball and Bobby Hull in hockey have successfully switched leagues without completing the obligations of long-term contracts.

*Again, to be technical, a basketball player's contract does not contain an actual option clause, but instead has a provision that is worded almost identically with baseball's reserve clause. The basketball owners simply interpret the clause as giving a team "option" rights instead of "reserve" rights.

**In football, arbitration is done by a committee, whereas in basketball the Commissioner decides.

The key to the successful operation of the player reservation system is an agreement among the teams in a league not to compete for players. Each sport has an elaborate set of operating rules governing relations among teams, including prohibitions against negotiating with players whose rights are held by other teams. A team that contacts a player to determine if he might be interested in changing teams is guilty of "tampering" and can be severely punished by the league. The prohibition against tampering has two purposes. Obviously, it is designed to prevent interteam competition for players, but it also is said to maintain public confidence in the honesty of play. If a player were known to be negotiating with other teams and a misplay on his part led to a crucial defeat for his current team, the question could arise whether the player had intentionally committed the misplay or, at least, had been playing with something less than full dedication to victory. Sports entrepreneurs believe that there would be less public interest in professional sports if contests were regarded as "exhibitions" rather than "competitions"—that is, if the outcome were either predetermined or not the paramount concern of the teams.

During periods of interleague competition, the agreements not to compete within a league cease to be effective in preventing competitive bidding for players. When a new league is formed, the following sequence of events normally occurs. First, the financial strength of the new enterprise is tested during several years of increasingly intense competition for players, which cause player salaries to rise substantially. Eventually, the new league proves that its financial backing is adequate to survive the competition—and to cause financial losses to the established league. The second phase is then entered, during which the leagues negotiate a merger. To the fans, a merger means an interleague championship playoff and, in all sports but baseball, interleague play during the regular season. To tne owners, a merger brings about an agreement among all teams in the sport to limit the competition for players. Thus, the reserve and option clauses, with their limited efficacy during interleague competition, become secure again through mutual agreement.

Acquisition of new players. The arrangements for the entry of new players into professional sports are similar to the rules governing competition for veterans. Each sport has a "drafting" system whereby teams select "free agents," that is, players who have yet to sign a professional contract. As presently constituted, the order of selection is roughly inversely related to the quality of the team.* Once a team drafts a player, it acquires exclusive rights to negotiate with

*Priority in making draft choices is based on the standing of the teams in their leagues at the end of the season. Since leagues differ both in average team strength and in the distribution of strength among teams, the team ranked second or third from last in one league can actually be weaker than the last-

him.* Again, the effectiveness of this system rests on an agreement among the teams to respect exclusive bargaining rights. During periods of interleague competition, however, two teams, one in each league, have legitimate negotiating rights to any given player, and they engage in competitive bidding for his services. Often this leads to a breakdown in the agreement not to compete *within* a league, since each league wants to prevent the other from signing the best new players. Some football and basketball players, for example, have reportedly been signed by teams other than those holding their draft rights. Successful completion of a merger reinstates the effectiveness of a drafting system.

Nonroster veteran players. In all sports, teams have more players under exclusive contract than they normally have on their active rosters. For example, a baseball team can, for most of the season, carry only twenty-five players on its major-league roster, but it may have a total of forty players under exclusive contract; the fifteen extra men play for minor-league teams affiliated with the parent club. In football, although occasionally a nonroster player does play in the minor leagues, the rules once allowed a team seven nonroster players who were usually placed on the "taxi squad"—a group of players that practiced with the regular forty-man team but does not play in the games. In hockey, a team may have twenty-five players under contract, but normally only twenty are on the playing roster.* Thus, players with the greatest promise of developing major-league talent can be protected.

Two situations may arise in which teams might wish to compete for players even though a draft system or a reserve or option clause is in effect. First, a player who was not skilled enough to make the active roster of a team when originally signed to a professional contract may improve his skills over a period of several years until he becomes major-league material. Second, a player whose skills are not adequate to secure a position on one team may be acceptable to another. Each professional sport has provisions for limiting competition for these marginal players.

One such provision is the waiver rule. When a team gives up its exclusive rights to a player, the player does not at once become free to negotiate with all other teams. He must first "clear waivers," which means that each team in the league must have the opportunity to purchase from his old team, at a fixed price stated in league rules, exclusive rights to bargain with him. Even if he clears waivers,

ranked team in another, but the latter will receive a higher position in the selection order.

*Depending on the sport, the exclusive rights can be permanent or of as short as six months' duration. Obviously, the shorter the term of the exclusive rights, the greater the bargaining strength of the player.

he may still not be free unless, as in baseball, he has played in the major leagues for several years or his team has already assigned him to the minor leagues the maximum permissible number of times.

Another important arrangement is the minor-league draft. In baseball and hockey, players not on the protected roster of major-league teams can be claimed by other teams at the end of each season. Furthermore, when a team drafts a new player it must place him on the protected roster, thereby displacing a formerly protected player and making him available for drafting by other teams. This drafting procedure is, however, subject to important limitations. In baseball, a team cannot lose all of its unprotected players at once. And the payment exacted for a drafted player is $30,000 in hockey or $20,000 in baseball, which is a stiff price for a player who has not yet achieved major-league status.

While the veteran-player drafting procedures constitute a mechanism for circulating marginal players among teams, direct competition is discouraged. For example, a team that values a player more highly than his current team does may get the opportunity to draft him (and be obliged to compensate the team that loses him), but it is prevented from obtaining his services simply by offering him a higher salary or, if he is a minor-leaguer, by promising him a place on its major-league roster at his current salary.

The aggregate effect of all of the rules that limit competition for marginal players is more than just to prevent competitive bidding, although certainly they do achieve that as well. The other effect is to reduce the disparity in quality between the best and worst teams in a league. While a weak team that obtains rights to the rejects of championship teams is not likely to turn into a powerhouse, it probably will be stronger than if top-ranked teams were permitted to retain exclusive rights to an unlimited number of players. Whether the effect on competition is more far-reaching than this—that is, whether a system that prevents direct competition but permits drafting and acquisition through waivers actually produces more equally balanced sporting competition than a purely competitive system—is an unresolved controversy.

Exclusive Marketing Rights

Just as league rules limit competition in the acquisition of players, so, too, do they limit competition in selling the product of the industry. Teams have three important sources of income: admissions, broadcasting, and concessions. In all three areas, teams are essentially monopolisitic: for each sport, only one team in any city normally has the right to sell tickets to major-league professional contests, to offer broadcasts of contests, and to sell food, beverages, and souvenirs to those in attendance at its games. The rights to concessions are not covered by league rules and so are not treated in this book. Usually they are held either through contracts with stadium owners or because the team itself owns the stadium; teams then sell their concessions rights to catering companies through a competitive bidding process. The monopolies on contests and broadcasting in a particular sport do result from league rules and practices, and they raise important issues of public policy.

Team franchises. Each professional sport has rules governing the location of teams in the league. Although the rules vary among the leagues, the general effect is to prohibit a member team from locating in a city that another team has already designated as its home unless the latter gives its approval. Thus, each team has an exclusive right to sell admissions to major professional contests in the sport in its home territory.* Leagues also control the movement of existing franchises to cities without teams. A team wishing to relocate its franchise must obtain the approval of most of the other teams in its league (though the details differ from sport to sport). Established teams control the addition of new teams to the league by requiring not only that new teams pay multimillion-dollar fees to join the league, but also that they must locate in areas approved by the established teams.

As with the player reservation system, the exclusivity of franchise rights is threatened only by the emergence of interleague competition, and even this threat is minimal. The new football and basketball leagues that emerged in the 1960s failed, with the exception of the New York Jets of the American Football League, to survive the competition in the home cities of established teams. Two other teams, the Oakland Raiders and the New York Nets, survived competition with teams in the same metropolitan area but different cities. The World Hockey Association has attempted to challenge the National Hockey League in six cities, and its strongest franchise initially was in Boston, but moved to Hartford.

Whether the rules on franchising are legally enforceable is an interesting and debatable question. In the cases of the Milwaukee (now Atlanta) Braves and the Seattle Pilots (now Milwaukee Brewers), the courts have agreed that teams can move. But whether a team could be prevented from moving into an area already occupied by another team in the same sport, or, for that matter, from moving without receiving league approval, has never been tested in the courts, nor has a league's close control of expansion. In 1980 the Oakland Raiders caused this issue to be confronted by attempting a move to Los Angeles without League approval.

*The major exception to this generalization is in baseball, where a team in one league can locate in the home territory of a team in the other league as long as the stadiums are separated by five miles.

Again, the key to the success of the franchising rules is the mutual agreement among teams, and even among those who seek to acquire teams, to abide by the decisions of the league. Regardless of the legal standing of the rules, they are effective as long as all concerned agree that the number of franchises should be limited and that teams should not compete for the same fans.

Broadcasting rights. The limitations on competition in the broadcasting of games have two major features. First, rights to national broadcasts of games in each sport are controlled by the leagues. This situation resulted from legislation passed in the early 1960s that exempted sports from antitrust laws when teams in a sport combine sell national broadcast rights (P.L. 87-331, Sept. 30, 1961). Second, each team has exclusive rights to broadcast all home games that are not part of the league's national broadcasting package and to prevent the broadcast in its home territory of any game not in the package. Since all teams either have local monopolies or compete with only one other team in their sport, these rules create a local monopoly in broadcasting that can be more important to a team than league arrangements for national telecasts.* Teams may compete for broadcast rights outside of the home territory of any other team, but since nearly all large cities have teams in all sports, this competition is for a relatively limited market.

As the preceding discussion makes clear, professional sports leagues have a remarkably complex set of rules and practices that all but eliminate business competition among their members. The extent of the anticompetitive practices is made especially apparent by the contrast between normal operations and conditions during the occasional periods when a new league emerges, when, until one league fails or a merger is consummated, competition prevails. During these "wars," player salaries, especially for rookies and superstars, are considerably higher, team profits appear to be much lower, and the number of major-league teams is greater. Only twice has the end of a period of competition not been accompanied by a reduction in the number of major-league teams: at the turn of the century, the American League "war" ended when the National League accepted its competitor as an equal; and, in the mid-1960s, the American Football League merged with the National Football League without the loss of any teams.

The other major consequence of competition is that formation of a new league has *always* meant that some owners in the new league

---

*For all sports except football. A football team can sell radio rights for all games and television rights for exhibition games; television rights for regular-season and playoff games are sold only through the league. In the other sports, a team can televise as many games as it wants, as long as it does not infringe on any other team's local monopoly rights in broadcasting.

will obtain major-league franchises when peace is restored. The Federal League (baseball), the All-America Conference (football), and the American League (basketball) all folded, and the Continental League (baseball) never even began to play, but in each instance at least one team owner in the new league obtained the franchise of a team in the old after the new enterprise had gone out of business. This consistent pattern bodes well for owners and fans of the WHA.

POLICY ISSUES AND SPORTS OPERATIONS

The concerns of fans are related to many other subsidiary issues of sports operations and government policy. This section connects the more important operating procedures of sports—franchise location decisions, the player reservation system, and broadcasting policy—with the interests of fans, owners, and players, and proposes some alternatives to the current rules and policies that leagues have voluntarily adopted or that have been imposed by government.

Franchise Locations

Citizens and sportswriters are quick to express outrage when their home city loses a sports franchise. The public policy issue that usually arises is whether the government ought to prevent, or at least control, the movement of teams. But this is a highly superficial response to the problem. One must first ask why citizens become so concerned over losing a team. The answer is simply that it is very difficult to find a replacement, even if one could be profitable, because the leagues carefully control both the number and the location of franchises. A city can spend literally decades convincing the management of sports that it should have a team.

It does not make sense to force the owner of a business to continue to sustain financial losses operating in one location when he believes he could do much better elsewhere, so it is unlikely that the government will ever decide to prevent the transfer of franchises. But that does not mean that it should continue to be next to impossible for a city to gain a franchise. The central issue of public policy—and the one that seems most likely to result in government action—is whether existing teams should be permitted to maintain a scarcity of franchises.

The scarcity of franchises accomplishes two ends.. First, it enhances the value of existing teams. This occurs because it reduces competition for fans; causes revenues from national broadcasting rights to be divided among fewer teams; allows the market of both existing and expansion teams to be higher; preserves a few potentially lucrative franchise sites so that an existing team that begins to fail financially has an attractive alternative site; and, because of the threat of moving, gives a team additional bargaining power when negotiating stadium agreements or local broadcasting rights. The last point is illustrated by the attempts of the operators of Robert F. Kennedy Memorial Stadium in Washington, D.C., to keep the Senators, and later to lure the Padres, by promising a better rental agreement. Second, with fewer teams, and, consequently, fewer openings for major-league players, the average quality of play is probably higher—how much higher, and whether fans care about absolute quality of teams (rather than close competition or the presence of a few superior players), is uncertain.

Another important question related to the transfer of franchises is why a team would suffer financial losses in the first place. The reason usually given is that the team does not receive adequate support from its hometown fans, but it must be small comfort to a city the size of Seattle that it lost a baseball team because its team did not draw as well as teams in New York or Los Angeles. If each team must depend largely upon the revenues it can generate from admissions and broadcasting in its home territory, the charge of inadequate hometown support will persistently recur in all but the largest cities. The financial success of teams in smaller cities depends critically on the arrangements within its league for dividing revenues.

The effect of tax policies on franchise locations is also important. The practice of allowing owners to capitalize and depreciate half of the purchase price of a franchise has created a significant incentive for fairly rapid turnover of franchises. If a team is resold every few years, it is likely that occasionally the highest bidder will be someone from another geographical area who wishes to acquire the team. Furthermore, since only rich people with diverse business interests can take full advantage of the tax benefits of ownership, an owner is less likely to be interested in building a durable market for his team. His main concern is that he have a salable asset when his depreciation runs out, and as long as the number of franchises is scarce, businessmen in other cities will continue to be willing to purchase no matter how bad the team's local operation.

Finally, the instability of franchise locations is further magnified by the competition among local governments to promise ever lower rents for increasingly expensive facilities in order to attract teams. Since these subsidized rents bear no relation to true costs, a city that holds out for a cost-based rental agreement can lose its team to a city in which the true economic value of the team, measured by the excess of revenues over true costs, is actually lower.

Both forms of public subsidy of sports—tax breaks and stadium rents below cost—can have an effect on the number of financially viable teams. Several teams benefit from these subsidies by more than $1 million annually. In baseball, this is roughly the net gain to a team from attracting an additional 500,000 fans during a season,* which represents nearly half the average attendance of major-league baseball teams. These indirect subsidies are also about two-thirds the size of the average baseball team's total revenues from broadcasting. Thus, it is reasonable to conclude that many teams are financially viable only because of the subsidies they receive.

Whether subsidies of sports enterprises are socially desirable depends upon one's view of several related issues. The first is the overall equity of the system of taxes and expenditures. The tax provisions used by sports teams are a small part of the much larger issue of tax reform, and the expenditures of local governments on sports facilities are rarely more than a small part of the debate over local government priorities. Second is the social merit of subsidizing sports as a means of increasing the number of economically viable sports enterprises. Third is the effectiveness of indirect subsidization through taxes and low rent as compared to other methods of increasing the profitability of sports enterprises. Among the alternatives are direct subsidies, more liberal rules governing league expansion, and more even revenue-sharing arrangements among the teams in a league.

The principal disadvantage of tax subsidies as compared with these alternatives is that they apply to all teams, regardless of the amount of subsidization the franchise requires in order to survive. In fact, since the more remunerative franchises sell for higher prices and therefore have a larger basis for calculating player depreciation expense, the subsidy provided to them through the tax system is actually somewhat larger than for the less successful teams.

With these thoughts in mind, several other possibilities for dealing with the franchise problem emerge. All appear to make more sense than either the present system or direct government prohibition of or restriction on the relocation of teams.

—Government could require some minimum degree of revenue sharing among teams in a league. This would at least partially alleviate the wide disparities in the economic potential of franchise sites that contribute to the instability of franchises.

—Government could eliminate or severely restrict the extent to which franchise costs could be allocated to players and depreciated. The upper limit should be the reasonable profit expectations of

*With an average price of $4 per ticket, a team captures $2.0 million in gross revenues from 500,000 fans. But about 20 percent of this goes to the visiting team, and about a third more goes to rent, admissions taxes, and the other costs to the team that depend upon attendance (such as ushers, ticket sellers, and maintenance). Each fan generates about 50 cents in concession profits to the team, so that 500,000 fans produce a net gain of about $1 million.

teams in sport. This would eliminate the present incentive to use ownership of a sports enterprise as a shelter from income taxation revenues earned in other business activities. It would also tend to return sports ownership to individuals whose primary motivation for owning a team is to operate the team successfully, and who are thus less interested in selling the team within a few years. But to preserve many of the existing teams, this measure would have to be accompanied by more even revenue sharing.

—Government could insist that leagues expand whenever someone is willing to put up a reasonable amount of money for a franchise. What would be "reasonable" is, of course, debatable. Existing owners have some claim to compensation, to the extent that expansion reduces the income of existing teams. This will happen if more teams share in a fixed national broadcasting contract, if attendance at games in the expansion city is below the league average (the existing teams then receive a diminshed visitor's share for games in the new city), or if the new team goes bankrupt, forcing the league to operate the franchise until a new owner can be found or the team can be disbanded in an orderly fashion (certainly not in the middle of a season). To the extent that the new arrangements continued to permit reserve or option clauses in player contracts, owners would have a financial stake in the contracts they controlled. New teams would still be required to purchase these contracts. In order to forestall the possibility that owners might thwart a relatively open expansion policy by setting player prices unrealistically high, limits could be set on the price of a contract: two or three times the player's salary might be a reasonable limit, and would establish at least a rough correlation between the price of a contract and the quality of the player, a characteristic that current expansion prices do not have.

Player Reservation and Comparative Team Strengths

The "Player Reservation System," though differing from sport to sport, is in some form used by all team sports to reduce competition for players. Sports officials argue that without limitations on the competition for players, playing talent would tend to be concentrated in the biggest cities and in the teams whose owners are willing to spend the most money. The greater earning potential of the big cities and the economically irrational drive to win regardless of the cost that is said to motivate some owners would give a few teams an enormous advantage in bidding for players. Other teams would then be left with weak players and poor playing records, which would further erode their revenues and cause them to fail financially.

None of the research on the economics of sports, even by authors who favor maintaining some form of reservation system, lends any support to the view that player reservation has a significant effect on the balance of competition. The theoretical conclusion is that the reserve clause could balance competition only if player trades and sales were prohibited—certainly an undesirable and unenforceable proposition. Empirical investigations find no discernible relation between the closeness of competition on the field and the degree of competition in the market for players. They also find no evidence that the prime motivation of the vast majority of owners is any consideration other than profits.

Support for the reserve clause, or a similar measure, can be based on two grounds. First, it improves the financial position of teams in the less lucrative markets by lowering their costs and by giving them assets—exclusive rights to their players—that can be sold to richer teams. Second, it offsets to some degree the tendency in the competitive market to pay a player in relation to his contribution to team revenues rather than to revenues for the entire league. Since some of the revenues a player generates for a team arise because he improves the relative standing of his team, the net contribution of the player to his sport must reflect the declining revenues his performance causes for other teams whose relative quality he causes to decline. Thus, the reserve clause does operate to increase the number of financially viable teams and compensates for an inherent inefficiency in the player market.

Perhaps more important than the debate over the exact effects of the reserve clause is the fact that all three of its alleged benefits—more balanced competition, greater financial security for weaker teams, player salaries more in line with a player's value to a league—could be obtained by mechanisms other than the reserve clause.

All three objectives would be served if teams divided income more evenly. In order to preserve an owner's incentive to maintain the quality of a team, a team's financial success must depend heavily on its ability to attract fans. But the dependence need not be total, as it is in most sports. At the minimum, other sports might be required to copy football's lead, by sharing gate receipts relatively evenly between home and visiting teams. For sports that are heavily dependent on local broadcasting fees, similar sharing arrangements could be required for these revenues. Even more effective than splitting revenues between the home and visiting team would be to divide a share of the revenues equally among all teams. For example, the home team might receive 50 percent of gate and broadcast receipts, the visiting team 25 percent, and a league-wide fund, to be divided equally among all teams, the remaining 25 percent. This would reduce the financial disparities among teams and would also result in lower player salaries than would a competitive system with less even revenue sharing. Since a team would receive half of the increase in revenues attributable to a player (the rest being shared), the maximum it would be willing to pay to a player is less than if it received all the hometown revenue he generates.

Interteam financial disparities could also be reduced by increasing competition among teams for revenues. More teams could be placed in the most lucrative markets, and prohibitions on broadcast competition could be removed. Competition in a single market cannot be expected to result in a roughly equal division of revenues among all the teams in each year. Since some fans will give their loyalties to the more successful team, in a given year wide disparities in attendance and revenues would result. But over a long period of time, a capable owner should field the most attractive team in his city a reasonable fraction of the time, so that long-run revenues would be more evenly balanced. In any event, it is difficult to see the justification for preventing an owner from attempting to capture a share of a big-city market should he want to try. If he fails, the team can always move back to a smaller market. If he succeeds, the effect on league financial and playing balance can only be beneficial.

An effective mechanism for preventing an overzealous owner from monopolizing playing talent is to place a ceiling on a team's total budget for player salaries. Suppose that no team could spend more for player salaries than 150 percent of the league average expenditure in the previous year, and that each year every player was free to play for any team that offered him a job. The limit on total salaries would prevent a single team from signing a large number of superior players, would still permit substantial annual growth in the average compensation of players, and would substantially narrow the spread among teams in total player salaries (and, presumably, playing quality). An argument against the proposal might be that it is difficult to enforce: how would the league prevent illegal extra payments to players? The best protection against this is competition. The previous contracts of each player would be available for inspection, as would all the other offers that a player rejected. If a team persistently succeeded in signing players at salaries lower than other teams were offering, it would arouse suspicion that it was violating the rule. Furthermore, detection would be aided by the fact that if a team were substantially exceeding the league salary limit, either several players would have to be receiving payments on the side or a few players would have to receive much more than called for by their contracts. Investigations of the records of the teams and players, together with the information on past and rejected salary offers, should make enforcement of this rule feasible.

Broadcasting Rights

For most fans, televised sports are the most important source of sports entertainment. And fans, sportswriters, and even a President of the United States have spoken out against various aspects of current broadcasting policy, particularly the local blackout of games.

The proposal to make local blackouts illegal raises knotty economic issues. First, the broadcasting rights to a performance by two teams are clearly the property of the teams. Some teams do not now sell rights to televise their home games locally because they believe, rightly or wrongly, that the revenues they would receive from local telecasts would be more than offset by a decline in gate receipts. A requirement that these rights by given or sold to a local station is a rather arbitrary confiscation of personal property.

Second, to force a local team to allow a local station to carry a local game that was being televised elsewhere is to provide an economic boon to the station. A home game of the local team will draw larger audiences than another game, and thereby increase the advertising revenues of the station that carries it. Some of this increase in audience and advertising revenues will come at the expense of other stations in the same locality.

Third, the value of local broadcasting rights is likely to increase significantly in the near future with the development of pay-TV or, as it is more politely known, subscription television (STV) (Noll, et al. 1973). Many cable television systems have already begun to offer STV channels that, for some charge in addition to the monthly subscription fee for cable television, give viewers access to programs not normally televised—principally recent movies and sports events. In addition, over-the-air STV is likely to develop in several of the largest cities during the mid-1970s. The regulatory rules established by the Federal Communications Commission to control STV provide that no sports event that appears locally on free TV can switch to STV until it has been off the free TV airwaves for two years. Thus, to require teams to televise their home games locally would be to deny them access to the potentially lucrative STV market, and to deny the emerging STV industry what is likely to be one of its more attractive offerings. In smaller cities, revenues from local sports events on STV might be the determining factor in whether the area could support a major-league team, or whether STV would be financially viable. Even in the biggest cities, the viable number of teams and competing STV channels on cable systems will be affected by whether home games are allowed to be shown on STV.

The preceding arguments are not necessarily definitive ones against a rule to lift blackouts, but they do show that the issue has important financial consequences for the sports industry, broadcasters, and the emerging STV industry, in addition to its obvious relation to the welfare of sports fans. Lifting blackouts would clearly benefit some fans and some broadcasters; would clearly harm some teams, some broadcasters, and STV; and might harm some sports fans, to the extent that it prevented the emergence of new teams.

Another complicated issue is the restriction on broadcast competition. The principal effect of the current arrangements—pooled national rights, exclusive local markets— is to create a series of broadcast monopolies that increase broadcast revenues for sports and advertising costs for sponsors, while reducing the number of broadcasts available to the fan. Although national broadcast revenues are evenly split among the teams in a league, the overall effect of broadcast practices probably contributes to disparities in the financial health of teams. This is because a team's monopoly in broadcasting in its home territory is more important the larger the broadcasting market in which the team is located. The wide variance among teams in local broadcasting revenues, which reflects market sizes, also increases financial disparities, particularly since the visiting team does not receive a share of the revenues from local broadcasts.

Elimination of monopoly rights in broadcasting would, by itself, reduce the broadcast revenues of sports, and might reduce the revenues of every team, including those whose financial condition is weakest (although this is not certain). If a team in a small city could broadcast games into the home territory of a team in a larger city, two possibilities for additional revenue would arise. First, the current practice of granting a visiting team the right to broadcast games back home could be ended, and a team like Kansas City could broadcast its home games against the Yankees back to New York, thereby gaining access to the lucrative New York broadcast market. Second, one or a few teams might produce a package of games to be broadcast either nationally or in nearby major-league cities, in competition with the games and broadcasts of the home teams in the latter area. Thus, San Diego might broadcast games into Los Angeles, or Milwaukee might broadcast into Chicago, or Baltimore might broadcast into Philadelphia. These practices would probably reduce the revenues of teams in big cities, but the benefit to teams in smaller areas could more than offset the losses they would suffer from losing national and local monopoly positions. In any event, the net effect would be to narrow the spread in financial resources among teams. An ancillary benefit would be the added possibilities for competition in broadcasting. Stations that currently cannot broadcast games because of present restrictions, particulary independent stations, would be free to enter the field.

The preceding discussion suggests the following arrangement as a reasonable alternative to the present system, or to the present system modified by a prohibition of blackouts.

—Relatively even sharing of broadcast revenues, along the lines recommended above for gate receipts: either a 60–40 split between home and visiting teams, or a 50–25–25 split among the home team, the visiting team, and a fund to be divided equally among all teams.

—Repeal of the 1961 sports broadcasting act, which exempts leagues from antitrust laws when they pool broadcasting rights to form a single national package, the 1973 bill that lifts the blackouts of sold-out home games, and the rules that inhibit placing home games on STV.

—Prohibition of league rules that grant each team the right to exclude the broadcasts of other teams from its home territory.

INSTITUTIONAL ALTERNATIVES IN SPORTS

All sports have essentially the same governing structure. Baseball, football, soccer, basketball and hockey each have a single commissioner who, together with a committee of owners, decides upon the operating rules of the sport. Occasionally, governmental institutions exercise some influence: Congress has passed a few laws defining the legal boundaries of policies within sports, the Department of Justice has occasionally intervened in sports operations by invoking antitrust statutes, and the Federal Communications Commission has laid down a few rules that affect sports broadcasting. But, for the most part, serious attempts to change the operating procedures of sports have come from within the industry, when players, new leagues or a maverick owner have used labor relations and antitrust laws as the basis for attacks on the restrictions on competition for players and on the number and location of franchises.

The major development in the institutional organization of sports over the past several decades has been the rise of militant, strong player associations. This has had a significant effect on the operating rules of sports. Before analyzing alternative institutional structures, it is worthwhile to examine how player associations are likely to affect the present system, in the absence of intervention by the federal government and assuming that mergers between competing leagues are allowed to proceed.

Where the Player Associations Are Taking Sports

The principal effect of the player associations has been to raise all salaries while narrowing salary differentials between the least and most able major-league atheletes. In the short run, they have achieved this by raising minimum pay, increasing fringe benefits (such as pensions, per diem allowances on road trips, moving allowances, and health coverage), and obtaining greater job security (higher severance pay, arbitration of disputes between players and management, easing requirements for players to be placed on the disabled list, and so forth). In the longer run, they have attacked the player reservation system. Gains thus far include salary arbitration, eligibility of some players for a limited free agent status, the requirement that a veteran player approve an assignment of his contract to another team, and, in basketball, the delay of a merger, the terms of which would substantially reduce competition for players.

The attack on the player reservation system can be expected to continue, through new antitrust suits against teams and leagues and through periodic negotiations of the agreements between leagues and player associations. It is reasonable to predict that the current institutional structure of sports will produce a significant weakening of the player reservation system in all four major sports. The prediction will prove incorrect only if the internal strength of the player associations is not great enough to prevent management from destroying them before they achieve this goal. If the associations' strength is in doubt, there will probably be protracted labor disputes in at least some sports before the player reservation system is dismantled (as is most likely) or the associations are emasculated.

The effect of the player associations on the welfare of the fans is likely, in the long run, to be minimal. The dispute between players and management is over the profit in sports, much of which arises from monopolistic practices in the marketplace: broadcasting, home games, control over the number of franchises, concessions, and, in the future, subscription television. Practices that increase the total revenues of sports will be favored by players and owners alike. Thus, player associations will not try to change monopolistic practices that do not directly affect competition for players.

Even the part of the player reservation system that governs competition for new and minor-league players is unlikely to be changed through negotiations between leagues and player associations. Both owners and veteran players will have higher incomes if salaries for minor leaguers and new players are depressed. Since the player associations represent the veteran major-league players, they are likely to agree on the desirability of eliminating competition in the market for nonveteran players. In basketball, for example, owners and players have agreed that the draft system for players coming out of college should be retained, with the drafting team having exclusive negotiating rights to a drafted player for two years.

Increased player salaries would affect fans adversely if they led to increased ticket prices. This result seems unlikely, since the price-setting process in sports is not closely related to player salaries. If a team is maximizing its profits, ticket prices and team quality will be set so that the changes in the team's revenues and costs associated with attracting and serving one more fan are equal. The cost to the team of increasing attendance has two components. First is the direct cost of providing a seat, involving expenditures on ticket sales, ushers, and stadium rent and maintenance. These costs account for one-third to one-half the costs of a sports enterprise, and obviously are unrelated to the salaries of players. Second is the cost of attracting additional fans by improving the quality of the team, which is related to player salaries since, in general, better players receive higher salaries. But the cost of improved quality has other components as well—the cost of purchasing the contract of a player from another team, and the cost implicit in not taking advantage of the possibility of selling player contracts to other teams. Competition in the player market transfers the latter two costs to the player salary category, but does not change the total cost of improving quality. Consequently, it has no effect on the costs that enter into the price-setting mechanism.

The preceding argument rests on the assumption that outcomes in the player market are governed by the quest for profits by teams. The evidence suggests that this is an apt characterization of most sports operations but that some exceptions clearly exist. Where it holds true, profit orientation insulates fans from paying for higher player salaries. The relatively few teams that appear to be operated according to other motives, and that tend to set prices to cover costs but not to create maximum profits, will respond to higher costs of any kind by raising prices. An important consequence of the rise of player associations is that it will tend to make all teams set prices as if they were profit oriented, regardless of their actual motivation, with the increased revenues then going to the players.

Finally, player associations are not likely to try to reduce the financial disparities among teams. While players have an interest in keeping financially troubled franchises operating, they also have an interest in making the value of players as high as possible in the most financially lucrative markets. The greater the disparity in the markets of the members of a league, the higher player salaries will be. Thus, player associations are likely to try to preserve weak franchises by seeking governmental susidies, by gaining pledges from owners that the league will continue to operate a failing franchise, or by increasing the monopoly power of teams in selling games and broadcasts, but not by adopting more equal sharing of revenues within the league.

One can only conclude from the preceding analysis that the present structure of sports is not likely to produce any material change in the procedures that most affect the welfare of fans. In most cases, the interests of the players coincide with the interests of the owners, and both tend to benefit from the restrictive practices that are costly to fans.

If player associations are unlikely to alter significantly sports operations outside the player market, the only remaining question is whether attempts to enter the industry by those now excluded could do so. But this, too, is not likely to be particularly effective. First, the cost of fighting court battles with established teams to break monopolistic practices is significant; only if entry promises exceptionally good returns is it worth attempting. Second, entrants, being astute businessmen, are not likely to want to make permanent changes in the operating rules of sports; instead, their interests lie in gaining membership in a restored cartel, which can then reinstitute its restrictive practices. Baseball, basketball, hockey, and football have survived periods of competition without making significant long-term changes in operating structure (other than in the number of teams).

If new entrants into sports are unlikely to change sports operations, then the remaining alternative is governmental action.

Federal Regulation of Sports

One proposed response to the public concern about sports operations is to establish a federal agency to regulate sports, much as other regulatory agencies oversee such industries as transportation, telecommunications, broadcasting, drugs, and financial services. In 1972, Senator Marlow W. Cook introduced legislation that would create a federal commission within the Department of Commerce to regulate sports broadcasting arrangements, drafting procedures, the sale and movement of franchises, and the limitations on competition for players, U.S. Congress 2 sess. March 30, 1972: 3445.

One advantage of the proposal is that Congress could delegate to others the difficult task of writing detailed operating rules for sports. A second advantage is that the operations of sports would be subject to continual scrutiny, whereas reliance on congressional intervention would be likely to result in only intermittent investigations and actions. Ideally, a federal regulatory agency would be a highly expert body that would monitor day-to-day developments in sports, vigilantly protecting the public interest by adjusting the operating rules of sports as new policy issues arose.

Whether it is realistic to expect federal regulation of sports to achieve this ideal is debatable. Experience with public regulation in other agencies gives reason to doubt the wisdom of establishing a federal sports commission. In general, regulatory bodies tend to give most of their attention to the arguments and interests of groups that are effectively represented in the formal proceedings of the agency, while overlooking the interests of groups that are not effectively represented (Noll 1971; Berstein 1955; Lowi 1969). In the sports business, three groups are certain to be well represented:

owners of teams, veteran major-league players (through player associations), and broadcasters. Two other groups are almost certain not to be effectively represented. One is sports fans. Only when a city loses a franchise and the city officials act to protect the interests of their constituents is a group of fans likely to have substantial resources available to argue its case. The other unrepresented group consists of players without major-league experience, including free agents and minor leaguers.

As argued above, on a surprisingly large number of issues regarding the operation of sports the interests of the three represented groups either coalesce or at least are not competitive. All three groups probably benefit from the limitations to competition in broadcasting, since scarcity increases the total income each earns from broadcasts. Similarly, the scarcity of franchises is probably in the interests of all three, for it reduces or eliminates competition in each local market and thereby increases the total profitability from admissions and broadcasts. Some of this increased profitability probably accrues to the veteran ball player as a higher salary.

The unrepresented groups are the only ones that might benefit from more competition in the selling of sports contests. If there were more teams, fans would have more choice in attending contests, and more jobs in major-league sports would be open to marginal players. More competition in broadcasting would probably have little effect on unrepresented players, but it would give fans more choice in viewing and listening.

Regardless of the merits of the case for increasing competition in the sale of sports contests, a federal regulatory authority is not likely to take significant steps in that direction, for it will be subject to little if any organized pressure to do so.

The principal source of disagreement among the well-represented groups are the reservation system (players versus owners) and the blackout rule (broadcasters versus owners). Experience indicates that a regulatory agency faced with adjudicating a conflict of interests between two well-represented groups will seek to strike a compromise, even if the merits of the case, based upon either arguments of justice or the consequences of decisions for the general public, indicate that one side should win a clear victory. One might expect that a regulatory agency would settle the issue of player reservation by easing, but not eliminating, the limitations to competition, such as by establishing in all sports an option-clause system that was applicable only to players with a few years' experience and that placed an upper limit on the compensation paid to the team losing a player. This is probably a less liberal outcome than would ultimately emerge from negotiations between players and owners without government interference, and would be a step backward in baseball. One might also expect that some, but not all, aspects of the blackout rule would be eliminated, such as by permitting telecasts of playoff games in the cities in which they are located even if they are not sold out, but maintaining blackouts for regular-season games for which tickets are still available.

These types of compromises will undoubtedly strike many as reasonable resolutions of sticky policy issues, and perhaps they are. But it is not the basis of their merits that their adoption is predicted. In planning a regulatory agency for an industry, including sports, the nature of the decisions the agency is likely to make should be recognized. If the public interest would be reasonably well served by reaching compromises on the issues that divide the three major special interests in sports, while maintaining the status quo on practices that generate criticism only among groups that are not as well represented, then a regulatory authority for sports is a desirable instrument for making public policy. If, however, the interests of society dictate fundamental changes in the procedures by which franchises are granted and located and by which broadcasting rights are obtained, a regulatory authority for sports is not likely to be effective.

Legislation on Sports Operations

The alternative to regulation of sports is to pass legislation that specifically delimits the extent to which sports enterprises can engage in anticompetitive behavior. Instead of avoiding the responsibility either by inaction that implicitly ratifies continuation of the present system of selfregulation or by establishing a regulatory agency, Congress would undertake to identify the public interest in sports operations and then set forth operating rules for teams and leagues that served that interest.

Congress has engaged in several investigations of sports enterprises, but has succeeded in passing only bills that make matters worse, such as those that authorized league-wide pools of national broadcasting rights and the merger of the two football leagues in the 1960s. Congressman Emanuel Celler, in particular, carried out two exhaustive investigations in the 1950s, but never succeeded in obtaining the kind of comprehensive legislation he thought desirable.

Despite the rather sorry historical record, there is reason to believe that the performance of Congress in this area is improving, and that balanced, comprehensive sports legislation will eventually emerge. Congress did not rush to approve the proposed merger in professional basketball as it had done a few years earlier with the football merger. Many factors contributed to the change in attitude: football is a more popular sport and its owners are probably more influential (although, on the other hand, basketball was represented by Senator

Thomas H. Kuchel, whose standing in Congress is high); and the NBA Basketball Players Association in the 1970s, led by Oscar Robertson and Lawrence Fleischer, was a far more potent force against merger than the NFL Players Association was in the mid-1960s, before John Mackey became president and Edward R. Garvey became executive director. But also important was the increasing public concern that had been brought about by franchise shifts, construction of several expensive stadiums, player strikes, and the self-destructive feud between the National Collegiate Athletic Association and the Amateur Athletic Union over control of American participation in international competition. All of these served to weaken the prestige of the individuals responsible for sports operations.

The Senate Subcommittee on Antitrust and Monopoly, at the conclusion of its hearings on the basketball merger in mid-1972, reported out a bill establishing several conditions under which the leagues could obtain an antitrust exemption for their merger. (S. 2373, Sept. 18 1972). The bill was not passed and eventually died, but its provisions were unique in the history of sports legislation and suggest an important direction that government sports policy might follow. The most important provisions of the bill were:

1. The contracts of all veteran players were to have a fixed duration that was negotiated by the player and his team, with no limitation on the right of a player to switch teams after the expiration of his contract.

2. The free-agent draft was to be retained, but a rookie was obligated to play for the team that drafted him for only two years, after which he would be free to negotiate with any team.

3. National broadcasting revenues were to be shared equally (the merger agreement had stipulated that the American Basketball Association would not share until the expiration of the then current national contract held by the National Basketball Association), and gate receipts were to be split, 70 percent to the home team and 30 percent to the visitors.

The bill did not deal with the pooling of local broadcast revenues, which would more appropriately be dealt with in the context of all sports, nor did it establish rules governing expansion, sharing of local broadcasting rights, territorial rights, and the relocation of teams. Nevertheless, the bill was the first in the history of sports to establish conditions for granting sports an antitrust exemption, and thus may prove to be an important precedent.

More recently, Congressman John Seiberling has proposed legislation removing various antitrust exemptions from sports, and eliminating some of the restrictions on expansion and territorial rights. In mid-1979, hearings were held on these proposals, although Congressional action would still appear to be a long shot.

In any event, the most likely source of significant changes in sports operations, other than in player relations, is Congress. Only Congress can undo the effects of past legislation, and only Congress is likely to take steps to reduce the financial disparities among teams and to ease the procedures controlling expansion. Finally, only Congress has the power and the resources to undertake a thorough examination of the financial aspects of sports. The information on which this chapter is based is incomplete in important respects because a great deal of the relevant data is not publicly available. A necessary first step in reaching firm conclusions on what changes would be in the public interest is for Congress to conduct a definitive investigation of all aspects of sports operations. It could then write comprehensive legislation, covering all the restrictive business practices in sports, spelling out which practices, and with what modifications, should be given antitrust exemption. This would go a long way toward eliminating the present considerable uncertainty over the future of sports, would probably prevent several years of serious labor relations problems punctuated by strikes and lockouts, and would undoubtedly reduce significantly the number of expensive, protracted, and often inconclusive lawsuits that have become characteristic of sports.

REFERENCES

Bernstein, M.H. 1955. *Regulating Business by Independent Commission.* Princeton: Princeton University.

Lowi, T.J. 1969. *The End of Liberalism: Ideology, Policy, and the Crisis of Public Authority.* Boston: Norton.

Noll, R.G., Peck, M.J., and J.J. McGowan. 1973. *Economic Aspects of Television Regulation.* Washington, D.C.: Brookings Institution.

Noll, R.G. 1971. *Reforming Regulation: An Evaluation of the Ash Council Proposals.* Washington, D.C.: Brookings Institution.

Noll, R.G. 1971. The behavior of regulatory agencies. *Review of Social Economy* 29, 1:15–19.

In major part previously published in R. Noll, ed. 1974. *Sport and the Government.* Washington: Brookings Institution. Reprinted with permission.

THE FUNCTION OF SPECTATOR SPORTS

William Spinrad

Most of the published material on the "Sociology of Sport" concentrates on the actual participants. After some early discussion at the beginning of this century (Howard 1912) only a few analyses have emphasized the spectators. Among the tentative ideas that have appeared, several of which will be mentioned, a common failing is the lack of distinction within the audience. To understand the meaning of spectator sports in contemporary society, as well as its popularity, it is necessary to direct attention to what in English is termed the "fan" rather than the casual observer.

The fan is loosely definable as the person who thinks, talks about and is oriented towards sports even when he is not actually observing, or reading, or listening to an account of a specific sports event. As such, he comprises only a minority of the population, even a minority of those who attend the contests. Of course, it is a very sizeable minority, enough to supply a mass audience. Yet, this immersion in a mass culture is somewhat atypical. The fan's exposure and response is not partial, passive, or superficial. Like those who are devoted to "high culture," he tries to learn about every facet of the sport and participates, if vicariously, in every aspect. The precise characteristics that distinguish the fan should more clearly emerge after further discussion, but one essential feature is that observing a contest, in person or via the media, is a small part of his involvement, and, may, in fact, serve primarily to reinforce and stimulate the other forms of participation to be described.

Some features of a "fan" orientation have been observed in many diverse societies, for instance, among the Samoans and the Pueblo Indians (Dunlap 1969; Fox 1969). However, the complete pattern is associated with urbanization, industrialization, and pervasive mass media. Although the observations that follow are based primarily on North American experiences, with which the author is naturally most acquainted, most of them are applicable to other countries, if in modified form. Among these American sports, each may encourage a slightly different type of fan perspective, as, for instance, baseball versus football (Ross 1971). As will be illustrated the mass media are particularly important. The total "fan" culture is impossible without the regular communication of information and ideas from the media "experts" (Edwards 1973: 249; Givant 1978). The "fan" not only absorbs accounts of contests from the media, but gossip, analyses, a multiplicity of statistics—in general finds the material that will structure his conversations, even his thinking about sport. To reiterate a prevailing theme, one important characteristic of the fan is that he talks and thinks sports. Actually, the relationship between "cultivated fans" and the participants is usually very "onesided." To the performer, the fans are generally only an audience, not a group of "co-participants" (Kahn 1956).

Whatever data are available support the supposition that fandom is widely distributed across the socio-economic spectrum, and one study surprisingly reveals a correlation with higher education (Sutton-Smith et al. 1969). The old are as likely to be involved as the young, if, for no other reason, because they have more opportunity for contact with the culture of fandom (Anderson, Bo-Jensen, Elkaer-Nansen and Sonne 1969).

The principle thesis of this article is that "fandom" brings a type of involvement in popular culture with most of the virtues and few of the defects of this kind of experience. It encourages a peculiar type of active rather than passive participation. The comparative superficiality does not diminish its meaning, but, in fact, helps produce the unique functions and eliminates possible dysfunctions. The fan experience suggests an analogy to what Huizinga and Caillois observed about "play" and Simmel about "pure sociality"—they all constitute "frivolous" areas of activity, sharply demarcated from but contributing to more satisfactory participation in the "serious" social activities. (Huizinga 1955; Caillois 1961; Simmel 1949; Endleman 1967). This feature is typically ignored or minimized in many discussions of fandom, as for instance, Edwards' elaborate and "overserious" analysis (Edwards 1973).

Spectator sports represents a particular kind of "playful" experience which can satisfy the needs of the "players" by performing the following functions:

Vicarious Combat

The most obvious and frequently noted feature is that spectator sports allow an immersion in vigorous physical contest in which one is never personally hurt. The participants may, of course, be injured, even destroyed, as in the extreme case of Roman gladiators. The delight in physical destruction may be a dominant part of the appeal, as in automobile "demolition derbys," and personal annihilation may be an ever present danger, as in the case of auto racing. But,

the spectators at most sports do not possess the desire for blood-
letting of the gladiator enthusiast nor the fascination with death of
the bull fighting audience. They want to see the opponent bested,
which may involve some physical violence, but maiming for its
own sake is not the typical objective, and home team fans will
applaud when the injury to an opposing player turns out to be
minor. The fan wants the most vigorous physical assault against the
other side, as in American football and boxing, but he somehow
hopes that it will be enough of a "mock" experience even for the
contestants, i.e. they will end up physically almost as they were
before. This is essentially the justification that philosopher Morris
R. Cohen offered for his own baseball fandom—that it supplied the
oft-sought "moral equivalent for war" (Cohen 1919).

Others have expressed somewhat contrary views. The World War
II German general Von Reichenau referred to sports as "war with
friendly arms." (Natan 1969: 204) A psychiatrist has described the
spectator's drive as tantamount to a desire for physiological destruction of the loser (Beisser 1967). These comments miss the
uniqueness of this type of contest—for the spectators and probably
for many participants. Unlike what is typical of many other rivalries,
one wants the opponent to be as capable as possible, in order for
victory to be meaningful. Furthermore, since it is so playful, it is
hardly appropriate to ruin the game by reducing any of the participants to insignificance.

The spectator is, indeed, vicariously involved in a public drama,
but one without a precise script and, thus, one with an element of
genuine suspense. It is, in this sense, more akin to the real world
than any prewritten drama. Of course, the drama must contain
its appropriate heroes, whose actions "telescope the human struggle
for power." (Morton 1969: 199). But, as will be pointed out, they
are special brands of heroes, the power struggle is playful, and the
stakes, especially for the spectator, are minimal. Above all, they
have no relevance for the spectator's position in society. Despite
the intensity of the immediate contest, any lasting psychic impact
is rare. Attempts to politicalize sports, as in Soviet Russia, generally
fail, for sports represents one area of social life where there are no
"party truths" (Morton 1969: 199). They are, in the fullest sense,
only games.

Even more than the actual physical participants, the spectator
deals with "manageable success" and "manageable failure" (Sutton-
Smith et al. 1969: 256). One's ego is at stake only in a peripheral
and transitory manner. To feel otherwise implies a serious path-
ology and probably derision by actual fans. One analysis of American baseball points out that, in comparison with bull fighting,
the aggressive drives of the spectator are "distant and safe," in

fact, appear to resemble an "intellectualized" orientation to a "severely regulated conflict" Zurcher and Meadow, 1967). The involvement of the fan is, in many cases, very distant, that is only via the mass media.

As a partial rebuttal of these contentions, a critic may point to the tumultous spectator riots that sometimes accompany sports events. Such occurences are, indeed, rare, considering the vast number of contests regularly seen throughout the world and the apparent frenzied excitement of so many spectators. They are no more inherent accompaniments of watching sports than "party brawls" are inevitable results of drinking at social gatherings.

Although the contest is so vicarious, removed, and peripheral, the fan is personally involved in many other ways. He participates through his identification with specific *heroes* and particular *teams,* his assumption of expertise in *folklore* and a multiplicity of statistics, *his experiences in* mock rational arguments, *his efforts at* mock adminstration.

Hero Identification

Much of the popularity of spectator sports is obviously based on the psychic gratifications from identification with sports heroes, as well as with particular teams. In fact, no aspect of their appeal and function has received more attention. What is the basis of choice? An essential ingredient is the vicarious assumption of athletic skill among all the frustrated would-be athletes. The skill includes more than physical prowess, may, in fact, be skill in administration— managing, coaching, and so on. But, this is hardly a sufficient explanation. It cannot, for instance, account for the identification of women with male sports figures. In any case, only some can be chosen for identification.

One widespread interpretation emphasizes the common objects of identification for many—the "super star" who is a folk hero, frequently extolling the person from a humble background who achieves widespread fame (Andreano 1965). This doesn't explain the heroes of the genuine "fan," whose personal heroes may not even be celebrities under any definition. Both fans and the mildly interested mass public learn about their heroes from the mass media. But the fans' use of the media is selective, the mass publics' response is very passive. The latter will, therefore, be only interested in those athletes widely publicized to a mass audience by constant reiteration, who, if among the best, are not the only stellar performers. The fan may choose to identify with the lesser known greats, but also with others who are not so great.

The fans' choice of heroes is actually quite personal, even idio-syncratic. The supposed basis is achievement, which, as a presumed expert, the fan is supposed to know something about. The ingredient of "color," so important to the non fan, may sometimes affect the fan's choices, but is not an essential ingredient. The selections are often largely sentimental, with all the vagaries and variety expected from a large number of heterogenous individuals. Of course, the choice is usually legitimized in terms of the rational canon of achievement. Whatever the choice, it is always possible to find some rational justification for one's decision.

Hero identification is specific rather than diffuse. It is, in most instances, completely *situational,* i.e. the hero is no model for anything apart from the contest itself, and the vicarious empathy is usually limited to his supposed achievements. It does not extend to any other feature of his person; with very special exceptions, he is not deemed a leader or sage in any other area of social existence, his ideas are not given any special attention. Even his possible role as an object of emulation disipates very early in the maturation process of fans. What all this implies is that the situational feature of sports hero identification has few of the dysfunctions of other types of hero worship. Adulation of sports heroes will not result in any manipulation of the fan for other purposes, either by the hero himself or by those who would utilize him as a symbolic mechanism. A presumed refutation of this proposition for the U.S. is the apparent success of sports figures in winning elections for public office. In the absence of any systematic investigations of such elections, the most that can be said is that any kind of celebrity status can enhance one's viability as a candidate. But, it hardly assures victory. It would be easy to develop a list of sports heroes who have lost elections.

One generic basis for personal hero identification does exist; the ethnic factor. It can perhaps be considered a special manifestation of the humble background theme. The psychic gratification that comes from having a similar background to the great performer is very widespread, and is obviously utilized in promotional efforts, particularly in the United States: That professional athletics often offer one of the most available methods for upward social mobility for a relatively deprived group has been sufficiently noted. That this supplies a method of collective success or "arrival" for fellow ethnics is a logical corollary. To take the most publicized American examples, the vast upsurge in the number of baseball stars with Italian names and football luminaries with Polish names in the 1930's was, to many, the most apparent evidence that their groups were a significant part of the American scene. Many American Jews have felt that their presumed non-muscular image might be alleviated by the athletic prowess of Jewish athletes, particularly Jewish boxers. In the case of Blacks and Spanish speaking Americans, the patterns have been most recent and most dramatic. Boxing champion Joe Louis was probably the most important symbol for many young American Blacks in his day, tennis star Pancho Gonzales for Mexican Americans.

Critics of spectator sports might insist that this illustrates the dysfuntion of such spectator identification. Making sports figures the leading group representatives, to the group members and outsiders, seems a trivialization of the group's needs, aspirations, etc. Sports would thus seem another opiate. The historical evidence indicates that this is hardly the case. Actually, the sense of "arrival" through sports heroes may provide one small spur towards accentuating collective possibilities. In any case, the limited situational character of the identification minimizes any possible injurious effects.

The identification with a particular team is one of the few completely altruistic sentiments that many people exhibit. This form of "patriotism" again provides a moral equivalent for the intense xenophobia of war-like emotions. Typically, one doesn't actually hate the other team, one merely wants one's own team to come out on top. The most intense feelings are probably those associated with one's own school, club, or work place, which, again, is not likely to prod any demands for the subjugation and destruction of other groups. As a result, athletes may be given special privileges, often by circuitous methods. In the United States, the fervent efforts of some alumni to develop winning teams can have corrupting concommitants, as has been sufficiently enough documented on the allocation of school resources, the semi-clandestine methods of recruiting and subsidizing athletes, the possible alteration of their academic requirements and even their academic records. Nevertheless, this devotion to the athletic glory of their "Alma Maters" is one of the few efforts of many calculating businessmen that is completely without any economic self-interest.

For many metropolitan residents, identification with the home team can be the most prominent, perhaps the sole, sentimental nexus to the larger community, the major source of civic pride. Again, the genuine fan seems to have a freer rein than the casually interested, also along the lines of idiosyncratic – sentimental choices. His choice of a favorite team may have no apparent connection with anything in his personal life. Of course, the usual "mock" rational arguments for choice are always available, illustrating the characteristic style of legitimation after the fact.

Participation in Folklore

The fan participates in a special sub-cultural folklore, also mediainduced and reinforced by personal conversations. This includes, first of all, an amazingly accurate historical orientation—an acute awareness of particular contests, particular players and teams, the organization of the sports themselves throughout their histories, the vast number of statistical details. Because it is so historical, the sense of time and time sequences is essential. A serious mistake about time factors is a mark of incompetence in fandom. An important feature of history is the list of legends—about a season, a game, a series of games, a particular moment.

The contest itself contains its intrinsic lore—the rules, the rituals, the "inside" details. The fan participates, or feels he participates, in all of this. He likes to believe that he is completely cognizant of what goes on and why. He has picked up, from the media and from other fans, the appropriate language, the nuances of strategy and appropriate "tricks," and converses with other fans about them. In the case of involved games like American football and basketball, such knowledge, or at least a show of knowledge, is both a reflection of a profound sense of personal involvement and a mark of membership in the inner fan circle. Finally, the fan participates in the folklore of statistics and administration, which are left for separate discussions.

The Comprehensive Lore of Statistics

Without the complex and varied set of statistics, a sport does not possess a sufficient hold for genuine fandom. The rest of the folklore is insufficient, the basis for conversation and argument is reduced, media discussion is limited, efforts at mock rational appraisals become more difficult. Many sports do not command the complete fandom absorption because they have only a few available statistics, for instance, auto racing. Even basketball and American football, with their long-time spectator appeal, did not have as wide a coterie of genuine fans in North America as baseball until they developed a range of applicable statistics, becoming initially prominent in professional leagues.

Baseball offers the appropriate example because of the variety of statistics utilized, and because the comparative slowness of the game permits concentration on the statistics. A baseball broadcaster, on radio or television, has sufficient open-time to discuss the statistics in some detail. In fact, without them he might have to struggle to make every moment interesting enough to keep the audience's attention.

Statistics describe the individual game, the player, the team, the season, the long range trend. A corrollary element is the contest for being the *best* in some statistic for the season in one's league. Furthermore, each statistic is more than an entity unto itself. It becomes part of the historical lore of players and teams, and provides the legitimation for mock rational arguments. Some statistics, however, assume a transcendental aura because they become a "record," i.e. a mathematical expression of some all-time achievement. The "records"—for a game, a series of games, a season, several seasons, lifetime—are at least as varied as the number of statistics available. The assaults on records can provide contests as exciting and as publicized as the game itself, the race to win the championship, or the rivalry among individual players to be best in a specific statistic in a single season. The record or series of records may become the most prominent identifying marks of a particular player, what ever else he did.

Statistics contain another somewhat transcendental feature, a group of "magic numbers" that set the threshold for ascent into genuine excellence—in baseball the .300 batting average, the pitcher's 20 games won in a season, the team's 100 games won in a season. There are more ultimate pantheons available only to a very few—the .400 batting average, the 30 games won, the 50 home runs in a season or 500 in a lifetime.

Baseball represents the statistical potentialities of fandom par excellence. Though other sports offer possibilities, few are as varied. Fans thus become *ad hoc* mathematicians and, since they are then dealing with the "hard," objective data of human knowledge, they possess the ready equipment for mock rational arguements.

Mock Rational Argumentation

Statistics supply the objective rational justifications for sentimental choices of players and teams. No matter who your favorite is, you can find the appropriate statistic. Arguments include more than mere affirmations of faith or personal idiosyncracy. They assume the character of rational dialogues, conducted with playful fervor but typically without any sense of genuine ego involvement in the outcome. Some rational justification is always available. If the statistics seem to bolster the other side's position, one can always find some less measurable but seemingly rational argument. In baseball, a player with a comparatively low "batting average" is a "money player," that is he gets his "hits" when they really count. A favorite ritual in comparing teams is the position by position comparison which automatically assures an interesting, extensive, and apparently passionate conversation piece with so many justifications at hand for "proving" the superiority of a particular performer.

The use of rational legitimations for choices made on other grounds is of course typical of many aspects of contemporary society. The director of an advertising campaign utilizes market research to lend an official credence to a decision already made.

Interviewed voters frequently look for acceptable explanations for their choices, made on the basis of such typical determinants as family traditional voting or class and ethnic background. In fact, much of the campaign rhetoric is designed to permit all types of voters to find some official justifications for their choices, even though the overwhelming majority already made their decisions before the campaign started. Much political propaganda is a set of ideological legitimations for decisions made for very crude practical reasons.

The situation for the sports fan, however, possesses one important distinction. Because the entire experience is so playful, he tends to know what he is doing. In essence, he is not "deceiving anyone, especially himself. Whether educators should strive to point out that the fan's type of argumentation is a frivolous replica of what so frequently occurs in serious affairs is a debatable question. Perhaps the disenchantment would not be worth the price, but the resulting insight could ultimately produce a more realistic appreciation of the nature of public disputes. Fandom could thus encourage a more meaningful socialization into the complex macroscopic society, suggesting a similarity to George Herbert Mead's analysis of the function of active participation in sports games for the microscopic interpersonal society. (Mead, 1934). In any case, fans can simulate the rational arguments of public debate without any self-manipulation or cynical disillusionment.

Playing at Mock Administration
The fan participates in one other mock experience. He plays at being an administrator. He simulates running the team, tries to design the appropriate strategy of the game or moment, decides which players should be playing, who should be traded for whom. He may play at selecting managers and coaches, deciding which city should have a team, even determining the proper salary for performers.

A more elaborate form of mock administration is the selection of "all star" teams. Presumably one plays at being the top administrator, determining the most excellent performers at every position (which, of course, does not necessarily mean creating the best team). "All stars" permit the realization of the functions of both mock administration and mock rational argumentation. The potential proliferation of "all teams" provides a very wide range of options. Actual "all star" games create a specific institutionalized manifestation once a year in many American sports. But, so many other variants are possible: all league, all time, all time for team, all decade, etc. American college football, having so many teams and players, offers a very wide potential: all league, all Eastern, all Midwestern, all Senior, etc. The selections that are actually institutionalized offer a basis for comparison with one's own personal choices, but the latter are all important to the fan. Performance, buttressed by statistics, provide the rationale, but the sentimental grounds for choice remain the essential ingredient.

CONCLUSION

Spectator sports represent, to the fan, a special form of playful experience with a unique relation to the real world. The trivial but engaging experiences of fandom are, in the truest sense, an escape from the profound personal and social problems. Unlike most popular culture involvements it is a viable escape, partly because the experiences suggest a caricature of so many unstated features of regular societal processes. The result is a respite, a small-scale catharsis. Since it is not a genuine replica of the real world, the direct impact on one's serious behavior is generally minimal. In this respect it also differs from other involvements in popular cultures, for sports fandom does not produce any distortion of personal and social perspectives.

Perhaps its major potential dysfunction, at least in the United States, is its impact upon some young people and their parents, who conceive of sports heroes as models whose performances should be emulated in actual participation sports. The result can mean a strain in the enjoyment of active sports, as illustrated in the "little league" syndrome with its drive towards unattainable excellence on the part of many young performers.

Other possible dysfunctions have been suggested. James Coleman indicated, by empirical research, that some of the potentially "best" high school students did not strive for the highest grades because athletics provided a more likely avenue to school popularity. (Coleman 1960). At most, his interpretation seems to suggest an emphasis on high academic grades as a primary value. He does not show that high school sports generally have any deleterious effect on intellectual interests per se. In England sport fandom has taken on rather disruptive features in the case of soccer hooliganism, which has become a general concern of the government. (I. Taylor 1971). The possible corrupting effects from college sports over emphasis have already been described. Whatever may be "wrong" with institutions of higher education, sport, by now, typically plays a minor role in the total situation. The special favors given to some athletes in many countries represents a minor example of the advantages available to the publicly renowned in most societies.

One writer claims that international sports competition has become so politicized that it exacerbates national hostilities. (Natan 1969). This interpretation is as simplistic as the belief that the Olympic Games foster international harmony. Both approaches casually and naively identify sports playfulness with the serious business of international relations.

Finally, some have feared that a spectator approach to sports might diminish the amount of genuine active participation. This contention is not supported by any evidence. In one study in Denmark the overwhelming majority of those identified as spectators were also participants. (Andersen, Bo-Jensen, Elkaer-Nansen, Sonne 1969). If there is any correlation between active sports participation and spectator (or fan) interest, positive or negative, it is probably very complex, i.e. there are so many other relevant variables. In general, it is unlikely that sports fans who do not engage in active sports would do so if there were no basis for fandom around.

None of these possible dysfunctions seems too important for most sports fans. The special, if limited, gratifications, the absence of significant injurious consequences, are rare phenomena in modern popular culture.

REFERENCES

Andersen, H.; Bo-Jensen, A.; Elkaer-Nasen, H. and A. Sonne. 1969. Sports and games in Denmark in the light of sociology. Pp. 166-92 in J.W. Loy and G.S. Kenyon, eds. *Sport, Culture, and Society.* London: Macmillan.

Andreano, R. 1965. *No Joy in Mudville: The Dilemma of Major League Baseball.* Cambridge, Mas.: Schenkmann.

Beisser, A.R. 1967. *The Madness in Sports.* New York: Appleton-Century Crofts.

Brill, A.A. 1929. The why of the fan. *North American Review.* 228,4:429-34.

Caillois, R. 1961. *Men, Play and Games.* New York: Free Press.

Cheska, A. 1979. Sport spectacular: a ritual model of power. *IRSS* 14,2:51-72.

Cohen, Morris R. 1919. Baseball and religion. *Dial* 26, July: 57-58.

Coleman, J. 1960. The adolescent subculture and academic achievement. *AJS* 65,2:337-47.

Dunlap, H. 1969. Games, sports, dancing, and other vigourous recreational activities and their function in Samoan culture. Pp. 101-15 in Loy and Kenyon, *op. cit.*

Edwards, H. 1973. *Sociology of Sport.* Homewood, Ill.: Dorsey. Resp. 237-72.

Endleman, R. 1967. Personality and Social Life. New York: Random House. Resp. 415-21.

Fox, J.B. 1969. Pueblo baseball: a new use for old witchcraft. Pp. 136-44 in Loy and Kenyon, *op. cit.*

Givant, M. 1978. Pro football and the mass media. *Review Sport and Leisure* 3, Winter: 69-92.

Howard, C.E. 1912. Social psychology of the spectator. *AJS* 18,1:33-50.

Huizinga, J. 1955. *Homo Ludens.* Boston: Beacon.

Kahn, R. 1956. Intellectuals and ball players. *American Scholar* 26, Winter: 349- .

McPhail. C. and D.L. Miller. 1973. The assembling process. *ASR* 38,6:721-35.

Mead, G.H. 1934. *Mind, Self, and Society.* Chicago: University of Chicago Press. Resp. 150-55.

Michener, J. 1976. *Sports in America.* New York: Random House.

Morton, H.W. 1969. Soviet sports in the 1960. Pp. 192-202 in Loy and Kenyon, *op. cit.*

Natan, A. 1969. Sport and politics. Pp. 203-210 in Loy and Kenyon, *op. cit.*

Ross, M. 1971. Football red and baseball green. *Chicago Review* Jan.-Febr.: 30-40.

Simmel, G. 1949. The sociology of sociability. *AJS* 55, Nov.: 254-61.

Sutton-Smith, B.; Roberts, J.M. and R.M. Kozelka. 1969. Game involvement in adults. Pp. 246-50 in Loy and Kenyon, *op. cit.*

Taylor, I. 1971. Football mad. Pp. 352-77 in E. Dunning, ed. *The Sociology of Sport.*

Zurcher, L.A. and A. Meadow. On bullfights and baseball: an example of interaction of social institutions. *Int.J.Comp.Sociology* 8, March: 113-17.

PART V

SOCIAL PROBLEMS

AND DEVIANCE

IN SPORT

Lenk

Edwards

Eitzen

Lang

SPORT ACHIEVEMENT, AND SOCIAL CRITICISM

Hans Lenk

COMPENSATION AND ADAPTATION

Participation in sport activities has often been explained by philosophers and sociologists as a compensating reaction against requirements and impacts of industrial society and its conditions of life. The compensation function was identified as

1) a *vital-motorical* one against the minimal physical demands and the deforming impact of modern work, traffic, etc.,
2) a *psychic-integrating* one against boredom and existential impoverishment in the process of labour,
3) a *personality developing and identifying* one against lack of opportunity of the specialized workers' identification with a self-created product or with an achievement which can be ascribed to him personally,
4) a *social-integrative* one against the anonymity in modern labour differentiation and the "alienation" of everyone towards anyone in abstract role relations, intellectualization, bureaucracy of present life, etc., or
5) an *instinct-releasing* one against the lack of opportunity, e.g., for relieving aggression (Lorenz, 1963) or for satisfying "robber instincts" (Veblen, 1899; Adorno, 1955) within the otherwise domesticated and relatively even life of modern civilization.

Plessner (1952/3, 1967) suggested sport is a most attractive "ideal compensation," because of the opportunities it provides for overcoming freely chosen artificial obstacles; and it combines the "element of non-work with the principle of achievement," with no one able or wishing to dispense with the latter. Since achievements in sport apart from the voluntary nature of participation, are subject to the same or similar rules associated with professional work, sport is, according to Plessner, "a copy of the industrial world." "Two areas of labour" confront one another. Therefore, sport does not offer a "genuine alternative," but compensation only in the "sense of an equivalent" of a very similar structure (Plessner, 1967). Gehlen (1965) believes sport "a modified blueprint of the case of earnestness and of work life" because of "inner similarity in structure"—e.g., rules, discipline, and special morals which are to be deemed as traits of collective work organisation. Habermas (1958) accepted this "reduplication of the world of labour" thesis and developed a more precise version, namely, that "sport...has long been a sector of rationalized labour. That is, it is already shaped by most rationalized endeavours to maximize efficiency, and by market-conforming display and consuming attitudes."

Adorno (1955, 1969) fully replaces the compensation function by one of constraint in the interests of adaptation: sport only apparently serves to liberate the body. In fact, "the body itself tends to become assimilated to the machine." It serves to make man "remorselessly fit for handling the machine." "Fitness for work is apparently one of the hidden aims of sports." Ellul (1965), a French philosopher of technocracy, similarly discovers in sport an "extension of the technical spirit of efficiency, ending in complete functionalization of movements and bodies and in brute exploitation of the latter. Sport makes the massman of totalitarian cultures." Similarly, Peters (1927) ascribed disciplined nihilism to the athletes to whom sport offers only narcotic surrogate satisfaction for inner vacancy in only "functionalized industriousness."

The compensation reaction, considered at first as a functional one, now is seen as dysfunctional; i.e., it is understood as constraint and/or compulsion for adaptation. There is a remarkable difference in evaluation, if one is speaking of "compensation function" or of "surrogate satisfaction." This difference may reveal that the sketched analyses are not purely empirical ones, but that they represent normative (validating) interpretations, which are to be classified as such by so-called "critical" macro-sociology, or, still more precisely, by an ideology-criticizing social philosophy. (Incidently, neither Plessner, nor Gehlen, nor Ellul, are representative of the social critics of the New Left. Intellectual criticism of sport, especially of high achievement sport, apparently is remarkably unanimous on this point. Such conformity might be worth an intriguing analysis, but that is not the theme here).

Linde (1967) developed a criticism of the compensation thesis by means of limited empirical material—especially regarding the social-integrative and the personality-identifying part of this complex functional hypothesis. The results amounted to the statement that those workers most highly suppressed to anonymity in their tasks were significantly (about one-half) less active in sports than those whose professional work challenged them as persons. Moreover, the latter more often attended sports competitions as spectators. The "hallucination of 'dictation of work' " cannot be upheld. The process of selection is much more determined by biography. "Engagement in sports" is characterized by Linde as "a component of personality structure…, which is functionally favoured in a statistically significant measure by achievement competition in our industrial society" and which is given growing opportunities of articulation parallel with increasing leisure time. Instead, especially high frustration and aggressiveness "throughout conformistic activity and sociability" are more characteristic of sportsmen, than non-sportsmen. The compensation thesis, in its strict general version, is refuted by such empirical findings. Nevertheless, it may be justified in a reduced form and area of application, in cases of socially active and upward-mobility oriented persons. Only he who is somehow motivated toward social advancement and achievement (chiefly stemming from middle classes, and often of marginal personality or aspiration), will suffer from the anonymity of the working process and differentiation of the bureaucratic role, etc. Compensation, accordingly, is required only by such a marginal man.

In general, every monolithic, all-inclusive interpretation of the function of sport is missing the social phenomenon in its complexity and differentiation. The compensation function is too easily and quickly raised to be the essential feature of sport—in a *"post hoc ergo propter hoc"* fallacy, where a limited, partially relevant factor would be upgraded to be the only explanation.

Habermas (in Plessner-Bock-Grupe, 1967) as well as representatives of the latest social critics of sports (Böhme *et al* 1971; Rigauer 1969) curiously and quickly tried to reject Linde's criticism, but without serious arguments. They only pointed to the limitations of the empirical material and to methodological considerations, without, however, showing any readiness to submit the general compensation thesis of their own to any methodological criticism; or to try to vindicate and justify the thesis against such criticism, except by the decision simply to uphold it, simply on the basis that what *should* be so, must be so. This example alone, provides evidence for the necessity of methodological criticism by philosophers of science regarding so-called "critical theory" in sociology.

The later version of left social criticism (reflecting, incidently, the discovery of sport as a subject of interest several years late), has not presented new arguments above and beyond the mentioned theses of compensation and adaptation. The new critics combined criticism against sport with the general criticism of the "Achievement Principle" (following Marcuse 1955) and with criticisms of the existing system of society. Besides, they added some theses of psychoanalysis, concerning collective behaviour, some of them being generalized up to the point of curiosity.

First, one upholds the thesis of duplication of labour—whether in an unaltered and very over-all manner (Böhme *et al* 1971) or in the following limited and weakened version: "Worklike patterns of behaviour and ideas are integrated in the action system and the established power and control system" (Rigauer 1969: 67, 82). If one understands the notion of "labour" or "work" in such an extended sense as an activity, governed by aim-oriented rationality and need-satisfying goals, and directed to maximization of efficiency (*ibid.,* 15, 19, 65), then this weakened version of the conformity thesis is devoid of empirical content. It is a logical implication of the respective definition (or explication) of "work" (or "labour") and of each definition (or explication) of achievement sports, though the latter is circumscribed still relatively loosely. This further suggests that epistemological censorship and correction of theses comprising "critical" social philosophies are urgently needed.

The adaptation thesis has been taken over also, but it is developed further. Sports, as regarded by these critics, not only serve to train individuals to adapt to behaviour patterns and dispositions which are governing the work process, but also present a means of diverting, channelling, and neutralizing potentials which might turn out to be dangerous for the system; e.g., aggressive or sexual impulses, which could develop "social explosive power," if banked up or jammed. Likewise, the especially effective collective, regressive identification by the onlooker with the hero in the arena serves as a substitute and compensation for frustration in day-to-day work and deprivation of objects for libido as well as of libido beset on objects. The masses, being manipulated in collective narcissism—satisfied, narcotized, "apathized," and "apoliticized"—experience a secondary identification with the repression of the established system as a whole. They are reduced to infantile adaptation with respect to the existing circumstances—especially via chauvinistic emotions and mechanisms of group identification—big sport meetings guarantee system-wide conformity and loyalty. Even the athletes themselves are brought to a similar identification by means of piecemeal success and social and/or material gratifications in sport. Reduction of fear and anguish by means of outward projection of the respective sources of Oedipus-like fears of castration and father-son conflicts is deemed to be an important factor in the identification mechanisms (cf. Deutsch 1926; and Stokes 1956). According to the new critics of sport, authoritarian behaviour and training for competition combined with masochistic ideals of harshness, and "patterns of brutality" are internalized so effectively, that a "repressive adaptation" evolves and the development of a "critical consciousness" is prohibited (H. Adam 1966; Vinnai 1970; Böhme *et al* 1971).

In sum, the adaptation thesis is advanced from a twofold perspective:

a) *Adaptation* to sporting rules favours adaption to norms of labour, to behaviour structures, dispositions, and attitudes which are necessary in and for the *working process;*
b) The compensation for day-to-day frustrations in favouring pseudo-satisfaction, social quiescence, and identification with the social conditions at large; that is, it is favouring *adaptation* to the *established system whole.*

The latter version is the new thesis going beyond the older criticism of sport. Sport is "affirmative," system stabilizing, conformative to established powers and interests, drive diverging, and a "weakener" and harmonizer of conflict.

ACHIEVEMENT AND HIGH PERFORMANCE IN SPORT

The two versions of the adaptation thesis are especially applicable to the achievement orientation of sport, particularly high performance sport. The imperative of continuously increasing achievements in sport—of "achievement at all costs"—has, according to the new criticism of sport, grown to be an ideology of achievement; for it serves to justify and legitimate high achievement sport, which in turn would likely induce the achievement motivation necessary for professional work. Further, sports would divert the athlete away from legitimate "emancipatory" motivations and goals of achievement, particularly from those which are political, or class-conflicting in character. Equal opportunity would not be offered, in the first place. Achievements would be judged and remunerated according to their contribution to established power interests and to the stabilizing of privileges. Therefore, the Achievement Principle would prove an ideology of justificaton in capitalistic countries. Are there no privileges of the New Class, etc. to be established and guaranteed in socialistic countries? Are there no cases of decorating high sport functionaries for achievements which the athletes, indeed, did alone accomplish? Is there no sanctioned impulse or pressure or obligation for achievement nor an Achievement Principle? Is there no reward at all for exceeding achievement standards, records, etc.?

Achievement as an intrinsic value, as an "absolute measure," as a sufficient instance of legitimation seems to be a universal formal-functionalistic value substituting for other "material" ones that were in a sense socially discarded, indeed. Orientation and legitimation by pointing to achievement, and increase of achievement by itself exert motivating and normative influences. The ideal "Achieving Society" is sometimes presented as a total model for today's industrial world. The model character of an ideal type with all its contrasting profiles and limited applicability is occasionally overlooked. High achievement sport in turn is taken by some (Krockow 1962; K. Adam 1970) as "the symbolically most concentrated representation" of the principles of an achieving society. Each social philosophical model, however, when extended over all social areas and all concerns, will become ideological. That is undoubtedly the case. But it is very doubtful that the proponents of this model thesis did at all mean such a universal total extension of the thesis. A total achieving society concerning all regards would be inhuman. On the other hand, the undifferentiated, purely negative criticism against the Achievement Principle in the name of the only alternative, i.e., the "Pleasure Principle," as it is practised by Marcuse, who is in part, repeating, but at the same time modifying, Freud, is ideological as well, if it is universally extended over social life.

Who might responsibly think in a period of explosively growing populations, suffering from hunger in large part, that the Achievement Principle had done its historical task? Who might rely on the proper dynamics of scientific and technological progress alone—so that nutrition and catering for future mankind would be guaranteed, if only means and products were distributed and allocated in another way? But this obsolescence thesis is utopian even in altering allocation, e.g., of armament costs, on a humane and meaningful task. But without achievement motivation mankind cannot survive in the future. This does not constitute a plea for a total achieving society, for pressures to or constraints for achievement in all affairs. Neither is this a criticism of Marcuse's criticism of armament expenditure, or of waste production or of superfluous luxury production of certain goods. Marcuse (1955), however, did not define the term "Achievement Principle" in a clear way: on one hand he means by it the economical stratification and status differentiation in society according to economic success. The "definition" of life standard in terms of cars, TVs, and tractors is, after his statement, the "definition" of the Achievement Principle itself. On the other hand, he signifies by the "Achievement Principle" only the "additional," superfluous suppression and repression *beyond* guaranteeing the adequate necessary standard of life or minimum conditions of life, i.e., compulsory "alienated work." In contrast to that, in turn, Marcuse understands the Achievement Principle as the principle of personal identity, of self-constitution, self-presentation, and self-confirmation in our society and cultural tradition. Achievements in art and probably in sport, too, are, according to him, classified among the "criticisms of the Achievment Principle" itself—a somewhat contradictory conclusion regarding the last mentioned interpretation. According to this latter version he must have reckoned achievements in arts and sports under articulation forms of the Achievement Principle. Regarding the first interpretation, indeed, achievements in sports would not classify among the elements of the Achievement Principle, if one does fairly neglect some cases of big business of sporting athletes determining and elevating their status partly by selling their merchandise called "achievement" on the "achievement market." Also in the second version, achievements in sport are not to be reckoned under the Achievement Principle, if one does not take into account directing and "dirigibilistic" authoritarian and compulsory steps, sanctions, and threats on national federations to exclude an athlete from sport scholarships or supporting funds, only if he did not participate in a special training course or competition, etc. According to the second interpretation achievement sports have to be classified as "libidinous work" in the sense of Marcuse: the athlete does indeed strive for achievement and does endow it with intensive values, emotions and experiences of "pleasure." As such, any achievement in sport has to be deemed as "criticism of the Achievement Principle" in Marcuse's words, which evidently constitutes a paradox compared with the ordinary use of language.

Is there no emancipation of the athlete in achievement sports? Do presentation, development, and constitution of self-discipline in the light of achievement goals, for which the athlete himself aims and strives, and, does confirmation of self by experiences of achievement, not at all reveal emancipatory effects, i.e., are they not enlightening and liberating ones? Do social contacts and social upward mobility by sporting success offer no chance for individual emancipation? Even so sharp a critic as Plack (1967: 185, 188f) assesses sport as a chance of liberating man from suppression of motor drives. Contrary to the new criticism against sport he also sees in sporting activites a beginning of "revitalisation" and "resexualisation": "only the man liberated as regards his body is free regarding his spirit, too." One may very well state and criticize that traditional taboos and rules in sports organisations constituted remarkable obstacles against meaningful social change and such a liberation. That, however, is not a fault of sport as such—but is caused by society itself.

Sport—as a school of achievement motivation (or at least of instantial actualisation of that motive), as a field of public presentation and experience of self against counterparts and obstacles, and as active self-constitution as well as a modern surrogate for adventure for the common man,—may offer an arena of life for spontaneous, wished, primary, active self-probing and testing experiences, which are indeed experienced as achievements of one's own self. Here are chances for emancipation, too. Goffman's (1959) social psychological results on the indispensability of achievements of one's own, and of personal self-presentation in interaction contexts of groups for the constitution of self and for avoiding and overcoming of phenomena of "alienation," may provide confirming knowledge for the aforementioned possibilities of sport achievements, also.

In the whole, it is clear now that the dichotomy, "Achievement Principle" versus "Pleasure Principle" does not, in that undifferentiated form, suffice to cope with the complex phenomena and problems of all types of achievement behaviour. Achievements in sport are particularly not adequately or sufficiently integrated into a theoretical explanation and descriptive system by means of these categorical instruments alone.

A philosophical theory of achievement behaviour, by the way, does not exist up till now—perhaps one reason for the quick success of such an inconsistent and undifferentiated social philosophical criticism against the Achievement Principle?

TOWARD MORE ANALYTIC DIFFERENTIATION

Three factors are augmenting difficulties: in several sports, those with a special strain on the cardio-pulmonary system, actual feelings of displeasure are taken into account and are consciously disciplined in view of an expected confirmation of self and a kind of abstract "pleasure" in the future: experiences of success or a conscious "to have achieved something," "to have managed it" are felt as "satisfactions." Sometimes such deferred gratification or even light "self-torture" are experienced as "pleasure." Displeasure because of pleasure, pleasure of displeasure—a masochistic perversion? As in most cultural phenomena (in the students' rebellion e.g., too) there are also masochistic components and elements in some phenomena of sport. Are they or is it, respectively, to be refused therefore? Might it not be thought of as a characteristic feature of man that he is capable of being fond of, being pleased by, abstract goals requiring deferred gratification of needs?

As in professional achievement it is also true for achievement in sport, that there are other factors—depending on conditions which may be promoted by the state or society— such that it may be difficult to ascribe achievement itself to a single actor alone. The social, economic, cultural, and team conditions, and the state of scientific and technological development are not to be neglected as decisively determining factors of achievement. High achievements in sport also could be understood as products of perfect rationalization and preparation—as Habermas (1958) has already done exclusively. Nevertheless, the single athlete by himself must accomplish achievement in sport. In spite of perfect training and preparation, despite optimally arranged pacemaking by others he cannot obtain achievement by tricks alone. Only preconditions can be facilitated. The achievement itself is a personal feat, which is accomplished and experienced as a contrived and structured action of one's own self. For this reason it comprises and exerts its impressing value for constitution and development of personality.

Obviously, some "injustice," in a sense, is unavoidable. An athlete from a country without a generous commitment to fostering sport, or an athlete in a situation of not having available the necessary discretionary time or adequate devices, arrangements, and grounds for training, could not have accomplished special achievement. Does that fact diminish the achievement of the other athlete, who, by means of external advancement, did achieve? He who adheres to nationalistic categories in sport also, who thinks sport a proving field in the mutual competition of social and political systems, may deem this a failure of international comparability, or he may judge it as an indication of pre-established superiority of a system. But such an interpretation does not become more persuasive by being shared by millions. By the international records and championships of long distance runners from Kenya the social development of that country will hardly be advanced in a great leap.

A third factor involved indeed causes further complication in these affairs: we do not live in the publicly declared, idealized achieving society but in a *society of successes.* It is less the achievement effectively accomplished personally which determines gain in social status, but far more the social image of achievements, successes or sometimes alleged or pretended achievements respecting talents, and in some circumstances even the publicity of pseudo-achievements (e.g., in voting). Publicity as a surrogate of achievement? Does social success as such indicate or prove achievement? Achievements in sport may indeed be estimated as a counterweight against this trend towards fictitious publicity success (for they cannot be—as has been stressed above—obtained surreptitiously by tricks alone). But the fact is not to be overlooked that quasi-laws and norms of publicity in the entertainment industry even impress themselves on high achievement sports, too. The latter no longer complies with the ideal model of a pure achieving society. Why is the sprint star so much more known and sure of a higher social prestige than the walking champion?

Success and achievement can be, in the last analysis, only divided analytically. This distinction is as much idealized as is the model of an achieving society. In consequence, these tendencies and phenomena do not strictly contribute to a more precise and easier sociological and philosophical orientation, especially to one using over-all and vague concepts. Marcuse's simplifying analysis of social phenomena by a dichotomy of categories does not augment concurrence with reality—as little as the new left criticism of sport does, even if, admittedly, several vulnerable phenomena are rightly identified, although sometimes exaggerations in contrast can be accounted for as devices to augment the effectiveness of the criticism. Criticisms of concepts of social philosophies, of ideologies are necessary, as are bolder philosophical reconstructions of model features, especially because ideologists of sport and public opinion dwell on ideological simplifications which are socially effective. Indeed, in an indirect or figurative manner, they express social causes, in as much as one believes them, although committing a semantic fallacy à la Feuerbach's: "if it is in few heads, it is theory, if in many, practice."

THEORETICAL INTERPRETATION AND
EMPIRICAL RESEARCH

Criticism of ideologies, and on a par with it philosophical analysis, are necessary for effective criticisms of conceptions in social philosophy. That fact is more quickly and consistently understood by the new social critics of sport than by ideologists and scientists of sport themselves. One must follow the new criticism of sport in such detail—but one should not share the dogmatically upheld premises, for instance of neo-Marxism and the often adhered-to dogma of refusing detailed empirical studies, which were sometimes disqualified as "counting of fly-legs" ("Fliegenbeinzählerei"). Theoretical description and explanation of social phenomena of sport are to be accomplished neither on the basis of ideological premises, which one is not so ready to give up under any conditions, nor by neglecting representative empirical analyses. On the other hand, micro-sociological analyses cannot, by themselves, offer a *systematic* criticism of ideologies, but may at most punctiliously falsify prejudgements. Macro-sociology, in any case, cannot be sharply separated from philosophical premises. Even metaphysical ideas are hidden within or behind each scientific theory. That was proven by philosophy of science in cooperation with history of science in the last decade (cf. Feyerabend 1963; Lakatos 1970): metaphysical ideas are theories in their embryonic state. Whoever strives for fruitful theoretical advances, must not "positivistically" reject philosophical constructions. The positivism of unalterable "given" date, the ideology of data, is gone except within the fantasy of some polemic "criticizing" sociologists (better: social philosophers) or of many methodologically naive empirical and empiricist scientists. Data are always theory-impregnated; theoretical conceptions are always pregnant of philosophy. These are proven results of philosophy of science.

But back to the analysis of sport: here, also, a pure philosophical interpretation without empirical analysis and control would be empty (of empirical content and relevance). But on the other hand pure micro-sociological investigations without more macro-sociological theoretical conceptions and constructions and without philosophical interpretation would be blind, in no way suited to develop critical over-all estimations, analyses of goals and values of sports in whole, or to deliver systematically a philosophical criticism of ideology. Co-operation between sociology and philosophy as well as epistemology is necessary for the theoretical analysis of the social phenomenon of sport. Only in that way a realistic criticism of sporting ideologies and a criticism of ideological criticism against the latter in turn would be realizable. Only in that way would it be possible to deal empirically, "contentfully," and in a differentiated manner with the relatively undifferentiated criticisms of the new critics of sports (as sketched above) by using more objective, better tested and confirmed hypotheses, that is, to develop a well-founded critique of that criticism. Only in that way all-comprising, one-factor theories which do not fit the complexity of the phenomenon like the isolated theses of compensation and/or adaptation function might be effectively criticized and modified. Finally, only in that way the level of empirical analyses in detail are to be transcended towards a philosophical interpretation which might hopefully dissolve, invalidate, or at least weaken the pro-and-contra-ideologies in public opinion, in the ideological tradition of sports as well as in the likewise traditional intellectual anti-ideology. The well-worn-out ideology of "mens sana in corpore sano" alone does not fulfill such pre-conditions, neither do the isolated and "absolutized" theories of compensation, repression, manipulation or adaptation in and by sport.

Whereas the philosopher might generate ideas, foundations and beginnings of interpretation and constructions of theoretical hypotheses in a relative free and bold manner, the empirical sociologist within a cooperative relationship must be the realistic censor, whose task is, among others, to bring the high-altitude flight of trial-thinking and interpretation nearer to the ground again. The philosopher of science, in turn, is the methodological critic and "corrector" of sociological theory construction and empirical field work, including the methods of data-retrieval and data-evaluation. Then, the logical implications of definitions will not remain undiscovered, nor will it frequently happen that theoretical propositions containing inconsistent and vague notions be presented as well-confirmed empirical knowledge. Such mutual co-operation surely would be more fruitful than pure macro-sociological speculations about total society (though critical they may be), and also more fruitful than relatively isolated empirically detailed investigations without theoretical framework. Neither must sociology dispense with the possibly tentative handling macro-sociological problems which in part can be solved only from a philosophical point of view; nor must philosophy neglect the necessary contact and controlling confrontation with reality. Following the aim in the long run to reach a total interpretation of so complex a phenomenon as sport and to understand its social role and to develop a critical and detailed analysis, the cooperation of sport sociology and philosophy of sport is necessary, if guaranteeing mutual control, lest sport be taken over fatalistically like an occurrence of nature, rather than consciously changed according to goals. Also, this thesis is all the more valid, since there is no detailed philosophy of sport or of achieving behaviour in general, except some preludes. Social macro-problems and hidden philosophical, but historically extremely efficient preconditions and conceptions are too important to be simply neglected, to be pushed aside and/or to be uncritically rejected (if that were possible at all, without adhering to other ideologies)—or to be likewise naively adopted.

REFERENCES

Adam, H. 1966. Leibeserziehung als Ideologie. *Das Argument*. 398 ff.

Adam, K. 1973. Nichtakademische Betrachtungen zu einer Philosophie der Leistung. Pp. 22-31. In H. Lenk, et al., eds. op. cit.

Adorno, T.W. 1955. Veblens Angriff auf die Kultur. Pp. 82 in Adorno, *Prismen, Kulturkritik und Gesellschaft.* Berlin-Frankfurt (Suhrkamp).

Adorno, T.W. 1969. *Stichworte. Kritische Modelle 2.* Frankfurt:Suhrkamp.

Beisser, A.R. 1967. *The Madness in Sports.* New York: Appleton-Century-Crofts.

Böhme, J.O.; Gadow, J.; Güldenpfennig, S.; Jenson, J. and R. Pfister 1971. *Sport im Spätkapitalismus.* Frankfurt: Limpert.

Brohm, J.M. 1978. *Sport a Prison of Measured Time.* London: Ink Link.

Buytendijk, F.J.J. *Das Fussballspiel.* Würzburg (n.d.).

Deutsch, H. 1926. A contribution to the psychology of sport. *Int.J.Psychoanalysis* 7,2:223-227.

Edwards, H. 1968. *The Revolt of the Black Athlete.* New York: Free Press.

Ellul, J. 1965. *The Technological Society.* New York: Knopf.

Feyerabend, P. 1963. How to be a good empiricist? A plea for tolerance in matters epistemological. Pp. 3-39 in B. Baumrin, ed. *Philosophy of Science.* New York: Wiley.

Gebauer, G. 1972. Leistung als Aktion und Präsentation. *Sportwissenschaft* 2,2:182-203.

Gehlen, A. 1965. Sport und Gesellschaft. Pp. 22-31 in U. Schultz, ed. *Das grosse Spiel.* Frankfurt: Fischer.

Goffman, E. 1959. *The Presentation of Self in Everyday Life.* New York: Doubleday.

Graham, P. and H. Ueberhorst. 1976. *The Modern Olympics.* Cornwall, N.Y.: Leisure Press.

Habermas, J. 1958. Soziologische Notizen zum Verhältnis von Arbeit und Freizeit. Pp. 28 in *Konkrete Vernunft.* Bonn: Bouvier.

Hoch, P. 1972. *Rip of the Big Game. The Exploitation of Sports by the Power Elite.* Garden City, N.Y.: Doubleday.

Ichheiser, G. 1930. *Kritik des Erfolges.* Leipzig.

Ingham, A.G. 1976. *Sport and the New Left.* Pp. 238-48 in D. Landers, op. cit.

Jaspers, K. 1955. Die Situation der Zeit. Berlin (orig. 1931).

Krockow, C. von. 1962. Der Wetteifer in der industriellen Gesellschaft und im Sport. *Neue Sammlung.* 2, 4:297-308.

Krockow, C. von. 1972. *Sport und Industriegesellschaft.* München: Piper.

Krockow, C. von. 1973. *Sport. Eine Soziologie und Philosophie des Leistung-sprinzips.* Hamburg: Hoffmann und Campe.

Lakatos, I. 1970. Falsification and the methodology of scientific research pro-grammes. Pp. 91-96 in I. Lakatos and A. Musgrave, eds. *Criticism and the Growth of Knowledge.* Cambridge: Cambridge University Press.

Landers, D., ed. 1976. *Social Problems in Athletics.* Urbana, Ill.: University of Illinois Press.

Lenk, H. 1976. *Team Dynamics.* Champaign, Ill.: Stipes.

Lenk, H. 1964. *Werte—Ziele—Wirklichkeit der modernen Olympischen Spiele.* Schorndorf-Stuttgart: Hofmann.

Lenk, H. 1971c. *Philosophie im technologischen Zeitalter.* Stuttgart:Kohlhammer.

Lenk, H. 1972. *Leistungssport: Ideologie oder Mythos?* Stuttgart:Kohlhammer.

Lenk, H. 1973. Alienation, manipulation, and the athlete's self. Pp. 8-18 in O. Grupe, et al., eds. *Sport in the Modern World—Chances and Problems.* New York: Springer.

Lenk, H.; Gebauer, G. and E. Franke. 1972. Perspectives of the philosophy of sport. Pp. 29–58 in H. Baitsel, et al., eds. *The Scientific View of Sport.* New York: Springer.

Lenk, H. Moser, S. and E. Beyer, eds. 1973. *Philosophie des Sports.* Schorndorf/-Stuttgart: Hofmann.

Lenk, H. 1976. *Sozialphilosophie des Leistungshandelns.* Stuttgart:Kohlhammer.

Linde, H. 1967. Zur Soziologie des Sports. Versuch einer empirischen Kritik soziologischer Theoreme. Pp. 103-20 in H. Plessner, et al., eds. op. cit.

Lorenz, K. 1966. *On Aggression.* New York: Harcourt, Brace and World.

Marcuse, H. 1955. *Eros and Civilization.* Boston: Beacon.

McClelland, D.C. 1961. *The Achieving Society.* Princeton: Van Nostrand.

Michener, J. 1976. *Sport in America.* New York: Random House.

Morikawa, S. 1979. Fundamental problems in studies on amateur sport. *IRSS.* 14, 1:21-50.

Offe, C. 1970. *Leistungsprinzip und industrielle Arbeit.* Stuttgart: Europäische Verlagsanstalt.

Peters, A. 1927. *Psychologie des Sports.* Leipzig: Der neue Geist.

Plack, A. 1967. *Die Gesellschaft und das Böse.* München: List.

Plessner, H. 1952/53. Soziologie des Sports, Deutsche Universitätszeitung 7:22-24; 9-11; 22-23.

Plessner, H.; Bock, H.E. and O. Grupe, eds. 1967. *Sport und Leibeserziehung. Sozialwissenschaftliche, pädagogische und medizinische Beiträge.* München: Piper.

Rigauer, B. 1969. *Sport und Arbeit.* Frankfurt: Suhrkamp.

Risse. 1921. Soziologie des Sports. Berlin: Reher.

Schafer, W. 1976. Sport and youth counterculture. Pp. 183–100 in D. Landers. op. cit.

Scheler, M. 1927. *Preface* in A. Peters. op. cit.

Scott, J. 1971. *The Athletic Revolution*. New York: Free Press.

Slusher, H.S. 1967. *Man, Sports, and Existence*. Philadelphia: Lea and Febiger.

Stokes, A. 1956. The development of ball games. *Int.J.Psychoanalysis* 37,2/3: 185–192.

Tunis, J.T. 1928. *Sports, Heroes and Hysterics*. New York: John Day.

Vanderzwaag, H.J. 1972. *Toward a Philosophy of Sport*. Reading, Mass.: Addison-Wesley.

Veblen, T. 1899. *The Theory of the Leisure Class*. New York.

Vinnai, P. 1970. *Fussballsport als Ideologie*. Frankfurt: Europäische Verlagsanstalt.

Weiss, P. 1968. *Sport—A Philosophic Inquiry*. Carbondale, Ill.: Southern Illinois University Press.

Reprinted with permission of editor and publisher from *Man and World*. 1972, 5:179-92.

AUTHORITY, POWER, AND INTERGROUP STRATIFICATION BY RACE AND SEX IN AMERICAN SPORT AND SOCIETY

Harry Edwards

Both the public's acceptance of sport as separate from the serious realities of life and academicians' traditional substantiation of this perspective—i.e., that sport embodies activities and relationships legitimately consigned to the "toy department" of human affairs—at long last have been breached. Over the last decade, perspectives and definitions limiting the boundaries of sport's relevance to the field of athletic competition have persistently given way to the realization that sport is indeed a significant element of social reality, demonstrably anchored in and pervasively invested with the prevailing ideological blueprints of the established social order. Further, the contention here is that sport as a social institution has historically reflected, and thereby provided a means of exhibiting and celebrating, the major ideological emphases at the very foundations of the power and authority relationships in society, contributing in the process toward the affirmation, reinforcement and perpetuation of the legitimacy of these relationships. Consequently, a viable sport institution constitutes a major component of the societal machinery effectuating political solidarity, social control and general pattern maintenance imperatives.

Our purposes here, then, are to clarify the theoretical basis for this contention and to illuminate the dynamics and implications of authority and power relationships as manifest in American sport.

AUTHORITY AND POWER CLARIFIED

From the outset, we must be clear as to the distinction between *authority* and *power*. The need to delimit the boundaries of these concepts generates from significantly more than merely the requirement of academic precision or an urge toward intellectual gymnastics. For as employed in the examination of the sport institution the relative degree to which patterns of human interaction (role behavior) are predicated upon and sustained by *power* as opposed to authority relations has important implications.

From the writings of Weber, Blau and Scott, Simon and Homans, three criteria appear to differentiate authority from power. First, there exists under authority a certain minimum of *voluntary submission* and obedience; orders and directives are voluntarily obeyed (Weber 1947: 324). Secondly, authority implies *a priori acceptance* of an order or directive. Authority, then, is said to be in operation whenever a subordinate, as Simon says, "permits his behavior to be guided by a decision of a superior without indepenedently examining the merits of that decision (Simon 1957. II). And thirdly, authority is distinguishable from power in that authority is present only to the extent that there exists a *value orientation* among persons subject to the control that defines the exercise of that control as legitimate (Weber 1947: 328). Thus, Weber observes, "no system of authority voluntarily limits itself to the appeal to material or affectual or ideal motives as a basis for guarenteeing its continuance. In addition every such system attempts to establish and to cultivate a belief in its 'legitimacy.'" (Weber 1947: 325). The internalization of an established system of values (ideology) crystalizing in the form of attitudes and beliefs on the parts of individuals which motivate them to accept their places in the authority structure, provides the only sufficiently reliable basis for a stable and effective system of control (Simon: 1952). And to the extent that such a system of values is widely internalized among subordinates, the failure on the part of a subordinate to comply with the directives of established authority may elicit sanctions not only from his superior but from his peers as well (Blair and Scott 1962: 29). So as Homans observes, "authority depends not only on a [superior's] relations with his [subordinates] but also upon [subordinates] relations with each other" (Homans 1961: 295).

AUTHORITY AND POWER IN SPORT

From its inception, sport has grown increasingly to be characterized by Weber's "legal authority," particularly insofar as role relations on the field of competition and service contracts between individuals and sports organizations are concerned. In combination with this type of authority, one also finds instances of immense "charismatic authority" being rather broadly exercised as in the case of the late professional football coach, Vince Lombardi. But at the very foundations of conformity and control in day-to-day role interaction in sport has been "traditional authority," authority whose "legitimacy rests substantially upon the believed sanctity of the role order in sport and that of established authority relations among these roles largely because that order and those authority relations have come down from the past" (Parsons 1961: 646-7) are viewed as having "always" existed, as being "natural" and "normal."

Authority relations in the dominant sport institution, then, have elicited compliance partially because those in the authority system voluntarily conformed to rules perceived as formally correct and which presumably had been imposed by accepted procedure; and frequently because of subordinates' personal devotiion to some charismatic figure by whom authority was exercised; but most fundamentally because of an ingrained belief in the sanctity of a traditional role order and the established authority relations among those roles. But there have been sanctions for non-compliance in sport, and these have ranged in order of severity, from pressure toward compliance inflicted by peers to physical sanctions (extra practice or punative physical drills), symbolic sanctions (such as a denial of minor privileges), material sanctions (fines) and administrative sanctions (demotion or dismissal from the sports organization—all usually applied by a superior. In a strict sense, however, the actual use of sanctions of any kind has always been an indication of the erosion of the authority structure. For at that point where sanctions are applied to *compel* obedience and conformity, a shift, de facto, has occurred from the exercise of authority to a reliance upon "power"—the ability to coerce or induce certain desired behavior in reluctant or recalcitrant others.

As American society has increased in both population and complexity, the tendency has been toward the general expansion of legal authority as the basis of stable coordinated human interaction, particularly in the instrumental spheres of life; and also towards greater reliance upon power to compel conformity to directives in lieu of formal rules and contracts specifically stipulating the boundaries of authority. In short, because increasing population, urbanization, technological development and the general character and complexity of modern life have rendered tradition less and less relevant at an increasing rate, authority relations predicated largely upon tradition have likewise been eroded and, concommitantly, have increasingly come to be perceived by subordinates as less binding and less legitimate. In the sport institution this development has had a critical impact. For here, the dearth of formal and clearly specified criteria deemed requisite to role attainment is paralleled only by the morass of ambiguity regarding the character and boundaries of authority relations among sport roles in the wake of a diminution of compelling tradition. Mitigating the situation still further is the fact that in the institution of sport much of the interaction is, first, not readily amenable to the imposition of formal rules (owing, for example, to necessities of spontaneity in the fan role and vaguely bracketed realms so traditionally discretionary decision-making authority ac-

crued to the coaching role). Secondly, it is doubtful that a thorough
and all-encompassing formal system of binding and precise authority
and behavior guidelines which was both acceptable to incumbents
and consistent with broader, more fundamental ideological values
(i.e., democratic procedure, due process, individual rights, and so
forth) could be developed—even assuming that such a system was
desired in sport. Therefore, the vacuum created through the erosion
of traditional authority in sport has been filled largely by a greater
reliance upon *power relations* to compel desired behavior. Furthermore, in sport, the more generally relevant *intergroup conflicts*
within which power has been employed have reflected conflicts
emergent from the disruption of prevailing legal authority and the
erosion of traditional authority relations between groups in the
broader society.

POWER, SCARCITY AND STRATIFICATION
BY RACE AND SEX IN AMERICAN SPORT AND SOCIETY

Generally implicit in intergroup power relations are some fundamental postulates regarding the character of self- and group interests.
Here, the work of Gerhard Lenski is appealing in our efforts to clarify
the sources of intergroup stratification in sport within the American
context. In his theory of power and privilege, Lenski contends humankind by nature is a social being, obliged to interact with other
members of his species to more efficiently secure elemental necessities
of life (food, shelter, and protection) as well as other *emergent*, but
no less desired scarce valuables (e.g., status, prestige, wealth and
so forth). He also asserts that humankind, unlike plants and other
animal life, has an insatiable appetite for the emergent valuables in
particular. Thus in human societies, there exists an omnipresent and
ongoing [potential for] struggle toward the attainment of these
scarce valuables (Lenski 1966: 31-35). Because these valuables are
in short supply relative to the total aspiration pool and owing to
humankind's associative proclivities, *intergroup* conflict may emerge
out of interindividual competition as important individual decisions
and actions come to be increasingly prompted by an amalgam of
perceived self-interests and partisan group interests.

Now, perhaps more so than in any other modern western society,
in the United States the *potential* for a struggle toward the attainment of scarce valuables has been institutionalized as a legitimate
mechanism of mobility through this society's pervasive ideological
emphases upon interindividual competitiveness. Therefore, by applying Lenski's postulates to the consideration of race, sex and power
within the sports institution we may propose two arguments. First,
in sport as in the larger society, the history of intersex and inter-

racial relations has been substantially determined by white males' efforts to maintain control of scarce valuables in the face of a perceived threat or the actual attempt by Black males and by women to increase their own access to attainment of, and thus control over, these valuables. Secondly, owing to the latent functions of sport in society, we may also argue that, to the extent that they have been successful in sustaining their domination of sport, white males have concommitantly realized the latent accomplishment of reaffirming, reinforcing and thereby perpetuating the legitimacy of both the prevailing system of ideological beliefs in general and white males' own partisan group ideological defintions in particular, i.e., those conducive to sustaining white male dominance in both sport and the greater society. In sport, then, we may expect to find, in microcosm, structural and ideological manifestations of intersex and interracial authority and, subsequently, power relations consistent with those prevailing in society at large.

In an elaborate analysis of the interpenetration of social structure and intergroup relation, Pierre van den Berghe stipulates that "it is reasonable to accept that aspects of social structure exert a considerable degree of determinism on the prevailinig type of [intergroup] relations" (van den Berghe 1967: 26). In line with this astute observation, he proceeds to develop a typology relating dominant-subordinate group interaction patterns to basic structural variables such as the economy, the division of labor, and the character of social stratification. He terms his first polar type of patterned interaction *paternalistic* intergroup relations.

PATERNALISTIC INTERGROUP RELATIONS IN AMERICAN SPORT AND SOCIETY

Paternalistic relations are, according to van den Berghe, most characteristic of fairly complex but pre-industrial societies wherein agriculture and handicraft production constitute the basis of an "individual achievment" oriented society. In such a society, the dominant group, a numerical minority in the total population, develops an ideology of "benevolent despotism" and regards members of subordinate groups as "inferior, but loveable, as long as they stay in their place." An elaborate system of etiquette marked by assymetrical manners of dress and speaking, stringent regulations and continuous manifestations of subservience and dominance maximize the distinctions between the statuses of dominant and subordinate group members (van den Berghe 1967: 28). This ideology of "benevolent despotism" is widely internalized by subordinates as legitimate *or* if subordinates come to accept, by tradition, definition of the *power potential* of the dominant group as being so great as to compel compliance a priori, then a kind of "role symbiosis" and relatively harmonious dominant-subordinate status complementarity is likely to emerge. Furthermore, if sustained over an extended period of time, such status complementarity may evolve into a pervasive pattern of traditional authority relations between dominant group and subordinate group members. As applied to the interface of sport and stratification by sex, van den Berghe's paternalistic form of intergroup relations is instructive. (Owing the space considerations and because, in any event, only the most fragmentary information on antebellum Black sport involvement survives—an artifact perhaps of both the severity of slavery and the extent of white paternalism toward enslaved and free Blacks—we will be concerned here only with manifestations of paternalism in male-female relations in sport and society.)

In her insightful work "Symbolic Forms of Movement: The Feminine Image in Sports," Eleanor Metheny (1970) argues persuasively that biological distinctions provide no logical basis for the restriction of access by women to the full range of roles within the sport institution. While she focuses primarily upon athlete roles in strenuous Olympic sports, the implications of her analysis would most certainly apply also the secondary level role involvement in all realms of sport (for example, they would apply to control and authority roles such as coach and manager and also involving ideological interpretations such as sports editor and sports reporter). She observes that while it is a truism that "on the average men are stronger than women, this generalization does not hold for individual representatives of the two sexes. Some women may be very much larger and stronger than some men." As a group, women's achievements in sport may be less spectacular than those of men; however, in terms of individual achievement, some women may well excel most of the male competitors in any given event. And though intermittent pregnancies, and possibly menstruation, may constitute mitigating episodes, "they do not vitiate the biological fact that women appear to be fully as competent as men to fulfill even the most strenuous of sport roles," (Metheny 1970: 292). In her view, the subjugation of women in sport is tracable to social definitions that rationalize the division of labor in Western societies, particularly as this bears upon differences between the ways men and women may use their bodies. Metheny notes, for example, that force is a male preogrative and correspondingly, from the act of procreation to the waging of war, in the Western world it has been widely regarded, by social tradition, as inappropriate for the female to coerce or subdue another person to her will. Thus, while in every society biology contributes to some degree toward differentiating the roles men and women play in the social order, the status and authority relationships vested in these roles are *socially* determined.

Consistent with ideological definitions shared commonly between sport and society, then, the western tradition of paternalistic male-female role realtions have come to be manifest in the character of this nation's sport institution. As the work of Sutton-Smith, et al. demonstrates, from puberty onwards sport has been a predominantly masculine phenomenon in this culture. Boys proceed from pastimes to athletic participation, but girls, by comparison do not. "....sports have always been positively associated with the male role, but negatively associated with female role" (Sutton-Smith et al. 1963: 126). Marie Hart observes that traditionally the woman who dared pursue athletic involvement in any but those roles socially approved for females—cheerleader, beauty queen, pom-pom girl—has done so at risk of impuning her feminine image from the perspective of both males and her female peers (1972: 291). This, and the fact that so long after the onset of industrialization and urbanization, residues of a paternalistic tradition have persisted to such an extent that women have yet to achieve even the range of legitimacy in sport enjoyed by Blacks, is perhaps some indication of (1) the relative magnitude of threat posed by women, who constitute a numerical majority, to white male domination of status opportunities in both sport and society; (2) the degree and intensity of entrenched male chauvinistic ideology in the United States; (3) the extent to which this ideological tradition has crystalized into a symbiotic pattern of male-female status complementarity and (4) the probability that in the U.S., white intragroup distinctions in status predicated upon sex not only have greater tenure but greater tenacity than racially grounded status inequities. So while the United States appears most certainly to be a society with an intense counter-current of racist ideology, it would appear also that it is foremost and most committedly a sexist society with substantial, if not decisive, populations of both men and women acceding to the legitimacy of established paternalistic male-female authority relationships.

COMPETITIVE INTERGROUP RELATIONS AND POWER IN AMERICAN SPORT AND SOCIETY

The polar extreme of van den Berghe's paternalistic intergroup relations is the *competitive* form. This form is generally found to exist in industrialized urban societies, particularly those with a historical and continuing ideological tradition legitimizing interindividual competiton for scarce valuables. If such a society is also quite heterogeneous racially, intergroup competition tends to emerge along racial as well as sex lines. As Amos Hawley suggests, "...where population is   subdivided into racial groups, [legitimate interindividual] competition tends to shift from an individual to an intergroup basis. When this occurs, the fundamental competitive issue is altered; to the problem of how much [of the scarce values] each individual competitor will be able to obtain is added, the problem of how many individuals from each racial group will have the opportunity to even enter the competition" (Hawley 1944: 669).

Hawley further suggests that if only a small number of subordinate group individuals are involved in the competitions for scarce valuables in a particular societal sphere, competition is likely to remain more on an interindividual as opposed to an intergroup basis. But if a subordinate group increases the numbers of its members seeking, through interindividual competition, to obtain scarce valuables in a particular sphere, competition in that sphere may be expected to become increasingly more intergroup in character. As members of the subordinate group are perceived by dominant group members to loom as a progressively more threatening competitive force, then, members of the dominant group shift from an individual toward intergroup competitive orientation. Accordingly, intergroup tensions mount, restrictions on subordinate group members' behavior options, freedom of ideological expression and actual opportunities to participate in the competitive process accumulate, and there ultimately ensues a pattern of intergroup relations based upon differential group "power resources" (Wilson 1976: 16), and the ability of each group to apply its resources toward the achivement of partisan group goals.

Now, implicit in this formulation is not only the idea that both dominant and subordinate group members must attach the same status value to scarce valuables obtainable through competition but also the idea that the integrity of the interindividual competitive process itself is largely assessed by each group according to its collective judgement of the potential for successfully achieving or sustaining partisan group interests by way of that process. To the extent that the members of the dominant or the subordinate group, or both, define important partisan group interests as vulnerable at any given juncture under the established interindividual competitive process, they are likely to bring collective power resources to bear in an attempt to realize greater competitive advantage for involved members. Therefore, unlike under paternalism where subordinate groups tend to lack control of sufficient power resources, and in some instances even the incentive to seriously challenge the dominant group's virtual monopoly on means and authority to "define the situation," relations between groups in the competitive system are characterized by reciprocal rather than onesided vulnerability to the manipulation of power resources and also by relatively greater preeminence of expediency as opposed to established procedure in efforts to achieve desired ends.

As applied to the dominant sport institution, the competitive model allows us to diagramatically illustrate the changing character of intergroup relations by sex and race from the turn of the century to the present. Dates associated with the three stages of the competitive model are, of course, only approximate since it clearly would be impossible to establish a precise chronology of change in so dynamic a situation. Likewise, the diagram depicts the resultant cumulative changes regarding subordinate groups' achieved levels of involvement in sport toward the end of each period. The three stages portrayed are delimited according to certain events regarded as seminal: the *Early Stage* in the development of intergroup relations is stipulated to span a time period roughly from the late 1890's (the onset of major sports events and the final collapse of Reconstruction which threw Blacks into direct competition with whites for scarce valuables) to 1946—the year just prior to Jackie Robinson's entry into professional baseball; the *Middle Stage* covers a period from 1947 to 1967, the year just prior to widespread Black political activity in sport and the onset of the women's liberation movement; and the *Latest Stage* is dated from the revolt of Black collegiate and worldclass amateur athletes in 1968 and widespread legal and political action among women seeking greater athletic involvement from the late 1960's to the present.

The three stages portrayed clearly point up the changing character of Black males' and women's involvement opportunities and therefore, their potential access to scarce valuables in the dominant sport institution. But more importantly, they depict the continuity of changes in intergroup power relations as manifest in sport and the general society. In short, subordinate groups' abilities to organize, concentrate and deploy power resources toward the accomplishment of partisan group ends in the society at large have enabled them to use similar tactics and strategies (boycotts, protests, legalities, etc.) to more or less successfully challenge established intergroup authority and status relations, as well as supporting ideological rationalizations in sport. Thus, against the background of the competitive intergroup model, it would be reasonable to expect (1) that the subordinate group achieving the greatest success in challenging the established order would be that group whose potential in the interindividual competitive situation was perceived by the dominant groups as ideologically the most manageable, as the most exploitable in terms of the traditional structure and ends of sports, and therefore as the least threatening to the more central values defining status and authority relations; (2) that successful strategies and tactics employing subordinate group power resources in the general society

The Changing Character of Intersex and Interracial Relations in the Dominate Sport Institution

	*Interpretative Roles	*Control Roles	Athlete Roles	Fan Role
I **Early Stage** (Circa late 1890s to 1946) Period characterized by de facto and dejure Jim Crow and male chauvinism in sport and society	White Males Monopoly	White Males Monopoly	White Males Monopoly	White Males and Females — Institutional Integration by Sex; Black Males and Females — Segregation by Race
II **Middle Stage** (Circa 1947–1967) Period characterized by widespread Black Civil Rights Activities and emergence of new or modern Women's Liberation Movement	White Males Monopoly	White Males Monopoly	White Males, Black Males — Institutional Integration by Whites, Race/Position-al Segregation by Race; Women — Segregation by Sex	Blacks and Whites, Males and Females — Institutional Integration by Race and Sex
III **Latest Stage** (Circa 1968–Present)	Token Institutional In-	Institutional Integra-	Institution-al Integra-	

Period characterized by "revolt of the Black Athlete", legal and political activities among women toward the end of legitimizing their full involvement in Sport.

	White Males Black Males	tegration by Race/Positional Segregation by Race	White Males Black Males	tion by Race/Positional Segregation by Race	White Males Black Males Women	tion by Race/Token positional Integration by Race Token Integration in Sports by Sex	Blacks and Whites, Males and Females	Institutional Integration by Race and Sex
*Sports editors Sports reporters for major newspapers and sports magazines								
*Owner, manager, coach on the field control roles such as umpire, referee, field judge, etc.								
Radio and Television Sports Editors, producers, sportscasters, commentators, and announcers								
Sports Organization, Publicists, press relations agents, etc.								

Legend: (1) —— segregated (2) —— Token Integration by Race (3) —— Token Integration in some sports (4) —— Token Institutional Integration/positional segregation (5) – – – – Institutional Integration/position segregation —— Institutional Integration/Token Positional Integration would also be adapted for use in the sport institution; (3) that sub-ordinate groups would be most successful in altering relations at the bottom end of the status and authority hierarchy in sport; and (4) that each successful challenge to the established order would constitute a potential contribution to the power resources of the challenging group, thus generating dominant group efforts toward projecting a conciliatory posture, ostensibly granting some highly visible concessions, while simultaneously manipulating the confrontation situation so as to minimize the possibility of concessions being transmitted into subordinate group power resources.

Therefore, the most integrated role in sport is that of the fan. The tradition of males "taking" females to sporting events dates back to the earliest days of sport establishment as an institution in this society. Here the male has satisfied his own desires for female companionship both during and frequently after the sports event without endangering his dominant status. The character of the male role in this relationship is consistent with male roles in the larger society: he is the facilitator, solving the logistics and providing the means of getting to and into the sport event; he is the reigning authority on the correct interpretation of events on the field of competition, fully expecting his female companion to accept his judgements even over those of officials on the field.

By the end of the *Middle Stage* of development, there was both sex and racial integration in fandom. Though the latter was prompted primarily by Black efforts to desegregate public facilities and accommodations in all realms of societal life, racial integration in the stands was so quickly and so widely implemented largely because the money paid by Blacks for tickets to a sports event is indistinguishable from that paid by whites once it is in the coffers of the sports organization.

In terms of its traditional position in the sport status and authority hierarchy, the athlete role is superordinate only to that of the fan. Thus it is reasonable that the second most integrated role in sport should be that of the athlete. Next to the fan role, it is as athletes that both Blacks and women have achieved their greatest successes in challenging white male dominance in the sport institution. And in terms of their more fundamental significance, even these successes are not of the magnitude implied by consideration of mere quantitative increases in Black and female participation. Let us then look more closely at the phenomenon of increased female and Black male involvement as atheletes in sport.

The most obvious fact emerging from the diagramatic depiction of the *Middle* and *Latest Stages* of change in sport is that Black males have made substantially greater progress in sport at all levels than have women—most particularly as athletes. The contention here is that this occurred initially because (1) Blacks were able to marshal their power resources toward the end of challenging established intergroup status and opportunity relationships earlier and to a greater degree than women in the general society; (2) Black males constituted a smaller group in the general population than women; (3) Black males in the athlete role were more exploitable than women within the traditional athletic structure and in terms of the established goals of sports involvement; and (4) Black males were potentially more manageable than women as athletes in the sport milieu (for example, the Black male athlete's status continuity across sport and the larger society was more readily sustained within the context of established ideological rationalizations than that of women).

Thus, Black males fulfilling the athlete role were perceived by dominant white males as a lesser threat than women both to established ideological definitions and the sport structure, and so to the prevailing character of intergroup relations. The dominant group has both exploited Black male athletic skills toward traditional sports ends within the established structure and also manipulated the character of Black involvement opportunities (positional segregation) and developed ideological rationalizations (innate Black intellectual inferiority and physical superiority) sustaining white male status and authority dominance in sport and, by implication, in society.

And because of the nature of the interdependence extant between sport and society, the dominant group has also realized an additional accomplishment. It has effectively transmuted increased Black involvement in sport—a potential power resource and an ostensible advance toward full Black integration in American life—into a mechanism forestalling Black challenges to the integrity of the system of interindividual competition in the broader society. And recall, so long as subordinate group members do not question the integrity of that system, they are unlikely to perceive competition as "intergroup" in nature and to bring power resources to bear in pursuit of partisan group interests. The dynamics of this latent accomplishment bears upon the relationship between sport and the fan role.

In accordance with ideological values shared commonly between sport and society, each individual is presumed to be accountable for his own failings and to deserve rewards and status according from his successes. Yet in this highly complex society, no individual can hope to control all of the intricate and impersonal relationships that impact upon his outcomes, even though he might rigorously adhere to the American ideological ideals emphasizing individual competitiveness. Rewards all too often fall short of expectations, producing "strain" and dissatisfaction in the disappointed striver. When "normal" frustrations are compounded by categorical impediments to achievement—impediments emerging out of intergroup competition based upon racial distinctions—individual dissatisfaction may crystalize into group hostility and even violence.

Sport because of its value reinforcement function (social control) in society offers not only a balm for individual frustrations but a means toward social stability within the context of established dominant-subordinate group status relations. The Black fan finds in the success of the Black athlete reinforcement of those values which define established means—interindividual competition—as legitimate, and by implication, that define the resultant configuration of inter-group status and authority relationships as just and correct.

Furthermore, because of the relatively greater concentration and visibility of Black athlete role models, a disproportionately high number of young Black males have been channeled toward athletic pursuits as career interests, thereby diminishing the number of Black males motivated early in life toward competing with white males for high status occupational positions in other realms of society. Also, because the number of strivers and because of quotas and other forms of discrimination against Blacks in sport, the overwhelming majority of those who pursue sport are doomed to failure regardless of their achieved levels of athletic proficiency.

The relatively meager involvement of Blacks in control and inter-pretative roles therefore becomes understandable. When, in the late 1960's, Black amateur and collegiate athletes staged protests, boycotts, and sit-downs in order to organize demands for Black coaches and athletic administrators, Black *assistant coaches* were hired in every major amateur sport organization in this society which exploited Black athletic talent—colleges, universities, athletic clubs, and even the United States Olympic Committee. At colleges and universities a new position was established specifically to accommodate Black demands for Black athletic administrators—*Assistant to* the Athletic Director. Unlike the traditional "Assistant Athletic Director," Black Assistants *to* the Athletic Director typically had few responsibilities beyond cooling out potentially disruptive activities and attitudes among Black athletes, Black students and the Black public to the degree that these might impact negatively upon white male defini-tions of the interests of the sport organization. Black assistant coaches fulfilled parallel responsibilities on the field—their main duty being to cool out Black athletes' concerns over such issues as posi-tional segregation (or stacking) and to manage any Black-white interpersonal disputes that might have emerged out of or held the potential for expanding into intergroup conflict. The dominant group also took care to hire "team men," Blacks who were "safe" in so far as their potential for using their acquired positions to further challenge white male dominance in sport.

Logically, the most segregated roles in sport are the interpretative roles. It is through these roles that prevailing ideological definitions come to be subjectively applied toward characterizing and interpreting relations, events and activities in the sport institution. For this reason, those filling interpretative roles exercise the greatest power in sport. By sustaining a white male domination of these roles, those definitions of the situation conducive to the perpetuation of white male superordination are more readily sustained. Thus, major metropolitan newspapers, or sports magazines, television or radio stations have Black people permanently functioning as sports columnists, commentators, or broadcasters in the tradition of print and electronic journalism (as opposed to celebrity assignments as "color men" commenting on sports with which they are widely identified as athletes). Not a single major sports organization has hired a Black person as head publicist or press relations agent. So, with the exception of their token integration as "color men" and occasionally as sports reporters given three to five minutes to report box scores on local television news programs serving areas with substantial Black populations, Blacks are almost totally excluded from significant interpretative roles.

Women, for the most part, have fared even worse. Indeed, beyond the fan role, women have been only minimally integrated into the sport hierarchy. And even though there *is* an occasional and highly pubiciized venture by a woman into auto and horse racing into the "no-woman's land" of coaching or officiating, or into the locker room as a sport reporter, these are exceptions that prove the rule. As Metheny notes, for the most part even in athletic endeavors "approved" for women, competition is still largely woman to woman, while males dominate control and interpretative roles. Even in tennis—a sport long approved for women—mixed doubles are played woman to woman and man to man, the most common strategy emphasizing the man's strength of arm while the woman uses her skill to support his efforts within a smaller part of their common court area.

IMPLICATIONS

Aside from those implications already cited in the corpus of this work, a fundamental implication of our analysis here is that a thorough and accurate interpretation of human relations in sport can yield valuable insights into the character, bases and dynamics of social organizations in society. More specifically, the extent to which any changes ostensibly affecting the basic structure and ideological foundations of intergroup authority and status relations are more cosmetic than real, can be readily assessed through an analysis of changes in the proportionality of group representation throughout the authority hierarchy in sport.

Also, to the extent that prevailing confrontation of subordinate group members' involvement opportunities in sport are predicated upon the dominant group's superior power ability rather than upon subordinate groups' definitions legitimizing prevailing authority relations, intergroup relations in the institution of sport, and by implication in society, will remain "unstable." Thus, through an analysis of sport we can determine changes in the degree of intergroup ideological consensus and differential power ability in society, since significant ideological dissensus and changes in power ability across competing groups in society is likely to find expression in sport by way of challenges to existing authority, status, and opportunity relations.

In the future, as the energy crisis, technological development and the reality of a shrinking world continue to compound the effect of expanded populations and increased societal complexity in Western nations, sport will loom more and more significant as a barometer of both social stability and radical discontinuities in ideological and structural tradition.

REFERENCES

Blau, P.M. and M.G. Scott. 1962. *Formal Organizations.* San Francisco: Chandler.

Curtis, J. and J. Loy. 1978. Positional segregation in professional baseball. *IRRS* 13, 1:67-80.

Edwards, H. 1969. *The Revolt of the Black Athlete.* New York: Free Press.

Edwards, H. 1973. *Sociology of Sport.* Homewood, Ill.: Dorsey Press.

Edwards, H. 1975. Desegregating sexist sport. *Intellectual Digest.* Nov.

Edwards, H. 1972. The myth of the racially superior athlete. *Intellectual Digest.* March.

Cheffers, J. 1975. *A Wilderness of Spite.* New York: Vintage.

Gerber, E.W. et al. eds. 1974. *The American Woman in Sport.* Reading, Mas.: Addison-Wesley.

Gruneau, R.S. 1975. Sport, social differentiation and social inequality. Pp. 121-84 in D. Ball and J. Loy, eds. *Sport and Social Order.* Reading, Mas.: Addison-Wesley.

Hart, M. ed. 1972. Sport in the Socio-Cultural Process. Dubuque, Iowa: Brown.

Hawley, A. 1944. Dispersion versus segregation: a propos of a solution of race problems. *Papers of Michigan Academy of Science, Arts and Letters.* 30: 669.

Hoch, P. 1972. *Rip Off the Big Game.* New York: Doubleday.

Homans, G.C. 1961. *Social Behavior. Its Elementary Forms.* New York: Harcourt, Brace and World.

Lenski, G. 1966. *Power and Privilege: A Theory of Social Stratification.* New York: McGraw Hill.

Loy, J.W. and J.F. McElvogue. 1970. Racial segregation in American sport. *IRRS* 5, 1:5–24.

McClendon, M. and D.S. Eitzen. 1975. Interracial contact on collegiate basketball teams. *Social Science Quarterly* 55, 5:926–38.

Metheny, E. 1970. Symbolic forms of movement: the feminine image in sports. Pp. 291-303 in G.H. Sage, ed. *Sport in American Society*. Reading, Mas.: Addison-Wesley.

Noll, R. ed. 1974. *Government and the Sports Business*. Wash.: Brookings.

Oglesby, C. 1978. *Women and Sport*. Philadelphia: Lea and Ferbiger.

Olsen, J. 1968. The black athlete. A shameful story. *Sports Illustrated*. August.

Parsons, T. 1961. *The Structure of Social Action*. Glencoe, Ill.: Free Press.

Picou, J. 1978. Race, athletic achievement, and educational aspiration. *Sociological Quarterly*. 19, 3:429-38.

Scully, G.W. 1974. Discrimination. The case of baseball. Pp. 221-273 in R.Noll, ed. *Government and the Sports Business*.

Simon, H.A. 1957. *Administrative Behavior*. New York: Macmillan.

Simon, H.A. 1952. Comments on the theory of organizations. *American Pol. Sci. Review* 46, 6:1130-39.

Stone, G.P. 1973. American sport: play and display. Pp. 65-85 in J. Talamini and C. Page, eds. *Sport and Society*. Boston: Little, Brown.

Stone, G.P. 1969. Some meanings of American sport. Pp. 5–16 in G.S. Kenyon, ed. *Sociology of Sport*. Chicago: Athletic Institute.

Sutton-Smith, B.; Rosenberg, B. and E. Morgan. 1963. Development of sex differences in play choices during preadolescence. *Child Development* 34, 1:119–126.

Thompson, R. 1964. *Race and Sport*. London: Oxford University Press.

Thompson, R. 1975. *Retreat from Apartheid: New Zealand's Sporting Contacts with South Africa*. New York: Oxford University Press.

Van den Berghe, P. 1967. *Race and Racism*. New York: Wiley.

Voigt, D.Q. 1976. *America through Baseball*. Chicago: Nelson-Hall.

Weber, M. 1947. *The Theory of Social and Economic Organization*. Glencoe, Ill.: Free Press (orig. 1923).

SPORT AND DEVIANCE

D. Stanley Eitzen

Sport and deviance would appear on the surface as antithetical terms. After all, sport contests are bound by rules, school athletes must meet rigid grade and behavior standards in order to compete, and there is a constant monitoring of athletes' behavior because they are public figures and because there are officials and organizations whose primary function is to curb their illegal behaviors. Moreover, sport is assumed by many to promote those character traits deemed desirable by most in society: fair play, sportsmanship, obedience to authority, hard work, goal orientation, and the like.

The thesis of this paper is, to the contrary, that the structure of sport in society actually promotes deviance. Deviance is defined here as behavior that: (1) violates the rules of the game; (2) offends the universal values of sportsmanship and fair play; and (3) illegitimately brings harm to persons or property (violence). The first meaning is self explanatory. The rules of a sport create deviance by negatively labeling and punishing rule breakers. A fight among players in a soccer game, for example, is easily defined as rule breaking and the punishment for such conduct is easily dispensed. The other two meanings are normative ones and require further elaboration. These meanings include as deviance those behaviors that violate ideals which are presumed to have universal acceptance. It is assumed that those activities that give an athlete or team an unfair advantage in a sports event are generally abhorred throughout the world of sport. "Unfair" is meant to connote those means that enhance the chances of victory other than skill, luck, strategy, and ability. In addition to unfairness, the deliberate harming of people and property is generally decried and defined as deviant behavior.

This paper examines the relationship between sport and deviance, emphasizing four areas: (1) sport as festival; (2) sport and violence; (3) the interference of outsiders in the outcome of contests; and

(4) the corruption of the ideals of sport. The first three sections deal primarily with the mechanisms by which sport promotes deviance among spectators. The last one focuses on the deviant behavior of athletes and coaches in their drive to succeed-at-any costs. Drug abuse, cheating, the corruption of education, and the abuse of the athlete are highlighted in that section.

SPORT AS FESTIVAL

Sporting events share characteristics with such non-sporting events as Mardi Gras and New Year's Eve celebrations, rock concerts, and conventions. The shared characteristics found typically at these seemingly different events (which classify them as festivals) are: music, costuming, ostentatious displays of material possessions, the use of alcohol as a "social lubricant," the buying and selling of memorabilia, and the *existence of "routinized" deviance* (Koval, 1974).

Apparently festivals serve several related "escape valve" functions for the members of a society: (1) they provide excitement in an otherwise routine world (Elias and Dunning 1970); (2) they allow adults to react against their over-socialization and retreat at least momentarily to a fantasy world of their youth; and (3) they provide a release from the constraints of the social world. Festivals provide an antidote to normal social life that is bound by pressures to conform in relatively rigid ways. Festivals allow the individual to participate in relatively unstructured and spontaneous behaviors. At sporting events, spectators can deviate from society's norms (within reasonable limits) without penalty. The individual can drink to excess, shout obscenities, destroy property (e.g., goal posts), act hysterically, and generally make a fool of himself/herself. In other words, individuals may behave in ways that they would consider deviant in other social contexts. The game, as a festival, is legitimized by society and its agents of social control as a time to act illegitimately, to be released from the standardized forms of social relationships of the everyday world.

SPORT AND VIOLENCE

Normative Violence in Sport

The most popular sports in many societies actually encourage player aggression. Not only is the nature of these sports to hit an opponent but the sport can encourage excessive violence with little or no penalty. For example, a player willfully injuring another player can be reprimanded, fined, removed from the contest, or banished from the sport forever. Hockey, especially, is well known for its minimal penalties and in effect condoning violence as a crowd-pleasing part of the game. Player fights routinely result in cuts, concussions, and fractures not only in the professional leagues (Kennedy 1975), but also in amateur (McMurtry 1974), and in youth hockey (Smith 1974). But why do these athletes participate in violence? Smith (1974) has argued that violence in hockey, as in war, is a socially rewarded behavior. The players are convinced that aggression (body checking, intimidation, and the like) is vital to winning. Thus, the behavior is approved by fans, coaches, and peers. Younger athletes, of course, idolize the professionals and attempt to emulate their aggressive behaviors at their level of play, thereby perpetuating violence in the sport.

Violence is also an integral part of a sport such as football (Underwood 1978). Players are expected to be "hitters." They are taught to lower their heads to deliver a blow to the opponent. They are taught to gang tackle—to make the ball carrier "pay the price." The assumption is that physically punishing the other player will increase the probability of the opponent fumbling, losing his concentration and executing poorly the next time, becoming exhausted, or having to be replaced by a less talented substitute. These brutal, win-at-any-cost tactics are almost universally held among coaches, players, and fans in the United States. The unfortunate result is a very high injury rate. The probabilities of injuries for any season are that 1,000,000 high school players will be hurt enough to miss one game, as well as 70,000 college players and a 100 percent injury rate (at least one per player) for the professionals (Underwood 1978; Surface 1974). Every year 100,000 to 130,000 knees are damaged with 30,000 to 50,000 of them requiring surgery (Treaster 1979). Some of these injuries are very serious. The data show that from 1971 to 1977 there were 77 football related fatalities and from 1971 to 1977 there were 1,129 serious neck or spinal injuries, 176 of which resulted in permanent quadriplegia (Middleton 1979).

The high injury rate is a function of playing a violent game. Most important for our purposes is that this violence is considered a "normal" part of the game. The athletes are expected to behave in ways that in nonsporting and non-warlike contexts would be considered deviant.

The Function of Violent Sports for the Athletes, Spectators, and Society

We can only speculate as to why violent sports thrive in some societies (for a history of sporting violence, see Atyeo 1979). Do violent societies need violent sports? Gladitorial combat on the athletic field reflects the emphasis, perhaps, of militarized societies. Or is it possible that violent sports act as a catharsis, ridding the individuals (and, therefore, society) of pent-up aggression, thereby lessening the possibility of war? The rationale for each position follows (Sipes 1973; Tandy and Laflin 1973).

The drive discharge theory begins with the assumption that aggression by individuals and groups is innate (instinctive). Aggressive tension is further assumed to accumulate in the individual and society and must be discharged. War results when these tensions become too great. Warlike sports will serve to discharge accumulated aggression (catharsis) and serve as a legitimate alternative to war.

The alternative approach, the culture pattern theory, argues that aggression is primarily a learned behavior. Therefore, societies will emphasize activities that promote either competitiveness and aggression or cooperation and passivity. Warlike sports, then, will be the rule in aggressive societies. Such sports, rather than providing a catharsis effect, lead to the enhancement of aggression in the society.

The study by Sipes (1973) was a direct test of these two theories. Two methods were used. First, 20 tribal societies were randomly selected to determine whether warlike societies had combative sports or not. This analysis strongly supported the culture pattern model. Nine of the 10 warlike societies had combative sports while only two of the 10 peaceful societies had combative sports. The second test examined the popularity of combative sports in the United States from 1920 to 1970 and also supported the culture pattern model. Sipes found that combative sports (football, boxing, hockey) increased in popularity in time of war while baseball decreased. His conclusion was that sports are not alternative channels for the discharge of aggressive tensions. Combative sports, rather than lessening aggression, appear to intensify it. This conclusion is supported also by the research of others on the effects of watching violent sports on spectator (Goldstein and Arms 1971; Geen and Berkowitz 1966; Turner 1968).

Despite these studies, there is not a definitive answer as to whether the existence and popularity of violent sports does or does not drain off aggressive tendencies in the populace. The existence of violent sports in a violent society is not proof that one causes the other. Such sports may indeed perform a safety valve function. Just because there is a high level of aggression in the United States, for example, does not mean that the violent sports do not work as safety valves. It may mean that participants in society are overwhelmed by too many sources of frustration and aggression. It may mean, in fact, that without violent sports, spectators and players would be all the more aggressive. Clearly, more research is needed before we can answer this interesting speculation with any certainty.

Spectator Violence

1. Rowdyism. This type of spectator violence refers to interpersonal and property vandalism associated with sports contests. Unlike the other forms of spectator violence, rowdyism (or hooliganism as it is sometimes called) occurs regardless of what occurs on the field. It refers to hostile acts aimed at whatever targets are handy. Apparently sports events provide a locale where angry people can congregate and take out their frustrations individually and collectively.

Such behavior connected with soccer matches has become a major social problem in England (Taylor 1972) and is a rising concern in the United States. Even at baseball games (where the game itself is essentially nonviolent), spectators have engaged in such outrageous behavior as setting off firecrackers, interrupting the game by running out on the field of play, throwing objects at players, attacking players as they enter or leave the field, pouring beer on injured players, stealing equipment, damaging the stadium, and the like. Fimrite has provided several possible reasons for the increased incidence of such offensive behavior (1974): (1) increased drinking at games (one ugly incident by rowdy fans occurred at a Cleveland Indians baseball game in 1974 when the management had a 10¢ beer night—selling some 60,000 ounce cups of beer to the 25,134 fans in attendance); (2) we are living in an age of free expression and youth, especially, are accustomed to venting their emotions; (3) there is a general contempt for the establishment and authority figures; (4) there has been a trend toward a widening breach between the fans and the professional athletes, as the latter demand ever higher salaries and evidence little loyalty to the fans; (5) many professional teams have shown contempt for the fans by moving to other cities where more money can be made. Fimrite's reasons for rowdyism include both societal factors and sport related factors. Research is needed to determine whether sport is a source of the frustration or just a convenient outlet for its expression.

2. Sports riots. Sports related riots can be divided into two types depending on the intent of the participants. One type is a celebration where the participants exult in a victory by destroying property. A prime example occurred following the New York Mets improbable winning of the National League pennant when their fans literally stripped the stadium of anything they could carry (signs, bases, turf, lumber, seats). The other type of riot, and the one we will emphasize, is characterized by hostility rather than exuberance.

Since sports riots occur in a social and cultural context, we need to examine the specific social structural strains present in the situation that may lead to these riotous episodes (Smith 1973; 1975; 1978). If there are ethnic, political, economical, class, religious or other cleavages present in the society, then the potential for intergroup conflict is great. In other words, collective violence tends to erupt when the representatives of groups already in conflict meet in a sport contest. The following are some examples:

item: a massive brawl with over 500 injuries occurred in 1962 when a lower class school was defeated by an affluent private school in the Washington, D.C. high school championship football game.

item: in 1971 a major outbreak of violence occurred when the predominantly black Camden High School lost to mostly white Bishop Eustace High School of Pennsanken, New Jersey.

item: In the best two out of three soccer match between Honduras and El Salvador in 1969 for the right to represent the region in the World Cup, much rioting took place resulting finally in the severing of diplomatic and commerical relations and in the attack by the El Salvadorean army on the Honduras border. The soccer matches that resulted in this war were not responsible for the war because the games took place in an atmosphere of great tension and hostililty because of a long standing dispute between the two countries.

Another structural strain that may lead to sports related riots is the unavailability of alternate avenues of protest for grievances. As a general rule, the more underdeveloped the society industrially, the fewer the channels for expressing grievances. This may explain the relatively widespread existence of violence associated with soccer matches in Latin America. One soccer riot in Lima, Peru, for instance, ended with 293 fans killed and over 500 injured. A reasonable hypothesis is that where the majority of fans are very poor and there are no outlets for expressing grievances, riots will be relatively commonplace. The poor identify strongly with the players who most often come from similar origins. Defeats in important matches, where the fans have a strong emotional attachment, may be an intolerable deprivation by an already deprived group. A typical result is aggression toward the supporters of the opposing team.

Given these structural conditions ("structural conduciveness"), riots emerge when a precipitating event occurs. The spark may be violence by players, the antics of the opponents, individual or small scale spectator fights, or a disputed judgment by an official. As an example of the latter, in 1950 an official was beaten to death by players and fans following his controversial decision in a Buenos Aires soccer match.

In addition to the riots emerging in an already divisive and therefore ripe context, there are sports related riots that are not related to underlying strains in the society. Lewis calls these "issueless" riots in that they are strictly related to the sports event itself. He lists four hypotheses that specify the variables accounting for this type of sports riot (Lewis 1975: 9):

(1) The severity of a sports riot varies directly with the importance in the status of the competition (e.g., playoff game or championship game versus a regular season game).
(2) The more important the sporting event in terms of traditional rivalries the greater the severity of the sports riot.
(3) There is a direct relationship between the severity of sports riots and the crowd's perception of an officiating error.
(4) There is a direct relationship between the violence of sport *per se* and the severity of a sporting riot (see also Lang 1980).

ILLEGITIMATE ATTEMPTS BY NON–ATHLETES TO INFLUENCE THE OUTCOME OF SPORTS CONTESTS

Spectators at a sports contest essentially have two avenues to influence outcome. The method considered appropriate is to support one's team through organized cheers, music, random shouts of encouragement, and various other displays of loyalty. There are also unsportsmanlike (illegitimate) means of affecting a game's outcome. Efforts to distract opponents by unusual noises or through racial/ethnic slurs are unacceptable means of support. Also the excessive booing of an opponent or the cheering of an opponent's injury are considered by most persons to be inappropriate actions. Clearly, a contemptible example of foul tactics by spectator is the attempt to harm an opponent physically by throwing objects or tripping the athlete.

Another form of deviance generated by sport is the corrupting of athletes by individuals interested in fixing the outcome of games to insure gambling profits. A number of scandals from around the world have shown that gamblers have bribed or attempted to bribe athletes to either lose a contest or to manipulate the point spread. The athletes most vulnerable to these attempts are those who participate in individual sports (e.g., jai alai, tennis, golf, boxing and track) or who play at especially crucial positions in team sports (e.g., goalie, field goal kicker, quarterback, pitcher).

DEVIANCE BY PLAYERS, COACHES, AND ADMINISTRATORS

The *sine qua non* of sport is competition. The goal is winning. In the drive to succeed athletes, coaches and athletic administrators may use illegal and unfair methods. This section will examine three of these illicit activities: drug abuse, cheating, and the corruption of education to accommodate winning teams.

Drug abuse. Aside from the influence of living in a drug oriented age, the modern athlete is subject to other pressures to take drugs. If s/he is a marginal athlete, there will be pressures to take drugs in order to make the team. If s/he is near the top in the sport, the use of drugs may make the winning difference. Finally, drug use may be strictly an act of self defense because the athlete assumes that his or her opponents are taking drugs to enhance their performances.

The drugs used by athletes can be roughly divided into two categories by their function: restorative and additive (cf. Gilbert 1969; Scott 1971). Restorative drugs are used to restore an injured athlete's skill to what it normally would be. Drugs in this category are painkillers, muscle relaxers, and anti-inflammatants. Ordinarily these drugs are not controversial unless they are given to allow the athlete to participate when medically s/he should not because of further damage.

Additive drugs (e.g., amphetamines and anabolic steroids) are used to enhance an athlete's performance beyond his or her "normal" capacity. There are two fundamental issues with the use of additive drugs: (1) an ethical one involving the artificial stimulation of performance; and (2) the physical and psychological damages that can occur.

The ethical issue is clear (Bueter 1972). Sport is intended to be a competition between athletes for the joy of participation and to determine supremacy on the basis of ability, strategy, and skill. By introducing drugs that artificially enhance performance beyond normal limits, the question is not whether one athlete is better than another but which one has the better pharmacist—clearly a perversion of the meaning of sport.

The problem is that additive drugs, especially amphetamines, are used commonly by athletes. Amphetamines are stimulants and are used by runners, cyclists, football, basketball, and soccer players to increase endurance, quickness of reactions, speed, and confidence. Although the exact extent of their usage is unknown, there are numerous examples of its use by athletes (Mandell 1979). At the 1970 world weight lifting championships, for instance, nine of the first 12 medalists were disqualified when urine tests revealed they had taken amphetamines.

The negative side effects from the use of additive drugs should, in addition to the ethical problem, preclude their use in sport. The use of amphetamines is dangerous for several reasons. They can be psychologically addictive. Overdoses or regular usage can cause ulcers, cerebral hemorrhage, paranoia, cardiovascular collapse, nutritional problems, aggressive behavior, and irritability (Scott 1971). By masking fatigue and overstimulating the heart, death is always a possibility as evidenced by the occasional deaths of cyclists in Europe.

Anabolic steroids are male hormones that increase weight and strength. They are used primarily by linemen in football, weight lifters, and weightmen in track. Although researchers are unsure, there is a strong indication that these hormones have dangerous side effects such as cancer of the prostate, testicular atrophy, liver damage, and edema.

The use of drugs in sport is probably to be expected in societies that are already drug oriented and where winners are demanded. The result is the widespread use of uppers, painkillers, and muscle-builders that harm athletes and subvert the ideal of sport.

Cheating. The goal of winning is so important that many athletes and coaches use illegal means to gain unfair advantage over their opponents (cf. Lüschen 1976). We have noted elsewhere in this paper three types of cheating: illegal recruiting practices by schools, the use of drugs to enhance performance artificially, and manipulation of the point spread. In this section, additional illicit modes will be examined pointing to the wide range of unfair practices that occur in sport.

Cheating in sport takes many forms. For analytical purposes these can be divided into two types: institutional cheating and deviant cheating. Institutional cheating refers to those illegal acts that are, for the most part, accepted as part of the game. Coaches encourage them or look the other way and the enforcers (referees, league commissioners, and rule making bodies) rarely discourage them, impose minimal penalties, or ignore them altogether. This type of cheating is widespread and more prevalent than deviant cheating. Some examples are:

item: Attempts to put the opponent off-balance psychologically through heckling and "gamesmanship."

item: Pretending to be fouled in basketball in order to receive an undeserved free throw and give the opponent an undeserved foul (cf., Ramsey and Deford, 1963).

item: Wrestlers and boxers who dehydrate themselves just prior to a contest in order to fight at a weight lower than their true weight.

item: Using a loophole in the rules to take unfair advantage of an opponent. For example, in 1973 the University of Alabama was playing the University of California in football and had the ball on the California 11 yard line. Alabama sent in their field goal kicker with a tee but a player did not leave the field. California countered by sending in its defensive team against the kick. As the huddle broke, the field goal kicker picked up his tee and dashed off the field, leaving the defense at a distinct disadvantage. Alabama scored on the play and the NCAA Rules Committee later declared such plays illegal (in the future) because a team cannot simulate a substitution designed to confuse an opponent.

item: The practice is common in baseball for the home team to "doctor" its field to suit its strengths and minimize the strengths of a particular opponent. A fast team can be neutralized, for example, by slowing down the basepaths.

item: In baseball, the application of a foreign substance to the ball in order to disadvantage the hitter has been a common, but illegal occurrence.

item: Basketball players are often coached to bump the lower half of a shooter's body because referees are likely to be watching the ball and the upper half of the shooter's body.

item: Offensive linemen in football are typically coached to use special but illegal techniques to hold or trip the opponent without detection.

These commonplace occurrences in sport are cheating because they take unfair advantage of opponents. But they are coached and acceptable practices, and therefore what we might call "routinized deviance" or "institutional deviance."

"Deviant" cheating occurs also in sport but is not accepted and is subject to stern punishment. The use of illegal equipment, drugging a race horse, a golfer improving his lie, accepting a bribe, tampering with an opponent's equipment, throwing lime in an opponent's face, are a few examples of this mode of cheating.

An interesting research question is to determine under what conditions cheating of both types is most likely to occur in a contest. Lüschen has hypothesized that the probability of cheating increases as: (1) the level of uncertainty of the outcome increases; (2) the greater the rewards for winning; and (3) the greater the proportion of participants with lower class origins. The bases for this last hypothesis are that the norms and values of sport are essentially those of the middle class and because the poor realistically assess their chances for upward social mobility as relatively limited (Lüschen 1976).

Sport, because cheating occurs, should not be disproportionately reprimanded for at least two reasons. First, where cheating is endemic to society, it will also occur in sport. And second, chances are that cheating in sport probably occurs *less* than in other institutional areas of society. This is because: (1) sport is more visible; (2) sport is closely monitored by various agents of social control; (3) the rules in sport are usually quite explicit; and (4) the penalties for getting caught may deprive the athlete from further participation. However, cheating does occur in sport and is largely ignored by officials and often encouraged by coaches. This raises the important question of whether exposure to sport teaches wholesome character traits as it is so often purported to do.

The corruption of higher education. School sports, especially at the intercollegiate level, have become increasingly dominated by high pressure, commercialism, and a philosophy of winning at any cost (Nyquist 1978). These are manifested in a strong tendency for schools in the "big time" or those striving for that level to use illegal recruiting practices and to abuse athletes, physically and psychologically, for the good of the program. In short, intercollegiate athletics has, in very fundamental ways, corrupted the goals and ideals of higher education.

When the pressure to win becomes too great, the result can be a policy of cheating—offering athletes more than the legal limit to lure them to your school. In a 1929 report, the Carnegie Foundation decried the widespread illegal recruiting practices of American colleges and universities (Savage 1929). Not only has the problem continued but it has intensified because the economic rewards for winning are now so much greater than 50 years ago. A losing season can mean a considerable loss of alumni contributions (as well as gate receipts). When the Ohio State football team went from a 7-2 record in 1966 to 4-5 the next year, alumni contributions dropped by almost $500,000. Conversely, a winning team can dramatically aid a program financially, as evidenced by the contributions in excess of $1 million to North Carolina State's athletic scholarship fund after that school won the 1974 NCAA basketball championship (Denlinger and Shapiro 1975).

The extent of recruiting irregularities is unknown. A reasonable speculation is that recent scandals involving such schools as Long Beach State, Southwest Louisiana, Minnesota, Oklahoma, and Michigan State are only the visible portion of the iceberg.

> A 1974 survey by the National Association of Basketball Coaches said that one of every eight major colleges made illegal offers to prospects, that all the cheaters were offering money, 80 percent were offering cars, and more than half were offering clothing. The survey was conducted among 25 recently graduated college players, 25 current high school standouts, 25 sets of parents, and 25 athletic directors of major-college basketball programs. Of the 50 players interviewed, 40 percent said they had received illegal offers.
>
> (Denlinger and Shapiro 1975: 42)

In addition to the illegal offering of material things, coaches have also altered transcripts to insure an athlete's eligibility, had substitutes take admissions tests for athletes of marginal educational ability, provided jobs for parents, paid athletes for non-existent jobs, illegally used government work studies monies for athletes, and the like.

Clearly, such behaviors not only corrupt coaches and athletes alike, but they demean the ideals of higher education.

In such a climate athletes are bound to become cynical about their education (Black 1978). Coaches proclaim that their athletes are students first and only secondarily athletes. This is the typical recruiting speech to prospects and their parents. But in practice the reverse often is true. The athlete has signed a contract and is paid for his athletic services. He is an employee and the relationship between a coach and his athlete is essentially employer-employee. Athletes are often counseled to take easy courses whether or not they fit their educational needs. Because the demands on their time are so great in the season, athletes frequently must take a somewhat reduced load, which means they will not usually graduate in the normal amount of time. Study halls and tutors are frequently available, even required, for college athletes, but their primary function is to insure athletic eligibility, not necessarily the education of the athlete. If the athlete achieves an education in the process, it is incidental to the overriding objective of a winning athletic program.

Some coaches, in their zeal to be successful, are also guilty of behaviors that brutalize and demean their athletes—actions that in other contexts would not be tolerated. The common charge of critics of these practices is that the athletes have become tools of the schools. The athlete is dehumanized as s/he works endless hours to develop machinelike precision. S/he is dehumanized as coaches demean and belittle them in an effort to increase the athlete's performance. The athlete is dehumanized further when s/he is forced to participate in incredibly rigorous conditioning drills or drills designed to get marginal players to quit in humiliation and pain (Shaw 1972; Putnam 1973).

The athlete is also dehumanized by being treated as a perpetual adolescent, as someone who cannot be trusted. Ironically, this control of the athlete occurs at the very time that the myth is perpetuated by schools and coaches that participation in sports is teaching the athlete to be a self-disciplined, mature, and responsible person (Sauer 1971: 24-27).

The sociological explanation for cheating, hypocrisy, brutality, and authoritarianism by some coaches lies not in their individual psyches but in the intensely competitive system within which they operate. In American society the success or failure of a team is believed by most persons to rest with the coach. This pressure to win brings some coaches to use illegal inducements to attract athletes to their school, or coach their linemen to hold without getting caught, or to look the other way when athletes (who face the same pressures to succeed) use drugs to enhance their performance. The absolute necessity to win also explains why some coaches drive their players so hard. Thus, what some persons might label brutality has been explained by some coaches as a necessity to get the maximum effort from players (Edwards 1973: 135-141).

The abuses of athletes have occurred at some of America's most prominent universities. The administrators at these schools have tended to avoid careful scrutiny of their programs because "winning" and the money and prestige that come in its wake are considered so important. As long as the coaches win games and avoid getting caught in illegal activities, then administrators will not fire or even censure them. The players in such a situation, if they are relatively conscious, must realize that they are just pieces of machinery to be used, abused, and when worn out or broken, to be replaced by another replaceable part for the good of the school. Clearly, schools that allow such practices to exist have prostituted their ideals for the sake of the prestige and money that accrues from a "winning" athletic program.

CONCLUSION

The overriding thesis of this paper is that sport is not an island of purity—a privileged sanctuary from real life. That myth must be put aside (Cosell 1971). Sport is a reflection of society. It has within it the same maladies as the society in which it resides. If the society is beset with problems of poverty, racism, and other cleavages, then sports contests will not be just a means of escape but also an occasional battleground. If violence rages in society, then sport will also be afflicted. If politicians and businessmen seek the grail of success by any means, then players and coaches will also succumb to these pressures and use drugs, bribes, and illegal recruiting to insure success.

To stress that sport mirrors society does not excuse sport or justify the wrongdoings that are common to both. Sport needs reform. School sports need to be put in perspective and promoted for their educational values. The original purpose of sport—the pleasure in the activity—needs to be recaptured. Sportsmanship must be a universal goal. Unfair competition is the enemy of true sport. But while the reform of sport is a laudable goal, we must recognize that it is a futile effort without concomitant efforts to change the other institutions of society.

REFERENCES

Athletics and Education: Are They Compatible? The entire issue of *Phi Delta Kappan.* 56 (October, 1974).

Atyeo, D. 1978. *Blood and Guts.* New York: Paddington Press.

Black, S. 1978. The most ruthless game in sports. *New West.* 24, Nov.: 81-102.

Bueter, R.J. 1972. The use of drugs in sports: an ethical perspective. *The Christian Century.* 89, Apr, 5:394-398.

Cosell, H. 1971. Sports and good-by to all that. *New York Times.* April 5, 1971: 33.

Denlinger, K. and L. Shapiro. 1975. *Athletes for Sale: An Investigation into America's Greatest Sports Scandal—Athletic Recruiting.* New York: Crowell.

Edwards, Harry, 1973. *Sociology of Sport.* Homewood, Ill.: Dorsey.

Elias, N. and E. Dunning. 1970. The quest for excitement in unexciting societies. Pp. 31-51 in G. Lüschen, ed. *The Cross-Cultural Analysis of Sport and Games.* Champaign, Ill.: Stipes.

Fimrite, R. 1974. Take me out to the brawl game. *Sports Illustrated.* June 17: 10-13.

Geen, R. and L. Berkowitz. 1966. Name-mediated aggressive cue properties. *Journal of Personality.* 34:456-465.

Gilbert, B. 1969. Drugs in sport. *Sports Illustrated.* June 23:64–72; June 30: 30–42; July 7:30–35.

Goldstein, J. and R.L. Arms. 1971. Effects of observing athletic contests on hostility. *Sociometry.* 34, March: 83-90.

Hanford, G.H. 1974. *The Need for and the Feasibility of a National Study of Intercollegiate Athletics.* Washington, D.C.: American Council on Education.

Kennedy. R. 1975. Wanted: an end to mayhem. *Sports Illustrated.* November 17: 17-21.

Koval, J. 1973. Football as a social festival: a videotape essay. Paper. *Midwest Sociological Society Meetings.* Omaha, Neb.

Lang, G.E. 1980. Riotous outbursts at sport events. Pp. 413–434 in this Handbook.

Lewis, J.M. 1975. Sports riots: some research question. Paper. *American Sociological Association Meetings.* San Francisco.

Lüschen, G. 1976. Cheating in sport. Pp. 67-77 in D. Landers, ed. *Social Problems in Athletics.* Urbana: University of Illinois Press.

Lüschen, G. 1971. Delinquency. Pp. 1391-93 in *Encyclopedia of Sport Sciences and Medicine.* New York: MacMillan.

Mandell, A. 1979. The Sunday syndrome. National Amphetamine Conference, San Francisco (September, 1978). *Science.* 203, Feb. 16: 626-628.

McMurtry, W.R. 1974. *Investigation and inquiry into Violence in Amateur Hockey.* Report to the Ontario Minister of Community and Social Services. Toronto.

Middleton, L. 1979. Football under pressure to reduce injuries. *Chronicle Higher Education.* April 16: 7.

Nyquist, F.G. 1978. The future of collegiate athletics *College Board Review.* 109 Fall: 10-17.

Putnam, P. 1973. A case of volunteer—or else. *Sports Illustrated.* July 23: 22-25.

Ramsey. F. and F. Deford. 1963. Smart moves by a master of deception. *Sports Illustrated.* December 9: 57-63.

Sauer, G. 1971. Interview by Jack Scott with George Sauer on the Reason for Sauer's Retirement from Professional Football While at the Height of His Career. Hayward, Cal.: California State College, Department of Physical Education.

Savage, H.J. 1929. *American College Athletics.* New York: The Carnegie Foundation. Bulletin 23.

Scott, J. 1971. It's not how you play the game, but what pill you take. *The New York Times Magazine.* October 17: 40-41, 106-109.

Scott, M.B. 1968. *The Racing Game.* Chicago: Aldine.

Shaw, G. 1972. *Meat on the Hoof: The Hidden World of Texas Football.* New York: St. Martin's Press.

Short, J.F.; Tennyson, R.A. and K.I. Howard. 1963. Behavior dimensions of gang delinquency. *ASR.* 28, June: 411-428.

Sipes, R. 1973. War, sports and aggression: an empirical test of two rival theories. *American Anthropologist.* 75, Feb.: 64-86.

Smith, M.D. 1973. Hostile outbursts in sport. *Sport Sociology Bulletin.* 2, Spring: 6-10.

Smith, M.D. 1974. Significant others; influence on the assultive behavior of young hockey players. *IRSS.* 9: 45-56.

Smith, M.D. 1975. Sport and collective violence, Pp. 281-330 in D. Ball and J. Loy, eds. *Sport and Social Order: Contributions to the Sociology of Sport.* Reading, Mass.: Addison-Wesley.

Smith, M.D. 1978. Precipitants of crowd violence. *Sociological Inquiry.* 48,2: 121-131.

Surface, B. 1974. Pro football: is it getting too dirty? *Reader's Digest.* November: 151-154.

Tandy. R.E. and J. Laflin. 1973. Aggression and sport—two theories. *JOHPER.* 44, June: 19-20.

Taylor, I. 1971. Football mad: a speculative sociology of football hooliganism. Pp. 352-77 in F. Dunning, ed. *Sociology Sport.* London: Cass.

Thrasher, F. 1927. *The Gang.* Chicago: University of Chicago Press.

Treaster, J.G. 1979. Violence in sports. *Penthouse.* 10, March: 73-76; 144-145.

Turner, E.T. 1968. The effects of viewing college football, basketball and wrestling on the elicited aggressive responses of male spectators. Pp. 325-28 in G. Kenyon, ed. *Contemporary Psychology of Sport.* Chicago: Athletic Institute.

Underwood, J. 1978. An unfolding tragedy. *Sports Illustrated.* August 14: 69-82; August 21: 32-56; August 28: 30-41.

Weis, K. 1976. Abweichung und Konformität in der Institution Sport. Pp. 296–316 in G. Lüschen and K. Weis, eds. *Die Soziologie des Sports.* Darmstadt: Luchterhand.

Previously published in S.Eitzen, ed. 1979. *Sport in Contemporary Society.* New York: St. Martin's.

RIOTOUS OUTBURSTS AT SPORTS EVENTS

Gladys Engel Lang

Riotous outbursts at sports events serve as strategic research sites both for studying problems fundamental to the sociology of sport—concerning spectator behavior, player-fan interaction and the social function of spectator sports—and to the study of collective behavior—for instance, the dynamics of collective violence and its linkages to social structure.

There has been, until recently, little sociological interest in or systematic research into riots—like disturbances at sports events—that occur on "happy occasions" and appear, superficially, to be "riots without a cause or Cause." This article which emerges from a sociological concern with collective behavior and a long-standing spectator interest in sports behavior, is programmatic in intent; its purpose is to examine a number of outbursts connected with a variety of sports-games, to suggest a heuristic typology and to indicate the lines along which systematic study and analysis might proceed (K. and G. Lang 1961). Where disturbances at sports events become a matter of public concern, it may provide some suggestions about questions that need answering and how one might go about getting some answers.

SPORTS CROWDS AND THE RIOT POTENTIAL

Psychologists and "psychologizers" refer to the socio-psychological satisfactions derived from sports spectatorship (Beisser 1967). Thus spectatorship is said to furnish therapeutic release through vicarious (sublimated) aggression; to provide an opportunity for fantasy—a kind of dream or wish-fulfillment—in which the fan becomes the "star player" to fulfill needs for identification with a group and, especially, for the social isolate, a means by which to satisfy his need for belonging. In line with these interpretations of individual satisfaction, the function of spectator sports for the *group* is variously interpreted as a mechanism through which morale is built and sustained as individuals identifying with the team are tied to each other in momentary fraternity. Such loyalty can be readily transferred and attached to larger social units—like an educational or industrial institution, a city, or a nation. And, according to the uses to which this loyalty is put by the larger unit, the enthusiasm and fervor aroused on behalf of a team can operate to maintain the status-quo—in line with other forms of bread-and-circuses—or to mobilize support for reform.

Whatever else it is, the sports contest has to be considered one of many ritualized occasions through which the society provides the individual with defenses against anxiety and the build-up of tension. It acts as a "safety-valve." Like other public events that draw large audiences it is a much-approved way of "letting off steam," a socially-sanctioned occasion during which otherwise deviant behavior may be tolerated or behavior that is usually tolerated at a given level is permitted to intensify (Madge and Harrison 1967).

Since the sports audience operates within loosely drawn boundaries of permissible deviance and self-indulgence while focusing on a game in which group tensions are often on the verge of exploding, it is not surprising that it sometimes "gets out of hand" and, going beyond approved boundaries, acts in ways that result in damage to persons and/or property. Like data on other volatile and sometimes unanticipated and transitory phenomena, the details necessary to our understanding of these collective disturbances usually must be reconstructed post factum from data gathered by investigative commissions, from newspaper or other mass media accounts and from police records. It is only when disturbances at sports events become sufficiently frequent and potentially serious in their consequences to threaten the future of the sport that social scientists are called to help through systematic inquiry. The investigation of "soccer hooliganism" in England is a case in point. (Taylor 1971).

The understanding of riotous outbursts at sports events should be especially important for students of collective behavior. For, research on riots, and especially inquiries into student protest, ghetto uprisings and anti-war demonstrations focused attention on conditions of widespread social unrest or intergroup tensions as a precondition for collective violence. *But all occasions,* where through the convergence of individuals large numbers of persons are assembled together, under conditions of great excitement, should be viewed as having a high violence potential. It *is* true that sports events only infrequently lead to fullfledged rioting but the potential is always there and attested to by provisions local governments make for "crowd control" on such occasions, with plans specially tailored to such factors as the expected size of the crowd, the "origins" of the crowd and the type of event. For instance, the still-cited Report of the Departmental Committee on Crowds in Great Britain pointed, to the greater difficulty of dealing with crowds who find themselves in strange surroundings—like fans who travel to out-of-town games (1924). It also considered football crowds particularly difficult to handle because of the short duration of the event, the confined space, and the excitement the game seemed to muster.

The research question becomes: under what conditions is the potential for violence realized? The first need is for objective and reliable descriptions of riotous outbursts on sports occasions that allows us to link the predispositions and expectations (including fears, demands and hopes) of participants to the conditions under which the crowd comes together and the pattern of behavior that develops. Among the factors that have to be examined and about which we seek data are these:

(1) the larger social context surrounding the event;
(2) the ecology of the specific situation, i.e. the setting in which the outburst occurs, including the composition and distribution of the audience in relation to space;
(3) the type of event, including the characteristics and dynamics of the sport-game;
(4) the social psychology of the audience situation;
(5) the provisions for audience control and responses of control agents to events as they develop;
(6) the specific occurrence or episode precipitating the outbreak of disorder;
(7) the epidemiology of the disorder, i.e. the pattern by which it spreads and/or is contained, and finally
(8) any replication of the occurrence at a distance in time or space that can be linked to the initial outburst.

The kinds of data sought are discussed in more detail later in this article.

A TYPOLOGY OF SPORTS RIOTS

My initial attempt was to collect data, as outlined above, on a multiplicity of riotous outbursts or spectator disorders occurring in different places at different times at different types of sports events. In accord with the main working hypothesis, riotous outbursts were classified as football riots, basketball riots, hockey riots, etc., on the assumption that explanations for the differential patterns and frequency of collective violence should be sought in the dynamics of the sport—including the rules of play, the amount and kinds of aggression involved, the extent to which the game involves a contest for territory, and some aspects of player–fan interaction.

But the collection of descriptive materials—at this stage of research dependent mainly on availability of documentary and newspaper materials—soon led to the conclusion that the pattern of development and response in a particular "soccer riot," for instance, might be more like a particular riot during water polo than like the rioting accompanying another soccer match. While the pattern of response in *any* particular disorder does depend in some way and to some extent on the dynamics of the sport which attracts spectators to the scene, it soon became apparent that there are different types of riotous outbursts connected with sports events, each characterized by different response patterns and requiring different explanations. At least theoretically any type of sports event (game) can be the occasion for any type of riotous outburst.

I would like to propose, then illustrate in some detail, a working typology of sports riots, distinguished by the *predominance of different response patterns.* Riots that follow other "joyful occasions" —i.e. riots that occur on theatrical occasions, boat rides, rock-and-roll concerts, etc. can also be classified in this way. I am neither saying (a) that these are the only types of response patterns nor (b) that any riotous outburst can always be clearly depicted as one type or another.

(1) A *fanatic public* "extends" its support of a player or team through some form of *collective protest* against a decision or act it views as damaging to the reputation (or chance for victory) of the player or team

(2) An *acquisitive crowd* acts spontaneously in a form of *anomic protest* against a decision or act it defines as "against the rules of fair play" and/or incurring some kind of personal damage or loss of self;

(3) The *licentious (or exuberant) crowd* seizes an opportunity to indulge individual whims and appetites, resulting—whether willfully or accidentally—in *destructive behavior or public disturbance.*

(4) The *polarized audience* seizes the occasion to *continue a conflict that has its primary roots outside the sports arena.*

The Fanatic Public

This is the "classic" type of sports riot, the one that comes most readily to mind: The typical rioter is the "sports nut" to whom "life seems insignificant in comparison with the excitement at the stadium" and who is "emotionally, if not physically...ever ready if the call to play should come (Beisser 1967: 12). He sublimates his aggressive impulses by responding with cheers to the aggressiveness displayed on the field. He becomes one of a collectivity of supporters who band together at the train station to welcome back or give a rousing send-off to the team, at the stadium to provide moral support, and after the game to express their admiration and support for "the team" or a particular "star" or athlete. Particularly the fans devoted to the individual player are apt to take on the characteristics of a "fanatic public" which sees its own "honor" and fate dependent upon the fate and fortune of the athlete who is the social object of their attention. His "enemies" are "their enemies" and, upon occasion, they extend their support through violent protest of a decision or act they define as damaging to his reputation or the chance the team (or player) has for victory.

Three examples of fanatic public riots follow: Two outbursts, beginning as fanatic public riots, led to city-wide rioting and destructive behavior; the third did not spread beyond the sports arena, though under other circumstances it might have. In all three instances—involving three different sport-games and three different countries—a decision defined as unfair was the spark that set off the protest. In two instances, the decision was against an individual, in the other, directly involved the fate of the team. In our own illustration:

> The annals of soccer are replete with examples of fanatic public riots. Disorders that lasted two full days were touched off in Italy during September 1969, according to accounts available in the American press, when the Italian Soccer Federation ruled that a Caserta player had tried to bribe a Taranto player before a game the previous May. That game had put Caserta in first place in the "C" league and thus qualified it for advancement to a better league, dropped Caserta to second place (cf. N.Y. Post—Sept. 10, 1969 and N.Y. Times Sept. 9 and 10). A demonstration of fans protesting the decision (initially about 500 in number) marched to the main square in Caserta, some of the demonstrators being 12 or 13 years of age. However, violence was touched off as the "mob" of "angry soccer fans," "armed with clubs and throwing stones" went on a rampage, burning down the railroad station near the central square, then burning other stores (including a tax office) as well as cars and trucks.
>
> After the rioting began (and towards the end of the first day) the City Council passed a resolution asking the League to review its decision and calling upon sports fans to refrain from further violence. When this message was broadcast to 3000 people gathered in a square near the Prefettura, it was greeted with boos and jeers.
>
> Troops were moved in, using tear gas bombs against the rioters barricaded behind commandeered busses. Many now participating were reported to be "gangs of youths streaming in from the country-side." And, in two days of fighting between demonstrators and police, more than 30 persons were injured, more than 75 arrested and formally detained—"mostly youths." About 2000 security officers and national policemen were utilized in the riot area which covered about 10 blocks in a town with a population of 70,000.

Reports that this was a political demonstration were denied by the
head of the public security forces who said any extremists played only
a marginal role. He called it a "sporting protest." A few days later several thousand demonstrators marched in Vittoria, Sicily to protest the
demotion of its local soccer club but there was no indication that this
remained more than a peaceful protest.

A second illustration of a *fanatic public* collectively protesting a
decision it deemed unfair comes from the annals of boxing; here the
protest was confined to the arena in which it erupted.

On March 10, 1967, at Madison Square Garden in New York City, a
Panamanian lightweight boxer won an unanimous decision (based on
clear decisions by three judges) in a twelve-round bout against his Puerto
Rican opponent. Despite the unanimity of the decision, its announcement set off a barrage of bottles, mainly liquor bottles, thrown by Puerto Rican supporters in the balcony. A number of persons, who had
watched the match from the most expensive ringside seats had to be
hospitalized.

This was the second riot at the Garden following an appearance by
Frank Narvaez, an idolized Puerto Rican lightweight. About two years
before on August 4, 1965, an "even bloodier riot" had occurred. This
time, anticipating the possibility of violence, the Garden had 20 city
policemen on call to assist its regular staff of 53 special policemen and
all quickly moved in after trouble began. They made no arrests as they
had on the prior occasion; such arrests, they believed, might provide a
rallying point for further protest among New York's large Puerto Rican
population.

One sports reporter, injured while writing his account of the fight,
claimed that a riot was liable to have occurred, even had the decision
gone the other way. The people from Panama and the Puerto Ricans in
the crowd were all fired up. An estimated 4600 Panamanians and possibly 5000 Puerto Ricans were among the near 12,000 spectators present;
New York City not only has a sizeable Puerto Rican community but
also had, among its residents at that time, about 18,000 Panamanians.
In addition, more than 400 fight fans had come directly from Panama
specifically to attend the fight. Between rounds many of the Panamanian's supporters stood and chanted the name of their hero, waving their
hands, handkerchiefs and flags in anticipation of a victory, especially
after Narvaez' face swelled from a blow near his right eye. Puerto Rican
fans similarly evidenced their fervor, carrying "Frankie by KO" signs.

In the dressing room, Narvaez—according to a sports reporter from
the *New York Post,* volunteered an explanation of the riot—"Maybe
those fans felt the way I did about the decision. I wouldn't have been
satisfied with a draw. I felt I won it clear."

The third example is of a "fanatic public" riot which was used by
some individuals and groups in the community as a cover for destructive activity.

Ice hockey is one of the most brutal of all sports. It is tremendously demanding on the players since there are no time outs and the action rarely ceases during the course of a game. It is a body contact sport and the aggressive, tough and fearless player is most successful. The intense action on the ice carries into the audience. Ice hockey fans are extremely devoted to their teams and to the sport itself. Hockey rules legitimate much of the violence in the game. A player is penalized for certain infractions but much is condoned (New York Times 9–9/10, 1967). Fights, tripping and body checking are *de rigueur.* Thus the crowd expects and lauds violent play.

The most avid ice hockey city in the world is Montreal, Canada. The fans in Montreal are known for their devotion to their team, the Canadiens. Montreal is also the home of the National Hockey League, the professional league which in 1955 was composed of six teams including Montreal, Toronto and four "American" teams. (In 1955 there were no players in the league who were from the United States). Montreal was a leading team in the league throughout the nineteen fifties.

On March 13, 1955, Montreal was visiting the Boston Bruin club. Montreal's superstar, Maurice (the Rocket) Richard was "high-sticked" (struck above the shoulders) by a Boston player. With blood streaming down his face he retaliated by smashing his opponent with his stick. Up to this point this was a typical sequence of events in this sport. It should be noted here that as a superstar, Richard was constantly provoked since violence would cost him valuable minutes on the ice. Thus Richard constantly suffered penalty assessments, and led the league in total time spent in the penalty box. However, this statistic enhanced his image in Montreal and he was by far the most popular player in the history of the Canadiens.

Had Richard been satisfied with his retaliation that would have ended the matter, but when an official tried to intervene Richard struck him with his fist. The official was not injured, yet Richard had committed a very serious infraction as far as the League was concerned. The sanctions for striking an official are grave and Richard was banned from continuing in the game.

On March 16 Maurice Richard was suspended by the League president, Clarence Campbell, for the remainder of the season. This meant that Richard would be unable to aid his team which was engaged in a battle for first place and would miss the playoffs that Montreal was sure of entering. "Montreal fans reacted angrily. The switchboard at the League office was swamped with calls. Many threats were made against Campbell's life" (N.Y. Times and N.Y. Post 3–11–67).

On March 17 the Detroit Red Wings, Montreal's competition for first place, came to the Montreal Forum for a scheduled game. All afternoon crowds milled around the Forum with placards denouncing Campbell's decision. Montreal radio stations fanned the flames of unrest by reporting this activity throughout the day. In addition Campbell announced that he was going to attend tha game that evening.

At game time there were thousands of people outside the Forum who tried in vain to gain entrance. There were no tickets available. This crowd did not disburse. The game began without incident. Richard was seated in the arena watching the action. Campbell arrived midway into the first period. He was immediately greeted with catcalls and epithets and the crowd started to "get out of hand" at this point. For fifteen minutes the emotions "grew to a fever pitch." At the intermission, a smoke bomb was exploded and hundreds of people ran in panic to the exits. In order to avoid further panic, the Montreal Fire Chief ordered the game suspended. Most of the 14,000 fans in the Forum were unaware of the smoke bomb so that the disturbance in the arena was slight. The only real disturbance in the Forum occurred around the League president's box. Campbell had been pelted with an assorment of rubbers, galoshes, programs, fruit and other missiles. One fan actually broke through a police line and struck Campbell.

The real trouble started when the fans coming out of the Forum incited the people who had been milling about outside. This crowd then went on a rampage. The turmoil lasted seven hours in the worst rioting that had occurred in Montreal since the early nineteen forties. Fifteen blocks of stores had been smashed and looted. Streetcar windows were pelted with ice and snow, corner newsstands were sacked and burned, automobiles were overturned, and windows were smashed indiscriminately. More than 100 people were arrested, many of them had pockets filled with small looted items. There were many injured people including spectators in the Forum who had been hit with flying objects.

The Acquisitive Crowd

This crowd acts spontaneously in a form of anomic protest. I use the term "anomic protest" in the sense of an "anomic interest group" (K. and G. Lang 1961: 133), indicating a strongly felt sense of powerlessness that exists in the absence of norms by which protest can be organized and directed strategically and effectively so as to attain desired goals. A decision is experienced among a sizeable number of those present at some sporting event as "going against the rules of fair play" and/or incurring some kind of personal damage or loss of self.

The collective process—wherein many individuals experience this sense of loss—is one of demoralization, a turning toward one's self in a form of panic response as prior expectations and hopes are suddenly undermined. On such occasions, what becomes crowd wrath, as despair explodes in anger, can quickly, given a sudden turn of events, result in group panic with each individual on his own and concerned with his own security. *Panic* represents a process of demoralization— with *anomic protest* a spontaneously shared defense wherein demoralized individuals—acting together—protect themselves against the perils of psychological withdrawal. The point here is that the acquisitive crowd can, given a fortuitous turn of events, quickly become an escape mob. It is always on the verge of panic and can go either way.

Acquisitive crowds most often form where the sports event is also a betting event with the organized gambling as much an attraction as the event itself. Thus, rioting that follows this pattern has occurred at racetracks—horse races, greyhound races, sports car races, etc. But such riots can also occur where crowds become impatient to acquire entry into the sports arena—at a football match, at a soccer match, etc. or, on almost any occasion, when fans feel they have been unjustly deprived of their due—when a "star" doesn't show up to play, when "trophies" promised to those attending prove to be in scarce supply, as at baseball games in the U.S.A. on "bat day" when not enough baseball bats are available for distribution, as promised, to every youth attending. On March 5, 1964 in London, two persons were killed in a crush as 100,000 persons sought admission to a soccer match at Sunderland, England. This is a converging, acquisitive crowd—pure and simple—with the process of convergence itself ending in disaster.

I have not yet read of a riot at a golf tournament. Still, a description of the "golf gallery" written many years ago by sociologist Emory S. Bogardus illustrates the process by which an acquisitive crowd may develop (1931). Such golf galleries—like spectators at racing matches (auto, horse, motorcycle, etc.)—could metamorphose into acquisitive crowds.

Bogardus explains how, during a golf tournament, many persons mill around trying to better their position to see a difficult putt. Between plays on different greens there is a rushing, occasionally a stampeding to obtain a vangtage point of observation at the next green. It is necessary to hold the crowd back by ropes, although there is rarely any rushing of the ropes.

Bogardus describes one gallery that spontaneously protested what it deemed to be "unsportsmanlike behavior" on the part of a nationally known player. "The gallery...groaned when he made a good stroke and applauded when his ball went into a trap." Newspaper writers condemned the behavior of the gallery, partly because they thought the spectators had misjudged the actions of the player, but mainly because they deplored the "unsportsmanlike role" of the gallery. Writing about the golf gallery, as it appeared in the 1920's, Bogardus described it as growing excited only when the players fail to measure up to expectations in their treatment of one another. He implies that the usual decorum of the tournament spectators is at least partially explained by the type of spectator who makes up the golf gallery.

[It] is composed for the most part of persons of manners, means prominence, travel. No rowdies or ruffians such as frequent baseball crowds are in evidence; the police are rarely if ever needed. Persons of leisure abound. Few if any children are present. The "lower classes" would consider a golf game a waste of time. Those who are present usually know something about the game from experience... [with] golfing knowledge limited largely to the professional and leisure classes who take pride in conducting themselves seemly... Since golf tournaments are generally played on private golf links, the reserve of the private golf club is maintained. The restraint of the well mannered is generally evident.

(Bogardus 1931)

The golf gallery in these affluent days when tournament grounds are more accessible to more people may be subject to more frequent lapses of sportsmanlike behavior with more physical and obvious competition for choice vantage points from which to follow the play. Still, at least in the U.S.A., golf is not a sport where interest in the sporting outcome is at least equaled by an interest in better odds and pay-off. Acquisitive crowds are most likely to be found acting in anomic protest at sports associated with gambling—in the U.S.A. especially at horse races.

Thus in the 1960's there were a number of riots at raceways. In May 1962 several hundred spectators at Yonkers Raceway, near New York City, voiced their protest when the odds on a horse dropped from 10-to-1 in the morning to 5-to-2 just before the race; they became increasingly vocal about their suspicions when the horse ran the race. For some time the officials debated the wisdom of starting the ninth race, as scheduled, but the anger of spectators seemed to be dissipating. Then, just as the horses were lining up at the starting gate, a group of spectators tore down a mesh fence that had prevented fans from approaching the track. One man slipped on the track, was struck on the head by the starting gate and had to be taken to the hospital. Other fans then poured onto the track, halting the race. Fences and the wooden railing were ripped down. Some persons set fire to the wooden seats. Still others threw bricks through the window of the track restaurant. Fifteen cash registers were damaged as well as ten refreshment stands and four cigar stands. Four cigar stands were stolen.

All this "rioting took place within a brief period of time. Four rioters were arrested and the fire department quickly put out the many minor fires that had been started.

Here follows our second illustration of a raceway riot indicating the acquisitive crowd:

In November 1963 at Rossevelt Raceway, a harness racing track near New York City, the "worst riot in the history of New York racing" took place in protest against a ruling about the outcome of the sixth race, the first race in the "twin double."

It must be explained that many racetracks provide an extra wagering situation in order to increase the amount of betting. These are usually in the form of a parlay (picking successive winners) and involve payoffs which are often quite large since there are so many combinations each time another condition is added to the bet. Daily double betting is one example of this system: at the Roosevelt Raceway, the holder of a winning ticket combining the sixth and seventh races was entitled to exchange the ticket for selections in the eighth and ninth races. The payoff potential was enormous: only two nights before the riot there was a payoff of $79,660.30 for a two dollar wager.

During the running of the sixth race—the first race of the first double, six of the eight participating horses were involved in an accident so that only two horses finished the race. A rule of the New York State Harness Commission states that so long as at least one horse finishes a race, that race is official. In keeping with this rule, the Racing Commissioner at the track declared the sixth race offical. This meant that all the money wagered on the six nonfinishers was lost, including the money bet in over 82,000 twin double-tickets. Immediately after the official sign went on announcing the winner, the fans started booing and jeering. Many apparently believed that the race should have been declared "no contest" and money refunded. (In 1965 at Yonkers Raceway a similar mishap had been declared "no race" and incipient rioting quickly halted).

When the sign flashed on, almost all the 23,127 fans began to boo and many threw debris onto the track. Four or five fans jumped over the railing onto the track and, when security police made no effort to stop them, others in the crowd followed. Soon, hundreds of people—at one point, described as "about 500"—were swarming onto the track. A track announcer appealed to the crowd: "The program can't be completed with you people on the track." But the protesters attacked the judges' booth, injuring one of the judges. They smashed the tote board and extinguished its lights, some crying "We want our money back. We want our money back."

Those in the stands set fire to program booths in the stands; others smashed windows and damaged cars in the parking lot adjacent to the track. During the height of the rioting the head of the security police at the Raceway collapsed and died of a heart attack. Even the announcement over the public address system that this popular ex-policeman had died, did not stop the destructive acts.

Nassau County police were called; several hundred policemen entered the track before the riot was brought under control at 11:55 p.m., about an hour and ten minutes after it started.

According to the *New York Times* as the first police cars rolled onto the track at the height of the riot, the patrolmen were engulfed by the crowd. Other rioters attempted to overturn the cars, and the police used their nightsticks. Some patrolmen pulled their revolvers, but no shots were fired. Tear gas guns were in evidence but were not used. More and more police arrived at the scene to join the hand–to–hand combat. Rioters tore out the plumbing and used the pipes as weapons.

The *New York Post* describes spasmodic fights between fans in the stands and "one woman pummelling a cop with her umbrella." While the fighting was going on, "three of the younger, and more active, fans stole a sulky from the paddock area. One of them climbed aboard, while his two companions pulled him back and forth across the finish line. Finally, they tired, broke up the sulky and set it on fire."

Shortly before midnight, police gained the upper hand and spectators began drifting off the track; many persons—fearful for their safety—left long before the remaining races were called off. Fifteen persons were hospitalized; fifteen persons arrested. Almost all those present had vented their anger at the decision in one way or another; those arrested were booked on charges of resisting arrest, assault on policemen, malicious mischief; there is no mention of whether all had tickets on the twin double. Of the 15 arrested, two were brothers, and another two were father and son. Their ages ranged from 19 to 53, with seven being 30 years of age or older. Their names reveal diversity of ethnic background— Italian, Jewish, German, Chinese, and Anglo-Saxon; they came from all parts of New York City and the surrounding counties. Whatever else they did *not* have in common, they were angry beyond reason and devastatingly demoralized by this damaging decision to declare a "winner;" and they struck out to protest and somehow reverse what seemed irreversible.

The Licentious Crowd

The Licentious (or exuberant) Crowd seizes an opportunity to indulge its whims or appetites. Whether purposely or accidentally, their indulgence in behavior that is usually not tolerated or even forbidden results in destructive behavior or public disturbance.

Accounts of such behavior surrounding sports events are easy to come by. The British investigation of "sports hooliganism" is in large part an inquiry into the behavior of licentious individuals. The licentious crowd is the image people have in mind when they think of a "crowd getting out of hand" with fans "overdoing it." There are *two sub-types of licentious crowds* connected with sports-events. *In the first,* many individuals or groups of individuals use the occasion as an opportunity for indulging in deviant or forbidden behavior. Many sports-games attract such individuals—the boisterous drunk, the raucous fan loudly booing the umpire, the souvenir hunter who insists on running onto the field before the play ends, the school boy in the bleachers who tosses cartons, programs or what-have-you onto the field or onto those occupying more favorable seats. A *licentious crowd*—as we are using the term here—exists when a sufficient number of persons so indulge themselves as to threaten the well-being of others in the audience or to threaten the continuance of the game or, even the sport itself. This variety of licentious crowd thus results from the spontaneous coalescence of unrestrained behavior on the part of many individuals.

The exuberant crowd represents the most spontaneous, volatile and transitory form of the licentious crowd. Events on the field stir emotions so as to cause many individuals in the crowd to abandon—at least momentarily—their usual restraints and together, create a public disturbance. What happened following the first victory of New York Mets baseball team in 1969 and what happened when Barzil's soccer team won the World Cup in 1958 are illustrative:

> The New York Mets, beloved by their fans, were nevertheless, the laughing stock of the National League, one of the two major leagues in American baseball. They had never finished better than ninth in the ten-team league. And in 1969 they were rated 100-to-1 longshots to win the pennant. Early in this first year, in which each league had been divided into two divisions, the Chicago Cubs had pulled away to what seemed like a sure win. But, by September, the Mets had reduced the Cubs' lead of eight games to 1-1/2 games; the two teams met for a crucial two-game series. The Mets won, took over first place, and never gave it up. On September 24, at their home in Shea Stadium, the Mets clinched the division championship. At the last out, the Met fans swarmed onto the field. Estimates of the number of people who ran onto the field went as high as 55,000—an unlikely number since the total attendance was only 54,928. Still, it seemed that "almost everyone" joined in the "ecstasy." Several fans were injured: one teen-ager fell from the scoreboard while attempting to scale it. Seven fans suffered broken bones. Two bases and home plate were missing when the crowd was finally dispersed. Between 1000 and 1500 square feet of sod was torn up, taken home for souvenirs, when it had not been used for "confetti." The fans also took the pitchers' mound and the American flag.
>
> Two days later a group of over 100 young fans who had been standing in line outside the stadium for two days to buy tickets to the play-off series grew bored with their long sedentary idleness. They managed to enter the Stadium and take it over. Some rode around in the relief pitcher's cart screaming, "We're Number One!" Others used hoses to stage a water fight. A few took over the lighting booth and illuminated the field; some others indulged their imaginations by announcing "the World Series" from the broadcasting booth.
>
> On October 16th when the Mets—incredibly—won the World Series against the Baltimore Orioles, the National League champions, there was a repeat of the exuberant outburst that followed the Division win. Fans tore up the sod and this time managed to take home all four bases. Still, though 300 policemen and 332 ushers were unable to prevent the charge onto the field, there was some resistance by spectators who tried to keep other fans from reaching the field. One elderly fan was seen to trip—intentionally—a boy climbing through his section to join the throngs.

The response in Brazil to its team soccer victory over Sweden was more deadly. According to a report from Rio de Janeiro, *"Brazilians exploded today in their greatest demonstration of joy since the end of World War II."* It touched off an impromptu carnival with strangers embracing on the streets, Roman candles exploding in the skies, Samba lines snake-dancing their way through Cinelandia, Rio's Times Square, to the beat of carnival drums. The *New York Times* reported the words of a new samba march chanted by the crowd and composed for the occasion, *"Brazil's hour has at last arrived; there are no Russians, English, Swedes or French."* But an excess of exuberance also brought tragedy. In Rio, a millionaire was shot and killed by the driver of a car he pounded in his enthusiasm. In Recife, a newspaperman was fatally shot in an altercation over the triumph. Two small children were killed by stray bullets and a man who was "celebrating too boisterously" was shot by a policeman with whom he argued.

Licentious crowds have coalesced on all kinds of sports occasions—at baseball games, soccer, motorcycle racing, football, basketball, etc. American high school administrators, worried about disorders at secondary school athletic events,—specifically, fights among "thug spectators," found that the highest incidence of spectator misbehavior occurred during basketball games where spectators were sitting close to the players and could easily observe the behavior of players, coach, etc. Studies of student disorders at the University of California at Berkeley led two sociologists to wonder about fluctuations between some types of riots and others: "Why do some periods like the late '20's and early '50's seem to produce mainly short-run displays of footloose animal spirits, lacking much political content, while others, like the present/1964 produce sustained, organized political activity?" Were the kind of Big-Game (football) disturbances that occurred regularly each Fall, according to them, alternatives to organized protest—just a different way of working off excess energy (Heinrich and and Kaplan 1967)?

According to a number of writers, hooliganism has always been associated with soccer games in Scotland but only much later became a source of concern in England. Disorders have erupted both at the game themselves and in the course of travel to and from games. John Harrington, writing in the *Guardian* (11–16–67) described how:

> A mob of about 150 youths sweeps wildly through the streets damaging cars, plundering shops, and smashing things within reach, after an apparently orderly soccer match between West Ham and Fulham. At least 35 people are injured as Manchester City and Manchester United fans hurl bottles and pint glasses in wild scenes before the start of the game.

Wilfred Sheed, writing about "This Riotous Isle" describes a *"normal English soccer crowd warming up for an average game"* (Sports Illustrated. 1969, 4–21):

> Gray, bleak, cold. The fans are jammed so close that you can't get your hand to your mouth to move the cigar in or out. The crowd sways sideways and lifts you five feet to the right. "God bless our gracious team," they sing, And "...the sodding visitors." Toilet rolls whistle and flap past your ear to clutter the field like ticker tape. Someone drips his tea on you for a giggle...Down below, the police keep a baleful eye on certain spots...This may be the stadium that fate has chosen for Monday's headline, *Disgusting Outbreak of Violence in Leicester*...Or it may be routine bedlam, two bloody noses and a broken umbrella.....
>
> For some hooligans, fighting has simply displaced the game altogether...The fighters are the most straightforward and sociable of hooligan–hooligans. You know where to find them—directly behind the goal—and if you get caught up in their revels you have only yourself to blame. There has been some scare talk about how they terrorize football games and keep innocent folk away. But statistics suggest that innocent folk are coming in ever larger numbers, possibly to watch the fighters from a safe distance.

One of the recent examples of a licentious crowd appeared at the occasion of the European Soccer Finals in the game between *Leeds United* and *Bayern Munich*. The extent of licentiousness was obviously facilitated because the game occurred in Paris at a neutral location and in a different country. Consequently, social controls were even more absent and it fits this interpretation, when the French police stood idly by. The disturbances and riotous outbursts had already started in Dunkirk, when the fans arrived by ship from England, and they lasted long into the night, when the game was over. Property damage to the stadium, to shops in the area was excessive. An expensive TV camera was destroyed and a camera-man lost an eye. It was reported that most of the *Leeds United* followers were deeply embarrassed trying in vain to restrain a minority of rioters (Green 1975).

The worry that the introduction of hooliganism, rowdyism, and vandalism into sport, especially football, might spell the end of the game, led the British Minister of Sport to ask a Birmingham research group to investigate possible avenues of research into the problem. A survey of public response to the problem indicated that 3/4 of the public thought hooliganism constituted a serious threat to the future of football and some evidence was obtained that the rowdy element is driving away the older and more law-abiding citizens—including the "older regular supporters" (Harrington in The Guardian. 1967, 11-16).

The preliminary report of this group used "soccer hooliganism" as a blanket term covering several types of misbehaviour by spec-

tators before, during, or immediately after a football match, including rowdyism on crowded terraces, horseplay and threatening behavior, foul support, soccermania ("an excitable mob of 50 or more
youths who collectively misbehave before or generally after the match
or on their way home) and football riots (like those in Turkey, where
many people were reported killed where supporters of one team
fought with supporters of the other team).

This last no longer represents a "licentious crowd" but a "polarized crowd" (the last to be discussed). "Soccermania" and situations
where rowdyism and horseplay become so widespread as to threaten
the welfare of other spectators or the continuance of the game exemplify the first type of licentious crowd.

A *second* sub-type of *licentious crowd* is more conventionalized.
The crowd that gathers for the event is as much attracted by the
opportunity the event affords for indulging in deviant behavior as
by the event itself. The event can be a drag car race, a motorcycle
meet—or it can be a "pep rally" the night before a big game, meant
to demonstrate support for the team. In either case, the event (the
sport itself or the ritual surrounding the sport) itself may come to
be viewed as so disruptive that it falls into disrepute among many
potential fans or even, is banned by the community or groups which
it threatens. Where licentious crowds "spontaneously" and frequently
begin to coalesce in connection with a given sport, the licentiousness
can become conventionalized so that one sub-type gives rise to the
other.

A riot that took place in Garnett, Kansas, July 6, 1963, during a
sports car race illustrates the more conventionalized type of licentious
crowd. To sum the events (Schul 1963):

> The race course was 2.8 miles of macadam road bordering Lake Gar-
> nett in the city park, a public road closed two days each year to the
> public in order to be used as a race course. The race, sponsored by the
> sports car association, was a national championship SCCA event.
> Most of the early arrivals were young people who established camp
> nearby in what came to be called "Tent City." In the early morning
> hours of the day on which the races were to begin, partying began with
> "Beer for Breakfast," as one observer put it. Most would-be spectators
> were of college age, "a number apparently from upper middle class
> families as expensive sports cars and high powered vehicles were preva-
> lent...most were from Kansas, that is, natives of the area. By noon the
> heat had become intense and incidents began to occur, with occasional
> fights and outbursts of profanity as the social contact became a little
> strained." While a large number of the young people were attending the
> afternoon trial runs at the track, others were sunbathing, stripping their
> clothes, etc. By afternoon two youths had been arrested on charges
> of indecent exposure. People milled around Tent City and on the court-

house square, where some friends had tried unsuccessfully to win their release, grumbling, shouting, and now and then shouting, "Freedom!" A score of peace officers patrolled the town. Three local taverns were packed with—according to the official report "drunkenness increasing, boisterousness rampant, with confusion developing against the syncopated beat of voices, laughter, screaming tires and fireworks.

When the Garnett taverns all closed by 11 p.m. the troopers had to be called to quiet a disturbance by protesting youth. More arrests were made as some lay down in the streets to block traffic or threw firecracks, cherry bombs and beer cans. By midnight a full-fledged riot was in process, with additional help sought from neighboring towns and with the National Guard called in by dawn. By midmorning peace was restored and the main day of the races "came off like clockwork."

The average age of 29 youths arrested, was 20—the range being from 16 to 27; two were high school students and 18 about to start or returning to college in the Fall. Most came from middle class families and, with three exceptions, had never been in trouble before with the law. Most admitted having drunk too much beer.

It should be apparent that most were attracted less by the chance to attend the sports car race than by the opportunity the event offered to join their peers for a good time away from home.

Shellow and Roemer (1966) writing about *"The Riot That Didn't Happen"*—told how they helped the police in a Maryland County prevent a potentially similar riot among a crowd gathered for motorcycle races over Labor Day weekend, 1965.

The Polarized Crowd

Finally, the sports event can become the occasion which polarized audiences or subgroups in the population seize to engage in violent behavior. There are many such instances to be drawn from accounts of sports events but there are two subtypes to be distinguished:

(1) those where the game itself becomes the site for continuing or furthering past feuds, and
(2) those where the outcome of events during a game (or contest) touches off fighting or other forms of conflict between two polarized groups.

In the United States, for instance, ethnic or inter-racial conflicts have, at times, erupted into disorders and violence at the sports arena; participants in some of the riots developing around desegregation of Southern campuses in the 1960's—like that at 'Ole Miss' in 1962— first attended the football game, then joined the jeering mob (Barnett 1965). But the pattern extends to other countries: rioting in Shanghai, in 1946 was, in part fueled by the "whites only" policy at the

British-owned Polo Grounds (K. and G. Lang 1961, ch. 5). Conflicts between nations have been played out on the field and in the stands at international meets. At the Winter Olympics in 1956, just after the Hungarian uprising, a water polo match where Hungary defeated the USSR 4–0, was reported to have been marked by fist fights and bloodshed between players and disorderly and sustained booing by the fans. When a Hungarian star was injured, according to Henry Morton in *Soviet Sport,* the "pro-Hungarian crowd, including many Hungarian emigrés, rushed to the pool and had to be dispersed by the police." The *New York Times* (August 1, 1961) carried a story about anti-Soviet riots on the field and in the stands during a Soviet–Polish soccer match in May 1961. The Polish goalie, carried off in an ambulance after fouling a Russian player, was forced to leave the field under heavy police protection.

Further descriptions covering a range of such sports–connected rioting by polarized crowds could be added. Perhaps best known is the so-called Honduras–El Salvador "soccer war" in 1969; another would be the "post-hockey victory riots" in Czechoslovakia in 1969, or the race riot during a high school football game in Washington, D.C. during Thanksgiving Day weekend, 1962. Finally, there was the rioting that followed the victory of Jack Johnson, the first black world boxing champion, over Jim Jeffries, the "Great White Hope" of pre-World War I America in 1910 (Batchelor 1956).

DISCUSSION

Systematic examination of riotous outbursts should help interpret the meaning of sports events to spectators as well as to the larger society. Many *clichés* can be reexamined—for instance, about the function of sports as safety valves. When do these events become not so much "collective pacifiers" as anxiety-evoking occasions that spill over to add to other sources of individual and group tension? Can we talk about the social function of "sports" or only about the social function of different types of sporting events? How has the meaning of spectatorship changed over periods of time? And can we even talk about "spectatorship" but only about different types of spectators? What can we learn about the nature of social control—for instance, under what circumstances will spectators abide by the "rules of the game" or go beyond limits that have been long maintained?

One methodological procedure might be to take each sport (for example, soccer) and examine various types of riotous outbursts connected with it: fanatic publics (such as the Caserta rioting), acquisitive crowds (the Sutherland tragedy), the licentious crowd (the Brazil victory carnival and/or "soccermania"), and the polarized audience ("the soccer war" or the riots in Turkey). A non-exhaustive but supporting list of data to be collected in order to illuminate the relations between collective violence at sports events and social structure would include:

On the *larger social context,* such relevant information as the past history of the general event, that is, the Olympics, the World Series, the World Cup, and any more time-bound developments, such as the history of any build-up of tensions over the specific event and the expectations built by mass media coverage.

On the *ecology of the situation;* the numbers assembled, the field of vision of spectators seated in given areas (i.e. how visible are the players, coaches, referees, score board, etc?); the amount and intensity of crowding; the amount and velocity of movement among spectators; the humidity–temperature index; the physical layout of the sports arena—its size, exits, standing areas sheltered or not sheltered? enclosed or not enclosed?; arrangements within the sports arena, such as segregation or integration of locals and non-locals among the spectators; the grouping of spectators—do they come as individuals or in family or informal peer groups? or in organized groups?; are spectators seated or standing? what is the hierarchy of seating?—at what distance are spectators from the field of action?

On the *type of sports event* and characteristics of the game, an indication of the *level of competition* (local, national, international; amateur, semi-professional, professional; adolescent, adult; preliminary, semi-final, final; etc.) the *amount and kinds of physical violence* permissible and provisions for controlling tensions engendered; the *dynamics* of spectator–team interaction; including spectator–player interaction, spectator–coach interaction, spectator–referee interaction; the *flexibility–rigidity dimension* of game or contest rules; the *ambiguity–clarity dimension* of game or contest rules; *rewards for players and spectators,* including trophies, gifts and the provisions and importance of legalized, illegal or informal wagering on outcomes.

On the *social psychology of the spectator situation,* there is a need to classify and examine the motivations and behavior of the spectators in their roles as members of the sports audience *but* also according to the role played in the disorders that develop (initiators, followers, rallying points, victims, resisters, etc.). Most needed are systematically collected, multi-observational data and/or survey data providing information on demographic characteristics of individuals—sex, color, ethnic background, socio-economic level, age, education, juvenile or adult arrest records, association with past sports events, membership in fan clubs, participation in sports, etc.—and on interaction (behavior) among those assembled. Questions to be answered through these methods of data collection concern the *meaning of attendance at the event* [are these regulars or newcomers? how scarce are tickets? does the event have a larger audience listening to or viewing the event at a distance? In other words, how much and what kind of value does attendance have for various types of individuals?] ; *familiarity with and acceptance of rules of spectator behavior* including sanctions for misconduct; and, finally, the *expectations of game outcome and its importance.*

On the *provisions for audience control,* we have to look both at the activities of agencies organized to control crowds, such as police and private guard and ushering services as they plan for and respond to developments at the game but also at the control exercised by sports officials and team members. The referee and other officials at the sports game have to be viewed as control agents, whether they so define themselves or not. If the behavior of coaches and players towards the referee and umpire affects the attitude of the crowd—if the coach heckles the referee, can the crowd do so?—, the administrator, by controlling the coach, becomes an agent of crowd control as is illustrated in a description of what happened at the 1970 World Cup match:

> In the first game, when Mexico confronted Russia, the German referee plied his whistle to finicky excess, taking names liberally and brooking no argument...[he] set the level for the tournament and curbed in advance the more cantankerous of the players...[the] authority of the referee was acknowledged.
>
> (Reid 1970)

Finally, it is necessary to secure as reliable descriptions as possible about the *specific occurrence or episode precipitating the outbreak of disorder,* and about *its recurrence or replication.* Only by linking the emerging behavior in these situations to what has been learned about the larger social context, participant expectations and predispositions of the sports audience, the ecology of the situation, the type of event, and the provisions for control can we understand the dynamics of the collective violence that occurs on these "happy" occasions.

REFERENCES

Barrett, H.H. 1965. *Integration at Ole Miss.* Chicago: Quadrangle Books.

Batchelor, D. 1956. *Jack Johnson and His Times.* London: Ferndale.

Beisser, A.H. 1967. *The Madness in Sports.* New York: Appleton–Century–Crofts.

Berk, A.R. 1972. The controversy surrounding analyses of collective violence: some methodological notes. Pp. 112–18 in J. Short and M. Wolfgang, eds. *Collective Violence.* Chicago: Aldine.

Bogardus, E.S. 1931. Golf galleries as a social group. *Sociology and Social Research* 4:270–276.

Crowds Committee Report. 1924. London: H.M. Stationary Office.

Elias, N. and E. Dunning. 1966. Dynamics of sport groups with special reference to football. *British Journal of Sociology* 17,4:388–402.

Elias, N. and E. Dunning. 1970. The quest for excitement in unexciting societies. Pp. 31–51 in G. Lüschen, ed. *The Cross–Cultural Analysis of Sport and Games.* Champaign, Ill.: Stipes.

Elias, N. 1976. Sports and violence. *Notes Recherche Sciences Sociales* 2,6:2–20.

Fox, J.R. 1961. Pueblo baseball: new use for old witchcraft. *Journal of American Folklore* 74, 1:9–18.

Goldstein, J.H. and R.L. Arms. 1971. Effects of observing athletic contests on hostility. *Sociometry* 34, 1:83–90.

Green, G. 1975. Leeds supporters bottom of League. *The Times.* May 30.

Harrington, J.A. 1968. *Soccer Hooliganism.* A Preliminary Report to Mr. Denis Howell. Minister of Sport. London: John Wright.

Hastorf, A.H. and M Cantril. 1954. They saw a game: a case study. *Journal of Abnormal and Social Psychology* 44, 2:129–34.

Heinrich, N. and S. Kaplan. 1967. Yesterday's discord. Pp. 10–35 in S. Lippet and S. Wolin, eds. *The Berkley Student Revolt.* Garden City, N.Y.: Doubleday Anchor.

Heinlä, K. 1966. Notes on the intergroup conflicts in international sport. *IRSS.* 1:49–69.

Howard, G.S. 1912. Social psychology of the spectator. *AJS.* 18, 1:33–50.

Kleinman, S. 1960. *Factors that Influence Behavior of Sports Crowds.* Ph.D. Thesis. Ohio State University.

Kuhlmann, W. 1975. Violence in professional sports. *Wisconsin Law Review.* 3:771–790.

Lang, G. and K. Lang. 1961. *Collective Dynamics.* New York: Crowell.

Lang, G. and K. Lang. 1968. Collective Behavior. *International Encyclopedia of the Social Sciences* II:556–565.

Lang, G. 1976. Der Ausbruch von Tumulten bei Sportveranstaltungen. Pp. 273–295 in G. Lüschen and K. Weis, eds. *Die Soziologie des Sports.* Darmstadt: Luchterhand.

Madge, C. and T. Harrison. 1939. *Britain by Mass Observation.* Middlesex: Penguin.

Marsh, P. 1978. *Aggro.* London: Dent.

Morton, H. 1963. *Soviet Sport.* New York: Collier.

Reid, A. 1970. The sporting scene: shades of Tlachtli. *New Yorker.* 46,2:50–71.

Schachter, N. 1960. The administrator, the coach and the riot. *Journal of Secondary Education* 35,2:155–160.

Schul, B.D. 1963. *A Study of the Garnett Riot.* Topeka: Kansas State Attorney General. (unpublished).

Shellow, R. and D.V. Roemer. 1966. The riot that didn't happen. *Social Problems* 14,2:221–233.

Silberstein, R. 1969. *Sports Riots.* Paper. Department of Sociology. Columbia University, New York.

Smith, M.D. 1974. Violence in sport. *Sportwissenschaft* 4,2:164–173.

Smith, M.D. 1975. The legitimation of violence: hockey players' perceptions of their reference groups' sanctions for assault. *Canadian Review of Sociology and Anthropology* 12,1:72–80.

Smith, M.D. 1975. Sport and collective violence. Pp. 281–300 in D. Ball and J. Loy, eds. *Sport and Social Order*. Reading, Mass.: Addison-Wesley.

Taylor, I. 1971. Football mad. A speculative sociology of football hooliganism. Pp. 352–77 in E. Dunning, ed. *The Sociology of Sport*. London: Cass.

Turner, R. and I. Killian. 1972 *Collective Behavior*. Englewood Cliffs, N.J.: Prentice-Hall.

PART VI

PLAY,

SPORT AND

PERSONALITY

Riezler

Sutton-Smith

Ellis

Martens

PLAY AND SERIOUSNESS

Kurt Riezler

We say: this is merely play; he is merely playing. We differentiate between play and something that is not merely play but is serious. What does this "merely" mean?

But is not the answer obvious? We say "merely playing" whenever we are not serious. We say we are not merely playing so far as we are serious though playing. Unfortunately, the simple answer does not get us very far. What, for heaven's sake, is serious, and why? The "merely" points to a deficiency, to something that is absent in playing. When we say "not merely play" we indicate that this something is present despite our playing. Thus explaining this something whose absence the "merely" asserts, the "not merely" denies, means explaining our seriousness. The question grows.

That seems to be an inquiry into the usage of a word. But the "merely," asserted or denied, accompanies all playing throughout the countries, ages, and languages. It tends to indicate something in man, the queer being, that is able to play and bound to be serious.

The "merely" or "not merely" resides in the attitude of man, not in things, matters, actions, that we could subsume under play and seriousness. The "merely" differentiates attitudes. Man may decide according to his own will or mood whether he should deal playfully or seriously with a person, a thing, a task, a situation, or a game. Man does not decide which attitude of his is playful and which serious. Though man's mood can move things to and fro over the borderline between play and seriousness, he can not move the borderline itself, which demarcates attitudes, not things.

I begin with the most simple case. We play games such as chess or bridge. They have rules the players agree to observe. These rules are not the rules of the "real" world or of "ordinary" life. Chess has its king and queen, knights and pawns, its space, its geometry, its laws of motion, its demands, and its goal. The queen is not a real queen, nor is she a piece of wood or ivory. She is an entity in the game defined by the movements the game allows her. The game is the context within which the queen is what she is. This context is not the context of the real world or of ordinary life. The game is a little cosmos of its own.

We may call this little cosmos a world—the "playworld." The term, however, is misleading. "World" suggests certain features the playworld lacks. "World" means or should mean the totality of a something "in" which we live. We ourselves are part of this something. Though the world is always our world, it is intended to mean a world that is not and never will be ours. It means everyone's world. It embraces all other worlds of all other beings. So it is the real world.

We are free to play or not to play, to enter or to leave the "playworld." Our relation to the real world is of a different kind. We have been thrown into it willy-nilly; we can leave but never reenter it. As the real world differs from the playworld, so a real queen differs from the queen in chess. In the real world all things are connected with all things, every effect is a cause, every end a means. Not so in the playworld. Here the chains of causes and effects are thought of as having limits. Events within the game are separated from events in the real world. The "merely" may have to do with this separation.

In playing chess we can be more or less serious. A bridge player may be chided by his partner for lack of seriousness. She feels he is not paying sufficient attention to the game or that he does not live up to its spirit. Still, mere lack of seriousness should not be called a playful attitude toward the game. Play or playfulness is not a negative term. We could speak of a playful attitude if a player were to play a game within the game itself, whether by pursuing a goal of his own or by superimposing rules of his own on the rules of the game—replacing the spirit of the game by the caprices of his mood, which are at odds with the spirit of the game although not forbidden by its rules. For example, a bridge-player might try to get as many kings as possible in his tricks. He could be said to play with the play. We say that he merely plays so far as he substitutes demands of his own for the demands of the game. Here playfulness stresses the detachment of a sovereign mood—which in this case is detachment from the spirit of the game. Thus the "merely" seems to indicate a detachment from demands that seriousness commands us to respect.

The story of our playing has still other aspects. Though the playworld may be separated from the real world, the goal of the game can be connected with the real world, our ordinary life, our substantial interests. Money, honor, even life, may depend on our winning or losing. The gambler can raise his stakes to a point at which losing would mean serious harm. He has not much use for the "merely," though we might say that he deals seriously with the play but playfully with his money. It is he himself who links his serious interests with the play. To the football champion the victory of Lions over Tigers may be the only thing that matters. Glory, honor, career may depend on his success, according to the customs and codes of the society in which he lives. Since he has to submit to these codes, his football is not merely a play, perhaps no play at all—at least to him. It is an institution of the real world or ordinary life. The playful attitude, if there is any, is on the side of a society that connects a mere play with the glory, honor, and career of its members.

A fashionable gentleman trifles away his day and gambles at night. His gambling is his only seriousness. Here at least he faces the reality of life: fear and hope, risk, action, passion, need for caution and self-control. It may even be that the very thirst for real concern drives him to the gambling table—away from his day of non-committing trifles. Now play and seriousness exchange places. We may conclude: play can be serious, ordinary life need not be serious at all. The "real world" or "ordinary life" may be used to differentiate things belonging to play from those belonging to seriousness; they cannot be used to differentiate a playful from a serious attitude.

There are, however, many games of another sort. In some the emphasis lies not on obeying but on inventing or changing rules. After all, chess and bridge also were invented in a playful mood. We might even dare to say that in the present American form, bridge has taken on the character of work by being fettered to so many elaborate rules and conventions that obedience to them threatens to suffocate the playful mood. We never enjoy a playful attitude more than when making or changing the rules or conventions to which we submit. We do it rarely, because we are lazy or lack inventiveness.

This is clear in the case of children's play. What they enjoy most is their own inventive activity. Long before they play games children play with or without toys. They invent and perform stories, determine the meaning of things, assume for themselves the role of a king or queen. This chair is a mountain, the doll in the blue dress and with pink cheeks is Aunt Geraldine. The child disregards the fact that Aunt Geraldine has neither a blue dress nor pink cheeks. She enjoys her activities in determining the meaning of the doll or in forcing Aunt Geraldine to sit straight in her doll chair.

Grownups, watching the child, say: she plays. In their world the child's play is "merely" play. There may be, however. no "merely" for the child herself—no playful attitude, no "merely" that could hint at deficiency. The distinction between play and seriousness is still in the making, the real and the imaginary world are not yet separated. For the child, things do not yet have their own definite meaning, which demands to be respected and is put aside when we merely play. Things, as separated from their meanings, are as yet unknown. They are what they mean. To children their little activity in playing seems to share in a seriousness in which, in between anxiety and curiosity, they discover the world and its things, themselves and their relation to the world, their power and its limitations. It is the share they enjoy, since in playing alone are they acting.

The "merely" enters the scene when children begin to be capable of, and granted, a first consistent activity in a consistent reality. Now the things of the real world begin to raise their voices, impose their demands, and be conceived in the horizon of an order in which things are no longer what you choose them to be. Now the doll and Aunt Geraldine, play and seriousness, part company. This process may take considerable time.

A four-year-old boy plays railroad with a series of chairs. He sits on the first chair and is the engine. His father enters the room and kisses him. "Don't kiss me," protests the boy, "the chairs could see it and forget that they are railroad cars." Huizinga (1938) uses the case to support his thesis that children realize that they merely play. The example, however, is dubious. It shows only how the real and the imaginary world still interpenetrate each other.

A girl, we say, plays around with the boys. Or this man merely plays with that girl. We may pity the girl who takes herself or her love seriously and demands to be not merely played with. The girl or the social group sets a standard of love to which this man should but does not conform. His merely playing means disregarding this standard. In some cases both the male and the female merely play. They play with each other a very old play, each knowing that the other merely plays and both enjoying the charm of the game. "Why not? After all, it is not so serious a matter." We say they merely play though they may pretend or even believe themselves to be serious. We say so if we know that neither would go a few steps out of his way for the other's sake. We set a standard of love to which intimate relations between a boy and girl should conform. The "merely" means that an obligation inherent in the relations between the sexes has been disregarded. In some languages, such as older Low German and Dutch, the term for an illegitimate child is "playchild," suggesting that only marriage is serious. But play is not the mere negation of seriousness. A love affair that lacks seriousness need not even be play. The amorous life of societies that succeeded in bestowing some charm on love as a game tells another story. There are winners and losers, goals and rules. The two players may play with each other; the prize may be to be loved and not love. It may be mere vanity, honor, reputation, in a leisure class engaged in a collective battle against boredom. Or the lovers may play not only with each other but with the danger that at any moment one may commit him- or herself seriously and really fall in love. The game has its rules. These rules—the moral code of illicit love—tend to separate the game from ordinary life, its commitments, its interests, titles, rights, and its knowledge. The rules demand "discretion" in all the shades of the term, which range from separation through freedom to courtesy. It may happen that both players lose and really fall in love. Then they no longer merely play, though they may go on observing some rules of the game and try to isolate their love from ordinary life. Out of mutual respect for their self-defense they may even go on pretending to play, using the ruse of a playful attitude to cloak their seriousness.

In some Catholic countries of an old tradition a few weeks of carnival festivities put the relations between the sexes under the exceptional rules of a play. Visitors from countries without such a tradition usually assume that all they have to do is to rid themselves of an habitual restraint. Though nowadays the actual practice of the natives themselves does not quite live up to the idea, the natives still dislike these visitors because their failure to observe the rules spoils the game. Here a social code demands the playful attitude. You are in disguise, wearing a mask and a costume. You are not yourself. You play a role. No one is expected to ask or answer serious questions. The stories you tell, the promises you make, the love you profess, need be true but for the moment—in a fictitious world. No consequences should be drawn, no obligations remembered, beyond Mardi Gras. The favors you may consummate give you no titles. They do not count in ordinary life. A really jealous husband who does not merely act the part of a jealous husband violates the rules of the play.

Here a society plays, watching in common agreement over rules meant to separate the game from the real world or ordinary life and its chains of causes and effects, ends and means.

The example of love is ambiguous—the ambivalence of love between play and seriousness being the charm of the game. Other examples are simpler.

A writer's cunning and skill may be remarkable. He forces the language to follow his moods. Yet we blame him for merely playing with the language. What do we mean? He only wants to display his skill, enjoys moving along the boundary of what is still allowed, startles us by his artifices. He is an acrobat, not an artist. He merely plays so far as he disregards, for purposes of his own mood, obligations that the correlation of subject-matter and language silently imposes.

We say that a conductor deals but playfully with a Beethoven symphony. We mean that the desire to show off his craftsmanship overpowers the devotion the work demands.

Statesmen, whose job it is to consider all sides of a situation, often complain of experts who isolate the interests of their fields. Once in a while they may sigh angrily; the generals or the diplomats are merely playing their game. The statesman may be right or wrong; he means that the diplomat, educated in the traditions of the European balance of power, the rules of diplomacy and its craftiness, looks at

Europe as the playground of a diplomatic game that is an end in it-self, and is unable to realize demands beyond his game or require-ments of a situation that can not be mastered by his means, methods, or goals, In an analogous way the general, educated as a staff officer by playing war games on maps or in manoeuvres, regards the surface of the earth as a playground for moving armies and navies. Both sepa-rate a playworld from the real world, absolutize their own rules and goals, and disregard every horizon that is beyond the limited horizon of their game. Even in such cases play and its "merely" retain the shadow of their meaning. Such examples can be multipled; the "mere-ly" continues to accompany the playful attitude.

I venture a preliminary thesis. The diversity of our playing seems to suggest two ways of defining the "merely," the one starting from the player, the other from the play. In a playful attitude the manner of our being concerned has specific features, as has the object with which we are concerned. Since these two sorts of specificity corre-spond to each other the two ways of defining the "merely" converge; they explain each other.

In a playful attitude we are "not really" concerned. But it is just this "not really" that must be explained. Moreover, "not really" is wider than "merely playfully." We are "not really" concerned in many cases when there is no playfulness in our attitude. We may try to say: in a playful attitude things do not matter so much—we are only partly concerned, not with the whole of our interest. But this again is doubtful.

We are often partly concerned in matters of ordinary life, yet this our partial concern need not be playful. If "partial" is to be used this partialness must be of a peculiar kind. We are partly concerned but without linking this partial concern to other parts or to the whole of our concern. It does not count. In severing the link that connects this part with other parts we treat a "partial" concern as if it were no part of anything. Thus the part, not being conceived of as part, is not a part. In the seriousness of ordinary life all partial concern remains partial because it is connected with some of or all our other concerns. The "merely" in our playing seems to point not to a partial concern, but to a distinction in which our concern in playing is separated from our other concerns.

If we start from the game or from the object with which a playful attitude is concerned, a different aspect tells the same story. An area of playing is isolated by our sovereign whim or by man-made agree-ment. Things within this area mean what we order them to mean. They are cut off from their meanings in the so-called real world or ordinary life. If there still are such chains they are disregarded. So far as we do not disregard them our attitude is no longer merely playful. An area that under the aspect of ordinary life would be conceived of as only a part is regarded not as part of a wider area but as a cosmos of its own. Thus the two aspects tell the same story.

In merely playing we forget the "real world," our ends, our dependence on things. We often play only for the sake of diversion. At any rate, we disregard the context of ordinary life, the meaning of things, their demands, our obligations, and put in their place meanings, demands, and obligations of our own making. In playing we enjoy being our own masters.

Playing, if it is merely playing, is never a means. The goal of playing is part of the game. It is not an end to which our playing is the means—it serves only to direct our activity, to measure the skill, to differentiate between winner and loser. Playing, our activity in playing is its own end, though we are capable of linking the goal of the game to means and ends in our life outside the game. If we do, we usually drop the "merely." The chains of causes and effects, means and ends, are meant to be cut at the boundaries of the play. No more than causes from outside are allowed to interfere, lest they spoil the game, should consequences be drawn to the life outside the play.

So it seems that with respect to both the how and the what of our concern the "merely" could be explained as follows: things, in their relation to us, are surrounded by a horizon that depends on our attitude toward them. In different attitudes we see things in different horizons. The horizon makes things what they are to us. In the seriousness of our daily activity we look at things within the horizon of our interests in the various concatenations of causes and effects, means and ends. Here every horizon seems to be partial, pointing beyond itself, intended to mean something in connection with other things and other possible horizons. When in serious life we say that we are only partly concerned, we look at our own concern as but a greater or smaller part of our concernedness—in the horizon of something that is more than this part. In a playful attitude the horizon does not point at anything beyond itself, though it is the horizon of a limited area or of a limited concern that is not yet connected with, and not a part of, a wider area or a broader concern: the horizon of a play that is merely a play.

This thesis, however, is preliminary indeed. It may be of some service to differentiate playfulness from the average seriousness of our daily life. But it has no reason to offer why this kind of ordinary life should be serious at all. Why should or could a man not deal playfully with all the chains of means and ends in this dubious seriousness? The question grows out of the answer.

Ere I proceed, I permit an antithesis to speak and to sweep the thesis away in a burst of rage.

At last, so the argument runs, you seem to discover the shortcomings of a thesis that takes for granted the seriousness of ordinary life.

In starting from the "merely" you presuppose a standard of serious-ness that may be only the standard of the kind of society that thinks in terms of means and ends, in terms of business. It may be that the "merely" is only a habit of speaking. There need not be an absolute "merely" in playing as such—no deficiency. If there is deficiency it may be a deficiency not in play but in the man who utters the "mere-ly" and thus shows that he can not rid himself of his puny sort of seriousness. Your start from the "merely" distorts the story of play.

There is no "merely"—rather an "even." Play is man's triumph—he, the greatest of all beings, can even play. Only the lowest animals do not play. All higher animals, wild or tame, play. The reasons for which we call them higher or lower may account for their playing and not playing. We assume that worms do not play, though we can not know what movements, actions, things are to worms in their worm world, if there is such a thing. We think of worms as closely tied up with their actual environment at any given moment. They live in the dark. The demands they put upon and receive from their environment are dumb pressures. They can not detach themselves from their environ-ment, change the meaning of things and their functions, as play im-plies. Dogs and cats, most higher animals, undoubtedly can. They can fight for the love of fighting and not "mean it seriously." They chase a ball, push it away and capture it again, for the fun of chasing; give it importance for a while and leave it as something that is of no inter-est. Their playing is detachment from the environment and its de-mands, a sort of freedom the worm seems to lack. The way from worm to cat is but the first and minor part of the way from slavery to freedom. From dog to man is another, and the history of man's culture is again another part. Man's playing is his greatest victory over his dependence and finiteness, his servitude to things. Not only can he conquer his environment and force conditions to comply with his needs and demands far beyond the power of any other animal. He can also play, i.e., detach himself from things and their demands and replace the world of given conditions with a playworld of his own mood, set himself rules and goals and thus defy the world of blind necessities, meaningless things, and stupid demands. Religious rites, festivities, social codes, language, music, art—even science—all con-tain at least an element of play. You can almost say that culture is play. In a self-made order of rules man enjoys his activities as the maker and master of his own means and ends. Take art. Man, liber-ated from what you call the real world or ordinary life, plays with a world of rhythms, sounds, words, colors, lines, enjoying the triumph of his freedom. This is his seriousness. There is no "merely."

The antithesis plays havoc with our preliminary thesis. If the shat-tered thesis is to survive, it must be reshaped in order to withstand the violent assault.

We must make a new start. The "merely" may be misleading. What about the "not merely"? There are cases in which play, though play, is not merely play; and not only because the result of the play is connected by agreement with means and ends in ordinary life, such as money or honor, but in itself, by its inherent seriousness, which is not the seriousness of the real world or ordinary life. But is there such a thing? Why is it serious?

Art is play, though not merely play. Some put the emphasis on play, others on the "not merely." To the artist, if he is a real artist, it is deadly earnest, as earnest as religion to the religious man. But what is art? If we define art as the class of things called art—by some minimum conditions to which the elements of this class must submit, —we find works of art that are not even play, others that are merely play, and again others that certainly are not merely play. In search of the "not merely" we can not start from a definition of minimum conditions. There is something—whatever it may be, call it quality or value,—by virtue of which a work of art is "real art" or "great" or more or less "good." Toward this something both the artist and the art connoisseur are looking, the one in creating, the other in judging, the work. Though both may be equally unable to say what this mysterious something is, they presuppose that there is some thing. Whoever honestly denies it is not an artist or an art connoisseur. Obviously the "not merely" refers to this mysterious something.

If we apply to art the standards of the preliminary thesis, art is merely play. It separates things from the real world, disregards their demands, puts things in an imaginary context, within which they mean what art orders them to mean. The artist is the creator of his own rules and laws, which are not the rules and laws of ordinary life and are conceived of as being severed from its endless chains of means and ends, causes and effects. Thus, he merely plays.

And yet he does not play. There is not and can not be a playful attitude, be it in the artist who creates or in the connoisseur who enjoys and judges a work of art. It seems even that this play can not be played in a playful attitude. There is, in art itself, a demand, an ultimate obligation, with which no artist plays. It is devotion to this demand and detachment from all other demands that makes him an artist. With respect to this detachment you may say that he merely plays; with respect to this devotion, he simply can not help being serious indeed. This obligation is there ere the artist becomes an artist and creates his particular style and his works. It is the supreme lead, taken on in reverence and obeyed in judging, choosing, rejecting. It is not man-made, not the creation of any arbitrary mood, not part of the rules of the play, but prior to any rules. There is no such thing in playing games. Thus, art is not play. The "not merely" points at an unconditional obligation.

Here, however, we are likely to run into a peculiar difficulty. We use and certainly need the term "playful" to characterize a style, a work, the individuality of an artist. Mozart is more playful than Beethoven. Rafael sometimes seems to be; Michelangelo is never playful. The history of art abounds in examples. The term, used in this way within art, need not have any bearing on "good" or "bad"—there is no "merely" in this playfulness, no differentiation of any kind. We mean only an apparently effortless ease that makes creativity look like the play of a sovereign mood. Both *King Lear* and *Midsummer Night's Dream* are called plays, though the former is certainly less playful than the latter. We are tempted to say that compared with *King Lear, Midsummer Night's Dream* is "merely" a play: it is a dream in a playworld that does not claim to represent the real world. But we certainly do not mean that Shakespeare's attitude toward his poetry and its inherent demands is merely playful.

In the *Merchant of Venice* the relation itself between play and seriousness is the core of the work. Hence its difficulties. In most performances the tragedy of Shylock is put to the fore as the center of the work framed by a playworld of love, fun, music, and sweetness. Such performances can hardly be convincing. If the relation is reversed the performance convinces—a world of play and love put to the fore against the background of a world in which Shylocks hate and suffer. The poet, however, does not deal playfully with the tension between play and seriousness or with human life, of which this tension is part, or with his poetry.

Whenever in the history of art artists not only seem to have but really have an attitude toward their art that could be called merely playful, this "merely" indicates decay, second-rate work, or the end of a style. Playfulness in art is "not merely" playful at the beginning and "merely" playful at the end of a stylistic period—not in all but in many cases.

Art, whether playful or not, is never merely play. If the mysterious something we call good or quality or value means an obligation that is unconditionally serious, this seriousness is certainly not the seriousness of ordinary life and its horizons of means and ends. If the lead of the term "horizon" is to be followed the "horizon" in art is of another kind.

Listen to a Beethoven symphony. You are in a world of sounds—nowhere else. This world embraces you. It is present as a whole. There is nothing beyond. The "real world" or ordinary life with all its endless chains of aspects, causes, means, in which every step is finite and none the last, disappears. Something else appears—which can be grasped with your senses but not put into words. If unfortunately a philosophical context or a question that continues to grow compels you to describe it you search for words in a kind of despair. One of the words you are likely to hit upon is "horizon."

This horizon includes a whole. This whole seems present at whatever point we touch this horizon. It is just this that the term "horizon" suggests or should suggest. We apply the term to the sky: south or north, west or east—only one horizon borders the sky. It is the same horizon all around. Thus the term implies the oneness of a whole. Here "whole" does not mean completeness of several elements. It means a Gestalt, present in every part, and not only by virtue of the presence of all other parts. You look only southward and yet the horizon you see embraces a whole. In art the horizon of the whole can still be visible in a torso or a fragment.[1]

The horizon embracing a whole is an ultimate horizon. It does not limit a part as part. It is not a particular horizon, pointing beyond itself. If there is infinity this infinity is within the horizon—an inward infinity.

While you listen to the symphony you are not partly concerned—the whole of your being is listening, you are moved to the core, open to something the term "ultimate horizon" is intended to indicate. The term does not claim to answer the unanswerable question of the mysterious something by virtue of which a work of art is more or less good. Its only claim is descriptive power. We might say that Leonardo or Michelangelo or Shakespeare in their Mona Lisa or Adam or Caesar succeeded in making visible an ultimate horizon that forces the human cosmos as a whole to become transparent in the portrait of a lady, in the movement of a body, in verses uttered by actors that are not Caesars on the boards of a stage that is not the world.

Reformulating the preliminary thesis I may say: Man acts and is acted upon as being directed in itself toward a "whither" whatever this whither may be or at any given moment seems to be. He lives in a world on which he depends. His life is his relation to his world. The world, however, is not merely the sum total of the things in the world. Nor is our relation to our world the sum total of our relations to the things in the world. Single things are to us what they are in the context of our world as a whole. In all our meddling and wrestling with things we wrestle with and woo the world as a whole in a loud or mute give and take, understanding and misunderstanding, power and devotion. So far as we deal with single things, all our "whithers" are finite, though behind each stands another that again is finite—in an

---

[1] I refer to the logical tools of Gestalt psychology which realizes the insufficiency of a logic that starts from a multitude of elements and their relations.

endless finiteness. So far as we relate single things to the whole of our being or to our world as a whole (we can not do the one without the other) an ultimate horizon and in it an ultimate whither become visible, which is not the next step. In fact, it is no step at all, not even the last one, because it is not an element of a sequence.

Art is but an example. Though nowadays registered under entertainment business, it was born as a child of religion and entrusted with making visible its ultimate horizon. Art could outlive any religious faith but never the ultimate horizon. The ultimate horizon is not a monopoly of either religion or art. You love someone. The ultimate horizon is present though your theories about love may prevent you from recognizing its presence. You are confronted with a cause you would fight for, whatever words you choose to use. It is by referring the cause to an ultimate horizon, embracing your world as a whole, that you would fight for it. You "evaluate." You do it in two ways: by relating single things or actions to other things or actions in the endless finiteness of your chains of means and ends; or by referring one thing to the whole of your world, to an ultimate horizon bordering this whole. In the second, you may happen to use the term "value." Again it does not matter which terms you use. Let us assume that a social scientist tries honestly to prove that there are no values, but only wants and desires that bring about valuations. He may even succeed. Yet he can not help either looking at his own honesty in an ultimate horizon or admitting that he is not serious.

At any moment any link in one of the endless chains of our ordinary life can be referred to an ultimate horizon of our world as a whole. Without such reference it need not be serious. None of our games that are merely play, such as bridge or chess, has an ultimate horizon; nor have the endless chains of causes and effects, means and ends, in the so-called seriousness of our ordinary life, as far as you conceive of life as a linkage of chains in which any horizon is only particular and no end ultimate. Whenever an ultimate horizon grips the whole of our being our playing is no longer "merely" playing, ordinary life is bound to be serious, and our concern with whatever it is is really real concern.

It is the ultimate horizon that lets both our play and ordinary life be serious—as the one thing nobody can play with, unless it disappears.

Thus the preliminary thesis, reshaped, can deal with the antithesis. Play may be a triumph of freedom; culture may contain an element of play. Since, however, the very life of culture is nothing else than an ultimate horizon, made visible, this playing never acknowledges a "merely." But the question goes on growing and the thesis remains preliminary. Heracleitus, watching boys playing in the holy grove of the temple of the Ephesian Diana, said: "Aeon is a boy who plays and moves the pawns to and fro." Though you may think of the world as God's play, you are not God. What is "merely" to such a God is "not merely" to you.

REFERENCES

Buytendijk, F.J.J. 1933. *Wesen und Sinn des Spiels.* Berlin.

Caillois, R. 1958. *Les jeux et les hommes.* Paris: Gallimard. English 1961 as *Men, Play and Games.* Glencoe, Ill.: Free Press.

Caillois, R. ed. 1967. *Jeux et Sports.* Paris: Encyclopedie de la Pléiade.

Groos, K. 1899. *Die Spiele der Menschen.* Jena: Fischer. English 1916 as *The Play of Man.* New York: Appleton.

Gulick, L.H. 1920. *A Philosophy of Play.* New York: Scribners.

Hall, G.S. 1920. *Youth.* New York: Appleton.

Huizinga, J. 1938. *Homo Ludens.* Utrecht. English 1955 as *Homo Ludens.* Boston: Beacon.

McDougall, W. 1918. *Social Psychology.* Boston: Luce.

Mead, G.H. 1934. *Mind, Self, and Society.* Chicago: University of Chicago Press.

Piaget, J. 1951. *Play, Dreams and Imitation in Childhood.* New York: Norton.

Schmalenbach, H. 1939. *Geist und Sein.* Basel: Haus zum Falken. 1977. Excerpts as Human existence, play and seriousness. Pp. 215-25 in Schmalenbach on *Society and Experience.* G. Lüschen and G. Stone, eds. Chicago: University of Chicago Press.

Simmel, G. 1917. *Grundfragen der Soziologie.* Berlin: De Gruyter.

Simmel, G. 1950. *Essays on Sociology,* K. Wolff, ed. Glencoe: Free Press.

Originally published in *The Journal of Philosophy* 38, 1941: 505–517 (references added by the editors).

THE SOCIAL PSYCHOLOGY AND
ANTRHOPOLOGY OF PLAY AND GAMES

Brian Sutton-Smith

There are basically two classes of theory in the study of play. There are those which view play as a formative phenomenon preparing the players for other forms of adaptation. And there are those which see play as an expression of other more fundamental forces in life, but do not view it as being of a basically formative character. We would include in this latter category the theories of play as surplus energy, recreation, relaxation and recapitulation. In all these theories play has a relatively subsidiary role in biological or psychological existence.

Beginning with Groos' theory as espoused in the *Play of Animals* (1898) and *The Play of Man* (1916), the theory of animal or children's play as a preparation and practice for adult life became an important part of the tradition of play theorizing. Most works on animal play still view it in these terms. In a recent work on *Play Fighting* (1975), for example, Owen Aldis presents the view that those animals play more that must spend more of their adult energy in skillful attempts to overcome their prey. He contends that the exercise of muscle and the co-ordination of skill in the play period is correlated direcly with requirements of adult adaptation. In 1938 a Dutch historian, Huizinga, presented the even more radical thesis that culture itself begins as play. Culture is first "played" before it settles down into the institutional forms that we know as language, war, law, and art. While his speculative thesis was at first greeted with some skepticism, there has been increasing evidence that would tend to support his view that play is a creative center for subsequent growth. In anthropology we have discovered that in those tribes where children play most, in subsequent years they have the greatest requirements for complex and flexible responses. In psychology we have discovered that those who play most are also the most creative (Sutton-Smith 1974).

All of these developments, therefore, strongly suggest that play is prepatory for subsequent life. Despite their emphasis however, no one has been able to tie such play behaviors directly into adult adjustment. There appears to be some sort of indirect connection but not a direct one. The characteristics of expressiveness, of lightheartedness, of relaxedness and of bubbling energy which were noted by the earlier non-prepatory theories are still there. Play may be some sort of a preparation but as theories emphasize it also is some sort of a relaxed and inconsequential phenomena.

One way to resolve these contradictions, which are inherent in these two trends in play theory, is to say that play does not directly prepare but only that it is preadaptive. That is, play gets responses ready, but does not decree that they shall ever be used beyond the play itself. Or to put it another way, play potentiates responses, rather than prepares them. This has been called play as *adaptive potentiation* (Sutton-Smith 1975). As an essential part of this theory it can be pointed out that the player cannot experiment with his potential future unless he feels completely free to do whatever he wishes to do. He must feel unconstrained by everyday requirements. He must have the freedom to be ridiculous or inventive. Unless one feels such freedom it is difficult to try out all the response combinations and response permutations that real experimentation requires. From this point of view prior theories have selectively attended either to the ultimate consequences of this sort of experimentation (and called play a preparation) or they have attended to the mood or attitude within which the play itself must operate (and called play free expression). Evidence in favor of the view that play is preadaptive comes from recent findings that children are more developmentally advanced in play than in other adaptations. This comes from the work of Nicolich (1975); Overton and Jackson (1973); Dansky and Silverman (1973). Petersen (1976) for example, has shown that children telling stories in response to the instruction "tell me any story you have made up" tell a story of a higher level of cognitive complexity than the same children telling stories to pictures or inkblots. The freer the circumstances the higher the developmental level of the product.

When play is viewed in such a "creative" way it becomes very important to distinguish within children's activity just what is play and what is not. In the pages that follow, therefore, we deal in turn with the antecedents of play (biological, psychological and anthropological) which are often confused with play, but are instead merely the circumstances that precede it. Then we deal with the transition into play, that is, with the way in which such earlier circumstances lead to play. Finally we attempt to define the essential nature of play as well as some of the changes that take place in children's development through play. These characteristics of play structure and play development help, in our view, to describe why play has the preadaptive function that we assign to it.

ANTECEDENTS

This section focuses upon the nature of the necessary preconditions for play to occur. It is assumed that some circumstances may be required to support play, even though these conditions do not actually cause it to occur; they are necessary but not sufficient. Evidence of these antecedent conditions is derived from research in animal psychology, child psychology and anthropology. The biological and psychological studies refer mainly to play, whereas those in anthropology are more often about games.

Biological Antecedents

Although this work is concerned primarily with psychological and anthropological issues in the study of play, some mention must be made of the increasing body of work on the biological antecedents of play. Students of animal behavior (comparative psychologists and ethologists) make it clear that diverse species show differences in their amounts of play, and that certain general conditions underlie the amount of playfulness which we find. The Australian anthropologist Peter Reynolds (1972) has spoken of these conditions as the "flexibility complex." He says, "There is reason to believe that the history of man consists largely of a progressive phylogenetic elaboration of the flexibility complex." He includes in this complex an increased delay in maturation, a condition of semi-domestication and the dependence of the infant on the parents for caretaking. To these he adds the capacity for observational learning, imitation, exploration, and the development of play group subcultures with institutions of their own. In a number of articles Jerome Bruner has spoken to the same general set of conditions, but with a greater emphasis on the functional value for skill acquisition of the particular conditions surrounding play. He says, for example, "There is a well-known rule in the psychology of learning, the Yerkes-Dodson Law, that states that the more complex a skill is, the lower the optimum level of motivation required to learn it. That is, too much motivation arousal can interfere with learning. By de-emphasizing the importance of the goal, play may serve to reduce excessive drive and thus enable young animals and children to learn more easily the skills they will need when they are older" (1975, p. 82). Elsewhere he speaks of play as a program of variation, and points out that even animals, when provided with caretaking, increase innovation (1972, 1973). Therapeutic work with the disabled, disturbed and deficient child also indicates that only when the child is reassured that he is protected and safe does he attempt to reach out and express himself freely in play behaviors. Safety, protection, security and trust seem to be as important to animals as they are to humans. This thesis is supported by Mary Main's (1975) demonstration that secure babies, as compared with the insecure, explore more intensively and with longer duration; they also smile and laugh and play more willingly with their playmates. Obviously as individuals mature and their playing and gaming capacities strengthen and become internalized, the need for secure external circumstances may be considerably reduced. Studies in humor, for example, indicate that it is the more secure individual who is able to use humor for anxiety reduction in a stressful situation. There are common reports of soldiers at play on the eve of battle. Extremes of motivation (starvation, the midst of battle) may still preclude play, but for some adults play is no longer the tentative competence it was in the early years. The conditions of audience behavior under which some modern sports such as soccer are played, show the extent to which adults can go in maintaining their play under quite severe circumstances. Only further research will show whether there are culture specific ratios of security and anxiety in the play of particular games and sports.

Psychological Antecedents

Despite the examples just given, it is generally agreed that young players do not play when in states of emergency. Usually other psychological drives (hunger or fear) or cultural emergencies (war or revolution) must be dealt with first. The psychological paradox is how such initial states of relaxation or boredom can then lead to the high states of motivation we associate with play and games. The internal conflict theories of psychoanalysis or the child rearing conflict theory of Roberts and Sutton-Smith (1966) must deal with the fact that such conflicts, if at a high point, interfere with play. They do not facilitate it. Only after the play occurs can the conflict be introduced into its content. Apparently, therefore, the conflicts do not explain the game structure, though they may ultimately affect its content.

Recent work in the psychology of play, however, has focused less on the inference of such internal states, than on the observations of the antecedent contingencies for play in stimulus conditions, social conditions and in communication. We take these up in turn.

(1) Mastery of stimulus conditions. There is considerable consensus that the person who plays is at some ease with his environment and his fellows. Sometimes this state of quiescence is conceptualized as (a) a state of equilibrium, or (b), in behaviorist terms, as a state of stimulus-redundancy, or (c), in motivational terms, as the absence of drive urgency or (d), in neurological terms, as a below normal level of arousal (boredom) or (e), in affective terms, as a state of relaxation.

The problem for play theory is how these preceding states of quiescence (however they may be conceptualized) give way to the high

states of alertness and arousal that constitute play. To explain the
occasional exceptions when those who play become so involved that
they ignore the usual biological indicators of stress (hunger, elimination, pain) is still another problem.

In recent years increasing research work has clarified certain points.
First, it is clear that although play is a voluntary activity (the subject
is doing what he chooses to do and is not compelled or driven by internal or external need to do this), not all such voluntary activity is
play. There are other voluntary activities, such as exploration, which
usually precede play. It is argued that despite the voluntariness of
exploration, the subject's activity during exploration is still very much
dictated by the stimulus conditions in the environment, whereas the
essence of play is that it is an activity in which the subject imposes
his own idea (schema, fantasy, image, response) upon the surrounding circumstances.

It has become increasingly clear, from recent research, that we can
describe the *phases* in a continuum of voluntary activity that begins
with exploration and may end with play. Researchers working with
primates as well as with children have observed parallel sequences.
Thus Chevalier-Skolnikoff writes:

> ". . . primates also react to novel objects first with fear then with care-
> ful inspection, which is visual, tactile, and olfactory, and sometimes even
> includes tasting, and finally with experimentation and play, which will
> give the animals maximal information about the object. Note that the ex-
> ploratory sequence is similar in the raven and in the primate." (1973: 2)

In Hutt's (1971) work with children the transitions made across
four phases in this continuum of voluntary behavior are the examination of a novel object, the repetition of an adequate response, the
combination of responses, then finally the transformation into a play
response. The point is that children do not generally play in a novel
setting or with novel materials until they have established mastery
over that setting and with those materials.

There is no theoretical difference between saying one must master
the physical setting and mastering the stimulus conditions in a setting.
This is just a difference in the level of analysis applied. However, we
can use this difference to make a further point. Namely, that although
the player must first be master of the setting, this does not mean he
completely transcends it in his play. Though he may impose his schema
or his fantasy on his environment, he nevertheless assimilates that
environment into the contents of the fantasy as he proceeds. By and
large psychologists have gradually reduced their concern with environments or playgrounds from a molar to a molecular level. They have
been far less at home with settings than with stimuli. Although an

interesting exception is the work of Gump, Schoggen and Redl which shows a variety of interesting relationships between play and physical setting (Herron & Sutton-Smith 1971).

One way of clarifying the apparent contradiction in saying both that the environment influences play and yet that play transcends the environment, is to be found in the data of Beatrice and John Whiting (1975) which involves a study of children in six cultures. They have shown that children in more complex cultures play more and with more complexity. Their findings here parallel those of Roberts and Sutton-Smith (1966) in finding more types of games in cultures of higher complexity. These findings may be read to mean that the culture makes a direct impact on the structure of the play and games to be found within it. Technological, social and economic complexity is paralleled by game complexity. But the Whiting (1975) study also showed that within the complex groups themselves, there was relatively more play and games in the group in which the children had the greatest freedom to play. Thus there was more play amongst the Taira of Okinawa than amongst the Rajputs of India although both were complex societies. In Taira the children were much freer to roam about the community and to play with whomsoever they chose, whereas the Rajputs were confined to their backyards and sibling playmates. This suggests, that the "cultural leeway" which permits play is of greater scope in Taira than Rajput. The idea that there must be leeway for play to develop, so that the child is given scope to react back on his cultural circumstances has been suggested by the leading exponent of play analysis, Erik Erikson (1972). All of which may be summed by saying that culture and ecology make a direct impress on play, but only to the extent that the players are free to make use of it. Just what determines which parts of their culture they make use of is considered later.

Much of this information fits the type of thinking espoused by Berlyne (1962) in which the activation of the organism is seen as a function of the degrees and kinds of stimulus novelty. In those terms, more complex societies, or more freedom to move around in any society, would bring the subject into contact with more stimuli (more novel, complex and conflicting stimuli) which would in turn lead to more voluntary response on his part. Efforts have been made to interpret most of children's play in these terms and more recently to interpret the activities of sportsmen also in terms of their need for such stimulation (Loy and Ingham 1973). While there is undoubted truth to these interpretations, they fail to distinguish between exploration and play. Novel stimuli are certainly arousing and effect exploratory activity. Do they also effect playful activity? One suspects that there is a correlation between the two. That the organism aroused to exploratory activity also plays more. But there is certainly no one-to-one relationship between the two, so other critical variables are apparently involved.

An important consequence of the distinction being made between exploratory mastery and play is that it may serve to sharpen future observation in cross cultural work. The two forms of activity appear to have diverse adaptive consequences as we will argue in the rest of this review.

(2) The management of social power. The child must be not only master of objects and physical setting, he must also be master of the other players, remembering that we use the word "mastery" here for some unspecified degree of sufficient familiarity and freedom from anxiety in the presence of these players. To do this, he must develop techniques of social influence. Between the ages of two and seven years there is a great increase in children's skill in social tactics. In our own observation of playground play we have noticed that children must solve the management problems before they can begin to play. Freedman (1974) has asserted that the differences between the sexes in the development and use of power tactics are common both to primates and man. Females are to be found in smaller groups and to be more concerned with affiliation and grooming. Males are to be found in larger groups and to be concerned with dominance and subordination. Whether such sex differences in dominance interests are cross cultural universals in children's societies has yet to be investigated. Recent work on primates showing great variations in dominance practices contradicts Freedman's assertions about universality. Tindall (1975) has argued that even at the adult level, unless the underlying matters of power are dealt with, which he terms "the hidden curriculum of sport," true play cannot proceed. What we can be sure of is that in every society, although in different ratios, the relationship between power outside the game and power modelled within it, must be resolved.

(3) Management as communication. Knowing how to communicate is one part of knowing one's place in the dominance hierarchy. Following the stimulus of Bateson, there has been an increasing amount of work on the different signal systems (or metacommunications) used within different species to indicate that they intend to play with each other. Thus, Bekoff has contrasted the play of beagles, wolves and coyotes and found that with the beagles these play signals are less critical, whereas they are most critical with the very hostile coyotes. For the coyotes there was no play that was not preceded by the correct signal. It is tempting to infer that more hostile humans have to get their signals very much clearer than less hostile ones. Chevalier-Skolnikoff (1973) has contrasted the various types of face used by macaque, apes and man to indicate the message "This is play." Paradoxically, man sometimes signals that he is about to make a joke by

looking more serious than usual. A key to play at such higher levels of playfulness is indicated by a subtle manipulation of these signals. It is most probable that there are differences cross-culturally in these signals for play.

Cultural Antecedents

Although it is clear in the ethnological data that play usually occurs first in the vicinity of the mother, later with other infants, then with peers and juveniles, there has been no systematic study of the particular kinds of protections that each of these relationships provide nor of the implications that each has for the kind and nature of play which ensues. One would assume some setting of boundaries in each case to ensure safety which would then be followed by specific patterns of stimulation. There is certainly abundant anecdotal evidence, both on the primate and human level, of difference between mother-infant play, toddler play, and the play of peer groups or juveniles.

Typically the investigator has been content to show that there is, in fact, some global relationship between play and other cultural variables. In significant association with play we find included cultural customs, cultural complexity, cultural differentiation, social class, economic or adaptive strategy, family structure, sex role value, child rearing practices, etc. We will deal with some examples of these, keeping in mind that the demonstration of a correlation between the variable and play may justify the view that play is "functional" to the culture in some way, but otherwise tells us very little about the relationship. We may assume either that these variables truly antecede play and are necessary to it, or that these variables and play are implicated in some other pattern of variables which is not determined by this analysis. By and large the research on cultural antecedents has focused on games and sports.

(1) Antecedent Customs. Historically, the favorite cultural explanation for games was their occurrence on ritual occasions. It was argued that the game came into being because it fulfilled a religious or magical function. Thus Simri (1966), after an exhaustive survey of the evidence, came to the conclusion that ball games were originated in most cases as a part of fertility cults. The passing of the ball back and forth, he said, signified a tension between man and the power of nature. Unfortunately for this kind of explanation, there are too many ball games that seem to thrive without this particular set of circumstances. This takes nothing away from the possibility that games of a given sort were used on such ritual occasions, but it does limit the persuasiveness of that type of argument. In his survey of North American tribes, Salter (1967) found games associated with various rituals, such as death, weather, sickness and fertility. Some games were restricted to one ritual, some served for several. Considerable

differences in usage between tribes were also observed. In general he concluded that it was the manner of playing the game rather than the outcome that was believed by the people themselves to have the greatest "spiritual" effect. Games of physical skill and strategy were more often found in these ritual contexts than were games of chance. A more illuminating survey, also by Salter (1967), of records of Australian aboriginal games, showed that out of 94 games the associations with cultural domains were as follows:

Economic pursuits: 29
Social interation: 22
Political activity: 13
Cultural identification: 13
Domestic aspects: 9
Ceremonial rituals: 8

While there is nothing final about Salter's classifications there can be little argument with the major outcome: that games as such can be associated with almost any cultural institution or social purpose. Surveys of the games of Melanesia and Polynesia have led to similar findings. Even when any particular game or sport is studied as, for example, Frederickson's examination of wrestling in various cultures (1960), a similar result follows. In some cultures she found wrestling used as a legal and judicial mechanism for settling the boundaries of rice fields, elsewhere as a part of puberty rites, as a means of selecting a mate, as a demonstration of prestige and power and finally, in ritual context, as a means of ensuring a successful harvest. Other general surveys of the function of games in culture also add up to the view that games and sports are multi-functional and may be found in association with a wide variety of antecedent circumstances. While it is probable that there are some limits to the lability of games and sports, the available evidence provides us with no surety as to what these limits are. All we can say is that they may be found in association with many cultural situations and perform many diverse functions and that, therefore, their explanation cannot be reduced to an account of associated customs.

(2) *Cultural complexity.* To date the most satisfactory empirical correlations between games and culture have been established with indices of cultural complexity. Thus Roberts (1959) and co-workers in a series of cross-cultural studies involving hundreds of tribal cultures, discovered a relationship between the number of *types* of competitive games in a culture and other measures of complexity in that culture, for example, social stratification, political organization etc.

In these papers a game was defined as a "recreational activity characterized by: (a) organized play, (b) competition, (c) two or more sides,

(d) criteria for determining the winner, and (e) agreed upon rules" (Roberts, Arth and Bush, 1959: 597). Three types of games were dealt with, those of physical skill, chance and strategy. Games of *physical skill* were defined as those in which the outcomes are determined by the player's motor activities (marathon races, darts, etc); games of *chance* were those in which the outcome is determined by a guess or some external artifact such as a die or wheel (bingo, roulette); games of *strategy* were those in which the outcome is determined by rational choices (checkers, chess, go, etc.).

There were some cultures on record in which no such competitive games were reported; but there is considerable doubt about the validity of these records, which may well have derived from inadequate ethnographic coverage. The few cultures that were reported to have strategy or chance or both but not physical skill were also regarded as doubtful. Physical skill is so pervasive in world cultures that its absence is suspicious. There are, however, cultures with games of physical skill and strategy but without games of chance.

The results are quite extensive, and cannot be cited here but in summary, cultures which appeared to lack these competitive games were of very low complexity. Those with physical skill only were of simple technology and subsistence economics. Those with games of chance were of wide ranging complexity but noted for various forms of economic and social uncertainty. Those with strategy were noted for their complexity of social organization and severity of child rearing. The most complex of all societies possessed all three types of games. In a subsequent series of studies Roberts and Sutton-Smith (1966) sought to show that these cross cultural correlations could be used to make predictions to game and personality relationships within American society, a validation technique they called *sub-system replication*.

In a reconsideration of the Roberts game and cultural complexity data, Ball (1972) argued that the relationships between games and cultural variables could be handled in a statistically more sophisticated manner by weighting the complexity of each form of game and game combination (change with strategy, physical skill with chance, etc.), rather than simply comparing the absence or presence of the various basic types. Using this ordinal technique he discovered higher relationships between game complexity and variables involving social organization (social class, political integration and size of community), than variables involving economic-technological complexity, although, as he points out, it is not actually easy to differentiate the two. Still his data are important in the light of the classic controversy between those who interpret games in economic terms and those who find their basis in social behavior. In a subsequent study Ball (1974) developed a new scale of gaming based not on game complexity, but on the degree of risk involved in the game. In this scale, games of skill and strategy are at the highest end of the scale and games of chance at the lowest end. He calls this a *game control scale,* the general idea being that at the highest end the players exercise more control over risk and at the lowest more acceptance of the risk involved. His notion of game control is very much like that to be found in the large literature on "locus of control" studies in psychology. What is interesting is that, although the same units of games are used in both the scales, the results are quite different. Once again the game complexity scale covaries with measures of social complexity. But now, the game control scale covaries with economic measures. Ball argues that the game control scale varies negatively with the more fatalistic activities of hunting, fishing and gathering where success depends upon climate, nature, luck, etc. and it varies directly with the more manipulative intervention practices of animal husbandry and agriculture where efforts are made to conquer and control the vicissitudes of the environment (1974: 176).

Ball argues that what is important about the relationship of games to economics, is not the structure of the organization (fishing, occupational specialization, etc.) but the attitude of rationality and control that is associated with it. Not surprisingly games as expressive models are capable of modelling both this aspect of the social structure as well as its sheer complexity.

There are many other evidences of relationships between cultural complexity and the character of games. Most of these are anecdotal, or ethnographic and although they support the general proposition that games model society, they do not really explicate the relationship in any definitive way. In these works, various explanations for the relationships are offered. It is said that more complex games go with more complex cultures because of the higher levels of stimulation offered (as above); because there is simply more money and opportunity for play and for the purchase of more complex apparatuses; because higher status groups induce higher achievement motivation; or because complexity in adult social relationships is modelled by complexity in child social relationships.

In the Whitings' (1975) studies there were a number of other clues about the association between cultural complexity and game complexity.

> "The work on the Nyansongo of Kenya, for example, shows that in cultures where the children are an important cog in a fragile economic machine, there is little scope for them to play. The major job for these children is herding the cattle. It is reported that "fantasy play is almost non-existent among these children" (1963: 173). All that was observed was some fairly desultory physical play such as blocking streams

and swimming, climbing trees, shooting birds with slings, fighting with each other, tussling, chasing and exchanging blows, watching cars on the roads. This is consistent with the studies of Dina Feitelson who reports that in the carpet weaving cultures of the Middle East where children are an economic asset, they also begin early in direct imitation of adult activity and do not indulge greatly in what you or I might call play (1974). The studies of Sarah Smilansky of hierarchical cultural groups in Israel are of similar importance (1967). This does not mean that all relatively simple cultures do not play, because the records of play amongst Australian aboriginal groups are very extensive. What seems to be critical is whether or not the adults have a direct economic need to train the children in highly normalized means of survival. In such cultures the "work ethic" makes real sense. The adults know what must be done to survive and they cannot afford the wasted time of child play. Children are an important cog in the machine. The same position prevailed in England in the early half of the nineteenth century when pauperism was widespread and young children were exploited in mines and factories as a necessary way of helping each family to survive. The Australian aborigines have an open ended environment for their children. There is much they can teach but much also the child must learn through self reliance, including the fact that he must deal with novel circumstances. Play seems to be most relevant in such "open" societies, and much less relevant in "closed ones" (Sutton-Smith, 1974).

Our point at the moment, is that in some cultures and with some segments of complex society, complexity of games cannot develop because the children's labor is needed elsewhere. If we contrast the society studied by the Whitings et al. with the greatest amount of observed play (the Taira of Okinawa) against the society with the least (the Nyansongo of Africa) the following differences also occur:

The family unit in Taira is nuclear, there are private courtyards (so privacy is possible), children can wander in an open and friendly society of other children, they meet more children who are not their kin, there is a school and there are competitive games at the school, there is more interaction with the father, there are more outsiders in the playgroups, children under five are seldom given chores, they do not have to look after younger children to any extent, there are various specialized buildings such as shops, etc., children are self assertive. In the Nyansongo by contrast where subsistence agriculture prevails the children must help with the work, they must help with the care of the younger children. Under the mother's control they help with many chores, getting fuel, cooking. They are members of an extended family and they are discouraged from leaving their immediate home environment. There is no school and no organized play (there is some dirt throwing and roughhousing by boys). There is little interaction with the father. They are very much under the mother's control and dominance. These are all interesting contrasts. It is simply not possible yet for us to know which of these

variables is intrinsic to the difference in play, and which merely an
accidental associate. Intuition suggest the complexity, the play groups,
the privacy, the father stimulation, the lack of chores might all be important contributors (Sutton-Smith, 1974).

(3) Methods of child rearing. The record of parallels between forms
of cultural or social complexity and game complexity is quite substantial. At a minimal level of explanation, we have suggested that
some of the differences cited may reflect only the amount of opportunity available for play by these different groups. Some groups, usually the simpler ones, are needed in the work force and there is less
opportunity for complex play. Traditional female socialization requires the girl to be more concerned with family maintenance and
restricts her freedom for outdoor play. Still, throughout the studies
cited there is hint of a more direct connection between the cultural
structure and the game structure. The ball game-control measure implies that an attitude of readiness for greater risk taking may be engendered in the family or origin. This is consistent with Lüschen's
(1970) finding of relationships between sub-cultural value orientations (for example, of achievement) and interest in sports and it is
consistent with Glassford's explanation of Eskimo games in terms
of basic types of economic strategies (1970). In comparing these
generations of McKenzie Delta Region Eskimoes he found that the
older Eskimoes, following their collaborative economic behavior,
showed a greater interest both in cooperative games and in games
of individual self testing, which were of a low order of complexity
and involved few step sequences. The younger Indians favored more
complex, highly competitive games. Glassford states the difference in
terms of the game theory contrast between "Maximin" strategy
(security before gain) and "Minimax" strategy (gain before security).
Other cultures have also been compared in these cooperative v.
competitive game playing terms.

These value systems, as they apply to games, might be carried by
the character of the family structure: the more authoritarian that
structure, the greater the preference for arbitrary power games. A
number of studies of games have pursued that type of parallel by
contrasting in particular the more authoritarian Mexican family with
the more egalitarian American one. In all these studies, however, we
are once again dealing with implied relationships between the parents,
parent values, child rearing practice and the childrens' play at games,
when in fact we are usually correlating only two points on this continuum, often those at the furthest remove. In a recent interview and
observational study Watson (1977) has attempted to transcend these
lacunae by contrasting the different approaches of lower and middle
class parents to their boys playing Little League Baseball.

Here the children were playing the same game. What Watson found, however, was that parental values and the nature of the boys' play differed markedly between the groups. The lower class parents showed more involvement in the game, emphasized its value as authority over the boys and the importance of the boys' conformity. The lower class boys also emphasized belonging to the group, and developed a much more highly structured and ritualistic game. By contrast, the middle class parents emphasized the learning of cooperation and the middle class boys the display of their skills in a competitive setting. One gets a clear contrast between a game used by the middle class boys as an enhancement of personal status, and a game used by the lower class boy and parent as a means of collective integration into a community. It is not difficult to believe that it is the latter role that games and sports have performed historically in integrating lower class and immigrant groups into the larger system of cultural values; in due course these particular "collective" values have given way to the individualistic ones which are more characteristic of the middle class achiever. The major importance of this study however, is that it shows a consistency between parent values, child values and child practices which is meaningful in terms of the socio-economic status of the parents. It confirms the expectancies which are implicit in most of the studies already cited, that children are directly *socialized* as they play games.

To date, however, the only direct study of child training and games on a large scale cross cultural basis is that carried out by Roberts and Sutton-Smith (1966) and, more recently, Barry and Roberts (1975). In all of these studies significant relationships were established between patterns of child rearing and distinctive types of games. In general the more types of games present the more severe the socialization process. Most illuminating is the recent paper of Roberts and Barry showing that cultures with games of strategy and skill present are more likely to require more industry, obedience and responsibility from their children and yet be low in the inculcation of self-reliance, honesty and trust. The authors conclude that "If games build character, that character may be less than ideal" (1975: 39).

Another reading of the same data could simply imply that in more complex societies more effort must be spent in assessing the motives of other people. Distrust and dishonesty may be associated with learning how to achieve some distance from as well as insight into other people. We have to remember that these characteristics are part of a complex which also includes restraint and obedience as well as industry and responsibility. These characteristics may only imply the importance of avoiding fallibility. Children in Western culture between the ages of four and seven years usually have a critical socialization in not being gullible. In simpler societies, where direct and personal collaboration is often critical for survival, there may, in consequence, be a greater emphasis on trust and honesty, and self reliance is important because survival depends on the physical skills of the individual. In modern society personal physical skill is often irrelevant to survival in the professions, business or politics.

On the basis of the data presented it seems most probable that there is a chain of mediated relationships between types of social or economic institutions and games played. Parents, as members of these institutions, convey their own values to children through the forms of child training that are relevant to their own lives in those institutions (obedience, distrust, etc.). These values are then also modelled by the games they teach and approve of in the children's play. Strategy games require deception of the opponent and distrust of his moves. They also require considerable restraint, obedience to rules, and industrious application of an intellectual sort. Still we must confess the cross cultural study in which all these variables (institutional, parental, child training and method of play) are carefully assessed has not yet appeared.

THE TRANSITION TO PLAY

Although it has been popular to interpret play as a "projection" of its preconditions (stimulus conditions, drive states, aggression, etc.), such explanations are clearly insufficient. We may suppose that play is at least as universal as language, noting that language itself always implies certain sustaining conditions of either a biological or social nature, as the cases of deafness and autism indicate. We may suppose that the potentiality for play is universal even though we do not, therefore, have to hold that children everywhere play the same way or even the same games. As the Whitings' *Six Culture Study* (1975) shows, there are important cultural differences in ways of playing. There is no one language of play or games. There is evidence also of the more obvious fact, that, within our own culture, there are quite different social class as well as individual patterns of play. What needs to be achieved in anthropology is an investigation of these different patterns of play and games and the way in which they enter differentially into their appropriate cultural life. Cultures in which self-reliance is very important (Australian aboriginal, Amerindian), put a great stress on self-testing though not always on contesting. The children spend great amounts of time in the rehearsal of physical skills. Again, cultures in which traditional ways of managing the economy are important emphasize strict imitation. In these cultures, children's play appears to be meticulously imitative. In Western Society however where achievement through symbolic means has become important, children are occupied with creative sociodramas and make-believe constructions, as well as with competitive victories. We would expect the play in each culture to reflect these preferences for certain modes of adaptation over others.

The major implication of these cultural differences is that the greater part of children's play is learned from others. And indeed a host of recent experimentation on the modelling of children's play would support this argument. In a way, such a thesis should be obvious except for the fact that many researchers have assumed for so long that play and games were universally everywhere the same. Many books have been written with that theme in mind. Unfortunately, most of the recent modelling research on play has had as its aim the increase of children's verbal interactions, or their imaginative or fantasizing competences, etc., as assets in normal schooling. There is not really any detailed research on the naturalistic ways in which children *imitate* the play behavior of others. The classic exception is Piaget's (1948) study on marble playing, in which the various steps through which children proceed in their identification with older players are outlined.

In a recent study of the Kpelle, Lancy outlines some of the steps which such modelling can take over a period of time. He says:

> "Make believe play seems to be one step in an alternatively collapsing and expanding process. A child of three spends hours observing a blacksmith at work. A child of four brings his stick down on a rock repeatedly and says he is a blacksmith. A child of eight weaves with his friends elaborate reconstruction of the blacksmith's craft, all in make-believe. The child of ten is a blacksmith's helper in reality; he fetches wood for the forge and no more. At twelve he begins learning the actual skills of smithing, adding a new one every few months or so. At eighteen he is a full fledged blacksmith with his own forge. Parallel patterns can be observed for virtually every class of work" (1976: 75).

In this account of Lancy's we get a hint of the *timing* of the play modelling. A series of cumulative steps is observed. First there are the years of exploratory observation; then there is explor-imitation; then there is the play transformation; then there is real life behavior. The transition to play modelling seems to have its basis in a regular series of earlier steps in the acquisition of understanding through exploration and imitation. There may be some principle here. We recollect that Parten's classic series of play steps outlined in her articles of the 1930's involved first, observation, solitary play, parallel play and then association and cooperation. More recently, Burton White (1973) and others have estimated that approximately 60% of a young child's voluntary time is spent in observational behavior.

It seems probable therefore, that there is some lawfulness in the relationship between the preceding phases of observation, exploratory activity and the transformation into make-believe play. The immediately prior mastery behavior may well be the final stimulus for the play. In the above example, beating a stick in imitation of the blacksmith precedes the make-believe expansion into blacksmith life.

It is possible to suggest therefore that what stimulates the play is the attempt to bring the immediately prior accommodation into accord with early forms of response, a process termed "assimilation" by Piaget (1948). The virtue of this explanation is that it can also take into account the classic Freudian conflict theory, insofar, as what will persist in play are conflicting responses that have been difficult to assimilate on earlier occasions because they are at variance with the responses usually required of the child and rewarded by others. In these terms the most persistent content for play would be long standing conflicts over love, separation, and power. Much of the anecdotal early childhood evidence seems to suggest that this is true.

THE STRUCTURES OF PLAY

Cognitive structure

To this point we have attempted to deal with conditions that occur prior to the occurrence of play. It has been suggested that the child must first be master of his physical and social conditions before he can play. Secondly, it has been argued that those prior processes of attempted mastery may be themselves the immediate instigations for the content of the play itself.

But play, like language or humor, also has its internal organization, and it is to this organization that we now turn. There are many ways in which the structures of play and games can be conceptualized and most of these have already been surveyed.

In more recent work, there is increasing recognition of the view that play itself is a structuring or rule engendering process. Vygotsky (1962) speaks of it as a process of abstraction; Fein (1976) discusses the prototypes formed in play. What seems to be implied in these approaches, is that although the content of play may be derived from past experience (indeed be a projection of it), the organization of play is not. The organization itself is unique and novel in the child's experience, and as such it anticipates the organization the child will use in later problem solving and communication. In a number of recent studies, it appears that the way children play in the second year of life may anticipate the type of pivot grammar which they will use when they begin to speak. There are other evidences that children are developmentally further ahead in play which is additional reason for thinking of play structures as prototypic. They are prototypic because they are anticipatory. In these terms, we may suppose that each culture gives rise in the child to an alphabet of play anticipations.

Unfortunately we do not have any very well described accounts of the "play grammar" used by children of different ages as they develop, nor any accounts of the ways in which these grammars change relative to culture. However there are many descriptions of the general character of the stages through which children proceed in complex societies, and we do have indications that there is no universality of these stages, even in complex societies.

Two free play areas which have come under more systematic study recently have shown their susceptibility to sequential structural analysis. Work on the freely told fantasy stories of children between the ages of 2 and 12 years has shown that they are susceptible to a variety of folkloristic, anthropological and Piagetian paradigms of structural analysis. For example, a system developed by the Marandas (1971) derived from Lévi-Strauss involves a series of four steps in which a story is told (a) about a state of threat or deprivation (b) which if first reacted to unsuccessfully (c) but the threat is then nullified, and finally (d) the total situation is transformed and a hero emerges. The approximate ages at which children tell stories involving these elements in succeeding order are five years, seven years, nine years and eleven years. It is possible to argue on these grounds that story telling habit in childhood is the underbelly of mythology, a point of view quite consistent with Kirk's (1970) analysis of mythology.

Children's play with riddles has also been analyzed in sequential structural terms. It has been shown that riddles can be viewed as exercises in classification, reclassification and multiple classification and that this approach successfully manages about 70% of the riddles although is not sufficient for the description of all varieties, for example, riddle parodies. In more recent work Sutton-Smith, Botvin and Mahony (1976) have sought to show that the development of all expressive systems (play, games, toys, sports, graphics, narrative, plastics, humor, music, etc.) is susceptible to analysis in terms of Piagetian structural approach. Their approach seeks to discover structural constancies across different media, as for example, when at the age of about five years, children play games of reversible characters as in hide and seek, tell stories in which characters reverse their picaresque travels through space quitting and returning to a home base, sing songs of a similar a-b-a palindromic structure, and carry out cognitive operations called "concrete operations" involving the same maintenance of identity through reversible phases. It is pointed out, however, that the use of the Piagetian cognitive system as an analogue for expressive structures in this way involves putting it to quite different functional use, in which the aesthetic issues of tension arousal and resolution as discussed by Berlyne (1960) become central rather than peripheral modes of functioning. In an aesthetic reversible structure the focus is upon the tension generated by the opposing forces within the expressive media: whereas in the type of cognitive structure which Piaget discusses the tension is between the structure and the external referent, so that any tension internal to the system is purely an instrumental method of arriving at an appropriate solution. In addition, the resolution that occurs in the aesthetic structure is also internal to the system. Its functional referent is the audience that entertains it rather than a change of adaptation in the external world.

While structural analyses of fluid play and expressive behavior are relatively novel, (apart from work on children's drawings), structures in games have more often been described. Since game rule structures are overt a great deal of game playing is available, even to the players, and can be reported to the investigator. Current literature on games most often refers to two systems. The first is that of Roberts et al, (1959) which has been previously described. It has been suggested by this group that there is a cultural evolutionary order to these games with physical skill games preceding, the combinations of skill and chance or skill and strategy and with both these preceding the combinations of all three types. It is also believed by this group that this is probably the order of their evolution in child development. It should be noted, however, that this conceptualization of game structure applies only to game outcome determinants. There are many other aspects of games which are not dealt with in this system, and might prove equally fruitful if they could be included. The other system often referred to is that of Caillois (1961) who classifies games into the categories of competition, chance, simulation and vertigo. Within each category there is an evolutionary and developmental order, earlier games are characterized more by lack of control and later games by more precise rule behavior. Thus, in competitive games, at the less organized end there is racing while at the more organized end there is checkers; in chance, there is heads or tails versus lotteries, in simulation, there is make-believe versus theater; in vertigo, there is whirling about versus scuba diving. The advantages and limitations of each of these systems as applied to Sudanese children's games has been decribed by Royce (1972).

Once again, as in the case of the more fluid expressive behaviors of play, it is possible to apply a Piagetian type of analysis to game and sports evolution. As Piaget has pointed out, structural analysis requires an accounting of the systems of self regulation and transformation which govern the entity to be described. In these terms it is possible to divide game evolution into four systems of regulation corresponding to pastimes (Farmer in the Dell), central person games (Tagging), competitive games (Marbles) and sports.

Figure I: Levels of structured interaction in games

Wholeness (type of gestalt)	Self-Regulation (type of coordination)	Transformation (type of reversability)
I. Primary Interactions (Actions)		
Game type A. Prescriptive games		
Level 0 (Farmer in the Dell")	Ritual codes	Ritual reversal
Game type B. Central Person Games		
Level 1 ("Tag")	Uncoordinated roles and actions	Role reversal
Level 2 ("Release")	Uncoordinated roles and actions	Action reversal
II. Secondary Interactions (Signals)		
Game Type C. Competitive Games (Group & Individual)		
Level 3 ("Dodge Ball")	Coordinated actions role & signals in one group	Central role reversal
Level 4 ("Prisoners Base")	Coordination between groups	Group reversal in size
III. Tertiary Interactions (Meta Signals)		
Type D. Sports (Team & Individual)		
Level 5	Coordinated external relationships (coaches–audiences) Coordinated team play with specialists	Team reversals
Level 6 (Batting Games)	Differentiated & coordinated defense	Defense reversal
Level 7 (Kicking Games)	Differentiated & coordinated attack and defense	Attack & defense reversals

From Sutton-Smith, B. "A structural grammar of games and sports," Paper presented at International Society for the Sociology of Sport Meeting, Heidelberg, Oct., 1975.

Each stage is governed by a different system of coordinations. At the first level these are prescriptive, at the second level they involve actions only, at the third level they involve signals as well as actions; and at the fourth level, they involve a meta signal system. In addition each stage involves characteristic forms of transformation. Once again these are at the first stage prescriptive, at the second stage role and action reversals, at the third stage group character and success reversals; and at the fourth stage attach and defense reversals. This tentative system has been applied to both developmental and cultural data with considerable success, in terms of its ability to order children's play chronologically and cross cultural data in terms of complexity. The games of Pygmies (Mbutu), Australian aborigines, and Amerindian hunters involve dominantly the first two levels, whereas American Villagers, Polynesians, Melanesians and Africans show a striking increase in the latter two levels. Within this system sports are defined by the appearance of vicarious groups circumjacent to the game event which are characterized by the marked influence of meta game activity (rule discussion, referees, judges, audience evocation, etc.).

It is not meant to argue that these structural levels imply universality. They imply only that where games evolve in complexity these are useful general systems of analysis. We would suggest however that there is a psychologically universal competence *to game* which like the competence *to speak* is a part of the human condition. While this gaming competence is not used extensively by some tribal groups (pygmies) it is not absent amongst them. In these terms gaming is seen as a generative social procedure whereby oppositions between people, or within a person, are transformed into a set of alternating ludic behaviors. Games in these terms are a cognitive-social device for the management of conflict. As we have seen, the greater the socialization pressure cross-culturally (and implicitly the conflict), the greater the presence of games. While the conflicts can be quite mild, such as an inability to master a set of conditions, as when most children play schooling only for the first several years of schooling, they can also be quite severe as in the case of those adult game addicts who spend most of their life in a driven motivational pursuit of their chess or chance. This then is the ultimate source of games; the binary quality of emotional life and the structuring quality of mind which allows it to reconcile these ambivalent pressures by stating them as alternatives within one system of ludic behaviors, the game. In these terms a game always involves an opposition between forces and proceeds according to rules which allow the oppositions to be resolved in favor of one or other of the parties. A definition at this level can include mother-infant finger play as well as football.

Conative Reversals

There are two other aspects of play as structure that are essential to any adequate conceptualization. These are the conative and affective aspects. When it was stated above that a state of conflict is translated in play into a set of oppositions, the important thing about those oppositions is that they are reversible. Reversibility is a key to play just as it is to many rituals. It is useful to unite the concept of play with the anthropological concept of ritual. In fact, play may be thought of as a miniature rite. Victor Turner (1974) has discussed ritual in terms of Van Gennep's rites of passage, that is as transition and reintegration. Our first section on antecedents may be thought of as dealing with separation. There we were concerned with getting the play started. The present section deals with the transitional yet circumscribed state which Turner calls liminal. In these terms the player goes apart from society into a special sphere defined, as Huizinga (1949, p. 28) does, by its limits of time and place, its rules and its being different. Here, as in all other rituals, the conditions of society may be reversed (Babcock-Abrahams, 1978). Those who are lowly may become high and those who are high may be debased. Above we have discussed the structural sequencing of these reversals in games of increasing complexity. In play there is at first a reversal of intention (one imposes oneself on external conditions, rather than being subject to them); then when a group plays together running their own playtime—there is a reversal of social control (they, not their parents are in charge). Next, about age three when they learn to take turns, there can be a reversal of turn taking (taking turns at being first!). When proper games begin, role reversal is essential as well as the other kinds discussed in the prior section. In competitive games tactical reversals become pronounced as a way of reaching success. By that age also children become capable of engineering new games, so intentional rule reversal is possible, although it has always been present idiosyncratically in cheating. Cheating is an innovative source of change with players of all ages.

From a cultural point of view, however, perhaps the most interesting form of play reversal occurs when the reversals inherent in the game dictate new adaptations in the culture. Conventional sociological theorizing contends that the culture dominates the game proclivities of the individual. Actual examples show that this is sometimes true and sometimes not. The game may bolster other social systems or it may reverse them. If a game is introduced into a culture which is not in a state of uncertainty, the game will tend to be adapted to local norms. Maccoby et al. (1964) illustrate the way in which an egalitarian chasing game from the U.S.A. which was introduced into a Mexican village became, over a short period of time, converted into an authoritarian form, similar to other local games with which the players were more comfortable. On the other hand, there were also examples in which a game introduced from outside is used by one group to express its dissatisfaction with local group norms. Sometimes the game is merely an expressive form of dissatisfaction—a compensation if you will. Sometimes the game becomes a rallying point and is actually the focus for a realistic revolt against the prevailing institutions.

It is in these latter cases, where there is some existing cultural conflict, that the different or alternative form suggested by the game can become the basis for a change in cultural customs. In a way we do not need any esoteric examples from the literature to illustrate the way in which games change culture. The history of modern sports and the changes they have brought first to college life and later to the lives of the masses is an indication of vast cultural change. It is reasonable to argue that they brought a message of the rationality of personal and corporate achievement to many who had not hitherto considered themselves within this domain. In due course this same ideology became normative and sports became more conservative in import. However we still find that for members of lower social classes sports can still have that life transforming function, whereas for established members of the culture they do not. By way of warning it should be mentioned here that the present notion that game participation can change the life of an individual, or of a group of individuals within the larger culture, is not meant to imply that it normally will. The relationship between play and life is probabilistic not irrevocably rehearsive. Play potentiates; it does not itself actualize. Thus the Olympic Games make theoretically potential a universal world of cooperating nations. Some of their sponsors envisage that possibility. They create a fantasy of unity. The relationship of that fantasy to what may actually happen is however determined, even overwhelmed, by many other variables. But at least the play is a communicative form that can be understood by many who were formerly completely entrapped within their more parochial boundaries.

We thus argue that play as conative reversal is the seed of alternative attitudes to society. In a paper, "Games of order and disorder" we have described how even the very youngest children assimilate into their play the first opposition, that of order and anarchy. Games of all circling together then falling down together, or of building blocks and smashing them down, they make fluid and reversible these two fundamental aspects of the children's society. Nursery school teachers frequently find these anarchic aspects quite chaotic, because they do not realize the consensual and collaborative achievements that are also involved.

Affective Qualities

It has been usual to identify the emotional quality of play as being that of fun. It is doubtful if this is correct. In a series of studies of players and workers, from rock climbers to surgeons, Csikszentmihalyi (1974) has sought to identify the phenomenology of the player. What stands out is their involvement in what he calls the "flow" of activity. He says that they are very aware but not self-conscious; they are in control of the situation but nevertheless in a state of uncertainty. The stimulus field is limited; the feedback is immediate. From many hours of watching young children at play we have elsewhere identified the same affective state as one of *vivification*. The feeling of euphoria seems to be an affective state that arises only after periods of vivid involvement or in between such states. The same notion of vividness is conveyed in Freudian descriptions of primary process; it is even conveyed by linguistic descriptions of play as "light and quick movement". According to Huizinga's survey of linguistic usages cross culturally this is about the most general connotation that the word play receives in different languages.

We may summarize these comments on the cognitive, conative and affective aspects of play by attempting a structural definition appropriate to the materials that have been presented. First, it is clear from the discussion of antecedents that we define play only as a subset of voluntary behavior. There is much voluntary behavior (exploration, etc.) that is not play. Essential to play is the reversal of the usual contingencies of power. The player is always in charge. In addition, when play begins the player's integration of his life experiences is unique to him, and that organization is a forecast of his future competencies, so we call it a prototypic organization. Again what seems to draw the player into these unique autonomous experiences are the vivid and summarized living that is possible within them. Briefly then *play may be defined* as a subset of voluntary behaviors in which the individual reverses the usual contingencies of power by enacting prototypes of experience in a vivifying manner. In these terms *games are themselves* defined as a subset of play in which a rule governed system of oppositional lucid behaviors, mediated through different phases of activity or playing sides produces a disequilibrial outcome. *Sports are defined* as that subset of games in which meta-game participation of vicarious groups exercises an influence over the outcome.

These are meant to be basically structural, not functional distinctions. It is clear, however, from the review of antecedents presented that we view a definition of play and games relationship to antecedents as involving a response in both cases to either modelled behavior or prior states of conflict. Play arises out of stimulus discrepancy or affective or cognitive conflict. Whether the conflict is the epistemic stimulus couched kind discussed by Berlyne, the more affective variety discussed in psychoanalysis, or in the cognitive disequilbria of Piaget, we are of the view that the motivation for play lies at that point. Although as we are trying to make very clear, that motivation does not itself explain the autonomous nature of play as a processing and generative language is not determined by the content of speech although that content may be its occasion for emergence. Similarly play structure is not explained by conflict, although such conflict may be the occasion for its emergence.

REFERENCES

Aldis, O. 1975. *Play–Fighting.* New York: Academic Press.

Babcock-Abraham, B. 1978. *The Reversible World: Essay on Symbolic Inversion.*

Ball, D. 1974. Control versus complexity—continuities in the scaling of gaming. *Pacific Sociological Review.* 17, 1:167–184.

Barry III, H. and J.M. Roberts. 1972. Infant socialization and games of chance. *Ethnology.* 11, 2:296–308.

Berlyne, D.E. 1960. *Conflict, Arousal and Curiosity.* New York: McGraw-Hill.

Bruner, J. 1972. Nature and uses of immaturity. *American Psychologist.* 27, 1:1–22.

Bruner, J. 1973. Organization of early skilled action. *Child development.* 44, 1:1–11.

Bruner, J. 1975. Play is serious business. *Psychology Today.* 8,81–83.

Caillois, R. 1961. *Man, Play and Games.* Glencoe, Ill.: Free Press.

Chevalier-Skolnikoff, Susanne. 1973. The primate play face: A possible key to the determinants and evolution of play. Paper. *Meeting of the American Anthropological Association.* New Orleans.

Csikszentmihalyi, M. 1974. *Flow: Studies of Enjoyment.* P.H.S. Report. University of Chicago.

Dansky, J.L. and I.W. Silverman. 1973. Effects of play on associative fluency in preschool children. *Developmental Psychology.* 9, 1:38–43.

Erikson, E.H. 1972. *Childhood and Society.* New York: Norton Books.

Fein, R. 1976. The social competence of play. Paper, *A.E.R.A.–Meeting,* San Francisco.

Feitelson, D. and G.S. Ross. 1973. The neglected factor play. *Human Development* 16, 2:202–223.

Frederickson, F.S. 1960. Sports and the cultures of man. Pp. 633–646 in W. Johnson, ed. *Science and Medicine of Exercise and Sport.* New York: Harper.

Freedman, D.G. 1974. *Human Infancy, an Evolutionary Perspective.* New York: Wiley.

Glassford, G. 1970. Organization of games and adaptive strategies of the Canadian Eskimo. Pp. 70–84 in G. Lüschen, *op.cit.*

Groos, K. 1898. *The Play of Animals.* New York: Appleton.

Groos, K. 1916. *The Play of Man.* New York: Appleton.

Herron, R. and B. Sutton-Smith. 1971. *Child's Play.* New York: Wiley.

Huizinga, J. 1949. *Homo Ludens: A Study of the Play Element in Culture.* London: Routledge and Kegan Paul. (orig. 1938).

Hutt, C. 1971. Exploration and play in children. Pp. 231–51 in R.E. Herron and B. Sutton-Smith, eds. *Child's Play*. New York: Wiley.

Kirk, G.S. 1970. *Myth*. London: Cambridge University Press.

Lancy, D.F. 1976. The play behavior of Kpelle children during rapid cultural change. Pp. 72–79 in D. Lancy and B. Tindall, eds. *The Anthropological Study of Play*. Cornwall, N.Y.: Leisure Press.

Loy, J.W. and A.G. Ingham. 1973. Play, games and sports in the psychosocial development of children and youth. In L. Rarick, ed. *Physical Activity*. New York: Academic Press.

Lüschen, G. 1970. *The Cross-Cultural Analysis of Sport and Games*. Champaign, Ill.: Stipes.

Maccoby, M. et al. 1964. Games and social character in a Mexican village. *Psychiatry* 27,1:150–162.

Main, M. 1975. Exploration, play, cognitive functions and the mother-child relationship. Paper. *Society for the Research in Child Development*. Denver, Colo.

Maranda, E.K. and P. 1971. *Structural Models in Folklore and Transformational Essays*. The Hague: Mouton.

Nicolich, L.M. 1975. A longitudinal study of representational play in relation to spontaneous imitation and development of multi-word utterances. *Final Report, National Institute of Education*. Rutgers, N.J.

Overton, W.F. and J.P. Jackson. 1973. The representation of imagined objects in action sequences: A developmental study. *Child Development*. 44, 2:309–314.

Parten, M. 1933. Social play among preschool children. *J.Abnormal Social Psychology* 28,1:136–147.

Peterson, L. 1976. Constraining the child's storytelling situation: Does it make a difference. Ph.D. Thesis. New York: Columbia University.

Piaget, J. 1948. *The Moral Judgment of the Child*. Glencoe, Ill.: Free Press. (orig. 1932).

Reynolds, P. 1972. Play, language and human evolution. Paper, *AAAS-Meeting*, Washington, D.C.

Roberts, J.M.; Arth, M.J. and R.R. Bush. 1959. Games in culture. *American Anthropologist*. 61:597–605.

Roberts, J.M. and H. Barry III. 1975. Inculcated traits and games type combinations: A cross-cultural view. Paper. *American Medical Association*. Atlantic Beach.

Roberts, J.M. and B. Sutton-Smith. 1962. Child training and game involvement. *Ethnology* 1,1:166–185.

Roberts, J.M. and B. Sutton-Smith. 1966. Cross-cultural correlates of games of chance. *Behavior Science Notes*. 3:131–144.

Royce, J. 1972. 'Validation' of game classification models against Sudanes children's games. *Anthropos* 67,1:138–151.

Rüssel, A. 1953. *Das Kinderspiel*. Munich: Beck.

Salter, M. 1967. *Games and Pastimes of the Australian Aboriginals*. Edmonton: University of Alberta.

Scheuerl, H. 1962. *Das Spiel* Weinheim: Beltz.

Simri, U. 1966. *The Religious and Magical Functions of Ball Games in Various Cultures*. PhD-Thesis. Morgantown: West Virginia University.

Smilansky, M. and S. 1967. Intellectual advancement in culturally disadvantaged children *Int.Review Education* 13,4:410–431.

Sutton-Smith, B. 1972. *The Folk Games of Children.* Austin: University of Texas Press.

Sutton-Smith, B. 1974. The anthropology of play. *Association for the Anthropological Study of Play.* Volume 2:8–12.

Sutton-Smith, B. 1975. Play as adaptive potentiation. *Sportwissenschaft.* 5, 1: 103–118.

Sutton-Smith, B. 1978. *Die Dialoktik des Spiels.* Schorndorf: Hofmann.

Sutton-Smith, B. ed. 1979. *Play and Learning.* New York: Gardner Press.

Sutton-Smith, B.; Botvin, G. and D. Mahony. 1976. Developmental structures in fantasy narratives. *Human Development* 19,1:1–13.

Tindall, B.A. 1975. Ethnography and the hidden curriculum in sport. *Behavioral and Social Science Teacher* 2:

Turner, V. 1974. *Dramas, Fields and Metaphors.* Ithaca: Cornell University Press.

Vygotsky, L.S. 1962. *Thought and Language.* London: Cambridge University Press.

Watson, G. 1977. Games, socialization and parental values. *IRSS* 12,1:17–48.

White, B.L. 1973. *Experience and Environment.* Englewood Cliffs: Prentice-Hall.

Whiting, B.B. and J. Whiting. 1975. *Children of Six Cultures, a Psychocultural analysis.* Cambridge, Mass.: Harvard University Press.

MOTIVATIONAL THEORIES OF PLAY: DEFINITIONS AND EXPLANATIONS

Michael J. Ellis

Sport and Physical Education have benefited from the accumulation of a body of knowledge that supports the activities of those involved with them. A firmer knowledge base has been acquired. As a result the practices of those professing to be physical educators have become less dependent on intuition and dogma, and more firmly rooted in objective knowledge and theory. The continued professionalization of the practitioners in the field depends on the establishment of theories explaining and predicting the phenomena associated with people engaging in sport, dance, exercise and play.

One of the major and fundamental theoretical questions for the professional in this field must be, "Why do people play?" That question has been asked for centuries and the literature abounds with attempted answers. Yet there is dangerously little questioning of the answers at the moment in both the fields of research and practice. It is important for professionals dealing with the play of the peoples of the world to make serious attempts to understand the motives for the great variety of human play behavior.

Theories are important because they are simplifying explanations of previous experiences and data that seem to have the capacity to predict what will come about. Therefore, a theory is good if it seems to explain and predict phenomena. The more inclusively and reliably it does this, the more useful it is as a tool. A theory has no worth beyond its value to promote insights into and predictions of outcomes. A theory, then, is an ordered way of moving from previous experience into the future.

The question, "Why do we play?" has spawned many theories that try to establish the basic nature and motive for play. Our job is to evaluate these theories and to put them to work so that as the result of analysis they become more reliable, explain more behavior, and allow an increasing professionalism in our search for better leisure opportunities for everyone.

At my last count there were at least 15 identifiable theories purporting to explain why people play. Most of them are old, some of them are mutually exclusive, and they all live on. As a field we have not yet had the courage to face the reality that most of those theories are unacceptable as guides to action in research and in practice. They have lingered on, presumably because they were seen as innocuous cognitive artifacts cluttering only the introductory chapters of our textbooks. However, they clutter our professionalism. It is time to eliminate as many of them as we can so that we can get on with the task of determining why people play. That new knowledge may then contribute to the management of sport, exercise, dance and play.

Play Definitions.
"Play" as a word is often used to mean the trivial activities of the young and is not applied to the leisure activities of adults. In this paper the meaning of the word is extended to apply to activities that are not immediately critical for the survival of any human—young or old—and to simplify the problem the play of animals will be ignored. Play itself has always proved difficult to define and this entire article could be devoted to arguing the toss on definitions of play.

Despite our verbal difficulties we can, without trying to get to the semantic roots of the problem, recognize play when we see it. A dog can recognize when its master is playful and vice versa, and this capacity leads logically to a major subclass of definitions of play. These are definitions of the attributes of the behavior called play. Such explantations characterize play as behavior used out of context, that is, incomplete and usually emitted by the young. Play behavior seems to produce the continuation of a behavior rather than its completion (*Poole* 1966; *Loizos* 1966).

This method of defining play is usually applied to animals, but can be applied to humans. These definitions may vary across circumstances and they require extensive analysis and observation to arrive at a definitive answer concerning the content of play. This approach seems circular in fact. For the contents of play to be analyzed the observer must already be able to recognize the characteristics that set playful behavior apart. The process then becomes one of establishing what particular people do when they are recognizably playing.

The characteristics of one playful response that engender a playful response in another, rather than an earnest one, is communicated by gesture, intonation, posture. The grin, the jocular tone of voice, the wagging tail are all meta-communications containing information about the mode of the upcoming interaction (*Bateson* 1956). By experience and example we learn how to interpret the messages from others concerning their intentions. It is the same process that allows those that define play by content to proceed. Thus it can be seen that even though some observers claim to define play by content they are only describing what happens once they have decided an interaction is playful. Their decision depends on the signals broadcast by the players concerning their motives. Thus, the process of defining play by content is rooted in motivation.

The other major method of defining play is directly dependent on the imputation of the motive of the player. For example, "Play is instinctive," is such a definition. This kind of statement takes the general form "Play is the behavior motivated by...." In these definitions the uncertainty concerning the nature of play is shifted down the sentence and onto its motive. Evaluation of these definitions must wait until the various motives that vie for placement at the end of the sentence have been considered. This kind of definition of play is only as good as the delineation of its motive.

THE MOTIVES FOR PLAY

Let us consider the predictive value of the various theories of motivation to play that could be placed in the general form of the definition. Each of the theories or motives should be tested by each professional who should ask whether it helps in the processes of his profession. Each worker must assume responsibility for evaluating the worth of these cognitive tools to him as a professional. Those that seem to explain and predict the behavioral phenomena of interest should be kept. Those that do not should be eliminated.

Play theories, or the explanations of the cause of play, cannot all be considered in detail here, that required a book (*Ellis* 1973). However, they can be classified into groups and their essential evaluations can be achieved by the tabulation of concise statements of their assumptions and criticisms (*Gilmore* 1966; *Ellis* 1973). With limited space this seems the most sensible way of arriving at a judgment on the worth of a theory or explanation.

Classical Theories of Play

The best known class of play theories are the classical theories that are regularly treated in introductory texts and courses in the field. The classical theories of surplus energy, instinct, recapitulation, preparation, and relaxation originated before the turn of the century. They were all concerned with those elements in the nature of man in general that led him to play and with the purposes that play served. They were not concerned with differences between people and peoples but were really only global armchair explanations for behavior that was not work. Despite the fact that their tenets often led to testable hypotheses they have not spawned much research but they often appear in our arguments for the constructive use of leisure and in the justifications for sport.

Table 1: CLASSICAL THEORIES OF PLAY

Name	Play is caused:	This explanation assumes:	It can be criticized because:	Verdict:
Surplus Energy I	by the existence of energy surplus to the needs of survival.	1. energy is stored 2. storage is limited 3. excess energy must be expended. 4. expenditure is made on play, by definition.	1. children play when fatigued or to the point of fatigue so a surplus is not necessary for play. 2. the process of evolution should have tailored the energy available to the energy required.	Inadequate
Surplus Energy II	by increased tendency to respond after a period of response deprivation.	1. response systems of the body all have a tendency to respond. 2. response threshold is lowered by a period of leisure.	after periods of disuse, eventually all available responses should reach a low enough threshold to be discharged. Some responses available to the person are never used.	Inadequate as written but has been incorporated in learning theory.
Instinct	by the inheritance of unlearned capacities to emit playful acts.	1. the determinants of our behavior are inherited in the same way that we inherit the genetic code that determines our structure. 2. that some of those determinants cause play.	1. it ignores the obvious capacity of the person to learn new responses that we classify as play. 2. the facile naming of an instinct for each class of observed behavior is to do no more than to say "Because there is play, there must be a cause which we will call an instinct."	Inadequate

Preparation	by the efforts of the player to prepare for later life.	1. play is omitted only by persons preparing for new ways of responding, and in general in the preserve of the young. 2. the player can predict what kinds of responses will be critical later. 3. instincts governing this are inherited imperfectly and are practiced during youth.	1. it requires that the player inherit the capacity to predict which responses will be critical. This requires the inheritance of information about the future. 2. play occurs most frequently in animals that live in rapidly changing circumstances. 3. when acceptably prepared the person should stop playing.	Inadequate. However play may have by-products that are advantageous later.
Recapitulation	by the player recapitulating the history of the species during its development.	1. critical behaviors occurring during evolution of man are encoded for inheritance. 2. person emits some approximation to all these behaviors during his development. 3. since they are currently irrelevant they are play. 4. the stages in our evolution will be followed in the individual's development.	1. no linear progression in our play development that seems to mirror the development of a species. At one point, late boyhood and adolescence, there may be similarity between sports and games and the components of hunting, chasing, fighting, etc., but before and after there seems little relation. 2. does not explain play activities dependent on our advanced technology.	Inadequate
Relaxation	the need for an individual to emit responses other than those used in work to allow recuperation.	1. players work 2. play involves the emission of responses different to those of work.	1. it does not explain the play of children — unless they are clearly working some part of their day. 2. does not explain the use in play of activities also used in work.	Inadequate

484   *Play, Sport and Personality*

Table 1 lays out as a skeleton the essential arguments and contents of these classical theories. It can be seen that they are all open to serious criticism. In the absence of much data in the literature to support them this analysis would reject them all as worthy theoretical bases for the leisure professions.

The intriguing question is why have they continued for so long unchallenged? A major explanation for the survival of these theories must rest on the extent to which they seemed to explain the puzzling behavior of play to the old thinkers. Also, recently it has not been considered very important to challenge the theories of play. Play, in a puritan setting, was considered trivial and did not attract much attention from established disciplines. However, times have changed and many are now concerned directly with the play of man and the search for satisfactory theoretical systems to underpin our practices.

Recent Theories of Play

The period after the turn of the century spawned many additional explanations of play. These recent theories, generalization, compensation, catharsis, psychoanalytic, development and learning, had a different character than the classical theories. They were concerned with the content of the play behavior and attempted to link antecedent and subsequent events, causes and effects in the stream of behavior. Thus, they attempt to account for the play of an individual. These theories are more difficult to reduce to a simple taxonomy because they have not been winnowed by the passage of time. They have not been simplified and compacted. Some of them are partial explanations and they are still essentially in the process of being worked out. However, they deserve similar consideration (see Table 2).

The tabulation for the recent theories does not allow such a simple summary as did the classical theories. Only one theory, catharsis, can be rejected and then only within the limitations that it is used to purge unacceptable aggression. Other emotions and behaviors might be disorganizing, subject to frustration of expression, and be satisfactorily expressed via substitute behavior. No evidence for its value for other behaviors is available. However, the picture is clear for hostility catharsis which the field has traditionally used to validate its use of contact sports *(Berkowitz* 1969; *Mallick and McCandless* 1966).

The explanations of generalization and compensation stem from notions that play is a generalization of or a compensation for behaviors emitted at work. These notions are still being tested yet they have some appeal since work still figures as a powerful influence in the lives of schoolchildren and adults. They can explain some aspects of leisure behavior for all but preschoolers and retirees. However, these notions at heart exhibit the same problems as play. Work has been operationalized as the responses occurring either during sold-time or sold directly. Yet clearly work is complexly motivated and until these simplistic definitions of work are passed over in favor of definitions based upon the intentions of the worker these approaches are of limited value.

Psychoanalytic theories exist that seem to contain two variants, one involving coming to terms with experiences and the other purging them. There is no clear-cut recognition of this contradiction, and as yet there is no clear-cut contribution to the play behavior of people not driven to play by an unpleasant experience. To the extent that the client is "normal" and is not "beyond the pleasure principle" then the psychoanalytic view of play behavior does not seem helpful —particularly since it does not look forward to predict future behavior. We await clear formulations that permit public test before this kind of explanation can serve as a theoretical base for our practice.

The psychoanalytic theories which are concerned with actions beyond the pleasure principle are counterbalanced by the opposite view of play as learned behavior. This view of play is a powerful one and stems directly from theories of learning which claim that the organism acts in such a way as to maximize the likelihood of pleasant outcomes and vice versa. Thus, the child plays because he learns to play. This is related to developmentalist views of play which claim that play produces learning in the sense that as the child accumulates experiences he becomes more complex and eventually approximates adult behavior. The stages or changes in the characteristics of a child as it grows older follow a common path. These characteristics modify the content of the behavior and need to be taken into account.

To summarize, some of these explanations seem to be useful. However, they are limited to certain circumstances and to the previous experiences of an individual. Thus, they only have explanatory power if you know something about the subject.

Modern Theories of Play

There are only two modern theories of play: play as competence motivation (*White* 1959) and play as information seeking (*Ellis* 1973). They are quite modern and have their origin in objective data rather than in the armchair. This does not necessarily make them better in the end, but they get a better start. They are both concerned with the existence of surplus behaviors that seem to be omitted even though the emitter does not seem to be driven by the necessary responses of survival. They try to answer the question why do children, adults or animals continue to behave when their needs are apparently all satisfied.

Play as information-seeking is the most recent attempt at explaining play and has been elaborated upon swiftly to the point where it can be used to make predictions and be tested. In essence, play is

Table 2: RECENT THEORIES OF PLAY

Name	Play is caused:	This explanation assumes:	It can be criticized because:	Verdict:
Generalization	by the players using in their play experiences that have been rewarding at work.	1. that there are at least two separable categories of behavior. 2. that the players transfer to play or leisure, behaviors that are rewarded in another setting. 3. that to be useful we understand what rewards an individual at work.	1. it seems to exclude play of preschool children. 2. it assumes that at least some aspects of work are rewarding.	1. Data tend to support this as a view of leisure behavior preferences in adults, providing a chronic or long-term view of their behavior is taken. 2. We must wait for more data.
Compensation	by players using their play to satisfy psychic needs not satisfied in or generated by the working behaviors.	1. that there are at least two separable categories of behavior. 2. the player avoids in play or leisure behaviors that are unsatisfying in the work setting. 3. the player selects leisure experiences that meet his psychic needs. 4. that to be useful we understand the mismatch of needs and satisfactions in the work setting (or vice versa).	1. it seems to exclude the play of preschool children. 2. it assumes that work is damaging, does not satisfy some needs.	1. Such data as exists gives support to the idea in the long term. 2. We must wait for data.
Catharsis	in part by the need to express disorganizing emotions in a harmless way by transferring them to socially sanctioned activity. This concept has almost entirely been limited to questions of aggression, and will be so here.	1. frustration of an intention engenders hostility towards the frustrator. 2. this hostility must be expressed to reduce psychic and physiological stress. 3. this frustration or hostility can be redirected to another activity.	1. it is a partial explanation for only the compensatory behavior engendered by hostility. 2. the data show conclusively that sanctioning aggression increases it. 3. the planning of activities to provide outlets for aggression constitutes its sanctioning.	As an explanation for some aspects of play and leisure pursuits (usually vigorous games), it has no support in the aggression literature.

Psycho-analytic I	in part by the players repeating in a playful form strongly unpleasant experiences, thereby reducing their seriousness and allowing their assimilation.	1. simulating unpleasant experiences in another setting reduces the unpleasantness of their residual effects.	both ignore play that is not presumed to be motivated by the need to eliminate the products of strongly unpleasant experiences.	There are few data, or conceptual analyses of these tenets. The work is strongly clinical and concerned with individuals. We need clear formulations of what the psycho-analytic view of play is, so that it may be tested.
Psycho-analytic II	in part by the player during play reversing his role as the passive recipient of strongly unpleasant experience, and actively mastering another recipient in a similar way, thus purging the unpleasant effects.	1. achieving mastery, even in a simulated experience, allows the elimination of the products of an unpleasant experiences by passing similar experiences on to other beings or objects.		
Developmentalism	the way in which a child's mind develops. Thus play is caused by the growth of the child's intellect and is conditioned by it. That play occurs when the child can impose on reality his own conceptions and constraints.	1. that play involves the intellect. 2. that as a result of play, the intellect increases in complexity. 3. that this process in the human can be separated into stages. 4. that children pass through these stages in order.	1. it doesn't account for play when and if the intellect ceases to develop.	The best known thinker in this school is Piaget who is concerned with the cause of play, but more importantly with its content. This concept must be integrated with a more precise theory of motivation and learning.
Learning	the normal processes that produce learning.	1. the child acts to increase the probability of pleasant events. 2. the child acts to decrease the probability of unpleasant events. 3. the environment is a complex of pleasant and unpleasant effects. 4. the environment selects and energizes the play behaviors of its tenants.	1. it doesn't account for behavior in situations where there are no apparent consequences. (However this theory would maintain that there are no such settings.) 2. it doesn't account for the original contributions to behaviors made by an individual's genetic inheritance.	Cultural, sub-cultural and familial differences support the view that quantity and content of play behavior is learned. The theory can account for the content of an individual's play if not his inherited tendencies to play.

seen as a class of behaviors that are concerned with maintaining the flow of information through the organism (*Ellis* 1978). It is speculated that the mechanisms responsible for modulating this behavior involve arousal mechanisms and the maintenance of optimal arousal levels. Some of the data are reviewed in *Ellis* (1973, 1978).

The assumptions of this explanation for play behavior are fundamentally different from those of the traditional homeostatic drives which assume that the organism acts to reduce the level of stimulation created by a need like hunger, thirst, etc. The older drives depend on the assumption that the natural state of the organism is quiescence, and consequently they have always had difficulty explaining surplus behavior.

Need-reduction theorists always had to postulate a further unsatisfied need to drive manipulatory, exploratory, and play behaviors. They now have one—the need to maintain arousal. However, the new need is fundamentally different in that it leads to increases in stimulation. The postulation of an incessant need for interaction with the environment in a way that produces arousing stimuli is an attractive way to handle the surplus behaviors so obviously and continuously emitted by man.

The kinds of stimuli that are arousing, those that are novel, complex, or dissonant, can only remain so for a while. There comes a time when this information load is exhausted and when they cease to be arousing. Then the need for continued stimulation causes the person, or animal, to search for and generate other interactions that are stimulating. As the process proceeds the person becomes more complex and so do the necessary interactions. This idea draws attention to the fact that when the more potent needs of survival have been satisfied the organism is then driven into interactions of increasing complexity with the environment. This is an optimistic statement for recreation professionals. The natural state of man requires arousing interactions with the environment, and to the extent that these are not met by work, they will have to be met through play. More simply put, the physical education and recreation professional is involved in facilitating the delivery of opportunities for man to optimize his arousal level.

Competence motivation was advanced early in the process of the theorizing that led to a modern theory. It is possible to make a case that competence motivation is merely a subclass of arousal-seeking behaviors. Since it has not been elaborated, it may go the way of many theories and wane as others wax. At this time it does not add anything to the arousal-seeking model (see Table 3).

At this point the question becomes what is it about information bearing interactions that is rewarding. Looking backward across the history of our evolution it can be seen that we have emerged from a

Table 3: MODERN THEORIES

Name	Play is caused:	This explanation assumes:	It can be criticized because:	Verdict:
Play as Arousal-Seeking	by the need to generate interactions with the environment or self that elevates arousal (level of interest or stimulation) towards the optimal for the individual.	1. stimuli vary in their capacity to arouse. 2. there is a need for optimal arousal. 3. change in arousal towards optimal is pleasant. 4. the organism learns the behaviors that result in that feeling and vice versa.	1. it is very general and handles equally well questions of work and play. In fact it questions the validity of separating work from play.	Together with learning, and developmentalism as a package is a very powerful theoretical base for our professional operations.
Competence/ Effectance	by a need to produce effects in the environment. Such effects demonstrate competence and result in feelings of effectance.	1. demonstration of competence leads to feelings of effectance. 2. effectance is pleasant. 3. effectance increases the probability of tests of competence.	1. for the organism to constantly test whether it can still competently produce an effect seems to require uncertainty as to the outcome. Uncertainty or information seem to be the very attributes of stimuli that are arousing. 2. thus it can be argued that competence/effectance behavior is a kind of arousal-seeking.	Is best subsumed as an explanation that developed as theorists moved towards the arousal seeking model.

process whereby we as a species (and like many others) have become behaviorally more complex. We exploit changing circumstances in an entrepreneurial sense. The propensity to be curious, to explore, investigate, manipulate and wonder, have conveyed a selected advantage upon our forebears. Clearly, our propensity to play and the mechanisms that sustain it, have been constructed by the evolutionary process.

The nature of the reward, a feeling of enjoyment, and the circumstances which make for it, have been elegantly developed by *Csikszentmihalyi* (1975). Here the interaction between the challenges (questions, problems, uncertainties) of a setting and the ability of the person to deal with them have been explored in chess players, surgeons, climbers, and sports people. The process of being instrumental and creatively dealing with the flow of information leads to enjoyment. *Csikszentmihalyi* dissects the affect that results. It is intense, time-free and where, for the interlude, the player is merged or at one with the environment. These *FLOW* experiences, as they were labelled, are quite often given as the sustaining experiences of individual's lives. They are highly prized.

The arousal or information seeking model and the *FLOW* experience belong together. The former concentrates on the circumstances, the input, and the play behavior, the output, while the latter attends to the subjective interpretations of the affective state that results from successful playful episodes.

Integrating the Theories

Three of the theories that have survived this winnowing process can be integrated. Piaget's developmentalism, play as learned responding, and the arousal-seeking model can be fitted together. Moving from the general model to the more specific, the information-seeking model provides us with a motive for the continuance of surplus behavior. In fact, we can now no longer call it that. The organism has a need for optimal arousal and arousal-elevating behaviors are necessary not surplus or trivial. In fact the research on sensory deprivation and the use of solitary confinement as the most serious punishment attests to its importance.

As a result of reinforcement of certain behaviors the organism learns to emit the responses that will generate optimal arousal without adverse side effects. Thus, in any particular culture, setting, or family, etc., there will be a host of contingencies that will pressure the choice of the interactions that will be learned in response to the joint action of the drive for stimulation and the drive to avoid adverse outcomes.

Finally, in the case of the child, a further restraint is imposed on the interactions that can produce appropriate arousal—the cognitive complexity of the child. Early in its life it has fewer experiences and knowledges, and simple interactions are arousing. The nature of the upward passage in individual complexity seems to be essentially common across children. This common pathway of development has identifiable attributes or stages, hence Piaget's and others' theories of development.

SUMMARY

Now, to leave the specific theories and summarize the points of this article. Theories of play are too important to us to be ignored. We need to develop an approach to theory as professionals so that we are constantly testing and evaluating the fundamental theoretical bases of the profession—one class of which concerns play. The play theories are legion and many are logically or empirically inadequate. It behooves us to critically evaluate them, actively rejecting those that are of no use, and using those that are in our everyday practice.

REFERENCES

Bateson, G. 1956. The message, "This is Play". Pp. 145-246 in B. Schaffner, ed. *Group Processes: Transactions of the Second Conference.* New York: Josiah Macy Foundation.

Berkowitz, L. 1969. Simple view of aggression: an essay review. *American Scientist* 57:372-382.

Csikszentmihalyi, M. 1975. *Beyond Boredom and Anxiety.* San Francisco: Jossey-Bass.

Ellis, M. 1971. Play and its theories re-examined. Pp. 48-55 in *Parks and Recreation.* Washington: NRPA.

Ellis, M.J. 1973. *Why People Play.* Englewood Cliffs, N.J.: Prentice-Hall.

Ellis, M.J. 1976. Play: a paradox for teacher and scientist. *Quest, Monograph 26: "Learning How to Play":*128-139.

Ellis, M.J. and G.J.L. Scholtz. 1978. *Activity and Play of Children.* Englewood Cliffs, N.J.: Prentice-Hall.

Gillmore, J.B. 1966. Play: a special behavior. Pp. 343-355 in R.N. Haber, ed. *Current Research in Motivation.* New York: Holt, Rinehart and Winston.

Loizos, C.A. 1966. Play in mammals. Pp. 1-9 in P.A. Jewell and C.A. Loizos, eds. *Play, Exploration and Territory in Mammals.* London: Academic Press.

Mallick, S.K. and B.R. McCandless. 1966. A study of catharsis of agression. *Journal of Personality and Social Psychology.* 4:591-596.

Poole, T.B. 1966. Aggressive play in polecats. Pp. 23-28 in P.A. Jewell and C.A. Loizos, eds. *Play, Exploration and Territory in Mammals.* London: Academic Press.

Riezler, K. Play and Seriousness. Pp. 437-449 in this Handbook.

White, R.W. 1959. Motivation reconsidered—the concept of competence. *Psychology Review.* 66:297-333.

Modified version of "Play and its theories re-examined" published in *Parks and Recreation.* August, 1971.

SPORT PERSONOLOGY

Rainer Martens

For years coaches have thought it would be a tremendous asset to be able to identify through personality assessment the probability of success for a given athlete. In turn, athletic administrators have thought it equally advantageous to know from the results of a personality profile the probability of a coach being successful or of a referee being competent. The lure of such useful knowledge has motivated sport psychologists to tenaciously seek to identify the unique personality traits of successful athletes, coaches, and even the much maligned sport official.

From the annals of sport psychology, Coleman Griffith stands as a pioneer in the study of personality characteristics of athletes. In 1938, when sport psychology was a mere illusion, Griffith conducted a comprehensive analysis of the personalities of the Chicago Cub players while ostensibly serving as a batting practice pitcher. From his participant observation research with the Cubs and his study of "Big Ten" football players, including interviews with the immortal Knute Rockne, he concluded that the desirable traits of "great athletes" included ruggedness (defined as high achievement motivation and determination), courage, and intelligence. In addition he felt that good players must have such traits as exuberance, buoyancy, good powers of emotional adjustment, a leaning toward optimism, conscientiousness, loyalty, alertness, and respect for authority. While Griffith was indeed a pioneer of sport psychology, his conclusions were predicated on the methods (global, unreliable observations) and attitudes of that era (sport was all-virtuous). Since the time of Griffith many sport psychologists have continued to seek to identify those inner qualities that personify the successful athlete.

Although delineating the personality profile of the successful sport participant has always had first priority, more recently some sport psychologists have become interested in determining whether sport participation changes a person's personality. This interest has surfaced as a result of the frequent claim by physical educators and sport aficionados that sport does wonders not only for the body but for the mind, including the person's social and emotional behavior. Because experimental evidence to substantiate such claims was nonexistent, sport psychologists began seeking to determine if participation in sport does in fact affect participants' personalities.

Before proceeding to recount the answers that sport psychologists have obtained to these two broad concerns, it will be helpful to clarify briefly what is meant by the term personality. In addition, a brief sketch of the conceptual approaches to the study of personality will be presented and the general methods used to assess personality differences will be identified.

AN ORIENTATION TO PERSONALITY RESEARCH

The major reason for studying the personality of sport participants is to identify the consistencies and the idiosyncracies in behavior among participants in order to predict their future behavior. The term personality is used here to mean "the sum total of an individual's characteristics which make him unique" (Hollander 1967), or as Allport (1961) has stated "...the dynamic organization within the individual of those psychophysical systems that determine his characteristic behavior and thought."

Personology is rich with theory: some of the more prominent theories are Freud's psychodynamic theory, Lewin's field theory, Sheldon's constitutional theory, Cattell's factor theory, Rotter's social learning theory, and Roger's and Maslow's humanistic theories of personality. These theories differ on the relative importance given to conscious and unconscious determinants of behavior, hereditary factors, learning, rewards, and the uniqueness of the individual. Most of these theories are pregnant with implications for sport, but most sport personality research has not been guided by these or other theories. While personologists normally permit theory to determine method, sport personologists have far too often permitted method to unwittingly prescribe their theoretical orientation. The predominant orientation has been a trait approach, as exemplified by the frequent use of Cattell's 16 personality factor inventory.

Every man is "...like all other men, like some other men, and like no other men" wrote Kluckhohn and Murray (1949). Based on this observation, Carlson (1971) developed a typology for the methods used in the study of personality: experimental methods (like all other men), correlational methods (like some other men), and clinical methods (like no other men). The *experimental* approach seeks to discover general laws of human nature through an emphasis on situational factors as major sources of variation in human nature and a de-emphasis on genetic variation and constitutional bases of individuality. *Correlational* methods seek to discover the differences in psychological processes by identifying group differences on the basis of pre-existing subject variables. The correlational approach has placed emphasis on intrinsic intrapersonal structures as base lines for further inquiry, and on both genetic variation and cultural determinism as sources of critical differences. The *clinical* method seeks to discover the intricate organization of psychological processes within the unique individual. Both the experimental and correlational approaches are also known as nomothetic approaches to the study of personality and the clinical approach is known as the idiographic approach to personality. The *nomothetic* approach seeks to uncover consistent behavior patterns that generalize across persons. The *idiographic* approach seeks to uncover consistent behavior patterns for a particular individual in order that generalizations can be made about the person in a variety of situations. The idiographic personologist, who usually functions as a clinical psychologist, assesses personality by acquiring a profile of an individual's life history through interview and observation as well as through objective and projective personality inventories. The objective and projective inventory has been the predominant means of assessing personality by personologists using the nomothetic approach.

In a recent review of the sport personology literature, Martens (1975) reported that for 160 data-based studies investigating the personality of sport participants, 10% were experimental, 89% correlational, and 1% were clinical in their methods. All of the experimental and correlational studies used objective and projective inventories to assess personality.

THE TRAIT APPROACH

As stated above, one of the major objectives of sport personology has been to determine if sport participants differ in personality. In pursuit of an answer, sport psychologists have asked these questions: (a) Do sport participants differ in personality from non-sport participants? (b) Do participants in one sport or certain types of sports differ from participants in another sport or other types of sports? (c) Do highly successful sport participants differ in personality from less successful sport participants? (The term sport participant is used here not only to refer to the players or athletes, but to coaches and officials as well.) The second objective in sport personology has been to determine if sport participation affects the person's personality. In this section the research pertinent to these two objectives is evaluated.

Literally hundreds of published and unpublished studies have investigated these three questions. The vast majority of these studies have examined the personality of the athlete, but more recently interest has increased in identifying the personalities of coaches and officials. Space limitations render it impossible to review all of the research in detail, thus it is necessary to provide a global impression based substantially on existing reviews. The conclusions drawn about these three questions are based entirely on studies using the correlation approach—i.e., the studies have sought to identify the personality profiles of one group compared with another by measuring a series of traits using a personality inventory. Hereafter this method is referred to as the *trait approach* or trait psychology.

The research investigating the personality profiles of *athletes* has culminated in a quagmire of findings that has obfuscated all of sport personology. For almost every study identifying a positive relationship between personality traits and sport participation, another study can be found that fails to substantiate it. The equivocality of findings is not the only demise of the empirical literature—the methodological ineptness of many studies voids any possibility of deriving valid conclusions. To add to the plight, reviewers of essentially the same literature have disagreed markedly in their generalizations about the accumulated evidence.

To illustrate, Ogilvie (1968) concluded that a general "sport personality type" existed, and this was not restricted by the type of sport participated in or the sex or age of the participant. Harris (1973) and Morgan (1972) concurred in attributing the sport personality type to pre-existing differences among persons selecting to participate in sport rather than changes arising from participation in sport. Other reviewers of essentially the same literature, and in some cases of more recent literature, concluded that the evidence was insufficient to support the existence of a sport personality type (Fisher 1975; Johnson and Cofer 1974; Kroll 1970; Martens 1975; Rushall 1973). With specific reference to the female athlete, Berlin (1974) also concluded that there is insufficient evidence of a female sport personality type. She states, "To seek some unique factor(s) that would permit typifying sportswomen with any reasonable degree of confidence or predicting athletic success is like searching for a pot of gold at the end of a rainbow."

Conflicting conclusions also have been drawn about the relationship between extroversion-introversion and success in sport. Kane (1964) and Harris (1973) concluded that success in sport was positively related to Eysenck's extrovert typology, but Hardman (1973) has made a convincing case for this not always being true. Hardman suggested that extroverted persons are more likely to be successful in certain sports and introverted persons are more likely to succeed in other sports. He outlined the characteristics of those sports that extroverts and introverts were more likely to succeed in based on deductions from Eysenckian theory, but to date evidence has not substantiated these hypotheses.

When scholarly reviews of the sport personology literature arrive at such contradictory conclusions, it gives the justifiable impression that anarchy prevails. Not only is this true for athletes, but also for coaches and officials. Although substantially less research has been completed with these sport participants, indications are that this research will be equally unproductive in yielding useful generalizations.

Some important reasons exist as to why the trait approach has led to both equivocal evidence and equivocal conclusions. The first and more obvious reason that the empirical evidence using the trait approach has not led to decisive conclusions is that much of the research is methodologically inadequate. Several reviewers have presented comprehensive discussions of the methodological indequacies (Kroll 1970; Martens 1975; Morgan 1972, Rushall 1973). In brief, these problems include the failure to clearly operationalize important variables (e.g., defining who is an athlete or a successful athlete), deficient sampling procedures (particularly when studying team sport participants), inappropriate statistical analyses, and inappropriate or weak measurement of personality traits. These methodological weaknesses are easily discernible in the empirical literature and have been acknowledged by reviewers. What apparently has occurred in some reviews though, is that after reviewers acknowledge these methodological errors the deficiencies were ignored in deriving conclusions.

Perhaps the most fundamental reason for the inconclusive findings is that the trait approach as used by most sport personologists has not been based on any conceptual or theoretical framework of personality. Almost no justification is found among the research studies for the use of the trait approach. In fact there is reason to suspect that many researchers using this approach were unaware of the underlying assumptions of trait psychology.

Trait psychology is based on the assumption that personality traits are relatively stable, consistent attributes that exert generalized causal effects on behavior. This approach considers the general source of behavioral variance to reside within the person, minimizing the role of situational or external environmental factors. Mischel (1968, 1973) has made a convincing case that the environment or situational variables, are important determinants of behavior. He and others have advocated what is known as situationism—the study of personality by accounting for human behavior largely in terms of the situation in which it occurs.

Personologists such as Bowers (1973) and Carson (1969) have made impressive cases that both trait psychology and situationism are too simplistic for the study of the human personality. Instead, these people advocate the interactional paradigm—the study of personality by accounting for human behavior in terms of both the person and the situation in which the behavior occurs. Elsewhere Martens (1975) has presented an in-depth discussion as to why interactionism is a superior paradigm for the study of personality in sport. Interactionism considers situational factors and person variables (traits or dispositions) as co-determinants of behavior without specifying either as primary or subsidiary. Instead the primacy of a situational variable and a person variable is dependent upon the sample of people studied and the particular situation they are in.

The demise of the trait approach is not entirely unexpected. What has been unexpected is the tenacity with which sport psychologists have continued to pursue the trait approach in light of evidence that in other areas of psychology the trait approach has failed to provide the simplistic conclusions for which it was hoped. A cogent example is in the field of leadership behavior, where the early research sought to identify a "leadership type" personality by using the trait approach. No such type was found, of course, and leadership research today is based primarily on an interactional approach which considers leadership behavior to be a function of both the person (individual attributes) and the leadership situation.

A third reason the trait approach has proved inadequate is due to the tremendous diversity in persons studied, sports participated in, and personality instruments used in the research. With such variation across studies it is almost impossible to compare results, particularly when the research has no underlying theoretical framework. Unquestionably the absence of theory is the dominant reason that research using the trait approach has lacked direction. In fact, considering the almost chaotic course the trait approach has followed, it would be surprising if the results revealed anything but inconsistencies.

There is one noteworthy exception to the atheoretical sport personality research completed within the trait paradigm. Several investigators (Hardman 1973; Morgan 1972; Warburton and Kane 1966) have used Eysenckian theory as a basis for their investigations. While these researchers believe this trait-based theory has considerable utility within sport, the theory is subject to the criticisms of any trait-based theory. At present there is no evidence that Eysenckian theory is leading to meaningful generalizations pertinent to sport participation. But, in fairness, there is little evidence at present that any theory is leading to meaningful generalizations in sport personology. Several interactional theories, however, are discussed in the following section that are not subject to the same criticisms of trait-based theories.

The research directed toward the second objective of sport personology—determining if sport participation affects the personality of sport participants—is not replete with equivocality. Although this objective has not been investigated extensively, sport personologists are nearly unanimous in their conclusions. Morgan (1972) for example wrote: "The findings relative to the psychological effects of sport

and physical activity are easily interpreted, and for the most part
they are in agreement with predictions from theoretic psychology.
As could be expected, personality traits remain largely unaffected as
a result of athletic participation. What differences have been observed
are likely due to genetic differences." Other reviewers (Kane 1970;
Ogilvie 1968; and Rushall 1973) also concluded that there was insufficient evidence to conclude that personality changes as a result
of sport participation. Fisher (1975) pointed out that it is unlikely,
using the trait approach, that changes in personality will be easily
observed because this approach ignores situational variables within
sport.

Thus while at the present time evidence does not indicate that
sport participation changes personality, this question has not been
sufficiently investigated. Noticeably absent in the research literature
are longitudinal studies completed over extended periods of time. It
is improbable that short term studies, resulting in minimal changes
of personality characteristics, can detect these changes by the crude
methods available for measuring personality.

In summary, only one conclusion may be drawn safely from the
extant literature—that no conclusion is warranted. It is of course dis-
couraging to sport psychologists to discount this abundance of research as meaningless. There is a strong motive to thrash through the
literature one more time in hope of uncovering some meaningful conclusion. But when the totality of evidence is weighed, it is clear that
the trait approach to the study of personality in sport has failed. The
failure, while in part due to methodological ineptness, is attributable
primarily to conceptual over-simplicity. While this is a somber conclusion to this research, on a more optimistic note it is quite evident
that currently a renaissance is underway in sport personology. Trait
psychology is deservedly dying and interactionism is assuredly emerging.

INTERACTIONISM

In the study of personality, whether in sport or other contexts,
the ultimate objective of the behavioral scientist is to explain and
predict *behavior*. There is a growing consensus among behavioral
scientists that this can be done better by not pitting nature against
nurture, heredity against environment, situational variation against
organismic variation, but pursuing the study of human behavior
through interactional paradigms. The interactional paradigm suggests
research designs in which the behavioral effects of situational factors
and variables, and their interactions, are studied concurrently. Experimental treatments are not applied to random samples, but to subjects
who differ on theoretically relevant dimensions. In this section three

interactional theories will be discussed briefly and the evidence pertaining to sport will be reviewed. The three theories are Atkinson's (1957) achievement motivation theory, Spielberger's (1972) trait-state theory of anxiety, and Rotter's (1954) social learning theory.

Atkinson's Theory of Achievement Motivation

According to Atkinson (1957) any achievement situation may arouse two different motives within a person—a motive to achieve success (M_s) and a motive to avoid failure (M_{af}). The actual tendency to achieve success (T_s), however, is not only a function of M_s (a personality variable conceived to be relatively general and stable), but also of two situational variables. These situational determinants are the expectancy of the outcome in terms of probability of success (P_s) and the incentive value of success (I_s). Thus, Atkinson theorized that T_s is a multiplicative function of M_s, P_s, and I_s or $T_s = M_s \times P_s \times I_s$. In turn he proposed that the same achievement situation produced an overall tendency to avoid failure (T_{-f}) which is a multiplicative function of M_{af} and the situational factors—the probability of failure (P_f) and the incentive value of failure (I_f). Thus $T_{-f} = M_{af} \times P_f \times I_f$.

In any given achievement situation, the difference between these two motives determines the strength of the resultant achievement tendency (T). Stated formally, $T = T_s + T_{-f}$. If the T_s is dominant, the resultant achievement oriented tendency will be to approach the task, but if the T_{-f} is stronger the resultant achievement tendency will be to avoid the task. Atkinson also postulates that P_s and I_s are inversely related as are P_f and I_f—i.e., a high P_s results in a low I_s. From this theory, oversimplified in its presentation here, a number of lines of research have emerged resulting in an extensive literature.

Sport psychologists have often voiced interest in achievement motivation and have seen the obvious applications of the theory to sport, but have not conducted as yet any extensive amount of research based on the theory. A few exceptions exist though, with the major concern centering on the performance differences between subjects differing in T_s and T_{-f}. The general prediction from the theory is that persons higher in T_s perform better in achievement contexts than persons higher in T_{-f}. Evidence has supported this proposition, with perhaps the most interesting finding being obtained by Ryan and Lakie (1965). They reported that the T_{-f} subjects performed better in noncompetitive situations and the T_s subjects performed better in competitive situations. Other studies (Healey and Landers 1973; Roberts 1972), however, have failed to confirm these performance differences.

These studies were laboratory experiments using fine and gross motor task. Atkinson and Feather (1966) have suggested that under conditions of very intense positive motivation, a strong tendency to avoid failure may actually enhance rather than hinder the efficiency of performance. It is unlikely that such positive motivation can be fabricated in the laboratory, but very likely to occur in sport. Thus research from laboratory experiments may not be of value in understanding the relationship between sport performance and achievement motivation. Weinberg (1976) recently reviewed the evidence concerning the relationship between sport performance and achievement motivation concluding that there is no support for the hypothesis that high motive-to-achieve-success subjects are superior in sport performance when compared to high motive-to-avoid-failure subjects. This may in part be due to the explanation of Atkinson and Feather—that both motives function to facilitate performance in highly motivating situations. Thus, while at present the relationship between achievement motivation and sport performance remains unclear, its potential for clarification is promising with additional research.

Another prediction from the theory is that persons higher in T_s are more likely to select tasks of intermediate risk and those higher in T_{-f} prefer tasks of very low or very high risk. This hypothesis has not been pursued within the sport context, but again it provides a guide for understanding individual differences in the preference for low and high risk sports. Many other facets of achievement motivation theory have implications for sport as well, but as yet remain uninvestigated. The theory makes predictions about the effects of long-term success and failure on the development of M_s and M_{af}; about the degree of persistence among persons differing in M_s and M_{af}; about the influence of extrinsic rewards on such persistence; and about sex differences in achievement behavior in the sport context.

With respect to this latter issue, Horner (1969) recently generated considerable enthusiasm about the finding that not only do women share with men the fear of failure motive, but they also have much higher motives to avoid success. Horner postulated that because success in competitive achievement situations may actually have negative consequences for women they become more anxious, not just when failing, but also when succeeding. In support of this premise, Horner and others presented a wave of evidence showing that the fear of success motive was much higher in females than in males. More recently, however, the empirical support for this supposition has been called into question (Tresemer 1974). In spite of this present state of confusion, understanding the fear of success and other achievement for both male and female participants in sport has eminent utility in sport psychology.

The achievement motive is closely related to the concept of competitiveness—competitiveness being a cluster of motives that predispose an individual to compete or not to compete in a social evaluative context as contrasted to non-social contexts. Scanlan (1974) has used Atkinson's theory and other achievement-related theories in formulating a model describing the development of competitiveness. If this model is an omen, future research likely will be directed toward understanding the *biocultural development* of competitiveness and other sport-relevant personality variables. Recent theories about the development of achievement motivation, such as those by Crandall (1969) and Veroff (1969), are being discussed as guides for such research programs.

Spielberger's Trait–State Theory of Anxiety.
Fundamental to Spielberger's (1972) theory of anxiety is the distinction between trait and state anxiety. Trait anxiety (A-trait) is a predisposition to perceive danger or threat in the environment; it is the proneness to manifest state anxiety. State anxiety (A-state) is the actual feeling of apprehension in response to the perception of danger and is associated with activation or arousal. The theory postulates that when stimuli, either internal or external to the person, are cognitively appraised as threatening they evoke an A-state reaction. The greater the threat perceived and the longer the threat perceived, the more intense and the more enduring the A-state reaction. The hypothesis of greatest interest, in terms of the interactional paradigm, is that high A-trait persons perceive more situations as threatening and respond with more intense A-state reactions than low A-trait persons.

As with Atkinson's achievement motivation theory, considerable research has substantiated parts of Spielberger's theory. The hypotheses predicting differences in A-state for persons varying in A-trait has received wide support. Evidence has also accrued indicating that situations involving potential failure or threat to self-esteem are more potent sources of threat than situations involving potential physical harm. This finding, although unexamined in a sport context, is a provocative avenue for future study. It would be particularly helpful to know if there are individual differences among sport participants in their fear of physical harm as contrasted with their fear of psychological harm.

Spielberger, Gorsuch, and Luschene (1970) developed two scales for measuring A-state and A-trait. These instruments have been used by several investigators in the sport context. For example, Griffin (1972) found that A-trait varied significantly for female athletes who competed in eight different sports. Gymnasts had the highest A-trait followed by swimmers, volleyball players, track and field athletes, softball, tennis, field hockey and basketball players. Among these athletes, 16-17 year-olds were highest in A-trait, while 19-and-over athletes were the lowest, and the 12-13 year-olds fell in between. Although these data are interesting descriptive findings within sport, they do not investigate Spielberger's theory. Klavora (1975) is one of the few investigators who tested the theory within sport, but his results were inconclusive.

From research concerned with test anxiety, audience anxiety, and social anxiety, evidence indicates that general anxiety is too broad a construct for accurate behavioral predictions and that situation-specific A-trait constructs are better predictors of behavior in those specific situations. Martens (1976) developed a sport-specific competitive A-trait scale known as the Sport Competition Anxiety Test. This scale, validated by laboratory and field studies, has been able to predict pre-competitive A-states almost three times more accurately than Spielberger's general A-trait scale. The accumulated evidence from a series of studies using this sport-specific A-trait scale reveals the utility of developing instrumentation specific to sport when wishing to predict behavior in sport.

Although considerable interest in anxiety is currently being shown by sport personologists, as yet all the interesting questions remain unanswered. How does anxiety relate to performance? How does the athlete, or the coach working with the athlete, effect change in competitive A-traits and A-states? What are the situational determinants within sport that precipitate high levels of A-state?

This latter question is where Spielberger's theory is most inadequate. The theory fails to specify any of the situational factors likely to elicit perceptions of threat. A definite direction for future research with competitive anxiety is determining what situational factors within sport influence the interaction between A-trait and A-state. For example success-failure experiences in sport at an early age is a situational outcome hypothesized to be a major determinant of a person's competitive A-trait level.

Understanding the antecedent conditions eliciting high A-states is a prerequisite to finding means to alleviate elevated A-states. More than ever before athletes are seeking effective means to reduce anxiety. Some have tried hypnosis, others transcendental meditation or yoga, and yet others have turned to drugs. Some have even reported that vigorous physical activity alleviates elevated A-states prior to competition.

Of course, the long standing interest in the relationship between anxiety and performance in sport will continue to be investigated. While this relationship has been elusive in the past, advances in methodology and theory are likely to facilitate the discovery of what obviously is a very complex relationship.

Rotter's Social Learning Theory.

Of the theories considered here, Rotter's (1954) social learning theory is by far the most comprehensive for the study of personality.

A basic premise of social learning theory is that the proper unit of investigation for the study of personality is the interaction of the individual with his meaningful environment. Rotter, Chance, and Phares (1972) stated this premise as follows, "...a sufficient basis for behavioral prediction lies in the statement that behavior directed toward the attainment of a learned goal, or external reinforcement, may be predicted through knowledge of the organism's situation and knowledge of his past learning experience (expectancies and reinforcement values)."

Within Rotter's social learning theory, the construct of greatest empirical interest has been locus of control or internality-externality. The concept of internal versus external control of reinforcement refers to the degree of control a person judges to have over his environment. A person at the internal end of the continuum perceives outcomes to be a consequence of his own actions and the person at the external end perceives outcomes to be a result of fate, luck, or powerful others, and, therefore are beyond his personal control. Several scales have been developed to measure this personality disposition.

At present only a few investigators have incorporated social learning theory into their study of sport. For example, Lynn, Phelan, and Kiker (1969) reasoned that athletes trained to cooperate in team sports would be more able to perceive reinforcements as dependent on their own behavior than participants in individual sports. They supported their hypothesis, finding that male junior high school basketball players were higher in internality than similar-aged gymnasts. Later studies, however, were unable to find any differences in locus of control for athletes in a variety of individual and team sports or for older age groups.

When making racial comparisons on internal-external control, blacks have been found to be higher in externality than whites, suggesting that blacks may have low expectancies with regard to the self-determination of reinforcements in achievement situations. Thurber Heacock, and Brown (1973) compared the locus of control for black and white athletes with their performance in basketball. Blacks were significantly more external than whites, and more interestingly, their externality correlated .95 with their performance as measured by the number of points scored. For the white players the correlation between internal control and performance was −.40, which was nonsignificant. This study suggests that external control, rather than being negatively related to achievement, is positively related to achievement with black basketball players. The authors suggested that because of the experiences of blacks (discrimination, segregation), external control is a realistic expectancy that is adaptive.

From the small sample of studies just discussed, it is apparent that sport psychologists are beginning to discover the utility of social learning theory. While the research as yet is meager and has concerned itself only with internal-external control, the potential application of this comprehensive theory to sport is vast.

A POTPOURRI

In this section brief mention is made of some other approaches to the study of personality and some conclusions are drawn about the future of sport personology. Sport personologists, along with many other personologists, have viewed the new-born person as a blank sheet upon which the learning process writes out its own formulas. Until the recent emergence of behavior genetics, personologists have neglected the role of heredity in the study of individual differences. Unquestionably genes set the limits for the behavioral capabilities or potentialities of the organism, but just how restricting these limits are remains an open question.

In early research concerned with the genetic determinants of behavior, Sheldon (1940) aroused much controversy with his constitutional theory. This theory described the relationship between morphology (physique) and temperament (personality). Sheldon reported an incredibly high correlation of .80 between physique and temperament, but later his research was found deficient for several reasons and other investigators never were able to obtain equally high correlations. As a result interest quickly died in constitutional theory. Although it is improbable that physique and personality are related to the extent reported by Sheldon, what has been forgotten is that many other investigators did find moderate correlations between morphology and temperament. This evidence, along with other research in behavior genetics and developmental psychology, is forcing behavioral scientists to recognize that the newborn child is not a blank sheet. Perhaps this recognition explains why there is a resurgence of interest in the relationship between morphology and personality, both in and out of sport (Hopkins, 1972).

As noted earlier, there is merit in the development of personality constructs specific to sport. Loy and Donnelly (1975) have found this to be the case, proposing a sport-specific personality construct called the need for stimulation. Individuals high in the need for stimulation seek out stimulating environments characterized by complexity, novelty, uncertainty and high information loads. Their preliminary conceptual model proposed that the interaction between individual differences in the need for stimulation and situational factors determines the degree of arousal manifested within an individual at any given moment. The resultant arousal influences the person's behavior in that situation. While empirical research with the need for stimulation construct is just beginning, what is particularly noteworthy is that these sport personologists have developed a sport-specific personality construct within an interactional paradigm.

The entire domain of perception and how it relates to personality has largely been neglected by sport personologists. Jones (1973) has noted that understanding individual differences in selective perception and dominant modes of information processing constitutes an important dimension of personality as it pertains to sport. Several people have suggested that the ability to selectively attend to the environment in certain ways is related to field dependent/field independent perceptual modes described by Witkin, Dyk, Faterson, Goodenough and Karp (1962). Stated more generally, persons differ in their cognitive styles and this is related to differences in selective attention abilities. Mischel (1973) has placed the study of cognitive styles on a high pedestal, considering cognitive styles to be one of the broader and more important personality constructs. While some research has examined the relationship between motor behavior and field dependence/independence, specific extension of this dimension to the sport context has not occurred.

Pertinent to the relationship between perception and personality is the currently popular area of causal attributions. For any particular behavioral event how people attribute causes to individual characteristics and to situational factors influences how they behave in related situations. Weiner (1972) has developed an important attributional theory describing how persons assign causes to their success and failure in achievement situations. Iso-Ahola (1975) and Roberts (1975) have tested this model within sport finding that players attribute failure more to external factors (luck and task difficulty) and attribute success more to internal factors (ability and effort), which supports Weiner's theory. Weiner has indicated that achievement motivation is an important personality variable affecting attributions. At present, however, researchers have not yet investigated how personality factors mediate the situational determinants of causal attributions about outcomes of success and failure.

And there are many other facets of personality that pertain to behavior in a sport context that have not been mentioned here. Attitudes are an important part of personality, particularly attitudes about the self. Some research has investigated the influence of sport participation on the self concept, but as yet no generalizations appear to be warranted. Intrinsic motivation, authoritarianism, hostility, and cooperativeness are all potentially important dimensions of sport participants' personality that need to be studied.

In conclusion, it is apparent that the major thrust of sport personality research—the trait approach—has not proven to be a functional approach for studying the complex nature of man. The trait approach relies on a very simplistic model of man, and has resulted in research attempting to answer questions that were too broad. For example, asking the question, "What are the consequences of sport on personality?" is dependent on many events that occur within sport. Success, failure, fun, violence, joy, pain, and many other experiences in sport are important determinants of behavior for persons differing in age, sex, abilities, and intelligence. Sport personologists are recognizing that the relationships between personality and sport participation is mediated by many variables, and that simple general relationships are non-existent.

While the evidence marshalled here may present a dismal picture, it must be recalled that over 95 percent of all sport psychology research has been completed in the last 15 years. The field is young and has shown its immaturity. But there is good reason for optimism in the area of sport personology—a renaissance is indeed underway. Promising new directions currently being undertaken by sport personologists have been briefly discussed in the last two sections of this article. Although at this point generalizations are premature, these new directions suggest that at least the answers obtained will not be immature.

REFERENCES

Allport, G.W. 1961. *Pattern and Growth in Personality.* New York: Holt, Rinehart and Winston.

Atkinson, J.W. 1957. Motivational determinants of risk-taking behavior. *Psychological Review. 64,3:* 359-372.

Atkinson, J.W. and Feather, N.T. 1966. *A Theory of Achievement Motivations.* New York: Wiley.

Berlin, P. 1974. The woman athlete. Pp. 100-200 in E.W. Gerber, et al. eds. *The American Woman in Sport.* Reading, Mass.: Addison-Wesley.

Bowers, K.S. 1973. Situationism in psychology: An analysis and a critique. *Psychological Review 80,2:* 307–336.

Carlson, R. 1971. Where is the person in personality research? *Psychological Review 75,2:* 203–219.

Carson, R.C. 1969. *Interaction Concepts of Personality.* Chicago: Aldine.

Crandall, V.C. 1969. Sex differences in expectancy of intellectual and academic reinforcement. Pp. 100-200 in C.P. Smith, ed., *Achievement-Related Motives in Children.* New York: Russell Sage.

Fisher, A.C. 1975. Sport personality assessment: facts, fallacies, and perceptives. Paper, *AAHPER National Convention,* Atlantic City, N.J.

Griffin, M.R. 1972. An analysis of state and trait anxiety experiences in sports competition by women at different age levels. *Foil:* 58-63.

Griffith, C. 1928. *Psychology and Athletics.* New York: Scribner.

Hardman, K. 1973. A dual approach to the study of personality and performance in sport. In H.T.A. Whiting et al. eds. *Personality and Performance in Physical Education and Sport.* London: Kimpton.

Harris, D.V. 1973. *Involvement in Sport: A Somatopsychic Rationale for Physical Activity.* Philadelphia: Lea and Febiger.

Healey, T.R. and Landers, D.M. 1973. Effect of need achievement and task difficulty on competitive and noncompetitive motor performance. *Journal of Motor Behavior 5,1:* 121-128.

Hollander, E.P. 1967. *Principles and Methods of Social Psychology.* New York: Oxford University Press.

Hopkins, B. 1972. Body-build stereotypes. In H.T.A. Whiting, ed. *Readings in Sports Psychology.* Lafayette, Ind., Balt.: 1969.

Horner, M. 1969. Fail: bright women. *Psychology Today. 3,1:* 36-38.

Iso-Ahola, S. 1975. A test of the attribution theory of success and failure with little league baseball players. *Proceedings Canadian Psycho-motor Learning and Sport Psychology Symposium:* 323-337.

Johnson, W.R. and C.N. Cofer. 1974. Personality dynamics: psychosocial implications. In W.R. Johnson and E.R. Buskirk, eds. *Science and Medicine of Exercise and Sport.* 2nd ed. New York: Harper & Row.

Jones, M.G. 1973. Personality and perceptual characteristics. In H.T.A. Whiting et al. eds. *Personality and Performance in Physical Education and Sport.* London: Kimpton.

Kane, J.E. 1964. Psychological correlates of physique and physical abilities. In E. Jokl and E. Simon, eds. *International Research in Sport and Physical Education.* Springfield, Ill.: Thomas.

Kane, J.E. 1970. Personality and physical abilities. In G.S. Kenyon and T.M. Grogg, eds. *Contemporary Psychology of Sport.* Chicago: Athletic Institute.

Klavora, P. 1975. Emotional arousal in athletics: New considerations. *Proceedings Canadian Psycho-motor Learning and Sport Psychology Symposium.* 279-287.

Kluckhohn, C. and H.A. Murray. 1949. *Personality in Nature, Society, and Culture.* New York: Knopf.

Kroll, W. 1970. Current strategies and problems in personality assessment of athletes. In L.E. Smith, ed. *Psychology of Motor Learning.* Chicago: Athletic Institute.

Loy, J.W. and P. Donnelly. 1975. Need for stimulation as a factor in sport involvement. Paper, National Conference *Mental Health Aspects of Sports.* American Medical Association, Atlantic City, N.J.

Lynn, R.W., Phelan, J.G., and Kiker, V.L. 1969. Beliefs in internal-external control of reinforcement and participation in group and individual sports. *Perceptual and Motor Skills 29,3:* 551-553.

Martens, R. 1975. The paradigmatic crisis in American sport personology. *Sportwissenschaft 5,1:* 9-24.

Martens, R. 1977. *The Sport Competition Anxiety Test.* Urbana, Ill.: Human Kinetics Publishers.

Mischel, W. 1968. *Personality and Assessment.* New York: Wiley.

Mischell, W. 1973. Toward a cognitive social learning reconceptualization of personality. *Psychological Review 80,2:* 252-283.

Morgan, W.P. 1972. Sport psychology. In R.N. Singer, ed. *The Psychomotor Domain: Movement Behaviors.* Philadelphia: Lea and Febiger.

Ogilvie, B.C. 1968. Psychological consistencies within the personality of high-level competitors. *Journal of the American Medical Association 205:* 156-162.

Roberts, G.C. 1972. Effect of achievement motivation and social environment on performance of a motor task. *Journal of Motor Behavior 4,1:* 37-46.

Roberts, G.C. 1975. Win-loss causal attributions of little league players. *Proceedings Canadian Psycho-Motor Learning and Sport Psychology Symposium:* 315-323.

Rotter, J.H. 1954. *Social Learning and Clinical Psychology.* Englewood Cliffs: Prentice-Hall.

Rotter, J.B., Chance, J.E., and Phares, E.J. 1972. *Applications of a Social Learning Theory of Personality.* New York: Holt, Rinehart, and Winston.

Rushall, B.S. 1973. The status of personality research and application in sports and physical education. *Journal of Sports Medicine and Physical Fitness 13,2:* 281-290.

Ryan, E.D. and W.L. Lakie. 1965. Competitive and noncompetitive performance in relation to achievement motive and manifest anxiety. *Journal of Personality and Social Psychology 1,2:* 342-345.

Scanlan, T. 1974. Antecedents of competitiveness. In M.G. Wade and R. Martens, eds. *Psychology of Motor Behavior and Sport.* Urbana, Ill.: Human Kinetics Publishers.

Sheldon, W.H. 1940. *The Varieties of Temperament.* New York: Harper & Row.

Spielberger, C.D., Gorsuch, R.L., and Luschene, R.E. 1970. *The State-Trait Anxiety Inventory.* Palo Alto, Calif.: Consulting Psychologists Press.

Spielberger, C.D. 1972. Conceptual and methodological issues in anxiety research. In C.D. Spielberger, ed. *Current Trends in Theory and Research.* Vol. 115. New York: Academic Press.

Thurber, S., Heacock, D. and B. Brown. 1973. The control orientation of black athletes in relation to unobtrusive tasks of skill. *Journal of Psychology 85,1:* 43-44.

Tresemer, D. 1974. Fear of success: popular, but unproven. *Psychology Today 7,1:* 82-85.

Veroff, J. 1969. Social comparison and the development of achievement motivation. In C.P. Smith, ed. *Achievement-Related Motives in Children.* New York: Russell Sage Foundation.

Warburton, F.W. and J.E. Kane. 1966. Personality related to sport and physical ability. In J.E. Kane, ed. *Readings in Physical Education.* London: Physical Education Association.

Weinberg, B. 1976. A comparison of resultant achievement motivation levels of college athletes and nonathletes. *Paper, National Convention, American Alliance Health, Physical Education, Recreation.*

Weiner, B. 1972. *Theories of Motivation.* Chicago: Markham.

Witkin, H.A. et al. 1962. *Psychological Differentiation.* New York: Wiley.

PART VII

INTERNATIONAL

CLASSIFIED

BIBLIOGRAPHY

ON

SOCIOLOGY OF SPORT

Lüschen

Hammerich

INTERNATIONAL CLASSIFIED BIBLIOGRAPHY ON SOCIOLOGY OF SPORT

Günther Lüschen
Kurt Hammerich

with the assistance of Zofia Ciupak, Eric Dunning, Fred Gras, Ference Hepp, Gerald Kenyon, Pekka Kiviaho (†), Oleg Milshtein, Takaaki Niwa, Kresimir Petrovich, Sandra Weis and Montrew Batson, Cynthia Hasbrook, Cläre Lüschen, Gerhard Lüschen, Leila Sfeir. The SIRLS at the University of Waterloo gave access to its reference system. Financial support was provided by the Federal Institute of Sport Science in Cologne/Germany.

I. Sociology of Sport as a Field of Study

1. Theory, Methodology, Methods

1001. Andresen, R. and G. Hagedorn. 1976. *Zur Sport-Spiel-Forschung.* Berlin: Bartels und Wernitz. 215 pp.

1002. Artiomov, R.N. 1978. Socio-linguistic research in sociology of sport *IRSS* 13,2:95–108.

1003. Asada, T. 1961. Taiikugaku kenkyu niokeru shakaigakuteki jikken (Sociological experiments in physical education research). *Bulletin Fac.Phys.Educ. Tokyo University of Education* 1:1–14.

1004. Ball, D.W. 1975. A note on method in the sociological study of sport. Pp. 39–49 in Ball/Loy.

1005. Bergman, H. ed. 1976. *Sport en wetenschap* (Sport and science). Haarlem: De Vrieseborch. 279 pp.

1006. Bird, A.M. 1976. Nonreactive research: applications for sociological analysis of sport. *IRSS* 11,1:83–90.

1007. Buggel, E. 1965. Über eine repräsentative komplex-territoriale Stichprobenerhebung in der DDR für den Bereich der Körperkultur. *Theorie und Praxis* 14,4:359–362.

Note: The bibliography is classified according to major subject areas. The subject index allows the identification of problems treated in individual publications as a second or third item. Such references are referred to by the number within the index from 1001 on. English, French and German publications are collected up to 1979. Material in other languages is covered only up to and including 1975.

1008.   Burdge, R.J. and D.J. Field. 1972. Methodological perspectives for the
         study of outdoor recreation. *J.Leisure Research* 4,Winter:63-72.
1009.   Dumazedier, J. 1964. Education physique, sport et sociologie. *Education
         physique et Sport* 15,69:7-10.
1010.   Dunning E. 1967. Notes on some conceptual and theoretical problems in
         the sociology of sport. *IRSS* 2:143-154.
1011.   Dunning, E. 1971. Some conceptual dilemmas in the sociology of sport.
         Pp. 34-47 in Albonico/Pfister-Binz. *German* 1976. Zum Dilemma
         theoretischer Ansätze in der Soziologie des Sports. Pp. 24-38 in Lüschen/
         Weis.
1012.   Erbach, G. 1965. Sportwissenschaft und Sportsoziologie. *Wissensch.
         Zeitschr.DHFK* 7,2:35-50.
1013.   Erbach, G. 1965. Sportwissenschaft und Sportsoziologie. *Theorie und
         Praxis* 14,10:877-883 and 11:950-963. *Engl.* 1966. The science of sport
         and sport sociology. *IRSS* 1:97-126.
1014.   Frenkin, A.A. 1962. Ekziestencializm i idiealisticskaja "sociologija
         sporta" (Existentialism and the idealistic "sociology of sport"). *Teorija
         i Praktika* 3:55-57.
1015.   Gras, F. 1974. Interaktionalismus und sozialer Konflikt in der bürgerlichen
         Sportsoziologie. *Theorie und Praxis* 23,5:392-396.
1016.   Gras, F. 1974. Zum Entwicklungsstand und zu einigen Entwicklungs-
         tendenzen der Sportsoziologie in der DDR. *Wissensch.Zeitschr.DHFK*
         15,2:69-82.
1017.   Gras, F. and B. Kleine. 1974. Stellung und Aufgaben der marxistisch-
         leninistischen Sportsoziologie in der Sportwissenschaft. *Theorie und
         Praxis* 23,11:1033-1037.
1018.   Gurvich, S.S. 1970. Znachenie lenisnkoj kritiki idealizma dlja razo-
         blachenija idealisticheskih teorij v zarubezhnoj medicine i sociologii
         sporta (The significance of Lenin's criticism of Idealism for the un-
         masking of idealistic theories in medicine and sociology of sport). Pp.
         29-43 in *Materialy nauchnoj knoferencii po itogam nauchnoissledo-
         vatelskoj raboty za 1969g.* Kiev. Part 1.
1019.   Heinemann, K. 1971. Zur Soziologie des Sports. Pp. 48-60 in H. Beyer,
         ed. *Reclams Sportführer.* Stuttgart: Reclam.
1020.   Jakobson, M.A. 1967. Nekotorye ishodnye principy formirovanija socio-
         logicheskoj teorii srednego urovnja dlja fizicheskoj kultury (Some initial
         principles of forming a sociological theory of the middle range for
         physical culture). Pp. 79-80 in *Sbornik nauchnyh rabot molodyh
         uchenyh.* Leningrad.
1021.   Kane, J.E. and C. Murray. 1966. Suggestions for the sociological study of
         sport. Pp. 111-127 in J. Kane, ed. *Readings in Physical Education.*
         London: Physical Education Association.
1022.   Kato, K. 1951. *Sports no shakaigaku* (Sociology of sport). Tokyo: Sekai-
         Shoin.
1023.   Kawanabe, A. 1972. Sport shakaigaku no genjo (An outline of the present
         situation in sociology of sport). *Tokyo University Foreign Area Studies*
         22:127-140.
1024.   Kawanabe, A. 1973. Taiiku to sport no shakaigaku niokeru riron to jissen
         (Problems of theory and practice in sport sociology). *Research J. Sport
         Sociology* 2:169-191.

1025. Kenyon, G.S. and J.W. Loy. 1965. Toward a sociology of sport. *JOHPER* 36,5:24–25 and 68–69.

1026. Kenyon, G.S. 1971. The use of path analysis in sport sociology with special reference to involvement socialization. Pp. 151–163 in Albonico/ Pfister-Binz.

1027. Knoop, J.C. 1979. Assessing equivalence of indicators in cross-national research. *IRSS* 14,3–4:137–156.

1028. Kondo, Y. 1972. Taiiku kenkyu niokeru shakaigaku no yakuwari (A methodological study of the sociological approach to physical education). *Research J. Sport Sociology* 1:1–22.

1029. Kövecses, Z. 1976. Toward the semantics of sport. *Semiotica* (The Hague) 18,4:313–318.

1030. Krawczyk, B. and Z. 1971. Socjologiczne Badania nad Sportem w Polsce (Sociological research on sport in Poland). *Studia Socjologiczne* (Warsaw) 40,1:223–235.

1031. Krawczyk, B. 1974. Use of sociology in competitive sport. *IRSS* 9,1: 141–146.

1032. Krawczyk, Z. 1977. Theory and empiricism in social sciences regarding physical culture. *IRSS* 12,1:71–91.

1033. Krawczyk, Z. 1977. Genesis of sociology of physical culture and sports. *Sociologicky Casopis* (Warsaw) 13,3:280–287.

1034. Kulinkovich, K.A. and O. Milshtein. 1972. Nekotorye metodologicheskie voprosy issledovanija socialnyh problem bolshogo sporta (Methodological aspects of studying social problems of sport). Pp. 7–9 in Materialy respublikanskoj konferencii. *Voprosy* teorii i praktiki fizicheskoj kultury i sporta. Minsk.

1035. Kun, L. 1970. Történet szociológiai célkitüzéseink (Our historical-sociological tasks). Pp. 33–34 in *Tanulmányok a testi neveles köréböl.* Budapest: Magyar Pedagógiai Társaság.

1036. Lenk, H. 1971. Bäume, Turniere und soziometrische Graphen. Zur Anwedbarkeit der mathematischen Graphentheorie in der Sportsoziologie. Pp. 163–183 in Albonico/Pfister-Binz.

1037. Lenk, H. and G. Lüschen. 1975. Epistemological problems and the personality and social system in social psychology. *Theory and Decision* 4,2:333–355.

1038. Lenk, H. and G. Lüschen. 1976. Wissenschaftstheoretische Probleme der Sozialpsychologie des Sports. *Sportwissenschaft* 6,2:121–143.

1039. Linde, H. 1967. Zur Soziologie des Sports. Versuch einer empirischen Kritik soziologischer Theoreme. Pp. 103–121 in *H. Plessner et al.*

1040. Linde, H. and K. Heinemann. 1971. Das Verhältnis einer Soziologie des Sports zu alternativen soziologischen Theorieansätzen. Pp. 47–51 in Albonico/Pfister-Binz.

1041. Loomis, C.P. 1960. *Social Systems.* Princeton: VanNostrand. 349 pp.

1042. Loy, J.W. and J.O. Segrave. 1973. Research methodology in the sociology of sport. Pp. 289–333 in L. Rarick, ed. *Physical Activity.* New York: Academic Press.

1043. Lüschen, G. 1960. Prolegomena zu einer Soziologie des Sports. *Kölner Z. Soziol.* 12,3:505–515.

1044. Lüschen, G. 1970. Soziologie des Sports. Pp. 158–168 in Groll/Strohmeyer.

1045. Lüschen, G. 1973. Critical remarks concerning the sociology of leisure. *Society and Leisure* (Prague) 1:165–175.
1046. Lüschen, G. 1976. Zur Strukturanalyse des Sports. Pp. 52–69 in Lüschen/ Weis.
1047. Lüschen, G. 1976. Toward a structural analysis of sport. *The Academy Papers* (Washington, D.C.) 10:80–87.
1048. Milsthein, O.A. 1971. Nekotorye problemy marksistskoj sociologii fizkultury i sporta kak nauchno-uchebnoj diszipliny (Problems of Marxist sociology of physical culture and sport as a scientific-didactic discipline). Pp. 96–101 in *Istorija, organizacija i sociologija fizicheskoj kultury i sporta*. Minsk.
1049. Novikov, A.A. 1966. Problemy teorii fizicheskogo vospitanija (Problems of theory of physical education). *Teorija i Praktika* 5:11–16.
1050. Novikov, A.D. and P.S. Stepnoj. 1966. K voprosu o predmete i metodah konkretnyh sociologicheskih issledovanij fizicheskoj kultury i sporta (On problems of subject and method in sociological studies of physical culture and sport). Pp. 28–38 in *Materialy I Vsesojuznoj konferencii po sociologicheskim problemam fizicheskoj kultury i sporta*. Leningrad.
1051. Novikov, A.D. and N.I. Rytberg. 1973. Ob osnovnyh hapravlenijah nauchnyh issledovanij marksistskih sociologicheskih problem fizicheskoj kultury i sporta (Main trends of scientific investigation on Marxist sociological problems of physical culture and sport). *Teorija i Praktika* 3:68–69.
1052. Olsen, A.M. 1971. Sociology of sport in relation to physical education and sport theory. Pp. 13–21 in Albonico/Pfister-Binz.
1053. Onishi, K. 1962 and 1963. Taiiku no shakaigakuteki kenkyu kadai (Topics of sociological research in physical education). *Bullectin Education Faculty Ibaraki University* 12,1:199–217 and 13,1:163–180.
1054. Onishi, K. 1972. Taiiku shakaigaku no kadai ryoiki (Scope of sociological research in physical education). *Research J. Sport Sociology* 1:47–67.
1055. Phillipps, J.C. 1977. Some methodological problems in sport sociology literature. *IRSS* 12,1:93–99.
1056. Ponomarev, N.I. 1978. About system analysis of sport. *IRSS* 13,1:7–28.
1057. Prosenc, M. 1971. Methodische Probleme der Beeinflussung und Planung. Pp. 147–150 in Albonico/Pfister-Binz.
1058. Rieder, H. ed. 1975. *Empirische Methoden in der Sportpsychologie*. Schorndorf: Hofmann. 226 pp.
1059. Rittner, V. 1974. Zur Konstitutionsproblematik der Sportwissenschaft. *Sportwissenschaft* 4,4:357–371.
1060. Rittner, V. 1976. Sociology, history and sport. *IRSS* 11,3:85–102.
1061. Saeki, T. 1969. Sport to sportshakaigaku kaidai (Examining sport and sport sociology). *Research Reports Kochi University* 18.
1062. Saeki, T. 1973. Shakaitaiiku no shakaigakuteki kenkyu no kadaito houho (Sociological problems and methods of sport and physical education in the community). *Research J. Sport Sociology* 1:69–87.
1063. Saunders, E.D. 1968. Sociological orientation to the study of physical education. *Physical Education* 60,179:21–26.
1064. Sawada, K. 1972. Rinenkei to gengo (Idealtypes and language). *Research J. Sport Sociology* 1:145–157.

1065.   Schiller, J. 1971. Kutatási módszerek a sportszociológiaban (Research methods in sociology of sport). *Sportvezetö* (Budapest) 10:20-21.
1066.   Schulz, R. 1961. Über Wesen und Methoden wissenschaftlicher Soziologie. *Theorie und Praxis* 10,2:108-114.
1067.   Schulz, R. 1971. Über theoretische Grundlagen einer marxistischleninistischen Soziologie des Sports. Pp. 23-27 in Albonico/Pfister-Binz.
1068.   Schutz, R.W. 1970. Stochastic processes: their nature and use in the study of sport and physical acitvity. *Research Quarterly* May: 205-212.
1069.   Schwalbe, J. 1975. Methodologische Überlegungen zu einer neuen Bestimmung des Begriffs 'Spiel' und erste Auswirkungen für die Praxis. *Neue Praxis* (Berlin) 3:218-228.
1070.   Shimazaki, J. 1972. Taiiku-shakaigaku to sport-shakaigaku tono kankei (A theoretical study of sport sociology and sociology of physical education). *Research J. Sport Sociology* 1:89-96.
1071.   Simmel, G. 1908. *Soziologie.* Berlin: Duncker und Humblot. 578 pp.
1072.   Simmel, G. 1917. *Grundfragen der Soziologie.* Berlin: DeGruyter. 98 pp.
1073.   Simmel, G. 1950. *Essays on Sociology.* K. Wolff, ed. Glencoe, Ill.: Free Press. 445 pp.
1074.   Snyder, E. 1974. Sociology of sport: concepts and theories. *J. Popular Culture* 8,Fall:361-369.
1075.   Steele, P.D. and L.A. Zurcher. 1973. Leisure sports as 'ephemeral roles': an exploratory study. *Pacif. Soc. Review* 16,3:345-356.
1076.   Stevenson, C.L. 1976. An alternative theoretical approach to sport socialization: a concept of institutional socialization. *IRSS* 11,1:65-76.
1077.   Stolàrov, V.I. 1976. The historical method in the sociology of sport. *IRSS* 11,3:103-111.
1078.   Takenoshita, K. 1957. Taiiku no shakaigakuteki kenkyuho (Social research methods in sport, recreation and physical education). *Research Methods Physical Education* (Tokyo) 11,4:297-349.
1079.   Takenoshita, K. 1967. The sociological research work of sport in Japan. *IRSS* 2:179-186.
1080.   Tichochoda, A.S. ed. 1969. *Metodizheskie razrabotki i ukazanija po voprosam sociologii sporta* (Methodical elaborations and instructions on problems of sociology of sport). Kiev. 101 pp.
1081.   Tichochoda, A.S. 1973. *Socialnye problemy fizicheskoj kultury i sporta* (Social problems of physical culture and sport). Moscow. 94 pp.
1082.   Trogsch, F. 1962. Marxistische Sozialforschung und ihre Anwendung auf dem Gebiet von Körperkultur und Sport. *Wissensch.Zeitschr.DHFK* 4,2:89-99.
1083.   Vrcan. S. 1971. Sociolog pred fenomenom nogometa (A sociologist looks at soccer). *Sociologia* (Beograd) 13,1:5-20.
1084.   Vsesojusnaja nauchnaja konferencija. 1971. *Istorija, organizacija i sociologija fizicheskoj kultury i sporta* (History, organization and sociology of physical culture and sport). March 9-13, 1971. Minsk: Tezisy dokladov. 284 pp.
1085.   White, L.A. 1965. Anthropology 1964: retrospect and prospect. *American Anthropologist* 67,3:629-637.
1086.   Whitson, D.J. 1976. Method in sport sociology: the potential of a phenomenological contribution. *IRSS* 11,4:53-68.

1087.   Whitson, D.J. 1978. *Research Methodology in Sport Sociology*. CAHPER-Monograph. Calgary: University of Calgary. 72 pp.
1088.   Wohl, A. 1965. Pojecie i zakres socjologii sportu (Concept and scope of sport sociology). *Kultura Fizyczna* 18,3:135–142.
1089.   Wohl, A. 1966. Conception and range of sport sociology. *IRSS* 1:5–27.
1090.   Wohl, A. 1975. Some remarks on the methodology of research on sociology of sport. *IRSS* 10,2:5–32.
1091.   Ziemilski, A. 1971. The contemporary sport—three aspects of sociological analysis and their methodological consequences. Pp. 74–78 in Albonico/Pfister-Binz.
1092.   Zoldak, V.I. 1971. O niekatorych voprosach organizacii konkrietnych sociologiceskich issledovanij fiziceskoj kultury (Some problems of organizing concrete-sociological studies of physical culture). Pp. 50–62 in *Fiziceskaja kultura i sport v sistiemie naucnoj organizacii truda*. Svierdlovsk.

2. *Programmatic Discussions and Reviews*

1093.   Albonico, R. 1966. Sport sociology in Switzerland. *IRSS* 1,1:209–217.
1094.   Albonico, R. 1967. Soziologie des Sports. *Jugend und Sport* (Bern) 24,5:131–133 and 6:163–165.
1095.   Anonymous. 1971. Research on sport sociology in the GDR. *Bulletin National Olympic Committee GDR* 16,4:20–32.
1096.   Artemov, V.A. 1963. Ob izucenii sociologiceskogo fiziceskoj kultury (Investigation of sociological aspects of physical culture). *Teorija i Praktika* 26,4:58–60.
1097.   Aveni, A.F. 1976. Man and machine: some neglected considerations on the sociology of sport. *Sport Sociology Bulletin* 5,1:13–23.
1098.   Brewster, P.G. 1956. The importance of the collecting and study of games. *Eastern Anthropologist* (Lucknow) 10,1:5–12.
1099.   Cauwels, A. 1965. Introduction à une sociologie du sport. Inleiding tot de sociologie van de sport. *Sport* (Brussells) 30,2:68–76.
1100.   Cikler, J. 1964. Vedecka sociologie a telesna kultura socialismu (Scientific sociology and physical culture under Socialism). *Teorija praxa Vychovani* (Prague) 12,7:295–297.
1101.   Ciupak, Z. 1965. O niektorych aspektach socjologii moralnosci sportowej w swietle dyskusij publicystycznej (Sociology of sport problems in the light of public discussion) *Kultura Fizyczna* 7-8:415–420.
1102.   Claeys, U. et al. 1975. *Sport sociaal gezien* (Sport in sociological perspective). Leuwen: Acco. 108 pp.
1103.   Claeys, U. and P. Suetens. 1976-77. *Sportbeoefning in Vlaanderen*. Deel I-IV. University of Leuwen. 158, 226, 200, 128 pp.
1104.   Cowell, C.C. 1937. Physical education as applied social science. *Educational Research Bulletin* 16,1:147–155.
1105.   Frenkin, A.A. 1962. Burzhuaznaja sociologija o roli sporta v obshchestve (Bouregeois sociology about the role of sport in society). *Teorija i Praktika* 12:16–22.
1106.   Frenkin, A. 1965. The bourgeois sport sociology and its reactionary role. *Teorija i Praktika* 28,2:5–9.

1107. Frenkin, A.A. 1965. Krizis burzhuaznoj sociologii sporta (The crisis of the Bourgeois sociology of sport). Pp. 23–86 in *Kritika burzhuaznoj sociologii sporta.* Moscow: Fizkultura i sport.

1108. Frick, E.A. 1961. Aspects sociologiques du sport. *Schweizerische Zeitschrift für Sportmedizin.* 9,1:35–48.

1109. Greendorfer, S.L. 1977. Sociology of sport: knowledge of what? *Quest* 28:58–65.

1110. Groenman, G.J. 1972. Sociologie van de sport (Sociology of sport). *De Lichamalijke Opvoeding* (Zeist) 60,5:103–107.

1111. Gruneau, R.S. 1978. Conflicting standards and problems of personal action in the sociology of sport. *Quest* 30, Summer:80–90.

1112. Hajek, M. 1970. Sociology of sport. *Sbornik Praci.* Brnenske University. 19,14:134–145.

1113. Hammerich, K. Critical remarks regarding the state of sociological research in the German Federal Republic. *IRSS* 1,1:229–236.

1114. Heinemann, K. 1974. Schwerpunkte für Lehre und Forschung im Bereich der Soziologie des Sports. *Gymnasion* 11,3:20–35.

1115. Heinemann, K. 1975. Gegenstand und Funktionen einer Soziologie des Sports. Pp. 9–20 in Hammerich/Heinemann.

1116. Heinemann, K. 1980. *Einführung in die Soziologie des Sports.* Schorndorf: Hofmann. 242 pp.

1117. Hendry, L.B. 1973. Sports sociology in Britain—career or commitment? *IRSS* 8,3–4:117–124.

1118. Hendry, L.B. 1975. Research trends in sports sociology. *Brit.J.Physical Education* 6,1:I.

1119. Ingham, A.G. 1973. Delineation of sport sociology in 1972. *IRSS* 8,1: 103–114.

1120. Japanese Society of Physical Education. Sociology Dpt. 1962–1965. *Taiikushakaigaku senmonbunkakai hokokusho* (Report of the Sociology Dpt. Assembly). Tokyo. 4 vols.

1121. Jensen, J. 1973. Bemerkungen zur Entwicklung der Sportsoziologie. Pp. 65–71 in K.J. Gutschke, ed. *Sportwissenschaft in der Entwicklung.* Berlin: Freie Universität.

1122. Kageyama, K. 1972. Taiiku shakaigaku no shomondai (Problems of sociology for physical education). *Research J. Sport Sociology* (Tokyo) 1:109–122.

1123. Kleine, B. and F. Trogsch. 1967. Die Sportsoziologie in der DDR. *Körpererziehung* 17,7:341–350.

1124. Langenfeld, H. 1971. Soziologische Grundlagen des Sports. Pp. 350–355 in ADL, eds. *Motivation im Sport.* Schorndorf: Hofmann.

1125. Lenk, H. 1973. Zur pädagogischen Bedeutung der Sportsoziologie. *Gymnasion* 10,3:16–26.

1126. Lloyd, F.S. 1937. The sociology of physical education. *JOHPER* 8,4: 204–205 and 266–267.

1127. Lowe, B. 1978. What do you know about sport sociology? *Olympic Review* Oct.:132–133, Nov.:601–611.

1128. Loy, J.W. 1972. Sociology and physical education. Pp. 168–236 in R. Singer, ed. *Physical Education.* New York: Macmillan.

1129. Loy, J.W. 1972. A case for the sociology of sport. *JOPHER* 43,6:50–56.

1130. Loy, J.W.; McPherson, B. and G. Kenyon. 1979. *The Sociology of Sport as an Academic Speciality.* CAPHER-Monograph: Calgary. 85 pp.

1131.   Loy, J.W. 1979. An exploratory analysis of the scholarly productivity of North Ameican based sport sociologists. *IRSS* 14,3-4:97-116.

1132.   Lüschen, G. 1968. *The Sociology of Sport.* A Trend-Report and Bibliography. Paris and The Hague: Mouton. Also as *Current Sociology* 1967,3. 140 pp.

1133.   Lüschen, G. and K. Hammerich. 1968. Sociologische Grundlagen von Leibeserziehung und Sport. Pp. 104-130 in O. Grupe et al. eds *Einführung in die Theorie der Leibeserziehung.* Schorndorf: Hofmann. Rev. 2nd, 3rd and 4th ed. 1974, 1976, 1980.

1134.   Lüschen, G. 1972. Zur Soziologie des Sports. Pp. 101-135 in O. Grupe Engl. On sociology of sport. Pp. 101-134 in O. Grupe.

1135.   Lüschen, G. 1975. The development and scope of a sociology of sport. *Am.Corr.Ther.Journal* 29,2:39-43.

1136.   Lüschen G. and K. Weis. 1976. Sport in der Gesellschaft. Standort und Aufgaben einer Soziologie des Sports. Pp. 9-21 in Lüschen/Weis.

1137.   Lüschen, G. 1980. Sociology of sport: present state and prospects. *Annual Review of Sociology* 6:315-347.

1138.   Malova, V.A. 1972. Osnovnye napralenija v rasvitii sociologiche-skih issledovanij v oblasti fizicheskoj kultury i sporta (Main trends in the development of sociological studies in the field of physical culture and sport). Pp. 106-125 in *Sbornik nauchno-metodicheskih rabot po organizacii fizkulturnogo drizenija i formam massovoj fizkulturnoj raboty.* Leningrad.

1139.   Marletti, C. 1967. Contributio per una defizione sociologica dello sport (Contribution toward a definition of sociology of sport). *Il Discobolo* 31,5:46-48.

1140.   Martin, D. 1971. Probleme und Theoriebildung einer Soziologie des Sports aus sportpädagogischer Sicht. *Die Leibeserziehung* 20,1:4-9.

1141.   Milsthein, O.A. 1966. Marksistskaja i burzuaznaja sociologija o roli i suscnosti svobodnovo vremieni v sfierie fizkceskovo vospitanija (The Marxist and bourgeois sociologies about the role and essence of leisure in physical culture). Pp. 140-142 in *Matierialy piervoj Vsiesojuznoj naucnoj konfierencii po sociologiceskim probliemam fiziceskoj kultury i sporta.* Leningrad.

1142.   Milsthein, O.A. 1974. Sociology of physical culture in the USSR. *IRSS* 9,2:137-146.

1143.   McIntosh, P.C. 1967. The Sociology of sports. *Sport and Recreation* 8,1:40-44.

1144.   McPherson, B.D. 1975. Past, present and future perspectives for research in sport sociology. *IRSS* 10,1:55-71.

1145.   McPherson, B.D. 1978. Avoiding chaos in the sociology of sport brickyard. *Quest* 30,Summer:72-79.

1146.   Nieuwenhuis, G.J. 1930. Soziologie der Leibesübungen. *Volksgesundheit* (Vienna) 4:1-3.

1147.   Nixon, H.L. 1976. *Sport and Social Organization.* Indianapolis: Bobbs-Merrill. 75 pp.

1148.   Page, C. 1973. The world of sport and its study. Pp. 3-39 in Talamini, J.T. and C. Page, eds. *Sport and Society.* Boston: Little, Brown.

1149. Petrak, B. 1966. Zakladni vymezeni problematiky sociologie telesne vychovy jako specialni sociologicke discipliny (Basic questions of sociology of physical education as a special sociological discipline). *Teory praxe telesne vychovy* (Prague) 14,1:16–20.

1150. Petrak, B. 1967. *Sociologie a telesna kultura* (Sociology of sport). Prague: Statui Pedagogicke Nakladatestvi.

1151. Pietersen, L. 1961. *Sociologie van de sport* (Sociology of Sport). Utrecht: Het Spectrum. 147 pp.

1152. Plessner, H. et al. 1967. *Sport und Leibeserziehung. Sozialwissenschaftliche, pädagogische und medizinische Beiträge.* Müchen: Piper. 400 pp.

1153. Rigauer, B. 1971. Inhaltliche und methodologische Bestimmungen einer kritischen Soziologie des Sports im Rahmen der Sportwissenschaften. *Die Leibeserziehung* 20,1:9–14.

1154. Rosenmayr, L. 1969. Probleme und Beispiele aus der Sportsoziologie. Pp. 62–73 in F. Tscherne, ed. *Leibesübungen in der technokratischen Welt von morgen.* Wien: Bundesverlag.

1155. Sage, G.H. 1977. Sport sociology: the state of the art and the implications for physical education. Pp. 310–319 in L. Gedvilas and M. Kneer, eds. *Proceedings of Orlando Conference 1977 NCPEAM/W.*

1156. Saunders, E.D. 1968. Sociological orientation to the study of physical education. *Physical Education* (London) 60,179:21–26.

1157. Schiller, J. 1965. A sportszocilogiai kutatasok problemai (Problems of sport sociological research). *Testneveles F. Tudomany Közl.* 4,2:77–81.

1158. Schiller, J. 1970. A Sportsociologia alkalmazasanak lehetösegei a telijesit-manyfokozasban (Prospects for application of sport sociology in performance increase). *Testneveles F. Tudomany Közl.* 2:402–413.

1159. Schiller, J. ed. 1970. *Sportszociologia.* Budapest: Tankönyvkiado. 143 pp.

1160. Schulke, H.J. 1977. Sociology in sport science: theoretical and methodological aspects of the research situation in the German Federal Republic. *IRSS* 12,3:63–73.

1161. Seikatsu Kagaku Chosakai, ed. 1962. *Sports no shakaigaku* (Sociology of sport). Tokyo: Ishiyaku Shuppan.

1162. Snyder, E.E. and E. Spreitzer. 1974. Sociology of sport: an overview. *Sociol.Quarterly* 15,4:467–487. Also 1975 pp. 9–34 in Ball/Loy.

1163. Staikof, Z. 1965. Sociologija na Fiziceska kultura i sporta (Sociology of physical culture and sport). *Voprosi na Fiziceskata Kultura* (Sofia) 10,4:202–205.

1164. Staikof, Z. 1966. Sociology of sport in Bulgaria. *IRSS* 1:410–413.

1165. Stepwoj, P.S. 1973. Nekotorye aktualnye problemy marksistskoj sociologii sporta (Actual problems of the Marxist sociology of sport). *Teorija i Praktika* 8,:5–6.

1166. Stoychev, A. 1970. Mezhdunaroden simpozium po sotsiologiya na sporta (Int. Symposium on Sociology of Sport in Sofia 1969). *Sotsiologicheski Problemi* 2,2:92–96.

1167. Takenoshita, K. and E. Isomura, eds. 1965. *Sports no shakaigaku* (Sociology of sport). Tokyo: Taishukan. Nr. 10.

1168. Takenoshita, K. and K. Sugawara. 1972. *Taiiku shakaigaku* (Sociology of physical education). Tokyo: Taishukan. 382 pp.

1169. Van Pelt, H. 1971. The beginning of a sociology of sport in Flanders.

Society and Leisure (Prague) 3,4:59–65.

1170.   Voigt, D. 1975. *Soziologie in der DDR. Eine exemplarische Untersuchung. Analyse der DDR-Soziologie am Beispiel des Forschungsgegenstandes Sport.* Köln: Verlag Wissenschaft und Politik. 335 pp.,

1171.   Voigt, D. and F. Grätz. 1977. Probleme der Sportsoziogie in der DDR. *Kölner Z.Soz.* 29,2:295–318.

1172.   Warszaw Seminar 1963. Über philosophische und sociologische Probleme der Körperkultur. *Theorie und Praxis* Sept. 1964. Supplement.

1173.   Yiannakis, A. et al. eds. 1976. *Sport Sociology: Contemporary Themes.* Dubuque, Ia.: Kendall/Hunt. 239 pp.

1174.   Zeigler, E.F. ed. 1971. *Research in the History, Philosophy and International Aspects of Physical Education and Sport.* Champaign: Stipes. 3xx pp.

1175.   Ziemilski, A. 1958. Florian Znaniecki a kultura fizyczna 1882-1958. (Florian Znaniecki on physical culture 1882-1958). *Kultura Fizyczna* 11,8:589-592.

3. Comprehensive and Systems Analyses

1176.   Asai, A., Kondo, H. and T. Niwa. 1973. *Taiiku shinron* (New theory of physical culture). Osaka: Times. 179 pp.

1177.   Benary, W. 1913. *Der Sport als Individual—und Sozialerscheinung.* Berlin: Wedekind. 128 pp.

1178.   Bouet, M. 1968. *Signification du sport.* Paris: Editions Universitaires. 671 pp.

1179.   Bouet, M. 1969. *Les motivations des sportifs.* Paris: Editions Universitaires. 239 pp.

1180.   Cattanei, G. 1973. *Analisi sociologica dello sport* (Sociological analysis of sport). Genova: Tilgher. 211 pp.

1181.   Coakley, J. 1978. *Sport in Society. Issues and Controversies.* St. Louis: Mosby. 349 pp.

1182.   Cratty, B.J. 1967. *Social Dimensions of Physical Activity.* Englewood-Cliffs, N.J.: Prentice-Hall. 139 pp.

1183.   Doros, G. 1932. *A sport szocialis es tarsadalmi conatkozasai* (Social and Sociological relations of sport). Budapest: Stephaneum. 137 pp.

1184.   Edwards, H. 1973. *Sociology of Sport.* Homewood, Ill.: Dorsey. 395 pp.

1185.   Eitzen, D.S. and G. Sage. 1978. *Sociology of American Sport.* Dubuque, Ia: W.C. Brown. 336 pp.

1186.   Georgescu, F. 1971. *Educatio fisica si sportul—fenomen social* (Physical education and sport as a social phenomenon). Bukarest: Stadion. 195 pp.

1187.   Grieswelle, D. 1977. *Sportsoziologie.* Stuttgart: Kohlhammer, 2 Vols.

1188.   Ibrahim, H. 1975. *Sport and Society: An Introduction to Sociology of Sport.* Whittier, Cal.: Whittier College. 243 pp.

1189.   Krawczyck, Z. 1970. *Natura, Kultura, Sport.* Warsaw: PWN. 387 pp.

1190.   Krockow, C. von. 1972. *Sport in der Industriegesellschaft.* Munich: Piper. 102 pp.

1191.   Krockow, C. von. 1980. *Sport, Gesellschaft, Politik.* Munich: Piper. 138 pp.

1192. Lenk, H. 1979. *Social Philosophy of Athletics.* Champaign, Ill.: Stipes. 227 pp.
1193. Loy, J.W.; McPherson, B. and G.S. Kenyon. 1978. *Sport and Social Systems.* Reading, Mass: Addison-Wesley. 447 pp.
1194. Lyra Filho, J. 1973. *Introducao a sociologia dos desportes* (Introduction to sociology of sport). Rio de Janeiro: Bloch. 390 pp.
1195. Magnane, G. 1964. *Sociologie du sport.* Paris: Gallimard. 190 pp.
1196. Risse, H. 1921. *Soziologie des Sports.* Berlin: Reher. 84 pp.
1197. Snyder, E. and E. Spreitzer. 1978. *Social Aspects of Sport.* Englewood-Cliffs: Prentice-Hall. 214 pp.

4. *Readers, Edited Collections, Proceedings, Bibliographies*

1198. Albonico, R. and K. Pfister-Binz, eds. 1971. *Soziologie des Sports— Theoretische und methodische Grundlagen/Sociology of Sport—Theoretical Foundations and Research Methods.* Basel: Birkhäuser. 208 pp.
1199. Ball, D. and J.W. Loy, eds. 1975. *Sport and Social Order.* Reading, Mass.: Addison-Wesley. 574 pp.
1200. Bratton, R., ed. 1978. *Sociology of Sport Monograph Series of CAPHER.* Calgary: University of Calgary. 13 volumes.
1201. Bulgarski Sujuz za Sport. 1970. *Sociologijata na sporta Bulgarija—Bibliografija 1959–1970.* Sofia. 138 pp.
1202. Dunning, E. ed. 1971. *The Sociology of Sport.* London: Cass. 382 pp.
1203. Eitzen, S. ed. 1979. *Sport in Contemporary Society.* New York: St. Martin's Press. 467 pp.
1204. Frey, J. ed. 1979. *Contemporary Issues in Sport.* Annals of AAPSS. Sept. 165 pp.
1205. Goldstein, J.H. ed. 1979. *Sports, Games, and Play.* Hillsdale, N.J.: Erlbaum. 456 pp.
1206. Groll, H. and H. Strohmeyer. eds. 1970. *Jugend und Sport.* Wien: Bundesverlag. 247 pp.
1207. Grupe, O. et al. eds. 1972. *Sport im Blickpunkt der Wissenschaften.* Berlin: Springer. *Engl. The Scientific View of Sport.* New York: Springer. 275 pp.
1208. Grupe, O. et al. eds. 1973. Sport in der modernen Welt. Berlin: Springer. 625 pp. *Engl. Sport in the Modern World.* New York: Springer.
1209. Hammerich, K. and K. Heinemann. eds. 1975. *Texte zur Soziologie des Sports.* Schorndorf: Hofmann. 292 pp.
1210. Hart, M. ed. 1972. Sport in the Socio-Cultural Process. Dubuque, Ia.: Brown. 4xx pp.
1211. Henze, P.W. ed. 1971. *Motivation im Sport.* Hilden: Buchpresse. 394 pp.
1212. Howell, M. 1971. A selected bibliography of sports and games in early and primitive societies. Pp. 46–87 in E. Zeigler, ed. *Research in the History, Philosophy, and International Aspects of Physical Education and Sport.* Champaign, Ill.: Stipes.
1213. Johnson, J.M. Ed. 1978. Sociology of Sport. *Urban Life* 7,2:147–280.
1214. Kenyon, G.S. ed. 1968. *Sociology of Sport. Aspects of Contemporary Sport Sociology.* Chicago: Athletic Institute. 213 pp.

1215.   *Konferencija po psihologii i sociologii sporta.* (Conference on psychology and sociology of sport). 1969. Tartu. 230 pp.

1216.   Krotee, M.L. ed. 1979. *The Dimensions of Sport Sociology.* West Point: Leisure Press. 256 pp.

1217.   Lancy, D.F. and B.A. Tindall, eds. 1978. *The Study of Play.* West Point, N.Y.: Leisure Press.

1218.   Landers, D. ed. 1976. *Social Problems in Athletics.* Urbana, Ill.: University of Illinois Press. 280 pp.

1219.   Landry, F. and W. Orban. eds. 1978. *Sociology of Sport. Proceedings of Quebec Olympic Congress.* Miami: Symposia Specialists. 609 pp.

1220.   Loy, J.W. and G.S. Kenyon. eds. 1969. *Sport, Culture, and Society.* London and New York: Macmillan. 464 pp.

1221.   Lüschen, G. ed. 1966. *Kleingruppenforschung und Gruppe im Sport.* Opladen: Westdeutscher Verlag. 280 pp.

1222.   Lüschen, G. ed. 1970. *The Cross-Cultural Analysis of Sport and Games.* Champaign, Ill.: Stipes. 192 pp.

1223.   Lüschen, G. and K. Weis. eds. 1976. *Die Soziologie des Sports.* Darmstadt: Luchterhand. 339 pp. Spanish 1979: *Sociologia del Deporte.* Valladolid: Minon. 294 pp.

1224.   Noll, R.G. ed. 1974. *Government and the Sports Business.* Washington, D.C.: Brookings Institution. 350 pp.

1225.   Salter, M.A. ed. 1979. *Play: Anthropological Perspectives.* West Point, N.Y.: Leisure Press. 200 pp.

1226.   Schwartzman, H.B. ed. 1980. *Play and Culture.* West Point, N.Y.: Leisure Press. 328 pp.

1227.   Stevens, P. ed. 1979. *Studies in the Anthropology of Play: Papers in Memory of B. Allan Tindall.* West Point, N.Y.: Leisure Press.

1228.   Stone, G.P. ed. 1972. *Games, Sport and Power.* New Brunswick, N.J.: Transaction Books. 228 pp.

1229.   Widmeyer, W.N. ed. 1978. *Physical Activity and the Social Sciences.* New York: MSS Information Corporation. 501 pp.

1230.   Yiannakis, A. et al. eds. 1976. *Sport Sociology: Contemporary Themes.* Dubuque, Ia.: Kendall/Hunt. 239 pp.

II. *Sport, Culture, Society and Social Institutions*

1. *Cross-Cultural and Cross-National Analysis* (including culturally indigenous sports and games)

2001.   Ahokas, J. 1959. Le pays de la compétition. Engl. The land of competition. Diogène/Diogenes 26,avr.-juin:115–125.

2002.   Allardt, E. 1970. Basic approaches in comparative sociological research and the study of sport. Pp. 14–30 in Lüschen.

2003.   Allardt, E. 1976. Vergleichende Sozialforschung und die Analyse des Sports. Pp. 72–86 in Lüschen/Weis.

2004.   Allison, M.T. and G. Lüschen. 1979. A comparative analysis of Navaho and Anglo basketball sport systems. *IRSS* 14,3–4:75–86.

2005. Anderson, R. and W. Bruce. 1967. On the comparability of meaningful stimuli in cross-cultural research. *Sociometry* 30,2:124–136.

2006. Artjemov, R.N. 1970. Vlijanie razvitija sporta na jazykkovuju kulturu (The influence of sport development on language culture). Pp. 21–24 in *Materialy nauchno-metodicheskoj konferencii.* Vilnus: Sovetskij Chelovek i fizicheskaja kultura.

2007. Balazs, E.K. 1977. A cross-cultural comparison of some outstanding sportswomen. Pp. 105–116 in M. Adrian and J. Brame, eds. *Research Reports of AAHPER.* Washington, D.C.

2008. Ball, D. 1972a. What the action is. *Theory Soc.Behavior* 2,Oct.:121–143.

2009. Ball, D. 1972b. Olympic Games competition. *Int.J.Compar.Sociol.* 15,1: 186–200.

2010. Ball, D. 1972c. The scaling of gaming. *Pac.Sociol.Review* 15,2:277–294.

2011. Ball, D. 1974. Control versus complexity: continuities in the scaling of gaming. *Pac.Sociol.Review* 17,2:167–184.

2012. Bennett, B.L. et al. 1975. *Comparative Physical Education and Sport.* Philadelphia: Lea and Ferbiger. 289 pp.

2013. Brewster, P.G. 1954. Some Nigerian games with their parallels and analogues. *Journal de la Société des Africanistes* 24,1:25–48.

2014. Brewster, P.G. 1955. A collection of games from India, with some notes on similar games in other parts of the world. *Zeitschrift für Ethnologie* 80,1:88–102.

2015. Brewster, P.G. 1955. The game of sahbi iddi zaiat: some parallels and analogues. *Hesperis* 42,1–2:239–244.

2016. Brewster, P.G. and J. Milojkovic-Djuric. 1956. A group of Jugoslav games. *Southern Folklore Quarterly* 20,3:183–191.

2017. Brewster, P.G. 1957. Some games from Czechoslovakia. *Southern Folklore Quarterly* 21,3:165–174.

2018. Brewster, P.G. 1959. Three Russian games and their Western parallels. *Southern Folklore Quarterly* 23,2:126–131.

2019. Brewster, P.G. 1960. A sampling of games from Turkey. *East and West* 11,1:15–20.

2020. Burridge, K.O.L. 1957. A Tangu game. *Man* 57, June:88–89.

2021. Caillois, R. 1957. Jogos e civilizacoes (Games and civilization) *Anhembi* 28,83:229–243 and 84:451–461.

2022. Curtis, J. 1971. Voluntary association joining: a cross-national comparative note. *ASR* 36,Oct.:872–880.

2023. Damm, H. 1960. Vom Wesen sogenannter Leibesübungen bei Naturvölkern. *Studium Generale* 13,1:3–10. Engl. 1970. The So-called sport activities of primitive peoples. Pp. 52–69 in Lüschen.

2024. Daniels, A. 1966. The study of sport as an element of the culture. *IRSS* 1:153–166.

2025. Dunlap, H. 1951. Games, Sports, dancing and other vigorous recreational activities and their function in Samoan culture. *Research Quarterly* 22,3:298–311.

2026. Elias, N. and E. Dunning. 1970. The quest for excitement in unexciting societies. Pp. 31–51 in Lüshcen.

2027. Frederickson, F.S. 1960. Sports and the cultures of man. PP. 633–646 in W.R. Johnson, ed. *Science and Medicine of Exercise and Sport.* New

York: Harper. Also 1969 pp: 87–115 in Loy/Kenyon.

2028.   Freitas de Castro, E.de. 1954. As cavalhadas de Vacaria (Equestrian sport). Porto Alegre: Impr. official. 32 pp.

2029.   Glassford, R.G. 1970. Organization of games and adaptive strategies of the Canadian Eskimo. Pp. 70–84 in Lüschen.

2030.   Hayner, N.S. 1953. Mexicans at play—a revolution. *Sociol.Soc.Research* 38,2:80–83.

2031.   Heinilä, K. 1974. *Ethics of Sport: Junior Football Players as Cross-National Interpreters of the Moral Concepts.* Research Reports. University of Jyväskylä. Nr. 4. 71 pp.

2032.   Herrigel, E. 1956. *Zen in der Kunst des Bogenschiessens.* Munich: Barth. 94 pp.

2033.   Hollander, P. 1966. Leisure as an American and Soviet value. *Soc. Problems* 24,1:179–188.

2034.   Hopkins, B. 1972. The sociology of sport. A cross-cultural model of physical activity and its application to the Old Order Amish society. *Anstey College of Education Monographs* Nr. 2.

2035.   Howell, M. 1970. Sports and games in certain primitive societies. *Canadian J.Hist.Sport Phys. Ed.* 1,1:17–32.

2036.   Jensen, A.E. 1948. Wettkampfparteien, Zweiklassensysteme und geographische Orientierung. *Studium Generale* 1,1:38–48.

2037.   Jokl, E. 1956. *Sports in the Cultural Pattern of the World: A Study of the 1952 Olympic Games.* Helsinki: Institute Occupational Health. 126 pp.

2038.   Kenyon, G.S. 1970. Attitude toward sport and physical activity among adolescents from four English speaking countries. Pp. 138–155 in Lüschen.

2039.   Kiviaho, P. and P. Mäkelä. 1978. Olympic success: A sum of non-material and material factors. *IRSS* 13,2:5–22.

2040.   Laszlo, I. and F. Megyeri. 1960. A társaslpi fejlödés az olimpiai játékok tükrében (The social revolution reflected in the light of Olympics). *Sport és Tudomany* 8,4:227–228.

2041.   Levine, N. 1974. Why countries win Olympic medals? Some structural correlates of Olympic Games success. *Sociol.Soc.Research* 58,4:353–360.

2042.   Lüschen, G. 1962. Der Leistungssport in seiner Abhängigkeit vom soziokulturellen System. *Zentralblatt Arbeitswissenschaft* 16,12:186–190.

2043.   Lüschen, G. 1967. The interdependence of sport and culture. *IRSS* 2,1: 127–141. Also 1970 pp. 85–99 in Lüschen.

2044.   Mannhardt, W. 1904 and 1905. *Wald-und Feldkulte.* Berlin: Borntraeger. 648 and 359 pp.

2045.   Marboc, E. ed. 1948. *The Book of Austria.* Wien: Österreichische Stattsdruckerei. 544 pp.

2046.   Masüger, J.B. 1955. *Schweizerbuch der alten Bewegungsspiele.* Zürich: Artemis 467 pp.

2047.   Mehl, E. 1948. Baseball in the Stone Age. *Western Folklore* 7:145–155.

2048.   Meldrum, K.I. 1971. Participation in outdoor activities in selected countries in Western Europe. *Comparative Education* 7,3:137–142.

2049.   Mendner, S. 1956. *Das Ballspiel im Leben der Völker.* Münster: Aschendorff. 170 pp.

2050.   Mindt, E. 1938. *Spiel und Sport als völkisches Erbe.* Berlin.

2051. Miyahata, T. 1962. General organization of physical education in Japan, with annotations regarding other countries in Asia. *Bulletin of FIEP* 3-4:14-28.

2052. McClintock, C.G. and J.M. Nuttin. 1969. Development of competitive game behavior in children across two cultures. *Journ.Exper.Soc.Psychology* 5,2:203-218.

2053. McClelland, D.C. 1961. *The Achieving Society.* New York: VanNostrand. 512 pp.

2054. Nduka, O. 1964. *Western Education and the Nigerian Cultural Background.* Ibadan.

2055. Nixon, J.E. 1969. Comparative, international and development studies in physical education. Pp. 114-123 in *Proceedings National College Phys. Ed.Assoc. Men.*

2056. Novikov, A.D. and A.M. Maximenko. 1972. The influence of selected socio-economic factors on the level of sports achievements in various countries. *IRSS* 7,1:27-43. German: 1972. *Sportwissenschaft* 3,2: 156-167.

2057. Pfetsch, F. et al. 1975. *Leistungssport und Gesellschaftssystem.* Schorndorf: Hofmann. 218 pp.

2058. Risset, R. 1951. Sport et culture. *Education physique et sport* 7,2:3-6.

2059. Roberts, J.M.; Arth, M.J. and R.R. Bush. 1959. Games in culture. *American Anthropologist* 61,4:597-605.

2060. Roberts, J.M. and B. Sutton-Smith. 1962. Child training and game involvement. *Ethnology* 1,2:166-185.

2061. Robinson, J.P. 1967. Time expenditure on sport across ten countries. *IRSS* 2,1:67-88.

2062. Robinson, J.P. 1970. Daily participation in sport across twelve countries. Pp. 156-173 in Lüschen.

2063. Rodgers, B. 1977. *Sport in Its Social Context.* International Comparisons. Strasbourg: Council of Europe. 64 pp.

2064. Rosenblatt, P.C. 1962. Function of games: an examination of individual difference hypotheses derived from a cross-cultural study. *Journal Soc. Psychology* 58,1:17-22.

2065. Seagoe, M. 1962. Children's play as an indicator of cross-cultural and intracultural differences. *Journ.Ed.Sociol.* 35,6:278-283. Also 1970 pp. 132-137 in Lüschen.

2066. Seppänen, P. 1968. Sport success and the type of culture. *Research Reports.* University of Helsinki. Nr. 151.

2067. Seppänen, P. 1971. O Papel dos Desportos de Competicao nas diferentes sociedades (Competitive sports and their role in different societies). *Educaco e movimento* 10,April-June:7-18.

2068. Seppänen, P. 1972. Die Rolle des Leistungssports in den Gsellschaften der Welt. *Sportwissenschaft* 2,2:133-155.

2069. Seurin, P. 1962. Comparative study of the organization of physical education and sport in Western countries. *Bulletin of FIEP* 3,4:139-185.

2070. Stejskal, M. 1954. *Folklig Idrott* (Folkloristic sport). Kobenhavn: Munksgaard. 224 pp.

2071. Stejskal, M. 1970. Folk-athletic games. *IRSS* 5,1:175-184.

2072. Sutton-Smith, B. et al. 1963. Game involvement in adults. *J.Social Psy-*

chology 60,1:15–30.

2073.   Sutton-Smith, B. and J.M. Roberts. 1970. The cross-cultural and psycho-logical study of games. Pp. 100–108 in Lüschen.

2074.   Webster, D. 1960. *Scottish Highland Games.* London.

2. Sport and Games in Tribal, Developing and Intermediate Societies

2075.   Ager, L.P. 1974. Play among Alaskan Eskimos. *Theory into Practice* 13,4:252–256.

2076.   Ajisafe, A.K. 1924. *The Laws and Customs of the Yoruba People* London: Routledge. 97 pp.

2077.   Anboyer, J. 1956. Archery: a royal sport and sacred game in ancient India. *Arts and Letters.* India, Pakistan, Ceylon 30,1:3–12.

2078.   Arimar, H. 1954. *Growing up in an Egyptian Village.* London: Routledge and Kegan Paul. 316 pp.

2079.   Aymonier, E.F. 1900. *Le Cambodges. Le Royaume Actual.* Paris: Leroux. 478 pp.

2080.   Baldwin, G.C. 1969. *Games of the American Indian.* New York: Norton. 150 pp.

2081.   Béart, C. 1955. *Jeux et jouets de l'Ouest africain.* Dakar: Ifan. 2 vols. 888 pp.

2082.   Béart, C. 1960. *Recherche des éléments d'une sociologie des peuples africains à partir de leur jeux.* Paris: Présence africaine. 147 pp.

2083.   Belgrave, J. 1953. *Welcome to Bahrain.* Stourbridge, W'shire: Moody. 154 pp.

2084.   Bell, M.J. 1948. *An American Engineer in Afghanistan.* Minneapolis: University of Minnesota Press. 335 pp.

2085.   Bell, C. 1928. *The People of Tibet.* Oxford: Clarendon Press. 319 pp.

2086.   Benneth, H. 1958. Games of the old time Maori. *Te Ao Hou* 6,22:45–47 and 24:52–53.

2087.   Blasig, R. 1933. The practice of sports among the Indians of America. *Mind and Body* 24,40:216–219.

2088.   Bogeng, G. 1926. *Geschichte des Sports aller Völker und Zeiten.* Leipzig.

2089.   Brown, E. 1861. *A Seaman's Narrative of His Adventures During a Captivity among Chinese Pirates.* London: Westerton. 292 pp.

2090.   Burton, R.F. 1856. *First Footsteps in East Africa or an Exploration of Harar.* London: Longman, Brown and Green. 648 pp.

2091.   Camble, D. 1957. *The Wolof of Senegambia, together with Notes on the Lebu and the Serer.* London: Int.African Institute. 110 pp.

2092.   Carneiro, R.L. 1970. Hunting and hunting magic among the Amahuaga of the Peruvian Montana. *Ethnology* 4,9:331–340.

2093.   Catlin, G. 1965. *Letters and Notes on the Manners, Customs and Conditions of the North American Indians.* Minneapolis: Ross and Haines (1841 reprint). 846 pp.

2094.   Centner, T.H. 1963. *L'enfant africain et jeux dans le cadre de la vie traditionelle au Katanga.* Elisabethville, Kat.: CEPSI. 412 pp.

2095.   Cheska, A. 1975. Guessing and gambling games: play patterns of North

American Indian cultures. In *Proceedings North Am.Society Sport History*. Windsor, Ont.

2096. Cheska, A. 1979. Native American games as strategies of societal maintenance. Pp. 227–247 in C. Farrer and E. Norbeck, eds. *Forms of Play of North Americans*. St. Paul: West.

2097. Cheska, A. 1979. Cross discipline research in the study of play. Pp. 119–134 in U. Simri, ed. *Comparative Physical Edcation and Sport*. Natanya: Wingate Institute.

2098. Chham-Chhom, M. 1949. Jeux Cambodgiens. *France-Asie* 1,4:881–888.

2099. Cimlette, J.D. 1929. *Malay Poisons and Sham Cures*. London: Churchill. 301 pp.

2100. Culin, S. 1907. *Games of the North American Indians*. Washington, D.C.: Bureau of American Ethnology. 846 pp.

2101. Culin, S. 1958. *Games of the Orient*. Rutland, Vt.: Tuttle. 177 pp.

2102. Cunningham, A. 1854. *Ladak, Physical, Statistical, Historical*. London: Allen. 485 pp.

2103. Damm, H. 1922. *Die gymnastischen Spiele der Indonesier und Südseevölker*. Leipzig: Spamer.

2104. Dennys, N.B. 1894. *A Descriptive Dictionary of British Malaya*. London: London and China Telegraph Office. 423 pp.

2105. Deraniyagala, P.E. et al. 1951. *Some Sinhala Combative, Field and Aquatic Sports and Games*. Colombo: National Museum of Ceylon.

2106. Deydier, H. 1952. *Introduction a la Connaissance du Laos*. Saigon: Impr. Française d'Outre-Mer. 140 pp.

2107. Diem, C. 1941. *Asiatische Reiterspiele*. Berlin Deutscher Archiv-Verlag.

2108. Eisen, G. 1976. Games and sporting diversions of the North American Indians as reflected in American historical writings of the 16th and 17th centuries. *Canadian J.History Sport Phys.Education* 9,1:58–85.

2109. Engert, C.V.H. 1924. *A Report on Afghanistan*. Washington, D.C.: Gvt. Printing Office. 225 pp.

2110. Evans-Pritchard, E.E. 1972. Zande string figures. *Folklore* 83,Autumn: 225–239.

2111. Ferrars, M. *Burma*. 1901.[2] London: Low, Marston. 237 pp.

2112. Finney, B.R. 1959. Fa`a he`e l`ancien sport de Tahiti. *Bulletin de la Société des Études Océaniennes*. 127–28, 1(2–3):53–56.

2113. Firth, R. 1930. A dart-match in Tikopia—a sociology of primitive sport. *Oceania* 1,1:64–96. *German*: 1976. Ein Speerspiel in Tikopia. Pp. 103–114 in Lüschen/Weis.

2114. Fox, E.F. 1943. *Travels in Afghanistan, 1937–38*. New York: Macmillan. 285 pp.

2115. Franck, H.A. 1926. *East of Siam: Ramblings in the Five Divisions of French Indo-China*. New York: Century. 357 pp.

2116. Fraser-Tytler, W.K. 1942. Afghanistan: a brief description. *Royal Central Asian Soc. Journal* 29,3–4:165–175.

2117. Gorer, G. 1935. Book one: Senegalese. Pp. 25–79 in *Africa Dances*. London: Faber and Faber.

2118. Gouin, A.J. 1891. Le costume annamite. *Société de Géographie Bulletin* (Paris) 7,12:242–251.

2119. Graham, W.A. 1924. *Siam*. London: La More Press. Vol. 1. 395 pp.

2120.   Griaule, M. and Z. Ligers. 1955. Le Bulu, jeu Bozo. *Journal de la Société des Africanistes* 25,1–2:35–37.
2121.   Griffis, W.E. 1882. *Corea: The Hermit Nation.* New York: Scribner. 462 pp.
2122.   Gurdon, P. 1907. *The Kasis.* London: Nutt. 227 pp.
2123.   Heber, A.R. and K.M. 1926. *In Himalayan Tibet.* Philadelphia: Lippincott. 283 pp.
2124.   Hervey, D.F.A. 1903. Malay Games. *Journal Anthropological Institute Great Britain and Northern Ireland* 33:284–303.
2125.   Hoàng-Yèn. 1919. La musique de Hué, Don-Ngnyet and Don-Tranh. *Bulletin Amis de Vieux Hué* 6:233–387.
2126.   Hoffmann, W.J. 1890. Remarks on Ojibwa ball play. *American Anthropologist* 3,2:133–135.
2127.   Howard, J.H. 1971. The Ponca shinny game. *Indian Historian* 4,3:10–15.
2128.   Hulbert, H.B. 1906. *The Passing of Korea.* New York: Doubleday Page. 473 pp.
2129.   Hummel, S. 1958. Das tibetanische Kungserspiel. *Acta Ethnographica* 7,1–2:219–221.
2130.   Hye-Kerkdal, K. 1955. Tika, an old mystery game in the Pacific. *Journal Polynesian Society* 64,2:197–226.
2131.   Hye-Kerkdal, K. 1956. Wettkampfspiel und Dualorganisation bei den Timbira Brasiliens. Pp. 504–533 in J. Haekel, ed. *Die Wiener Schule der Völkerkunde.* Wien: Berger. 568 pp.
2132.   Ikbal, A.S.S. 1939. *Modern Afghanistan.* London: Low, Marston. 341 pp.
2133.   Kagwa, A. 1934. *The Customs of the Baganda.* New York: Columbia University Press. 199 pp.
2134.   Kähler-Meyer, E. 1955. Spiele bei den Bali in Kamerun. *Afrika und Übersee* 39,4:179–190.
2135.   Kang, Y. 1931. *The Gray Roof.* New York: Scribner. 367 pp.
2136.   Kawaguchi, E. 1909. *Three Years in Tibet.* Adgar, Madras: Theosophist Office. 719 pp.
2137.   Keri, H. 1958. Ancient games and popular games. *American Imago* 15,1: 41–89.
2138.   Krieger, K. 1955. Knabenspiele der Hausa. *Baessler Archiv* 28,3:225–232.
2139.   LaFlamme, A.G. 1977. The role of sport in the development of ethnicity: a case study. *Sport Sociology Bulletin* 6,1:47–51.
2140.   Lévi-Strauss, C. 1966. *The Savage Mind.* Chicago: University of Chicago Press.
2141.   Levine, D.N. 1965. *Wag a Gold: Tradition and Innovation in Ethiopian Culture.* Chicago: University of Chicago Press.
2142.   Longrigg, S.H. 1953. *Iraq, 1900 to 1950.* London and New York: Oxford University Press. 436 pp.
2143.   Lorimer, E.O. 1939. *Language Hunting in the Karakoram.* London: Allen and Unwin. 310 pp.
2144.   Mackenzie, D.R. 1925. *The Spirit Ridden Konde.* London: Seeley Service. 318 pp.
2145.   Mair, L.P. 1934. *An African People in the 20th Century.* London: Routledge. 300 pp.
2146.   Mariw, G. 1931. Somali games. *Royal Anthropological Institute Great*

Britain and Northern Ireland Journal 1931:499–511.

2147.   Massé, H. 1938. *Croyanes et Coutumes Persanes.* Paris: Librairie Orientale et Américaine. 2 Vols. 539 pp.

2148.   Materi, I.T. 1949. *Irma and the Hermit: My Life in Korea.* New York: Norton. 256 pp.

2149.   Maurel, E. 1887. A scientific mission to Cambodia. *Popular Science Monthly* 30,71:310–322.

2150.   Mazur, A. 1967. Game theory and Pathan segmentary opposition. *Man* 2,3:465–466.

2151.   Mead, M. 1937. *Cooperation and Competition among Primitive Peoples.* New York: McGraw Hill. 151 pp.

2152.   Moncrieff, J. 1966. Physical games and amusements of the Australian Aboriginal. *Australian Journal Physical Education* 36,Febr.-March:5–11.

2153.   Mooney, J. 1890. The Cherokee ball games. *American Anthropologist* 3,2:105–132.

2154.   McDonald, D. 1929. *The Land of the Lama.* London: Seeley, Service. 283 pp.

2155.   Ngu Yen, v.K. 1930. Essai sur le Dinh et le Culte du Génie Tutélaire des Villages au Tonkin. *École Française d'Éxtrême-Orient Bulletin* 30: 107–159.

2156.   Nimuendaju, C. 1946. *The Eastern Timbira.* Translated and edited by R.H. Lowie. Berkeley: University of California Press.

2157.   Nordenskiold, E. 1910. Spiele und Spielsachen im Gran Chaco und in Nordamerika. *Zeitschrift Ethnologie* 42:427–433.

2158.   Omurzakov, D. 1958. *Kirgizskie nacionalnye vidy sporta i narodnyeigry* (Aspects of Kirghiz national sport and popular games). Frunze: Kirgizgosizdat.

2159.   Ory, P. 1894. *La Commune annamite au Tonkin.* Paris: Augustin Clallamel. 147 pp.

2160.   Overbeck, H. 1915. New notes on the game of 'Chongkak'. *Royal Asiatic Society Straits Branch Journal* 68:7–10.

2161.   Pennington, C.W. 1970. La carrera de bola entre los tarahumaras de Mexico. *American Indigena* 30,1:15–40.

2162.   Pina Chan, R. 1969. *Spiel und Sport im alten Mexiko.* Leipzig. 72 pp.

2163.   Polunin, I. 1952. Traditional beats of Malaya. *Geographic Magazine* (London) 25,1:334–345.

2164.   Porée, C. and E. Maspero. 1938. *Mœurs et costumes des Khmèrs* Paris: Payot. 270 pp.

2165.   Porée, C. and E. Maspero. 1949. *Cambodia. Commission des mœurs et coutumes.* Pnom-Penh: Imprimerte Portail. 84 pp.

2166.   Puccioni, N. 1936. Antropologia e etnografia delle genti della Somalia (Anthropology and ethnography of the peoples of Somalia). *Etnografia e paletnologia* (Bologna) 3:1–140.

2167.   Reinach, L.de. 1901. *Le Laos.* Paris; Charles Libraire. 2 vols.

2168.   Ribbach, S.H. 1940. *Drogpa Namgyal: ein Tibeterleben.* Munich: Barth. 263 pp.

2169.   Richard, P.C. 1867. Notes pour servir á l'ethnographie de la Cochinchine. *Revue Maritime et Coloniale* 21:92–133.

2170.   Rockhill, W.W. 1891. Notes on some of the laws, customs and superstitions of Korea. *American Anthropologist* Vol. N:177–187.

2171.   Rockhill, W.W. 1895. Notes on the Ethnology of Tibet. Pp. 665–747 in *Report U.S. National Museum for 1893.* Washington, D.C.: Smithsonian Institution.

2172.   Romero, E. 1954–56. Juegos infantiles tradicionales en el Peru (Traditional children's games in Peru). *Folklore Americano* 2,2:89–118. 3,3: 94–120 and 4,4:89–118.

2173.   Roscoe, J. 1911. *The Baganda: An Account of Their Native Customs and Beliefs.* London: Macmillan. 547 pp.

2174.   Salamone, F.A. 1979. Children's games as mechanisms for easing ethnic interaction in ethnically heterogeneous communities: a Nigerian case. *Anthropos* 74,1–2:202–210.

2175.   Saunderson, H.S. 1894. Notes on Corea and its people. *Journal Anthropological Institute Great Britain and Northern Ireland* 24:299–316.

2176.   Savage-Landor, A.H. 1895. *Corea or Cho-Sen. The Land of the Morning Calm.* London: Heinemann. 304 pp.

2177.   Schlenther, U. 1976. Sport und Spiel in Altamerika. *Das Altertum* (Berlin) 22,1:36–41.

2178.   Scott, J.G. 1910.[3] *The Burman, His Life and Notions.* London: Macmillan. 609 pp.

2179.   Shen, Tsung-hen and Shen-chi lin. 1953. *Tibet and the Tibetans.* Stanford: Stanford University Press. 199 pp.

2180.   Smith, E.W. *The Ua-speaking Peoples of Northern Rhodesia.* London: Macmillan. Vol. 2, 433 pp.

2181.   Stannus, H. 1910. Notes on some tribes of British Central Africa. *Journal Royal Anthropological Institute Great Britain and Northern Ireland* 40:285–335.

2182.   Stegmiller, P.F. 1925. Pfeilschiessen und Jagdgebräuche der Kasis. *Anthropos* 20:607–623.

2183.   Stevenson, M.C. 1903. Zuni games. *American Anthropologist* 5,3: 468–497.

2184.   Stumpf, F. and F.W. Cozens. 1947 and 1948. Some aspects of the role of games, sports and recreational activities in the culture of primitive peoples. *Research Quarterly* 18,2:198–218 (Maori). 20,1:2–30 (Fiji).

2185.   Suratgar, O.H. 1951. *I Sing in the Wilderness: An Intimate Account of Persia and the Persians.* London: E. Stanford. 222 pp.

2186.   Sykes, E.C. 1910. *Persia and Its People.* New York: Macmillan. 356 pp.

2187.   Taube, E. 1976. Die drei Wettspiele der Männer. Über die traditionellen Sportarten der Mongolen. *Das Altertum* (Berlin) 22,2:99–106.

2188.   Tessmann, G. 1913. *Die Pangwe: Völkerkundliche Monographie eines west-afrikanischen Negerstammes.* Berlin: Wasmuth. Vol. 2. 402 pp.

2189.   Thompson, V.M. 1937. *French-Indochina.* New York: Macmillan. 516 pp.

2190.   Thompson, V.M. 1941. *Thailand.* New York: Macmillan. 865 pp.

2191.   Tobe, J.H. 1963. Hunsa in the Himalayas. *Natural History* 72,8:38–45.

2192.   Vassal, G.M. 1910. *On and Off Duty in Aunam.* London: Heinemann 283 pp.

2193.   Weis, K. Die Funktion des Ballspiels bei den alten Maya. Pp. 115–129 in Lüschen/Weis.

2194.   Wheeler, L.R. 1928. *The Modern Malay.* London: Allen and Unwine. 300 pp.

2195. White, J. 1823. *History of a Voyage to the China Sea.* Boston: Wells and Lilly. 372 pp.

2196. Wilkinson, R.J. *Papers on Malay Subjects' Life and Customs.* Kuala Lumpur: Government Press. Part III. 97 pp.

2197. Winstedt, R.O. 1906. Some notes on Malay card games. *Royal Asian Society, Straits Branch Journal* 45:85–88.

2198. Witt-Siwasariyanon. 1954. *Life in Bangkok.* Bangkok: National Culture Institute.

2199. Yang, M.C. 1945. *A Chinese Village: Taiton, Shantung Province.* New York: Columbia University Press. 275 pp.

2200. Youd, J. 1961. Notes on kickball in Micronesia. *Journal American Folklore* 74,1:62–64.

2201. Young, E. 1898. *The Kingdom of the Yellow Rope. Being Sketches of the Domeshe and Religious Rites and Ceremonies of the Siamese.* Westminster: Archibald Constable. 399 pp.

3. Sport in Modern Society

2202. Aménagement du Territoire. 1975. Sport et société. *Deux Mille* (Paris) 33:1–56.

2203. Andersen, H. et al. 1957. Sporten i Danmark i Sociologisk belysning (Sport in Denmark in sociological perspective). København: Danske Forlag. 98 pp.

2204. Arai, S. 1971. Nihonjin to sport nitsuiteno ichikosatsu (A study of Japanese and sport with special reference to change of undo-kai). *Research of Physical Education Kyushu University* (Fukuoka) 4,4:1–6.

2205. Arai, S. et al. 1973. *Gendai seikatsu to taiiku* (Modern life and sport). Tokyo: Gakujitsutosho shuppansha.

2206. Asada, T. and A. Kataoka. 1975. Sport consciousness and behavior of Japanese people. *Research J.Phys.Education* 19,6:317–328 (Overseas edition).

2207. Boehme, J.O. et al. 1971. *Sport im Spätkapitalismus.* Frankfurt: Limpert. 160 pp.

2208. Bouet M. 1966. The function of sport in human relations. *IRSS* 1: 242–249.

2209. Bouet, M. 1969. Integrational functions of sport. *IRSS* 4,1:129–136.

2210. Boyle, R.H. *Sport: Mirror of American Life.* Boston: Little Brown. 293 pp.

2211. Brogan, D. 1944. *The American Character.* New York: Knopf 168 pp.

2212. Cagigal, J.M. 1975. *El deporte en la sociedad actual* (Sport in modern society). Madrid: Prensa Espanola. 160 pp.

2213. Charabuga, G.D. 1966. Zakonemiernosti Sviazi fiziceskoj kul'tury s drugimi storonami kul'tury obscestva (Patterns of relations between physical culture and other facets of culture). Pp. 48–50 in *Matierialy piervoj Vsiesojuznoj Konfierencii po Sociologiceskim Probliemam Sporta.* Leningrad.

2214. Claeys, U. 1977. Projecto de investigacao sobre a socializacad das funcoes algons resultados na Belgia (Research project in Belgium concerning social function of sport). *Antologia Deportiva* (Lisbon):1–11.

2215. Clouscard, M. 1963. Les fonctions sociales du sport. *Cahiers Int.Sociologie* 34, jan.–juin:125–136.

2216.   Coakley, J.J. 1978. *Sport in Society.* St. Louis: Mosby. 349 pp.
2217.   Conrad, W. and S. Strubel. 1971. *Frisch, fromm, fröhlich, frei. Sport und Gesellschaft.* Reinbek: Rowohlt. 93 pp.
2218.   Cozens, F.W. and F.S. Stumpf. 1953. *Sports in American Life.* Chicago, Ill.: University of Chicago Press. 366 pp.
2219.   Crepeau, R.C. 1976. Punt or bunt: a note on sport in American culture. *J.Sport History* 3,3:205–212.
2220.   Daley, R. 1963. *European Sports.* New York: Morrow. 180 pp.
2221.   Denney, R. 1957. *The Astonished Muse.* Chicago: University of Chicago Press. 264 pp.
2222.   Diepenhorst, J.A. et al. 1955. *De sport in onze samenleving* (Sport in our society). Rapport Nederlands Gesprek Centrum ll. Utrecht: Van Stockum. 32 pp.
2223.   Driel, K.V. 1954. De sociaale functie van de sport (The social function of sport). *Schalm* (Utrecht) 11,5:187–200.
2224.   Dunning, E. 1973. The structural-functional properties of folk-games and modern sports. *Sportwissenschaft* 3,3:215–232.
2225.   Eichberg, H. 1975. Spielverhalten und Relationsgesellschaft in West Sumatra. *Arena* 1,1:1–48.
2226.   Eichberg, H. 1976. Zur historisch-kulturellen Relativität des Leistens in Spiel und Sport. *Sportwissenschaft* 6,1:9–34.
2227.   Eitzen, D.S. and G.H. Sage. 1977. *Sociology of American Sport.* Dubuque, Ia.: Grown. 336 pp.
2228.   Esashi, S. 1969. 'Matsuri' ni kansuru sport shakaigakuteki kenkyu (A sport sociological study of English 'festivals' in modern times). *Research of Physical Education Kyushu University* (Fukuoka) 4,2:65–71.
2229.   Esashi, S. 1973. Taishu sport no shakaiteki tokusei to kadai (A sociological study of mass sport) *Research J.Sport Sociology* (Tokyo) 2:85–99.
2230.   Frenkin, A.A. 1960. *Sport i obshchestvo* (Sport and society). *Voprosy Filosofii* 2:105–116.
2231.   Fujita, N. 1972. Gendai no shakai to sport (Modern society and sport). *Bulletin Doshisha Hokentaiiku* (Kyoto) 12:15–35.
2232.   Geblewicz, E. 1962. Kultura fizyczna w kulturze wspolxzesnej (Physical culture in contemporary culture). *Kultura Fizyczna* 4:264–266.
2233.   Gehlen, A. 1965. Sport und Gesellschaft. Pp. 22–33 in U. Schultz, ed. *Das grosse Spiel. Aspekte des Sports in unserer Zeit.* Frankfurt: Fischer.
2234.   Grieswelle, D. 1973. Die sozio-politische Funktion des Hochleistungssports. *Civitas* 12:105–115.
2235.   Grube, F. and G. Richter, eds. 1973. *Leistungssport in der Erfolgsgesellschaft.* Hamburg: Hoffmann und Campe. 233 pp.
2236.   Gruneau, R.S. and J.G. Albinson, eds. 1976. *Canadian Sport. Sociological Perspectives.* Don Mills, Ont.: Addison-Wesley. 433 pp.
2237.   Gryspeerdt, A. 1972. Appartenance socio-culturelle et intérêts sportifs. *Recherches sociologiques* (Louvain) 3,2:226–246.
2238.   Hack, L. 1972. Alle haben doch die gleiche Chance. Leistungssport-Leistungsgesellschaft-Gerechtigkeit? Pp. 105–127 in G. Vinnai, ed. *Sport in der Klassengesellschaft.* Frankfurt: Fischer.
2239.   Hagimitov, B.D. 1965. Otnosenie na selskoto naselenie kam II-ta repub-

likanska spartakiada (Attitudes of people towards the second republican Spartakiada). *Vaprosi na Fiziceskata Kultura* 10,12:715-721.

2240. Halldén, O. 1970. *Idrotten i det svenska samhället* (Sport in Swedish society). Stockholm. 260 pp.

2241. Hamano, Y. 1970. Kenpo dai 89 jyo tp shakaitaiiku (The 89th article of the constitution and out-of-school physical education). *Annual Report Physical Education, Waseda University* (Tokyo) 1,3:63-73.

2242. Hammerich, K. 1969. Leibesübung in einer 'kopflastigen' Gesellschaft. *Anstösse* (Berlin) 16,5-6:184-195.

2243. Hammerich, K. 1970. Zur Frage einer gesundheitsfördernden Wirkung des Sports. Versuch einer soziologischen Analyse. *Sportcahiers* (Hertogenbosch) 6,1:4-17.

2244. Heinemann, K. 1975. Leistung, Leistungsprinzip, Leistungsgesellschaft. *Sportwissenschaft* 5,2:119-146.

2245. Heinemann, K. 1976. Soziale Determinanten des Sportengagements. *Sportwissenschaft* 6,4:374-383.

2246. Heinilä, K. 1963. Urheilu rationallistuvassa maailmassa (Sport in the rationalistic world). *Stadion* (Helsinki) 1:13-17.

2247. Heinilä, K. 1974. *Urheilu-Ihminen-Yhteiskunta* (Sport, man and society). Jyväskylä: Gummerus. 290 pp.

2248. Horkheimer, M. 1964. New patterns in social relations. Pp. 173-185 in E. Jokl and E. Simon, eds. *International Research in Sport and Physical Education*. Springfield, Ill.: Thomas.

2249. Howell, R. and M. 1969. *Sport and Games in Canadian Life*. Toronto: Macmillan.

2250. Isaacs, N.D. 1978. *Jock Culture USA*. New York: Norton 211 pp.

2251. Jaeggi, U. 1967. Sport und Gesellschaft. *Sociologia Internationalis* 5,1:57-80.

2252. Jakobson, M.A. 1971. Sociologicheskie problemy fizicheskoj kultury (Sociological problems of physical culture). *Socialnye issledovanija* (Moscow) 7:128-136.

2253. Jeu, B. 1973. La contre-société sportive et ses contradictions. *Esprit* 10,Oct.:391-416.

2254. Jokl, E. 1964. Sport and culture. Pp. 1-24 in *Doping*. Oxford: Pergamon Press.

2255. Kloehn, G. ed. 1961. *Leibeserziehung und Sport in der modernen Gesellschaft*. Weinheim: Beltz. 108 pp.

2256. Kondo, Y. 1966. Gendaishakai niokeru tairyoku no mondai I. (Sociological approach to problems of physical fitness for modern living I). *Bulletin Miyagi University of Education* (Sendai) 1:69-85.

2257. Krawczyk, Z. 1970. Konciepcija za czowieka i niegoboto otnoszienie km fizkulturata (The concept of man and his attitude toward physical culture). *Medicine i Fizkultura* (Sofia):41-47.

2258. Krawczyk, Z. ed. 1973. *Sport w spoleczenstwie wspolczesnym* (Sport in modern society). Warszawa: PWN. 382 pp.

2259. Krawczyk, Z. et al. 1973. The dialectics of transformation in modern sport. Pp. 55-60 in Grupe et al. German 1976. Die Dialektik des Wandels im modernen Sport. Pp. 165-172 in Lüschen/Weis.

2260. Kriukov, V.Y. 1978. Mass sport, personal contacts and integration. *IRSS*

13,3:65-74.

2261.   Krockow, C.v. 1958. Die Bedeutung des Sports für die moderne Gesellschaft. *Jahrbuch des Sports* (Frankfurt):28-37.

2262.   Krockow, C.v. 1962. Der Wetteifer in der industriellen Gesellschaft und im Sport. *Neue Sammlung* 2,4:297-308.

2263.   Krockow, C.v. 1972. *Sport und Industriegesellschaft.* Munich: Piper. 103 pp.

2264.   Krockow, C.v. 1974. *Sport.* Hamburg: Hoffman und Campe.

2265.   Krockow, C.v. 1975-76. Faszinosum Sport. *Schweizer Monatshefte Politik, Wirtschaft, Kultur* (Zürich) 55,6:468-477.

2266.   Krockow, C.v. 1980. *Sport, Gesellschaft, Politik.* Munich: Piper. 138 pp.

2267.   Krüger, A. 1976. Der Leistungssport als Subsystem der Gesellschaft. *Leistungssport* 6,1:4-11.

2268.   Kukushkin, G.I. 1963. Sociologicheskie problemy sovetskogo fizkulturnogo dvizenija (Sociological problems of the movement of physical culture). *Teorija i Praktika* 10:7-12.

2269.   Kukushkin, G.I. 1964. Eiziceskaja kul'tura i vsiestoronnieje razvitije sovietskovo celovieka (Physical culture and the all-around development of Soviet man). Pp. 5-10 in *Matierialy k itogovoj naucnoj sessii instituta za.* Moscow.

2270.   Kunath, P. 1972. Die Veränderung der Leistungsmotivation in Abhängigkeit von gesellschaftlich-sozialen Bedingungen. *Theorie und Praxis* 21,12:1089-1091.

2271.   Lasch, C. 1979. *The Culture of Narcissm.* New York: Norton. 447 pp.

2272.   Lersch, P. 1960. Der Sport als Aufgabe unserer Zeit. *Jahrbuch des Sports* (Frankfurt):7-16.

2273.   Lever, J. 1969. Soccer: opium of the Brazilian people. *Trans-action* 7,Dec.:36-43. German: 1976. Fussball in Brasilien. Pp. 222-237 in Lüschen/Weis.

2274.   L'Heureux, W.J. 1964. Sport in modern Canadian culture. *JOHPER* 35,3:28-29 and 61.

2275.   Lüschen, G. 1963. Die Funktion des Sports in der modernen Gesellschaft. *Leibeserziehung* 12,12:383-387.

2276.   Lüschen, G. 1964. Die gesellschaftliche Funktion des modernen Sports. *Krankengymnastik* 16,8:209-213.

2277.   Maheu, R. 1962. Sport and culture. *Int.J.Adult Youth Education* 14,4: 169-172.

2278.   Manders, T. and J.A. Kropman. 1974. *Sportbeœfning en zijn organisatiegraad in Nederland* (Sport and its degree of organization in Netherland). Nijmegen: University of Nijmegen. 4 vols. 234, 365, 381 and 44 pp.

2279.   Megyeri, F. 1961. A tömegek véleménye a tömegek sportjáról (The opinion of the masses about sport of the masses). *Sport és Tudomány* 10:291-292 and 11:328-329.

2280.   Michener, J.A. 1976. *Sports in America.* New York: Random House. 466 pp.

2281.   Miermans, C.G.M. 1956. De waadering van de sport in onze samenleving (Evaluation of sport in our society). *Mens en Maatschappij* (Amsterdam) 31,6:329-334.

2282.   Milshtein, O.A. 1970. Otnoshenie raslichnyh socialnodemograficheskih grupp k fizicheskoj kulture i sportu kak sociologicheskaja problema

(The attitude of various socio-demographic groups to physical culture and sport as a sociological problem). Pp. 14 in *Sovetskaja Sociologiche-skaja Associacija.* Varna Int.Congress.

2283.   Milshtein, O.A. 1971. Attitude of various socio-demographic groups to sports and physical culture as a sociological problem. *IRSS* 6,1:63–78.

2284.   Minabe, M. 1963. *Nippon no sports* (Sports in Japan). Tokyo: Sanichi-Shobo. 270 pp.

2285.   Miscol, O. 1970. Sport, contributii la culture de masa (Sport and its contribution to mass culture). Pp. 253–284 in *Sociologia culturii de masa.* Bucarest.

2286.   Mitscherlich, A. 1972. Heutige Gesellschaft. Arbeitsformen und Sport-bedürfnisse. *Universitas* 27,8:793–800.

2287.   Montagu, I. 1956. Sports and pastimes in China. *United Asia* 8,2:150–152.

2288.   Morton, H.W. 1963. *Soviet Sport. Mirror of Soviet Society.* New York: Collier Books. 221 pp.

2289.   Mottana, G. et al. 1974. Inchiesta sulla condizione dello sport nazionale (Investigation of determinants of national sport). *Vita e pensiero* (Milano) 57,4–6:233–236.

2290.   Mrozek, D.J. 1978. Image of the West in American sport. *Journal of the West* 17,July:71–82.

2291.   Murray, L. 1977. Value categories for Australian sport. *IRSS* 12,3:97–105.

2292.   McIntosh, P.C. 1958. The British attitude to sport. Pp. 13–24 in A. Natan, ed. *Sport and Society.* London: Bowes.

2293.   McIntosh, P.C. 1966. Twentieth century attitudes to sport in Britain. *IRSS* 1:27–48.

2294.   Nagai, Y. and K. Kodama. 1965. Sports ni tsuiteno ishiki ni kansuru kenkyu (A public opinion study of sport on amateurism). *Bulletin Shimane University* (Matsue) 15:1–25.

2295.   Nagai, Y. and K. Kodama. 1966. Taiiku ni kansuru ishiki ni tsuite no kenkyu (A study of public opinion for physical education). *Bulletin Shimane University* (Matsue) 16:91–114.

2296.   Naison, M. 1972. Sports and the American Empire. *Radical America* 6,4:95–120.

2297.   Natan, A. ed. 1958. *Sport and Society.* London: Bowes. 208 pp.

2298;   Naus, M.H.J. et al. 1963. *Lichamalijke opvoeding en sport in noord-brabant* (Physical education and sport in North Brabant). Tilburg: Provinciaal Opbouworgaan Noord-Brabant. 72 pp.

2299.   Naus, M.H.J. et al. 1964. *Nippon sports no genjo.* (The status quo of in Japan). Tokyo: Kyorin-Tosho.

2300.   Niwa, T. et al. 1964. Gendaini okuru sports no shakaiteki kino (Social function of sport at the present time). *Research Journal Physical Education* (Tokyo) 9,1:431–434.

2301.   Niwa, T. 1970. Gendai shakai ni okeru sport no kino (The function of sport in modern society). Pp. 100–219 in A. Asai, ed. *Taiikugaku Ronso.* Osaka: Times.

2302.   Niwa, T. 1973. The function of sport in society today. *IRSS* 8,1:53–68.

2303.   Okonashvili, P.F. 1972. Gruzinskij nacionanyj sport v programme narodnyh i religioznyh prazdnikov i nekotorye voprosey sovremennosti (Georgian national sport and the program of national and religious holidays and some modern problems). Pp. 81 in *Materialy I nauchno-*

metodicheskoj konferencii institutov fizicheskoj kultury respublik Zakavkazja. Tiblisi.

2304. Peters, A. 1927. *Psychologie des Sports.* Mit einem Vorwort von Max Scheler. Leipzig: Der neue Geist. 93 pp.

2305. Peters, A. 1928/29. Sport und Hygiene. *Archiv angewandte Soziologie* (Berlin) 1,6:38–45.

2306. Physical Education Association of Great Britain. 1956. *Britain in the World of Sport.* An examination of factors involved in participation in competitive international sport. London: Phys.Ed.Assoc.Great Britain and Northern Ireland. 68 pp.

2307. Plessner, H. 1952. Soziologie des Sports. *Deutsche Universitätszeitung* 7, Nov.–Dec.:9–11, 12–14, 22–23.

2308. Plessner, H. 1956. Die Funktion des Sports in der industriellen Gesellschaft. *Wissenschaft und Weltbild* (Wien) 9,4:262–274.

2309. Plessner, H. 1967. Spiel und Sport. Pp. 17–28 and 121–122 in H. Plessner et al. eds. *Sport and Leibeserziehung.* Munich: Piper.

2310. Ponomarev, N.I. 1973. K voprosu o predmete marksistskoj sociologii fizicheskoj kultury i sporta (The Problem of the subject area of the Marxist sociology of physical culture). *Teorija i Praktika* (Moscow) 1:62–65.

2311. Ponomarev, N.I. 1974. *Sotsialie functsii fizicheskoj kultury i sporta* (The social function of physical culture and sport). Moscow: Fizkultura i Sport.

2312. Redmond, G. 1978. *Sport and Ethnic Groups in Canada.* CAHPER Monograph. Calgary: University of Calgary. 93 pp.

2313. Rijsdorp, K. 1973. *Sport en maatschappij: een confrontatie van de sport met maatshappelijke vragen* (Sport and society: a confrontation of sport and social problems). Alphen-aan-den-Rijn: Samson. 187 pp.

2314. Riordan, J. 1976. Sport in Soviet society. *Stadion* 2,1:90–120.

2315. Riordan, J. 1977. *Sport in Soviet Society.* Cambridge: Cambridge University Press. 435 pp.

2316. Rodichenko, V.S. 1972. Sportivnoe sorevnovanie kak social'noe javlenie (Sport competition as a social phenomenon). *Teorija i Praktika* 8:7–10.

2317. Sage, G.S. ed. 1980.[3] *Sport and American Society.* Reading, Mas.: Addison-Wesley. 395 pp.

2318. Schultz, W. ed. 1965. *Das Grosse Spiel.* Frankfurt: Fischer. 154 pp.

2319. Schwank, W. 1975. *Sport und Gewerkschaft in der BRD.* Ahrensburg: Czwalina. 144 pp.

2320. Sieger, W. 1964. Zur Körperkultur in der sozialistischen Gesellschaft. *Deutsche Zeitschrift für Philosophie* (Berlin) 12,8:923–934.

2321. Spreitzer, E. and E. Snyder. 1975. The psychosocial functions of sport as perceived by the general population. *IRSS* 10,3–4:87–93.

2322. Stepovoj, P.V. 1972. *Sport i Obshchestvo* (Sport and society). Tartu. 221 pp.

2323. Stevenson, C.H.L. and J.E. Nixon. 1972. A conceptual scheme of the social functions of sport. *Sportwissenschaft* 2,2:119–132.

2324. Stevenson, C.H.L. 1974. Sport as a contemporary social phenomenon: a functional explanation. *Gymnasion* (Schorndorf) 11,3:8–19.

2325.   Stoljarov, V.I. et al. 1975. Sportivnaja nauka v. GDR (Sport in the GDR). *Teorija i Praktika* 38,4:67–69.

2326.   Stone, G.P. 1955. American sports: play and display. *Chicago Review* 9,3:83–100.

2327.   Stone, G.P. 1957. Some meanings of American sport. Pp. 6–29 in *60th Annual Meeting College Phys.Ed.Assoc.* Columbus, Ohio. Revised 1969 pp. 5–16 in Kenyon. Revised 1976 in German: Soziale Sinnbezüge des Sports in der Massengesellschaft. Pp. 132–145 in Lüschen/Weis.

2328.   Struna, N.I. 1977. Sport and societal values: Massachusetts Bay. *Quest* 27:38–46.

2329.   Suchodolski, B. 1959. Perspektywy rezwoju kultury fizicznej w warunkach nowoczesnej cywilizacij (Perspectives of physical culture under conditions of modern civilization). *Wychowanie Fizyczne i Sport* (Warsaw) 3:429–436. Summary in English. Résumé en francais.

2330.   Sykora, B. 1973. La culture physique en tant qu'élément de la vie de la société (in Czech). *Nova Mysl* (Ostrava) 27,8–9:1171–1180.

2331.   Takenoshita, K. 1953. Gendai ni okeru recreation no shomondai (Problems of recreation in modern society). *Soc.Education* 12,2:189–201.

2332.   Takenoshita, K. 1972. *Play, sport and taiiku ron* (Play, sport and physical Education). Tokyo: Taishukan. 252 pp.

2333.   Tanaka, S. 1963. Olimpic no uketomekata (The attitudes of the Japanese to Tokyo Olympics). *JOHPER* (Tokyo) 13,11:616–619.

2334.   Tendances culturelles. 1977. Le livre et la culture. Les sociétés. Le sport. *Cultures Suisse* 4,2:7–198.

2335.   Tyszka, A. 1964. Kilka hipotez o roli sportu we wspolczesnosci (Some hypotheses on the role of sport in contemporary life). *Kultura Fizyczna* 11–12:673–675.

2336.   Tyszka, A. 1973. Komunikacja symboliczna jako jedna z funkcji sportu (Symbolic communication concerning the functions of sport). Pp. 143–169 in Z. Krawczyk, ed. *Sport w spoleczenstwie wspolczesnym.* Warsaw: PWN.

2337.   Van den Berghe, P.L. 1975 *Man in Society.* New York: Elsevier. 300 pp.

2338.   Van Driel, K. 1954. De sociale functie van de sport. *Schalm* 11,5:187–200.

2339.   Vita e Pensiero. 1974. Sullo sport in Italia (On sport in Italy). *Vita e Pensiero* 57,4–6:1–232.

2340.   Wasilewski, E. 1961. Stan zainteresowan sportowych w Polsce w swietle opracowan statystycznych (The level of sport interest in Poland in light of statistical research). *Kultura Fizyczna* 14,12:880–894.

2341.   Wein, D. 1905-1906. Nemzeti kulturánk és a testi nevéles (Our national culture and physical education). *Tornaügy* (Budapest) 23,19:423–427.

2342.   White, C.M. 1974. Sport as a social phenomenon. *Social Studies* 4,Sept.: 403–409.

2343.   Wohl, A. 1970. Competitive sport and its social functions. *IRSS* 5,1: 117–130.

2344.   Wohl, A. 1971. Die Integrationsfunktionen des Sports. Pp. 94–105 in Albonico/Pfister-Binz.

2345.   Wohl, A. 1975. Der Leistungssport und seine sozialen Funktionen. *Sportwissenschaft* 5,1:56–67.

2346.   Zikmund, A.A. 1924. Osnovy sovetskoj sistemy fizicheskoj kultury
         (The foundations of the Soviet system of physical culture). Pp. 144 in
         Molodaja Gvardija. Moscow.
2347.   Zoldak, V.I. 1970. Svjaz' razvitija fizicheskoj kul'tury s niekatorymi
         social'no-diemograficheskimi faktorami (The linkage between physical
         culture and some socio-demographic factors). Pp. 69–71 in *Matierialy
         itogovoj naucnoj sessii instituta za 1968.* Moscow.

         4. *Sport and Social Institutions*

         a. *Polity, political behavior, ideology, conflict*

2348.   Arndt, H. et al. 1971. Das marxistisch-leninistische Grundlagenstudium
         als Kernstück der klassenmässigen Erziehung der Studierenden. *Wis-
         sensch.Zeitschr.DHFK* 13,3–4:33–42.
2349.   Arndt, H. and G. Eichler. 1972. Der moderne Sozialdemokratismus und
         Probleme der Sportpolitik in der BRD. *Theorie und Praxis* 21,5:419–42.
2350.   Arnold, P.J. 1968/69. The 1968 Olympics and their aftermath. Pp. 21–3ϲ
         in *Physical Education Yearbook.* London: Phys.Ed.Assoc.
2351.   Baillie-Grohman, W.A. 1919. Sport: a mirror of national character. *Nine-
         teenth Century and After* 86, Dec:1125–1139.
2352.   Belberov, D. 1976. L'Education physique et les sports: objets d'attention
         de la part d L'UNESCO. *Problemi na Visseto obrazovanie* (Sofia) 14,3:
         61–62.
2353.   Bernett, H. 1966. *Nationalsozialistische Leibeserziehung.* Schorndorf:
         Hofmann. 232 pp.
2354.   Bernett, H. 1971. *Sportpolitik im Dritten Reich.* Hilden: Buchpresse.
         132 pp.
2355.   Bernett, H. 1975. Die innenpolitische Taktik des nationalsozialistischen
         Reichssportführers. *Arena* (Leyden) 1,1:140–178.
2356.   Betts, J.R. 1971. Home front, battle field, and sport during the Civil
         War. *Research Quarterly* 42,2:113–132.
2357.   Bonacossa, C. 1942. L'idea olimpia e la realta politica (Olympic idea
         and reality of politics). *Olympische Rundschau* 18:2–4.
2358.   Boserup, A. and A. Mack. 1975. *War Without Weapons: Non-Violence
         and National Defense.* New York: Schocken.
2359.   Bruns, W. 1972. Ist der Sport ein Mittel der Völkerverbindung? Eine
         Problemanalyse. *Die Leibeserziehung* 21,8:279–283.
2360.   Bugrov, N.N. 1969. Socialnoe znachenie mezhdunarodnyh sportivnyh
         svazej (Social significance of international sport connections) Pp.
         225–229 in *Materialy nauchnoj konferencii po istorii, organizacii i
         sociologii fizicheskoj kultury i sporta.* Tashkent-Samarkand.
2361.   Carr, G. 1974. The use of sport in the German Democratic Republic for
         the promotion of national consciousness and international prestige.
         J.Sport History 1,2:123–136.
2362.   Cone, C.B. 1975. Parliamenteering and racing. *Historian* 37,May:407–420.
2363.   Czula, R. 1978. The Munich Olympics Assassinations: a second look.
         Journal Sport and Social Issues 1,Spring-Summer: 19–23.

2364. Dabschec, B. 1976. Economics, power and sportsmen. *Politics* 11,2: 212-213.

2365. Davila, L. 1972. *Politica y deporte* (Politics and sport). Andorra Ca Vella: Editorial Andorra. 221 pp.

2366. DeKoff, I. 1962. The role of government in the Olympics. Pp. 189-194 in *Educat.Doctorate Project Report.* New York: Columbia Teachers College.

2367. Deutsch, J. 1928. *Sport und Politik.* Berlin: Dietz. 72 pp.

2368. Digel, H. 1975. Sport und nationale Repräsentation. *Der Bürger im Staat.* (Stuttgart) 25,3:239-242.

2369. Dobozy, L. 1959. A sport szerepe a falu szocialista átszervéséber. (About the role of sport in the socialist reorganization of the village). *Sport és Tudomány* 3,6:3-5.

2370. Dolkart, E.I. 1973. K voprosu o vsaimosvjazi sostjazanij, igr i fizicheskih uprazhneij s narodnymi tradicijami respublik Srednej Asii i Kazahstana (Problems of linkage between matches, games and physical activity with the national traditions of the Middle Asia Republics and Kasahstan). Pp. 193-196 in *Materialy po istorii, organizacii i sociologii fizicheskoj kultury.* Moscow.

2371. Drake, B. and R.E. Rockvian. 1912. *British Somaliland.* London: Hurst and Blackett. 334 pp.

2372. Elashvili, V.I. 1966. Tradicii nazionalnoj fizicheskoj kultury i sovremennost (Traditions of national physical culture and modern times). Pp. 154-156 in *Materialy I Vsesojusnoj konferencii po sociologicheskim problemam fizkultury i sporta.* Leningrad.

2373. Ennis, T.E. 1936. *French Policy and Developments in Indo-China.* Chicago: University of Chicago Press. 230 pp.

2374. Erbach, G. and E. Buggel. 1972. Sociological problems in the presentation of development tendencies of socialist physical culture in the GDR. *IRSS* 7,1:103-110.

2375. Erbach, G. 1972. Körperkultur und Sport im gesellschaftlichen Planungsprozess unter besonderer Berücksichtigung des Hochleistungssports. *Theorie und Praxis* 21,12:1059-1071.

2376. Erbach, G. 1973. High performance sport as a social problem. Pp. 409-416 in Grupe.

2377. Fabrizio, F. 1976. *Sport e fascismo* (Sport and Facism). Rimini-Firenze: Guaraldi. 181 pp.

2378. Flynn, P. 1971. Sambas, soccer and nationalism. *New Society* (London) 18,464:327-330.

2379. Frenkin, A. 1961. Autinrodnye teorii burzuaznoj sociologii sporta (Economy-theories in the bourgeois sociology of sport). *Teorija i Praktika* 6:457-459.

2380. Frenkin, A.A. 1962. Fizicheskoj kulture—vsenarodnyj kharakter (The national character of physical culture). *Teorija i Praktika* 9:6-10.

2381. Frenkin, A.A. 1963. Sport i politika (Sport and politics). *Sport za rubezom* (Moscow) 4,14:2-6.

2382. Frenkin, A. 1964. Celovek, tehnika, sport (Man, technics and sport). *Sport za rubezom* (Moscow) 5,1:14-16.

2383. Frenkin, A. 1971. *Kapitalizm i lichnost* (Capitalism and personality).

Moscow. 35 pp.

2384.   Geyer, H. 1972. Lokaler Sport, internationaler Sport, Sportnationalismus. *Das Parlament* (Bonn) 9. Beilage.

2385.   Gieseler, K. 1966. *Sport als Mittel der Politik.* Mainz: Hase und Köhler. 88 pp.

2386.   Gieseler, K.H. 1969. Medaillenjagd und Massensport. Eine Analyse des sowjetischen Sports mit mexikanischem Akzent. *Osteuropa* 19,2:81–96.

2387.   Goodhart, P. and C. Chataway. 1968. *War Without Weapons.* London: Allen.

2388.   Goodhue, R.M. 1976. The development of Olympism, 1900–1932: technical success within a threatening political reality. Pp. 27–38 in P. Graham and H. Ueberhorst, eds. *Modern Olympics.* Westpoint: Leisure Press.

2389.   Grace, M. 1974. The origin and development of governmental sport policies in the Republic of South Africa. Pp. 107–117 in *Proceedings Society History Phys.Educ. and Sport Asia and Pacific.*

2390.   Güldenpfennig, S. 1979. Gewerkschaftliche Sportpolitik. Köln:Pahl Rugenstein. 219 pp.

2391.   Güldenpfennig, S. 1980. *Texte zur Sporttheorie und Sportpolitik.* Köln: Pahl-Rugenstein. 198 pp.

2392.   Hagimitov, B.D. et al. 1962. *Ucim se rabotim i ziveem po kommunistisceski* (learning to work and live according to the communistic way). Sofia: Narodna Mladezh. 240 pp.

2393.   Hagimitov, B.D. 1964. Fiziceskata kultura i sportat v brigadite za kommunisticeski trud (Physical culture and sports in the brigades for communistic work). *Voprosi na Fiziceskata Kultura* 9,8:561–565.

2394.   Hagimitov, B.D. et al. 1967. *Geroi na socialisticeskia trud i ordenonosci* (Heroes of socialistic work and supporters of order). Sofia: Protizdat. 165 pp.

2395.   Hanna, W.A. 1962. The politics of sport. *Southeast Asia Series Nr. 10.* Washington D.C.: American Universities Field Staff. 19 pp.

2396.   Heiniläa, K. 1966. Notes on the inter-group conflicts in international sport. *IRSS* 1:49–69. Also 1970 pp. 174–182 in Lüschen, 1971 pp. 343–351 in Dunning.

2397.   Henderson, V.C. 1969. The role of government in leisure time activity. *Australian J.Phys.Educat.* 47,Oct-Nov.:5–11.

2398.   Hermier, G. 1976. *Le sport en questions?* Paris: Ed.Sociales.

2399.   Hirt, E. 1955. Jugend, Sport und Politik. *Politische Rundschau* 34,7: 201–207.

2400.   Hoernlé, R.F.A. 1945. *South African Native Policy and the Liberal Spirit.* Johannesburg: Wiitwatersrand University Press.

2401.   Hönle, A. 1972. *Olympia in der Politik der griechischen Staatenwelt.* Bebenhausen: Rotsch. 212 pp.

2402.   Howell, R. 1975. The USSR: Sport and Politics Intertwined. *Comp. Education* 11,2:137–145.

2403.   Kakó, G. 1962. A politika és sport és politika kölcsönös kapcsolata (Interdependence between sport and politics). Nésport (Budapest) 227:3.

2404.   Kanin, D. 1978. China Rapture and American sport studies. *Journal Sport Behavior* 1,Febr.:37–41.

2405. Kiviaho, P. 1968. Urheilipolitiikkaa vai poliittista urheilna (Sport politics and political sport). Pp. 9–28 in Pirinen, ed. *Terve urheilun maa.* Helsinki.

2406. Kiviaho, P. 1974. The regional distribution of sport organizations as a function of political cleavages. *Sportwissenschaft* 4,1:72–81. Also 1975 in *IRSS* 10,1:5–14.

2407. Kolatsch, J. 1972. *Sports, Politics and Ideology in China.* New York: David. 400 pp.

2408. Kolokova, V.M. 1962. Sport kak odno iz sredstv vospitanija novogo celoveka-aktivnogo borca za kommunism (Sport as a means of education of new man, the active fighter for communism). *Teorija i Praktika* 25,5:8–15.

2409. Kondo, Y. 1967. Gendaishakai niokeru tairyoku no mondai II (Sociological approach to problems of physical fitness for modern living II). *Bulletin Miyagi University of Education* (Sendai) 2:53–75.

2410. Kradman, D.A. 1924. *Fizicheskaja kultura kak chast kulturnoprosveti-telnoj raboty* (Physical culture as part of cultural enlightenment work). Leningrad: GUBONO. 87 pp.

2411. Krockow, C.v. 1972. Leistungsprinzip und Herrschaft. Betrachtungen aus Anlass der Olympischen Spiele. *Das Parlament.* Beilage 33:3–15.

2412. Krüger, A. 1972. *Die Olympischen Spiele 1936 und die Weltmeinung. Ihre aussenpolitische Bedeutung unter besonderer Berücksichtigung der USA.* Berlin: Bartels und Wernitz. 244 pp.

2413. Krüger, A. 1975. *Sport und Politik. Von Turnvater Jahn zum Staats-amateur.* Hannover: Fackelträger. 261 pp.

2414. Kukushkin, G.I. 1965. Socialnaja rol fizicheskoj kultury v sozdanii materialno-technicheskoj bazy kammunisma (The social role of physical culture and the making of the material-technical base of Communism). Pp. 9–14 in *Materialy k itogovoj nauchnoj sessii instituta za 1964.* Moscow.

2415. Kukushkin, G.A. 1966. Fizicheskaja kultura i stroitelstvo kommunizma (Physical culture and the building of Communism). Pp. 3–13 in *Materialy I Vsesojuznoj Konferencii po sociologicheskim Problemam Fizicheskoj Kultury i Sporta.* Leningrad.

2416. Laky, L. and L. Klész. 1963. A burzsoá sport mai tendenciái (The present tendencies of bourgeois sport). *Testneveles F.Tudomany Közl.* (Budapest) 3,2:58–75.

2417. Laskiewicz, H. 1968. Dzialalnosc socjalistycznych i rewolucyjnych zwiazkow mlodziezy Polski w dziedzinie kultury fizycznej w latach 1918-1939 (The activities of socialist and revolutionary youth unions in Poland in physical culture in the years 1918-1930). *Roczniki Naukowe* (Warsaw) 9:27–55.

2418. Lemke, W. 1971. *Sport und Politik.* Ahrensburg: Czwalina. 113 pp.

2419. Lipsky, R. 1978. Toward a political theory of American sports symbolism. *American Behavioral Scientist* 21, Jan.: 345–360.

2420. Lowe, B. et al. eds. 1978. *Sport and International Relations.* Champaign, Ill.: Stipes. 627 pp.

2421. Lund, Sir A. 1972. Sports and politics. Pp. 482–485 in Hart.

2422. Mandell, R.D. 1971. *The Nazi Olympics.* New York: Macmillan. 316 pp.

2423.   Mateev, D. 1949. *Fiziceskata Kultura v svetlinata ne Marksizma-Leninizma* (Physical culture under aspects of Marxism-Leninism) Sofia: Medicina i Fizkultura. 50 pp.

2424.   Mazrui, A.A. 1977. Boxer Muhammed Ali and soldier Idi Amin as international political symbols: the bioeconomics of sport and war. *Compar. Studies Sociol.History* 19,April:189–215.

2425.   Meyer, H. 1972. Das Bündnis mit dem Militär. Historisch-soziologische Anmerkungen zur Konstituierung des olympischen Reitsports als eines Militärsports. Pp. 11–18 and 199 in H. Wagner and H. Meyer, eds. *Kavalkade*. Mönchengladbach: Lapp.

2426.   Meynaud, J. 1966. Aspectos generales de movimiento olimpico (General aspects of the Olympic movement). *Revista del Instituto de Ciencias Sociales* 8:11–38.

2427.   Meynaud, J. 1966. *Sport et Politique.* Paris: Payot. 321 pp.

2428.   Meynaud, J. 1966. L'Intervention de la politique dans le sport. *Economie et Humanisme* (Calnire) 18mar-avr.:40–56.

2429.   Molyneux, D.D. 1962. *Central Government Aid to Sport and Physical Recreation in Countries of Western Europe.* Edgbaston: University of Birmingham. 51 pp.

2430.   Moustard, R. 1971. Sport et idéologie. *Nouvelle Critique* (Paris) 43,1: 68–76.

2431.   Nafziger, J.A.R. and A. Strenk. 1978. The political uses and abuses of sports. *Connecticut Law Review* 10,2:259–289.

2432.   Niscocks, R. 1953. *The Rebirth of Austria.* London and New York: Oxford University Press. 263 pp.

2433.   Oelschlägel, G. 1968 and 1969. Karl Marx und die Körperkultur. *Theorie und Praxis.* 17:394–401, 587–594. 18:388–400, 511–519 and 681–691.

2434.   Ortega y Gasset, J. 1954. Der sportliche Ursprung des Staates. Pp. 428–449 in *Gesammelte Werke I.* Stuttgart: Deutsche Verlagsanstalt.

2435.   Petrie, B.M. 1975. Sport and politics. Pp. 187–238 in Ball/Loy.

2436.   Petrie, B.M. 1977. Examination of a stereotype: athletes as conservatives. *IRSS* 12,3:51–62.

2437.   Podvojskij, N.I. 1923. *Kakaja fizkultura nuzna proletariatu SSSR u kak ona dolzna sozdavat'sja?* (What kind of physical culture does the proletariat of the USSR need and what organization?). Moscow. 18 pp.

2438.   Pointu, R. and R. Fidani. 1975. *Cuba: Sport en révolution.* Paris: Editeurs Français Réunis. 218 pp.

2439.   Ponomarev, N.I. 1973. Nacionalnoe i internacionalnoe v sporte (The national and international in sport). *Teorija i Praktika* 5:6–10.

2440.   Pooley, J.C. and A.U. Webster. 1975. Sport and politics: Power play. *J.Canadian Assoc.Health, Physical Education Recreation* 41,3:10–19.

2441.   Purcell, V. 1954. *Malaya: Communist or Free?* Palo Alto: Stanford University Press. 288 pp.

2442.   Ray, H.L. 1970. Let's have a friendly game of war! *Quest* 14, June:28–41.

2443.   Rigauer, B. Et al. 1974. Beitrag des Sports zur politischen Sozialisation. Pp. 117–129 in ADL, eds. *Sozialisation im Sport.* Schorndorf: Hofmann.

2444.   Riordan, J. 1974. Soviet sport and Soviet foreign policy. *Soviet Studies* 26,July:322–343.

2445.   Riordan, J. 1977. Sport and the military. *Co-Existence* 14,2:299–323.

2446.   Ritter, P. 1978. The Olympic movement in the service of peace and brotherhood. *Olympic Review* 130-131, Aug.-Dept.:503-505 and 526-527.

2447.   Röblitz, G. 1962. Freizeit und Körperkultur der Menschen im Sozialismus-Kommunismus. *Wissensch.Zeitschr.DHFK* 4,3:121-127.

2448.   Röblitz, G. 1965. Zu den Funktionen der Freizeitbetätigungen und speziell des sportlichen Tuns im Lebensvollzug der Menschen der sozialistischen Gesellschaft. *Wissensch.Zeitschr.DHFK* 7,2:51-60.

2449.   Rostas, G. 1963. Sport és politika (Sport and politics). *Testneveles F. Tudomany Kösl.* 3,1:287-301.

2450.   Rowe, D.N. 1955. *China: an Area Manual.* Vols. I and II. Johns Hopkins University. Washington, D.C.: Operations Research Office.

2451.   Schelsky, H. 1973. *Friede auf Zeit.* Die Zukunft der Olympischen Spiele. Osnabrück: Fromm.

2452.   Schiller, J. and F. Takács. 1970. *Sportpolitika* (Sport politics). Budapest: Tankönyv Kiadó. 83 pp.

2453.   Schulke, H.J. ed. 1975. *Sport, Wissenschaft und Politik.* Köln: Pahl-Rugenstein.

2454.   Schulke, H.J. 1976. Olympia und Breitensport. Ein Beitrag zu den ökonomischen und politischen Grenzen der olympischen Bewegung. *Blätter für deutsche und internationale Politik* 21:671-689.

2455.   Semashko, N. 1924. Oktjabr i fizkultura (The great October and physical culture). *Izvestija fizicheskoj kultury* 20:2-3.

2456.   Sipes, R.G. 1973. War, sports and aggression: an empirical test of two rival theories. *American Anthropologist* 75,1:64-86.

2457.   Smulders, H. 1977. Sports and politics: the Irish scene. *Review Sport Leisure* 2,June:116-129.

2458.   Stepovoj, P.S. 1966. O probleme 'Sport i politika' (On the problem 'Sport and politics'). Pp. 39-42 in *Materialy I konferencii po sociologicheskim problemam fizicheskoj kultury i sporta.* Leningrad.

2459.   Stolbov, B.B. 1965. Bor'ba kommunisticheskih partij kapitalisticheskih stran za molodjezh i sport (The struggle of Communist parties in Capitalist countries for youth and sport). *Teorija i Praktika* 7:44-48.

2460.   Stranai, K. 1974. Education physique dans le système de l'éducation communiste. *Pedagogika* (Prague) 24,2:195-203.

2461.   Strenk, A. 1978. Thrill of victory and the agony of defeat: sport and international politics. *Orbis* 22,Summer:453-469.

2462.   Swierczewski, R. 1978. The athlete: the country's representative as a hero. *IRSS* 13,3:89-100.

2463.   Talalaev, J. A. 1973. Sport—oblast mirnogo sorevnoyanija (Sport a field of peaceful competition). *Teorija i Praktika* 1:7-10.

2464.   Thompson, R.W. 1978. Sport and ideology in contemporary society. *IRSS* 13,2:81-94.

2465.   Tunis, J.R. 1941. *Democracy and Sport.* New York: Barnes. 52 pp.

2466.   Vydrin, V.M. 1973. Kulturnaja revolucija v USSR i fizicheskaja kultura (Cultural revolution in the USSR and physical culture) pp. 31 in *Obshchestvo Znanie.* Leningrad.

2467.   Wagner, H. 1959. *Humanismus, Militarismus und Leibeserziehung.* Munich: Barth. 140 pp.

2468.   Waller, K. und H. Michels. 1974. *Sport, Profit, Politik.* Frankfurt: Verlag Marxistische Blätter.

2469.   Weinberg, P. 1973. Staatsmonopolistische Formierung, Sport und demo-kratische Bewegung in der BRD. *Blätter deutsche und internationale Politik.* 18,10:1072–1094.

2470.   Wiehl, J.V. 1972. *Olympische Spiele wozu?* München: Schneekluth. 124 pp.

2471.   Wildt, C.C. 1960. Sport im Spiegel des Nationalcharakters. *Studium Generale* 13,2:96–104.

2472.   Winkler, H.J. 1972. *Sport und politische Bildung. Modellfall Olympia.* Opladen: Leske. 192 pp.

2473.   Wohl, A. 1953. Zagadnienia rozwoju kultury fizycznej w ustrojo socjalis-tycznum (Problems of development of physical culture in the socialist system). *Kultura Fizyczna* 6,3:182–187.

2474.   Wohl, A. 1955. W sprawie tak zwannego amotorstwa panstowowego (On the question of state-sportsmen) *Kultura Fizyczna* 8,3:552–560.

2475.   Wonneberger, G. and L. Kleine. 1972. Bemerkungen zur Struktur des Profisports im System des staatsmonopolitischen Kapitalismus. *Theorie und Praxis* 21,12:1081–1083.

2476.   Wright, S. 1977. Are the Olympics games? The relationship of politics and sport. *Millennium* 6,Spring:30–44.

2477.   Wright, S. 1978. Nigeria: the politics of sport, a channel for conflict and a vehicle for national self-expression. *Commonwealth J.Int.Affairs* 272,Oct.:362–367.

2478.   Wright, G. 1978. The political economy of the Montreal Olympic Games. *Journal Sport Social Issues.* 2,Spring–Summer:13–18.

2479.   Zholdak, V.I. 1967. Dvizhenie kommunisticheskogo truda i fizicheskaja kultura (The Communist labor movement and physical culture). *Teorija i Praktika* 5:4–7.

2480.   Zoller J.O. 1972. Sport, Gesellschaft und Politik. *Politische Studien* (Munich) 23,20:352–360.

b. *Law*

2481.   Aikens, C. 1971. The struggle of Curt Flood. *Black Scholar* Nov.:10–15.

2482.   Anonymous. 1976. Sex discrimination and intercollegiate athletics. *Iowa Law Review* 61,2:420–457.

2483.   Berry, R.C. and L.S. Sobel. 1977. Professional sports and law. *Trial* 13,5:37–38.

2484.   Binder, R.L. 1975. Consent defense—sports, violence and criminal law. *American Criminal Law* 13,2:235–248.

2485.   Brody, B.F. 1978. Impact of litigation on professional sports. *Trial* 14, June:34–38.

2486.   Flakne, G.W. and A.H. Gaplan. 1977. Sport violence and prosecution. *Trial* 13,1:33–35.

2487.   Furuya, T. 1956. Sports rule no hoteki igi ni kansuru kenkyu (Studies on the legal meaning of sport rules). *Research J.Physic.Education*

(Tokyo) 2,2:85–89.

2488. Hallowell, L. and R.I. Meshbesher. 1977. Sports violence and the criminal law. *Trial* 13,1:27–32.

2489. Hogan, J.C. 1974. Sports in the courts. *Phi Delta Kappan* 56,2:132–135.

2490. Jedruel, S. 1973. Odpowiedzialnosc za szkody zwiazane z uprawianiem sportu (Responsibility for damages caused during sport participation). *Sport Wyczynowy* (Warsaw) 4:40–44.

2491. Kuhlmann, W. 1975. Violence in professional sports. *Wisconsin Law Review* 3:771–790.

2492. Leavell, J.F. and H.L. Millard. 1975. Trade regulation and professional sports. *Mercer Law Review* 26,2:603–616.

2493. Letourne, G. 1977. Legality of violent sports and criminal code. *Canadian Bar Review* 55,2:256–288.

2494. Lowell, C.H. 1975. Federal administrative intervention in amateur athletics. *George Washington Law Review* 43,3:729–790.

2495. Nelson, S. 1978. Bringing sports under legal control. *Connecticut Law Review.* 10,2:251–258.

2496. Rivkin, S.R. 1974. Sports league and the federal antitrust laws. Pp. 387–410 in R. Noll.

2497. Robinson, W.C. Professional sports and the anti-trust laws. *Southwestern Social Science Quarterly* 38,2;133–141. Also 1969 pp. 223–231 in Loy/Kenyon.

2498. Szwarc, A.J. 1972. Postulaty karania sportowcow wypadkow sportowych (Postulates of penalty for the causes of sport accidents). *Sport Wyczynowy* (Warsaw) 2:42–47. 3:44–49. 4:44–49. 7:39–44.

2499. Topkis, J.H. 1949. Monopoly in professional sports. *Yale Law Review* 58:692–712.

2500. Topkis, J.H. 1967. The Super Bowl and the Sherman Act: professional team sports and the Antitrust Laws. *Harvard Law Review* 81:418–434.

2501. Vigorita, A. 1971. Doping of athletes in ordinary and sports law (in Italian). *Quaderni Dello Sport* 9:21–27.

2502. Warren, A. ed. 1973. Athletics. *Law and Contemporary Problems* 38,1: 1–171.

c. *Economy*

2503. Baumann, H. 1973. *Wirtschafts—und verkehrsgeographische Auswirkungen von Sportveranstaltungen hohen Publikumsinteresses.* Ahrensburg: Czwalina. 103 pp.

2504. Berezovskij, A.P. 1973. Fizicheskaja kultura i sport—sredstvo obshchenija narodov Sovetskogo Sojuza (Physical culture and sport as means of communication of the nations of the Soviet Union). *Teorija i Praktika* 4:47–49.

2505. Brouhon, H. 1964. Le sport dans son contexte économique et social. Pp. 175–191 in *Int.Congress Sport and Leisure of Workers.* Brussels.

2506. Brouwer, J.J. 1977. Professional sports team ownership: fun, profit and ideology of the power elite. *IRSS* 12,4:89–98.

2507.   Ciampi, A. 1974. Consumo dello spettacolo in Italia e industria culturale (Entertainment in Italy and the cultural industry). *Spettacolo* 24,2:3–59.

2508.   Crawford, V.P. 1977. A game of fair division. *Review Economic Studies* 44,June:235–247.

2509.   Danielsson, K.F. and S. Hausson. 1953. Idrotten En Samhällsekonomisk Faktor (Sport, a socio-economic factor). Pp. 301–356 in SRF, ed. *Svensk Idrott*. Malmö: Allhem.

2510.   Dumazedier, J. 1977. Les athlètes sont-ils propriété d'état? *Esprit* (Paris) 1,Jan.:83–89.

2511.   Durso, J. 1971. *The All-American Dollar*. Boston: Houghton Mifflin. 294 pp.

2512.   Durso, J. 1975. *The Sports Factory: An Investigation into College Sports*. New York: Quadrangle. 207 pp.

2513.   Eichler, G. 1972. Falsch getrimmt. Sport für alle? Pp. 47–59 and 139–140 in J. Richter, ed. *Die vertrimmte Nation*. Reinbek: Rowohlt.

2514.   Friedrich, W. 1978. Sport and its economic and social importance. *Olympic Review* 128,June:373–377 and 383.

2515.   Furst, R.T. 1971. Social change and the commercialization of professional sports. *IRSS* 6,1:153–173.

2516.   Geyrhofer, F. 1972. *Sport als Industrie*. *Neues Forum* (Wien) 20,224: 22–28.

2517.   Griffiths, I. 1971. Gentlemen suppliers and with-it consumers. Pp. 53–59 in Albonico/Pfister-Binz.

2518.   Grimes, A. et al. 1974. A socioeconomic model of national Olympic performance. *Soc.Science Quarterly* 55,3:777–783.

2519.   Groenman, S. 1966. Menswaardige sportbeoefening: Een sociologische benadering (Humanistic sports: a sociological consideration). *Richting* (Hilversum) 20,4:85–91.

2520.   Herskovitz, D.L. 1971. Techniques to shield the high income of the superstar. *Journal of Taxation* 34,5:270–274.

2521.   Jackson, M. 1969. College football has become a losing business. Pp. 232–242 in Loy/Kenyon.

2522.   Johnston, W.E. and G.H. Elsner. 1972. Variability in the use among ski areas: a statistical study of the California market region. *Journal Leisure Research* 4,1:43–49.

2523.   Kahn, R. 1957. Money, muscles and myths. *Nation* 185,1:9–11.

2524.   Koch, J.V. 1971. The economics of 'big-Time' intercollegiate athletics. *Soc.Science Quarterly* 52,2:248–260.

2525.   Krockow, C.v. 1972. Leistungssportler als Kleinunternehmer? Die Grenzen einer Analogie. *Leistungssport* 2,5:382–385.

2526.   Krüger, A. 1972. Der Leistungssportler als Kleinunternehmer. Eine sozioökonomische Interpretation des Verhältnisses von Sport und Arbeit. *Leistungssport* 2,3:211–216.

2527.   Littlechild, S.C. 1975. Common costs, fixed charges, clubs and games. *Review Economic Studies* 42,June:117–124.

2528.   Mahoney, S. 1964. Pro football's profit explosion. *Fortune* 70,5:153–155 and 218–230.

2529.   Malenfant-Dauriac, C. 1977. *L'économie du sport en France. Un compte satellite du sport.* Paris: Centre d'etud de des techniques économiques modernes. Ed. Cujas. 326 pp.

2530. Model, O. 1955. *Funktionen und Bedeutung des Sports in ökonmischer und soziologischer Sicht.* Winterthur: Keller. 180 pp.

2531. McPherson, B.D. 1975. Sport consumption and the economics of consumerism. Pp. 243–275 in Ball/Loy.

2532. Neale, W.C. 1964. The peculiar economics of professional sports. *Quarterly J.Economics* (Cambridge) 78,1:1–14. Also 1969 pp. 211–222 in Loy/Kenyon. *German* 1975 in Hammerich/Heinemann.

2533. Nixon, H.L. 1974. The commercial and organizational development of modern sport. *IRSS* 9,2:107–131.

2534. Noll, R.G. 1974. The product market of sport. Pp. 13–24 in *National Football League Players Association Conference.*

2535. Noll, R.G. 1974. The U.S. team sports industry: an introduction. Pp. 1–35 in Noll.

2536. Nosova, G.I. 1972. O normah racionalnogo potreblenija sportivnoj odezhdy, obuvi (On standards of rational consumption of sporting clothes and footwear). Pp. 102–104 in *Nauchny trudy za 1970* Moscow: T.I.

2537. Okner, B.A. 1974. Subsidies of stadiums and arenas. Pp. 325–348 in Noll.

2538. Okner, B.A. 1974. Taxation and sports enterprises. Pp. 159–184 in Noll.

2539. Quirk, J. 1974. Professional sport franchise values. Pp. 25–32 in *National Football League Players Association Conference.*

2540. Reeve, A.B. 1910. What America spends for sport. *Outing* 57,Dec.: 300–308.

2541. Rigauer, B. 1971. Die Eigentore der Beherrschten. Fussball-Bundesliga-affäre 1971. *Olympische Jugend* 16,11:4–6.

2542. Rust, H. 1972. Thesen zur gesellschaftlichen Bedeutung sportlicher Grossveranstaltungen. *Leibeserziehung* 21,10:345–349.

2543. Scheuch, E.K. 1976. Die Vielzweck-Schau genannt Olympia. *Merkur* 30,4:395–400.

2544. Shingleton, R.G. 1972. The utility of leisure: game as a source of food in the Old South. *Mississippi Quarterly* 25,4:429–445.

2545. Stoessel, H. 1973. *Sport und Fremdenverkehr.* Bern and Stuttgart: Haupt.

2546. Tunis, J.R. 1934. Changing trends in sport. *Harper's Magazine* 170,Dec.: 75–86.

2547. Vickerman, R.W. 1975. *The Economics of Leisure and Recreation.* London: Macmillan. 229 pp.

2548. Weinberger, J. 1937. Economic aspects of recreation. *Harvard Business Review* 15:448–463.

2549. White, D. 1972. Spending in sport. *New Society* (London) 22,534: 724–725.

2550. Wohl, A. 1960. Sport a zagadnienie produkcji (Sport and production) *Kultura Fizyczna* 13,12:841–846.

2551. Zoldak, V.I. 1969. Niekatoryje rezultaty konkretnych issledovanij social'no-ekonomiceskich funkcii fiziceskoj kultury sredi trudjacichsja promyslennych priedprijatij (Results of empirical studies of the socio-economic function of physical culture among industrial workers). Pp.

24–28 in *Fiziceskaja Kultura i proizvodstwo.* Moscow.

2552.   Zoldak, V.I. 1970. Trud i fiziceskaja kultura (Work and physical culture).
        Pp. 10–18 in *Matierialy naucno-mietodiceskoj konfierencii.* Vilnus.

d. *Religion and Church*

2553.   Ballou, R.B. 1970. The role of the Jewish priesthood in the expansion of
        Greek Games in Jerusalem. *Canadian J.History Sport Phys.Educ.* 1,2:
        70–81.
2554.   Bell, Sir C. 1946. *Portrait of the Dalai Lama.* London: Collins. 414 pp.
2555.   Bickel, J. 1960. *Sport und Religion.* Recklinghausen: Paulus. 103 pp.
2556.   Browridge, D. 1975. Karate and Christianity: parallels on different planes.
        Sport Sociology Bulletin 4,1:56–59.
2557.   Brunner, E.de S. 1928. *Rural Korea. A Preliminary Survey of Economic,
        Social and Religious Conditions.* New York: Int. Missionary Council.
2558.   Clarke, J.D. 1944. Three Yoruba fertility ceremonies. *Royal Anthro-
        pological Institute Great Britain and Northern Ireland* 74:91–96.
2559.   Coles, R.W. 1975. Football as a surrogate religion? *Sociol.Yearbook
        Religion* 8:61–77.
2560.   Dallet, C. 1874. *Histoire de l'Eglise de Corée.* Paris: Palmé. Vol. I. 387 pp.
2561.   Das, S.C. 1902. *Journey to Lhasa and Central Tibet.* London: Murray.
        285 pp.
2562.   Davis, T. 1970. Some notes on historians' treatment of Colonial American
        sport. *Canadian J.History Sport Physical Educ.* 1,2:37–51.
2563.   Davis, T.R. 1972. Puritanism and physical education: the shroud of gloom
        lifted. *Canadian J.History Sport Phys.Educ.* 1,2:1–7.
2564.   Dirksen, J. 1975. The place of athletics in the life of the Christian. *Sport
        Sociology Bulletin* 4,1:48–55.
2565.   Dobrov, A. and B. Lisicin. 1966. Sport i religija (Sport and religion).
        Nauka i religija (Moscow) 8:43–46.
2566.   Esashi, S. 1968. Sport, Shukyo, shakai—seikyoto kakumeiki o chushinni
        (Sport, religion and society—with emphasis on Puritan revolution).
        Research Phys.Educ.Kyushu University (Fukuoka) 4,1:63–67.
2567.   Freischlag, J. 1974. Ethnic and religious difference in sport choice, success
        and position. *Sport Sociology Bulletin* 3,1:12–23.
2568.   Geldbach, E. 1975. *Sport und Protestantismus.* Wuppertal: Brockhaus.
2569.   Goellner, W.A. 1953. The court ball game of the aboriginal Mayas. *Re-
        search Quarterly* 24,2:147–168.
2570.   Gyimesi, T. 1965. A sport és vallásörténetelméleti kapescolata (History-
        theoretical relations of sport and religion). *Testneveles F. Tudomany
        Közl.* 4,2:193–196.
2571.   Henderson, R.W. 1947. *Ball, Bat and Bishop.* New York: Rockport. 220
        pp.
2572.   Hortzfleisch, S.v. 1970. Religious Olympism. *Social Research* 37,2:
        231–236.
2573.   Hurlbut, F. 1939. *The Fukinese: A Study in Human Geography.* Published
        by the author. 143 pp.
2574.   Jakobi, P. and H.E. Rösch. 1977. *Sport. Dienst am Menschen.* Mainz:
        Grünewald.

2575. Körbs, W. 1960 Kultische Wurzel und frühe Entwicklung des Sports. *Studium Generale* 13,1:11–21.

2576. Krasnowoski, J. 1973. Sport wspolczesny a proces desakralizacji (Contemporary sport and the process of desacralization). Pp. 83–103 in Z. Krawczyk, ed. *Sport w spoleczenstwie wspolczesnym.* Warsaw: PWN.

2577. Krickeberg, W. 1948. Das mittelamerikanische Ballspiel und seine religiöse Symbolik. *Paideuma* 3,3–5:118–190.

2578. Kun, L. 1962. Az egyhazak és a sport (Churches and sport). *Sport és Tudomány* 6,7:193–194.

2579. Löffler, L.G. 1955. Das zeremonielle Ballspiel im Raum Hinterindiens. *Paideuma* 6,2:86–91.

2580. Meyer, H. 1971. Puritanismus und Leibesübungen. *Olympische Jugend* 16,1:12–13.

2581. Meyer, H. 1973. Puritanism and physical training: ideological and political accents in the Christian interpretation of sport. *IRSS* 8,1:37–52.

2582. Müller, H. 1955. *Papst Pius XII und der Sport.* Düsseldorf: Haus Altenberg. 27 pp.

2583. Narita, J. and T. Setoguchi. 1976. A study on the Religious character of "Sumo." *Bulletin Phys.Ed. Tokyo Univ. Education* 15:15–21.

2584. Neale, R.E. 1969. *In Praise of Play—Toward a Psychology of Religion.* New York: Harper and Row 187 pp.

2585. Netherland Protestant Church. 1963. *Kerk en sport* (Church and sport). DenHaag: Boekencentrum.

2586. Pombo, A.F. 1960. *El deporte en la palabra de los Papas* (Sport in the speeches of the Popes). Madrid: Estades.

2587. Price, F.W. 1948. *The Rural Church in China: A Survey.* New York: Agricultural Missions Inc. 274 pp.

2588. Schroeteler, R.P.J. 1936. Leibeskultur im Lichte des Christentums. *Bildung und Erziehung* (Vienna) 31,2:82–90.

2589. Shcheulov, I.V. and E.I. Kaimazova. 1965. Cerkov i fizicheskaja kultura. (Church and physical culture). Pp. 125–147 in *Kritika Burzhuaznoj Sociologii Sporta.* Moscow.

2590. Simri, U. 1975. The religious and magical dimensions of play involving physical activities. Pp. 121–127 in U. Simri, ed. *International Seminar on Play.* Natanya: Wingate Institute.

2591. Skidmore, R.A. 1948. *Mormon Recreation in Theory and Practice: A Study of Social Change.* Philadelphia: University of Pennsylvania. 137 pp.

2592. Söll, M. 1959. *Sport in katholischer Gemeinschaft.* Düsseldorf: Haus Altenberg. 125 pp.

2593. Söll, M. 1964. *Kirche zum Sport. Stimmen der Päpste.* Düsseldorf: Haus Altenberg. 80 pp.

2594. Suchockij, V.I. 1964. Reakcionnaja rol klerikalizma v fizicheskom vospitanii (The reactionary role of Clericalism in physical education). *Teorija i Praktika* 7:61–65.

2595. Swanson, R.A. 1968. The acceptance and influence of play in American Protestantism. *Quest* 11,Dec.:58–70.

2596. Tanikeev, M. 1968. Reakcionnaja sushchnost sovremennogo islama v razvitii fizicheskoj kultury i sporta v stranah Vostoka (The reactionary essence of modern Islam in the development of physical culture and

sport in Oriental countries). Pp. 166–170 in *Istorija fizicheskoj kultury.*
Rasshirennoj konferencii. Erevan.

2597. Tsybikov, G.T. 1919. *A Buddhist Pilgrim to the Holy Places of Tibet.*
Petrograd: Russian Geographical Society. 472 pp.

2598. Utz, A.F. and J.F. Groner. 1954. *Aufbau und Entfaltung des gesellschaftlichen Lebens.* Fribourg: Paulus. 254 pp.

2599. Vlot, N.G. 1964. A sociological analysis of sport in the Netherlands. Pp.
198–212 in E. Jokl/Simon, eds. *International Research Sport Physical
Education.* Springfield, Ill.: Thomas.

2600. Zeiss, K. 1962. *Christ und Sport.* Gladbeck: Schriftenmissions—Verlag.
96 pp.

2601. Zöld, J. 1962. Sport és világnézet (Sport and ideology). *Világosság* (Budapest) 7–8:85–89.

e. *Education, school; educational attainment*

2602. Albonico, R. et al. 1963. *Sport, Student und Studium.* St. Gallen: Wein-
hold. 24 pp.

2603. Albonico, R. 1967. Modern university sport as a contribution to social
integration. *IRSS* 2,1:155–164.

2604. Arai, S. 1973. Daigaku taiiku no shakaiteki seikaku (A sociological study
of university physical education). *Research J.Sport Sociology* 2:
119–138.

2605. Baker, G. 1962. Survey of the administration of physical education in
public schools in the United States. *Research Quarterly* 33,4:632–636.

2606. Bäskau, H. 1972. Stand und Entwicklungstendenzen des ausserunter-
richtlichen Sports an den allgemeinbildenden Schulen der DDR. *Wis-
sensch.Zeitschr. DHFK* 21:861–869.

2607. Bene, E. 1959. Some differences between middle-class and working-class
grammar school boys in their attitudes towards education. *Brit.J.Sociol.*
10,2:148–152.

2608. Berryman, J. and J. Loy. 1976. Secondary schools and Ivy League letters.
Brit.J.Sociol. 27,1:61–77.

2609. Binnewies, H. and K.J. Gutsche. 1976. *Strukturen im Hochschulsport—
eine Bestandsaufnahme.* Ahrensburg: Czwalina. 181 pp.

2610. Bloss, H. 1970. Die sportliche Aktivität von Berufsschülern. *Die Leibeserziehung* 19,2:48–52.

2611. Bojko, J. and P. 1971. Fizicheskaja kultura i sport v svobodnom vremeni
uchashchihsja shkol zapadnyh oblastej Ukrainy (Physical culture and
sports in the free-time of the pupils of West Ukrainian secondary schools).
Pp. 199–201 in *Istorija, organizacija i sociologija fizicheskoj kultury i
sporta.* Minsk: Tezisy dokladov.

2612. Buhrmann, H.G. 1972. Scholarship and athletics in junior high school.
IRSS 7,1:119–131.

2613. Christenson, A. 1958. *The Verdict of the Scoreboard.* New York: American Press. 190 pp.

2614. Clark, E.H. 1964. The Olympic Games and their influence on physical
education. *JOHPER* 35,6:23–25.

2615. Coleman, J.S. 1961. Athletics in high school. *Annals of AAPSS* 338: 33–43.
2616. Coleman, J.S. 1962. *The Adolescent Society.* Glencoe: Free Press. 368 pp.
2617. Coleman, J.S. 1969. Sports and studies as paths to success. Pp. 287–305 in Loy/Kenyon.
2618. Conkov, V. 1970. Szocialsita orságok testnevelési rendszereinek nemzetközi lényege és nemzeti arculata (The national profile and international essence of physical education systems in socialist countries). *Testneveles F. Tudomany Közl* 2:156–167.
2619. Davis, A.M.F. 1883. College athletics. *Atlantic Monthly* 51:677–684.
2620. Dewing, R. 1977. History of American sports: academic featherbedding or neglected area? *Social Science Journal* 14,3:73–81.
2621. Diem, C. 1957. Die Aufgaben des Sports und die moderne Kultur. Pp. 493–503 in Festschrift Spranger. *Erziehung zur Menschlichkeit.*
2622. Eggleston, J. 1965. Secondary schools and Oxbridge Blues. *Brit.J.Sociol.* 16,3:232–242.
2623. Eitzen, D.S. 1976. Sport and social status in American public secondary education. *Review Sport Leisure* 1,Fall:139–156.
2624. Elahi, S.D. 1972. L'Education physique et le sport en Iran. *Education physique et sport* (Paris) 114:29–32.
2625. E.S.F. 1977. *Questions—reponses sur l'éducation physique et sportive.* Paris: Edition E.S.F. 176 pp.
2626. Fagin, R. and P. Brynteson. 1975. The cohesive function of religion and sport at a sectarian university. *Sport Sociology Bulletin* 4,1:33–47.
2627. Fichter, J.S. 1958. *Parochial School: A Sociological Study.* South Bend, Ind.: University of Notre Dame Press. 494 pp.
2628. Goncalves, M. 1969. Relacoes humanas na escola e prevencao dos desajustamentos sociais. *Educaciao Fisica Desportes* 5,19:12–25.
2629. Güldenpfennig, S. 1972. Anmerkungen zum politischen Bewusstsein der Sportstudenten. Pp. 174–190 in G. Vinnai, ed. *Sport in der Klassengesellschaft.* Frankfurt: Fischer.
2630. Haerle, R.K. 1975. Education, athletic scholarships, and the occupational career of the professional athlete. *Sociology Work and Occupations* 2,4:373–403.
2631. Heinilä, K. 1962. *The Preference of Physical Activities in Finnish High Schools.* Institute of Sociology Publication Nr. 14. University of Helsinki. 42 pp.
2632. Heinilä, K. 1964. *Voimistelunopettajat ja liikuntakasvatus oppikonlon sosiaalisessa Järjestelmässä* (Physical education teachers in high schools) Institute of Sociology Publication Nr. 39. University of Helsinki. 105 pp.
2633. Heinilä, K. 1964. The preference of physical activities in Finnish high schools. Pp. 123–151 in E. Jokl and E. Simon, eds. *International Research.* Springfield, Ill.: Thomas.
2634. Hentig, H.v. 1977. Fahrstuhl, Kniebeuge, Goldmedalle—oder die Dialektik des Sportunterrichts. *Neue Sammlung* 17,2:118–132.
2635. Howell, M.S. and M.L. VanVliet. 1965. *Physical Education and Recreation in Europe.* Ottawa: Dpt. National Health Welfare. 30 pp.
2636. Hughes, W.C. 1950. The place of athletics in the school physical education program. *JOPHER* 21,Dec.:23–37.

2637.	ICHPER. 1969. *International Questionnaire Report on Physical Education Programs.* Washington, D.C. 3 vols.

2638.	Jaeggi, U. et al. 1963. *Sport und Student.* Bern and Stuttgart: Haupt. 144 pp.

2639.	Jakobson, M.A. 1966. O nekotoryh osnovnyh chertah amerikanskoj sociologii fizicheskoj kultury (Some traits of American sociology of physical culture). Pp. 91–103 in *Uch jenye zapiski.* Leningrad.

2640.	Japan. 1964. *Japan Mombusho taiikukyoku* (Physical education and sports in Japan). Tokyo. 220 pp.

2641.	Japanese Society Phys.Educat. 1958 and 1959. Kôtôgakkô undôbu narabini senshu ni kansuru kyôiku-shakaigakuteki kenkyû (A sociological study on athletes and sport clubs of high schools). *Research J. Phys.Educat.* 3,1:271–289 and 4,1:278–295.

2642.	Johnson, W. ed. 1966–1971. *Physical Education Around the World.* Indianapolis: Phi Epsilon Kappa Fraternity. 30 vols. 2nd compreh. edition 1980 Champaign, Ill.: Stipes.

2643.	Kado, O. 1971. Taiikukakyoiku no shomondai—Taiiku girai no haikei kara (Problems of physical education—The viewpoint and background of physical education detesters). *Bulletin Tokyo Gakugei University* V,23:227–240.

2644.	Kado, O. 1972. Meijiki ni okeru gakukotaiiku no tokushitu—Wagakuni no kindaika no shiten kara (School physical education since Meiji and modernization in Japan). *Bulletin Tokyo Gakugei University* V,24:210–221.

2645.	Kalmánchey, Z. 1966. A testnevelés szerepe a világnézeti nevelésben (The role of physical education in ideological education). *Testneveles Tan.* (Budapest) 1:1–6.

2646.	Kiskin, N.P. 1973. Fizicheskaja kultura i sport v srednih specialnyh uchebnyh zavedenijah Zapadnoj Sibiri (Physical culture and sports in technical schools of West Sibiria). Pp. 239–243 in *Materialy po istorii, orgnaizacii i sociologii fizicheskoj kultury.* Tashkent: Medizina Publishing House.

2647.	Kobayashi, A. 1968. Structure of factors determining the attitudes of college students toward required health and physical education. *Research J.Phys.Educat.* (Tokyo) 12,3:147–156.

2648.	Kobayashi, A. 1969. Hokentaiikukamoku ni taisuru gakusei no kachitaido (Value attitudes of college students toward required health and physical education). *Research Bulletin Nagoya University* 13:41–49.

2649.	Kobayashi, A. 1970. Taiikujitsugi ni taisuru gakusei no taido no kozo to henyo (Attitude structure and attitude change of students toward required health and physical education). Pp. 54-74 in A. Asai, ed. *Taiikugaku Ronso II.* Osaka: Nihonjisho.

2650.	Krawczyk, B. 1966. Attitude toward studies and professional aspirations of the students of the Academy of Physical Education. *IRSS* 1:195–208.

2651.	Krawczyk, B. 1968. Social specificity of higher schools of physical education. *IRSS* 1968,3:97–116.

2652.	Landers, D. and D.M. Landers. 1978. Socialization via interscholastic athletics: its effects on delinquency and educational attainment. *Sociol. Education* 51,4:299–303.

2653.	Leslie, B. 1976. Response of four colleges to rise of intercollegiate athletics. *J.Sport History* 3,3:213–222.

2654. Linde, H. 1970. Sind gute Sportler schlechtere Schüler? Pp. 148–158 in H. Groll and H. Stohmeyer, eds. *Jugend und Sport*. Wien: Bundesverlag.

2655. Linde, H. and K. Heinemann. 1974. *Leistungsengagement und Sportinteresse*. Schorndorf: Hofmann. 114.

2656. Lueptow, L.B. and B.D. Kayser. 1973/74. Athletic involvement, academic achievement, and aspiration. *Sociological Focus* 7,1:24–36.

2657. Mandić, O. 1967. Sociologijski aspekti fizicke kulture studenata (Sociological aspects of students' physical culture). *Fizicka kultura* (Beograd) 21,7–8:247–252.

2658. Michaux, J. and M. Declerck. 1959. L'Organisation de l'éducation physique dans les écoles de cités de la Région Nord de la S.N.C.F. *L'Éducation physique* 51,17:23–26.

2659. Nakashima, T. 1971. Gakko taiiku to shakaitaiiku no setten ni kansuru kenkyu (Sports activities in adult life as related to prior physical activities at Nagoya University). *Research Bulletin Dpt.General Education of Nagoya University* 15:61–85.

2660. Németh, J. 1972. Egyetemi hallgatók tevékenységi strukturájának alakuláse (The development of activation structure of university students). *Testneveles Tan.* (Budapest) 3:85–87.

2661. Ohashi, Y. 1972. Sport no taiiku shakaigakuteki kenkyu (A sociological study of physical education and sport). *Bulletin School of Education Okayama University* 33:217–224.

2662. Otsuka, A. 1956. Gakusei no seikatsu jikan to taiiku no ichi (The position of physical education in daily student life) *Annual Reports of Studies of Doshisha Women's College* 7:287–292.

2663. Otto, L.B. and D.F. Alwin. 1977. Athletics, aspirations and attainments. *Soc.Education* 50,2:102–113.

2664. Pangle, R. 1956. Scholastic attainment and the high school athlete. *Peabody J.Education* 33:360–364.

2665. Petrovic, K. 1971. Merjenje nekaterih psihicnih in socialnih dimenzij ucencev osnovne sole (Measurements of some physical and social dimensions of elementary school students). *Telesna kultura* (ljubljana) 19:7–8 and 29.

2666. Phillips, J.C. and W.E. Schafer. 1971. Consequences of participation in interscholastic sports: a review and prospectus. *Pacif.Soc.Review* 14,3: 328–338.

2667. Ponomarev, N.I. 1961. Fizicheskoj vospitanie i avtomatizacija proizvodstva (Physical education and mechanization of production). *Teorija i Praktika* 24,10:773–775.

2668. Red Flag. 1976. Educational guidelines in 1975. Documents from Red Flag. *Chinese Education* 9,3:3–77.

2669. Redl, S. 1972. Bemerkungen zur Schulbildung österreichischer Leistungssportler. *Leibesübungen-Leibeserziehung* (Vienna) 26,7:150–155.

2670. Rehberg, R.A. and W.E. Schafer. 1968. Participation in interscholastic athletics and college expectations. *AJS* 73,6:732–740.

2671. Rehberg, R.A. 1969. Behavioral and attitudinal consequences of high school interscholastic sports: a speculative consideration. *Adolescence* 13,4:69–88.

2672. Ripa, M.D. and A.M. Maksimenko. 1973. Physical education and sport in the life of urban school youth. *IRSS* 8,2:35–46.

2673.   Roper, L.D. and K. Snow. 1976. Correlation studies of academic excellence and big-time athletics. *IRSS* 11,3:57–69.

2674.   Sack, A.L. and R. Thiel. 1979. College football and social mobility: a case study of Notre Dame football players. *Soc.Education* 52,Jan.:60–66.

2675.   Schafer, W.E. and J.M. Armer. 1966. Athletes are not inferior students. *Trans-action* 6,1:21–26 and 61–62. Also 1972 pp. 97–116 in Stone.

2676.   Schafer, W.E. and R.A. Rehberg. 1970. Athletic participation, college aspirations and college encouragement. *Pacif.Soc.Review* 13,1:182–186.

2677.   Schafer, W.E. and J.M. Armer. 1971. On scholarship and interscholastic athletics. Pp. 198–229 in Dunning.

2678.   Schmitz, J.N. 1963. Soziologische Aspekte der Leibesübungen. *Die Leibeserziehung* 12,12:383–392.

2679.   Schneiter, C. 1970. Direction of studies and sport interests. *IRSS* 5,1: 185–190.

2680.   Shadman, S.F. 1937. Education in Iran. *Asiatic Review* 33:165–173.

2681.   Stensaasen, S. 1974. School sport on a voluntary basis. *IRSS* 9,3–4: 33–44.

2682.   Stensaasen, S. 1975. Pupils liking for physical education as a school subject. *Scandinavian J.Educational Research* 19:111–129.

2683.   Snyder, E. 1969. A longitudinal analysis of the relationship between high school student values, social participation, and educational-occupational achievement. *Soc.Education* 42,2:261–270.

2684.   Snyder, E. 1975. Athletic team involvement, educational plans and coach-player relationship. *Adolescence* 38,10:191–200.

2685.   Snyder, E. and E. Spreitzer. 1977. Participation in sport as related to educational expectations among high school girls. *Soc.Education* 50, Jan.:47–55.

2686.   Solley, W.H. 1961. Relationship between participation in inter-school sports and extraclass play activities in college. *Research Quarterly* 32,1: 93–108.

2687.   Spady. W.G. 1970. Lament for the letterman: effects of peer status and extra-curricular activities on goals and achievements. *AJS* 75,4:680–702.

2688.   Spreitzer, E. and M. Pugh. 1973. Interscholastic athletics and educational expectations. *Soc.Education* 46,2:171–182.

2689.   Start, K.B. 1966. Substitution of games performance for academic achievement as a means of achieving status among secondary school children. *Brit.J.Sociol.* 17,3:300–306.

2690.   Start, K.B. 1967. Sporting and intellectual success among English secondary school children. *IRSS* 2,:47–54.

2691.   Sugiyama, T. 1957. Gakkôsports no jittaichôsa (A research report on sports in schools). *Research J.Phys.Educ.* 2,4:190–198.

2692.   Sviridova, A.J. 1970. Izuchenie fizicheskogo vospitanija shkolnikov metodom konkretnoj sociologii (A study of pupils' physical training through empirical sociology). Pp. 94–101 in *Materialy nauchnoj konferencii po itogam nauchnoissledovatelskoj raboty za 1969*. Kiev. Part I.

2693.   Texier, A. 1979. La notion d'opposition en éducation physique. *Education Physique et Sport* 155:56–59.

2694.   Thomson, I. 1965. Sociology and physical education. *Bulletin Brit.Assoc. Sport and Medicine* 2,2:35–43.

2695.   Todorov, I. 1974. Enseignement appliqué de l'éducation physique dans les instituts d'enseignement supérieur (Bulgaria) *Problemi na visseto obrazovania* (Sofia) 3:27–30.
2696.   Ulrich, C. 1968. *The Social Matrix of Physical Education.* Englewood Cliffs: Prentice-Hall. 144 pp.
2697.   UNESCO. 1956. *La place du sport dans l'éducation. Étude comparative.* Paris: UNESCO. 66 pp.
2698.   Vajksaar, A. and T. Kyresaar. 1969. Otnoshenie studentov k fizicheskoj kulture i sportu (The attitude of students to physical culture and sport). Pp. 51–53 in *XI Respubikanskaja nauchno-metodicheskaja konferencija.* Tallin: Tezisy.
2699.   VanDalen, D.B. 1961. Cultural impact on physical education. *JOPHER* 32,Dec:15–17.
2700.   Verebélyi, F. 1948. Tanulányi és sportszociográfia (Study and sociography of sport). *Testultura* (Budapest) 2:27–29.
2701.   Vumsai, M.L. 1951. *Manich Compulsory Education in Thailand.* Paris: UNESCO. 110 pp.
2702.   Waller, W. 1932. *The Sociology of Teaching.* New York: Wiley. 467 pp.
2703.   Werner, A.C. and E. Gottheil. 1966. Personality development and participation in college athletics. *Research Quarterly* 1,March:126–131.
2704.   Wolf, D. 1972. The growing crisis in college sports. Pp. 445–472 in M. Hart.
2705.   Yoshiato, T. 1957, 1958 and 1959. Kôtôgakko undôbu no kyôiku shakaigakuteki kôsatsu (Inter-school athletics in senior high school from the viewpoint of educational sociology). *Bulletin Nagasaki University* 3:109–115. 4:107–122. 5:75–85.
2706.   Yuchtman-Yaar, E. and M. Semyonov. 1979. Ethnic inequality in Israeli schools and sports: an expectation–status approach *AJS* 85,3:576–590.
2707.   Znaniecki, F. 1928 and 1930. *Socjologia wychowania* (Sociology of education). Warszaw: Naukowe Towarzystwo Pedagogickne. 2 vols.

f. *Family, Kinship*

2708.   Adam, S. 1969. Several characteristics of students at the Faculty of Physical Training and Sport in Prague. *IRSS* 4,1:31–52.
2709.   Buck, J.L. 1930. *Chinese Farm Economy.* Chicago: University of Chicago Press. 476 pp.
2710.   Choate, J.E. 1957. Recreational boating: the nation's family sport. *Annals AAPSS* 313:109–112.
2711.   Cousins, A.N. 1960. The failure of solidarity. Pp. 412 in N. Bell and E. Vogel, eds. *The Family.* Glencoe, Ill.: Free Press.
2712.   Dowell, L.J. 1973 Attitudes of parents of athletes and non-athletes toward physical activity. *Psychological Reports* (Missoula, Mont.) 32,3:813–814.
2713.   Famaey-Lamon, A. 1977. Some aspects of social status culture and promotion factors of the family in relation to sport practice. *IRSS* 12,4:5–15.
2714.   Hammerich, K. 1963. Funktionen des Sports in der Familie von heute. *Die Leibeserziehung* 12,12:392–397.

2715. Houdous, L. 1929. *Folkways in China.* London: Probstham. 228 pp.

2716. Kemper, F.J. and K. Prenner. 1974. Talentförderung und Elternverhalten als Sozialisationsfaktor. Pp. 323–327 in ADL, eds. *Sozialisation im Sport.* Schorndorf: Hofmann.

2717. Lang, O. 1946. *Chinese Family and Society.* New Haven: Yale University Press. 395 pp.

2718. Levy, M.J. 1949. *The Family Revolution in Modern China.* Cambridge, Mass.: Harvard University Press. 390 pp.

2719. Mi Mi Khaing. 1946. *Burmese Family.* Bombay: Longmans, Green. 138 pp.

2720. McPherson, B. 1976. Consumer role socialization: a within-system method. *Sportwissenschaft* 6,2:144–154.

2721. Orlick, T.D. 1974. An interview schedule designed to assess family sports environment. *Int.J.Sport Psychology* (Rome) 5,1:13–27.

2722. Rosenmayr, L. 1963. *Familienbeziehungen und Freizeitgewohnheiten jugendlicher Arbeiter.* Wien: Verlag Geschichte und Politik. 431 pp.

2723. Skorodnumova, A.P. 1969. Otnoshenie semej trudjashchihsja k fizicheskoj kulture i sportu v zavisimosti ot sostava semej (The attitude of worker's families to physical culture and sport with reference to family composition). Pp. 189–190 in *Konferencija po psychologii i sociologii sporta.* Tartu.

2724. Start, K.B. 1960. Influence of a boy's home background upon his level of performance in games at a Grammar School. *Educational Review* 13:216–233.

2725. Watson, G.G. 1974. Family organization and Little League Baseball. *IRSS* 9,2:5–32.

2726. Wohl, A. 1976. The contribution of women and girls in sport in the light of the evolution of the social structure of the Polish countryside. *IRSS* 11,2:105–116.

2727. Wolanska, T. 1963. Sport w rodzinie, wazny element sportu rekreacyjnego (Sport in the family, an important element of sport for recreation). *Kultura Fizyczna* (Warsaw) 16,9:575–578.

2728. Zurcher, L.A. and A. Meadow. 1967. On bullfights and baseball. An example of interaction of social institutions. *Int.J.Comp.Sociol.* (Leiden) 8,1:99–117. Also 1970 pp. 109–131 in Lüschen, 1971 pp. 175–197 in Dunning. German 1975 pp. 110–130 in Hammerich/Heinemann.

5. *Community, Social Region*

2729. Akiyoshi, Y. 1973. Chiiki recreation ni kansuru kenkyu (A study of community recreation). *J.Leisure Recreation Studies* (Tokyo) 3.

2730. Amiot, M. et al. 1972. *Les groupements socio-culturels et les pouvoirs locaux dans le département des Alpes-Maritimes.* Université de Nice: Laboratoire de Sociologie. 228 pp.

2731. Arai, S. and S. Esashi. 1974. Kinkōnōson ni okeru saikin 6nenkan no taiiku sports no henka to sonomondai (Changes in physical recreation activities during the recent six-year span and its problems in an urban community). *Research J.Phys.Education* 18,4:173–184.

2732.   Asada, T. 1961. Noson no recreation-teki shudan ni kansuru jisshoteki (Research on recreational groups in rural communities). *JOHPER* (Tokyo) 11,11:551–553.

2733.   Asada, T. 1962. Noson recreation no genjo to kasai (The present condition and problems of recreation in rural communities). *JOHPER* (Tokyo) 12,9:456–461.

2734.   Bobev, S. 1964. Prinos kam formite za podobrjavane organizaciata na svobodnoto vreme na mladezhta va gradovete (A contribution to the forms of improving the organization of leisure of youth in towns). *VIF* (Sofia) 3,3:77–93.

2735.   Borisov, J.V. 1973. Otnoshenie selskogo naselenija k fizicheskoj kulture i sportu (The attitude of the rural population to physical culture and sport). Pp. 40–64 in *Problemy upravlenija fizkulturnym dvizheniem.* Moscow.

2736.   Brockmann, D. 1969. Sport as integrating factor in the countryside. *IRSS* 4,1:151–176.

2737.   Cabral, S.L. 1977. Ethnic impact on American sports scene. *Urban Anthropology* 6,2:339–343.

2738.   Ciupak, Z. 1967. Spoleczne warunki sportu wiejskiego (Social conditions of rural sport). *Kultura Fizyczna* 10:455–459.

2739.   Claeys, U. 1977. Sport voor allen. Sportrecreatie in de Stadwijk (Sport for all. Recreational sport in the city). *Sport* (Brussels) 10:422–429.

2740.   Crepeau, R.C. 1975. Urban and rural images of baseball. *J.Popular Culture* (Bowling Green) 9,Fall:315–318.

2741.   Drazdzewski, S. 1964. O dobrowolnym ruchu sportowo-turystcznym na wsi (Voluntary sport and tourist activities in the Polish countryside). *Kultura Fizyczna* 17,4:217–221.

2742.   Dumazedier, J. and N. Samuel. 1973. Etudes des processus de décision dans le développement culturel d'une collectivité locale. Paris: CNRS. *CORDES* Sept. 75 5091 and 75 5092.

2743.   Escobar, G. 1969. The role of sports in the penetration of urban culture to the rural areas of Peru. *Kroeber Anthropological Society.* Papers 40:72–81.

2744.   Florl, R. 1966. Zur komplex-territorialen Analyse des Volkssports in Landgemeinden. *Wissensch.Zeitschr.DHFK* 8,1.

2745.   Forbes, A. 1938. *Sport in Norfolk County.* Boston: Houghton Mifflin. 274 pp.

2746.   Foskett, J.M. 1955. Social structure and social participation. *ASR* 20,4: 431–438.

2747.   Frankenberg, R. 1957. *Village on the Border.* London: Cohen and West. 136 pp.

2748.   Geyer, H. 1972. Stellvertreter der Nation. Repräsentation und Integration durch Sport. Pp. 75–87 and 143 in J. Richter, ed. *Die vertrimmte Nation.* Reinbek: Rowohlt.

2749.   Gomes de Freitas, L.G. 1957. Antigos jogos desportivos da Campanha (Old time rural sportive games). *Revista do Museo Julio de Castillos* (Porto Allegre) 6,7:12–19.

2750.   Gubarev, J.F. 1970. Ob otnoshenii trudjashchihsja i chlenov ih semej k sanjatijam fizkulturoj i sportom vo vremja otdyha v zagorodnyh zonah i v uslovijah goroda (On the attitude of working people and their families to practising sports at out-of-town leisure and in urban communities). Pp. 115–116 in *Nauchnye trudy za 1970*. Moscow: T.I.

2751.   Hayakawa, Y. and H. Kaga. 1963. Nagoya-shi ni okeru shakaitaiiku shi-setsu riyo no jittaichose (A report of a survey concerning stages in the use of public sport facilities in Nagoya City). *Research J.Phys.Educ.* 7,2: 49–57.

2752.   Heinilä, K. 1967. Kuntien liikuntatoiminnan suunnitellu (Community planning in sport and physical activity). Pp. 163–180 in *Kunnan kult-tuuripolitiikka Suomen Kultuurirahasto*. Helsinki: Vammala.

2753.   Hendricks, J. 1971. Leisure participation as influenced by urban residence patterns. *Sociol.Social Research* 55,July:414–428.

2754.   Herzfeld, G. 1959. *Turn—und Sportvereine in Wiesbaden*. Wiesbaden: Statistisches Landesamt. Sonderheft 4.

2755.   Ikeda, T. 1958. Noson shuraku ni okeru recreation ni kansuru ichi kosatsu (A consideration of recreation in a rural area). *Bulletin Yamaguchi University* 8,3:41–50.

2756.   Janisova, H. 1971. The leisure time of city residents in the light of urban living conditions and environment. *Society and Leisure* (Prague) 1,1: 121–144.

2757.   Japanese Society Phys.Education. 1958 and 1959. Noson recreation no shakaigakuteki kenkyu (A sociological study of recreation in rural communities). *Research J.Phys.Educ.* 3,1:290–293. 4,1:296–300.

2758.   Jesohko, K. 1969. *Sport in Wien*. Munich: Verlag Jugend und Volk. 90 pp.

2759.   Kato, K. and S. Ebashi. 1952 and 1953. Iwayuru 'sports mura' no shakaitekisekatsu (The sociological study of the influence of sports for the rural Community). *Research J.Phys.Education* 1,3:203–208, 4: 245–250. 1,5:353–357.

2760.   Kawanabe, A. 1968. Noson chiikishakai niokeru sport no shakaigaku-tekikenkyu (The sociological study of sports in rural community). *Research Report Tokyo University of Foreign Studies* 1–11.

2761.   Komarovsky, M. 1946. The voluntary associations of urban dwellers. *ASR* 11,6:686–698.

2762.   Kraft, K. 1966. Sportabzeichen und Bevölkerung. *Wissensch.Zeitschr. DHFK* 8,1:59–68.

2763.   Krawczyk, B. 1962. O specyfice spolecznej sportu wiejskiego (On social specification of rural sports). *Wychowania Fizycznego* 2:277–293. Summary in English. Résumé en francais.

2764.   Lundberg, G.A. et al. 1934. *Leisure: A Suburban Study*. New York: Columbia University Press. 396 pp.

2765.   Lüschen, G. 1965. Sport e populazione rurale (Sport and the rural population). *Traguardi* (Rome) 9,8:3–11.

2766.   Lynd, R.S. and H.M. 1937. *Middletown in Transition*. New York: Harcourt. 604 pp.

2767.   Maekawa, M. and K. Takenoshita. 1957. Noson recreation ni kansuru kenkyu (A study of recreation in rural communities). *JOPHER* (Tokyo) 7,11:452–455.

2768.   Mansurov, I.I. 1973. Struktura zanjatij fizicheskoj kulturoj i sportom naselanija Karachaevo-Cherkessii (The structure of physical culture and sport practiced by the people of Karachaevo-Cherkessy). *Teorija i Praktika* 10:40–42.

2769.   Mead, M. 1962. Outdoor recreation in the context of American cultural values. Pp. 2–24 in *ORRRC-Report Nr. 22*. Washington, D.C.: Gvt. Printing Office.

2770.   Moose, J.R. 1911. *Village Life in Korea*. Nashville: M.E. Church. 242 pp.

2771.   Nadori, L. and G. Szilasi. 1976. The influence exerted by the local social milieu on extra-mural physical and sport activity of school youth. *IRSS* 11,1:49–64.

2772.   Nagai, Y. 1968. Kasochiiki no taiiku ni tsuite (Physical education in a rural community). *Memoirs of San-in Institute* (Matsue) 9:49–82.

2773.   Nagai, Y. 1970. Kasochiiki ni okeru taiiku no mondai (Problems of physical education in rural community). Pp. 114–141 in A. Asai, ed. *Taiikugaku Ronsō II*. Osaka: Nihonjisho.

2774.   Nesbitt, P.D. and S. Girard. 1974. Personal space and stimulus intensity at a Southern California amusement park. *Sociometry* 37,1:105–115.

2775.   Northam, J.A. and J.W. Berryman. 1978. Sport and urban boosterism in the Pacific Northwest: Seattle's Alaska-Yukon Pacific Exposition 1909. *Journal of the West* 17,July:53–60.

2776.   Olin, K. 1979. Sport, social development and community decision-making. *IRSS* 14,3–4:117–135.

2777.   Petrak, B. 1966. Sport activity in the life of the population of the Czecho-Moravian plateau. *IRSS* 1:250–263.

2778.   Planck, U. and G. Lüschen. 1956. Landjugend und Sport. Pp. 264–292 in U. Planck et al. eds. *Die Lebenslage der westdeutschen Landjugend*. Vol. 2. Munich: Juventa.

2779.   Pudelkiewicz, E. 1970. Sociological problems of sport in housing estates. *IRSS* 5,1:73–104.

2780.   Raymond, H. 1960. Recherches sur un village de vacances. *Revue française de Sociologie* 1,3:323–333.

2781.   Retel, J.O. 1974. *Vie communale et occultation du politique*. Paris: Centre de Sociologie Urbaine. 159 pp.

2782.   Rooney, J.F. 1975. Sports from a geographic perspective. Pp. 55–115 in Ball/Loy.

2783.   Rowntree, B.S. and G.R. Lavers. 1951. *English Life and Leisure: A Social Study*. London and New York: Longmans Green.

2784.   Saar, E. 1972. Competitive sport as a factor in social migration processes. *IRSS* 7,1:133–144.

2785.   Saeki, T. 1969. Kōkyō taiikushisetsu no shiyakaigakuteki kenkyu (Sociological research on public sport facilities). *Bulletin Faculty Phys.Educ. Tokyo University of Education* 8:35–49.

2786.   Seeley, I.H. 1973. *Outdoor Recreation and the Urban Environment*. London: Macmillan.

2787.   Staikof, Z. 1966. Svobodnoto vreme i fiziceskata kultura na gradskoto naselenie (Leisure and physical culture of the urban population). *VIF* (Sofia) 9,4:120–125.

2788.   Stiles, M.H. 1967. Motivation for sports participation in the community. *Canadian Medical Assoc.J.* 96:889–894.

2789.   Sugawara, R. 1956. Sports jinkō ni mirareru chiikikakusa (Regional differences among people engaged in sports). *Bulletin Faculty Phys. Educ. Tokyo University of Education* 3:45–60.

2790.   Sugawara, R. 1965. Kinkoshigaichi ni okeru recreation no genjo to mondai

(The present conditions of physical recreation and its problems in districts adjacent to cities). *Research J.Phys.Educ.* 9,3:1-12.

2791. Suonperä, M. 1970. *Palvelupistetutkimus* (research on sport service areas). Helsinki: Ministry of Education. Nr. 3.

2792. Takenoshita, K. 1960. Chiiki shakai to sports katsudo (Physical recreation and the community). *JOPHER* (Tokyo) 10,7:367-370.

2793. Takenoshita, K. 1962. Chiiki-shakai to taiiku sports no soshiki (The organization of physical recreation in communities). *Bulletin Faculty Phys.Educ.Tokyo University of Education* 2:68-81.

2794. Takenoshita, K. and R. Sugawara. 1963. Sports Jinko ni mirareru chiiki kakusa (Regional differences seen among people engaged in sports). *Bulletin Faculty Phys.Educ.Tokyo University of Education* 3:45-60.

2795. Terasawa, T. 1968. Chiikisport shūdan no shakaigakuteki kenkyu (Sociological research of community sports groups). *J.Toyota Technical College* 1:69-85.

2796. Tsujimoto, I. et al. 1971. Hekichi ni okeru taiiku sport no genjyo to mondai I (The present state of physical activities in rural areas I). *Bulletin Educational Research Institute,* Nara University 8:147-160.

2797. Tsujimoto, I. et al. 1972. Hekichi ni okeru taiiku sport no genjyo to mondai II (The present state of physical activities in rural areas II). *Bulletin Educational Research Institute,* Nara University 7:241-258.

2798. Tyszka, A. 1964. Einige soziale Probleme der Körperkultur in Plock. (Some social problems of physical education in Plock). *Theorie und Praxis* 3,Sept.:187-209.

2799. Tyszka, A. 1967. Kultura Fizyczna jako skladnik kultury wspólczesnej wsi w Polsce (Physical culture an element in rural Poland). *Wychowanie Fizyczne i Sport* (Warsaw) 11,3:113-127.

2800. Vidich, A.J. and J. Bensman. 1960. *Small Town in Mass Society.* Garden City, N.Y.: Doubleday. 337 pp.

2801. Wohl, A. 1966. Social aspects of the development of rural sports in Poland. *IRSS* 1,1:109-135.

2802. Wolfenden Committee. 1960. *Sport and the Community.* London: Central Council of Physical Recreation. 135 pp.

2803. Zelenov, I.I. and J.S. Tarabykin. 1969. Otnoshenie k fizicheskoj kulture i sportu selkoj molodjezi (The attitude of rural young people to physical culture and sport). *Teorija i Praktika* 3:43-45.

2804. Zürn, M. 1973. Sport i rekreaja fizyczna w czsie wolnym mieszkancow miast (Sport and physical recreation in the leisure of urban people). Pp. 333-355 in Z. Krawczyk, ed. *Sport Spoleczenstwie Wspolczesnym.* Warsaw: PWN.

6. Social Change and Evolution

2805. Adedidji, J.A. 1979. Social and cultural conflict in sport and games in developing countries. *IRSS* 14,1:81-88.

2806. Allison, M.T. 1979. On the ethnicity of ethnic minorities in sport. *IRSS* 14,1:89-96.

2807. Aronson, S.H. 1952. The sociology of the bicycle. *Social Forces* 30,3: 305-312.

2808. Barthel, S. 1961. Spiele der Osterinsulaner. Pp. 27–42 in D. Drost and W. König, eds. *Beiträge zur Völkerforschung.* Berlin: Akademie Verlag.

2809. Betts, J.R. 1953. The technological revolution and the rise of sport 1850–1900. *Mississippi Valley Historical Review* 40,2:231–256.

2810. Blanchard, E.S. 1956. The revolution in sports. *Harpers' Magazine* 212, 1272:77–79.

2811. Brailsford, D. 1969. *Sport and Society: Elizabeth to Anne.* London: Routledge and Kegan Paul. 279 pp.

2812. Brewster, P.G. 1958. The earliest known list of games: some comments. *Acta Orientalia* 23,1–2:33–42.

2813. Bruner, J.S. et al. 1976. *Play: Its Role in Development and Evolution.* New York: Penguin.

2814. Charlesworth, J.C. 1964. *Leisure in America: Blessing or Curse?* Monograph 4. Philadelphia: AAPSS. 90 pp.

2815. Chen, T. 1946. *Emigrant Communities in South China.* New York: Secretariat Institute of Pacific Relations. 287 pp.

2816. Clignet, R. and M. Stark. 1974. Modernization and the game of soccer in Cameroun. *IRSS* 9,3–4:81–96. Also 1974 *J.Modern Africa Studies* 12,3: 409–421.

2817. Colloque International F.S.G.T. ed. 1969. *Sport et développement social au XXe siècle.* Paris: Editions Universitaires. 235 pp.

2818. Deschner, R.B. 1946. *The Evolution of Sports and the Cultural Implications of Physical Education.* St. Louis: Medard. 40 pp.

2819. Dickinson, V. 1977. The cool and the lonely: conformity in changing American sport. *Quest* 27:97–105.

2820. Diem, C. and G. Engelhardt. 1955. Sport. Pp. 513–515 in W. Bernsdorf and F. Bülow, eds. *Wörterbuch der Soziologie.* Stuttgart: Enke.

2821. Dulles, F.R. 1965.[2] *A History of Recreation: America Learns to Play.* New York: Appleton-Century-Crofts.

2822. Dunning, E. 1971. Sport as a field of sociological enquiry. Pp. XVII–XXII in Dunning.

2823. Dunning, E. 1979. The figurational dynamics of modern sport. *Sportwissenschaft* 9,4:341–359.

2824. Dunning, E. and K. Sheard. 1979. *Barbarians, Gentlemen and Players.* New York: New York University Press. 321 pp.

2825. Edwards, H. 1976. Change and crisis in modern sport. *Black Studies* 8,Oct.:60–65.

2826. Eichberg, H. 1973. *Der Weg des Sports in die industrielle Gesellschaft.* Baden-Baden: Nomos. 172 pp.

2827. Eichberg, H. 1977. Strukturen des Ballspiels und Strukturen der Gesellschaft. Zur Kritik linearer Fortschrittshypothesen. Pp. 87–100 in G. Curl, ed. *International Seminar History Phys.Educ. and Sport.* Dartford, Kent.

2828. Esashi, S. 1970. Kindai sport no hassei, hatten ni kansuru kenkyū (The origin and development of modern sport). Pp. 182–198 in A. Asai, ed. *Taiikugaku ronsō II.* Osak: Nihonjisho.

2829. Eyler, M. 1961. Origins of contemporary sports. *Research Quarterly* 32,4:480–489.

2830. Fontana, H. 1978. Over the edge: a return of primitive sensations in play and games. *Urban Life* 7,July:213–229.

2831. Frenkin, A.A. 1960. Progress sporta rascvet lichnosti (Sport progress and prosperity of personality). *Teorija i Praktika* 23,2:853-856.
2832. Freund, E.H. 1971. The transition of a fertility rite to an indigenous spectator sport. *Quest* 16,June:37-41.
2833. Gregory, C.J. 1976. The rise of sport in Britain: an interpretative analysis of Inn signs and sporting emblems. *Canadian J.History Sport Phys.Educ.* 7,1:22-32.
2834. Gulick, J. 1955. *Social Structure and Culture Change in a Lebanese Village.* New York Wenner Gren Foundation for Anthropological Research. 191 pp.
2835. Guttman, A. 1978. *From Ritual to Record: The Nature of Modern Sport.* New York: Columbia University Press. 198 pp. German 1979 Schorndorf: Hofmann.
2836. Hamilton, L.C. 1973. Modern American rock climbing. *Pacif.Soc.Review* 22,3:285-308.
2837. Harris, H.A. 1975. *Sport in Britain. Its Origins and Development.* London: Paul. 224 pp.
2838. Henderson, R.W. 1953. *Early American Sport.* New York: Barnes. 234 pp.
2839. Hijmans, E. 1964. The impact of industrial change on the texture of recreation and physical education. Pp. 52-111 in *Int.Congress Phys. Educ.Sport and Leisure of Workers.* Brussels.
2840. Jaworski, Z.; Krawczyk, Z. and T. Ulatowski. 1972. Dialektyka przeobrazeń wspolczesndgo sportu (Dialectic of changes of modern sport). *Kultura Fizyczna* 9:386-389. *German* 1976 Die Dialektik des Wandels im modernen Sport. Pp. 165-172 in Lüschen/Weis.
2841. Kiviaho, P. 1978. Sport and intracultural social change. *Reports Physical Culture and Health.* Nr. 13. 38 pp.
2842. Kiviaho, P. 1978. Sport and intracultural social change: a longitudinal analysis. *Acta Sociologica* 21,1:3-21.
2843. Kolchin, N.T. 1966. Osobennosti razvitija fizicheskoj kultury v Tatarii (The peculiarities of development of physical culture in Tataria). Pp. 156-158 in *Materialy I Vsesojusnoj konferencii po sociologisheskim problemam fizicheskoj kultury i sporta.* Leningrad.
2844. Krawczyk, Z. 1973. Sport as a factor of acculturation. *IRSS* 8,2:63-76.
2845. Kukushkin, G.I. 1966. Sport isocial'nyi progriess (Sport and social progress). Pp. 8-14 in *Materialy k itigovoj naucnoj sessii instituta za 1965.* Moscow.
2846. Kun, L. 1964. A sportolásra caló társadalmi motiváltság fobb tendenciáinak alakulása hazánkban a századfordulótól napjainkig (Main developmental tendencies of motivation for sport from the end of the last century until today). *Testneveles F. Tudomany Közl.* 3:220-243.
2847. Landon, K.P. 1939. *Thailand in Transition. A Brief Survey of Cultural Trends since the Revolution of 1932.* Chicago: University of Chicago Press. 427 pp.
2848. Lenk, H. 1971. Notizen zur Rolle des Sports und der Leistungsmotivation in einer künftigen Gesellschaft. *Die Leibeserziehung* 20,1:82-87.
2849. Loy, J.W. 1966. A paradigm of technological change in the sports situation. *IRSS* 1,1:177-194.
2850. Loy, J.W. 1968. Sociopsychological attributes associated with the early adoption of a sport innovation. *J.Psychology* 70:141-147.

2851. Loy, J.W. 1969. Social psychological characteristics of innovators. *ASR* 34,1:73–82.
2852. Loy, J.W. 1976. Sozialpsychologische Faktoren der Innovation bei Trainern. Pp. 246–251 in Lüschen/Weis.
2853. Mandell, R. 1976. The invention of the sports record. *Stadion* 2,2: 250–264.
2854. Martin, T.W. and K.J. Berry. 1974. Competitive sport in post-industrial society: the case of the motocross racer. *J.Popular Culture* (Bowling Green) 8,Summer:107–120.
2855. Miermans, C.G.M. 1959. *Sport in een veranderence wereld.* (Sport in a changing world). Utrecht: Het Spectrum. 126 pp.
2856. Miermans, C.G.M. 1966. Situatie en ontwikkeling van de sport (Situation and trends in the development of sport). *Sportcahiers* 1,2:12–37.
2857. Mikhailov, S. and A. Stoichev. 1972. Fizicheskata kultura i izgrazhdancto na razvito sotsialistichesko obshchestvo (Physical culture and the construction of a developed socialist society). *Sotsiologicheski Problemi* (Sofia) 5,4:61–68.
2858. Minami, M. 1959. Miyazaki ken no taiiku sports no koshinsei ni tsuite no kenkyu (A study of the lag of physical education and sports in Miyazaki prefecture). *Bulletin Miyazaki University* 6,1:1–18.
2859. Mlodzikowski, G. 1970. Genealogia spoleczna i klasowe funkcje sportu w latach 1860–1928 (Social genealogy and class functions of sport from 1860 to 1928). *Roczniki Naukowe AWF* 12:250 pp.
2860. McCormack, T. 1966. Changing social structure and the concept of fitness. *J.Canadian Assoc.Health, Phys.Educ. and Recreation* 32,5:4 and 29–36.
2861. McIntosh, P. 1963. *Sport in Society.* London: Watts. 208 pp.
2862. MacPartlin, G.A. 1961. Sport in the Commonwealth. *J.Royal Society Arts* 109:279–297.
2863. Nakamura, T. 1968. *Kindai sports hihan* (Thoughts on sports). Tokyo: Sanseido.
2864. National Conference of Associations of Health, Physical Education and Recreation, eds. 1959. *American Social Changes and Sports.* Washington, D.C. 80 pp.
2865. Ponomarev, N.I. 1970. *Vozniknovenie i pervonazalnoe razvitie fizicheskogo vospitanija* (The rise and initial development of physical education). Moscow. 247 pp.
2866. Rader, B.G. 1977. Quest for subcommunities and the rise of American sport. *American Quarterly* 24,Fall:355–369.
2867. Renson, R. et al. eds. 1976. *The History, the Evolution and Diffusion of Sports and Games in Different Cultures.* Brussels: BLOSO. 591 pp.
2868. Rijsdorp, K. 1972. Die Verschiebung in der Bedeutung der Leistung in der westlichen Welt. *Gymnasion* (Schorndorf) 9,4:4–8.
2869. Rittner, K. 1976. Sport, Bedürfnisstruktur und sozialer Wandel. *Stadion* 2,2:159–195.
2870. Rittner, V. 1976. Sport und Arbeitsteilung. Frankfurt: Limpert. 282 pp. 2,2:159–195.
2871. Rodichenko, V.S. 1969. Omnogostoronnosti vozdeistvija nauchnotechnicheskoi revolucii na fizicheskuju kulturu i sport (About multiple influences of the scientific-technical revolution on physical culture and sport). *Teorija i Praktika* 2:4–6.

2872.   Rodichenko, V.S. 1972. *Technicheskij progress—sojusnik sporta* (Technical progress is an ally of sport). Moscow. 151 pp.

2873.   Roesch, H.E. 1976. Zur Situation des Sports heute. *Die neue Ordnung* 3,June:198–210.

2874.   Rosenstock-Huessy, E. 1958. *Soziologie.* Stuttgart: Kohlhammer. 2 vols. 329 and 760 pp.

2875.   Scotch, N.A. 1961. Magic, sorcery, and football among urban Zulu: a case of reinterpretation under acculturation. *J.Conflict Resolution* 5,1:70–74.

2876.   Stockvis, R. 1974. Traditionalisme in de sportwereld (Traditionalism in the world of sport). *Mens en Maatschappij* 49,2:185–207.

2877.   Stokes, A. 1956. Psycho-analytic reflections on the development of ball games. *Int.J.Psychoanalysis* 37,2–3:185–192.

2878.   Sumner, W.G. 1940. *Folkways.* Boston: Ginn. 692 pp.

2879.   Sutton-Smith, B. 1951. The meeting of Maori and European culture and its effects upon the unorganized games of Maori children. *J.Polynesian Society* (Wellington, N.Z.) 60,1:93–107.

2880.   Sutton-Smith, B. 1959. A formal analysis of game meaning. *Western Folklore* 18,1:13–24.

2881.   Tanikeev, M.P. 1972. Kulturnaja revolucija i nekotorye voprosy razvitija fizicheskoj kultury v Kazahstane (Cultural revolution and problems of development of physical culture in Kazachstan). Pp. 23–24 in *Voprosy teorii praktiki fizicheskogo vospitanija.* Alma-Ata: Vyp.I.

2882.   Tanikeev, M. 1973. Problema sootnoshenija nacionalnogo i internacionalnogo v razvitii fizicheskoj kultury (A problem of national and international relations of physical culture). Pp. 39–47 in *Materialy po istorii organizacci i sociologii fizicheskoj kultury.* Tashkent.

2883.   Tylor, E.B. 1878. On the game of patoli in Ancient Mexico and its probable Asiatic origin. *J.Anthropological Institute* 8,2:116–131.

2884.   Tylor, E.B. 1896. On American lot-games as evidence of Asiatic intercourse before the time of Columbus. *Int.Archiv Ethnographie* (Leiden) 9:55–67 (supplement).

2885.   Tyszka, A. 1963. Socjologiczne aspekty atanu kultury fizycznej i jeu rozqoju w Plocku wobec zagadnien intensywnego uprzemyskowienia miasta (Sociological aspects of physical education and its development in Plock under conditions of intensive industrialization of that town). *Kultura Fizyczna* 16,3–4:229–232.

2886.   Umminger, W. 1962. *Helden, Götter, Übermenschen.* Düsseldorf: Econ. 342 pp. Engl. 1963. *Superman, Heroes and Gods. The Story of Sport through the Ages.* London: Thames and Nudson.

2887.   Urukova, G.M. 1973. Dialekticheskoe edinstvo nacionalnogo i internacionalnogo v razvitii fizicheskoj kultury i sporta (The dialectical unity of the national and international in the development of physical culture and sports). Pp. 168–169 in *Materialy po istorii, organizacii i sociologii fizicheskoj kultury.* Taskent: Medizina Publishing House.

2888.   Vierkandt, A. 1931. Kultur des neunzehnten Jahrhunderts und der Gegenwart. Pp. 149–150 in *Handwörterbuch der Soziologie.* Stuttgart: Enke.

2889.   Volpicelli, L. 1960. *Industrialisme e sport* (Industrialization and sport). Roma.

2890. Walwin, J. 1975. *The People's Game: A Social History of British Football.* London: Allen Lane. 201 pp.
2891. Weule, K. 1926. Ethnologie des Sports. Pp. 1–116 in G. Bogeng, ed. *Geschichte des Sports aller Völker und Zeiten.* Leipzig.
2892. Wohl, A. 1953. Przyczyny upadku kultury fizycznej w okresie rozkladu feudalizmu (The reasons for the decline of physical culture at the end order of Feudalism). *Kultura Fizyczna* 6,8:561–575.
2893. Wohl, A. 1971. Prognostic models of sport in socialist countries on the background of changes in sport of People's Poland. *IRSS* 6,1:17–48.
2894. Wohl, A. 1975. The influence of the scientific-technical revolution on the shape of sport and the perspectives of its development. *IRSS* 10,1:19–34.
2895. Wohl, A. 1977. Sport and the quality of life. *IRSS* 12,2:35–48.
2896. Wohl, A. 1979. Sport and social development. *IRSS* 14,3–4:5–20.
2897. Zoldak, V.I. 1969. Nekotorye sociologicheskie aspekty razvitija fizicheskoj kultury i sporta (Some sociological aspects of the development of physical culture and sport). Pp. 258–263 in *Materialy nauchnoj konferencii po istorii, organizacii i sociologii fizicheskoj kultury i sporta.* Tashkent, Samarkand.
2898. Zoldak, V.I. 1971. Naucno-tiechniceskaja revoljucija i jejo vlijanije na razvitije fiziceskoj kul'tury (The scientific-technological revolution and its impact on the development of physical culture). Pp. 4–12 in *Fiziceskaja kultura i naucnaja organizacija truda.* Moscow.

III. *Social Processes and Sport*

1. *Social Stratification*

3001. Aveni, A.F. 1976. Alternative stratification systems: the case of interpersonal respect among leisure participants. *Sociol.Quart.* 17,Winter: 53–64.
3002. Baltzell, E.D. 1958. *Philadelphia Gentleman.* Glencoe: Free Press.
3003. Blalock, H.M. 1966. The identification problem and theory building: the case of status inconsistency. *ASR* 311,2:52–61.
3004. Bend, E. and B.M. Petrie. 1977. Sport participation, scholastic success, and social mobility. Pp. 1–44 in R.S. Hutton, ed. *Exercise and Sport Sciences Reviews.* Santa Barbara, California: Journal Publishing Affiliates.
3005. Bensman, J. 1972. Classical music and the status game. Pp. 217–228 in Stone.
3006. Beue, E. 1959. Some differences between middle-class and working-class grammar school boys in their attitudes towards education. *Brit.J.Sociol.* 10,2:148–152.
3007. Bishop, D.W. and M. Ideka, M. 1970. Status and role factors in the leisure behavior of different occupations. *Sociol.Soc.Research* 54,2:190–208.
3008. Boynton, P.D. and J.D. Wang. 1944. Relation of the play interests of children to their socio-economic status. *J.Psych.* 64:129–133.
3009. Burdge, R.J. 1969. Levels of occupational prestige and leisure activity. *J.Leisure Research* 2,3:262–274.

3010. Crawford, S. 1977. A comparative study of occupational prestige rankings of Ireland and New Zealand rugby touring teams in 1976. *Research Papers in Physical Education* 3,3:16–19.

3011. Crawford, S. 1977. Occupational prestige rankings of the New Zealand Olympic athlete. *IRSS* 12,1:5–16.

3012. Cunningham, D.A. et al. 1970. Active leisure activities as related to occupation. *J.Leisure Research* 2:104–111.

3013. Dauriac, C. 1975. Social hierarchies regarding sport expenditures and practices. *IRSS* 1,10:73–87.

3014. Dubois, P.E. 1978. Participation in sports and occupational attainment: a comparative study. *Research Quarterly* 49,1:28–37.

3015. Eichberg, H. 1975. Alternative Verhaltensnormen im Arbeitersport? *Sportwissenschaft* 5,1:69–80.

3016. Graham, W.A. 1908. *Kelantan: A State of the Malay Pennisula; A Handbook of 1908 Information.* Glasgow: J. Maclehose. 139 pp.

3017. Gruneau, R.S. 1975. Sport, social differentiation and social inequality. Pp. 119–183 in Ball/Loy.

3018. Gruneau, R. 1978. Elites, class and corporate power in Canadian sport. Pp. 201–242 in Landry/Orban.

3019. Gryspeerdt, A. 1972. Appartenance socio-culturelle et intérêts sportifs: analyse factorielle d'une douzaine d'intérêts sportifs. *Recherches Sociographiques* 3,2:226–246.

3020. Heinemann, K. 1971. Das Sportengagement von Gymnasialschülern verschiedener Sozialschicten. *Sportwissenschaft* 1,2:214–228.

3021. Heinilä, K. 1966. Istuva ja liikkuva ylioppilas (sedentary and mobile students). *Stadion* (Helsinki) 4:4–34.

3022. Hodges, H.M. 1964. *Social Stratification. Class in America.* Cambridge, Mass.: Schenkman. 307 pp.

3023. Hollingshead, A.B. 1957. *Two Factor Index of Social Position.* New Haven, Conn.: Hollingshead.

3024. Humen, W. 1965. Wiek, wyksztalcenie, zawod, a formy rekrecji fizycznej u doroslych (Educational level, occupation, age and forms of physical recreation for adults). *Roczniki Naukowe AWF* (Warsaw). 6:3–45.

3025. Knauth, W. 1976. Die sportlichen Qualifikationen der altiranischen Fürsten. *Stadion* 2,1:1–89.

3026. Kniveton, B.H. and C.L.R. Pike. 1972. Social class, intelligence and the development of children's play interests. *J.Child Psychology and Psychiatry* 13:167–181.

3027. Kohn, M.L. 1969. *Class and Comformity: A Study in Values.* Homewood, Ill.: Dorsey Press.

3028. Koslin, B.M. 1968. Predicting group status from members' cognitions. *Sociometry* 31,1:64–75.

3029. Kowet, D. 1977. *The Rich Who Own Sports.* New York: Random House. 271 pp.

3030. Landtman, G. 1938. *The Origin of the Inequality of the Social Classes.* Chicago, Ill.: University of Chicago Press. 444 pp.

3031. Loy, J.W. 1969. The study of sport and social mobility. Pp. 101–134 in Kenyon.

3032. Loy, J.W. 1970. Social origins and occupational mobility patterns of a selected sample of American athletes. *IRSS* 7,1:5–26.

3033. Lüschen, G. 1962. Sport et stratification sociale. *Revue d'Education Physique* (Bruxelles) 2,2–3:219–224.

3034. Lüschen, G. 1963. Soziale Schichtung und soziale Mobilität bei jungen Sportlern. *Kölner Z. Soziol.* 15,1:74–93. Eng. 1969. Pp. 258–276 in Loy/Kenyon. 1971. Pp. 237–258 in Dunning.

3035. Lüschen, G. 1974. Pp. 112–138 in Die Freizeit der Arbeiterschaft und ihre Beziehung zum Sport. *International Congress on Leisure Time and Physical Recreation of the workers.* Bruxelles.

3036. Lüschen, G. 1965. Soziale Mobilität bei Sportlern. *Sportarzt und Sportmedizin* 16,4:136–141.

3037. Morris, G.; R. Paseward, and J. Schultz. 1972. Occupational level and participation in public recreation in a rural community. *J.Leisure Research* 4,Winter:25–32.

3038. Mott, J. 1973. Miners, weavers, and pigeons. In S. Parker/M. Smith, eds. *Leisure and Society in Britain.* London: Allen Lane.

3039. Noe, F.P. 1974. Leisure, lifestyle and social class: a trend analysis 1900–1960. *Sociol.Soc.Research* 58,3:286–294.

3040. Nowak, W. 1969. Social aspects of Polish boxers and the environment. *IRSS* 4:137–150.

3041. Oppenheim, A.N. 1955. Social status and clique formation among grammar school boys. *Brit.J.Sociol.* 6,3:228–245.

3042. Perleberg, H. 1956. Über die soziale Schichtung der Sporttreibenden in den einzelnen Sportarten. *Theorie und Praxis* 6,8:738–742.

3043. Petrovic, K. and Hosek, A. 1974. The determination of sport activities in the canonical configuration of the latest stratification discussion. pp. 135–169 in *Yugoslav Papers ISA World Congress,* Toronto. Ljubljana.

3044. Petrovic, K. 1976. Effects of social stratification and socialization in various disciplines of sport in Yugoslavia. *IRSS* 11,2:95–103.

3045. Ponthieux, N.A. and D.G. Barker. 1965. Relationships between socioeconomic status and physical fitness measures. *Research Quarterly* 36:464–467.

3046. Saunders, E.D. 1970. Extra-curricular activities in the secondary school. *JOHPER* 1,1.

3047. Schafer, W.E. and N. Stehr. 1970. Participation in competitive athletics and social mobility. Pp. 184–196 in Groll/Strohmeyer.

3048. Starosta, W. 1967. Some data concerning social characteristics of figure skaters. *IRSS* 2:165–178.

3049. Steinberg, D.A. 1978. Workers' sport internationals 1920–1928. *J.Contemporary History* 13:233–251.

3050. Sutton-Smith, B. and P.V. Gump. 1955. Games and status experience. *Recreation* 48,4:172–174.

3051. Timm, U. 1971. Sport in der Klassengesellschaft. Kürbiskern (Berlin) 3,4:608–617.

3052. Timmermann, H. 1973. *Geschichte und Struktur der Arbeitersportbewegung.* 1893–1933. Ahrensburg: Czwalina. 193 pp.

3053. Veblen, T. 1899. *Theory of the Leisure Class.* New York, London: Macmillan. 400 pp.

3054.   Veblen, T. 1976. Sport als atavistisches Raubverhalten Pp. 146-154 in Lüschen/Weis.

3055.   Vinnai, G. 1970. *Fussballsport als Ideologie.* Frankfurt: Europäische Verlagsanstalt.

3056.   Vinnai, G. 1972. ed. *Sport in der Klassengesellschaft.* Frankfurt: Fischer.

3057.   Voigt, D. and M. Messing. 1977. Soziale Schichtung im Hochleistungssport der DDR. *Sportunterricht* 26,7:226–229.

3058.   Voigt, D. 1978. *Soziale Schichtung im Sport.* Berlin: Bartels und Wernitz. 104 pp.

3059.   Wagner, H. 1973. *Sport und Arbeitersport.* Köln: Pahl-Rugenstein.

3060.   Watson, G. 1977. Games, socialization and parental values: social class differences in parental evaluation of Little League Baseball. *IRSS* 12,1: 17–48.

3061.   Weber, E. 1971. Gymnastics and sports in fin de siécle France: opium of the classes. *American Historical Review* 76,1:70–98.

3062.   Wettan, R. and J. Willis. 1976. Social stratification in the New York Athletic Club: a preliminary analysis of the impact of the club on amateur sport in late nineteenth century America. *Canad.J.History Sport Phys. Educ.* 7,1:41–53.

3063.   Wohl, A. 1955. Uzrodel sportu burzuaryjnego (Sources of bourgeois sport). *Kultura fizyczna* 7,9:680–688. 8,1–2:13–25, 87–96.

3064.   Wohl, A. 1973. Die gesellschaftlich–historischen Grundlagen des bürgerlichen Sports. Köln: Pahl-Rugenstein. 204 pp.

3065.   Yiannakis, A. 1975. A theory of sport stratification. *Sport Sociology Bulltin* 4,1:23–32.

3066.   Young, M. 1970. Personal-social adjustment, physical fitness, attitude toward physical education of high school girls by socioeconomic levels. *Research Quarterly* 41:593–599.

3067.   Zingg, W. 1971. *Spitzensport und soziale Mobilitat.* Magglingen: Eidgenössische Turn-und Sportschule. 32 pp.

2. Age Stratification: Childhood, Youth, Adulthood, Aged

3068.   Al Hamdan, M. and B. Abulaban. 1971. Games involvement and sex-role socialization in Arab children. *Int.J.Comp.Sociol.* 12,3:182–191.

3069.   Allardt, E. et al. 1958. *Nuorison hassastusket ja yhteison rakenne* (Activities and hobbies of youth and the structure of society). Helsinki: Porvoo W. Soderstrom. 235 pp.

3070.   Ariés, Ph. 1960. *L'enfant et la vie familiale sous l'ancien régime.* Paris: Plon. 503 pp.

3071.   Artus, H.G. 1974. *Jugend und Freizeit—Sport.* Giessen: Achenback 248 pp.

3072.   Atchley, R.C. 1971. Retirement and leisure participation: continuity or crisis. *Gerontologist* 2,1:13–17.

3073.   *Avenirs* 1971. Le sport et les jeunes. *Avenirs* 226–227:27–76.

3074.   Bates, J.E. and P.M. Bentler. 1973. Play activities of normal and effeminate boys. *Developmental Psychology* 9,1:20–27.

3075.   Bloss, H. 1970. Sport and vocational school pupils. *IRSS* 5,1:25-58.
3076.   Blumenfeld, W.S. R.D. Franklin, and H.H. Remmers. 1962. Youth's attitudes toward sports, the Peace Corps, military service and course offerings. *Purdue Opinion Panel Poll Report* 21,3:1-22.
3077.   Bouet, M. 1967. Les facteurs de L'expansion du sport moderne et leur signification par rapport à la jeunesse actuelle. *L'Homme Sain* 18,2: 96-101.
3078.   Boynton, P.L., and Wang, J.D. 1944. Relation of the play interests of children to their economic status. *J.Genetic Psych.* 64,1:119-138.
3079.   Brace, D.K. 1954. Sociometric evidence of the relationship between social status and athletic ability among junior high school boys. *Professional Contribution number 3.* Washington, D.C.: American Academy of Physical Education.
3080.   Brown, R.H. 1975. Class, race and athletics: a study of adolescent aspiration, intention and interests. *Sport Sociology Bulletin* 4,2:84-86.
3081.   Buggel, E. 1963. Sport und Touristik im Urlaubsverhalten Jugendlicher und Erwachsener (Sport and touristics in the behavior during vacation of adolescents and adults). *Theorie und Praxis* 12,4:360-371. 12,8: 700-708.
3082.   Bultena, G. and Wood, V. 1970. Leisure orientation and recreational activities of retirement community residents. *J.Leisure Research* 11, Winter:3-15.
3083.   Cammaer, H. 1963. *De houding van de 16-17 jarigen in het Vlaamse Land tegenover het verenigingsleven* (The attitude of 16 to 17 year old adolescents towards clublife in Flanders). Louvain: Nauwelaerts. 233 pp.
3084.   Campbell, D. 1969. Analysis of leisure time profiles of four age groups of adult males. *Research Quarterly* 40,2:266-273.
3085.   Catabrano, D.A. 1975. La cultura, el deporte y la juventud chilena (Culture and sport of Chilean youth). *Cuadernos Americanos* 200,3:55-68.
3086.   Clark, F.L.G. 1966. *Work, Age and Leisure.* London: Michael Joseph. 152 pp.
3087.   Cohen, G.B. 1959. Jeugd en enkele vormen van vrijetjdsbesteding (Youth and some forms of the use of leisure). *Sociologische Gids* 6,3:137-143.
3088.   Coleman, J.S. 1960. The adolescent subculture and academic achievement. *AJS* 65,3:337-347.
3089.   Coleman, J.S. 1961. *The Adolescent Society.* Glencoe, Ill.: Free Press. 368 pp.
3090.   Coleman, J.S. 1961. The competition for adolescent energies. *Phi Delta Kappan* 42,6:231-236.
3091.   Corain, C. 1957. L'interesse etnografico di alcuni giochi dei fanciulli. (The ethnographic importance of boys' games). *Archivio per L'antropologia e la etnologia* 87:133-158.
3092.   Crichton, A., James, E., Wakeford. I. 1962. Youth and leisure in Cardiff. *ASR* 10,2:203-220.
3093.   Deutsches Jugendinstitut. 1971. *Spiel im kindesalter.* Munich: Deutsches Jungendinstitut.
3094.   De Young, J.E. 1955. *Village Life in Modern Thailand.* Berkeley, Los Angeles: University of California Press. 201 pp.
3095.   Dietz, H. 1963. *Jugend von heute—Gesellschaft von morgen.* Berlin:

Neuwied, Luchterhand. 211 pp.

3096. d'Orleans, H. 1894. *Around Tonkin and Siam.* London: Chapman and Hall. 426. pp.

3097. Elkin, F. and W.A. Westley. 1955. The myth of adolescent culture. *ASR* 20,6:680-684.

3098. Emmet, I. 1971. *Youth and Leisure in an Urban Sprawl.* Manchester: Manchester University Press. 107 pp.

3099. Engstrom, L.M. 1974. Physical activities during leisure time: a survey of teenage sport activities in Sweden. *IRSS* 9,2:82-102.

3100. Fabis, E. 1971. Motywy uprawiania sportu w okresie mlodosci. (Reasons of the practising of sports during the period of youth). *Roczniki Naukowe WSWF* (Poznan) 20:153-170.

3101. Fagot, B. and I. Littman. 1975. Stability of sex role and play interest from preschool to elementary school. *J.Psychology* 89:285-292.

3102. Felling, A.J.A. 1967. Sportbeoefening van een kategorie jeugdigen. (Sport participation of a categorie of youth). *Sportcahiers* (Hertogenbosch) 4:6-31.

3103. Foster, J.C. 1930. Play activities of children in the first six grades. *Child Development* 1,3:248-254.

3104. Fulcher, D. and D.G. Perry. 1973. Cooperation and competition in interethnic evaluation of preschool children. *Psychological Reports* 33,3: 795-800.

3105. Furuya, T. et al. 1960. Seinenki ni okeru shakaiteki kincho to sports ni kansuru chosakenkyu (A survey of social tension and sports in adolescence). *JOPHER* (Tokyo) 5,1:105.

3106. Geyer, H. 1969. Sport. Pp. 1099-1103 in W. Bernsdorf, ed. *Wörterbuch der Soziologie.* Stuttgart: Enke.

3107. Gras, F. 1974. The shaping of the interest in and the need for sport among children and adolescents. *IRSS* 9,3-4:75-80.

3108. Gras, F. 1976. Problems of the social structure of children and young people participating in youth Spartakiads. *IRSS* 11,4:47-52.

3109. Greifzu, W. 1942. *Spiel und Arbeit. Sozialpsychologische Untersuchungen an Kindern eines Dorfes.* Jena: Fischer.

3110. Groessing, St. 1970. Sportliche Betätigung und Sportinteressen bei berufstätigen Jugendlichen. Pp. 126-134 in Groll/Strohmeyer.

3111. Hales-Tooke, A. 1972. World attitudes to play. *Child Education Quarterly* 49,1:25-30.

3112. Hargreaves, D.H. 1967. *Social Relations in a Secondary School.* London: Routledge.

3113. Havighusrst, R.J. et al. 1969. *Adjustment to Retirement: A Cross-National Study.* New York: Humanities Press. 195 pp.

3114. Helanko, R. 1953. *Turun poikasakit* (Gangs of boys). Turku: Yliopiston Julkaisuja. 260 pp.

3115. Helanko, R. 1964. Urheilun syntysijet. (The birthplace of sport). *Soziologia* (Helsinki) 2:58-62

3116. Hille, B. 1976. Zum Stellehwert des Sports bei Jugendlichen in der Bundesrepublik und in der DDR. *Deutschland-Archiv* (Köln) 9,6: 592-601.

3117. Hobart, C.W. 1973. Active sports participation among the young, the middle-aged and the elderly. *IRSS* 3-4,10:27-40.

3118. Hollingshead, A.B. 1949. *Elmtown's Youth.* New York: Wiley. 480 pp.

3119. Humen, W. 1964. Wiek a udzial w rekreacji fizycznej osob doroslych (Age and the participation in physical education of adults). *Kultura Fizyczna* 17,11-12:661-663.

3120. Hurtig, M.C. and M. Paillard. 1971. Jeux et activités des enfants de 4 (Age and the participation in physical education of adults). *Kultura Fizyczna* 17,11-12;661-663.

3121. Ikbal, A.S.S. 1930. *Eastward to Persia.* London: Wright and Brown. 292 pp.

3122. Ionescu, V.N. 1972. Le sport, une nécessité de la jeunesse. *Analele Universitatii Bucuresti, Serie Sociologie* (Bucarest) 21:175-181.

3123. Jackson, D.W. 1973. Alienation and identity-role diffusion in late adolescence. *J.Psychology* 83:251-256.

3124. Johnson, J.C.A. 1940. The Kurds of Irak. *Geographical Magazine* 10: 382-393.

3125. Kocian, M. 1965. Telovychovna cinnost u nasi sedmatilete mladezevtah mezi pranim a skutecnosti (Sport activity of our 17 year old, relations between desire and reality). *Teorie a praxe telesne vychovy* 13,6: 254-257.

3126. Künkele, Ph. 1930. Vom Sporterleben unserer Vierzehnjährigen (Sport experience of 14 year old youth). *Die Leibesübungen* 12:337-340.

3127. Latham, A.J. 1951. The relationship between pubertal status and leadership in high school boys. *J.Genetic Psych.* 78,2:185-194.

3128. Lehman, H.C. 1951. Chronological age vs. proficiency in physical skills. *American J.Psychology* 64,2:161-187.

3129. Lewis, G. 1977. Sport, youth culture and conventionality 1920-1970. *J.Sport History* 4,2:129-150.

3130. Lüschen, G. 1961. Die deutsche Sportjugend in ihrer Struktur und ihren sozialen Verhaltensweisen. *Olympische jugend* 6,3:2-5.

3131. MacDonald, M.; G. McGuire and R.J. Havighurst. 1949. Leisure activities and the socio-economic status of children. *AJS* 54,6:505-519.

3132. Marivoet, M. and U. Claeys. 1975. *Sociale Determinanten van het Sportgedrag bij de Jeugd* (Social determinants of sport behavior of youth). *Sociologich Onderzoekinstitut.* Leuven. 204 pp.

3133. Marivoet, M. 1976. *Problem in de jeugdsport.* (Problems of youth sport). University of Leuven. Sociologich Onderzoekinstitut. 177 pp.

3134. Martens, R. 1970. Social reinforcement effects on preschool children's motor performance. *J.Perceptual Motor Skills* 31:787-792.

3135. Matza, D. 1961. Subterrenean traditions of youth. *Annals AAPSS* 338: 102-118.

3136. Matza, D. 1964. Position and behavior patterns of youth (Sports and athletes). Pp. 191-216 in R.E.L. Faris, ed. *Handbook of Modern Sociology.* Chicago, Ill.: Rand McNally.

3137. Meger, J. 1972. Der Anteil der Freien Deutschen Jugend an der Entwicklung des Jugendsports in der DDR. *Wissensch.Zeitschr. Universität Rostock* 21:883-889.

3138. Megyeri, F. 1964. A szociológia és a teskultura néhány összefüggése, a tizéves gyerekek testnevelésében. (Some relations of sociology and physical culture in the physical education of children ten years of age). Pp. 605-623 in *Unesco Nemzetközi Testnevelési Tudományos Kon-*

ferencia, Budapest.

3139. Merand, R. 1974. Problems of play and sports activity of the child. *IRSS* 9,1:93–104.

3140. Milshtein, O.A. 1974. Sport kak faktor formirovanija socialnoj aktivnosti i socialnogo oblika sovetskoj molodjezhi (Sport as factor of forming social activity and social appearance of Soviet youth). Pp. 127–128 in *Fizicheskoe vospitanie podrasta jushchego pokool enija.* Moscow.

3141. Mistry, D.K. 1958. The Indian child and his play. *Sociol.Bulletin* 7,2: 137–147.

3142. Moose, E.J. 1897. *Korean Interviews.* New York: O. Appleton Company. 16 pp.

3143. Müller, S. 1960. Die Sportfreudigkeit unserer Jugend. *Wissensch.Zeitschr. DHFK.* 3,1–2:121–138.

3144. McPherson, B.D.; L.N. Guppy and J.P. McKay. 1976. The social structure of the game and sport milieu. Pp. 161–200 in J.G. Albinson and G.M. Andrew, eds. *Child in Sport and Physical Activity.* Baltimore, Mar.: University Park Press.

3145. Nádori, L. 1972. Ausserunterrichtlicher Sport in der Volksrepublik Ungarn (Out-of-school sport in People's Republic of Hungary). *Wissensch. Zeitschr.Universität Rostock* 21:871–875.

3146. Nelson, L.L. and Spencer, K. 1972. Competition, the star-spangled scramble. *Psychology Today.* 6,4:53–56, 90–91.

3147. Nicholson, C.S. 1979. Some attitudes associated with sport participation among junior high school females. *Research Quarterly* 50,4:661–667.

3148. Niewiadonski, M. 1960. Zainteresowania mlodziezy szolnij Lubelszczyzny zagadnieniami sportu i wychowania fizycznego. (Interest in sport and physical education of Lublin district school youth). *Kultura Fizyczna* 10:717–726.

3149. Olsen, A.M. 1955. *Aktiv Ungdom* (Active Youth). Oslo: State Office of Sport and Youth Work. 120 pp.

3150. Opie, I. and P. Opie. 1969. *Children's Games in Street and Playground.* Oxford: Clarendon Press. 400 pp.

3151. Paillard, M.C. and M. Hurtig. 1969. Peut-on etudier le jeu de l'enfant? *Psychologie Française* 14:333–342.

3152. Patriksson, G. 1976. *Ungdomas Attityder Fill Olympiska Spiel* (Attitude of youth toward the Olympics). Lararhogskolan: Mölndal. 68 pp.

3153. Pereversin, I.I. 1968. Socialnyj progress ivospitanie sportivnyh interesov molodjezhi (Social progress and the training of sport interests of young people). Pp. 3–5 in *Materialy konferencii molodyh nauchnyh sotrudnikovza god.* Moscow.

3154. Petrak, B. 1965. Prispevek k sociologickemu, specialne socialnepsychologickemu rozboru telovychovne cinnosti dospivjici mladeze (Sociological, especially psychological aspects of research in sport). Pp. 192–229 in *Telovychovny Sbornik.* Praha, SPN.

3155. Petrak, B. 1965. Telovychoona cinnost dispirajici vuladeze na vesnici (Physical training activity of village adolescent youth). Pp. 112–113, 117 in Z. Sprynar, *Felsna Vychova Pracajicich.* Praha, Sportovini a juristicke Nakladatelstvi.

3156. Petrie, B.M. 1971. Achievement orientations in adolescent attitudes toward play. *IRSS* 6:89–99.

3157. Philipp, H. 1971. Skizze zum Subsystem Kinder—und Jugendsport in System der sozialistischen Köperkultur in der DDR. *Wissensch.Zeitschr. Universität Rostock* 15,3:453–478.

3158. Philipp, H. 1971. Zur köperlichen und sportlichen Vervollkommnung der Jugend in der sozialistischen Berufsausbildung. *Wissensch.Zeitschn. Pädagogische Hoehschule Potsdam* 15,3:479–486.

3159. Proudfoot, B.F. 1957. An Edinburgh Street Game. *Ulster Folk Life* 3,1:70–75.

3160. Raum, O.F. 1940. *Chaga Childhood: A Description of Indigenous Education in an African Tribe.* London: Oxford University Press. 422 pp.

3161. Rehberg, R.A. and M. Cohen. 1975. Athletes and scholars: an analysis of the compositional characteristics and image of these two youth culture categories. *IRSS* 10,1:91–107.

3162. Renson, R. and A. Vermeulen. 1972. Sociale determinanten van de sportpraktijk bij Belgische volwassenen (Social determinants of sport practice among Belgian adults). *Sport* (Brussels) 15:25–39.

3163. Rijsdorp, K. 1960. *Sport als jong-menselijke activiteit.* Groningen: Wolters. 304 pp.

3164. Ritchie, O. and M.R. Koller. 1964. *Sociology of Childhood.* New York: Appleton. 333 pp.

3165. Royce, J. 1972. Validation of game classification models against Sudanese children's games. *Antropos* (Freiburg) 67,1–2:138–151.

3166. Rüssel, A. 1953. *Das Kinderspiel.* München: Beck. 176 pp.

3167. Scott, Ph. M. 1953. Comparative study of attitudes toward athletic competition in the elementary school. *Research Quarterly* 24,3:352–361.

3168. Seeberger, M. 1956. Erwachsenenspiele in Lötschen. *Schweizer Archiv für Volkskunde* 52,1:35–48.

3169. Smith, M.D. 1979. Getting involved in sport: sex differences. *IRSS.* 14,2:93–102.

3170. Soviet Education. 1974. Physical education and sports for Soviet school age youth. *Soviet Education* 16,4:4–114.

3171. Spirescu, R. 1970. Soziologie des Sports und berufstätige Jugend. Pp. 197–212 in Groll/Strohmeyer.

3172. Stendler, C.B. 1949. *Children of Brasstown.* Urbana, Ill.: University of Illinois. 103 pp.

3173. Stensaasen. 1977. Sport involvement of Norwegian youngsters related to sex, age, social class, cleverness at and satisfaction with school. *Sportwissenschaft* 7,2:151–159.

3174. Stone, G.P. 1965. The play of little children. *Quest.* Apr.:23–31.

3175. Sumi Y. 1953. Yoji no yugishudan ni okeru ningenkankei ni tsuite (An experimental study of play groups of young children). *Research J.Phys. Educ.* 1,5:310–360.

3176. Sutton-Smith, B. 1959. *The Games of New Zealand Children.* Berkeley, Calif.: University of California Press. 193 pp.

3177. Sutton-Smith, B. and B.G. Rosenberg. 1960. Manifest anxiety and game preferences in children. *Child Development* 31,2:307–311.

3178. Sutton-Smith, B. and B.G. Rosenberg. 1961. Sixty years of historical change in the game preferences of American children. *Journal American Folklore* 74,1:17–46.

3179. Sutton-Smith, B. 1972. *The Folkgames of Children.* Austin, Texas: University of Texas Press. 559 pp.

3180.   Takenoshita, K. 1961. Seishonen modai to sports (Problems of youth and sport). *Municipal Government* Tokyo. 10,6:13–19.

3181.   Tan, G.G. 1963. Boys Olympic games. *Physical Education Today* (Manila) March-June:20–25.

3182.   Taves, M.J. 1962. Exploration in personal adjustment after age 65. *Geriatrics* 17,May:309–316.

3183.   Telama, R. 1970–1972. *Oppikoululaisten fyysinen aktivisuus ja liikuntaharrastukset* (Secondary school students' physical activity and leisure time sports). University of Jyväskylä. Research Reports Nr. 75, 102,107, 142.

3184.   University of Michigan Survey Research Center. 1955. *A Study of Adolescent Boys.* New Brunswick, N.J.: Boy Scouts of America. 183 pp.

3185.   University of Michigan Survey Research Center. 1960. *A Study of Boys Becoming Adolescents.* Ann Arbor, Mich.: University of Michigan. 260 pp.

3186.   Valbuena, C.J. 1970. Infantiles montaneses "Las Vecas." *Publicaciones Institut Etnografia y Folklore* II:95–148.

3187.   Van Dalen, D.B. 1947. A differential analysis of the play of adolescent boys. *Journal of Educational Research* 41,3:204–213.

3188.   Webb, H. 1969. Professionalization of attitudes toward play among adolescents. Pp. 161–188 in Kenyon.

3189.   Werner, J. 1926. Das Spiel der Kinder. *Kölner Vierteljahrshefte für Soziologie.* 5,4:411–444.

3190.   Zukowska, Z. 1973. Wpływ sportu na osobowość młodzieży (The influence of sport on the personality of youth). Pp. 211–224 in Z. Krawczyk ed. *Sport w spoleczenstwie wspolczesnym.* Warsaw, PWN.

3. Sex Stratification

3191.   Adedeji, J.A. 1978. The acceptance of Nigerian women in sport. *IRSS* 1,13:39–48.

3192.   Albonico, R. 1970. Die jungen Mädchen und ihr Sport—Situation der Lehrtöchter. Pp. 23–28 in Groll/Strohmeyer.

3193.   Angrist, S.S. 1967. Role constellation as a variable in women's leisure activities. *Social Forces* 45,3:423–430.

3194.   Bausenwein, J. and A. Hoffman. 1967. *Frau und Leibesübungen.* Mülheim: Gehörlosen-Verlag.

3195.   Bergman, S. 1938. *In Korean Wilds and Villages.* London: John Gifford, 232 pp.

3196.   Bird, A.M. 1975. Cross sex effects of subject and audience during motor performance. *Research Quarterly* 46,3:379–384.

3197.   Brehm, B.W. 1975. *Sport als Sozialisationsinstanz traditioneller Geschlechtsrollen.* Giessen: Achenbach.

3198.   Buhrmann, H.G. and R.D. Bratton. 1977. Athletic participation and status of Alberta school girls. *IRSS* 12,1:57–70.

3199.   Caskey, S.R. and D.W. Felker. 1971. Social stereotyping of female body image by elementary school age girls. *Research Quarterly* 42,3:251–255.

3200. Claeys, U. 1976. Vrouw en sport. (Female and sport). *Sport* 19,1:31–36.
3201. Coffey, M.A. 1956. The sportswoman—then and now. *JOPHER.* 36,1: 38–41.
3202. English, J. 1978. Sex equality in sports. *Philosophy and Public Affairs* 7,Spring:269–277.
3203. Feltz, D. 1978. Athletics in the status system of female adolescents. *Review Sport Leisure* 3,1:98–108.
3204. Felshin, J. 1974. The triple option for women in sport. *Quest* 21:36–40.
3205. Fukuoka, T. 1958. Noson fujin no recreation ni kansuru chosa (Study on women's recreational activities in agricultural village). *Liberal Arts Journal* 9:41–52.
3206. Geadelmann, P.L. et al. 1977. *Equality in Sport for Women.* Washington, D.C.: American Alliance for Health, Physical Education, and Recreation. 202 pp.
3207. Gerber, E.W. et al. 1974. *The American Woman in Sport.* Reading, Mass.: Addison-Wesley. 562 pp.
3208. Gold, S. 1977. Sex stereotyping in the school: some solutions to the problem of discriminatory attitudes. *Education Canada* (Toronto) 17,1:22–27.
3209. Greendorfer, S. 1977. Female sport participation patterns. Pp. 30–36 in M. Adrian and J. Brame eds., *Research Reports.* Washington, D.C.: AAHPER.
3209a. Greendorfer, S. 1978. Social class influence on female sport involvement. *Sex Roles* 4,4:619–625.
3210. Hall, M.A. 1977. The sociological perspectives of females in sport. Pp. 37–50 in M. Adrian and J. Brame eds. *Research Reports.* Washington, D.C.:AAHPER.
3211. Hall, M.A. 1978. *Sport and Gender. A Feminist Perspective on the Sociology of Sport.* CAHPER Monograph. Calgary: University of Calgary. 83 pp.
3212. Harris, D. 1971 and 1973. *Women in Sport.* Washington, D.C.: AAHPER.
3213. Hart, M.M. 1972. On being female in sport. Pp. 291–302 in Hart.
3214. Hawkes, P. et al. 1975. Sex roles in school sport and physical education: the state of play. *Australian J.Health Phys.Educ.Recreation* 67:8–17.
3215. Huckle, P. 1978. Back to the starting line: title IX and women's intercollegiate athletics. *American Behavioral Scientist* 21, January:379–392.
3216. Hulbert, H.B. 1902. The status of women in Korea. *The Korean Review.* Seoul: Methodist Publishing House, 159 pp.
3217. Kennedy, L. 1977. Mother—daughter relationships and female sport socialization. *Canadian Assoc. Health, Physical Education, Recreation.* 43,3: 22–26.
3218. Kidd, T.R. and W.F. Woodman. 1975. Sex and orientation toward winning in sport. *Research Quarterly* 46,4:476–483.
3219. Knapp, B.N. 1969. Sex differences in the declared leisure interests of the 14–15 year age group. *Research in Physical Education* 1,8.
3220. Krawczyk, B. 1973. The social role and participation in sport: specific social features of women's sport. *IRSS.* 8,3–4:47–62.
3221. Kröner, S. 1976. *Sport und Geschlecht.* Ahrensburg: Czwalina. 265 pp.
3222. Landers, D.M. 1970. Psychological femininity and the prospective female physical educator. *Research Quarterly* 41:164–170.

3223.   Landers, D.M. 1970. Sibling-sex status and ordinal position effects on females' sport participation and interest. *J.Soc.Psych.* 80:247–248.

3224.   Landers, D.M. and G. Lüschen. 1970. Sibling-sex-status and ordinal position effects on the sport participation of females. Pp. 411–418 in Kenyon, ed., *Psychology of Sport*. Chicago: Athletic Institute.

3225.   Langlois, J.H. and N.Y. Gottfried. 1973. The influence of sex of peer on the social behavior of preschool children. *Developmental Psychology* 8,1:93–98.

3226.   Lekarska, N. 1973. Women in the Olympic Games and movement. Pp. 63–81 in Lekarska, N. *Essays and Studies on Olympic Problems*. Sofia, Bulgaria: Medicina and Fizcultura.

3227.   Lever, J. 1976. Sex differences in the games children play. *Social Problems* 23:478–487.

3228.   Lever, J. 1978. Sex differences in the complexity of children's play and games. *ASR* 43,4:471–483.

3229.   Loktionova, Z.I. 1972. Fizicheskaja kultura i sport v svobodnom vremeni zhenchchin, prozhivajushchih v selskoj mestnosti (Physical culture and sports at leisure time of women, living in the country). Pp. 38–39 in *Voprosy teorii i praktiki fizicheskogo vospitanija*. Alma-Ata.

3230.   Malmisur, M.C. 1978. Title IX dilemma: meritocratic and egalitarian tension. *J.Sport Behavior.* 3:130–138.

3231.   Metheny, E. 1965. Symbolic forms of movement: the feminine image in sports. Pp. 43–56 in E. Metheny, *Connotations of Movement in Sport and Dance*. Dubuque, Iowa: William C. Brown Co, Publishers.

3232.   McCandless, B.R. and J.M. Hoyt. 1961. Sex, ethnicity and play preference of pre-school children. *J.Abnormal Soc.Psychology* 62:683–685.

3233.   Nigg, F. and O. Heiderich. 1967. *Die jungen Mädchen und ihr Sport.* Bern: Eidgenössische Turn-und Sportschule. 106 pp.

3234.   Nigg, F. and O. Heiderich. 1968. Young girls and their sport. *IRSS* 3:125.

3235.   Oglesby, C.A. 1978. *Women and Sport: From Myth to Reality.* Philadelphia: Lea and Ferbiger. 256 pp.

3236.   Ohashi, Y. 1971. Kateifujin no sport ni kansuru shakaigakuteki kenkyu (A sociological study on sport activity of housewives). Pp. 29–39 in *Bulletin of the Faculty of Physical Education.* Tokyo: Tokyo University of Education.

3237.   Patel, J.S. and P.G. Brewster. 1957. The indian game of sagargote. *Zeitschrift für Ethnologie* 82,2:186–190.

3238.   Rijsdorp, K. Die sportliche Betätigung des Mannes und der Frau aus sozialwissenschaftlicher Sicht. Pp. 103–115 in *Sportliche Betätigung des Mannes—sportliche Betätigung der Frau.* Basel: Reinhardt.

3239.   Rosenberg, B.G. and B. Sutton-Smith. 1959. The measurement of masculinity and feminity in children. *Child Development.* 30:373–380.

3240.   Rosenberg, B.G. and B. Sutton-Smith. 1960. A revised conception of masculine-feminine differences in play activities. *J.Genetic Psych.* 96, March:165–170.

3241.   Saito, N. 1961. Shufu no yoka-katsudo ni kansuru kenkyu (Study on leisure-time of housewives). *Bulletin of Tokyo Gakugei College* 12:1–14.

3242.   Seffer, B. 1965. Vynzitie sociologickeko prieskumu v telesnej vychove pracujucik zien (Sociological investigations in connection with physical education of working women). *Teorie a praxe telesne vychovy.* 13,3: 117-122.

3243. Selby, R. and J.H. Lewko. 1976. Children's attitudes toward females in sports. *Research Quarterly* 47,3:453-463.

3244. Shimazaki, J. and Y. Ohashi. 1971. Kateifujin no sport ni kansuru shakai-gakuteki kenkyu (A sociological study on sport activity of housewives). Pp. 29-39 in *Bulletin of the Faculty of Physical Education.* Tokyo: Tokyo University of Education.

3245. Sisters in sport. 1975. *Human Behavior* 4,10:1-54.

3246. Smith, R.A. 1970. The rise of basketball for women in colleges. *Canadian J.History Sport Phys.Educ.* 1,2:18-36.

3247. Snyder, E. and J.E. Kiulin. 1977. Perceptions of the sex role among female athletes and non-athletes. *Adolescence* 12,45:23-29.

3248. Snyder, E. et al. 1978. Socialization comparisons of adolescent female athletes and musicians. *Research Quarterly* 49,Oct.:342-350.

3249. Stein, P.J. and S. Hoffman. 1978. Sports and male role strain. *J.Social Issues* 34,1:136-150.

3250. Sutton-Smith, B.S. and J.M. Roberts. 1967. Studies of an elementary game of strategy. *Genetic Psychology Monographs* 75,1:3-42.

3251. Szilasi, G. 1975. A nök tesnevelesnek es sportjanak nehany szociologiai problemaja (Some sociological problems of gymnastics and female sports). *Sport és Testneveles* 1:21-36.

3252. Tiger, L. 1969. *Men in Groups.* New York: Random House.

3253. Uesugi, T. and W.E. Vinacke. 1963. Strategy in a feminine game. *Sociometry* 26,1:75-88.

3254. Voigt, D.Q. 1978. Sex in baseball: reflections of changing taboos. *J. Popular Culture* 12,Winter:389-403.

3255. Wasilewski, E. 1962. Proba analizy zainteresowan sportowych mlodziezy szkolnej a akademickiej (Attempt to an analysis of sports interest of school children and college students). *Roczniki Naukowe AWF* 1: 91-122.

3256. Wonneberger, I. 1968. Physical culture and sport in leisure pursuit of women as compared with men. *IRSS* 3:117-124.

4. *Socialization and Social Control*

3257. AAHPER. 1951. *Democratic Human Relations.* Washington, D.C.: AAHPER. 562 pp.

3258. Adam, Y. et al. 1975. *Sport et Développement Humain.* Paris: Editions Sociales.

3259. ADL. 1974. *Sozialisation im Sport.* Schorndorf: Hofmann. 475 pp.

3260. Albinson, J.G. and G.M. Andrew. 1976. *Child in Sport and Physical Activity.* Baltimore, Maryland: University Park Press. 250 pp.

3261. Andrews, J.C. 1970. Sport and the socialization of the secondary school-boy. *Australian J.Phys.Educ.* 50:5-12.

3262. Bailey, I.C. 1977. Socialization in play, games and sports. *Physical Edu-*

cation 34,4:183–187.

3263. Ball, D.W. 1967. Toward a sociology of toys: inanimate objects, socialization, and the demography of the doll world. *Sociological Quarterly* 8,Autumn:447–458.

3264. Barry, H. III and J.M. Roberts. 1972. Infant socialization and games of chance. *Ethnology* 11,3:296–308.

3265. Baumann, H. 1974. Überlegungen zur Sozialisationfunktion des Spiels. *Sportunterricht* (Schorndorf) 23,9:302–311.

3266. Belorusova, V.V. 1971. Osnovnye problema nravstvennogo vospitanija sovetskogo sportsmena (The main problems of the ethical education of a Soviet sportsman). Pp. 32 in *Doklad na Vsesojuznom seminare lektorov po propagande fizicheskoj kultury i sporta.* Moskow: Znanie.

3267. Bernstein, B. and D. Young. 1967. Social class difference in conceptions of the uses of toys. *Sociology* 1,2:131–140.

3268. Betts, J.R. 1968. Mind and body in early American thought. *J.American History* 54,4:787–805.

3269. Biancani, A. Childhood development through low organizational games. *Sport Sociology Bulletin* 6,1:52–54.

3270. Bohn, F. 1908–1909. A testnevelés társadalmi és szociális jelentösége (Social meaning of physical education). *Tornaügy* (Budapest) 26,20: 309–314.

3271. Bruner, J.S. 1975. Child development: play as serious business. *Psychology Today* 8,8:81–83.

3272. Cachay, K. et al. 1973. Sozialisation im Sport—6. Kongress des ADL in Oldenburg. *Sportwissenschaft* 3,4:387–413.

3273. Cachay, K. and C. Keindienst. 1976. Soziale Lernprozesse im Sportspiel. *Sportwissenschaft* 6,3:291–310.

3274. Cagigal, J.M. 1970. Social education through sport: a trial. Pp. 339–348 in G.S. Kenyon.

3275. Cagigal, J.M. 1972. Social education and Sport. *Bulletin of Physical Education* 9,3:13–17.

3276. CAHPER. 1971. Socialization in sport. *CAHPER Journal* 37,3.

3277. Carnee, H. 1968. Learning under competitive and collaberative sets. *J. Experim.Soc.Psychology* 4:26–34.

3278. Castine, S.C. and G.C. Roberts. 1974. Modeling in the socialization process of the black athlete. *IRSS* 9,3–4:59–73.

3279. Ciuciu, G. 1974. The socialization process of children by means of extemporized and organized games. *IRSS* 9,1:7–22.

3280. Collard, R.R. 1971. Exploratory and play behavior of infants reared in an institution and in lower and middle class homes. *Child Development* 42,4:1003–1015.

3281. Cook, N.C. 1949. The theater and ballet arts of Iran. *Middle East J.* 3:406–420.

3282. Cowell, C.C. 1960. The contribution of physical activity to social development. *Research Quarterly* 31,2:286–306.

3283. Denzin, N.K. 1975. Play, games and interaction: the contexts of childhood socialization. *Sociological Quarterly* 16,4:458–478.

3284. Diem, C. 1963. The importance of sport to juvenile education in modern society. *Physical Education Today* (Manila) March-June:15–19.

3285. Du Quin, M.E. 1977. Differential sex role socialization toward amplitude appropriation. *Research Quarterly* 48,2:288–292.
3286. Eichler, G. 1974. Arbeit und Spielziehung: Versuch einer soziologischen Kritik der Spielideologie und der Spielerziehung. Pp. 301–303 in ADL, eds. *Sozialisation im Sport.* Schorndorf: Hofmann.
3287. Feitelson, D. 1975. Developmental functions of play. Pp. 135–140 in U. Simri *International Seminar on Play in Physical Education and Sport.* Netanya, Israel: Wingate Institute for Physical Education and Sport.
3288. Flitner, A. et al. 1975. Spiel. *Zeitschrift für Pädagogik* (Weinheim) 21,3: 325–405.
3289. Fraleigh, W.D. 1946. The influence of play upon social and emotional adjustment, with implications for physical education. Pp. 268–273 in *59th Annual Proceedings of College Physical Education Association.* San Fransisco, Calif.
3290. Frank, L.R. and R.E. Hartley. 1951. Play and personality formations in pre-school groups. *Personality* 1:149–161.
3291. Frank, L.R. 1955. Play in personality development. *American J.Orthopsychiatry* 25:576–590.
3292. Frank, L.R. 1964. Role of play in child development. *Childhood Education* 41:70–73.
3293. Franke, E. 1976. Imagebildung und Sozialisation im Welkampfsport. *Sportwissenschaft* 6,3:277–290.
3294. Frenkin, A.A. 1962. Vsestoronnee razvitie lichnosti i voprosy fizicheskogo vospitanija (The all-development of personality and the problems of physical education). *Voprosy Filosofii* 3:39–49.
3295. Frenkin, A.A. 1963. Jedinstvo duchovnovo i fiziceskovo vospitanija (The unity of physical and spiritual education). Pp. 103–107 in *Probliemy esteticeskovo vospitanija i souriemiennost'.* Moskau.
3296. Fujiwara, K. 1974. Shakaikihan to kachi no hokyō ni oyobosu sports no seikinō ni kansuru ichikōsatsu (A study of the function of sports for the reinforcement of social norms and values). *Research J.Phys.Educ.* 19, 4–5:175–188.
3297. Fujiwara, K. 1975. Shakaikihan to kachi no hokyo no oyobosu sports no gyaku kinō ni kansuru ichikōsatsu (A study on the dysfunction of sports to the reinforcement of social norms and values). *Research J. Phys.Educ.* 20,2:91–107.
3298. Fuxloch, K. 1930. *Das Soziologische im Spiel des Kindes.* Leipzig: Barth. 96 pp.
3299. Gorinevskij, V.V. 1945. Fizicheskaja kultura i zdorovje (Physical Culture and Health). *Fizkultura i Sport.* Moskau. 128 pp.
3300. Green, R. et al. 1972. Playroom toy preferences of fifteen masculine and fifteen feminine boys. *Therapy* 3:425–429.
3301. Greendorfer, S. 1977. The role of socializing agents in female sport involvement. *Research Quarterly* 48,2:304–310.
3302. Greendorfer, S. et al. 1978. Role of family members in sport socialization of children. *Research Quarterly* 49,May:146–152.
3303. Hammerich, K. 1971. Bemerkungen zu Thesen über eine Sozialisationsfunktion von Spiel und Sport. Pp. 127–137 in Albonico/Pfister-Binz.
3304. Heinemann, K. 1974. Sozialisation und Sport. *Sportwissenschaft* 4,1:

49–71.
3305.   Heinemann, K. et al. 1974. Podiumsdiskussion zum Kongressthema "Sozialisation im Sport." Pp. 11–43 in *ADL*, eds. *Sozialisation im Sport.* Schorndorf: Hofmann.
3306.   Helanko, R. 1957. Sports and socialization. *Acta Sociologica* 2,4:229–240.
3307.   Helanko, R. 1958. *Theoretical Aspects of Play and Socialization.* Turku: Universitas Turkunsis. 48 pp.
3308.   Helanko, R. 1966. Sport und Sozialisierung in Banden und Aggregaten. Pp. 254–280 in Lüschen.
3309.   Helanko, R. 1969. The yard community and its play activities. *IRSS* 4,1:177–187.
3310.   Henning, W. 1960–1961. Idealerleben bei Kindern und Jugendlichen. *Wissensch.Zeitschr.DHFK.* 3,4:385–409.
3311.   Herron, R. and B. Sutton-Smith. 1969. *Child's Play.* New York: Wiley.
3312.   Hilton, L. and J.H. Korn. 1964. Measured change in personal values. *Educational and Psychological Measurement* 24,3.
3313.   Hitchcock, J.L. 1978. Game preferences and child-training attitudes. *J.Soc.Psychology* 106,December:279–280.
3314.   Hoffmann, V. 1965. Vergleichende Untersuchungen über die Wirksamkeit verschiedener Leistungsmotive im Schulsport der Ober–und Berufsschule. *Wissensch.Zeitschr.DHFK* 7,3:39–50.
3315.   Humphrey, J.H. 1975. Child learning through active play. Pp. 61–68 in U. Simri, ed.: *International Seminar on Play.* Natanya, Israel: Wingate Institute.
3316.   Immig, F. and W. Immig. 1974. Sozialisationsprozesse in leistungsorientierten Kleingruppen. *Ausschuss Deutscher Leibeserzieher* Summer: 193–201.
3317.   Inbar, M. 1972. The socialization effect of game playing on pre-adolescents. *Leisure Today* 23–25.
3318.   Informations Sociales. 1977. Discours sur le corps. *Informations Sociales* (Paris) 5:5–114.
3319.   Ionescu, V.N. 1970–1971. Culture physique et formation professionnelle des étudiants (in RUMANIAN). *Annalele Universitatii Bucuresti.* Serie Sociologie (Bucuresti) 19–20:129–136.
3320.   Johnson, G.E. 1907. *Education by Play and Games.* Boston: Ginn. 234 pp.
3321.   Kenyon, G.S. and B. McPherson. 1973. Becoming involved in physical activity and sport. Pp. 304–332 in G.R. Rarick, ed. *Physical Activity.* New York: Academic Press.
3322.   Kenyon, G.S. and B.D. McPherson. 1974. An approach to the study of sport socialization. *IRSS* 9,1:127–139.
3323.   Keogh, J. 1962. Analysis of general attitudes toward physical education. *Research Quarterly* 33,2:239–244.
3324.   Klein, M. 1974. Sozialisation durch Sport. Pp. 10–18 in Landessportbund Nordrhein-Westfalen, ed. *Dokumentation.* Duisburg: Landessportbund.
3325.   Krawczyk, Z. 1970. Florian Znaniecki's humanist approach to physical culture. *IRSS* 5,1:131–161.
3326.   Krawczyk, B. 1973. Rola spłeczna a uczestnictwo w sporcie (The social role and the participation in sport). Pp. 297–317 in Z. Krawczyka, *Sport w społeczeństwie wspolczesnym.* Warsaw: PWN.

3327.   Kukushkin, G.I. Fizicheskaja kultura i vsestoronnee razvitie lichnosti
        (Physical culture and the all-round development of personality). *Teorija
        i Praktika Fizicheskoj Kultury* 6:1–9, 7:8–15.
3328.   Kunath, P. 1975. Der Sport als gesellschaftlich-sozialer Bereich der Ent-
        wicklung sozialistischer Persönlichkeiten. *Theorie und Praxis* 24,5:
        441–455.
3329.   Landers, D. et al. 1978. Socialization via interscholastic athletics: its
        effects on educational attainment. *Research Quarterly* 49,December:
        475–483.
3330.   Larson, D. et al 1975. Youth hockey programs: a sociological perspective.
        Sport Sociology Bulletin 4,2:55–63.
3331.   Laskiewicz, H. 1973. Ideowo-wychowawcze funkcje sportu robotniczeog
        (The ideological and education functions of the workers' sport). Pp.
        55–83 in Z. Krawczyk ed.: *Sport w spoleczeństwie współczesnym.*
        Warsaw: PWN.
3332.   Liecht, D. and A. Riom. 1972. Le jeu comme conduite sociale. *Vers
        l'Education Nouvelle* (Paris) 264:34–37.
3333.   Lindeman, E.C. 1941. Recreation and morale. *AJS* 47,3:394–405.
3334.   Lott, B. 1978. Behavioral concordance with sex role ideology related to
        play areas, creativity, and parental sex typing of children. *J.Personality
        Soc.Psychology* 36,October:1087–1100.
3335.   Lotz, F. 1971. Sport und Sozialisation. Pp. 153–172 in Festgabe für
        H. Fleckenstein, *Funktion und Struktur christlicher Gemeinde.*
        Würzburg.
3336.   Lowe, B. and M.H. Payne. 1974. To be a red-blooded American boy.
        J.Popular Culture 8,Fall:383–391.
3337.   Lowe, M. 1975. Trends in the development of representational play in
        infants from one to three years: an observational study. *J.Child Psychol.
        Psychiatr. allied Discipl.GB* 16,1:33–47.
3338.   Mahler, F. 1974. Play and counter-play. *IRSS* 9,1:105–116.
3339.   Malmisur, M. and N. Schmitt. 1975. Social adjustment differences between
        student athletes and student non-athletes as measured by ego develop-
        ment. *Sport Sociology Bulletin* 4,2:2–12.
3340.   Martinello, M.L. 1973. Play grounds for learning. *Elementary School
        Journal* (Chicago) 74,2:106–114.
3341.   Mead, G.H. 1934. *Mind, Self and Society.* Chicago, Ill.: University of
        Chicago Press. 401 pp.
3342.   Milshtein, O.A. 1968. Rol fizicheskoj kultury i sporta v rasvitii duhovnoj
        kultury rabochih (The role of physical culture in the development of the
        spiritual culture of workers). Pp. 24–28 in *Materialy Vsesojusnogo
        simposiuma.* Sverdlovsk.
3343.   Moore. O.K. and A.R. Anderson. 1967. Puzzles, games, and social inter-
        action. Pp. 234–245 in G. Levitas and G. Braziller, *Culture and Con-
        sciousness.* New York.
3344.   Marković, M. 1971. Utjecaj sistematskog bavljenja tjelesnim vezbanjem na
        strukturo stavova licnosti (The influence of systematic engagement in
        physical education on the structure of personality and attitudes).
        Kineziologija (Zagreb) 1,1:25–28.
3345.   Niranen, P. 1976. Leikin kehityspsykologiaa (on developmental psycho-

logy of play). *Psykologia* (Finland) 5-6:15-24.

3346.   Nixon, H.L.II. 1976. Growing up with hockey in Canada. *IRSS* 11,1: 37-48.

3347.   Novikov, A.D. and O.A. Milshtein. 1971. Nekotorye metodologicheskie principy izuchenija prozessa socializacii v sportivnok dejatelnosti (Some principles of the methods of study of the process of socialisation in sporting activities). Pp. 52-53 in Annotacii. *Sport i socializacija.* Vaterloo.

3348.   Oetinger, F. 1956. *Partnerschaft.* Stuttgart: Metzler. 319 pp.

3349.   Orlick, T.D. 1974. Sport participation: a process of shaping behavior. *Human Factors* 16,5:558-561.

3350.   Parlebas, P. 1977. Sports collectifs et socialization. *Vers l'Education Nouvelle* (Paris) 315:10.

3351.   Patriksson, G. 1979. *Sociolisation och involvering idrott* (Socialization and involvement in sport). Göteborg: Acta Universitas Gothoburgensis. 234 pp.

3352.   Pease, D.A. et al. 1971. Athletic exclusion: a complex phenomenon. *Quest* 16,June:42-47.

3353.   Piaget, J. 1945. *La formation du symbole chez l'enfant; imitation, jeu et rêve, image et représentation.* Neuchatel: Delachaux et Nieslé. 310 pp.

3354.   Piaget, J. 1965. *The Moral Judgement of the Child.* New York: Free Press. 417 pp.

3355.   Piers, M.W. ed. 1972. *Play and Development.* New York: Norton. 176 pp.

3356.   Ponomarev, I.N. 1974. The social phenomenon of game and sports. *IRSS* 9,1:117-126.

3357.   Rehberg, R.A. and M. Cohen. 1976. Political attitudes and participation in extracurricular activities. Pp. 201-211 in Landers.

3358.   Remans. 1976. *Socialisering van Vrijtijds y Rollen* (Socialization of Leisure Roles). Vol. I-III. University of Leuven Sociologisch Onderzoek Instituut. 113 pp., 153 pp., and 67 pp.

3359.   Rijsdorp, K. 1963. Physical education in the modern world. *Gymnasion* 1,Summer:16-19.

3360.   Rofer, R. and R.A. Hinde. 1978. Social behavior in a play group: consistency and complexity. *Child Development* 49,September:570-579.

3361.   Ruoppila, I. 1974. The significance of play for the cognitive development. *IRSS* 9,1:83-92.

3362.   Rudzińska, M. 1974. Sterotyp sportowca w opiniach dzieci, członków szkólek i klas sportowych (The stereotype of the athlete as seen by children—members of sports club and classes). *Kultura Fizyczna* 6:1-11.

3363.   Schafer, W.E. 1975. Sport and male sex-role socialization. *Sport Sociology Bulletin* 4,2:47-54.

3364.   Schafer, W.E. 1976. Sport and youth counter culture: contrasting socialization themes. Pp. 183-200 in Landers.

3365.   Secrétariat d'Etat. 1976. *Les Lycéens et les collégiens face aux activités sportives éducatives of culturelles.* Paris: Ministère Jeunesse et Sport. 90 pp.

3366.   Silying, S. 1962. The social preparation of the young footballer. *J.Sports Medicine Physical Fitness* 4,2:237-238.

3367.   Snyder, E. 1970. Aspects of socialization in sports and physical education. *Quest* 15:1-7.

3368.   Snyder E.E. 1972. Athletic dressing room slogans as folklore: a means of socialization. *IRSS* 7,1:89–102.

3369.   Sofranko, A.J. and M.F. Nolan. 1972. Early life experiences and adult sports participation. *J.Leisure Research* 4,Winter:6–18.

3370.   Spencer, H. 1896. Physical education. Pp. 219–283 in H. Spencer, *Education*. New York: Appleton. 301 pp.

3371.   Staniford, D.J. 1978. *Play and Physical Activity in Early Childhood Socialization*. CAPHER Monographs. Calgary, Alberta. 93 pp.

3372.   Start, K.B. 1960. A social implication of the games performances of a grammar school boy. *New Zealand J.Physical Education* 21,July:15–18.

3373.   Start, K.B. 1961. The relationship between the games performance of the grammar school boy and his intelligence and streaming. *Brit.J.Educ. Psychology* 31,3:208–211.

3374.   Stevenson, C.L. 1975. Socialization effects of participation in sport: a critical review of the research. *Research Quarterly* 46,3:287–301.

3375.   Stevenson, C.L. 1976. Institutional socialization and college sport. *Research Quarterly* 47,March:1–8.

3376.   Stone, G. 1962. Appearance and the self. Pp. 86–118 in A.M. Rose ed., *Human Behavior and Social Processes: An Interactionist Approach*. Boston: Houghton, Mifflin.

3377.   Stone, G. 1976. Ritual as game: playing to become a Sanema. *Quest* 26: 28–47.

3378.   Stransky, B.S. 1967. Personality in sport activity. *Ceckoslovenska Psychologie* 11,1:29–36.

3379.   Suetoshi, H. and M. Hayakawa. 1968 & 1972. Kagaikatsudō ga personality kiesei ni ataeru eikyō ni tsuiteno tsuisekiteki kenkyu—sono 1, sono 2— (Longitudinal study about the influence of sport activities on personality of school boys and girls who take part in sports—1), 2)). *Bulletin Kyoto University of Education* 33 and 41.

3380.   Sutton-Smith, B. and J.M. Roberts. 1964. Rubrics of competitive behavior. *J.Genetic Psych.* 105:13–37.

3381.   Sutton-Smith, B. 1973. Games, the socialization of conflict. *Sportwissenschaft* 3,1:41–46.

3382.   Taiban, M. 1971. Le jeu, moyen de socialisation des enfants d'âge préscolaire (in ROMANIAN). *Invatamintul Prescolar* (Bucuresti) 3,4:61–65.

3383.   Takács, F. 1967. A világnézeti nevelés néhány lehetósége és módszere (Some possibility and method of ideological education). *Testn.Tan.* 3:65–72.

3384.   Takenoshita, K. 1961. Taiiku no okeru Shakaisei (Socialization through physical education). *JOHPER* 11,5:219–222.

3385.   Takeuchi, K. 1972. Taiiku gakushū ni okeru shūdan kōsei (Groups, learning and physical education). *Bulletin of Kyoto University of Education* (Kyoto) 40.

3386.   Thomas, D.L. and A.J. Weigert. 1971. Socialization and adolescent conformity to significant others: a cross-national analysis. *ASR* 36,October: 835–847.

3387.   Ward, E. 1970. Research in socialization and physical activity. *Brit.J. Phys.Educ.* 1,2:11–15.

3388.   Watson, G.G. 1975. Sex role socialization and the competitive process in little athletics. *Australian J.Health, Physical Education, Recreation*

70:10–21.

3389.   Watson, G.G. and S. Murray. 1976. *Psycho-Social Study of Play, Games and Recreation.* Nedlands: University of Western Australia.

3390.   Wohl, A. and E. Pudelkiewicz. 1972. Theoretical and methodological assumptions of research on the processes of involvement in sport and sport socialization. *IRSS* 7,1:69–87.

3391.   Woody, T. 1955. School athletics and social good. *J.Educational Sociology* 28,2:243–248.

3392.   Yu, K. 1976. Strengthen ideological molding of ranks of athletes. *Chinese Education* 9,3:62–67.

3393.   Zern, D. 1979. Child-Rearing practices and games of strategy. *J.Soc. Psychology* 107,April:169–176.

3394.   Zimmermann, H.M. 1954. Physical activity experience and interests of college women. *Research Quarterly* 25,1:109–118.

5. Mass Communications

3395.   Belson, W.A. 1959. Effects of television on the interests and initiative of adult viewers in greater London. *Brit.J.Psychology* 50:145–158.

3396.   Berger, A.A. 1972. Authority in the comics. Pp. 217–228 in G.P. Stone ed., *Games, Sport and Power.* New Brunswick, N.J.: Transaction Books.

3397.   Betts, J.R. 1953. Sporting journalism in the nineteenth-century America. *American Quarterly* 5,1:39–56.

3398.   Binnewies, H. 1975. *Sport und Sportberichterstattung.* Ahrensburg: Czwalina. 227 pp.

3399.   Birrell, S. and J.W. Loy. 1979. Media sport: hot and cool. *IRSS* 14,1:5–20.

3400.   Bogart, L. 1956. *The Age of Television.* New York: Ungar. 348 pp.

3401.   Braddock, J.H. 1978. Television and college football: in black and white. *J.Black Studies* 8,3:369–380.

3402.   BBCARD. 1965. *The People's Activities.* London:BBC. 206 pp.

3403.   Cauwels, A. et al. 1976. *Menselijke begeleiding in de sport.* Leuven: Acco. 88 pp.

3404.   Clearing House, Brussels. 1977. *The Role of Television in Promoting the Practice of Sport.* Brüssels. 101 pp.

3405.   Dumazedier, J. 1955. *Télévision et éducation populaire.* Paris: Unesco. 281 pp.

3406.   Economist. 1978. Hooligans, researchers and the press (Great Britain). *Economist* 266,March,19.

3407.   Famaey-Lamon, A. and F. van Loon. 1978. Mass media and sports practice. *IRSS* 4,13:37–46.

3408.   Fasting, K. 1976. *Sports and TV.* Oslo: Norwegian Confederation of Sports. 77 pp.

3409.   Florl, R. 1972. Funktion und Wirkungsweise der Massenkommunikationsmittel bei der Gewinnung der DDR—Bevölkerung für Köperkultur und Sport. *Theorie und Praxis* 21,12:1095–1096.

3410.   Fujiwara, F.K. 1975. The special qualities of the local sport paper. *Shakai-gaku Hyoron* (Japanese Sociological Review) 26,2:53–73.

3411.   Gritti, J. 1975. *Sport à la une.* Paris: Colin. 224 pp.

3412. Hackforth, J. 1975. *Sport im Fernsehen,* Münster: Regensburg. 389 pp.

3413. ICSPE. 1973. *Mass Media, Sport, International Understanding.* Paris: Unesco.

3414. Jordan, J.M. 1951. *The Long Range Effect of Television and Other Factors on Sports Attendance.* Washington, D.C.: Radio and Television Manufacturers Association. 112 pp.

3415. Kato, K. et al. 1958. Mass communication wa taiiku ni ikanaru eikyô o ataeteiruka (The effects of mass communication upon physical education). *Research J.Phys.Educ.* 3,1:256–258.

3416. Kiseleva, V.A. 1969. Televidenie, socialnyj stereotip i obshchestvennoe mnenie (Television, social stereotype and public opinion). Pp. 140–143 in *Konferencija po psychologii i sociologii sporta.* Tarty.

3417. Kiseleva, V.A. and M.F. Gogulan. 1969. Televidenie i sport (Television and Sport). Pp. 239–244 in *Materialy nauchnoj konferencii po istorii, organizacii i sociologii fizicheskoj kultury i sporta.* Tashkent-Samarkand.

3418. Krauss, P.G. 1961. Anglo-American influence of German sport terms. *American Speech* 36,1:41–47.

3419. Krauss, P.G. 1962. English sports terms in German. *American Speech* 37,2;123–129.

3420. Laskiewicz, H. 1962. Problemy moralne sportu polskiego w swietle prasy polskiej 1961 (Moral problems of Polish sport in the Polish Press). *Kultura Fizyczna* 15,4:311–313.

3421. Licht, K. 1964. Ergebnisse einer soziologischen Untersuchung über die Rolle der Rundfunk—und Fernsehgymnastik im Rahmen des Volkssports. *Theorie und Praxis* 13,4:311–322.

3422. Lowenthal, L. 1956. Biographies in popular magazines. Pp. 63–118 in W. Peterson ed. *American Social Patterns.* Garden City, New York: Doubleday. 263 pp.

3423. Meyersohn, R. 1968. Television and the rest of leisure. *Public Opinion Quarterly* 32,1:102–112.

3424. Milshtein, O.A. and S.V. Molchanov. 1976. The shaping of public opinion regarding sport by the mass media as a factor promoting international understanding. *IRSS* 11,3:71–84.

3425. McCartney, E.S. 1938. Alliteration on the sports page. *American Speech* 13,1:30–34.

3426. McIntosh, P.C. 1974. Mass media: friends or foes in sport. *Quest* 22: 33–44.

3427. Naudin, P. 1970. Le sport, il cinema e la vita. *Spettacolo* 20,2:113–123.

3428. Noguchi, Y. et al. 1957. Taiiku to mass communication (Relation of mass communication to physical education). *Research of Physical Education* (Kyushu University) 2,1:21–41.

3429. Nugent, W.H. 1929. The sports section. *American Mercury* 16,March: 328–338.

3430. Nühlen, K. 1952. Das Publikum und seine Aktionsarten. *Kölner Z.Soziol.* 5,4:446–474.

3431. Nunfio, O. 1970. Radiografia de la guerra del futbol o de las cien horas. (Geography of football war, or 100 hours war). *Revista Mexicana de Sociologia* 32,3:659–690.

3432. Parente, D.E. 1977. Interdependence of sport and television. *J.Communi-*

cation 27,3:128–132.

3433.   Pelt, H. van. 1977. *Stijlveranderingen in de sport journalistiek.* University of Antwerpen. 33 pp.

3434.   Pelt, H. van. 1978. Voetbal op Televise. *Sport* (Leuven) 32,3:43–47.

3435.   Propaganda Bureau. 1965. *Sports ni kansuru seron chôsu* (The investigation of the public opinion on sport). Tokyo: Propaganda Bureau of the Prime Minister's Office.

3436.   Quanz, L. 1974. *Der Sportler als Idol.* Giessen: Focus. 174 pp.

3437.   Reczek, S. 1968. O stylu Polskiej prasy sportowej (On the style of Polish sport reports). *Zeszyty Prasoznawcz* 9,3:43–48.

3438.   Reuther, H. 1960. Umfang und Wertung des Sports in der modernen Publizistik. *Jahrbuch des Sports* (Frankfurt) 92–100.

3439.   Ripa, M.D. 1973. Massovye kommunikacii i sport ivnye interesy trudjascihsja (mass communications and sports interests of the worker). *Organ Uprav fizkultury dvizeniem* 1:166–174.

3440.   Robinson, J.P. 1969. Television and leisure time: yesterday, today and (maybe) tomorrow. *Public Opinion Quarterly* 33,2:210–222.

3441.   Salinnikova, N.G. 1970. Opyt sociologicheskogo issledovanija propagandy fizicheskoj kultury i sporta sredstvami massovoj informacii (A case of sociological research of the propaganda of physical culture and sports by mass media). Pp. 6–7 in *Texisy dokladov XVII Vsesojuznoj nauchnoj konferencii studentov po voprosam fizicheskoj kultury i sporta.* Moskau.

3442.   Schmidt, H.D. 1965. Versuch einer Inhaltsanalyse nationaler Tendenzen in Sportreportagen. *Psychologische Rundschau* 16,1:43–51.

3443.   Shishigin, M.V. 1973. Sportivnaja pechat—aktivnoe sredstvo propagandy fizicheskoj kultury i sporta (Sport press, active means of physical culture and sports propaganda). *Teorija i Praktika* 5:10–14.

3444.   Smith, G.J. and C. Blackman. 1978. *Sport in the Mass Media.* Vanier City, Ontario: CAHPER Monograph. 86 pp.

3445.   Tannenbaum, P.H. and J.E. Noah. 1959. Sportugese: a study of sports page communication. *Journalism Quarterly* 36,2:163–170.

3446.   Tuemmler, S. 1974. Zur Rolle und Funktion des Sports in den imperialistischen Massenmedien. *Theorie und Praxis* 25,11:977–981.

3447.   Tyszka, A. 1965. Wzor powodzenia osobistego sportowcow w opinii prasy. Analiza tresci wybranuch czasopism z lat 1960–63 (The pattern of personal success of the athlete in the opinion of the press. The content analysis of the selected journals 1960–63). *Roczniki Naukowe AWF* 4:285–299.

3448.   Tyszka, A. 1966. Sportowcy jako bohaterowie wspolczesni analiza tresci prasowych (Sportsmen used as modern heroes. A content analysis of sport press). *Studia Socjologiczne* 21:253–276.

3449.   UNESCO. 1971 and 1973. *Mass Media, Sport and International Understanding.* Paris: International Council for Sport and Physical Education. 48 pp. and 34 pp.

3450.   University of Tampere. 1973. *Instructional Inventory of Television Program Structure.* Tampere: Institute of Journalism and Communication.

3451.   Vinogradov, P.A. et al. 1970. Fizicheskaja kultura kak odin iz faktorov, sposobstvujushchih aktivizacii potreblenija obshchestvenno-politicheskoj informacii cherez sredstva massovoj kommunikacii (Physical culture as one of the factors, promoting the activization of consuming socio-political information by means of mass communication medium). Pp. 151-152 in *Nauchnye trudy za 1970*. Moscow.

3452.   Woodward, St. 1949. *Sports Page*. New York: Simon and Schuster. 229 pp.

IV. *Sport as a Subsystem and Its Structure*

1. *Theory and General Analysis of Sport, Play and Games*

4001.   Alexander, F.A. 1958. A contribution to the theory of play. *Psychoanalytic Quarterly* 27:175-193.

4002.   Amsler, J. 1963. Sociologie du temps sportif. *Éducation physique et Sport* 15,67-68:80-83.

4003.   Arai, S. and Y. Matsuda. 1977. Sportskodo ni kansuru jitsushotekikenkyū (2) (A positive research on the sport behavior–2). *Research J.Physical Education* 22,3:137-152.

4004.   Arnold, D.O. 1970. *The Sociology of Subcultures*. Berkeley: The Glendessary Press.

4005.   Asai, A. and S. Onishi. 1954. *Taiiku to ningen kankei* (Physical education and human relations). Kyoto: Ran Shobo.

4006.   Asai, A. 1956. *Taiiku to shakaiteki-ningenkankei* (Physical education and man as social being). Kyoto: Ran Shobo. 328 pp.

4007.   Asai, A. 1957. *Taiiku to Shakaisei* (Physical education and sociability). Tokyo: Kyorin-Shoin.

4008.   Barth, F. 1959. Segmentary opposition and the theory of games: a study of Pathan organization. *Journal Royal Anthropological Insitute* 89,1: 5-21.

4009.   Boroff, D. 1969. A view of skiers as a subculture. Pp. 453-455.

4010.   Brewster, P.G. 1957. Voorrang en vrijstelling in Kinderenspelen (Priority and exemption in children's games). *Volkskunde* (Antwerpen) 58,1: 21-30.

4011.   Britt, S.H. and S.Q. Janus. 1941. Toward a social psychology of human play. *J.Soc.Psychology* 13:351-384.

4012.   Brohm, J.M. 1973. Vers l'analyse institutionelle du sport de competition. *Homme et la Societé* (Paris) 29-30:177-199.

4013.   Bureau of Advertising. 1963. *A Survey of Sports Interest and Activities Among Men*. New York: American Newspaper Publishers Association. 117 pp.

4014.   Buytendijk, F.J.J. 1933. *Wesen und Sinn des Spiels*. Berlin.

4015.   Caillois, R. 1955. Structure et classification des jeux. *Diogène* 12, Oct.: 62-75.

4016.   Caillois, R. 1956. Estructura e classificacao dos jogos. *Anhembi* 24,72: 446-459.

4017.   Caillois, R. 1957. Unité du jeu, diversité des jeux. *Diogène* 19,July: 117-124.

4018.   Caillois, R. 1957. Para una teoria ampliada de los juegos (For a broader theory of games). *Revista de la Universidad de Buenos Aires* 2,2: 350-357.

4019.   Caillois, R. 1958. *Les jeux et les hommes*. Paris: Gallimard. 307 pp.

4020.   Caillois, R. 1958. Classification des jeux. *Synthesis* 13,140–141:18–39.
4021.   Caillois, R. 1958. Théorie des jeux. *Revue de Métaphysique et de Morale* 63,1:83–102.
4022.   Cailois, R. 1961. *Man, Play and Games*. Glencoe, Ill.: Free Press. 220 pp.
4023.   Caillois, R. 1963. *Die Spiele und die Menschen*. Munich: Langen-Müller. 222 pp.
4024.   Caillois, R. 1967. Jeux et Sports. *Encyclopédie de la Pléiade* (Paris).
4025.   Caillois, R. 1971. The classification of games. Pp. 17–39 in Dunning.
4026.   Caillois, R. 1976. Über Wesen und Einteilung der Spiele. Pp. 39–51 in Lüschen/Weis.
4027.   Claeys, U. 1976. Beschowingen by the Sport in 1975 (Examination of sport in 1975). *Sportcahiers* 6:63–68.
4028.   Claeys, U. 1976. De menselyke begeleiding in de sport (Human participation in sport). *Sport* 19:120–125.
4029.   Daniels, A.A. 1961. Some reflections on sport as an element of the culture. *The Ohio High School Athlete* 21:1–3.
4030.   Deportes (Sports). 1971. *Revista Espanola de la Opinion Publica* 25, July-Sept.:508–517.
4031.   Dickinson, J. 1977. *A Behavioral Analysis of Sport*. Princeton: Princeton Book Company. 134 pp.
4032.   Digel, H. 1977. Kommunikation und kommunikative Kompetenz. *Sportwissenschaft* 7,2:115–138.
4033.   Dumazedier, J. 1973. Sport and sports activities. *IRSS* 9:7–34.
4034.   Ellis, M.J. 1972. Play: practise and research in the 1970's. *JOHPER* 43,6:29–31.
4035.   Frankenberg, R. 1964. People at play. Pp. 212–225 in M. Douglas ed., *Man in Society*. London: MacDonald.
4036.   Fukuoka, T. 1969. Research on student athletes. *IRSS* 4:53–62.
4037.   Giddens, A. 1964. Notes on the concepts of play and leisure. *Sociological Review* 21,2:73–89.
4038.   Goffman, E. 1961. Fun in games Pp. 16–81 in E. Goffman *Encounters*. Indianapolis, Ind.: Bobbs-Merrill. 152 pp.
4039.   Groos, K. 1899. *Die Spiele der Menschen*. Jena, Germany: Fischer. 538 pp.
4040.   Gulick, L.H. 1920. *A Philosophy of Play*. New York: Scribners. 291 pp.
4041.   Harper, H. 1973. Playfulness: the art of not taking things too seriously: symposium; with editorial comments, bibliog. *Harper* 246:5–12.
4042.   Häusler, W. and K.H. Lehmann. 1956. Sport. *Handwörterbuch der Sozialwissenschaften* (Stuttgart) 13:718–725.
4043.   Heckhausen, H. 1964. Entwurf einer Psychologie des Spielens. *Psychologische Forschung* 27:225–243.
4044.   Heinilä, K. 1963. *Kilpaurheilun Theoria* (Theory of competitive sport). Helsinki: University of Helsinki, Department of Sociology. 26 pp.
4045.   Helanko, R. 1973. Pihaleikkien systematiikka (classification of field games). *Universität Turku* 63.
4046.   Helanko, R. 1974. Classification of children's outdoor games. *IRSS* 9,2:103–106.
4047.   Hessen R. 1908. *Der Sport*. Frankfurt: Rütten und Löning.
4048.   Howes, J.R. 1966. Play. *The Australian J.Phys.Educ.* October-November: 5–8.

4049.   Huizinga, J. 1939. *Homo ludens: Versuch einer Bestimmung des Spielele-
         mentes der Kultur.* Amsterdam: Pantheon. 345 pp.
4050.   Ivanov, G.T. 1969. Filospfiaja, sociologija i fizicheskaja kultura (Philo-
         sophy, sociology and physical culture). *Metodicheskie razrabotki i
         ukazanija po voprozam sociologii sporta* (Kiev) 53–61.
4051.   Jensen, A.E. 1942. Spiel und Ergriffenheit. *Paideuma* 2,3:124–139.
4052.   Jeu, B. 1972. Définition du sport. *Diogène* 80:153–167.
4053.   Jeu, B. 1972. Toute-puissance et immortalité ou les arriére-pensées du
         sport. *Ethno-Psychologie* 27,1:15–37.
4054.   Jeu, B. 1977. *Le Sport, L'émotion, L'espace: Essai sur la classification des
         sports et ses rapports aves la pensée mythique.* Paris: Vigot.
4055.   John, E. 1958. Kultur und Gesellschaft–Kultur und Körperkultur. *Theorie
         und Praxis* 7,3:201–212, 7,4:305–316.
4056.   Kawaguchi, T. 1965. Sport taishuka no sogai jyoken (A study on the
         obstructing conditions of sport popularization). *Annual Report of
         Hitotsubashi University* (Tokyo) 7:28–69.
4057.   Kawaguchi, T. 1966. Problems in "sports culture." An analysis of interior
         factors. *Hitosubashi J.Arts and Science* 7,1:47–58.
4058.   Kenyon, G.S. 1966. The significance of physical activity as a function of
         age, sex, education, and socio-economic status of Northern United
         States adults. *IRSS* 1:70–96.
4059.   Kenyon, G.S. 1969. A conceptual model for characterizing physical
         activity. Pp. 71–81 in Loy/Kenyon.
4060.   Kleine, L. and J. Schafrik. 1972. Ideologische Probleme der Identifikation
         des Menschen im Sport. *Theorie und Praxis* 21,12:1077–1080.
4061.   Knop, S. 1976. The social context of games: or when is play not play?
         Sociol.Education 49,4:265–271.
4062.   Krawczyk, Z. 1970. *Natura, Kultura, Sport* (Nature, culture, sport).
         Warsaw: PWN. 387 pp.
4063.   Krawczyk, Z. 1974. Antinomies of play and work and changes in the
         social structure. *IRSS* 9,27:73–82.
4064.   Krawczyk, Z. 1974. *Filozofia i socjologia kultury fizycznej* (Philosophy
         and sociology of physical culture). Warsaw, PWN.
4065.   Kuchevskij, V.B. 1972. Sport kak sovokupnost obshchestvennyh otno-
         shenij (Sport as a total combination of social relations). *Teorija i praktika*
         9:5–8.
4066.   Kuchevskij, V.B. 1974. Sport als Gesamtheit gesellschaftlicher Verhältnisse.
         Theorie und Praxis 23,9:838–842.
4067.   Landry, F. et al. 1966. Le Canada français et les grands jeux interna-
         tionaux. *Mouvement* 1,2:115–129.
4068.   Lenk, H. et al. eds. 1973. *Philosophie des Sports.* Schorndorf: Hofmann.
4069.   Lenk, H. 1975. *Pragmatische Philosophie.* Hamburg: Hoffmann und
         Campe.
4070.   Lenk, H. 1976. *Sozialphilosophie des Leistungshandelns.* Stuttgart:
         Kohlhammer.
4071.   Lisicyn, B.A. 1969. Socialnyj sostav sportsmenov vysokoj kvalifikacii
         (Social structure of sportsmen of high skill). Pp. 28–30 in *Materialy
         itogovoj nauchnoj sessii instituta za 1967.* Moscow.
4072.   Lowe, B. 1977. *The Beauty of Sport.* Englewood Cliffs: Prentice Hall.
         327 pp.

4073.   Loy, J.W. 1969. The nature of sport. Pp. 56–70 in Loy/Kenyon.
4074.   Loy, J.W. 1969. Game forms, social structure, and anomie. Pp. 181–199
         in R.Brown and B. Cratty. Englewood Cliffs: Prentice Hall.
4075.   Loy, J.W. and A. Ingham. 1974. The structure of ludic action. *IRSS* 9,1:
         23–62.
4076.   Loy, J.W. 1975. The professionalization of attitudes toward play as a
         function of selected social identities and level of sport participation.
         Pp. 77–106 in U. Simri ed., *International Seminar on Play in Physical
         Education and Sport.* Natanya, Israel: Wingate Institute.
4077.   Lunacharskij, A.V.1930. *Mysli o sporte* (Thoughts on Sports). Moscow.
         44 pp.
4078.   Meyer, H. 1973. Der Hochleistungssport—Ein Phänomen des Showbusi-
         ness. *Zeitschrift für Soziologie* 2,1:59–78.
4079.   Meyer, H. 1975. Der Sport als Medium der Selbstverwirklichung und
         Entfremdung. *Zeitschrift für Soziologie* 4,1:70–81.
4080.   Milshtein, O.A. 1969. Fizicheskaja kultura i sport kak sfera socialnoj
         dejatelnosti (Physical culture and sports as a sphere of social activities).
         Pp. 27–29 in *Materialy XIX nauchno-metodicheskoj konferencii po
         itogam raboty za 1968.* Omsk.
4081.   Mitscherlich, A. 1967. Sport—kein pures Privatvergnügen. Pp. 58–66 in
         H. Plessner et al. eds.: *Sport und Leibeserziehung.* München: Piper.
4082.   Nakamura, T. 1973. *Sports towa nanika?* (What is sports?). Tokyo:
         Popurasha.
4083.   Nettleton, B. 1967. Sport and social values. *Physical Education* (London)
         59:35–41.
4084.   Niwa, T. 1967. Sports no gainen (The concept of sport). Pp. 153–184 in
         A. Asai ed., *Taiikugaku Ronsō.* Osaka: Times.
4085.   Niwa, T. 1972. Yūgi riron no kentō (Examination on the theory of play of
         E.D. Mitchell). *Research J.Sport Sociology* (Tokyo) 1:125–144.
4086.   Niwa, T. 1973. Yūgi riron no kentō (2) (Examination on the theory of
         play of J. Huizinga). *Research J.Sport Sociology* (Tokyo) 3:141–167.
4087.   Novikov, A.D. and V.G. Grishin. 1973. Igra i sport (Game and sport).
         Teorija i Praktika 2:5–8, 3:8–12.
4088.   Ōhashi, Y. 1972. Gendai sport no gainen shiron (A trial theory of concept
         on modern sport). *Bulletin School of Education, Okayama University*
         34:157–165.
4089.   Ōhashi, Y. 1972. Eric Dunning no sport-ron to sono ichikosatsu (A con-
         sideration of sport theory by Eric Dunning). *Bulletin School of Edu-
         cation, Okayama University* 33:225–232.
4090.   Ōhashi, Y. 1973. Gendai sport no bunkateki kōsatsu (A cultural con-
         sideration on mondern sport). *Research J.Sport Sociology* 2:63–84.
4091.   Omvedt, G. 1966. Play as an element in social life. *Berkeley Journal
         Sociology* 11:1–13.
4092.   Ōnishi, K. 1973. Taishyu sport ron (Social approach on mass sport).
         Research J.Sport Sociology 2:17–44.
4093.   Parlebas, P. 1977. Sport et jeux. Extrait du livre "Questions reponses sur
         l'éducation physique." *Vers l'education nouvelle* (Paris) 314:24–31.
4094.   Phillipps, J.C. and W.E. Schafer. 1971. Subcultures in sport—a conceptual
         and methodological approach. Pp. 66–73 in Albonico/Pfister-Binz.

4095.   Popplow, U. 1951. Zu einer Soziologie des Sports. *Sport und Leibeser-ziehung* 11:2-4.
4096.   Popplow, U. 1953. Der Sport als kultursoziologisches Problem. *Olympisches Feuer* 3,3:1-7.
4097.   Rainwater, C.E. 1924. Play as collective behavior. *J.Applied Sociology* 8,2:217-222.
4098.   Read, D.W. and C.E. Read. 1970. A critique of Davenport's game theory analysis. *American Anthropologist* 72,2:351-355.
4099.   Renson, R. 1973-74. Symbol analysis of sport and games. An anthropo-logical-methodological approach. *Hermes* (Leuven) 7,5:379-386.
4100.   Riezler, K. 1941. Play and seriousness. *J.Philosophy* 38:505-517.
4101.   Roberts, J.M. et al. 1963. Strategy in games and folk tales. *J.Soc.Psychology* 69:277-289.
4102.   Roos, L.L. 1966. Toward a theory of cooperative experiments using nonzero-sum games. *J.Soc.Psychology* 69:277-289.
4103.   Schlosberg, H. 1947. The concept of play. *Psychological Review* 54: 229-231.
4104.   Schnellback-Nordmann, M.L. 1970. Psychology and sociology of games. Pp. 427-438 in Kenyon, ed. Psychology of Sport. Chicago: Athletic Institute.
4105.   Schroeter, H. 1972. Soziale Organisation. *Wissensch.Zeitschr.DHFK* 14,2-3:43-79.
4106.   Seppänen, P. 1967. Huippu-urheilun sosiaalisista edyllytyksistä ja funktiosta (Social determinants and functions of top-athletes). *Stadion* 1:2-17.
4107.   Shimazaki, J. 1971. Top-athletes ni kansuru shakaigakuteki kenkyu (A sociological study concerning top-athletes of Japan). *Bulletin Physical Education Tokyo University of Education* (Tokyo) 10:11-28.
4108.   Shimazaki, J. 1973. Gendai jin no sport shikō (A general tendency of sporting activities in Japan). *Research J.Sport Sociology* (Tokyo) 2: 45-62.
4109.   Specht, K.G. 1960. Sport in soziologischer Sicht. *Studium Generale* 13,1:28-37.
4110.   Stark, W. 1967. Play figures and play forms: a functional approach. *Revista International de Sociologia* 23:91-92 365-376.
4111.   Steele, P. and L. Zurcher. 1973. Leisure sports as "ephemeral" roles. *Pacific Soc.Review* 16,3:345-356.
4112.   Steinitzer, H. 1910. *Sport und Kultur.* Munich: Verlag Deutsche Alpen-zeitung. 79 pp.
4113.   Stranai, K. 1965. Teoria telesnej vychovy v sustave vied (The theory of physical education in the system of science). Pp. 153-294 in *Sbornik Institutu Telesnej Vychovy.* Bratislava: Slovenske pedagogicke nak-ladatelstvo. 320 pp.
4114.   Sugawara, R. et al. 1963. Wagakuni ni okeru sports jinko no kozo to hendo (The social structure of the sport population and its variation in Japan). *Research J.Physical Education* 8,1:404-406.
4115.   Suits, B. 1967. Is life a game we are playing? *Ethics* 77:209-213.
4116.   Suits, B. 1967. What is a game? *Philosophy of Science* 34:148-156.
4117.   Sutton-Smith, B. 1968. Games-play-daydreams. *Quest* 10,May:47-58.

4118.   Sutton-Smith, B. 1969. The two cultures of games. Pp. 135–160 in Ken-
        yon.
4119.   Sutton-Smith, B. 1971. Children at play. *Natural History* 60,10:54–59.
4120.   Sutton-Smith, B. 1971. The sporting balance. Pp. 105–113 in Albonico/
        Pfister-Binz.
4121.   Sutton-Smith, B. 1972. Play as a transformational set. *JOHPER* 43,6:
        32–33.
4122.   Sutton-Smith, B. 1973. Play: the mediation of novelty. Pp. 557–561 in
        Grupe.
4123.   Sutton-Smith, B. 1974. Development—structural aspects of play and
        games: an ideology for play. Pp. 50–55 *Brit.Commonwealth Conference
        Phys.Ed.Proceedings.*
4124.   Sutton-Smith, B. 1975. Play as adaptive potentiation. *Sportwissenschaft*
        5,2:103–118.
4125.   Sutton-Smith. B. 1976. A structural grammar of games and sports. *IRSS*
        11,2:117–137.
4126.   Sutton-Smith, B. 1978. *Die Dialektik des Spiels.* Schorndorf: Hofmann.
        236 pp.
4127.   Takenoshita, K. 1961. Nippon ni okeru sports jinko no kozo to sono
        hendo ni tsuite no kenkyu (The social structure of the sport population
        and its change in Japan. *JOPHER* (Tokyo) 11,11:547–550.
4128.   Takenoshita, K. 1964. Social factors affecting sports participation. *Re-
        search Jounral Phys.Educ.* (Tokyo) 7,4:10–20.
4129.   Takenoshita, K. 1965. Nippon no sports jinko (Population of sporting
        activities in Japan). *JOHPER* 15,2:64–67.
4130.   Takenoshita, K. 1967. The social structure of the sport population in
        Japan. *IRSS* 2,1:5–18.
4131.   Takenoshita, K. 1969. La structure sociale de la population qui pratique
        le sport au Japon. *Roczniky Naukowe AWF* (Warsaw) 8:557–570.
4132.   Thompson, R.W. 1977. Subcultural analysis in sport. *Canadian J.Applied
        Sport Sciences* 2,4:195–199.
4133.   Tscherne, F. 1966. Sociological work in the field of gymnastic exercises in
        Austria. *IRSS* 1:237–241.
4134.   Uesugi, T. 1975. The meaning of play. *Shonen Hodo* 10,2:9–17.
4135.   Ulrich, H.E. 1976. The social structure of high-level sport. *IRSS* 11,2:
        139–152.
4136.   Wischmann, B. 1955. *Der moderne Sport.* Waldfischbach: Hornberger.
        116 pp.
4137.   Wohl, A. 1956. Die Theorie der Körperkultur als gesellschafts-wissen-
        schaftliches Problem. *Theorie und Praxis* 5,7:492–504.
4138.   Wohl, A. 1968. Społeczne problemy kultury fizycznej (Social problems of
        physical culture). Pp. 1–288 in *Institute of Scientific Aid of Academy of
        Physical Culture.* Warsaw.
4139.   Wohl, A. 1974. The social conditioning of play in motion. *IRSS* 9,1:
        63–82.
4140.   Wuolio, J. 1963. Huippu-urheilijat tutkimuskohteena (Investigation of
        top-athletics). *Stadion* 1:32–35.
4141.   Yokoyama, I. 1968. Undobu shudan no shakaigakuteki kenkyu (A socio-
        logical study of sport groups). *Memoirs of the Faculty of Education,
        Fukui University* (Fukui) 18:1–32.

4142. Yokoyama, I. 1969. Sport jinko no shakaigakuteku kenkyu (A sociological study of the structure in the sport population). *Memoirs of the Faculty of Education, Fukui University* (Fukui) 19:1–40.

4143. Yokoyama, I. 1973. Nihon bunka ni okeru sport to sport gengo no kenkyu (A sociological study of the sport and sport language in the Japanese culture). *Research J.Sport Sociology* (Tokyo) 2:215–234.

4144. Zauli, B. et al. 1958. *Civieta sportiva* (Sport as culture). Roma: Ed. Mediterranee.

4145. Ziemilski, A. 1961. Sport a socjologiczna teoria gier-kilka hipotez wyjsciowych (Sport and the sociological theory of games-some initial hypothesis). *Wychowanie Fizycne i Sport* 5:77–83.

4146. Ziemilski, A. 1963. Sport jako rola spoleczna-proba analizy strukturalnej (Social role-sets in sport, an attempt of structural analysis). *Wychowanie Fizyczne i Sport* 7,3:362–372.

4147. Ziemilski, A. 1964. Sport stadionow a rzeczywistosc spoleczna hipotezy i watpligosci (Stadium sport and social reality: hypotheses and doubts). *Kultura i Spoleczenstwo* 8,4:135–146.

4148. Ziemilski, A. 1965. Niektore zalozenia ogolne i pierwsze wyniki badan nadd elita sportowa w Polsce (General principles and initials results of investigations on sport elite in Poland). *Wychowanie Fizyczne i Sport* 9,3:341–355.

4149. Ziemilski, A. 1965. Sport jako instytucja spolexzna. Uwagi wyjsciowe do analizy struktural nej (Sport as a social institution, a contribution to structural analysis). *Kultura Fizyczna* 18,1:5–6.

2. *Values, Norms and Behavioral Patterns in Sport*

4150. AAHPER. 1963. *Values in Sports; Report of a National Conference.* Washington: AAHPER 130 pp.

4151. Ames, C. and D. Feller. 1979. Evaluations in competitive, cooperative, and individualistic reward structures. *J.Educ.Psychology* 71,4:413–420.

4152. Ashworth, C.E. 1971. Sport as a symbolic dialogue. Pp. 40–46 in Dunning.

4153. Bernard, J. 1954. The theory of games of strategy as a modern sociology of conflict. *AJS* 59:411–414.

4154. Best, D. 1975. The aesthetic in sport. *J.Human Movement Studies* 1,1: 41–47.

4155. Biliński, B. 1969. Agony gymniczne oraz komponenty intelektualne i artystyczne w agonistyce starożytnej (Gymnic agonies and artistic components of ancient agons). *Kultura Fizyczna* 6,7,8:246–250.

4156. Bishop, T. 1962. Values in sports. *JOPHER* 33,6:45–46.

4157. Boreyer, G. 1963. Children's concepts of sportmanship in the 4th, 5th, 6th grades. *Research Quarterly* 34:282–287.

4158. Bouet, M. 1963. Pour une psychologie des intérêts compétitifs dans la pratique du sport. *Education physique et Sport* 13,65:7–10.

4159. Chase, S. 1928. Play. Pp. 332–353 in C.A. Beard, ed. *Wither Mankind.* New York.

4160. Ciupak, Z. 1974. O sporcie jako zjawisku moralnym (On sport as a moral phenomenon). Pp. 403–409 in Z. Krawczyk ed., *Filozofia i socjologia kultury fizycznej.* Warsaw: PWN.

4161. Ciupak, Z. 1974. Turystyka jako czynnik modyfikacji zbiorowych zacho-
       wań (The tourist movement as an instrument to modify group behavior).
       Roczniki Naukowe AWF 16:1–30.
4162. Cohen, J. 1964. *Bahaviour in Uncertainty.* New York: Allen. 208 pp.
4163. Copeland, I.C. 1972. The function of sport in secondary education.
       Educational Review 25,1:34–45.
4164. Crombag, M.E. 1966. Cooperation and competition in means interdepen-
       dent triads: a replication. *J.Personality Soc.Psychology* 4:692–695.
4165. Csikszentmihalyi, M. and S. Bennett. 1971. An exploratory model of
       play. *American Anthropologist* 73,1:45–48.
4166. Csikszentmihalyi, M. 1975. Play and intrinsic reward. *J.Humanistic
       Psychology* 15,3:41–63.
4167. Czula, R. 1978. Sport and Olympic idealism. *IRSS* 2,13:67–80.
4168. Devereux, E.C. 1976. Backyard versus Little League Baseball: the impover-
       ishment of children's games. Pp. 37–57 in Landers.
4169. Dowell, L.J. 1968. Effect of 'game strategy' on winning selected two-
       person zero-sum, finite strategy games involving a motor skill. *Research
       Quarterly* 38,3:496–504.
4170. Dussek, O.T. 1919. Notes on Malay indoor games. *Royal Asiatic Society,
       Straits Branch Journal* 80:68–71.
4171. Eibl-Eibesfeldt, I. 1970. *Liebe und Hass.* München: Piper. 420 pp.
4172. Eichberg, H. 1974. Mass und Messen in der frühen Neuzeit. Der Sport als
       Beispiel. Pp. 128–141 in R.E. Vente, ed. *Erfahrung und Erfahrungs-
       wissenschaft.* Stuttgart: Kohlhammer.
4173. Faroqui, M.A. 1958. Cooperation, competition and group structure.
       J.Psychological Research (madras) 1,May:68–70.
4174. Feger, H. 1978. *Konflikterleben und Konfliktverhalten.* Bern: Huber.
4175. Goldstein, B. and R.L. Eichhorn. 1961. The changing Protestant ethic:
       rural patterns in health, work and leisure. *ASR* 27,August:557–565.
4176. Gorskij, L.P. 1973. The role of physical education and sport in the system
       of social values. Pp. 18–24 in Grupe.
4177. Haerle, R.K. 1974. Athlete as moral leader. *J.Popular Culture* 8,Fall:
       392–401.
4178. Hahn, E. 1977. Magisches Denken im Sport. *Leistungssport* 7,1:68–71.
4179. Hammerich, K. 1971. Soziologische Analysen zur Leistung im Sport.
       Eine Nachbetrachtung. *Leibeserziehung* (Schorndorf) 21,2:15–22.
4180. Heinilä, K. 1967. Jakapalloilun tienviitoja-Sosiologin Käsityksiä (Football
       at the cross-roads-sociological conceptions). Pp. 10–50 in *Suomen
       Palloiitto.* Helsinki: Suomalaisen Kirjallisuuden Kirjapaino.
4181. Heinilä, K. 1969. Football at the crossroads. *IRSS* 4,1:5–30.
4182. Heinilä, K. 1974. Suomalainen Urheiluideologia (Finnish sport ideology).
       University of Jyväskylä Research Report 8. 163 pp.
4183. Hemming, J. 1972. The morality of sport. *New Society* (London) 22,532:
       628–630.
4184. Huizinga, J. 1971. The play element in contemporary sports. Pp. 11–16 in
       Dunning.
4185. Ingram, A.G. 1978. Dance and sport. *IRSS* 13,1:85–97.
4186. Jantz, R.K. 1975. Moral thinking in male elementary pupils as reflected by
       perception of basketball rules. *Research Quarterly* 46,4:414–421.

4187. Jech, M. 1962. *Moralnikodex budovateln Kommunismu va telesne vychove* (The moral codex of the founders of Communism in physical education). Praha: Sportovni a Juristiczé Nakladatelstvi. 14 pp.

4188. Jost, E. 1970. *Die Fairness.* Ahrensburg: Czwalina. 133 pp.

4189. Keating, J.W. 1964. Sportsmanship as a moral category. *Ethics* 75,1: 25-35.

4190. Keating, J.W. 1965. The heart of the problem of amateur athletics. *J. General Education* 16,4:261-272.

4191. Kenyon, G.S. 1968. A conceptual model for characterizing physical activity. *Research Quarterly* 39,1:96-105.

4192. Klapp, O.E. 1948. The creation of popular heroes. *AJS* 54,2:135-141.

4193. Krockow, C. von. 1974. Selbst-Bewusstsein, Entfremdung, Leistungssport. *Sportwissenschaft* 4,1:9-20.

4194. Kuchler, W. 1969. *Sportethos. Eine moraltheologische Untersuchung des im Lebensbereich Sport lebendigen Ethos als Beitrag zu einer Phänomenologie der Ethosformen.* München: Barth.

4195. Lenk, H. 1963. "Olympische Idee"—Vieldeutigkeit einer sprachlichen Form als Ursache ihrer sozialen Wirksamkeit. *Olympisches Feuer* 13,1: 22-28.

4196. Lenk, H. 1964. Die Olympische Amateurregel. *Jahrbuch des Sports* (Frankfurt) 24-66.

4197. Lenk, H. 1964. Values, aims and reality of the modern Olympic games. *Gymnasion* 4:11-17.

4198. Lenk, H. 1964. *Werte, Ziele, Wirlichkeit der modernen Olympischen Spiele.* Schorndorf: Hofmann. 368 pp.

4199. Lenk, H. 1976. Toward a social philosophy of the Olympics: values, aims, and reality of the modern Olympic movement. Pp. 107-167 in P. Graham and H. Ueberhorst, eds. *The Modern Olympics.* Cornwall, N.Y.: Leisure Press.

4200. Lenk, H. 1976. Zu Coubertins olympischem Elitismus. *Sportwissenschaft* 6,4:404-424.

4201. Lewis, H. 1974. The Baltimore Orioles, the Edmonton Eskimos, the Detroit Pistons, the Seattle Totems: Lévi-Strauss and the nature-culture dichotomy. *Western Canadian Journal of Anthropology* 4,1.

4202. Linde, H. and K. Heinemann. 1974. *Leistungsengagement und Sportinteresse.* Schorndorf: Hofmann. 125 pp.

4203. Lorenz, K. 1965. *Das sogenannte Böse. Zur Natur der Aggression.* Wien: Borotha-Schöler. Engl. *On Aggression.* New York.

4204. Lüschen, G. 1970. Cooperation, association, and contest. *J.Conflict Resolution* 14,1:20-34. German. 1975. Pp. 225-244 in Hammerich/Heinemann.

4205. Lüschen, G. 1971. Kooperation und Assoziierung. Zwei Formen sozialer Beziehungen im sportlichen Wettkampf als sozialer Konflikt. Pp. 136-142 in Albonico/Pfister-Binz.

4206. Lüschen, G. 1973. Psychologischer Reduktionismus und die informellen Beziehungen im Wettkampf. Pp. 753-759 in G. Albrecht, et al. ed. *Soziologie.* Opladen: Westdeutscher Verlag.

4207. Mai, H. 1974. Einige grundlegende Thesen zur Rolle und Bedeutung der Kategorie Leistung in Körperkultur und Sport. *Wissensch.Zeitschr.DHFK* 15,2:105-114.

4208.   Marshall, O. 1958. Epic motifs in modern football. *Tennessee Folklore Society Bulletin* 24,4:123–128.

4209.   Martens, R. 1976. Competition: in need of a theory. Pp. 9–17 in Landers.

4210.   Matejko, A. 1975. The diagnosis of conflict in sport. *Rev. Internationale Sociol.* (Madrid) 33,1:63–87.

4211.   Matsuda, I. and M. Kondo. 1966. Sports ni okeru kodokihan (Norms of behavior in sport). Pp. 35–64 in I. Matsuda and K. Kiyohara, eds., *Psychology of Sport.* Tokyo: Taishukan.

4212.   Melnick, M.J. 1974. The values of social conflict for sport. *Physical Educator* 31,2:82–86.

4213.   Metheny, E. 1965. Symbolic forms of movement: the Olympic Games. Pp. 35–42 in E. Metheny, *Connotations of Movement in Sport and Dance.* Dubuque, Iowa: Brown.

4214.   Murnighan, J.K. and A.E. Roth. 1978. Large group bargaining in a characteristic function game. *J.Confl.Resolution* 22,June:299–317.

4215.   MacKay, A.F. 1975. Interpersonal comparisons. *J.Philosophy* 72,Oct.: 535–551.

4216.   Neidhardt, F. 1978. Zeitknappheit, Umweltspannungen, und Anpassungs-strategien im Hochleistungssport. *Sportwissenschaft* 8,4:333–349.

4217.   Nelson, K. and C. Cody. 1979. Competition, cooperation, and fair play. *IRSS* 14,1:97–104.

4218.   Nitsch, J. 1975. Sportliches Handeln als Handlungsmodell. *Sportwissen-schaft* 5,1:39–55.

4219.   Olmsted, C. 1962. *Heads I Win, Tails You Lose.* New York: Macmillan. 277 pp.

4220.   Ossowska, M. 1963. O penwnych przemianach etyki walki (On some transformations of ethics in competition). Pp. 220–252 in *Socjologia moralnosci. Zarys sagadnien.* Warszawa: PWN.

4221.   Rapoport, A. 1960. *Fights, Games and Debates.* Ann Arbor, Mich.: University of Michigan Press. 400 pp.

4222.   Raynar, J.O. and C.P. Smith. Achievement-related motives and risk taking in games of chance and skill. *J.Personality* 34:176–198.

4223.   Richardson, D. 1962. Ethical conduct in sport situations. *Proceedings College Physical Education Association* 66:78–107.

4224.   Rodionov, A.P. 1963. Niekatoryje voprosy estetiki fiziceskoj kul'tury i sporta (Some problems of aesthetics in Physical Culture and Sports). *Teorija i Praktika* 4:7–15 and 5:6–16.

4225.   Rodionov, A.P. 1965. Matierialisticeskaja estetika i fiziceskoje vospitanije (The materialistic aesthetics and physical education). *Teorija i Praktika* 6:17–21, 7:31–36 and 8:23–28.

4226.   Roszak, T. 1972. Forbidden games, an occasional paper on the role of technology in a free society 1966. Pp. 91–104 in Hart.

4227.   Saraf, J. 1977. Semiotic signs in sport activity. *IRSS* 12,2:89–101.

4228.   Sargent, D.A. 1915. Is a war a biological necessity? *American Physical Education Review* 20, March:135–142.

4229.   Schlenker, B.R. and T.V. Boroma. 1978. Fun and games: the velocity of games for the study of conflict. *J.Confl.Resolution* 22,March:7–38.

4230.   Schofield, N. 1978. Instability of simple dynamic games. *Review of Economic Studies* 45, Oct.:575–594.

4231. Sherif, M. 1967. *Social Interaction: Process and Products.* Chicago: Aldine.

4232. Skarzewska, J. 1963. Postaway uczniow sportowcow wobec wybranych zagadnien z dziedniny styki sportowcow (Attitude of pupils participating in sports toward some selected problems in the field of sports' ethics). *Kultura Fizyczna* 16,10:622–629.

4233. Start, K.B. 1966. Wettbewerb und Geschicklichkeit im Sport. Pp. 203–208 in Lüschen.

4234. Sussangkarn, C. 1978. Equilibrium payoff of configurations for cooperative games with transferability. *J.Confl.Resolution* 22:March:121–141.

4235. Talalaev, J.I. 1974. K voprosu o socialnoj sushchnosti i znachenija sportivnogo sorevnovaniha (To the problem of social essence and significance of sport competition). *Teorija i Praktika* 1:5–7.

4236. Tyszka, A. 1970. *Olimpia i Akademia Wydawnictwo Sport i Turystyka.* Warszawa. 168 pp.

4237. Vydrin, V.M. 1951. Degumanizacija burzhuaznogo sporta (Dehumanization of the Bourgeois sport). Pp. 68–73 in *Materialy nauchnoj konferencii vuzov po fizicheskomy vospitaniju st dentov.* Leningrad.

4238. Watson, G.G. and T.M. Kando. 1974. The meaning of rules and rituals in little league baseball. *Sport Sociology Bulletin* 3,2:68–70.

4239. Watson, G.G. and T.M. Kando. 1976. The meaning of rules and rituals in Little League Baseball. *Pacif.Soc.Rev.* 19,3:291–315.

4240. Weiss, P. 1973. Strategems and competition. *Sportwissenschaft* 3,1:47–54.

4241. Witt, G. 1966. Einige Probleme der Beziehungen zwischen Kunst und Sport in der DDR. *Wissenschaftl.Zeitschr.* DHFK 8,1.

4242. Witte, W. 1960. Sport als Spiel und seine Bedeutung für den modernen Menschen. *Studium Generale* 13,1:48–62.

4243. Wohl, A. 1972. Körperkultur als soziales Produkt und als sozialer Wert. *Sportwissenschaft* 2,4:351–365.

4244. Wohl, A. 1973. Physical culture as a social product and as a social value. *IRSS* 8,1:19–35.

4245. Wroczynski, R. 1954. O spoleczhym podlozu wychowania fizycznego i sportu (On the social background of physical education and sport). *Kultura Fizyczna* 7,5:325–332.

4246. Zöld, J. 1967–68. Dondolatok sportéletünk néhány erkölcsi problémájáról (Reflections on some moral problems of our sporting life). *Testneveles Tudomany* 3:50–55.

3. *Small Groups, Teams and Social Relations in Sport*

4247. Acković, T. 1968. Skolski puseh ucenika u odnosu na njihov polozaj u strukturi kosarkaske ekipe (School results and the position of students on basketball teams). *Fizicka kultura* (Beograd) 3–4:91–96.

4248. Anger, H. 1966. Kleingruppenforschung heute. Pp. 5–35 in Lüschen.

4249. Asai, A. 1958. Yugi shudan ni okeru group norm ni tsuite (Group norm in the play group). *Research J.Phys.Educ.* 3,1:99.

4250. Asai, A. 1960. Yugi shshudan ni oketu yakuwaribuntan no katei (Role assignment in small play groups). *Japan Science Review. Humanistic*

Studies 11:126–129.

4251.   Asai, A. 1966. Undo yugi shudan no kozo to kino (A study on structure and function of the play group in physical activities). *Research J.Phys. Educ.* 9,4–5:133–139.

4252.   Asai, A. 1967. *Undo yugi shudan no kozo to kino* (Structure and function of play group in physical activity). Osaka: Nihon Jisho. 372 pp.

4253.   Back, K.W. et al. 1964. The subject role in small group experiments. *Social Forces* 43,2:181–187.

4254.   Bakonyi, F. 1966. A tesnevelés katása a 15–16 éves közepiskolai tanulók társas kapcsolataira (The influence of physical education on social relations of high school students 15 to 16 years of age). *Testneveles Tudomany* (Budapest) 1:4–15.

4255.   Bakonyi, F. 1970. A testnevelés és spotr katára a 10–14 éves tanulók társas kapcsolataira és osztályközösségeik alakulására (Effects of physical education and sport on social relations of students 10 to 14 and the development of class collectives) *Tudomany Közl.Testneveles F.* (Budapest) 1:218–252.

4256.   Ball, J.R. and A.V. Carron. 1977. The influence of team cohesion and participation motivation upon performance success in intercollegiate ice hockey. *Recreation Research Review* 5,1:53–58.

4257.   Becker, P. 1978. Einstellungskonvergenz bei Mitgliedern olympischer Sportgruppen. *Sportwissenschaft* 8,1:24–41.

4258.   Bernard, M. 1963. Une interprétation dialectique de la dynamique de l'équipe sportive. *Education physique et Sport* 13,63:7–10.

4259.   Biro, P. and L. Jáki. 1965. A sport hatása a Közepiskolai tanulok spontán társas kacsolataira (The influence of sport on the spontaneous group creation of pupils of middle class). *Testnevelés* 1,3:82–87.

4260.   Boering, S.A. and A.V. Bergen. 1960. Prestige en belangstelling (Prestige and interest). *Sociologische Gids* (Meppel) 7,2:70–77.

4261.   Bossard, J.H.S. and E.S. Ball. 1966. Peer groups: Preschool and later age. Pp. 386–403 in *The Sociology of Child Development*. New York: Harper and Row.

4262.   Boutin, L. 1960. Les groupes d'aptitude physique homogène au Lycée Marie Curie. *Education physique et Sport* 11(52):9–13.

4263.   Breck, S.J. 1950. A sociometric measurement of status in physical education classes. *Research Quarterly* 21,1:75–82.

4264.   Buggel, E. 1965. Die Struktur des Lebensvollzugs der Menschen nach Raum, Zeit und sozialen Gruppen. *Wissensch.Zeitschr.DHFK* 7,2:7–13.

4265.   Cagigal, J.M. 1966. Psicologia del groupo social y deporte (Psychology of the social group and sport). *Bulletin FIEP* 3–4:27–42.

4266.   Callahan, O.D. and S.S. Robin. 1969. A social system analysis of preferred leadership role characteristics in high school. *Soc.Education* 42,2:251–260.

4267.   Carron, A.V. and J.R. Ball. 1977. An analysis of the cause-effect characteristics of cohesiveness and participation motivation in intercollegiate hockey. *IRSS* 12,2:49–60.

4268.   Carron, A.V. 1978. Role behavior and the coach-athlete interaction. *IRSS* 2,13:51–66.

4269. Charnofsky, H. 1966. Die Aufgabe von Verteidigungsschichten in Druck-situationen. Pp. 237–250 in Lüschen.

4270. Cho, M.Y. 1966. A study on the factors to determine the social acceptance in sport groups. Seoul, Korea: Sookmyung Women's University. *Theses Collection* VI.

4271. Cikler, J. 1967. The rise, the development and the extinction of a soccer team of boys. *IRSS* 2,1:33–46.

4272. Cikler, J. 1970. Simultaneous research of the sports and creative artistic groups. *IRSS* 5,1:105–115.

4273. Cooper, R. and R. Payne. 1972. Personality orientations and performance in soccer teams. *Brit.J.Social Clinical Psychol.* 2,1:2–9.

4274. Corraze, J. and R. Nachache. 1965. Dynamique de groupes en com-pétition. *Education physique et Sport* 77,11:9–11.

4275. Cox, F.N. 1953. Sociometric status and individual adjustment before and after play therapy. *J.Abnormal Soc.Psychology* 48,7:354–356.

4276. Curtis, J.E. and J.W. Loy. 1978. Positional segregation in professional baseball. *IRSS* 13,4:5–24.

4277. Dankers, M.F. vanVlug. 1971. Kreatief spel (Creative play). *Impuls* (Lou-vain) 11,July-Aug.:380–393.

4278. Despot, M. 1971. Fudbalski tim kao socialna grupa (Soccer teams as social groups). *Strucni bilten FSS* (Beograd) 1,5–6:54–59.

4279. Dietrich, K. 1974. Sportspiele und Interaktion. *Sportunterricht* (Schorn-dorf) 23,1:4–10.

4280. Donnelly, P. et al. 1978. *Group Cohesion and Sport.* CAHPER Mono-graph. Calgary: University of Calgary. 83 pp.

4281. Dustin, D. 1966. Member reactions to team performance. *J.Social Psychol.* 69,2:237–243.

4282. Eitzen, S. 1973. The effect of group structure on the success of athletic teams. *IRSS* 8,1:7–17.

4283. Elias, N. and E. Dunning. 1966. Zur Dynamik von Sportgruppen. Pp. 118–134 in Lüschen.

4284. Elias, N. and E. Dunning. 1966. Dynamics of sport groups with special reference to football. *Brit.J.Sociol.* 17,4:388–402.

4285. Emerson, R.M. 1966. Mount Everest: a case study of communication feedback and sustained group goal-striving. *Sociometry* 29,3:213–227. *German* 1966. pp. 135–176 in Lüschen.

4286. Essing, W. 1971. Empirische Beiträge zur Analyse zwischenmenschlichen Verhaltens in einer interagierenden Gruppe—dargestellt am Beispiel einer Fussball-Bundesligamannschaft. Pp. 307–312 in ADL, ed. *Moti-vation im Sport.* Schorndorf: Hofmann.

4287. Essing, W. and H. Houben. 1973. Möglichkeiten und Grenzen der Anwen-dung der Soziometrie als Führungshilfe in Sportmannschaften. Pp. 24–27 in *Bericht 3 Europäischer Kongress für Sportpsychologie.* Schorn-dorf: Hofmann.

4288. Essing, W. and H. Eberspächer. 1974. Untersuchungen über Rollendif-ferenzierungen in Sportgruppen. Pp. 71–86 in *Kölner Beiträge zur Sportwissenschaft.* Vol. 2. Schorndorf: Hofmann.

4289. Famaey-Lamon, A. et al. 1979. Team-sport and individual sport. *IRSS* 14,2:37–50.

4290.   Fiedler, F.E. et al. 1952. *The Relationship of Interpersonal Perception to Effectiveness in Basketball Teams.* Bureau of Research and Service. Urbana, Ill.: University of Illinois. 23 pp. mimeo.

4291.   Fiedler, F.E. 1954. Assumed similarity measures as predictors of team effectiveness. *J.Abnormal Soc.Psychology* 49,3:381-388.

4292.   Fiedler, F.E. 1960. The leader's psychological distance and group effectiveness. Pp. 586-606 in D. Cartwright and A. Zander, eds. *Group Dynamics.* Evanston: Row Peterson.

4293.   Földesi, T. 1978. Investigation for the objective measurement of cooperative ability among the members of rowing teams. *IRSS* 13,1:49-70.

4294.   French, J.R.P. 1944. Organized and unorganized groups under fear and frustration. Pp. 229-308 in *Studies in Topological and Vector Psychology.* Iowa City: University of Iowa Studies of Child Welfare.

4295.   Fujita, N. 1965. Undobu shudan no seikaku ni tsuite (A study on the character of sport groups). *Bulletin Health, Physical Education Doshisha University* 5:37-51.

4296.   Fujita, N. 1970. Taiikukai undobu to sport dokokai nitsuiteno ichiko-satsu (A study on the university and private sport team). *Bulletin Doshisha University* 10:1-18.

4297.   Gill, D.L. and J.L. Perry. 1979. A case study of leadership in women's intercollegiate softball. *IRSS* 14,2:83-92.

4298.   Göldner, K.H. 1963. Über die Wirksamkeit von Beauftragungen im Turnunterricht auf die Struktur des Klassenkollektivs. *Theorie und Praxis* 12,11:987-995.

4299.   Goncharov, V.D. 1972. Liderstvo v sportivnyh komandah (Leadership in sport teams). *Teorija i Praktika* 2:11-14.

4300.   Gottheil, E. and D.P. Vielnaber. 1966. Interaction of leader squad attitudes related to performance of military squads. *J.Soc.Psychology* 68,1:113-127.

4301.   Greer, F.L. 1961. Leadership, indulgence and group performance. *Psychological Monographs* 75,516:1-35.

4302.   Gross, N. and W.E. Martin. 1952. On group cohesiveness. *AJS* 57,3: 546-554.

4303.   Hahn, E. 1970. Performance in sports as a criterion of social approach in school classes: a sociometric investigation. Pp. 395-404 in G. Kenyon, ed. *Psychology of Sport.* Chicago: Athletic Institute.

4304.   Hammerich, K. 1966. Leistungsforcierung im Sportunterricht und ihr Einfluss auf die Struktur von Schulklassen. Pp. 224-236 in Lüschen.

4305.   Hammond, L.J. and M. Goldman. 1961. Competition and noncompetition and its relationship to individual and group productivity. *Sociometry* 24,1:46-60.

4306.   Hanin, J.A. 1970. O vsaimosvjazi vnutrigruppovogo obshchenija i dejatelnosti (On correlation of group structure and activity) Pp. 169-170 in *Tezisy Vsesojusnogo simposiuma 1970.* Leningrad.

4307.   Harvey, O.J. 1953. An experimental approach to the study of status relations in informal groups. *ASR* 18,3:357-367.

4308.   Hawcroft, E.C. 1960. Group interaction in physical education. *Physical Education* (London) 52,3:15-18.

4309.   Hegg, J.J. 1975. Gruppendynamik im Sport. Pp. 111-115 in A. Uchtenhagen et al. eds. *Gruppentherapie und soziale Umwelt.* Bern: Huber.

4310.   Hendry, L.B. 1968. Assessment of personality traits in the coach-swimmer relationship and a preliminary examination of the father-figure stereotype. *Research Quarterly* 39,3:543–551.

4311.   Higashiyama, T. 1968. Undobuin no ikenhenyo ni oyobosu sociometory-kozo to communication-style no kumiwaseno kozo (The effects of sociometric structure and communication style upon the opinion-changes among members of athletic groups). *Bulletin Aichi Daigaku, Bungakubu Ronshv, Ippan-kyoikuben, Nagoya* 19:208–229.

4312.   Higashiyama, T. 1970. Gakko ni okeru sport shudan no kenyu–kyoiku teki shiten kara (The sport group in the school from the view point of education). *Aichi Kenritsu Daigaku Bungakubu Ronshu, Ippan-Kyoikuben, Nagoya* 21:91–108.

4313.   Ikuta, K. et al. 1960. Team games ni okeru team no gyoschusei no yoin ga teamseiseki ni oyobosu koka (The effect of cohesiveness of the team on team games). *Research J.Phys.Educ.* 5,1:43.

4314.   Immig, F. and W. 1976. Hochleistungssport und Rollenselbstbild. Darstellung einer Einstellungsbeurteilung in Hochleistungssportgruppen. *Leistungssport* (Berlin) 6,2:142–149.

4315.   Ingham, A.G. 1974. The Ringelmann effect: studies of group size and group performance. *J.Exp.Soc.Psychology* 10:371–384.

4316.   Iso-Ahola, S. 1976. Evaluation of self and team performance and feelings of satisfaction after success and failure. *IRSS* 11,4:33–46.

4317.   Jones, M.B. 1974. Regressing group on individual effectiveness. *Organizational Behavior and Human Performance* 11,3:426–451.

4318.   Julian, J.W. and F.A. Perry. 1967. Cooperation contrasted with intra-group and inter-group competition. *Sociometry* 30,1:79–90.

4319.   Kanezaki, R. 1973. Sports shonendanshidosha ni kansuru shakaigakuteki kenkyu (A sociological study of leaders in youth sport clubs in Japan). *Research Phys.Education Kyushu University* (Fukuoka) 5,1:1–8.

4320.   Klein, M. and G. Christiansen. 1966. Gruppenkomposition, Gruppenstruktur und Effektivität von Basketballmannschaften. Pp. 180–191 in Lüschen. *Engl.* 1969 pp. 397–407 in Loy/Kenyon.

4321.   Kobayashi, A. et al. 1960. Team game ni okeru seiin no undonoryoku to sogosayo no kata (An experimental study on the effect of individual athletic ability on status in a basketball team). *Research J.Phys.Educ. Kyushu University* 2,4:27–33.

4322.   Kobayashi, A. and S. Ikuta. 1961. Aite-team no rikiryo ni taisury yosoku to ninchi ga team ni oyobosu koka (The effects of anticipation and perception of opponent's power on team morale). *Research J.Phys. Educ.Kyushu University* 5,2:15–20.

4323.   König, R. 1966. Die Gruppe im Sport und die Kleingruppenforschung. Pp. 5–10 in Lüschen.

4324.   Kraus, U. 1976. Zur Analyse sozialpsychologischer Beziehungen in Sportgruppen. *Leistungssport* 6,6:428–432.

4325.   Landers, D.M. and T.F. Crum. 1971. The effect of team success and formal structure on interpersonal relations and cohesiveness of baseball teams. *Int.J.Sport Psych.* 2,2:88–95.

4326.   Landers, D.M. and G. Lüschen. 1974. Team performance outcome and the cohesiveness of competitive coacting groups. *IRSS* 9,2:57–71.

4327.   Lenk, H. 1965. Konflikt und Leistung in Spitzensportmannschaften.

Soziale Welt (Göttingen) 16,4:307–347.

4328.   Lenk, H. 1966. Maximale Leistung trotz inneren Konflikten. Pp. 168–172 in Lüschen. *Engl.* 1969 pp. 393–396 in Loy/Kenyon.

4329.   Lenk, H. 1971. Vergleiche von subjektiven Leistungsschätzungen und soziometrischen Wahlen am Beispiel der Weltmeisterachter von 1962 und 1966. Pp. 59–66 in Albonico/Pfister-Binz.

4330.   Lenk, H. 1968. Die Aufgabe von Wertbindungen bei westdeutschen Hochleistungsruderern unter soziodramatisch fingiertem Stress. *Soziale Welt* 19,1:66–73. *Engl.* 1968. The giving up of values in the case of top-class oarsmen under sociodramatic simulated stress. *IRSS* 3,1: 137–148.

4331.   Lenk, H. 1970. *Leistungsmotivation und Mannschaftsdynamik.* Schorndorf: Hofmann. 200 pp.

4332.   Lenk, H. 1977. *Team Dynamics.* Champaign, Ill.: Stipes. 180 pp.

4333.   Lott, A.J. and B. 1965. Group cohesiveness as interpersonal attraction: a review of relationships with antecedent and consequent variables. *Psychological Bulletin* 64,2:259–309.

4334.   Loy, J.W. and G.H. Sage. 1970. Effects of formal structure on organizational leadership. Pp. 363–374 in G. Kenyon, ed. *Psychology of Sport.* Chicago: Athletic Institute.

4335.   Lüschen, G. 1966. Leistungsorientierung und ihr Einfluss auf das soziale und personale System. Pp. 209–233 in Lüschen.

4336.   Lüschen, G. 1969. Small group research and the group in sport. Pp. 57–75 in Kenyon.

4337.   Martens, R. 1970. Influence of participation motivation on success and satisfaction in team performance. *Research Quarterly* 41,3:510–518.

4338.   Martens, R. and J. Petersen. 1971. Group cohesiveness as a determinant of success and member satisfaction in team performance. *IRSS* 6,1:49–61.

4339.   Matsuura, Y. 1973. Shudansogo no Rijisei to Tokushusei ni tsuite (Intergroup similarity and specificity among sport teams). *Research J.Phys. Educ.* 18,2:91–101.

4340.   Melnick, M.J. and M.M. Chemers. 1974. Effects of group social structure on the success of basketball teams. *Research Quarterly* 45,1:1–8.

4341.   Mihovilovic, M. 1966. Generationswechsel in Sportmannschaften. Pp. 173–179 in Lüschen.

4342.   Mills, T.M. 1965. Some hypotheses on small groups from Simmel. Pp. 157–170 in L. Coser, ed. Georg Simmel. Englewood-Cliffs: Prentice-Hall.

4343.   Mohás, L. 1969. Társas kaposolatok vizsgálata labdarugó gyerekeknél (Investigation of collective relations of pupils in a soccer team). *Testneveles Tan.* (Budapest) 5,2:39–44.

4344.   Momirovic, K. and K. Petrovic. 1972. Model strukture kinezioloskih skupin (The structural model of the kinesiological group). *Telesna kultura* (Ljubljana) 20,1–2:42.

4345.   Myers, A.E. 1962. Team competition, success, and the adjustment of group members. *J.Abnormal Soc.Psychology* 65,5:325–332. German Mannschaftswettbewerb, Erfolg und die Anpassung der Gruppenmitglieder. Pp. 272–287 in Hammerich/Heinemann.

4346.   Myers, A.E. and F.E. Fiedler. 1966. Theorie und Probleme der Führung. Pp. 92–106 in Lüschen.

4347.   McGrath, J.E. 1962. The influence of positive interpersonal relations on adjustment effectiveness in rifle teams. *J.Abnormal Soc.Psychology* 65,6:365-375.

4348.   McGraw, L.W. and J.W. Tolbert. 1953. Sociometric status and athletic ability of junior high school boys. *Research Quarterly* 24,1:72-80.

4349.   McIntyre, T.D. 1973. Judgemental measures as indices of interpersonal relationships. *IRSS* 8,2:103-110.

4350.   McPherson, B.D. 1978. Success in sport: the influence of sociological parameters. *Canadian J.Applied Sport Sciences* 3,1:51-59.

4351.   Nakamura, K. 1962. Taiiku-shakaigaku ni okeru ni tsuiteno ichikosatsu (A study of the group in sociology of physical education). *Bulletin Health, Phys.Educ.Doshisha University* 2:1-16.

4352.   Nakashima, T. 1972. Chiiki sport shudan noshakaigakuteki kenkyu (Sociological research of local sports groups. Rise and extinction of baseball teams). *Research Bulletin Dpt.General Education Nagoya University* 16:59-84.

4353.   Naul, R. and H. Voigt. 1972. Zur Problematik des Divergenztheorems für leistungsorientierte Ballspielmannschaften. *Sportwissenschaft.* 2,3: 300-306.

4354.   Nelson, J.K. and B.L. Johnson. 1968. Effects of varied techniques in organizing class competition upon changes in sociometric status. *Research Quarterly* 39,4:634-639.

4355.   Niwa, T. et al. 1961. Asobi no shudan nogyoshusei ni kansuru jikkenteki kenkyu (An experimental study of cohesiveness in the play group) *Research J.Phys.Educ.* 6,1:280.

4356.   Niwa, T. 1965. Undo shudan no kozo to kino (A study on structure and function of sport groups). *Studies in Humanities and Social Sciences Nara Women's University* 9:93-115.

4357.   Niwa, T. and A. Takemura. 1965 and 1966. Unbodu shudan to personality no kankei ni tsuite (The relationship between sport groups and personality). *Reseaarch J.Phys.Educ.* 9,2:9-17 and 11,1:1-8.

4358.   Niwa, T. and A. Takemura 1966. A longitudinal study on the effects of sport groups upon personality Pp. 510-512 in K. Kato, ed. *International Congress Sport Sciences.* Tokyo: University of Tokyo Press.

4359.   Niwa, T. 1966. Kleingruppenforschung in Anwendung auf Sportgruppen und Sportvereine. Pp. 259-267 in Lüschen.

4360.   Niwa, T. 1966. Sports shudan to ningenkankei (Sport group and human relations). Pp. 78-83 in I. Matsuda and K. Kiyohara, eds. *Psychology of Sport.* Tokyo: Taishukan.

4361.   Niwa, T. et al. 1966. Undobu no gyoshusei ni tsuite (A study of the cohesiveness of sport groups). *Research J.Phys.Educ.* 10,2:58-59.

4362.   Niwa, T. 1968. A methodological study on the group cohesiveness of sport groups based on sociometry. *IRSS* 3,1:57-71.

4363.   Niwa, T. and C. Higashiyama. 1968. Sociometry ni yoru undobu no gyoshyusei no kento (A methodological study on the cohesiveness of sport groups based on sociometry). *Research J.Phys.Educ.* 12,4; 226-236.

4364.   Niwa, T. and N. Yasumori. 1969. Leader ga shudanseiin no taido henyo ni oyobosu eikyo (The effects of leader on group members' attitude change). *J.Educational Soc.Psychology* (Fukuoka) 8,2:89–102.

4365. Niwa, T.; Odan, K. and K. Takeuchi, eds. 1972. *Taiiku shudan no kenkyu* (The study of groups for physical education). Osaka: Times. 492 pp.

4366. Nixon, H.L. 1974. An axiomatic theory of team success. *Sport Sociology Bulletin* 3,1,Spring:1–12.

4367. Odan, K. 1959. Yugi shudan sogo no koshokatei ni okeru shakaiteki katto (Social conflict in the negotiatory process of playing groups). *Research J.Phys.Educ.* 4,1:176.

4368. Odan, K. et al. 1961. Yugi shudan ni okeru hokenteki shudankozo to minshuteki shudankozo ni hikaky kenkyu (A comparative study of the feudalistic group constitution and the democratic group constitution in play groups). *Research J.Phys.Educ.* 6,1:276–279.

4369. Odan, K. and Y. Sato. 1964. Yugi shoshudan ni okeru shakaiteki seiryoku no keisei katei—Riida to shakaiteki seiryoku (The process of forming social power in play groups—The leader acting at the center). *Bulletin Faculty of Education Kobe University* 31:113–122.

4370. Odan, K. and Y. Sato. 1966. Yugi shoshudan ni okeru shudan kodo no hattatsu ni kansuru kenkyu I (Development of group behavior in a small group). *Bulletin Faculty of Education, Kobe University* 36: 107–113.

4371. Odan, K. and Y. Sato. 1966. Yugi shoshudan no ryoiki ni kansuru kenkyu (Division of group behavior in a small play group). *Bulletin Faculty of Education Kobe University* 36:115–121.

4372. Odan, K. and Y. Sato. 1967. Yugi shoshudan sogo no momiai no hassei ni tsuite no kenkyu (Fight for securing the soccer ball in small play groups). *Bulletin Faculty of Education Kobe University* 38:91–96.

4373. Odan, K. and Y. Sato. 1971. Yugi no ba ni okeru shudan kosei ga seiinkan no kyoryoku kodo no oyobosu eikyo (Influence of play-group constitution upon cooperative behavior of members). *Research J.Phys.Educ.* 15,2:125–130.

4374. Pavlovic, M. and K. Petrovich. 1969. Tehnika skaliranja in sociometrija pri ugotavljanju narave odnosov in procesov med igralci kosarkarskega kluba Olimpije (Measurement of relations between players of the basketball club 'Olimpia' through scaling techniques and sociometry). *Zbornik VSTK* (Ljubljana) 3:293–356.

4375. Pesquie, P. 1963 and 1964. La cohésion de l'équipe sportive. *Education physique et Sport* 67,Nov.:31–34. 68,Jan.:77–79.

4376. Petersen, J. and R. Martens. 1972. Success and residential affiliation as determinants of team cohesiveness. *Research Quarterly* 43,1:62–76.

4377. Petrak, B. 1964. Cleneni a zmeny telovychovnych skupin (The composition of sport groups and their change). Pp. 44–57 in *Metodickydopis o psychologicke priprave sportovce.* Prague: Ustredni Vybor.

4378. Petrovic, K. 1972. Kohezivnost sportne skupine in uspeh v tekmovanju (The cohesiveness of sport groups and its competitive achievements). *Telesna kultura* (Ljubljana) 20,7–8:44–47.

4379. Petrovic, K. 1973. Neki problemi povezani sa modelima primjenjenim u dosadasnijm istrazivanjima grupne dinamike u kineziologji (Problems related to recently applied models of group dynamics in sport). *Kineziologija* (Zagreb) 3,1:39–50.

4380. Reaney, M.J. 1916. *Psychology of Group Games.* Cambridge: University Press. 76 pp.

4381. Sato, Y. 1973. Shudan kino ni yoru sogo yuhatsu koka (Reciprocal effects and group function). *Bulletin Faculty of Education Kobe University* 49: 115-122.

4382. Schafer, W.E. 1966. Die soziale Struktur von Sportgruppen. Pp. 107-117 in Lüschen.

4383. Schiller, J. 1971. Csoportok és sportcsoportok (Groups and sport groups). *Sportvezetö* (Budapest) 6:18-19.

4384. Schubert, F. 1973. Probleme der Entstehung und Entwicklung der Rangstruktur in Sportgruppen. *Theorie und Praxis* 22,3:550-560.

4385. Sherif, M. and C.W. 1953. *Groups in Harmony and Tension.* New York: Harper. 316 pp.

4386. Sherif, M.; B. White and O.J. Harvey. 1955. Status in experimentally produced groups. *AJS* 60,3:370-379.

4387. Sherif, C.W. and M. 1961. *The Robber's Cave Experiment.* Norman: University of Oklahoma Press.

4388. Sherif, C.W. 1973. Intergroup conflict and competition. Pp. 60-69 in Grupe.

4389. Skubic, E. 1949. A study on acquaintanceship and social status in physical education classes. *Research Quarterly* 20,1:80-87.

4390. Slepicka, P. 1975. Interpersonal behavior and sports group effectiveness. *Int.J.Sport Psychology* 6,1:14-27.

4391. Snyder, E. 1972. High school athletes and their coaches. *Soc.Education* 45,2:313-325.

4392. Stendler, C. et al. 1951. Studies in cooperation and competition *J.Genetic Psychology* 79,1:173-197.

4393. Stogdill, R.M. 1963. *Team Achievement under High Motivation.* Columbus, Ohio: Ohio State University Business Research. 92 pp.

4394. Stone, G.P. 1966. Begriffliche Probleme in der Kleingruppenforschung. Pp. 44-65 in Lüschen.

4395. Sugawara, R. 1957. Social system toshiteno taiiku shudan no kzo ni tsuite (The group structure of physical education as a social system). *Research J.Phys.Educ.* 2,7:238.

4396. Sugawara, R. 1958. Gakkyu shudan no anteisei ni kansuru kenkyu (A study of the stability in a class group). *Literary Society of Tohoku University* 22,3:128-141.

4397. Sugawara, R. 1959. Taiiku no ba niokeru singen kankei ni kansuru kenkyu (The peculiarity of human relations in physical education). *Liberal Arts Review Tohoku University* 4:56-73.

4398. Szlatényi, B. 1971. Az edzö és a játékosok közötti viszony szociológiai viszgálata egy konkrét szakosztályon belül (Sociological investigation of player-coach relation within a sport club). *Testneveles F.Tudomany* 2:33-41.

4399. Takemura, A. 1972. Wagakuni ni okeru taiiku shudan kenkyu no doko to kadai (Trends and themes in group research in physical education). *Bulletin Nara University of Education* 21,1:161-176.

4400. Takeuchi, K. 1970. *Team work ron* (Team work theory). Osaka: Taimusha.

4401. Takeuchi, K. 1971. Game shakai ni okeru ningenkankei (Human relations in game society). *Bulletin Kyoto University of Education* 39.

4402.   Trogsch, F. 1966. Forschungsergebnisse im Bereich der Köperkultur und der Formierungsprozess von Sportgruppen. Pp. 268–272 in Lüschen.

4403.   Valentinova, N.G. 1969. Burzuaznaja socialnaja psichologija i probliema sportivnych grupp (Bourgeois society and sport groups. Pp. 233–239 in *Materialy naucnoj konfierencii.* Tashkent.

4404.   Valentinova, N.G. and V.V. Myedvyedyev. 1973. Selected problems of small groups in sport teams. *IRSS* 8,1:69–78.

4405.   Valentinova, N. and Y. Ryzkonkin. 1975. Experiences of a sociopsychological probing study of a sport team. *IRSS* 10,2:49–58.

4406.   Veit, H. 1971. Beitrag zu einer Typologie der Ballspielmannschaften. Pp. 184–197 in Albonico/Pfister-Binz.

4407.   Veit, H. 1971. *Untersuchungen zur Gruppendynamik von Ballspielmannschaften.* Schorndorf: Hofmann. 189 pp.

4408.   Vinacke, W.E. 1964. Intra-group power relations, strategy, and decisions in intra-triad competition. *Sociometry* 27,1:25–29.

4409.   Volkamer, M. 1971. Untersuchungen zur Bedeutung des Pareto-Koeffizienten in sozialen Systemen. Pp. 312–314 in ADL, eds. *Motivation im Sport.* Schorndorf: Hofmann.

4410.   Volkov, I.P. and V.M. Derevenskij. 1972. Liderstvo kak problema sportivnoj nauki i praktiki (Leadership as a problem of science and practice). *Teorija i Praktika* 9–13.

4411.   Vos, K. and W. Brinkman. 1967. Success en cohesie in sportgroepen (Success and cohesion in sport groups). *Sociologische Gids* (Meppel) 14,1:30–40.

4412.   Vos, K. and W. Brinkman. 1972. Erfolg und Zusammenhalt in Sportgruppen. *Leistungssport* 2,2:128–134.

4413.   Wegner, N. and D. Zeaman. 1956. Team and individual performances on a motor task. *J.General Psychology* 55,1:127–142.

4414.   Whyte, W.F. 1943. *Street Corner Society.* Chicago: University of Chicago Press. 284 pp.

4415.   Whyte, W.F. 1953. *Leadership and Group Participation.* Ithaca, N.Y.: Cornell University. 49 pp.

4416.   Widmeyer, W.N. et al. 1978. When cohesion predicts outcome in sport. *Research Quarterly* 49,3:372–380.

4417.   Woodman, W.F. and M.R. Grant. 1977. The persistence and salience of small group structures within a successful athletic team. *IRSS* 12,2: 73–89.

4418.   Yiannakis, A. 1977. Sport groups as subcultures: a conceptual analysis. *J.Sport Behavior* 1,3:105–117.

4419.   Yokoyama, I. 1970. Undobu shudan to sport taishu shakai (A study of relations in elite and mass sport). Pp. 5–22 in A. Asai, ed. *Taiikugaku ronso.* Osaka: Nihonjisho. Vol. 2.

4420.   Yokoyama, I. 1970. Undobu shudan noshakaitekikino ni kansuru kenkyu (Social functions in sport groups). *Memoir Faculty Education Fukui University* 2:21–42.

4421.   Yokoyama, I. 1971. Undobu shudan no morale no kenkyu (A study of morale in sport groups). *Memoirs Faculty Education Fukui University* 21:1–27.

4422.   Yokoyama, I. 1972. Undobu shudan no shakaiteki kino (Social functions of sport groups). Pp. 459–486 in H. Odan et al. eds. *The Studies of Groups for Physical Education.* Osaka: Times.

4423.   Yokoyama, I. 1973. Taiiku sport shudan no sogo katsudo no kenkyu I (A study of interaction process analysis in sport groups I). *Memoirs Faculty Education Fukui University* 23:1–23.

4424.   Zander, A. 1975. Motivation and performance of sports groups. Pp. 25–39 in D. Landers et al. eds. *Psychology of Sport and Motor Behavior.* University Park: Penn State University.

4. Sport Organizations, Administration, Planning, Policymaking

4425.   Amiot, M. 1969. Politique et administrations. *Sociologie du Travail* 11,2:113–144.

4426.   Andersen, H. et al. 1957. Sport and games in Denmark in the light of Sociology. *Acta Sociologica* 2,1:1–28.

4427.   Arai, S. 1973. Undōbu no shakaigakutekikenkyu niokuru shiten no settei ni tsuite (On setting of the view-point about the sociological research on "Undobu" (athletic club)). *Research of Physical Education Kyushu University* (Fukuoka) 4,3:13–21.

4428.   Artemov, V. 1971. Social planning of physical education and sports activity. *IRSS* 6,1:103–114.

4429.   Artemov, V.A. 1971. Nekotorye aspekty socialnogo planirovanija fizicheskoj kultury i sporta (Some aspects of the social planning of physical culture). Pp. 9–10, 59–60 in Annotacii, *Sport i Socializacija.* Vaterloo.

4430.   Artemov, V.A. 1971. Socialnoe planirovanie fizkulturno-sportivnoj dejatelnosti (The social planning of activities in the field of physical culture). *Teorija i Praktika* 9:38–40.

4431.   Arvisto, M. 1973. O podbore osnovnyh pokazatelej-kriteriev dlja socialnogo planirovanija fizicheskoj kultury (On selection of the main indices-critira for the social planning of physical culture). Pp. 35–37 in *Konferencija po problemam nauchnyh osnov organizacii sovetskogo dobrovolnogo fizkulturnogo dvizenija.* Tartu.

4432.   Babchuk, N. and A. Booth. 1969. Voluntary association membership: a longituditanal analysis. *ASR* 34,1:31–45.

4433.   BETURE. 1973. *Les nouvelles stations de sports d'hiver.* Paris: Départment Socio-Economie. 59 pp.

4434.   Binder, S. 1972. Nun siegt mal schön. Sportpolitik zwischen Milliarden und Medaillen. Pp. 87–100 in J. Richter, ed., *Die vertrimmte Nation.* Rowohlt: Reinbeck.

4435.   Boothby, J. and M.F. Tungatt. 1978. Amateur sports clubs. Their salient features and major advantages. *IRSS* 4,13:25–36.

4436.   Brundage, A. 1966. The Olympic movement: objectives and achievements. *Gymnasion* 3,1:3–4.

4437.   Bugrov, N.N. 1968. Kolonializm i sport (Colonialism and sport). Pp. 171–175 in *Materialy rasshirennoj konferencii, posvajshjennoj 50-letiju fizkulturnogo dvizhenija.* Erevan.

4438.   Bugrov, N.N. 1973. Moldjezh i olimpijskie igry (Youth and Olympic games). Pp. 56–59 in *Materialy po istorii, organizacii i sociologii fizicheskoj kultury.* Tashkent.

4439.   Cáp, A. 1969. Importance des "Universiades"; leur action sur le développement des relations dans le sport universitaire international et les résultats obtenus par les étudiants sportifs tchécoslovaques. *Telovichovny Sbornik* (Praha) 11:145–183.

4440.   Carr, G.A. 1976. The birth of the German Democratic Republic and the organization of East German sport. *Canadian J.History Phys.Ed.* 7,1: 1–21.

4441.   Claeys, U. et al. 1974. *Organisatie en financiering van de sport vor allen, explorend onderzock* (Organization and financing of sport for all, exploratory investigation). 2 vols. University of Leuven. 150 pp. and 142 pp.

4442.   Claeys, U. 1974. Financiering van de sport in Vlaanderen (Financing of sport in Flanders). *Sport* 17,4:316–222.

4443.   Claeys, U. 1976. Olympische spelen. Feest van het geweld (Olympic games. Festival of the world). *Sporta* (Leuven) 30:234–236.

4444.   Commission du 6ème Plan. 1972. Le développement du secteur socio-éducatif. *Cahiers Animation* 1:119–132.

4445.   Crase, D. 1972. The inner circles of intercollegiate football. *Sport Sociology Bulletin* 1,2:3–7.

4446.   Daume, W. 1963. Der Verein als Träger der deutschen Turn- und Sportbewegung. Pp. 17–37 in *Der Verein als Träger der deutschen Turn-Sportbewegung.* Dortmund: Deutscher Sportbund. 40 pp.

4447.   Department of Education and Science. 1968. *Enquiry into the State of Association Football at All Levels.* London: H.M.S.O.

4448.   Diem, C. 1953. *Deutsche und internationale Turn- und Sportverwaltung.* Cologne: Sporthochschule 160 pp.

4449.   Diem, C. 1955. Der Sport im heutigen Leben-Gefahren und Aufgaben. *Universitas* 5:485–493.

4450.   Dumazedier, J. et al. 1952. *Regards neufs sur les Jeux olympiques.* Paris: Éditions du Seuil. 129 pp.

4451.   Dunning, E. and K. Sheard. 1976. The bifurcation of Rugby Union and Rugby League: a case study of organizational conflict and change. *IRSS* 11,2:31–71.

4452.   Durso, J. 1975. *The Sports Factory.* New York: Quadrangle. 207 pp.

4453.   Erbach, G. 1977. Das Sportabzeichenprogramm der DDR. *Medizin und Sport* (Berlin-Ost) 17,2:33–37.

4454.   Espy, R. 1979. *The Politics of the Olympic Games.* Berkeley: University of California Press. 212 pp.

4455.   Euler, R. von. 1953. Idrottsörelsen av i Dag (Sport of today). Pp. 147–278 in *Svensk Idrott* 1903–1953. Malmö: Allhem 589 pp.

4456.   Europe, Council of. 1973. *Sport for all: Outline of a Methodology.* Stasbourg, France: Council of Europe. 103 pp.

4457.   Frey, J.H. 1977. The President's Commission on Olympic sports: implications of developing world class athletes. *Arena Newsletter* 1,6:13–18.

4458.   Frey, J.H. 1978. Organization of American amateur sport: efficiency to entropy. *American Behavioral Scientist* 21,January:361–378.

4459. Gallacher, O.R. 1957. Voluntary associations in France. *Social Forces* 36,2:153–160.

4460. Geller, E.M. 1971. Mesto i rol podvizhnyh igr v fizicheskom vospitanij uchashchihsja Belorusskoj SSR (The place and role of out-door games in physical education of the pupils of the Belorussian SSR). Pp. 191–194 in *Istorija, organizacija i sociologija fizicheskoj kultury i sporta.* Minsk.

4461. Genov, F. et al. 1955. *Organizacija na fiziceskata kultura i sporta v NR Bálgarija* (Organization of physical culture and sport in the peoples republic of Bulgaria). Sofia: Profizdat.

4462. Greendorfer, S.L. 1977. Intercollegiate football, an approach toward rationalization. *IRSS* 12,3:23–34.

4463. Groll, H. 1971. The situation of sports clubs within industrial communities. *Leibesübungen-Leibeserziehung* (Vienna) 25:170–173.

4464. Gross, E. 1979. Sport leagues: a model for a theory of organizational stratification. *IRSS* 14,2:103–112.

4465. Grousset, L.M. 1974. Le rattachement à l'Education Nationale du Secrétariat d'Etat à le Jeunesse et aux Sports. *Revue de l'Union Française des centres de vacances et de loisirs* (Paris) 116:6–7.

4466. Halldén, O. 1966. *Ungdomens förenings—och fritidsliv* (Youth organizations and Leisure). Stockholm: Statens offentliga utredningar. nr. 47. 302 pp.

4467. Harf, J.E. et al. 1974. Trans-societal sport associations: a descriptive analysis of structures and linkages. *Quest* 22:52–62.

4468. Heinilä, K. 1964. Ideologinen ja Instrumentaalisen Malli Urheilupolitisesa Päätoksenteossa (Ideological and instrumental models of political decisions in sport). Helsingfors: University of Helsinki, Institute of Sociology. 50 pp.

4469. Heinilä, K. 1972. Survey of the value orientation of Finnish sport leaders. *IRSS* 7,1:111–117.

4470. Heinilä, K. 1979. The value orientations of Finnish sport leaders. *IRSS* 14,3–4:59–74.

4471. Henderson, J.O. 1973. Professionalized attitudes of volunteer coaches toward playing a game. *IRSS* 8,2:77–87.

4472. Holló, Z. 1939–1940. Társadalmi sportszövetségek és egyesületek ügyvitele (Administration of sport associations and clubs). *Testnevelés* 12: 856–877, 964–985. 13:39–70,138–149.

4473. Hoyle, E. 1971. Organization theory and the sociology of sport. Pp. 82–93 in Albonico/Pfister-Binz.

4474. Hrandek, R.A. 1958. Beiträge zur Kenntnis des Wiener Vereinslebens. *Österreichische Zeitschrift für Volkskunde* 61,3:205–219.

4475. Hughes, W.C. 1944. *Sports: Their Organization and Administration.* New York: Barnes.

4476. Isomur, E. 1964. Olympic Tokyo taikai no shakaigakuteki kosatsu (Sociological consideration on the Tokyo Olympic games). *JOPHER* (Tokyo) 14,10:553–555.

4477. Ivanov, L.V. and I.I. Pereverzin. 1973. Sportivnaja programma pjatiletki (Sport programme of the 5-year plan). *Fizicheskaja Kultura i sport* 79.

4478. Jansen, O.J.A. 1966. Sport en sportbeoefening in sociologisch perspectief (Sport and sport activity in sociological view). *Sportcahiers* 1,1:22–33.

4479.   Johnson, A.T. 1978. Public sport policy. *American Behavioral Scientist*
        21,3:319-344.
4480.   Kageyama, K. et al. 1971. The social factors affecting the formation and
        development of baseball team in the community. *Research J.Phys.Ed.*
        (Tokyo) 16,6:309-318.
4481.   Kapitan, B. 1974. Sport i turystyka w polityce rozwoju spolecznego
        (Sports and tourism in development policy). *Nowe Drogi* (Warsaw)
        28,1:47-60.
4482.   Kiviaho, P. 1973. *Sport Organizations and the Structure of Society.*
        Report no. 4 Jyväskylä: University of Jyväskylä.
4483.   Kiviaho, P. 1973. *Contextual analytical study about environmental effect
        on organization membership and the choice of organization.* Report no
        2. University of Jyvškylä. Also 1976. *IRSS* 11,1:17-35.
4484.   Komuku, H. 1972. Meijiki ni okeru gakkō undōbu no henyō ni kansuru
        kenkyu (A research study of the changing process of university sport
        clubs in Meiji era). *Research Bulletin Phys.Educ.Tokyo Metropolitan
        University* 4.
4485.   Krout, J.A. 1929. *Annuals of American Sport.* New Haven, Conn.: Yale
        University Press. 360 pp.
4486.   Kulinkovich, K.A. 1963. Programma KPSS i voprosy rasvitija fizicheskogo
        dvizhenija (The CPSU programme and problems of the development of
        physical culture movement). *Nauka-sportu* (Minsk) 3-11.
4487.   Kumeno, Y. et al. 1965. Undobu tokuni kokoundobu no genjo to mondai
        (The present situation and problems in sport clubs in high school).
        Research J.Phys.Educ. 10,1:314-319.
4488.   Laskiewicz, H. 1962. Zadania i postawy ideowo-wychowawcze rovotniczej
        kultury fizycznej na lamach prasz komunistycznej i lewicowej w Polsce
        w latach 1918-1927 (Worker's movement in the field of physical culture
        and its ideological and educational task and basis in the columns of the
        communist and the leftwing press in Poland in the years 1918-1927).
        Roczniki Naukowe AWF (Warsaw) 1:310-315.
4489.   Laskiewicz, H. 1966. Dzialanosc Zwiazku Zawodowego Pracownikow
        Kolejowych w zakresie kultury fizycznej w latach 1918-1964 (The
        activity of the railroaders in the field of physical education in the years
        1918-1964). *Sport Robotniczy. Sport i Turystyka* (Warsaw) 3:70-110.
4490.   Laskiewicz, H. 1968. Niektóre problemy robotniczej kultury fizycnej
        (Selected problems of the workers' physical culture). *Wychowanie
        Fizyczne i Sport* 1:87-101.
4491.   Laskiewicz, H. 1970. Workers' sports and the Olympic games. *Wychowanie
        Fizyczne i Sport* 1:25-34.
4492.   Latten, W. 1933-34. Bürokratisierung im Sport. *Kölner Vierteljahrhefte
        für Soziologie* 12,3:297-304.
4493.   Leiper, J.M. 1976. The International Olympic Committee. Pp. 39-61 in
        P. Graham and H. Ueberhorst, eds. *The Modern Olympics.* Cornwall,
        N.Y.: Leisure Press.
4494.   Lenk, H. 1962. Sportverein—eine Brücke zur Öffentlichkeit. *Olympisches
        Feuer* 12,12:6-7.
4495.   Lenk, H. 1966. Zur Soziologie des Sportvereins. Pp. 253-314 in Ham-
        burger Turnerschaft von 1816, ed. *Der Verein.* Stuttgart: Hofmann.

4496. Lenk, H. 1966. Total or partial engagement? Changes regarding the personal ties with the sports club. *IRSS* 1:85–107.

4497. Lenk, H. 1972. *Materialien zur Soziologie des Sportvereins.* Ahrensburg: Czwalina. 147 pp.

4498. Leonard, W.M. and S. Schmidt. 1975. Observation on the changing social organization of collegiate and professional basketball. *Sport Sociology Bulletin* 4,2:13–35.

4499. Lowenfish, L.E. 1978. Tale of many cities: the westward expansion of major league baseball in the 1950's. *Journal of the West* 17,July:71–82.

4500. Lucas, J.A. 1974. The modern Olympic Games: fanfare and philosophy, 1896–1972. *Quest* 22:6–18.

4501. Lüschen, G. 1974. Policy-making in sport organizations and their executive personnel: a proposal for a cross-national project. Pp. 387–382 in M. Archer, ed. *Current Research in Sociology.* Mouton: The Hague.

4502. Lüschen, G. 1977. Die nationalen Wächter Olympias. Pp. 165–175 in H. Lenk, ed. *Handlungsmuster Leistungssport.* Schorndorf: Hofmann.

4503. Lüschen, G. 1979. Organization and policy making in National Olympic Committees. *IRSS* 14,2:5–20.

4504. Mandell, R.D. 1976. The modern Olympic Games: a bibliographical essay. *Sportwissenschaft* 1:89–98.

4505. Manders, W.M. and J.A. Kropman. *Kader behoefte bij sportverenigingen* (Personell needs of sport clubs). Nijmegen: Institut von Toegepaste Sociologie. 487 pp.

4506. Marsh, A.W. 1930. Athletics. Pp. 296–300 in E.R.A. Seligman, ed. *Encyclopedia of the Social Science.* London: Macmillan. vol. 2.

4507. Miermans, C.G.M. 1966. Het verschijnsel sport in organisatorisch perspektief (sport under organizational aspects). *Sportcahiers* 1:52–66.

4508. Misev, D. 1964. *Meet the Olympians.* Sofia: Medicine and Physical Culture Publishing House. 400 pp.

4509. Mlodzikowski, G. 1973. Filozoficzne i ideologiczne uwarunkowanie spolecznej doktryny neoolimpizmu (Philosophical and ideological determinants of the social doctrine of the neo-olympic idea). Pp. 29–55 in Z. Krawczyk. *Sport w spolczenstwie wspolczesnym.* Warsaw: PWN.

4510. Moriarty, D. et al. 1976. Change agent research: combining organizational development and organizational research. *Sport Sociology Bulletin* 5,1: 37–42.

4511. Nault, L.P. 1978. Canadian amateur hockey by the year 2000: projected problems and priority goals. *IRSS* 1,13:29–38.

4512. Nitsch, F. 1976. Warum entstand nach 1945 keine Arbeitersportbewegung? *Sportwissenschaft* 6,2:172–199.

4513. Niwa, T. and C. Higashiyama. 1967. Kihan keisei no kengen karamita undobu no kozo no kento (Examination of the structure in terms of the competence of decision of the norm and the goal in athletic club) *Research J.Phys.Educ.* (Tokyo) 12,2:8–16.

4514. Niwa, T. 1968. Undōbuin no seiinseikensa no sakusei (An attempt to construct a group membership test of the athletic club members). *Research J.Phys.Educ.* (Tokyo) 13,1:13–20.

4515. Oglesby, C. 1974. Social conflict theory and sport organization systems. *Quest* 22:63–73.

4516.   Osmulski, T. 1960. Spoleczno-organizacyjne aspekty kultury fizycznej
        w powiecie grojeckim (Social and administrative aspects of physical
        culture in Grojec district). *Kultura Fizyczna* 11:818–821.
4517.   Patrikksson, G. 1973. *Idrottens historia i sociologisk belysning* (Sport
        history in sociological view). Stockholm: Utbildningsförlaget. 128 pp.
4518.   Pereverzin, I. 1972. Prognozirovanie i planirovanie fizicheskoj kultury i
        sporta (Forecasting and planning of physical culture and sports). Mos-
        cow. 92 pp.
4519.   Petek, L. 1970. Klub sportowy jako srodowisko wychowawcza (Sport
        club as educational environment). *Roczniki Naukowe, Wyzxza Szkola
        Wychowanie Fizycznego Krakow* 9:263–308.
4520.   Petrak, B. 1971. Beitrag zu den Fragen der Bürokratie und des Büro-
        kratismus im Sport. Pp. 78–81 in Albonico/Pfister-Binz.
4521.   Pidoux, F. 1972. *Vers une politique de promotion sportive.* Basel: Birk-
        häuser. 70 pp.
4522.   Rigauer, B. 1972. Der programmierte Sport. Pp. 28–49 in A. Natan, ed.
        Sport—kritisch. Stuttgart: Hallwag.
4523.   Rigauer, B. 1972. Leistungssport als Arbeitsleistung. Zur gesellschaftlichen
        Dialektik sportspezifischer Leistung. Pp. 60–74, 140–142 in J. Richter,
        ed. *Die vertrimmte Nation.* Rowohlt: Reinbeck.
4524.   Riordan, J.W. 1969. The Olympic Games and Soviet society. *Anglo-Soviet
        J.* 29:7–15.
4525.   Riordan, J.W. 1972. The development of football in Russia and the
        U.S.S.R. *New Zealand Slavonic J.* 1,9:61–72. 2,10:114–131.
4526.   Röblitz, G. 1960. Zur gesellschaftlichen und psychologischen Grundlage
        der Aufgabe, die sportliche Betätigung als Lebensbedürfnis zu entwick-
        keln. *Wissensch.Zeitschr DHFK* 3,1–2:113–119.
4527.   Rücker, H. 1954. Vergleichende Untersuchungen über die Bundesjugend-
        spiele an ausgewählten Stadt- und Landschulen in Niedersachsen. *Sport-
        medizin* 5,4:553–555.
4528.   Sage, G.H. 1973. The coach as management: organizational leadership in
        American sport. *Quest* 19,Jan.:35–40.
4529.   Saito, S. and T. Azuma. 1958. Sykaitaiiku no hokosei no kansuru kenkyu
        (A study on the direction with proof of social physical education).
        Junetendo University Bulletin Health Phys.Educ. (Tokyo) 1,1.
4530.   Saito, S. and Y. Kitamori. 1971. Chyutosi ni okeru taiiku recreation—
        Keikaku sakutei no kizyun ni kansuru kenkyu ito (An experimental
        study of the method of establishing criteria for the basic planning of
        physical education and recreation-programs in middle-size urban com-
        munities). *Juntendo University Bulletin Health and Phys. Educ.* (Tokyo)
        15.
4531.   Saito, S. 1971–72. Chiiki no okeru taiiku sport jinko no keikakuka ni
        kansuru kenkyu ni ichijirei ni tsuite (A study on the basic planning of
        physical education, sports in urban communities). *J.Leisure Recreation
        Studies* (Tokyo) 1 and 2.
4532.   Sargent, D.A. 1910. History of the administration of intercollegiate ath-
        letics in the United States. *American Phys.Educ.Rev.* 15:252–261.
4533.   Savage, H.J. 1927. *Games and Sports in British Schools and Universities.*
        New York: Carnegie Foundation. 252 pp.

4534. Savage, H.J. et al. 1929. *American College Athletics.* New York: Carnegie Foundation. 383 pp.

4535. Savage, H.J. et al. 1931. *Current Development in American College Athletics.* New York: Carnegie Foundation. 58 pp.

4536. Scheuch, E.K. 1972. Der Sport in einer sich wandelnden Gesellschaft. Pp. 7–29 in *Jahrbuch des Sports.* Frankfurt: Limpert.

4537. Scheuch, E.K. 1972. Politikum Sport. Internationale und nationale Perspektiven. *Die Politische Meinung* 17,143:15–27.

4538. Schlagenhauf, K. and W. Timm. 1976. The sport club as a social organization. *IRSS* 11,2:9–30.

4539. Schlagenhauf, K. and J. Schiffer. 1979. The German and the Swiss club. *IRSS* 14,3–4:75–86.

4540. Seehase, G. ed. 1967. *Der Verein. Standort—Aufgabe—Funktion in Sport und Gesellschaft.* Schorndorf: Hofmann. 314 pp.

4541. Seppänen, P. 1967. *Liikunnan suunittelun sosiaaliset edellytykset* (Social conditions of planning in sport and physical activities). Helsinki: University of Helsinki, Institute of Sociology. 70 pp.

4542. Shneidman, N.N. 1978. *The Soviet Road to Olympus.* Toronto: Ontario Institute for Studies in Education. 180 pp.

4543. Smith, D.H. 1966. A psychological model of participation in formal organizations. *AJS* 72,3:249–266.

4544. Stern, R.N. 1979. The development of an interorganizational control network: the care of intercollegiate athletics. *Administrative Science Quarterly* 24,2:242–266.

4545. Sveriges Riksidrottsförbund. 1953. Svensk Idrott (Swedish sport). Malmö: Allhem. 591 pp.

4546. Takemura, A. and Niwa, T. 1968. Undobu no morale no kenkyu (1) (A study on the morale of athletic club (1)). *Research J.Phys.Educ.* 12,2: 77–83.

4547. Takenoshita, K. 1964. Kokutai-senshu no shakaiteki haikei (Sociological analysis of representative players in national sport festival). *JOPHER* (Tokyo) 14,6:347–350.

4548. Theberge, N. and J. Loy. 1976. Replacement processes in sport organizations: the case of professional baseball. *IRSS* 11,2:73–93.

4549. Troeger, W. 1965. Die Organisation des deutschen Sports. Pp. 44–59 in U. Schultz, ed. *Das grosse Spiel. Aspekt des Sports in unserer Zeit.* Frankfurt: Fischer.

4550. USSR 2nd Conference. 1973. *Materialy po istorii, organizacii i sociologii fizicheskoj kultury* (Materials on the history, organization and sociology of physical culture). II Respublikanskaja konferencija, posvjashchjennaja 50–letiju obrazovanija SSSR. Tashkent. 259 pp.

4551. Veen, P. 1969. *Meebeslissen. Een veldexperiment in een hockey club* (Participation in decision making. A field experiment in a hockey club). Utrecht: van Gorcum. 347 pp.

4552. Voronova, K.A. 1972. Racionalnaja struktura rabochego vremeni rukovodjashchih kadrov komitetov po fizicheskoj kulture i sportu (A rational structure of working time of the executives of sport commitee). *Teorija i Praktika* 1:53–56.

4553. Wheeler, R.F. 1978. Organized sport and organized labor: the workers'

sport movement. *J.Contemporary History* 13,April:191–210.
4554.   Wohl, A. 1967. 50 lat kultury fizycznej w ZSRR (The quingentory of physical culture in USSR). *Kultura Fizyczna* 11:497–505.
4555.   Wright, C.R. and H.H. Hymans. 1958. Voluntary association memberships of American adults. *ASR* 23,3:284–294.
4556.   Wurzbacher, G. 1963. Der Verein in der freien Gesellschaft. Pp. 5–14 in Deutscher Sportbund, ed. *Verein als Träger der deutschen Turn- und Sportbewegung.* Dortmund: Deutscher Sportubund.
4557.   Zetterberg, H. 1959. *Voluntary Organizations and Organized Power in Sweden.* New York: Columbia University, Bureau of Applied Social Research.
4558.   Zouabi, M. 1975. Physical education and sport in Tunisia. *IRSS* 10,3–4: 109–114.

5. *Sport Careers; Amateurism/Professionalism: Professionalization*

4559.   Akiyoshi, Y. 1972. Recreation shidosha ni kansuru kenkyu (A study of recreation leaders). *J.Leisure Recreation Studies* (Tokyo) 2.
4560.   Albinson, J.G. 1973. Professionalized attitudes of volunteer coaches toward playing a game. *IRSS* 8,2:77–88.
4561.   Anonymous. 1970. The balance of power in professional sports. *Maine Law Review* 22,2:1–14.
4562.   Ball, D. 1974. Replacement processes in work organization: professional football *Soc.Work Occupations* 1,2:197–217.
4563.   Ball, D. 1976. Failure in sport. *ASR* 41,4:726–739.
4564.   Beise, D. 1940. A comparative analysis of the physical education background, interest and desires of college students as an evaluation process. *Research Quarterly* 11,2:120–134.
4565.   Bernáth, J. 1909–1910. Amatör és professzionista (Amateur and professional). *Tornaügy* (Budapest) 27,17:263–266.
4566.   Blödorn, M. 1974. *Fussballprofis—die Helden der Nation.* Hamburg: Hoffmann und Campe. 186 pp.
4567.   Boersma, J. 1975. Arbeitspositie van professional voetballers (Work position of professional soccer players). *Sociaal Maandblad Arbeid* (The Hague) 30,11:689–698.
4568.   Börner, L. 1972. *Berufssportler als Arbeitnehmer.* Darmstadt: Stoytscheff.
4569.   Carik, A.V. 1970. K voprosu o prezhdevremennom uchode sportrsmenov iz sporta (The premature retirement of athletes from sport). Pp. 13–15 in *Voprosy teorii i praktiki fizicheskoj kultury i sporta.* Minsk.
4570.   Charnofsky, H. 1968. The Major League professional baseball player: self-conception versus the popular image. *IRSS* 3,1:39–55.
4571.   Daymont, T.N. 1975. The effects of monopsonistic procedures on equality of competition in professional sport leagues. *IRSS* 10,2:83–100.
4572.   DuWors, R.E. 1971. The amateur athlete as a source of understanding a society. *Philosophia* (Barcelona) 189–207.
4573.   Faulkner, R.R. 1974. Coming of age in organizations: a comparative study of career contingencies and adult socialization. *Sociol.Work Occupations* 1,2:131–173.

4574. Faulkner, R.R. 1975. Coming of age in organizations: a comparative study of career contingencies of musicians and hockey players. Pp. 525–558 in Ball/Loy.

4575. Funk, I.B. 1973. K voprosu obshchestvennogo pretizha trenerskoj raboty (The problem of social prestige of work of coaches) Pp. 63–66 in *Konferencija po problemam nauchnyh osnov organizacii sovetskogo dobrovolnogo fizkulturnogo dvizhenija*. Tartu.

4576. Furukawa, M. 1955. Sports ni okeru amateurism (Amateurism in sport) *Bulletin Education Faculty Kumamoto University* 3:106–113.

4577. Fuse, Y. 1971 and 1973. Kindai Beikoku sport no hatten to amateur kihan (Amateurism as a social institution in England and USA). *Bulletin Department General Education Tokyo Medical University* 1 and 3.

4578. Gamson, W.A. and N.A. Scotch. 1964. Scapegoating in baseball. *AJS* 70,1:69–76. With a reply by O. Grusky.

4579. Gowling, A. 1973. The place of luck in the professional footballer's life. In D. Weir, ed. *Men and Work in Modern Britain*. London: Fontana.

4580. Gregory, F.M. 1956. *The Baseball Player: An Economic Study*. Washington, D.C.: Public Affairs Press. 213 pp.

4581. Grusky, O. 1963. Managerial succession and organizational effectiveness. *AJS* 69,1:21–31.

4582. Grusky, O. 1963. The effects of formal structure on managerial recruitment. A study of baseball organization. *Sociometry* 26,3:345–353.

4583. Gutowski, J. 1972. The art of professional wrestling: folk expression in mass culture. *Pennsylvania Folklore Society* 1,2:41–50.

4584. Haerle, R.K. 1975. Career patterns and career contingencies of professional baseball players: an occupational analysis. Pp. 461–519 in Ball/Loy.

4585. Hammerich, K. 1972. Berufskarrieren im Spitzensport. *Sportwissenschaft* 2,2:168–181.

4586. Harper, D.D. and J. Hammon. 1977. The hypocrisy of amateurism. *Quest* 27:121–131.

4587. Heinilä, K. 1964. Tyytyväiset ja tyytymättömät voimistelunopettajat (The professional dissatisfaction of physical education teachers). *Stadion* (Helsinki) 1–2:3–17.

4588. Heinilä, K. 1973. Citius, altius, fortius: the Olympic contribution to the professionalization of sport? Pp. 351–355 in Grupe.

4589. Hendry, L.B. 1972. The physical education profession. *Education Today* 22,1:30–40.

4590. Hendry, L.B. 1975. Survival in a marginal role: the professional identity of the physical education teacher. *Brit.J.Sociol.* 26,4:465–476.

4591. Hill, P, and B. Lowe. 1974. The inevitable metathesis of the retiring athlete. *IRSS* 9,3–4:5–32.

4592. Hoyle, E. 1969. The role of the physical educationalist in contemporary society. *Bulletin Physical Education* (Liverpool) 7,6:7–12.

4593. Isaacs, S. 1964. *Careers and Opportunities in Sport*. New York: Dutton.

4594. Jackson, J.J. and B. Lowe. 1978. *Sport as a Career*. CAHPER Monograph. Calgary: University of Calgary. 88 pp.

4595. Janssen van Raaj, J.L. 1970. Beroepsvoetbal (Professional soccer). *Sociaal Maandblad Arbeid* (The Hague) 25,7–8:463–472.

4596. Jaworski, Z. 1974. Some phenomena connected with the employment of graduates of academies of physical education. *IRSS* 9,3-4:117-133.

4597.   Jones, F.E. and F.L. 1972. Occupational prestige in Australia and Canada: a comparison and validation of some occupational scales. *Australian and New Zealand J.Sociology* 8,June:75-82.

4598.   Jones, K.G. 1975. Developments in amateurism and professionalism in early 20th Century Canadian sport. *J.Sport History* 2,1:29-40.

4599.   Jung, A. 1956. De la désaffection de l'éducation physique dans les grandes classes. *L'Education physique* (Brussels) 48,3:31-35.

4600.   Karolczak, B. 1965. Profil kariery sportowej zawodnika (Profile of the athletic career of the competitor. A demographic analysis). *Kultura Fizyczna* 18,5:279-285.

4601.   Kaufman, M. and H. 1972. Henry Bergh, Kit Burns, and the sportsmen of New York. *New York Folklore Quarterly* 28,1:15-29.

4602.   Keating, J.W. 1972. Paradoxes in American sport and athletics. Pp. 17-29 in A. Flath, ed. *Athletics in America.* Corvallis, Ore.:Oregon State University Press.

4603.   Kenyon, G.S. 1965. Certain psychosocial and cultural characteristics unique to prospective teachers of physical education. *Research Quarterly* 36,1:105-112.

4604.   Kenyon, G.S. 1973. Careers in sport: patterns of role progression Pp. 359-365 in Grupe.

4605.   Korr, C.P. 1978. West Ham United football club and the beginning of professional football in East London. *J.Contemp.History* 13,April:211-232.

4606.   Krawczyk, B. 1963. Z badan nad aspicjami zawodowymi i wzorami kariery zawodewej studentow AWF (Professional aspiration and preferences of students of physical education academy). *Kultura Fizycznego* 16,3-4:237-241.

4607.   Krawczyk, B. 1964. Stocunek do zawodu kandykatow na studia i studentow AWF (Professional attitudes of candidates and students of academy of physical education). *Roczniki Naukowe AWF* 3:279-301.

4608.   Krawczyk, B. 1965. *Plany zyciowe i preferencje zawodowe absolwentow AWF* (Plans and occupational preferences of graduates of academy of physical education). Warsaw: Miedzyuczelniany Zaklad Badan nad Szkolnictwem Wyzszym.

4609.   Krawczyk, B. 1965. Przebieg procesow selekcij kandyato w na studia AWF w roku 1962-63 (Selection process of candidates for study at academy of physical educuation). *Roczniki Naukowe AWF* 4:267-284.

4610.   Krawczyk, B. 1965. *Spoleczne czynniki woboru Studiow wychowania fizycznego* (The social factors of selection of physical education studies). Warsaw: Miedzyuczelniany Zaklad Badan nad Szkolnictwen Wyzszym.

4611.   Krawczyk, B. 1966. Der Einfluss von Kameradschaftsgruppen auf die Einstellungen von Studenten. Pp. 251-253 in Lüschen.

4612.   Krawczyk, B. 1969. Spoleczny stereotyp zawodu trenera (The social image of the profession of coach). *Sport Wycznowy* (Warsaw) 7:1-6.

4613.   Krawczyk, B. 1973. Spoleczne wartosci kariery sportowej (Social values of the sports career). *Sport Wyczynowy* (Warsaw) 1:1-7.

4614.   Krawczyk, Z. 1973. System of education of the physical education teachers in Poland as the object of sociological research. *IRSS* 8,1: 121-125.

4615.   Krawczyk, Z. 1974. The profession of the physical education instructor.

IRSS 9,3-4:117-134.

4616. Krawczyk, Z. 1976. The social position of professional specialization in physical culture. *IRSS* 11,1:5-15.

4617. Krawczyk, B. 1977. The social origin and ambivalent character of the ideology of amateur sport. *IRSS* 12,3:35-49.

4618. Lüschen, G. 1973. Careers in sport. Pp. 358-359 in Grupe.

4619. Massengale, J.D. and S.R. Farrington. 1977. The influence of playing position centrality on the careers of college football coaches. *Review Sport Leisure* 2:107-115.

4620. Mihovilovic, M.A. 1968. The status of former sportsmen. *IRSS* 3,1:73-96.

4621. Milshtein, O.A. 1972. Obraz zhizni sportsmena kak sociologiches-kaja problema (The athlete's career as a sociological research problem) *Teorija i Praktika* 2:72-73.

4622. Mogull, R.G. 1975. Salary discrimination in major league baseball. *Review Black Political Economy* 5,3:269-279.

4623. Morikawa, S. 1977. Amateurism—Yesterday, today and tomorrow. *IRSS* 12,2:61-72.

4624. Morikawa, S. 1979. Fundamental problems in studies on amateur sport. Introduction to theories on 'sports labor.' *IRSS* 14,1:21-50.

4625. McPherson, B.D. 1976. Involuntary turnover: a characteristic process of sport organizations. *IRSS* 11,4:5-16.

4626. Ponomarev, N.I. 1951. Klassovaja sushchnost professionalizma i 'ljubitel-stva' v burzhuaznom sporte (Social class in professionalism and ama-teurism of Bourgeois sport). *Avtoreferat dissertacii pedagogicheskih nauk.* Moscow: 28.

4627. Pooley, J.C. 1975. The professional socialization of physical education students in the United States and England. *IRSS* 10,3-4:97-107.

4628. Roadburg, A. 1976. Is professional football a profession? *IRSS* 11,3:27-38.

4629. Ross, G.N. 1975. Determination of bonuses in professional sport. *American Economist* 19,2:43-46.

4630. Roth, A. 1971. Reflexions sur le sport. *Studia Universitatis* (Cluj) 16:73-80.

4631. Krawczyk, B. 1966. Attitude toward studies and professional aspirations of the students of the Academy of Physical Education. *IRSS* 1:195-208.

4632. Rychta, T. 1963. Badania na preferencijami zawodowymi w zakresie wychowania fizycznego i sportu (A study of professional preferences in physical education and sport). *Roczniki Naukowe AWF* 2:229-259.

4633. Sack, A.L. 1973. Yale 29-Harvard 4: the professionalization of college football *Quest* 19, Winter.

4634. Sack, A.L. and R. Thiel. 1979. College football and social mobility: a case study of Notre Dame Football players. *Sociol.Education* 52,Jan.: 60-66.

4635. Sage, G.H. 1975. An occupational analysis of the college coach. Pp. 395-455 in Ball/Loy.

4636. Sage, G.H. and J.W. Loy. 1978. Geographical mobility patterns of college coaches. *Urban Life* 7,2:253-277.

4637. Saito, N. 1960. Sports ni okeru amateurism no kosatsu (A study of ama-teurism in sport). *Bulletin Tokyo Teachers College* 5:9-22.

4638. Saunders, E.D. 1969. The role of the teacher. *Scottish Bulletin Physical Education* 7,2.

4639.   Scott, H.A. 1929. *Personnel Study of Directors of Physical Education.*
         New York: Columbia University. 90 pp.

4640.   Scoville, J. 1974. Labor relations in sports. Pp. 185–220 in Noll.

4641.   Sloane, P.J. Restriction of competition in professional team sports. *Bul-
         letin Economic Research* 44,3:330–339.

4642.   Smith, G.J. 1976. A study of a sports journalist. *IRSS* 11,3:5–26.

4643.   Snyder, E.E. 1973. Aspects of social and political values of high school
         coaches. *IRSS* 8,3–4:73–87.

4644.   Stebbins, R.A. 1977. The amateur: two sociological definitions. *Pacif.Soc.
         Review* 20,Oct.:582–606.

4645.   Sugawara, R. 1972. The study of top sportsmen in Japan. *IRSS* 7,1:45–68.

4646.   Talaga, J. 1971. An attempt to define the social position of football
         instructors and coaches in Poland. *IRSS* 6,1:125–152.

4647.   Tokunaga, M. and S. Arai. 1974. Gakusei no taiikujitsugi ni taisuru taido-
         henyo to sono yion—dai 2 ho (Changes in attitudes of college students
         toward physical education activities and contributing factors). *Research
         J.Phys.Educ.* 18,5:287–295.

4648.   Voigt, D. 1973. Die Soziologie in der Lehrer und Sportlehrerausbildung.
         Gymnasion 10,3:26–28 and 33–40.

4649.   Volkamer, M. 1967 and 1970. Zur Sozialpsychologie des Leibeserziehers.
         Die Leibeserziehung 16,12:404–410. 19,4:122–126.

4650.   Vuolle, P. 1977. Huippu-urheilun elamanura tutkimuksen kohteena (The
         career of the top athlete). *Stadion* (Helsinki) 14,4:129–131.

4651.   Weinberg, S.K. and H. Arond. 1952. The occupational culture of the
         boxer. *AJS* 57,5:460–469. Also 1971 pp. 285–300 in Dunning. *German*
         1976 pp. 253–260 in Lüschen/Weis.

4652.   Wilde, M.de. 1974. Le 'prof. de gym,' professeur principal? *l'Ecole des
         parents* (Paris) 4:19–28.

4653.   Wise, G.L. and M.K. Cox. 1978. Policy questions loom on the horizon
         as the consumer confronts selected aspects of major league baseball.
         American Behavioral Scientist 21,3:451–464.

4654.   Wohl, A. 1957. Jezcze raz w sprawie amatorstwa i zawodowstwa (Once
         more about amateurs and professionals in sport). *Kultura Fizyczna*
         10,1:552–560.

4655.   Woody, T. 1938. Professionalism and the decay of Greek athletics. *School
         and Society* 47,April:521–528.

4656.   Ziemilski, A. 1973. Satysfacja ludzi sukcesu sporzowego (Competitiors—
         their success and satisfactions). Pp. 251–277 in Z. Krawczyk, ed. *Sport
         w spoleczenstwie.* Warsaw: PWN.

4657.   Zuchara, K. 1971. Wzor osobowy trenera w swietle roznic pokoleniowych
         (Personality patterns of a coach in light of generation differences). *Sport
         Wyczynowy* (Warsaw) 3:20–27.

4658.   Zukowska, Z. 1975. Cultural and social activity of teachers of physical
         education. *IRSS* 10,1:109–116.

6. Collective Behavior, Spectatorship and Ritual

4659.   Baumann, N. 1974. Typische Verhaltensweisen der Zuschauer bei sport-
         lichen Grossereignissen. *Leistungssport* 4,4:298–300.

4660.   Beisser, A. 1972. *The Madness in Sports.* New York: Appleton-Century-Crofts.
4661.   Borhegyi, S. 1960. America's ballgame. *Natural History* 69,1:48–58.
4662.   Brill, A.A. 1929. The why of the fan. *North American Review* 228,4: 429–434.
4663.   Burkhardt, V.R. 1954. *Chinese Creeds and Customs.* Hongkong: South China Morning Post. 181 pp.
4664.   Cheffers, J. et al. 1976. Sports spectator behavior assessment by techniques of behavior analysis. *Int.J.Sport Psychology* 7,1:1–13.
4665.   Cheska, A.T. 1978. Sports spectacular: the social ritual of power. *Quest* 30,Summer:58–71.
4666.   Cheska, A.T. 1979. Sport spectacular: a ritual model of power. *IRSS* 14,2: 51–72.
4667.   Ciampi, A. 1972. Nuovi aspetti del consumo dello spettacolo in Italia (New aspects of consumption and spectatorship). *Spettacolo* 22,2: 77–96.
4668.   Ciupak, Z. 1970. Kulturni elementu na sportnata publuka (Cultural elements among sport spectators). Pp. 93–102 in *Medica i Fizkultura.* Sofia.
4669.   Ciupak, Z. 1970. Widownia sportowa/Komentarz socjologiczny (Sports audience). *Kultura Fizyczna* (Warsaw) 7:290–295.
4670.   Ciupak, Z. 1973. Sport spectators—an attempt at a sociological analysis. *IRSS* 8,2:89–101.
4671.   Ciupak, Z. 1973. Widownia sportowa (The sport audience). Pp. 317–333 in Z. Krawczyk, ed. *Sport w spoleczenstwie wspolczesnym.* Warsaw: PWN.
4672.   Cohen, M.R. 1946. *The Faith of a Liberal.* New York: Holt. 497 pp.
4673.   Deegan, M. and M. Stein. 1978. American drama and ritual: Nebraska football. *IRSS* 13,3:31–44.
4674.   Fox, J.R. 1961. Pueblo baseball: a new use for old witchcraft. *J.American Folklore* 74,1:9–16. *German* 1976 pp. 190–200 in Lüschen/Weis.
4675.   Freischlag, J. and D. Hardin. The effects of social class and school achievement on the composition of sport crowds. *Sport Sociology Bulletin* 4,2:36–46.
4676.   Geblewicz, E. 1960. Uwagi o psychologii widza sportowego (Remarks about the psychology of a sport spectator). *Wychowanie Fizycne i Sport* 4:409–413.
4677.   Gini, C. 1939. Rural ritual games in Lybia. *Rural Sociology* 4,3:283–299.
4678.   Harrold, R. et al. 1972. *The Student as a Sports Spectator.* Minneapolis: University of Minnesota.
4679.   Hastorf, A.H. and H. Cantril. 1954. They saw a game: a case study. *J. Abnormal Soc.Psychology* 44,2:129–134.
4680.   Herrmann, H. 1977. *Die Fussballfans.* Schorndorf: Hofmann. 117 pp.
4681.   Hill, A.H. 1952. Some Kilantan games-entertainments. *Royal Asian Society Malayan Branch* 25,1:20–34.
4682.   Howard, G.E. 1912. Social psychology of the spectator. *AJS* 18,1:33–50.
4683.   Howarth, P. 1973. *Play Up and Play the Game: The Heroes of Popular Fiction.* London: Eyre-Meuthuen.
4684.   Hunt, W. 1955. On bullfighting. *American Imago* 12,4:343–353.
4685.   Ingham, A. and M. Smith. 1974. Social implications of the interaction

between spectator and athletes. *Exercise Sport Sciences Review* 2,2: 189–220.

4686. Iso-Ahola, S. 1974. Social structure of spectator sport interest. *Research Report Nr.* 5. Jyväskylä: University of Jyväskylä.

4687. Ivanovskij, B. 1927. Boks kak zrelishche (Boxing as show). *Izvestija Fizicheskoj Kultury* 2:1–2.

4688. Kampf, L. 1977. Course on spectator sport. *College English* 38,8:835–842.

4689. Klapp, O. 1962. *Heroes, Villains, and Fools.* Englewood Cliffs: Prentice-Hall.

4690. Kenyon, G.S. 1969. Sport involvement: a conceptual go and some consequences thereof. Pp. 77–100 in G. Kenyon, ed. *Sociology of Sport.* Chicago: Athletic Institute.

4691. Lang, G.E. 1976. Der Ausbruch von Tumulten bei Sportveranstaltungen. Pp. 273–295 in Lüschen/Weis.

4692. McPhail, C. and D.L. Miller. 1973. The assembling process. *ASR* 38,6: 721–735.

4693. Oktavek, F.L. 1933. Spectator sports. *Recreation* 27,Oct.:320–322 and 347.

4694. Peterson, R. 1972. Audiences and all that Jazz. Pp. 55–73 in G. Stone, ed. *Games, Sport and Power.* New Brunswick, N.J.: Transaction Books.

4695. Petryszak, N. 1978. Spectator sports as an aspect of popular culture. *J.Sport Behavior* 1,Feb.:14–27.

4696. Pilz, G. 1973. Zur Frage der Motivation im Schausport. *Jugend und Sport* (Magglingen) 30,5:166–169.

4697. Popplow, U. 1955. Sportzeitschriften-soziologisch gesehen. *Olympisches Feuer* 5,11:7–11.

4698. Quas, H. 1966. Die Sozialstruktur des Grazer Sportpublikums. *Leibesübungen-Leibeserziehung* (Vienna) 20,5:3–6.

4699. Rodichenko, V.S. 1973. Sportliche Wettkämpfe als soziale Erscheinung. *Theorie und Praxis* 22,7:638–641.

4700. Rosenmayr, L. 1967. Sport as leisure activity of young people. *IRSS* 2,1:19–32.

4701. Rosenmayr, L. 1968. Der Sport als Freizeitaktivität von Jugendlichen. *Leibesübungen-Leibeserziehung* (Vienna) 22,8:1–6.

4702. Rosseau, E.L. 1958. Great American ritual: watching games. *Nation* 187,4:188–191.

4703. Schiffer, J. 1973. Soziologische Analyse des Schausports. *Jugend und Sport* (Magglingen) 30,5:170–175.

4704. Schwartz, B. and S. Barskey. 1977. The home advantage. *Social Forces* 55,3:641–662.

4705. Schwartz, J.M. 1973. Causes and effects of spectator sports. *IRSS* 8,3–4: 25–46.

4706. Silva, A.R. da. 1970. The role of the spectator in the soccer player's dynamics. Pp. 307–310 in G. Kenyon, ed. *Psychology of Sport.* Chicago: Athletic Institute.

4707. Singer, R.N. 1965. Effects of spectators on athletes and non-athletes performing a gross motor task. *Research Quarterly* 37,4:473–482.

4708. Snyder, E.E. 1975. *Sports: A Social Scoreboard.* Bowling Green, Ohio: Bowling Green State University Popular Press. 105 pp.

4709. Spettacolo. 1971. Dati statistici sullo spettacolo (Statistical data of spectator events). *Spettacolo* (Rome) 21,2:141–146 and 3:225–230.

4710. Spinrad, W. 1973. The sports fan in America. Pp. 419–421 in Grupe.

4711. Stone, G.P. and R.A. Oldenburg. 1967. Wrestling. Pp. 503–532 in R. Slovenko, and J. Knight, eds. *Motivations in Play, Games and Sports.* Springfield, Ill.: Thomas.

4712. Tunis, J.R. 1928. *Sports, Heroes and Hysterics.* New York: Day. 293 pp.

4713. Weaver, R.B. 1939. *Amusements and Sports in American Life.* Chicago: University of Chicago Press. 196 pp.

4714. Wecter, D. 1941. *The Hero in America.* New York: Scribner. 530 pp.

4715. Ziemilski, A. 1962. Psychologie trybun a spoleczenstwo mas (The psychology of the stadium and the society of masses). *Wychowanie Fizyczne i Sport* 3:363–371.

4716. Ziesmer, H. 1974. Phänomen ohne Wirklichkeit: Ein Kommentar zu H. Meyer. *Zeitschrift Soziologie* (Stuttgart) 3,1:99–101.

7. Attitudes, Motivation and Other Social-Psychological Variables

4717. Abel, G. and B.N. Knapp. 1967. The physical activity interests of secondary schoolgirls. *Bulletin Physical Education* 7.

4718. Abel, T.M. 1938. The influence of social facilitation on motor performance at different levels of intelligence. *American J.Psychology* 51,3: 379–388.

4719. Adler, Ł. and P.A. 1978. Role of momentum in sport. *Urban Life* 7,July: 153–176.

4720. Adzhemjan, S. et al. 1969. K voprosy o sportivnyh interesah uchashchihsja nekotoryh srednih shkol gorode Erevana (Sport interests of students in secondary schools of Erevan). Pp. 206–208 in *Konferencija po psychologii i sociologii sporta,* Tartu.

4721. Al-Talib, N. 1970. Effects of role playing on attitude change toward physical education courses. *Research Quarterly* 41,Dec:467–471.

4722. Alderman, R.B. 1970. A socio-psychological assessment of attitude toward physical activity in champion athletes. *Research Quarterly* 41,1:1–9.

4723. Andrews, J.C. 1971. Personality, sporting interest, and achievement. *Educational Review* 23,2:126–134.

4724. Antonelli, F. 1970. Psychological problems of top-level athletes. *Int.J. Sport Psychology* 1,1:34–39.

4725. Aronson, E. and J.M. Carlsmith. 1962. Performance expectancy as a determinant of actual performance. *J.Abnormal Soc.Psychology* 65,3: 178–182.

4726. Arvisto, M.A. Cennostnye orientacii kak metivacionnoe jadro sportivnoj dejatelnosti (Value orientations as motivation of sport activities). Pp. 164–166 in *Nauchnye trudy za 1970.* Moscow. Vol. 5.

4728. Bakonyi, F. 1959. A sportoló magatartása és külső vieslkedése (The athlete's attitude and his social behavior). *Sport és Tudomany* (Budapest) 3,8:16–17.

4729. Bakonyi, F. 1972. A sociálpszichológia kapcsolata a testneveléssel (Social

psychology and physical education). *Testneveles F. Tudomany Közl.*
1:145-150.

4730. Bala, G.S. 1975. The influence of primary social attitudes and normal
conative dimensions on the attitudes towards sport. *Gymnasion* 12,4:
26-35.

4731. Balazs, E. 1975. Psycho-social study of outstanding female athletes.
Research Quarterly 46,3:267-273.

4732. Ball, D.W. 1973. A politicized social psychology of sport: some assumptions and evidence from international figure skating competition. *IRSS*
8,3-4:63-72.

4733. Beisser, A.R. 1961. Psychodynamic observations of a sport. *Psychoanalysis
Psychoanal.Review* 48,1:69-76.

4734. Biddulph, L.G. 1954. Athletic achievement and the personal and social
adjustment of high school boys. *Research Quarterly* 25,1:1-7.

4735. Bojko, J.P. 1967. Sociologicheskie issledovanija voprosov fizicheskogo
vospitanija studentov pedagogicheskogo instituta (Sociological studies
concerning physical education among students of a college of education).
Teorija i Praktika 7:60-62.

4736. Borisova, L.G. and E.R. Podalko. Toward classification of motives. *IRSS*
10,3-4:45-60.

4737. Bouet, M. 1970. Aspects de la psychologie sociale du sport. *Int.J.Sport
Psychology* 1,2:105-116.

4738. Bruning, J.L. and D.R. Mettee. 1966. The effects of various social factors
on motivation in a competitive situation. *J.Social Psychology* 70,2:
295-297.

4739. Buggel, E. 1972. Grundgedanken zum Problem Sozialfaktoren und sportliche Leistung. *Theorie und Praxis* 21,12:1086-1088.

4740. Burch, W.R. 1965. The play world of camping: research into the social
meaning of outdoor recreation. *AJS* 70,5:604-612.

4741. Church, R.M. et al. 1968. Application of behavior theory to social psychology: imitation and competition. Pp. 135-168 in E.C. Simmel et al.
Social Facilitation and Imitative Behavior. Boston: Allyn and Bacon.

4742. Colby, K.M. 1953. Gentleman, the Queen. *Psychoanalytic Review* 40,2:
144-148.

4743. Cratty, B.J. and J.N. Sage. 1964. Effect of primary and secondary group
interaction upon improvement in a complex movement task. *Research
Quarterly* 35,2:265-274.

4744. Cratty, B.J. 1970. Coaching decisions and research in sport psychology.
Quest 13,1:46-53.

4745. Czikszentmihalyi, M. 1974. *Beyond Boredom and Anxiety.* San Francisco: Jossey-Bass. 320 pp.

4746. Dickinson, J. 1976. *A Behavioral Analysis of Sport.* London: Lepus.
134 pp.

4747. Dietz, H. 1968. *Sexus, Sport und geistiger Elan.* Berlin: Luchterhand.

4748. Doros, G. 1932. A sportmozgalom társadalmi lélektana (Social psychology
of sport movement). *Testnevelés* 5:8-10.

4749. Doros, G. 1943.[2] *A sport etikája és lélektana* (Ethics and psychology of
sport). Budapest: Stephaneum. 232 pp.

4750. Eichberg, H. 1974. Der Beginn des modernen Leistens. *Sportwissenschaft*
4,1:21-48.

4751. Ellis, M. 1973. *Why People Play.* Englewood Cliffs, N.J.: Prentice-Hall. 173 pp.

4752. Esprit. 1975. L'Education physique. *Esprit* (Paris) 5:641-928.

4753. Fielding, L. et al. 1976. The influence of spectator reaction and presence during training on performance. *Int.J.Sport Psych.* 7,2:73-81.

4754. Foot, N. 1951. Identification as the basis for a theory of motivation. *ASR* 16,1:15-16.

4755. Fournier, J. 1972. *l'animation sportive.* Paris: Les Editions Ouvrières. 206 pp.

4756. Gabler, H. 1972. *Leistungsmotivation im Hochleistungssport.* Schorndorf: Hofmann. 111 pp.

4757. Gebauer, G. 1972. Leistung als Aktion und Präsentation. *Sportwissenschaft* 2,2:182-203.

4758. Gomelauri, M.L. 1969. K voprosu o motivacionnom znachenii socialnyh oxhidanij (The problem of motivational significance of social expectations). *Materialy i soobshchenija* (Moscow) 25(40),2:100-123.

4759. Gottheil, E. 1955. Changes in social perceptions contingent upon competing or cooperating. *Sociometry* 18,1:132-137.

4760. Gras, F. 1976. About the way of life and development of personality of competitive sportsmen. *IRSS* 11,1:77-82.

4761. Gregory, C.J. and B. Petrie. 1975. Superstitions of Canadian intercollegiate athletes. *IRSS* 10,2:59-68.

4762. Griffith, C.R. 1928. *Psychology and Athletics* New York: Scribner. 281 pp.

4763. Hanada, K. et al. 1968. *Sportsmen teki seikaku* (personality of sportsmen). Tokyo: Fumaido-shoten.

4764. Healey, T.R. and D.M. Landers. 1973. Effect of need achievement and task difficulty on competitive and noncompetitive motor performance. *J.Motor Behavior* 5,2:121-128.

4765. Hendry, L.B. and H.T.A. Whiting. 1968. Social and psychological trends in national championship calibre junior swimmers. *J.Sports Medicine* 8,4: 198-203.

4766. Hendry, L.B. and L. Douglas. 1975. University students: attainment and sport. *Brit.J.Educ.Psychology* 45,2:299-306.

4767. Iso-Ahola, S. 1973. Liikunnen sosiaalipskologinen tutkimuskentta (The research area of social psychology of physical activity). *Stadion* (Helsinki) 10,1:84-86.

4768. Jones, J.M. and S.A. Williamson. 1976. A model of athlete's attitudes toward sports performance. *Int.J.Sport Psychology* 7,2:82-106.

4769. Julian, J.W. et al. 1966. Quasitherapeutic effects of intergroup competition. *J.Person. Soc. Psychology* 3,2:321-327.

4770. Kaniuk, R. 1972. Cialo jako wartosc. Rozwazania nad funkcjonalna teoria kultury B. Malinowskiego (The functional body as a value formulated by B. Malinowski's theory of culture). *Wychowanie Fizyczne i Sport* 2: 84-94.

4771. Karolczak, B. 1967. Kooperacja a wspolzawodnictwo (Cooperation and competition). *Wychowanie Fizyczne i Sport* 11,2:27-39.

4772. Karolczak, B. 1970. Z. badan nad stosunkiem zawodnikow do sportu (Research on the attitude of competitors to sport). *Wychowanie Fizyczne i Sport* 4:111-119.

4773.	Karolczak, B. 1973. Motywacynie interpretacje wynikow sportowych (Motivational interpretation of sport results). *Sport Wyczynowy* (Warsaw) 2:36–45.

4774.	Kelley, H.H. et al. 1962. The development of cooperation in the minimal social situation. *Psychological Monographs* 76, 538:1–19.

4775.	Kenyon, G.S. and J.W. Loy. 1966. Soziale Beeinflussung und Leistung bei vier psychomotorischen Aufgaben. Pp. 191–202 in Lüschen.

4776.	Kenyon, G.S. 1970. Social psychology of sport and physical activity. Pp. 331–338 in G. Kenyon, ed. *Psychology of Sport.* Chicago: Athletic Institute.

4777.	King, J.P. and P. Chi. 1974. Personality and the athletic social atructure: a case study. *Human Relations* 27,2:179–193.

4778.	Klausner, S.Z. 1967. Sport parachuting. Pp. 670–694 in R. Slovenko and J. Knight, eds. *Motivations in Play, Games and Sports.* Springfield, Ill.: Thomas.

4779.	Klein, M. 1967. Die Beziehung der Leistungsfähigkeit zur Form der Gruppenbeziehungen bei Spielern im Basketballteam. Pp. 165–169 in *Mezinarodi Kongres o Telesne Zdatnosti Mladeze Praha.* Prague: Olympia.

4780.	Klyszejko, W. 1960. Wstepne rozwazania z Zakresu reorii walki sportowej (Introductory remarks concerning sport competition). *Kultura Fizyczna* 5–6:285–290.

4781.	Knight, J.A. 1961. Motivation in Skiing. *Western Journal of Surgery, Obstetrics and Gynecology* 69,6:395–398.

4782.	Kotarbinski, T. 1957. *Wybor pieam* (On good work). Warsawa: PWN. *Engl. Praxeology.* London: Pergamon Press. 250 pp.

4783.	Krüger, A. 1974. Sozialpsychologische Untersuchungen in einem Trainingslager von Mittelstrecklern in der Vorbereitungsperiode. *Leistungssport* 3,6:456–462.

4784.	Kunath, P. 1974. Changes in performance motivations related to social conditions. *Int.J.Sport Psychology* 5,1:54–59.

4785.	Lehman, H.C. and P. Witty. 1927. *The Psychology of Play Activities.* New York: Barnes. 242 pp.

4786.	Martens, R. 1969. Effect of an audience on learning and performance of a complex motor skill. *J.Person.Soc.Psychology* 12,3:252–260.

4787.	Martens, R. 1970. A social psychology of physical activity. *Quest* 14,June: 8–17.

4788.	Martens, R. 1975. *Social Psychology and Physical Activity.* New York: Harper and Row. 180 pp.

4789.	Martens, R. 1975. Influence of win-loss ratio on performance, satisfaction and preference for opponents. *J.Exper.Social Psychology* 11,2:343–362.

4790.	Mead, G.H. 1964. *On Social Psychology.* Chicago: University of Chicago Press.

4791.	Milshtein, O.A. 1967. Fizicheskoe sovershenstvo lichnosti. Fizicheskiij i sociologicheskij aspekt problemy (Physical perfection of personality. Physiological and sociological aspects of the problem). Pp. 18–20 in *Materialy dokladow nauchno-metodicheskoj konferencii.* Omsk.

4792.	Milshtein, O.A. 1969. Rol svobodnogo vremeni v fizicheskom sovershenstvovanii lichnosti (The role of free time in physical perfection of personality). Pp. 327–338 in *Vsesojusnaja nauchno-technicheskaja konferencija.* Moscow.

4793. Milshtein, O.A. and I.A. Panfilov. 1973. K voprosu o sociologicheskoj tipologizacii lichnosti v sporte (Problems of sociological typology of personality in sport). Pp. 7–9 in *Materialy II Respublikanskoj konferencii.* Minsk. Part I.

4794. Milshtein, O.A. 1973. Issledovanie socialnogo oblika sportsmena kak osnovy tipologizacii lichnosti v sporte (Athlete's social character as determinant of personality type in sport). Pp. 66–70 in *Konferencija po problemam nauchnyh osnov organizacii sovetskogo debrovolnogo fizkulturnogo dvizhenija.* Tartu.

4795. Moede, W. 1920. *Experimentelle Massenpsychologie.* Leipzig: Hirtzel. 235 pp.

4796. Murray, C. 1971. Sociometry and athletic status of adolescents. *Perceptual and Motor Skills* 33,5:1143–1150.

4797. Myers, A.E. 1966. Performance factors contributing to the acquisition of a psychological advantage in competition. *Human Relations* 19,3:283–295.

4798. Myers, A.E. 1970. Psychological advantages in a competitive game. *IRSS* 5,1:163–174.

4799. McClintock, C.G. and S.P. McNeel. 1966. Reward and score feedback as determinants of cooperative and competitive game behavior. *J.Person. Soc.Psychology* 6,4:606–613.

4800. McClintock, C.G. and S.P. McNeel. 1967. Prior dyadic experience and monetary reward as determinants of cooperative and competitive game behavior. *J.Person.Soc.Psychology* 5,3:282–294.

4801. Nawrocka, W. 1960. Powstanie, rozwoj oraz ksztaltowanie sie zainteresowan sportowych (The origin and development of sport interests). *Kultura Fizyczna* 7-8:447–453.

4802. Nawrocka, W. 1966. Spdeczny charakter motywacij uprawiania sportu kwalifikowanego (The social character of motivation for participation in competitive sport). *Rozniki Naukowe AWF* 6:175–190.

4803. Nisbett, R.E. 1968. Birth order and participation in dangerous sports. *J.Person.Soc.Psychology* 8,4:351–353.

4804. Niwa, T. 1964. Factorial study of personality in the intercollegiate athletics. *Research J.Phys.Educ.* 7,4:21–37.

4805. Niwa, T. 1969. Undobu ni okeru buin no taidohenyo (Attitude change among members of an athletic club). *Studies Humanities Social Sciences Nara Womens University* 12:73–108.

4806. Niwa, T. 1975. Taidohenyo ni eikyo o ataeru joho teikyosha no shinpyosei no kento (Examination of communicator's credibility with influences on attitude change). *Studies Humanities Social Sciences Nara Womens University* 19:87–126.

4807. Noe, F.P. 1973. Coaches, players, and pain. *IRSS* 8,2:47–61.

4809. Noguchi, Y. 1960. Kagoshima daigaku no gakuyukai ni taisuru taido (Attitude of university students toward sport and cultural clubs). *Research Phys.Educ.Kyushu University* (Fukuoka) 12,4:15–26.

4810. Parlebas, P. 1970. L'éducation physique, une éducation des conduites de décision. *Education Physique et Sport* 21,103:25–30.

4811. Paulhus, D. et al. 1979. Control profiles of football players, tennis players and non-athletes. *J.Soc.Psychology* 108,Aug.:199–205.

4812.   Paulus, P.B. and W.L. Cornelius. 1974. An analysis of gymnastic performance under conditions of practice and spectator observation. *Research Quarterly* 45,1:56–63.

4813.   Pickford, R.W. 1941. Aspects of the psychology of games and sport.
         Brit.J.Psychology 31,4:270–293.

4814.   Portele, G. 1975. Überlegungen zur Verwendung von Spielen. *Gruppendynamik* (Stuttgart) 6,3:205–214.

4815.   Prenner, K. 1971. Leistungsgellschaft, Leistungsmotivation und Sport.
         Die Leibeserziehung 20,10:334–348.

4816.   Prenner, K. 1971. Leistungsmotivation im Spitzensport. Ein soziologischer
         Beitrag. *Die Leibeserziehung* 20,11:370–373.

4817.   Roberts, G.C. and R. Martens. 1970. Social reinforcement and complex
         motor performance. *Research Quarterly* 41,2:175–181.

4818.   Roberts, G.C. 1972. Effect of achievement motivation and social environment on performance of a motor task. *J.Motor Behavior* 4,1:37–46.

4819.   Röblitz, G. 1964. Das Verhältnis zum Sport und die Beweggründe für
         die sportliche Betätigung bei Jugendlichen als Ausgangswerte für ein
         regelmässiges Sporttreiben. *Theorie und Praxis* 13,7:601–612.

4820.   Rokusfalvy, P. et al. 1973. Achievement motivation: origin and development. Pp. 397–408 in Grupe.

4821.   Ryan, E.D. and W.L. Lakie. 1965. Competitive and noncompetitive
         performance in relation to achievement motive and manifest anxiety.
         J.Person.Soc.Psychology 1,4:342–345.

4821a.   Saraf, M. 1975. *Sport i Lichnost* (Sport and personality). Moscow: Fizkultura i Sport. 192 pp.

4822.   Schiller, J. 1973. Közvélemény kutatás az általános iskolások között
         (Investigation of opinions of elementary school pupils). *Sportélet* (Budapest) 9. Suppl. 4:1–20.

4823.   Schimel, J.L. 1970. The sporting and gaming aspects of love and war.
         Pp. 405–410 in G. Kenyon, ed. *Psychology of Sport.* Chicago: Athletic
         Institute.

4824.   Schleske, W. 1972/1973. Leistungsprinzip-Lustprinzip-Leistungssport.
         Leistungssport 2,6:458–459. 3,1:41–48.

4825.   Senters, J.M. 1971. A function of uncertainty and stakes in recreation.
         Pacif.Soc.Review 14,3:259–269.

4826.   Shaw, M.E. 1958. Some motivational factors in cooperation and competition. *J.Personality* 26,1:155–169.

4827.   Slovenko, R. and J. Knight, eds. 1966. *Motivation in Sports.* Springfield,
         Ill.: Thomas.

4828.   Stakienene, V.P. 1969. Dvigatelnye potrebnosti kak odno iz projavlenij
         lichnosti (Movement necessities as a condition for manifestation of
         personal activity). Pp. 165–175 in *Konferencija po psihologii i sociologii
         sporta.* Tartu.

4829.   Streubühr, J. 1971. Motivierung und Umwelteinfluss bei Spitzensportlern.
         Olympiateilnehmer der BRD. *Die Leibeserziehung* 20,11:374–378.

4830.   Suetoshi and G. Cooper. 1967 and 1968. A study of attitudes of British
         students towards sport. *Bulletin Kyoto University* 30 and 32.

4831.   Szot, Z. and B. Jurkewicz. 1979. An attempt at defining the influence of selected factors exerted on results in sport and gymnastics. *IRSS* 14,2:73-80.

4832. Takemura, A. 1963. Undobu senshu no seikakutokusei nioyobosu club no shojyoken noeikyo (Effects of conditions in athletic clubs upon personality traits of athletes). *J.Nara Gakugei University* 11:147-159.

4833, Takemura, A. 1966. Sports shudan to personality ni kansuru kenkyu (The relationship between sport groups and personality). *J.Nara University Education* 4:133-141.

4834. Takemura, A. 1971. Undobu shudan no kozo to morale ni kansuru kenkyu (The relationship between athletic club structure and morale). *Bulletin Nara University Education* 21,1:119-132.

4835. Thill, E. 1975. *Sport et personalité.* Paris: Editions universitaires. 216 pp.

4836. Tripplett, N. 1898. The dynamogenic factors in pacemaking and competition. *American J.Psychology* 9,4:507-533. *German* 1976. Schnelligkeit—soziale und psychische Faktoren beim Schrittmachen und Wettkampf. Pp. 174-184 in Lüschen/Weis.

4837. Tyszka, A. 1964. Socjologiczna analiza pojecia sukcesu sportowego (Sociological analysis of the concept of athletic success). *Kultura Fizyczna* 17, 5-6:320-324.

4838. Vanfraec, R. 1976. Study on social personality of athletes as a function of organization of their team. *Int.J.Sport Psych.* 7,3:169-186.

4839. Voigt, H. 1973. Sozialpsychologische Probleme im Mannschaftssport. *Sportunterricht* (Schorndorf) 22,4:125-130.

4840. Volkamer, M. 1971. Zur Aggressivität in konkurrenzorientierten sozialen Systemen. *Sportwissenschaft* 1,1:33-64.

4841. Veit, H. 1968. Die Bedeutung sozialpsychologischer Untersuchungen von Sportmannschaften für die Praxis. *Die Leibeserziehung* 17,3:80-87.

4842. Wasilewski, E. 1964. Problematyka motywaiji w dzialnosci sportowej (problems of motivation in sport activity). *Roczniki Naukowe AWF* 3:33-59.

4843. Wasilewski, E. 1968. Z badan nad niektorymi wlasciwosciami psychicznymi sportowcow wyczynowych (Research on psychological properties of top-athletes). *Roczniki Naukowe AWF* 9:105-131.

4844. Worthy, M. and A. Mackle. 1970. Racial differences in reactive versus self-paced sports activities. *J.Person.Soc.Psychology* 16,3:439-443.

4845. Wyer, R.S. and C. Malinowski. 1972. Effects of sex and achievement level upon individualism and competitiveness in social interaction. *J.Exper.Soc.Psychology* 8,4:303-314.

4846. Yiannakis, A. 1976. Birth order and preference for dangerous sports among males. *Research Quarterly* 47,1:62-67.

4847. Zurcher, L.A. 1970. The 'friendly' poker game: a study of an 'ephemeral' role. *Social Forces* 49,2:173-185.

8. *Sport Subcultures and the Structure of Single Sports*

4848. Adam, K. 1975. *Leistungssport. Sinn und Unsinn.* Munich: Nymphenburger.

4849. Andreano, R. 1965. The affluent baseball player. *Transaction* 2,4:10-13.

4850.   Andreano, R. 1965. *No Joy in Mudville.* Cambridge, Mas.: Schenkman. 191 pp.

4851.   Aran, G. 1974. Parachuting. *AJS* 80,1:144–152.

4852.   Bairam, M. 1957. Les sports équestres à Tunis au dix-neuviéme siècle. *Institut des belles-Lettres arabes* 20,77:31–36.

4853.   Bakonyi-Nádori, L. 1971. A magyar NB I-es labdarugók szociálpszichológiai viszgálata (Social-psychological examination of first national division soccer players). *Testneveles Tudomany* 1,1:4–47 and 2:3–28.

4854.   Betts, J.R. 1953. Agricultural fairs and the rise of harness racing. *Agricultural History* April:71–75.

4855.   Bouet, M.A. 1977. The significance of the Olympic phenomenon. A preliminary attempt at systematic and semiotic analysis. *IRSS* 12,3:5–21.

4856.   Boyle, R.H. 1971. Negroes in baseball. Pp. 259–278 in Dunning.

4857.   Bratton, R.D. et al. 1979. Why man climbs mountains? *IRSS* 14,2:23–36.

4858.   Brewster, P.G. 1955. A note on the Slovenian game 'Skarjice brusiti.' *Slovenski Etnografi* 8:255–258.

4859.   Brewster, P.G.1958. Bierki and other Polish games of chance and skill. *Zeitschrift Ethnologie* 83,1:83–85.

4860.   Brotjahn, M. 1959. Bullfighting and the future of tragedy. *Int.J.Psychoanalysis* 40,3–4:238–239.

4861.   Brown, C.C. 1928. Kelantan bull-fighting. *Royal Asiatic Society Malayan Branch J.* 6,1:74–83.

4862.   Buytendijk, F.J.J. 1952. *Het Voetballen* (The game of soccer). Utrecht-Antwerpen: He Spectrum. 39 pp. *German* 1953. *Das Fussballspiel.* Würzburg: Werkbund.

4863.   Cochran, R. 1976. Folk elements in a non-folk game: the example of basketball. *J.Popular Culture* 10,Fall:398–403.

4864.   Creighton, R.E. 1933. Jargon of 'Fistiana.' *American Speech* 8,3:34–39.

4865.   Cricher, C. 1971. Football and cultural values. *Working Papers in Cultural Studies* (Birmingham) 1:103–119.

4866.   Czula, R. et al. 1976. A multi-dimensional analysis of Olympic idealism. *Review Sport Leisure* 1,Fall:1–14.

4867.   De Borhegyi, S. 1960. America's ballgame. *Natural History* 69,1:48–58.

4868.   Dunning, E. 1971. The development of modern football. Pp. 133–151 in Dunning.

4869.   Dunning, E. 1975. Industrialization and the incipient modernization of football. *Arena* (Leyden) 1,1:103–139.

4870.   Edgell, S. and D. Jary. 1973. Football—a sociological eulogy. In S. Parker et al. eds. *Leisure and Society in Britain.* London: Allen Lane.

4871.   Elias, N. and E. Dunning. 1971. Folk football in medieval and early modern Britain. Pp. 116–132 in Dunning.

4872.   Esashi, S. et al. 1971. Bowling jinko zodai no yoin ni kansuru jirei kenkyu (Factors of the bowling boom: a case study). *Research Phys. Educ. Kyushu University* (Fukuoka) 4,4:7–13.

4873.   Esashi, S. and S. Arai. 1972. Gendai ni okeru honozumo no sonzaikeitai ni tsuite (A case study of the modern form of a dedicatory wrestling match). *Research Phys.Educ.Kyushu University* (Fukuoka) 4,5:37–42.

4874.   Essing, W. 1970. Team line-up and team achievement in European football. Pp. 349–354 in G. Kenyon, ed. *Psychology of Sport.* Chicago:

Athletic Institute.

4875. Ferrado, M.G. 1979. Problems and social values of top class Spanish athletes. *IRSS* 14,3–4:21–58.

4876. Fisher, A. 1966. Flexibility in an experience motivation: Sumo. *South Western J.Anthropology* 22,1:31–42.

4877. Fiske, S. 1972. Pigskin review: an American Initiation. Pp. 241-258 in Hart.

4878. Furst, R.T. 1974. Boxing stereotypes versus the cultures of the professional boxer: a sociological decision. *Sport Sociology Bulletin* 3,2:13–39.

4879. Geertz, C. 1972. Deep play: notes on the Balinese Cockfight. *Daedalus* Winter:1–37.

4880. Gmelch, G. 1972. Magic in professional baseball. Pp. 128-137 in Stone.

4881. Golias, R. 1959. Un sport se penche sur son passé: le golf. *Aesculape* 42,avr.:3–55.

4882. Goodger, B.C. and J.M. 1977. Judo in the light of theory and sociological research. *IRSS* 12,2:5–34.

4883. Greitbauer, K. 1962. Geistesgeschichtliche und soziologische Gesichtspunkte des Bergsteigens. *Leibesübungen-Leibeserziehung* (Vienna) 16,6:4–7.

4884. Grunwald, D.H. 1961. *Nieuwe wegen in de topsport* (New roads in topsport). Amsterdam: Born. 211 pp.

4885. Heinilä, K. 1975. *Kilpaurheilun säätelyjärjestelmä* (Synthesis and feedback in top-sport). Research Report Nr. 9. University of Jyväskylä.

4886. Hendry, L.B. 1971. Don't put your daughter in the water, Mrs. Worthington? A sociological examination of the subculture of competitive swimming. *Brit.J.Phys.Educ.* 2,3:17–19.

4887. Henricks, T. 1974. Professional wrestling as moral order. *Sociological Inquiry* 44,3:177–188.

4888. Henslin, J.M. 1967. Craps and magic. *AJS* 73,3:316–330.

4889. Herman, R.D. 1967. *Gambling.* New York: Harper and Row.

4890. Hopf, W. ed. 1979. *Fussball.* Bensheim: päd.extra. 280 pp.

4891. Hortleder, G. 1974. *Die Faszination des Fussballspiels.* Frankfurt: Suhrkamp. 161 pp.

4892. Huddle, F.P. 1943. Baseball jargon. *American Speech* 18,2:103–111.

4893. James, C.L.R. 1963. Cricket in West Indian culture. *New Society* 36,1: 8–9.

4894. Japanese Society of Physical Education. 1952. Shonen yakyu no kenkyu (A study of junior baseball). *Research J.Phys.Educ.* 1,3:236–244.

4895. Jarka, H. 1963. The language of skiers. *American Speech* 38,3:202–207.

4896. Kothari, U.C. 1962. On the bullfight. *Psychoanalysis and Psychoanalytic Review* 49,1:121–128.

4897. Lenk, H. 1972. *Leistungssport: Ideologie oder Mythos?* Stuttgart Kohlhammer. 192 pp.

4898. Mafud, J. 1967. *Sociologia del futbol* (Sociology of soccer). Buenos Aires.

4899. Manning, P.K. and B. Campbell. 1973. Pinball as game, fad and synecdoche. *Youth and Society* 4,3:333–358.

4900. Medina, F.O. 1970. Aspectos sociales de la caza (Social aspects of hunting). *Revista de Estudios agro-sociales* (Madrid) 70,19:7–23.

4901. Meyer, H. 1975. *Mensch und Pferd. Zur Kultursoziologie einer Mensch-*

Tier-Assoziation. Hildesheim: Olms. 306 pp.

4902.   Miermans, C.G.M. 1955. *Voetball in Nederland* (Soccer in Netherland). Assen: Van Gorcum. 339 pp.

4903.   Mihovilovic, M. 1974. *Vrhunski Sportasi* (Top sport). Institute of Sociology. University of Zagreb. 238 pp.

4904.   Misev, D. 1960. O vozraste i professi utcastnikov olimpiiskih igr (Age and profession of Olympic Games participants). *Teorie i Praktika* (Sofia) 23,6:458–460.

4905.   Mosteller, F. 1952. The world series competition. *J.American Statistical Association* 47,259:355–380.

4906.   Nagleer, B. 1964. *James Norris and the Decline of Boxing.* Indianapolis: Bobbs-Merrill. 252 pp.

4907.   Nelissen, N.J. and J.W. Foppen. 1972. *Topsport in het geding* (Top sport in action). Leyden: Meander. 203 pp.

4908.   Newman, O. 1972. *Gambling: Hazard and Reward.* London: Athlone.

4909.   Novak, M. 1976. Game's the thing: in defense of sports as ritual. *Columbia Journalism Review* 15,May:33–38.

4910.   O'Hare, J.R. 1945. *The Socio-Economic Aspects of Horse Racing.* Washington, D.C.: Catholic University Press.

4911.   Oldman, D. 1974. Chance and skill: a study of roulette. *Sociology* (London) 8,3:407–426.

4912.   Patrick, G.T.W. 1903: The psychology of football. *American J.Psychology* 14,3–4:104–117.

4913.   Patterson, O. 1969. The cricket ritual in the West Indies. *New Society* 352, June:988–989.

4914.   Pearson, K. 1979. The institutionalization of sport forms. *IRSS* 14,1: 51–60.

4915.   Polsky, N. 1967. *Hustlers, Beats and Others.* Garden City, N.Y.: Doubleday.

4916.   Polsky, N. 1967. Poolrooms: end of the male sanctuary. *Trans-action* 4,4: 32–40.

4917.   Ragot, M. 1972. *La saut en parachute. Aspects psychosociologiques.* Paris: Masson. 208 pp.

4918.   Rassem, M. 1970. Der Stabhochspringer: Ein Fragment zur Definition der Technik. *KAI* (Vienna) 1,3:10–12.

4919.   Reider, N. 1960. Chess, Oedipus and the Mater Dolorosa. *Psychoanalysis and Psychoanalytic Review* 47,2:55–82.

4920.   Riesman, D. and R. Denney. 1951. Football in America. *American Quarterly* 3,4:309–325. Also 1954 pp. 242–257 in Riesman. *Individualism Reconsidered.* Glencoe, Ill.: Free Press.

4921.   Rudzinska, M. 1971. Lucznictwo w swietle badan socjologicznych (Archery in light of sociological research). *Sport Wyczynowy* (Warsaw) 1:26–33.

4922.   Salamone, F.A. 1974. Gungawa wrestling as an ethnic boundary marker. *Sport Sociology Bulletin* 3,2:1–12.

4923.   Saunders, E.D. 1969. Sociological aspects of rugby football. *Physical Education* 61,182.

4924.   Schilling, G. 1975. Psychological aspects of play. Pp. 69–73 in U. Simri, ed. *International Seminar on Play.* Natanya: Wingte Institute.

4925. Scott, M.B. 1968. *The Racing Game.* Chicago:Aldine. 186 pp.

4926. Sheard, K.G. and E. Dunning. 1973. The rugby football club as a type of male preserve. *IRSS* 8,1:5–24. *German* 1975 pp. 186–203 in Hammerich/Heinemann. 1976 pp. 261–272 in Lüschen/Weis.

4927. Skubic, E. 1956. Studies of Little League and Middle League baseball. *Research Quarterly* 27,Oct.: 97–110.

4928. South African Rugby Board. 1964. *Rugby in South Africa.* Capetown: Johnston and Neville. 216 pp.

4929. Starosta, W. 1967. Social characteristics of figure skaters. *IRSS* 2,1: 165–178.

4930. Stone, G.P. 1971. Wrestling: the great American passion play. Pp. 301–335 in Dunning.

4931. Sztyma, G. 1971. Przycznek do badan karier sportowych w szermierce (Investigation on a sport career in fencing). *Sport Wyczynowy* (Warsaw) 2:57–61.

4932. Tunis, J.R. 1928. The great God football. *Harper's Magazine* 157,Nov.: 742–752.

4933. Vaughan, J.D. 1957. Notes on the Malays of Pinang. *J.Indian Archipelago and Eastern Asia* 2,2:115–175.

4934. Vaz, E.W. 1974. What price victory? An analysis of minor hockey league player's attitudes toward winning. *IRSS* 9,2:33–56.

4935. Veiga d Olivera, E. 1954. O jogo de toupiole em Portugal (The game of toupiole in Portugal). *Trabalhos de antropologia* 15,1–2:110–115.

4936. Voigt, D.Q. 1976. *America Through Baseball.* Chicago: Nelson-Hall. 221 pp.

4937. Vuolle, P. 1975. *Suomalaisen huippu-urhelijan yhteiskunnallinen orientoituminen* (The social orientation of Finnish top athletes). Jyväskylä: University of Jyväskylä.

4938. Wind, H.W. 1956. *The Story of American Golf.* New York: Simon and Schuster. 315 pp.

4939. Yaffe, M. 1974. The psychology of soccer. *New Society* Febr.:378–384.

V. *Sport, Social Problems and Deviance*

1. *Sport and Leisure; Participation Rates*

5001. Akiyoshi, Y. 1969. Kyoshi no seikatsu to yoka mondai no kenkyu (Study of leisure in life of the teachers). *Bulletin Fukuoka University Education* 19.

5002. Albrecht, O. 1977. Untersuchung zum Verhältnis von Leistungssport und Freizeitverhalten jugendlicher Spitzensportler. *Leistungssport* 7,1:54–67.

5003. Allardt. E. et al. 1958. On the cumulative nature of leisure activities. *Acta Sociologica* 3:165–172.

5004. Anderson, N. 1961. *Work and Leisure.* London: Routledge, Kegan Paul. 265 pp.

5005. Artemov, V. 1966. Physical education and leisure. *IRSS* 1:127–144.

5006. Artemov, V. 1971. Sovokupnyj fond vremeni fizkulturno-sporivnoj dejatelnosti naselenija goraoda (Joint time-budget of sport activities for urban people). Pp. 119–121 in *Istorija, organizacija i sociologija fiziche-skoj kultury i sporta*. Minsk: Tezisy dokladov.

5007.   Asada, T. 1965. Yoka kaiso no shorai yosoku ni kansuru kenkuy (Study on the estimation of leisure in the future). *JOPHER* (Tokyo) 15,9: 505–512.

5008.   Ashton, E.T. 1971. *People and Leisure*. London: Ginn. 81 pp.

5009.   Balog, M. 1974. The development of leisure time of married women with children in Hungary and their possibilities of acquiring further education. *Society and Leisure* 6,1:29–43.

5010.   Bishop, D.W. 1970. Stability of the factor structure of leisure behavior: Analysis of four communities. *J.Leisure Research* 2,3:160–170.

5011.   Blücher, V. 1956. *Freizeit in der industriellen Gesellschaft*. Stuttgart: Enke. 138 pp.

5012.   Bollaert, L. 1969. La promotion du sport de masse. *Sport* 12,Jan.:47–55.

5013.   Brightbill, C.K. 1961. *Man and Leisure*. Englewood Cliffs, N.J.: Prentice-Hall. 292 pp.

5014.   Buggel, E. et al. 1964. Sport und Touristik im Urlaub an der Ostee und im Mittelgebirge. *Wissenschaftl.Zeitschr.DHFK* 6,2:7–63.

5015.   Buggel, E. 1966. Die Urlaubsfreizeit und ihr Beziehungsgefüge im Lebens-vollzug erwachsener Menschen. *Theorie und Praxis* 15,12:1101–1110.

5016.   Buggel, E. 1967. Research on leisure pursuits in the form of sport activity regarding groups of holiday-makers. *IRSS* 2:55–66.

5017.   Buggel, E. 1971. Freizeit- und Erholungssport in der DDR. *Kürbiskern* 3,4:633–641.

5018.   Bull, C.N. 1971. One measure for defining a leisure activity. *J.Leisure Research* 3,2:120–126.

5019.   Bull, C.N. 1972. Prediction of future daily behaviors; An empirical measure of leisure. *J.Leisure Research* 4,4:119–128.

5020.   Campbell, F.L. 1970. Participant observation in outdoor recreation. *J. Leisure Research* 2,4:226–236.

5021.   Catton, W.R. 1971. The Wildland recreation boom and sociology. *Pacific Soc.Rev.* 14,3:339–359.

5022.   Cheek, N.H. and W.R. Burch. 1976. *The Social Organization of Leisure in Human Society*. New York: Harper and Row. 275 pp.

5023.   Claeys, U. and D. Veys. 1975. *Demografische Perspektieven en Sport*. Leuven: University of Leuven. 73 pp.

5024.   Clayre, A. 1974. *Work and Play: Ideas and Experience of Work and Leisure*. London: Weidenfeld and Nicolson. 261 pp.

5025.   Debreu, P. 1973. *Les comportements de loisirs des français*. Paris: Quai Branly. 200 pp.

5026.   Dee, N. and J.C. Liebman. 1970. A statistical study of attendance at urban playground. *J.Leisure Research* 2:145–159.

5027.   De Grazia, S. 1962. *Of Time, Work and Leisure*. New York: 20th Century Fund. 559 pp.

5028.   Delawska-Wyrobkowa, W. 1960. Z badan nad problematyka wolnego czasn (Some studies of leisure time problems). *Wychowanie fizyczne i sportu* 4,4–6:237–251.

5029.   Donald, M.H. and R.J. Havighurst. 1959. The meanings of leisure. *Social Forces* 37,4:355–260.

5030. Dumazedier, J. 1963. Contenu culturel du loisir ouvrier dans six villes d'Europe. *Revue français de Sociologie* 4,1:12–21.

5031. Dumazedier, J. 1964. The point of view of a social scientist. Pp. 212–217 in Jokl, E. and E. Simon, eds. *Research in Sport and Physical Education.* Springfield, Ill.: Thomas.

5032. Dumazedier, J. and A. Ripert. 1966. *Loisir et culture.* Paris: Editions du Seuil. 398 pp.

5033. Dumazedier, J. 1966. *Toward a Society of Leisure.* New York: Free Press. 256 pp.

5034. Dumazedier, J. 1968. Some remarks on sociological problems in relation to physical education and sports. *IRSS* 3,1:5–16.

5035. Du Toit, J.B. 1960. Work and leisure roles of young people. *Sociol.Soc. Research* 44,4:235–243.

5036. Eichler, G. 1979. *Spiel und Arbeit. Zur Theorie der Freizeit.* Stuttgart: Fromann-Holzboog. 223 pp.

5037. Eidgenössishe Turn- und Sportschule, eds. 1962. *Arbeit, Freizeit und Sport.* Bern: Haupt.

5038. Elias, N. and E. Dunning. 1969. The quest for excitement in leisure. *Society and Leisure* 2:50–85.

5039. Elias, N. and E. Dunning. 1971. Leisure in the sparetime spectrum. Pp. 27–34 in Albonico/Pfister-Binz.

5040. Erikson, E. 1972. The innocence of leisure: A gentle caution. *JOPHER.* 43,3:47.

5041. Esashi, S. and H. Noguchi. 1970. Gakusei no yokakatsudō ni kansuru kenkyū (Case study on student's leisure activites during three consecutive holidays). *Research Physical Education* 4,3:1–11.

5042. Esashi, S.; M. Ikeda and S. Morino. 1971. Gakusotsusha no yokaishki to yokakōdō ni kansuru chōsa kenkyū (Leisure time interests and activities among college graduates). *J.Leisure Recreation Studies* (Tokyo). 1 & 2.

5043. Etzkorn, P. 1964. Leisure and camping: The social meaning of a form of public recreation. *Sociol.Soc. Research* 49,1:76–89.

5044. Ferris, A.L. 1970. The social and personality correlates of outdoor recreation. *Annals AAPSS* 389:46–55.

5045. Fink, C.H. 1970. *Der Massentourismus.* Bern and Stuttgart: Haupt. 238 pp.

5046. Gerstl, J.E. 1961. Leisure, taste and occupational milieu. *Social Problems* 9,1:56–68.

5047. Groessing, St. 1968. Zusammenhänge zwischen Gesellschaftsform und Freizeitsport bei Berufstätigen. *Leibesübungen-Leibeserziehung* (Wien) 20,8:6–10.

5048. Groll, H. 1960. Psychologische und soziologische Ausblicke (Aspekte) auf die Bedeutung des Sports für die Freizeitgestaltung. *Leibeserziehung.* 9,11:349–357.

5049. Gross, E. 1961. A functional approach to leisure analysis. *Social Problems* 9,1:2–8.

5050. Güldenpfennig, S. 1974. Erweiterte Reproduktion der Arbeitskraft-Ein Ansatz zur Bestimmung des Verhältnisses von Sport und Arbeit. Pp. 12–59 in S. Güldenpfenning, et al. eds. *Sensumotorisches Lernen und Sport als Reproduktion der Arbeitskraft.* Köln: Pahl-Rugenstein.

5051. Gump, P.; P. Shoeggen and F. Redl. 1957. The camp milieu and its im-

           mediate effects. *Journal Social Issues* 13,1:40–46.
5052.   Hammerich, K. 1971. *Kritische Untersuchung zur Freizeitpädogogik.*
           Henn: Ratingen 250 pp.
5053.   Hanhart, D. 1963. Sport und Freizeit in der industriellen Gesellschaft.
           Pp. 13–68 in Eidgenössische Turn-und Sportschule, ed. *Arbeit. Freizeit
           und Sport.* Bern: Haupt.
5054.   Hanhart, D. 1963. *Arbeiter in der Freizeit.* Bern-Stuttgart: Haupt. 271 pp.
5055.   Hartley, H.M. and B.N. Knapp. 1971. *Riding for Recreation in the West
           Midlands.* London: Sports Council.
5056.   Heinilä, K. 1959. *Vapaa-aika ja urheilu* (Leisure and Sports). Helsinki:
           Porvoo. 215 pp.
5057.   Hertzfeld, G. 1963. *Freizeit. Problem und Aufgabe.* Schorndorf: Hofmann
           162 pp.
5058.   Hoar, J. 1961. A study of free-time activities of 200 aged persons. *Sociol.
           Soc. Research* 45:157–163.
5059.   Ibrahim, H. 1969. Recreational preference and personality. *Research
           Quarterly* 40,1:76–82.
5060.   Ibrahim, H. 1970. Recreation preference and temperament. *Research
           Quarterly* 41:145–154.
5061.   Ikeda, M. 1973. Rodo to yoka no tekio mechanism no bunseki (Analysis
           of the mechanical adjustment of leisure and work). *Journal Leisure
           Recreation Studies* (Tokyo) 3:1–6.
5062.   Isoguchi, A. 1964. Yoka bunseki to sonoigi (Study of Leisure and its
           meaning). *Bulletin Doshisha Hoken Taiiku* (Kyoto) 3:1–27.
5063.   Isoguchi, A. 1966. Recreation gainen eno sekkin (Approach to the concept
           of recreation). *Bulletin Doshisha Hoken Taiiku* (kyoto) 5:1–12.
5064.   Isoguchi, A. 1968. Recreationno kino (Function of recreation). *Bulletin
           Doshisha Hoken Taiiku* (Kyoto) 7:354–369.
5065.   Isoguchi, A. 1972. Leisure ni taisuru yokyuseiko (Needs for leisure).
           Bulletin Doshisha Hoken Taiiku (Kyoto) 16:1–14.
5066.   Iso-Ahola, S. 1975. Leisure patterns of American and Finnish youth.
           IRSS 10,3–4:63–81.
5067.   Jephcott, P. 1967. *Time of One's Own.* Edinburgh: Oliver and Boyd. 165
           pp.
5068.   Jordan, M.L. 1963. Leisure time activities of sociologists, attorneys,
           physists, and people at large from greater Cleveland. *Sociol.Soc.Research*
           47,3:290–297.
5069.   Jovan, L. 1968. Osebna svoboda v institucionalni obliki sportnega udej-
           stvovanja (Individual liberty in the institutional form of physical acti-
           vity). *Zbornik VSTK* (Ljubljana) 2:12–16.
5070.   Kaminski, A. 1964. Kultura pas a wczasy (Mass culture and leisure). *Kul-
           tura i Spoleczeństwo* (Warsaw) 3:95–110.
5071.   Kanezaki, R. 1973. Leisure kenkyu niokeru M. Kaplan no ichi (Standpoint
           of Kaplan on leisure studies). *Journal Leisure Recreation Studies*
           (Tokyo) 3:7–14.
5072.   Kaplan, M. 1960. *Leisure in America.* New York: Wiley. 350 pp.
5073.   Kawamura, H. 1970. "Yoka" to "Asobi" eno shiten (A point of view on
           leisure and play). Pp. 161–181 in A. Asai ed. *Taiikygaku ronso(2).*
           Osaka: Nihon-Jisho.

5074. Kelly, J.R. 1972. Work and Leisure: a simplified paradigm. *J.Leisure Research* 4:50–62.

5075. Knebel, H.J. 1960. *Soziologische Strukturwandlungen im modernen Tourismus.* Stuttgart: Enke. 178 pp.

5076. Knopp, T.B. 1972. Environmental determinants of recreational behavior. *J.Leisure Research* 4,2:129–138.

5077. Lascombe, P. 1955. Camping et auberges de jeunesse. *Urbanisme et Habitation.* 2:81–158.

5078. Leemans, E.J. 1964. A sociological approach to sports. Pp. 152–159 in E. Jokl and E. Simon, eds. *International Research in Sport and Physical Education.* Springfield, Ill.: Thomas.

5079. Levy, J. 1974. An applied intersystem congruence model of play, recreation, and leisure. *Human Factors* 15,5:545–547.

5080. Loos, P. 1970. Recreation in the open air. *Planning and Development in the Netherlands* (Assen) 4,1:107–122.

5081. Lüdtke, H. 1972. Sportler und Voyeursportler. Sport als Freizeitinhalt (Athletes and sport spectators. Sports as matter of leisure). Pp. 23–47, 137–139 in J. Richter, ed. *Die vertrimmte Nation.* Reinbek: Rowohlt.

5082. Marchlewski, S. and A. Ziemilski. 1964. Zwiad socjologiczny w Tatrach. Badania nad ruchem turystycznum wa rejonie Hali Gasienniecowej (The sociological reconnaissance in the Tatra Mountains. The inquiry in tourist movement in the Hala Gysiennicowa). *Wierchy* (Warsaw) 27: 51–76.

5083. Meyersohn, R. 1970. The charismatic and the playful in outdoor recreation. *Annals AAPSS* 389:35–45.

5084. Miermans, C. 1959. Sport en recreatie. *St. Thomas van Aquino* 10:1–14.

5085. Mihovilovic, M. 1969. *Evolution and influence of leisure in contemporary society.* Zagreb: University of Zagreb.

5086. Mihovilovic, M. 1974. 24 Sata Zivota i Rada Studenata Svencilista u Zagrebu (Leisure Time and work of students in Zagreb). University of Zagreb. 273 pp.

5087. Mueller, E. and G. Gurin. 1962. *Participation in Outdoor Recreation.* Washington, D.C.: Government Printing Office. ORRRC-Report Nr. 20. 180 pp.

5088. National Opinion Polls. 1971. *National Angling Survey.* London. 129 pp.

5089. Neulinger, J. and M. Breit. 1972. Attitude dimensions of leisure: A replication study. *J.Leisure Research* 3,2:81–107.

5090. Neumeyer, M.H. and E.S. Neumeyer. 1949. *Leisure and Recreation.* New York: Barnes. 411 pp.

5091. Oliver, D.B. 1971. Career and leisure patterns of middle-aged metropolitan out-migrants. *Gerontologist* 11,4:13–20. Part 2.

5092. Orlov, R.A. and I.B. Funk. 1969. Fizicheskaja kultura i sport v nedelnom bjudzhete vremeni studentov Kishinjevskogo politechnicheskogo instituta (Physical Culture and Sport in a week time budget of the students of the Kishinev College). *Teorija i Praktika* 3:57–58.

5093. Orthner, D.K. 1975. Leisure activity patterns and marital satisfaction over the marital career. *Journal Marriage Family.* 37,1:91–104.

5094. Otzuba, G. 1955. Kino-Theater-Sport. Die Freizeitinteressen von Wiener Berufsschülern. *Erziehung und Unterricht* (Vienna) 7,4:458.

5095. Outdoor Recreation Resources Review Commission. 1962. *Outdoor Recreation Resources.* Washington, D.C.: U.S. Government Printing Office. Reports 1–30.

5096. Polytechnic of Central London. 1975. *Sport and Leisure in Contemporary Society.* London.

5097. Ponomarev, N.I. 1966. Free time and physical education. *IRSS* 1: 287–304.

5098. Ponomarev, N.I. 1970. Fizicheskaja kultura kak potrebnost' obshchestvennogo razvitija (Physical culture as necessity of the social development). Pp. 5–7 in *Materialy nauchno-metodicheskoj konferencii.* Vilnus: Sovetskiji chelovek kultura.

5099. Prahl, H.W. 1977. *Freizeitsoziologie. Entwicklungen, Konzepte, Perspektiven.* Munich: Kösel. 152 pp.

5100. Robbins, F.G. 1955. *The Sociology of Play, Recreation and Leisure Time.* Dubuque, Ia: University Press.

5101. Roberts, K. 1970. *Leisure.* London: Harlow Longman. 133 pp.

5102. Röblitz, G.; G. Emmerich and G. Stübner. 1962. Zum Problem der Lebensgestaltung, des Freizeitverhaltens und der sportlichen Betätigung von Jugendlichen der 9. Klasse und Berufsschülern gleichen Alters. *Wissensch. Zeitschr.DHFK* 4,4:281–298.

5103. Röblitz, G. 1964. Die sportliche Betätigung im Freizeitverhalten von Jugendlichen swischen 17 und 18 Jahren. *Theorie und Praxis* 13,6: 498–510.

5104. Scherhorn, G. and G. Eichler. 1971. Der Wunsch nach sportlichen Erholungszentren in der Grosstadt. *Hochschule Wirtschaft Politik* (Hamburg). 49.

5105. Schiffer, J. 1971. Sport, Architektur, Soziologie. *Jugend und Sport* (Magglingen) 28,10:313–316.

5106. Schiller, J. 1973. Szabad idő és sport (leisure and sport). *Testneveles és Sport Időszerü Keŕdeśei* (Budapest) 1:65–81.

5107. Secrétariat d'Etat à la Culture. 1974. *Pratiques culturelles des Français.* Paris: Service des Etudes et de la Recherche. 2 Volumes. 182 and 175 pp.

5108. Seppänen, P. 1967. *Näkokohti työ—ja vapaa-ajan jakautumisesta modernissa yhteiskunnassa* (Notes on distribution of work and leisure in modern society). Publication 81. Institute of Sociology, University of Helsinki. 34 pp.

5109. Sessoms, H.D. 1963. An analysis of selected variables affecting outdoor recreation patterns. *Social Forces* 42,1:112–115.

5110. Skorzynski, Z. 1962. Podstawowe zajecia mieskancow Warszaway w codziennym buzecie czasu (The basic occupations in everyday budget of Warsaw inhabitants) *Biuletyn Osrodka Badan Opinii Publicznej* 1:1–36.

5111. Skorzynski, Z. and A. Ziemilski. 1964. Wakacje pracownicze w swietle badan nad czasem wolnym w Polsce (Vacations of the working-man in the light of empirical researches in Poland). *Kultura i Spoleczenstwo* 8,3:178–188.

5112. Skorzynski, Z. 1965. *Miedzy praca a wypoczynkiem. "Czaszajety" i "czaz wolny" mieszkancow miast w swietle badan empirycznynch* (Between work and leisure; town dwellers "busy" time and "free" time). Warszawa: Zaglad Narodowyim. Ossolińskich. 252 pp.

5113. Snyder, E. and E. Spreitzer. 1974. Orientations toward work and leisure as predictors of sports involvement. *Research Quarterly* 45,4:398–406.

5114. Staikof, Z. 1964. *Bjudget na vremeto na Trudestite se Bálgaria* (Time-budget of workers in Bulgarian people's republic.) Sofia: Nauke i Iskustvo. 80 pp.

5115. Standlee, L. and W.H. Popham. 1958. Participation in leisure time activities as related to selected vocational and social variables. *J.Psychology* 149–154.

5116. Stone, G. and M.J. Taves. 1960. Camping in the wilderness. Pp. 290–305 in E. Larrabee and R. Meyersohn, eds. *Mass Leisure.* Glencoe, Ill.: Free Press.

5117. Suonperä, M. and P. Paavola. 1971. *Liikuntatyyppinen vapaa-ajan käyttö* (The use of leisure-time as sportslike activity). Helsinki: Ministry of Education. 4.

5118. Sutherland, E.T. 1962. *Playtime in Africa.* New York: Artheneum. 56 pp.

5119. Takács, F. 1966. 6 kérdés, 600 felelet és néhány tanulság (6 questions, 600 answers and a few consequences). *Sportélet* (Budapest) 12:28–29.

5120. Takenoshita, K. 1964. Nipon ni okeru yoka-riyp no jittai (The present situation and problems of use of leisure in Japan). *Shakai Kyoiku* 18,8: 13–19.

5121. Takenoshita, K. 1965. Nippon ni okeru recreation kenkuy no genjo to kadai (The present situation and problems of study on leisure and recreation in Japan). *JOPHER* (Tokyo) 15,10:543–546.

5122. Van den Berg, S.A. 1974. Vakantie voorkeuren van jongeren in den leiftijd van 15 tot en ment 20 jaar (Leisure preferences of 15 to 20 year old young people). *Sociologische Gids* 21,5:318–325.

5123. Van Mechelen, F. 1964. *Vrijtijdsbesteding in Vlanderen.* (Leisure activity in Flanders). Antwerpen: Uitgiverij s.m. outvikkeling. 446 pp.

5124. Weir, L.H. 1937. *Europe at Play.* New York: Barnes. 589 pp.

5125. Wenkart, S. 1963. The meaning of sports for contemporary man. *Journal Existential Psychiatry* 3,12:397–405.

5126. Wennergren, E.G. and D.B. Nielson. 1970. Probability estimates of recreation demands. *J.Leisure Research* 11,Spring:112–133.

5127. Wilson, W. and M. Kayatani. 1968. Intergroup attitudes and strategies in games between opponents of the same or of a different race. *J.Person. Soc.Psychology* 9:24–30.

5128. Winkler, H.J. 1973. Politische Funktionen des nationalen Spitzensports. Pp. 40–45 in F. Grube and G. Richter, eds. *Leistungssport in der Erfolgsgesellschaft.* Hamburg: Hoffmann und Campe.

5129. Wohl, A. 1967. The problem of leisure in our times. *IRSS* 2:109–126.

5130. Zhukova, N.H. 1972. Fizicheskaja kultura i sport v bytu semej (Physical culture and sports in family everyday life). Pp. 21–22 in *Leningrad Konferencija Fizkultura i svobonce vremja.* Moscow.

5131. Ziemilski, A. 1958. Uwagi o problemie socjologii turystyki (Remarks on the problem of sociology of tourism). *Wychowanie Fizyszne Sport* 3:487–495.

5132. Zürn, M. 1971. Sport and physical recreation in the leisure-time culture of big-town dwellers. *Society and Leisure* 3,4:149–157.

5133.   Zűrn, M. 1973. Tourism and motor activity of Cracow inhabitants. *IRSS* 8,1:79–94.

2. Sport, Work and Industry

5134.   Ahtik, V. 1962. Industrial workers participation in cultural, social and physical leisure activities. Pp. 102–110 in *Evolution of the Forms and Needs of Leisure*. Hamburg: UNESCO Institute for Education.
5135.   Akiyoshi, Y. 1963. Shokuba taiiku ni kansuru kenkyu (Study on sports of industrial workers). *Research Phys.Educ. Kyushu University* (Fukuoka) 3,1:23–40.
5136.   Akiyoshi, Y. 1964. Tanko jyugyoin no recreation (A report of recreation activities of the coalmining workers). *Research Phys.Educ. Kyushu University* (Fukuoka). 3,2:54–69.
5137.   Akiyoshi, Y. 1967. Rodo nissu no tanshuku niyoru yokamondai no kenkyu (A study of leisure caused by shortening of labor hours). *Research Phys.Educ. Kyushu University* (Fukuoka). 3,5:79–97.
5138.   Asada, T. 1972. *Gendai shokuba recreation kisoriron* (Philosophy of industrial recreation). Tokyo: Romunkenkyusho.
5139.   Berdichevskij, J.I. and V.E. Ljamke. 1967. Fizicheskaja kultura sredi trudjashchihsja tekstilnyh predprijatij (Physical culture among the workers of the textile factories). *Teorija i Praktika* 10:58–61.
5140.   Borisov, J.V. 1972. Otnoshenie k fizicheskoj kulture i sportu trudjash- chihsja sovchoza (Attitude of the State farm workers to physical cul- ture). *Teorija i Praktika* 7:66–67.
5141.   Cahen-Salvador, M.J. 1957. La responsabilité des moniteurs d'éducation physique et des directeurs de grosses firmes ayant un terrain d'E.P., ou organisant pour leurs élèves ou employés des séances d'E.P. *L'Educa- tion Physique* (Brussels) 49,11:40–45.
5142.   Ciupak, Z. 1975. Rola zakladu pracy w upowszechnianiu kultury (The role of the work enterprise in the popularization of physical culture). *Rocz- niki Naukowe AWF* (Warsaw):75–102.
5143.   Dowell, L.J. 1967. Recreational pursuits of selected occupational groups. *Reseach Quarterly* 38,4:719–722.
5144.   Falaleev, A.N. and M.U. Sergeev. 1973. Fizicheskaja kultura i sport v plane socialnogo razvitija proizvodstvennogo kolleltiva (Physical Culture and sports in a plan of social development of a production collective). Pp. 94–117 in *Problemy fizicheskogo vospitanija, fiziologii, sociologii sporta*. Krasnojarsk.
5145.   Forands, I.F. 1974. Otnoshenija selskih truzhennikov k fizicheskoj kulture (The attitude of rural workers to physical culture). *Teorija i Praktika* 1:46–48.
5146.   Gras, F. 1966. Zu einigen Fragen des funktionellen Zusammenhanges zwischen der physischen Beanspruchung bei Berufsarbeit in der Land- wirtschaft und einer gezielten sportlich-kulturellen Betätigung. *Zeit- schrift für die gesamte Hygiene und ihre Grenzgebiete* 2,December.
5147.   Groll, H. 1971. Participation in high-level sports of young people working in industry and trade. *IRSS* 6,1:115–124.

5148. Güldenpfennig, S.; W. Volpert and P. Weinberg, eds. 1974. *Sensu-motorisches Lernen und Sport als Reproduktion der Arbeitskraft.* Köln: Pahl-Rugenstein. 139 pp.

5149. Hagimitov, B.D. et al. 1965. *Dvizenie za Komunisticeski trud v promis-lenostta* (The movement for communistic work in industry-a sociological investigation). Sofia: Profizdat. 330 pp.

5150. Hayakawa, Y. 1955. Shokuba taiiku no genjgyô to doko (The present conditions of physical education and the industrial workers). *JOPHER* (Tokyo) 5,10:405–408.

5151. Ingham, A.G. 1975. Occupational subcultures in the work world of sport. Pp. 33–389 in Ball/Loy.

5152. International Conference. 1960. *Sport, Work, Culture.* Helsinki: Government of Finland. 240 pp.

5153. International Labour Office. 1950. *Labour Conditions in the Oil Industry in Iran.* Geneva: ILO. 87 pp.

5154. Ishii, Y. 1954. *Shikuba taiiku* (Physical education of industrial workers). Tokyo: Kanazawa-Shoten.

5155. Jolivet, R. 1961. Work, play and contemplation. *Philosophy Today* 5:114–120.

5156. Kawamura, H. 1973. Shokuba recreation (Recreation in factories and offices). Pp. 155–168 in Japanese Society Phys.Educ. eds. *The Lifetime Sport and Physical Education.* Tokyo: Fumaido.

5157. Kornev, M.J. 1971. O meste fizichesko vospitanija v burzhuaznyh teorijah lichnosti (On the place of physical education in bourgeois theories of personality). Pp. 130–134 in *Materialy nauchnych konferencij vuzov po fizicheskoma vospitaniju studentov.* Leningrad.

5158. Kusolev, V.G. 1967. Fizicheskaja kultura v bytu trudjashchihsja (Physical education in workers everyday life). *Teorija i Praktika* 9:65–67.

5159. Le Fay, G. 1962. Incidence de l'éducation physique et du sport chez les ouvriers des houillères. *L'Education Physique* (Brussels) 54,29:14–20.

5160. Lopata, L. 1968. The structure of time and the share of physical education of industrial workers and cooperative farmers in CSSR. *IRSS* 3:17–38.

5161. Lucas, P. 1978. Le travail-gymnaste; rites mineurs du pays miniers. *Cahiers Internationaux de Sociologie* 64,1–2:84–102.

5162. Maier, H. 1975. *Vergesellschaftung des Sports. Zum Problem der Reproduktion der Arbeitskraft.* Lollar: Achenbach. 108 pp.

5163. Megyeri, F. 1962. Mit sportol és mit szeretne sportolni tizenthatezer dolgozó? (In what sport do 16000 workers participate and in what sport do they want to participate?) *Sport és Tudomany* 6,5:134–136.

5164. Megyeri, F. 1962. Munka, testnevelés és szabad idő néhány kérdése és a megoldás utja (Some problems of work, physical education and leisure and the way of solving them). *Sport és Tudomany* 6:178–179.

5165. Megyeri, F. 1967. A szabadidő és a testnevelés (Leisure and sport). Pp. 128–137 in F. Hepp. *A testnevelési tudományos kutató intézet 7 éve.* Budapest.

5166. Mukasa, Y. 1960. Kigyôtai no sports katsudô (Sport activity in the enterprise). *JOHPER* (Tokyo) 10,7:376–378.

5167. Nolan, M.F. and A.J. Sofranko. 1975. Influence of social, economic, and work-related factors on levels of sport participation. *Society and Leisure* 5,3:111–122.

5168. Noll, R. 1974. Alternatives in sports policy. Pp. 411–428 in Noll.

5169. Pakush, V.I. 1971. Fizicheskaja kultura v bytu naselenija kolchoza (Physical education in everyday life of the Kolchoz population). Pp. 154–156 in *Istorija, organizacija i sociologija fizicheskoj kultury i sporta.* Minsk.

5170. Philipp, H. 1972. Zur Situation des Lehrlingssports in der DDR. *Wissenschaftliche Zeitschrift Pädagogische Hochschule Potsdam* 16,3:469–477.

5171. Philipp, H. and G. Schott. 1973. Zur körperlichen Bildung und Erzichung der Lehrlinge in der DDR. *Wissenchaftliche Zeitschrift Pädagogische Hochschule Potsdam* 17,3:477–488.

5172. Ponomarev, N.I. 1962. Trud, svobodnoe vremja i Fizicesko vospitanie (Work, leisure and physical culture). *Teorija i Praktika* 25,11:17–21.

5173. Pudelkiewicz, E. 1971. Problemy sportu i kultury fizycznej w swietle opinii mlodych robotników i kobiet pracujacych (The problems of sports and physical culture: opinion of young male and female workers). *Roczniki Naukowe AWF* (Warsaw) 13:167–193.

5174. Pudelkiewicz, E. 1975. Dwa modele wczasów a realizacja wzoru spotowego Oczekiwania i rzeczwistość (Two models of workers holidays and the implementation of the sport model: Expectations and reality). *Roczniki Naukowe AWF* (Warsaw): 34–51.

5175. Rigauer, B. 1969. *Sport und Arbeit.* Frankfurt: Suhrkamp. 86 pp.

5176. Rodger, L.W. 1978. The games business people play. *Scottish Bankers Magazine* 70,May:41–49.

5177. Rutberg, N.I. 1971. K issledovaniju sozial'noj roli fizicheskoj kultury v razvitii lichnost sovetskogo cheloveka kak truzenika socialisticjeskogo proizvodstva (To the investigation of the social role of physical culture in the development of the personality of Soviet man as a worker of socialist production). Pp. 20–23 in *Materialy Vsesojusnogo simposiuma Riga 1971.* Moscow.

5178. Schaginger, E.M. 1960. Arbeit und Freizeit. *Psychologie und Praxis* 4,1:18–26.

5179. Schiller, J. and J. Zöld. 1965. A sportolók általános morális arculatának vizsgálata egy sportegyesületben (The examination of general moral profile in a sport club). *Testnevelés F. Tudomány Közl.* 5:34–44.

5180. Schiller, J. 1971. A munka ls a sporttevékenység (Work and sport activity). *Sportvezető* (Budapest) 9:10–11.

5181. Seligman, Ben B. 1965. On work, alienation and leisure. *American J. Economics Sociology* 24:337–360.

5182. Semecky, O. 1969. Nektere metodicke zkusenosti z vyzkumu spolecenskeho vyznamu sportovni cinnosti (Some methodical experiences obtained from the research into the social import of sporting activity). *Sociologicky Casopis* (CSSR) 5,1:58–64.

5183. Skavinsky, J.P. 1969. Fizkulturno-ozdorovitelnaja rabota v plane socialnogo razvitija kollektiva promyshlennogo predprijatija (Physical culture and health improvement in the plan of social development of the collective of an industrial enterprise). Pp. 200–204 in *Materialy k nauchnoj konferencii Lvovskogo Universiteta.* Lvov.

5184. Spirescu, R. 1969. L'activité sportive de la jeunesse ouvrière. *Tineretul*

Object de Cercetare Stiintifi (Bucarest) 1:248–251.

5185. Staikof, Z. 1964. Trud, svobodno vreme i perspectivi na fiziceskata kultura (Work, leisure and perspective of physical culture in the collective farms). *Vóprosi na Fiziceskata Kultura* 4:220–225.

5186. Takács, F. 1963. Az atlétakeret tagjai munkához való viszonyának vizsgálata (The examination of the relation of the members of the national track and field team to work). *Testnevelés F. Tudomány Közl.* 3,2: 49–57.

5187. Takenoshita, K. 1964. Shokuba no recreation to ningenkandei (Recreation and human relations in work). *Journal of Sciences of Labor* 19,10: 26–30.

5188. Tamasne, F. 1979. Involvement in sport and watching of sport events of workers of a large enterprise in Budapest. *IRSS* 14,1:61–80.

5189. Telama, R. 1975. *Meteli* (Metal workers). Jyväskylä: University of Jyväkylä.

5190. Terasawa, T. 1972. Shokuba taiiku no shinkō ni kansuru jireikenkyu (1) (A case study on the promotion of physical education in a company, Nr 1). *Journal of Toyota Technical College* (Toyota) 5:95–107.

5191. Terasawa, T. and Y. Itō. 1973. Shokuba taiiku no shinkō ni kansuru jirei kenkyu (2) (A study on the promotion of physical education in a company). *Journal of Toyota Technical College* (Toyota) 6:87–90.

5192. Wohl, A. 1954. Degredacja fizyczna ludnosci pracujacej w okresie kapitalistycznej industrializacji (Physical degeneration of working people in the period of capitalistic industrialization). *Kultura Fizyczna* 3:158–166.

5193. Wohl, A. 1962. Ideowe zalozenia sportu robotniczego (Ideological foundations of worker's sport). *Sport Robotniczy* (Warsaw):7–21.

5194. Wohl, A. 1969. Engagement in sports activity on the part of workers. *IRSS* 4,1:83–128.

5195. Zhvanija, D.K. 1973. O sochetanii zanjatij sportom s uchjeboj i trudovoj dejatelnostju (On combination of sport, studies and labour). *Teorija i Praktika* 6:46–48.

5196. Zoldak, V.I. 1967. Dvizenije kommunisticeskovo truda fiziceskaja kul'tura (The Communist labour movement and physical culture). *Teorija i Praktika* 5:4–7.

5197. Zoldak, V.I. and G.K. Karpovskij. 1971. Fiziceskaja kul'tura i podgotovka molodiezu k trudu (Physical culture and preparation of youth for work). *Fiziceskaja kul'tura i naucnaja organizacija truda:* 13–33.

3. Sport and Play of Handicapped Groups

5198. Boltanski, F. 1969. L'Éducation physique de l'enfant sain et handicapé. *Réadaptation* 165:4–8.

5199. Coleman, J.C. et al. 1963. Motor performance and social adjustment among boys experiencing serious learning difficulties. *Research Quarterly* 34:516–517.

5200. Gump, P. and B. Sutton-Smith. 1955. Activity-setting and social interaction. A field study. *American Journal of Orthopsychiatry* 25,4: 755–760.

5201. Kubie, L.S. 1954. Competitive sports and the awkward child. *Child*

         Study 31,1:10–15.

5201a.   Lewko, J. 1978. Significant others and sport socialization of the handi-
         capped child. Pp. 247–277 in F. Smoll and R. Smith, eds. *Psychological
         Perspectives in Youth Sport.* Washington, D.C.: Hemisphere.
5202.   Lonnoy, R. 1962. *Le sport-son role chez le sourd-muet.* Bruxelles. Mimeo.
5203.   Widdop, J.H. 1970. A comparative study of the motor performance of
         educable retarded children and normal children. Pp. 523–539 in G.S.
         Kenyon, ed. *Psychology of Sport.* Chicago: Athletic Institute.

4. Sport, Minorities and Discrimination

5204.   Babchuk, N. and R.V. Thompson. 1962. The voluntary associations of
         Negroes. *ASR* 27,5:647–655.
5204a.   Ball, D. 1973. Ascription and position: a comparative analysis of 'stacking'
         in professional football. *Canadian Rev.Sociol.Anthr.* 10,1:97–113.
5205.   Baron, H.M. 1968. Black powerlessness in Chicago. *Transaction* 6:27–33.
5206.   Blalock, H.M. 1962. Occupational discrimination: some empirical propo-
         sitions. *Social Problems* 9,3:240–247.
5207.   Brogneaux, J. 1955. Racial integration in high school interscholastic
         sports. *JOHPER* 26,April:26–37.
5208.   Brown, R.C. 1976. A commentary on racial myths and the black athlete.
         Pp. 168–173 in Landers.
5209.   Dodson, D.W. 1954. The integration of Negroes in baseball. *J.Educational
         Sociology* 28:73–82.
5210.   Dougherty, J. 1976. Race and sport: A follow-up study. *Sport Sociology
         Bulletin* 5,1:1–12.
5211.   Draper, M. 1963. *Sport and Race in South Africa.* Johannesburg: South
         African Institute of Race Relations. 109 pp.
5212.   Dubois, P. 1974. Sport, mobility, and the black athlete. *Sport Sociology
         Bulletin* 3,2:40–61.
5213.   Edwards, H. 1969. *The Revolt of the Black Athlete.* New York: Free
         Press. 202 pp.
5214.   Edwards, H. 1971. The sources of the black athlete's superiority. *The
         Black Scholar* Nov.:32–41.
5215.   Edwards, H. 1972. Desegregating sexist sport. *Intellectual Digest* 3,3:
         82–83.
5216.   Edwards, H. 1973. The black athletes: 20th century gladiators for white
         America. *Psychology Today* 7,6:43–44 and 47–52.
5217.   Eitzen. D.S. 1975. The segregation of blacks by playing position in foot-
         ball: Accident or design? *Social Science Quart.* 55,4:948–959.
5218.   Eitzen, D.S. and I. Tessendorf. 1975. Racial segregation by position in
         sports: The special case of basketball. Pp. 19–20 in D. Landers et al.
         eds. *Psychology of Sport and Motor Behavior II.* Pennsylvania: Univer-
         sity Park.
5219.   Eitzen, D.S. and N.R. Yetman. 1977. Sports: immune from racism? *Civil
         Rights Digest* 9:3–13.
5220.   Falkenstörfer, H. and H.O. Hahn. 1972. *Zwischenrufe.* Wuppertal: Jugend-
         dienst-Verlag. 102 pp.

5221. Govan, M. 1971. The emergence of the black athlete in America. *The Black Scholar* Nov.: 16–28.

5222. Hain, P. 1971. *Don't Play with Apartheid*. London: Allen and Unwin.

5223. Hare, N. 1971. A study of the black fighter. *The Black Scholar* Nov.:2–8.

5224. Hellman, E. and L. Abraham. 1949. *Handbook of Race Relations in South Africa*. Cape Town: Oxford University Press.

5225. Henderson, R.W. 1949. *The Negro in Sports*. Washington, D.C.: Associated Publishers. 507 pp.

5226. Henderson, E.B. 1968. *The Black Athlete—Emergence and Arrival*. New York: Publishers Company, Inc.

5227. Holloman, L.L. 1943. On the supremacy of the Negro athlete in white athletic competition. *Psychoanalytic Review* 30:157–162.

5228. Horrell, M. 1969. *South Africa and the Olympic Games*. Johannesburg: South African Institute for Race Relations.

5229. Horrell, M. 1960–1972. *A Survey of Race Relations*. Johannesburg: South African Institute for Race Relations. Annual Reports.

5230. Huddleston, C.R. 1957. *Sport: The Arts and the Colour Bar in South Africa*. London: The Africa Bureau.

5231. International Olympic Committee. 1967. *Report by the International Olympic Committee's Commission to South Africa*. Lausanne: IOC.

5232. Jones, J.M. and A.R. Hochner. 1973. Racial differences in sports activities: A look at the self-paced versus reactive hypothesis. *J.Person.Soc.Psych.* 27,1:86–95.

5233. Lapchick, R.E. 1975. *Politics of Race and International Sport: The Case of South Africa*. Westport, Connecticut: Greenwood. 268 pp.

5234. Lapchick, R.E. 1976. Apartheid and the politics of sport. *Africa Report* 21,Sept.: 37–40.

5235. Leonard, W.M. 1977. An extension of the Black, Latin, White report. *IRSS* 12,3:85–96.

5236. Leonard, W.M. 1977. Stacking and performance differentials of Whites, Blacks, Latins in professional baseball. *Review Sport Leisure* 2,June: 77–106.

5237. Loy, J.W. and J.F. McElvogue. 1971. Racial segregation in American sport. Pp. 113–127 in Albonico/Pfister-Binz.

5238. Loy, J.W. 1976. Race and sport. Pp. 157–167 in Landers.

5239. Madison, D.R. and D.M. Landers. 1976. Racial discrimination in football: A test of the "stacking" of playing positions. Pp. 151–156 in Landers.

5240. Manning, B.A.; J. Pierce-Jones and Parelman. 1974. Cooperative, trusting behavior in a "culturally deprived," mixed ethnic-group population. *J.Social Psych.* 92,1:133–141.

5241. Meade, G.P. 1952. The Negro in track athletics. *Scientific Monthly* 75,6: 366–371.

5242. Medoff, M.H. 1975. A reappraisal of discrimination against blacks in professional baseball. *Review of Black Political Economy* 5,3:259–268.

5243. Medoff, M.H. 1976. Racial segregation in baseball: the economic hypothesis versus the sociology hypothesis. *J.Black Studies* 6,4:393–400.

5244. Medoff, M.H. 1977. Positional segregation and professional baseball. *IRSS* 12,1:49–56.

5245. Mogull, R.G. 1974. Racial discrimination in professional basketball.

American Behavioral Scientist 18, Spring:11–15. Respective discussions in various issues 1975–1977.

5246. McClendon, M.J. and D.S. Eitzen. 1975. Interracial contact on collegiate basketball teams: a test of Sherif's theory of superordinate goals. *Soc. Science Quart.* 55,4:926–938.

5247. McPherson, B.D. 1975. The segregation by playing position hypothesis in sport: an alternative explanation. *Soc.Science Quart.* 55:960–966.

5248. McPherson, B.D. 1976. The black athlete: an overview and analysis. Pp. 122–150 in Landers.

5249. Olsen, J. 1968. The black athlete. *Sports Illustrated* 29,July,1:12–27. 8:18–31. 15:28–43. 22:28–41. 29:20–35.

5250. Phillips, J.C. 1976. Toward an explanation of racial variations in top-level sports participation. *IRSS* 11,3:39–55.

5251. Picou, J.S. 1978. Race, athletic achievement, and educational aspiration. *Sociol.Quart.* 19,Summer:429–438.

5252. Pudelkiewicz, E. 1973. The socio-historic background of the ideology of racism in sport. *IRSS* 8,3:89–115.

5253. Rainville, R.E. and E. McCornick. 1977. Extent of covert racial prejudice in pro-football announcers' speech. *Journalism Quart.* 54,Spring:20–26.

5254. Rainville, R.E. et al. 1978. Recognition of covert racial prejudice. *Journalism Quart.* 55,Summer:256–259.

5255. Rhodes, L. and J.S. Butler. 1975. Sport and racism: a contribution to theory building in race relations? *Social Science Quart.* 55,4:519–525.

5256. Ribalow, H.U. 1949. *The Jew in American Sport.* New York: Block. 288 pp.

5257. Rosenblatt, A. 1967. Negroes in baseball: the failure of success. *Transaction* 5:51–53.

5258. Scully, G.W. 1973. Economic discrimination in professional sports. *Law and Contemporary Problems* 38,1:67–84.

5259. Scully, G.W. 1974. Discrimination: the case of baseball. Pp. 221–274 in R. Noll.

5260. Simon, R.J. and J.W. Carey. 1966. The phantom racist. *Trans-action* 4,1:5–11.

5261. Steinkamp, E.W. 1976. *Sport und Rasse. Der schwarze Sportler in den USA.* Ahrensburg: Czwalina.

5262. Thompson, R. 1964. *Race and Sport.* London: Oxford University Press. 73 pp.

5263. Thompson, R. 1972.[2] *Race Discrimination in New Zealand.* University of Canterbury, N.Z.: Dept. Psychology and Sociology.

5264. Thompson, R. 1969. *Race Discrimination in Sport. A New Zealand Controversy.* Aukland, N.Z.: National Council of Churches.

5265. Thompson, R. 1975. *Retreat from Apartheid: New Zealand's Sporting Contacts with South Africa.* New York: Oxford University Press. 102 pp.

5266. Williams, R.L. and Z.I. Yousser. 1975. Division of labor in college football along racial lines. *International J.Sport Psychology* 6,1:3–13.

5267. Young, A.S. 1963. *Negro Firsts in Sports.* Chicago: Johnson.

5268. Zeigler, E.F. 1972. The black athlete's non-athletic problems. *Educational Theory* 22,4:420–426.

5. *Sport, Deviance, and Criminal Behavior*

5269.   Brickman, P. 1977. Crime and punishment in sports and society. *J.Social Issues* 33,1:140–64.

5270.   Brown, R.C. Jr. and D.W. Dodson. 1959. The effectiveness of a boy's club in reducing delinquency. *Annals AAPSS* 322, March:47–52.

5271.   Cohen, A.K. 1955. *Delinquent Boys.* Glencoe, Ill.: Free Press. 202 pp.

5272.   Cohen, S. ed. 1971. *Images of Deviance.* Harmondsworth: Penguin. 255 pp.

5273.   Cullen, F.T. 1974. Attitudes of players and spectators toward norm-violation in ice hockey. *Perceptual and Motor Skills* 38,3:1146.

5274.   Cullen, J.B. and F.T. Cullen. 1975. The structure and contextual conditions of group norm violation: some implications from the game of ice hockey. *IRSS* 10,2:69–78.

5275.   Fiutko, R. 1967. Wuchowanie fizyczne i sport—istotnym czynnikiem w reedukacij mlodocianych przestepcow (Physical education and sport as an essential factor in the education of juvenile delinquents). *Kultura Fizyczna* 20,5:210–213.

5276.   Griffin, M. 1937. *Fall Guys.* Chicago, Ill.: Reilley and Lee. 215 pp.

5277.   Heinemann, K. 1975. Sport als Instrument der Resozialization-eine ideologie-kritische Diskussion. Pp. 20–42 in *Sozialisation durch Sport.* Frankfurt: Deutsche Sportjugend.

5278.   Hosek, A. et al. 1973. Relacija socioloskih i demografskih karakteristika i kinezioloskih aktivnosti maloljetnih delinkvenata (Relations among sociological and demographic characteristics and kinesiological activity in juvenile delinquents). *Kineziologija* (Zagreb) 3,1:51–52.

5279.   Ingham, A.G. and J.W. Loy. 1973. The social system of sport: a humanistic perspective. *Quest* 19,1:3–23.

5280.   Khosla, T. 1968. Unfairness of certain events in the Olympic games. *British Medical Journal* 4,Oct.111–113.

5281.   Lüschen, G. 1971. Delinquency. Pp. 1391–1393 in *Encyclopedia of Sport Science and Medicine.* New York: Macmillan.

5282.   Lüschen, G. 1976. Cheating in sport. Pp. 67–77 in Landers.

5283.   Mahigel, E.L. and G.P. Stone. 1972. Making vs. playing games of cards. Pp. 74–93 in G.P. Stone, ed. *Games, Sport and Power.* New Brunswick, N.J.: Transaction Books.

5284.   Mahigel, E.L. and G.P. Stone. 1976. Hustling as a career. Pp. 78–85 in Landers.

5285.   Mrakovic, M.A. 1973. Hosek: Razlike izmedju maloljetnika kojima su izrecene vaninstitucionalne i institucionalne sankcije u kognitivnim i konativnim karakteristikama, stavovima prema sportu i angaziranosti kinezioloskim aktivnostima (The differences between juvenile delinquents with institutional and noninstitutional juridicial sanctions in cognitive characteristics, attitudes toward sport and participation in sport activities). *Kineziologija* (Zagreb) 3,1:83–92.

5286.   Newman, O. 1968. The sociology of the betting shop. *British J.Sociology* 19,1.

5287.   Newman, O. 1972. The gambling problem. Social Service Quarterly

(London), Spring.
5288.   Nolan, J.B. 1955. Athletics and juvenile deliquency. *J.Educational Socio-logy* 28,6:263-265.
5289.   Nyholm, T. and U. Lahtinen. 1974. *The Interest in Sports of Prisoners.* Publication Nr. 18. Jyväskylä: University of Jyväskylä.
5290.   Petrie, B.M. 1976. The athletic group as an emerging deviant subculture. Pp. 224-237 in Landers.
5291.   Polsky, N. 1964. The hustler. *Social Problems* 12,1:3-15.
5292.   Schafer, W.E. 1969. Social sources and consequences of interscholastic athletics. The case of participation and delinquency. Pp. 29-56 in Kenyon.
5293.   Schafer, W.E. 1969. Participation in interscholastic athletics and delinquency: a preliminary study. *Social Problems* 17,1:40-47.
5294.   Shanas, E. 1942. *Recreation and Delinquency.* Chicago: Chicago Recreation Commission. 284 pp.
5295.   Short, J.F. et al. 1963. Behavior dimensions of gang delinquency. *ASR* 28,3:411-428.
5296.   Short, J.F. and R.L. Strodtbeck. 1965. *Group Process and Gang Delinquency.* Chicago: University of Chicago Press. 294 pp.
5297.   Steele, P.D. 1976. The bowling hustler: a study of deviance in sport. Pp. 86-92 in Landers.
5298.   Thrasher, F.M. 1936. *The Gang.* Chicago: University of Chicago Press. 605 pp.
5299.   Truxal, A.G. 1929. *Outdoor Recreation Legislation and Its Effectiveness.* New York: Columbia University Press. 218 pp.
5300.   Weinberg, C. 1965. The price of competition. *Teachers College Record* 67,2:106-114.
5301.   Weis, K. 1976. Abweichung und Konformität in der Institution Sport. Pp. 296-315 in Lüschen/Weis.
5302.   Yiannakis, A. 1976. Delinquent tendencies and participation in an organized sports program. *Research Quarterly* 47,4:845-849.

6. *Aggression and Violence in Sport*

5303.   Cauwels, A. et al. 1977. *Geweld in de wereld, geweld in de sport* (Violence in the world, violence in sport). Leuven: Seco. 163 pp.
5304.   Denker, R. 1973. Sport and aggression. Pp. 381-388 in Grupe.
5305.   Denker, R. 1975. Sport und Aggression. *Der Bürger im Staat* (Stuttgart) 25,3:203-208.
5306.   Ekkers, C.L. and G.P. Hoefnagels. 1972. *Agressie en straf op het voetbalveld* (Aggression and punishment in the soccer world). Meppel: Born. 78 pp.
5307.   Elias, N. 1971. Sport en Geweld. Het Onstaan van de sport in de Antieke Wereld (Sport and violence. The development of sport in antiquity). *Sociologische Gids* 134,2:67-88.
5308.   Elias, N. 1971. The genesis of sport as a sociological problem. Pp. 88-115 in Dunning.
5309.   Elias, N. 1976. Sports and violence. *Actes de la Recherche en Sciences Sociales* (Paris) 2,6:2-20.

5310. Faulkner, R.R. 1974. Making violence by doing work: selves, situations, and the world of professional hockey. *Sociology Work Occupations* 1,3:288-312.

5311. Fourton, J. 1972. *Agressivité utile ou dangereuse.* Paris: Editions de la Tete de Fouilles. 200 pp.

5312. Gabler, H. 1976. *Aggressive Hanlungen im Sport.* Schorndorf: Hofmann.

5313. Gaskell, G. and R. Pearton. 1978. Aggression and Sport. Pp. 263-296 in Goldstein.

5314. Gluckman, M. 1973. Sport and conflict. Pp. 48-55 in Grupe.

5315. Goldstein, J.H. and R.L. Arms. 1971. Effects of observing athletic contests on hostility. *Sociometry* 34,1:83-90.

5316. Harrington, J.A. 1968. *Soccer Hooliganism.* London: Wright.

5317. Hatfield, F.C. 1973. Some factors precipitating player violence: a preliminary report. *Sport Sociology Bulletin* 2:1-21.

5318. Hughes, R. and J.J. Coakley. 1978. Player violence and the social organization of contact sport. *J.Sport Behavior* 1:155-168.

5319. Husman, B.F. 1955. Aggression in boxers and wrestlers as measured by projective techniques. *Research Quarterly* 26,4:421-425.

5320. Ingham, R. et al. 1978. *Football Hooliganism.* London: Inter-Action. 151 pp.

5321. Jacobson, S. 1975. Chelsea rule—okay. *New Society* 31,651:780-783.

5322. Jeu, B. 1972. *Le sport, la mort, la violence.* Paris: Ed. Universitaires. 208 pp.

5323. Kelly, B.R. and J.F. McCerty. 1979. Personality dimension of aggression: its relationship to time and place of action in hockey. *Human Relations* 32,March:219-225.

5324. Kingsmore, J.M. 1970. The effect of a professional wrestling and professional basketball contest upon the aggressive tendencies of spectators. Pp. 311-316 in Kenyon, ed. *Psychology of Sport.* Chicago: Athletic Institute.

5325. Klein, D. 1974. Body-contact: catharsis or reinforcement? *Accident Analysis and Prevention* 6:85-91.

5326. Lang, J. 1969. *Report of the Working Party on Cruel Behavior at Football Matches.* London: Her Majesty's Stationary Office.

5327. Layman, E.M. 1970. Aggression in relation to play and sports. Pp. 25-34. Kenyon, ed. *Psychology of Sport.* Chicago: Athletic Institute.

5328. Lefebvre, L.M. and M.N. Passer. 1974. The effects of game location and importance on aggression in team sports. *Inter.J.Sport Psychology* 5,2:102-109.

5329. Listiak, A. Legitimate deviance and social class: bar behavior during grey cup week. *Sociological Focus* 7,Summer:13-44.

5330. Marsh, P. 1975. Understanding aggro. *New Society* 32,3:7-9.

5331. Marsh, P. 1978. *Aggro, the Illusion of Violence.* London: Dent. 165 pp.

5332. Marsh, P. et al. 1978. *The Rules of Disorder.* London: Routledge and Kegan Paul. 140 pp.

5333. Naul, R. and H. Voigt. 1974. Aggression und Sport. *Soziale Welt* 25,3:347-369.

5334. Petryszak, N. 1977. The bio-sociology of joy in violence. *Review Sport Leisure* 2,June:1-16.

5335. Pilz, G.A. 1974. Fördert Sport aggressives Verhalten? *Die Umschau*

74,22:697-702.

5336.   Pilz, G. and A. Trebels. 1976. *Aggression und Konflikt im Sport.* Ahrensburg: Czwalina. 217 pp.

5337.   Plack, A. ed. 1973. *Der Mythos vom Aggressionstrieb.* München: List. 320 pp.

5338.   Prenner, K. 1972. Aggressivität und Gewalt im Sport. *Die Leibeserziehung* 21,10:340-344.

5339.   Runfola, R. 1975. Violence in sport: mirror of American society? *Vital Issues* 24,7:1-4.

5340.   Russell, G.W. 1974. Machiavellianism, locus of control, aggression, performance and precautionary behavior in ice hockey. *Human Relations* 27,9:825-837.

5341.   Ryan, E.D. 1970. The cathartic effect of vigorous motor activity on aggressive behavior. *Research Quarterly* 41:542-551.

5342.   Schleske, W. 1972. Der Sport in der Industriegesellschaft als Anlass für Aggression und Sublimation. *Die Leibeserziehung* 21,10:349-355.

5343.   Scott, J.P. 1970. Sport and aggression. Pp. 11-24 in G.S. Kenyon, ed. *Psychology of Sport.* Chicago: Athletic Institute.

5344.   Sipes, R.G. 1973. War, Sports and aggression: an empirical test of two rival theories. *American Anthropologist* 75:64-86.

5345.   Smith, G. 1971. Violence and sport. *JOHPER* 42,3:45-47.

5346.   Smith, M. 1973. Hostile outbursts in sport. *Sport Sociology Bulletin* 2:1-21.

5347.   Smith, M.D. 1974. Violence in sport. *Sportwissenschaft* 4,2:164-173.

5348.   Smith, M.D. 1974. Significant others' influence on the assaultive behavior of young hockey players. *IRSS* 9,3-4:45-58.

5349.   Smith, M.D. 1975. Sport and collective violence. Pp. 281-330 in Ball/Loy.

5350.   Smith, M.D. 1975. The legitimization of violence. *Canadian Review Sociology Anthropology* 12,1:72-80.

5351.   Smith, M.D. 1979. Towards an explanation of hockey violence: a reference other approach. *Canadian J.Sociology* 4,2:105-124.

5352.   Sprenger, J. 1974. Zum Problem der Aggression im Sport. *Sportwissenschaft* 4,3:231-257.

5353.   Taylor, I. 1969. Hooligans: soccer's resistance movement. *New Society* 358:204-206.

5354.   Taylor, I. 1971. Soccer consciousness and soccer hooliganism. Pp. 134-164 in S. Cohen, ed. *Images of Deviance.* Harmondsworth: Penguin.

5355.   Taylor, I. 1971. Football mad: a speculative sociology of football hooliganism. Pp. 352-377 in Dunning.

5356.   Turner, E.T. 1970. The effects of viewing college football, basketball and wrestling on the elicited aggressive responses of male spectators. Pp. 325-330 in Kenyon, ed. *Psychology of Sport.* Chicago: Athletic Institute.

5357.   Tutko, T.A. 1970. Conflict in sports. In G.S. Kenyon, ed. *Psychology of Sport.* Chicago: Athletic Institute.

5358.   Vrcan, S. 1971. La sociologie devant le football. *Soziologija* (Beograd) 13,1:5-20.

5359.   Weber, A. 1977. Aggressionskanalisierung durch sportliche Betätigung? *Sportwissenschaft* 7,2:181-190.

5360.   Zillmann, D. et al. 1974. Provoked and unprovoked aggression in athletes. *J.Research Personality* 8,2:139–152.

VI. *Varia and Miscellaneous*

   1. *Social Philosophy; Social Criticism; Humanist Analyses*

6001.   Adam, H. 1966. Leibeserziehung als Ideologie. *Das Argument* 40:402–407.
6002.   Bernett, H. 1977. Zum Problem der Fremdbestimmung und Instrumentalisierung des Sports. *Sportwissenschaft* 7,2:139–150.
6003.   Bernett, H. 1978. Die Ideologie der deutschen Gymnastik. *Sportwissenschaft* 8,1:7–23.
6004.   Brohm, J.M. 1978. *Sport a Prison of Measured Time.* London: Ink Link. 185 pp.
6005.   Bruns, W. 1973. Zur Kritik der Neuen Linken am Sport. Pp. 182–196 in F. Grube and G. Richter, eds. *Der Leistungssport in der Erfolgsgesellschaft.* Hamburg: Hoffmann and Campe.
6006.   Daempfert, E. 1974. Zur Leistungsinterpretation der "Neuen Linken" und ihren philosophischen Grundpositionen. *Wissensch.Zeitschr.DHFK* 15,2: 121–128.
6007.   Friedenberg, E.Z. 1968. Foreward to Man, Sport and Existence. In Hart.
6008.   Guillon, F. and A. Guillon. 1976. *Sport et créativité.* Paris: Delarge, Editions universitaires. 184 pp.
6009.   Guttmann, A. 1974. Sport in der amerikanischen Literatur: Bestätigung der neuen Sozialkritik. *Sportwissenschaft* 4,4:384–394.
6010.   Habermas, J. 1958. Soziologische Notizen zum Verhältnis von Arbeit und Freizeit. Pp. 219–231 in G. Funke, ed. *Konkrete Vernunft.* Bonn: Athenäum.
6011.   Henschen, H.H. et al. 1972. Anti-Olympia. *Ein Beitrag zur mutwilligen Diffamierung und öffentlichen Destruktion der Olympischen Spiele und anderer Narreteien.* München: Hanser. 148 pp.
6012.   Hoch, P. 1972. *Rip off the Big Game.* Garden City, N.Y.: Doubleday. 222 pp.
6013.   Ingham, A.G. 1976. Sport and the "New Left": some reflections upon opposition without praxis. Pp. 238–248 in Landers.
6014.   Keating, J.W. 1973. The ethics of competition and its relation to some moral problems in athletics. Pp. 157–198 in R.G. Osterhoudt, ed. *The Philosophy of Sport: a Collection of Original Essays.* Springfield, Ill.: Charles C. Thomas.
6015.   Kuntz, D.G. and P. Weis. 1977. On sport as performing arts. *International Philosophical Quarterly* 17,2:147–165.
6016.   Leguillaumie, P. 1972. *Pour une critique fondamentale du sport.* Paris: Petite maspero.
6017.   Lenk, H. 1971. Sport, Arbeit, Leistungszwang. *Leistungssport* (Frankfurt) 1,2:63–67.
6018.   Lenk, H. 1971. Sport, Gesellschaft, Philosophie. *Sportwissenschaft* 1,1: 19–32.
6019.   Lenk, H. 1972. Leistungssport und Leistungskritik heute. *Universitas*

(Stuttgart) 27,8:827–840.

6020. Lenk, H. 1972. Das Büroherz als revolutionäre Kraft?–Oder Leistungs-sport als Schule des Spätkapitalismus. *Olympische Jugend* 17,2:4-6.

6021. Lenk, H. 1973. Alienation, manipulation and the self of the athlete. Pp. 8-18 in Grupe.

6022. Lenk, H. 1973. Manipulation oder Emanzipation in Leistungssport. *Sportwissenschaft* 3,1:9–40.

6023. Lenk, H. 1976. Zur Kritik am Leistungsprinzip im Sport. Pp. 155-164 in Lüschen/Weis.

6024. Lenk, H. 1979. *Social Philosophy of Athletics.* Champaign, Ill.: Stipes. 227 pp.

6025. Lowe, B. 1973. A theoretical rationale for investigation into the relation-ship of sport and aesthetics. *IRSS* 8,1:95–101.

6026. Natan, A. 1972. *Sport-Kritisch.* Bern-Stuttgart: Hallwag. 224 pp.

6027. Neidhardt, H. 1966. Marxistisches Menschenbild und Körperkultur. *Wissenschaftliche Zeitschrift der DHFK* (Leipzig) 8,2:39–45.

6028. Osterhoudt, R.G. 1973. *The Philosophy of Sport: A Collection of Original Essays.* Springfield, Ill.: Thomas. 359 pp.

6029. Partisans. 1968. Sport, Culture et repressions. *Partisans* 43,July-Sept.: 5–152.

6030. Prokop, U. 1971. *Soziologie der Olympischen Spiele. Sport und Kapi-talismus.* München: Hanser.

6031. Richter, J. 1972. *Die vertrimmte Nation oder Sport in rechter Gesell-schaft.* Reinbek: Rowohlt. 144 pp.

6032. Sartre, J. 1960. Critique de la raison dialectique. Paris: Gallimard. 600 pp.

6033. Schmitz, J.N. 1974. *Sport und Leibeserziehung zwischen Spätkapitalis-mus und Frühsozialismus.* Schorndorf: Hofmann. 147 pp.

6034. Scott, J. 1971. *The Athletic Revolution.* New York: Free Press.

6035. Slusher, H.S. 1967. *Man, Sport and Existence; a Critical Analysis.* Phila-delphia: Lea and Flerbiger. 243 pp.

6036. Spady, W.G. 1976. A commentary on sport and the New Left. Pp. 212-223 in Landers.

6037. Stoijarok, V.I. 1977. On a humanistic value of sport. *IRSS* 12,3:75–84.

6038. Süenens, L. 1973. The alienation and identity of man. Pp. 3-8 in Grupe.

6039. Varga, S.F. 1936. *A sport. Kulturfilozofiai tanulmany* (Sport a study in cultural philosophy). Szolnok: Wachs nyomda. 68 pp.

6040. Weiss, P. 1969. *Sport: a Philosophical Inquiry.* Carbondale: Southern Ill. Press. 274 pp.

6041. Weiss, P. 1973. Records and the man. Pp. 537-544 in O. Grupe, et al. eds. *Sport in the Modern World.* Berlin: Springer.

6042. Wohl, A. 1964. Philosophische und soziologische Probleme im wissen-schaftlichen Bereich der Körperkultur. *Theorie und Praxis* 13,Sept.:3–9.

6043. Wohl, A. 1965. *Slowo a Ruch* (Word and Movement). Warsaw: PWN.

6044. Ziemilski, A. 1964. In der zweiten Hälfte des Jahrhunderts des Sports. Eine soziologische Skizze über den bürgerlichen Skeptizismus im Sport. *Theorie und Praxis* 13,3:170-178. (Supplement).

6045. Zöld, J. 1968. A testnevelés és sport a filozófiai és a társadalaomtudo-mányok érdeklödésének elöterében (Physical education and sport in the focus of interest of philosophy and sociological sciences). *Testn.Tan.* 4,3:76–81.

2. Historical Analyses

6046. Auguet, R. 1972. *Cruelty and Civilization: the Roman Games.* London: Allen and Unwin.

6047. Bengtson, H. 1972. *Die Olympischen Spiele in der Antike.* Zürich/Stuttgart: Artemis.

6048. Berryman, J.W. 1975. From the cradle to the playing field: America's emphasis on highly organized competitive sports for preadolescent boys. *J.Sport History* 2,2:112–131.

6049. Bruce, D.D. 1977. Play, work and ethics in the Old South. *Southern Folklore Quarterly* 41:33–51.

6050. Burgener, L. 1972. Die Geschichte der Leibesübungen und des Sports. *Körpererziehung/L'Education Physique* (Switzerland) 50,7-8:190–193.

6051. Crockett, D.S. 1961. Sports and recreational practices of Union and Conferederate soldiers. *Research Quarterly* 32,Oct.:335–347.

6052. Defrance, J. 1976. Esquisse d'une histoire sociale de la gymnastique (1760–1870). *Actes de la recherche en sciences sociales* 2,6:22–46.

6053. Diem, C. 1960. *Weltgeschichte des Sport und der Leibeserziehung.* Stuttgart: Cotta. 1123 pp.

6054. Drees, L. 1962. *Der Ursprung der Olympischen Spiele.* Schorndorf: Hofmann. 144 pp.

6055. Drees, L. 1967. *Olympia, Götter, Künstler und Athleten.* Stuttgart: Kohlhammer.

6056. Gillet, B. 1949. *Histoire du sport.* Paris: Presses Universitaires de France. 126 pp.

6057. Gradopolova, T.K. 1970. Otrazhenie socialnoj sushchnosti fizicheskogo vospitanija v russkoj hudozhestvennoj literature XIX–XX stoletija (The reflection of the social essence of physical education in Russian fiction literature of XIX–XX centuries). Pp. 17 in *Avtoreferat dissertacii.* Moscow.

6058. Graham, P.J. and H. Ueberhorst eds. 1976. *The Modern Olympics.* Cornwall, New York: Leisure Press. 236 pp.

6059. Kircher, R. 1927. *Fair Play. Sport, Spiel und Geist in England.* Frankfurt: Societäts-Druckerei.

6060. Kloeren, M. 1935. *Sport und Rekord.* Leipzig: Tauchnitz 294 pp.

6061. Lewis, G. 1969. Theodore Roosevelt's role in the 1905 football controversy. *Research Quarterly* 40,4:717–724;

6062. Manchester, H. 1931. *Four Centuries of Sport in America.* New York: Derrydale. 245 pp.

6063. McIntosh, P.C. et al. 1957. *Landmarks in the History of Physical Education.* London: Routledge.

6064. McIntosh, P.C. 1971. A historical view of sport and social control. *IRSS* 6,1:5–16.

6065. Pleket, H.W. 1974. Zur Soziologie des antiken Sports. *Medelingen van het Nederlands Instituut de Rome* 36:57–87.

6066. Pleket, H.W. 1975. Games, prizes, athletes and ideology. *Arena* (Leyden) 1,1:49–89.

6067. Renson, R. 1977. Play in exile: the Continental pastimes of King Charles II. Pp. 507–522 in G. Curl, ed. *International Seminar Phys. Ed. and Sport.* Dartford.

6068.   Wildt, C.C. 1957. *Leibesübungen im deutschen Mittelalter.* Frankfurt: Limpert. 44 pp.
6069.   Wohl, A. 1961. *Spoleczno historyczne odloze sportu* (Socio-historical foundations of sport). Warsaw: Sport i Turystyka. 150 pp.
6070.   Wohl, A. 1964. Die gesellschaftlich-historischen Grundlagen des bürgerlichen Sports. *Wissensch.Zeitschr.DHFK* 6,1:1-93.
6071.   Woody, T. 1949. *Life and Education in Early Societies.* New York: Macmillan. 825 pp.
6072.   Ylanan, R.R. 1965. *The History and Development of Physical Education and Sports in the Philippines.* Manila. 242 pp.

3. Miscellaneous and Late Entries

6073.   Alderman, R.B. 1974. *Psychological Behavior in Sport.* Philadelphia: Saunders. 280 pp.
6074.   Aldis, O. 1975. *Play Fighting.* New York: Academic Press. 319 pp.
6075.   Arms, R.L. et al. 1979. Effects on the hostility of spectators of viewing aggressive sports. *Social Psychological Quarterly* 42,Summer:275-279.
6076.   Beyer, E. 1964. *Die amerikanische Sportsprache.* Schorndorf: Hofmann. 108 pp.
6077.   Birrell, S. and A. Turowetz. 1979. Character work-up and display: collegiate gymnastics and professional wrestling. *Urban Life* 8,July: 219-246.
6078.   Brewster, P.G. 1970. A partial list of books and articles on games. *Southern Folklore Quarterly* 34,4:353-364.
6079.   Brower, J.J. 1979. Professionalization of organized youth sport: social psychological impacts and outcomes. *Annals AAPSS* 445:39-46.
6080.   Curtis, B. 1979. Scrutinizing the skipper: a study of leadership behaviors in the dugout. *J.Appl.Psychology* 64,August:391-400.
6081.   Dickinson, J. 1977. *A Behavioural Analysis of Sport.* Princeton, N.J.: Princeton Book Company.
6082.   Dietrich, K. et al. 1960. Untersuchungen über Bildungsstand und Meinungen verschiedener Berliner Bevölkerungsgruppen in Fragen der Gesundheitserziehung und des Sports. *Der Sportarzt* 8:193-196. 9: 224-229. 11:288-300.
6083.   Dumazedier, J. 1973. *Dinamica del tempo libero nelle societa industriali avanzate. The Dynamics of Free Time or Leisure in Advanced Industrial Societies.* Roma: Lo Spettacolo. 102 pp.
6084.   Ellis, M. 1973. *Why People Play?* Englewood Cliffs: Prentice-Hall. 173 pp.
6085.   Ellis, M. and G.J.L. Scholtz. 1978. *Activity and Play of Children.* Englewood Cliffs: Prentice-Hall. 173 pp.
6086.   Enz, F. 1976. *Sport im Aufgabenfeld der Kirche.* Schorndorf: Hofmann. 316 pp.
6087.   Frenkin, A. 1963. *Ästetika* Moscow: Fizkultura i Sport. 152 pp.
6088.   Hackforth, J. and S. Weichenberg, eds. 1978. *Sport und Massenmedien.* Frankfurt: Limpert. 272 pp.
6089.   Hall, M.A. 1979. Intellectual sexism in Physical Education. Quest 31,2: 172-186.

6090. Hanford, G.H. 1979. Controversies in college sport. *Annals AAPSS* 445: 66–79.

6091. Herron, R. and B. Sutton-Smith. 1971. *Child's Play.* New York: Wiley. 386 pp.

6092. Hu, Hsien Chin. 1948. *The Common Descent Group in China and Its functions.* New York: Viking Fund Publications in Anthropology. 204 pp.

6093. Johnson, A., ed. 1978. Political Economy of Sport. *American Behavioral Scientist* 21,3:315–464.

6094. Jokl, E. 1964. *Medical Sociology and Cultural Anthropology of Sport and Physical Education.* Springfield, Ill. : Thomas. 161 pp.

6095. Kjörmo, O. *Bibliografish Oversiht over Idrettssosiologisch Litteratur for Tidsrommet 1966–1978* (Bibliographical overview on sport sociology literature for the period 1966–1978. Oslo: Norges Idrettshogskole. 163 pp.

6096. Kofler, G. 1976. *Sport und Resozialisierung.* Schorndorf: Hofmann. 172 pp.

6097. Krawczyk, Z. 1978. *Absolwenci uczelni wychowania fizycznego* (Graduates of Academy of Physical Education). Warsaw: PWN. 136 pp.

6098. Kulp, D.H. 1925. *Country Life in South China.* New York: Columbia Teachers College. 367 pp.

6099. Lancy, D.F. and B.A. Tindall, eds. 1976. *The Anthropological Study of Play: Problems and Prospects.* Cornwall, N.Y.: Leisure Press. 245 pp.

6100. Latourette, K.S. 1934. *The Chinese: Their History and Culture.* New York: Macmillan. 389 pp.

6101. Lowe, B. 1977. *The Beauty of Sports.* Englewood Cliffs: Prentice-Hall. 327 pp.

6102. Malter, R. 1969. *Der 'Olympismus' Pierre de Coubertine.* Köln: Carl-Diem-Institut. 32 pp.

6103. Masüger, J.B. 1956. Vom Ringen und Schwingen in der Steiermark. *Schweizer Archiv für Volkskunde* (Basel) 46,4:56–61.

6104. Masüger, J.B. 1959. Über Gemeinsames in alten Bewegungsspielen Nordeuropas und der Schweiz. *Schweizer Archiv für Volkskunde* (Basel) 55:258–278.

6105. van Mechelen, F. 1964. *Vrijetijdsbesteding in vlaanderen* (Leisure activity in Flanders). Antwerpen: S.M. Ontwikkeling. 146 pp.

6106. Menke, F.G. 1969. *The Encyclopedia of Sports.* Revised 4th edition by R. Treat. South Brunswick, N.J.

6107. Moore, K. 1979. Campaign for athletes' rights. *Annals AAPSS* 445:59–65.

6108. Morgan, H.T. 1942. *Chinese Symbols and Superstitions.* South Pasadena, Cal.: P. and J. Perkins. 192 pp.

6109. McClintock, T. 1933. English and American sport terms in German. *American Speech* 8,4:42–47.

6110. Nielsen, H. 1972. *For Sportens Skyld.* (For sports' purpose). Kobenhavn: Nationalmuseet. 200 pp.

6111. Osgood, C. 1951. *The Koreans and Their Culture.* New York: Ronald. 387 pp.

6112. Parten, M. 1933. Social play among preschool children. *J.Abnorm.Soc. Psych.* 28,1:136–147.

6113.   Peirce, W.R. 1978. Sports versus the arts. *Nations Cities* 16,Febr.:26–27.
6114.   Petrak, B. 1967. *Sociologie a Telesna Kultura* (Sociology of physical culture). Prague: Statni Pedagogicke Nakldatestoi. 193 pp.
6115.   Rego, W.C.A. 1968. *Ensaio socio-ethnografica* (Socio-etnographic investigation). Rio de Janeiro: Campanhia Grafica Lux. 416 pp.
6116.   Riess, S.A. 1977. Race and ethnicity in American baseball: 1900–1919. *J.Ethnic Studies* 4,4:39–55.
6117.   Riordan, J. 1978. *Sport under Communism.* Montreal: McGill-Queens University Press. 177 pp.
6118.   Ryan, A.J. 1958. Humanism, athletics and the superhuman. *Medicina Sportiva* 12,July: 291–298.
6119.   Schleske, W. 1977. *Abenteuer, Wagnis, Risiko im Sport.* Schorndorf: Hofmann. 168 pp.
6120.   Schneider, G. 1968. *Puritanismus und Leibesübungen.* Schorndorf: Hofmann. 140 pp.
6121.   Simri, U. ed. 1976. *International Conference on Play.* Proceedings. Natanya, Israel: Wingate Institute.
6122.   Smilansky, S. 1968. *The Effects of Sociodramatic Play on Disadvantaged Children.* New York.
6123.   Spokas, A.A. et al. 1977. Nekotorye voprosy otbora i prognozirovanija ja sposobnestej junych sportsmenov (Problems of selection and prediction of ability of young athletes). *Teorija i Praktika* 3:40–43.
6124.   Szot, Z. 1978. *Kariera Sportova Gimnastykow* (Careers of male and female gymnasts). Gdansk: Wyzsza Skola Wychowanie Fizycznego. 147 pp.
6125.   Tetsch, E.J. ed. 1978. *Sport und Kulturwandel.* Stuttgart: Institut für Auslandsbeziehungen. 125 pp.
6126.   Tindall, B.A. 1975. Ethnography and the hidden curriculum in sport. *Behavioral and Social Science Teacher* 2.
6127.   Vygotksy, L.S. 1962. *Thought and Language.* Cambridge: Cambridge University Press.
6128.   Walser, R. 1971. Rodanthe's old buck. *North Carolina Folklore Society* 19,3:135–136.
6129.   Zeigler, E.F. ed. 1975. A History of Physical Education and Sport in the United States and Canada. Champaign: Stipes. 537 pp.
6130.   Zinkovskij, A.V. 1977. Dinamiceskaja model techniki sportivnych divizenij (Dynamic models of change in the sports movement) *Teorija i Praktika* 2:59–62.
6131.   Bud, A.M. 1975. Cross-sex effects of subject and audience during motor performance. *Research Quarterly* 46,3:379–384.
6132.   Daly, J.A. 1977. *Sport, Class and Community in Colonial South Australia.* PhD-Thesis. Urbana: University of Illinois. 243 pp.
6133.   Dieckert, J. ed. 1974. *Freizeitsport. Aufgabe und Chance für jedermann.* Gütersloh: Bertelsmann Universitätsverlag.
6134.   Eitzen, D.S. and N.R. Yetman. 1972. Managerial change, longevity and organizational effectiveness. *Adm.Sci.Quart.* 17,1:110–116.
6135.   Goodman, C. 1979. *Choosing Sides. Playground and Street Life on the Lower East Side.* New York: Schocken. 200 pp.
6136.   Iwanaga, M. 1973. Development of interpersonal play structures in three, four and five year old children. *J.Res.Devel.Education* 6,3:71–86.

6137.   Picou, J.S. and E.W. Curry. 1974. Residence and the athletic participation-educational aspiration hypothesis. *Soc.Sci.Quart.* 55,3:768–776.

6138.   Stolarov, W.I. and Z. Krawczyk, eds. 1979. *Sport i obras jisni* (Sport and life style). Moscow: Fizkultura i sport. 280 pp.

6139.   United States Senate. 1978 and 1979. *The Amateur Sports Act.* Senate Hearings. Washington, D.C.: Govt.Printing Office.

6140.   Allison, M.T. 1979. On the ethnicity of ethnic minorities in sport. *Quest* 31,1:50–56.

6141.   Farrer, C. and E. Norbeck eds. 1979. *Forms of Play of Native North American.* St. Paul: West Publishing Company. 290 pp.

6142.   Gould, P. and A. Gatrell. 1979/80. A structural analysis of a game: the Liverpool v. Manchester United Cup Final of 1977. *Social Networks* 2:253–73.

6143.   Hall, M.A. 1976. Sport and physical activity in the lives of Canadian women. Pp. 170–99 in Gruneau, R.S. and J.G. Albinson, eds. *Canadian Sport: Sociological Perspectives.* Don Mills, Ontario: Addison-Wesley.

6144.   Mead, M. 1975. Children's play style: potentialities and limitations of its use as a cultural indicator. *Anthropological Quarterly* 48,3,July: 157–81.

6145.   Silver, B.B. 1978. Social structure and games: a cross-cultural analysis of the structural correlates of game complexity. *Pacific Soc.Review* 21,Jan:85–102.

6146.   Stebbins, R.A. 1979. *Amateurs: On the Margin Between Work and Leisure.* Beverly Hills, Calif.: Sage. 280 pp.

6147.   Symons, D. 1978. *Play and Aggression: A Study of Rhesus Monkeys.* New York: Columbia University Press. 246 pp.

Abbreviations, Titles and Place of Appearance of Major Journals for the Social Science of Sport

AJS = American Journal of Sociology (Chicago, Ill.)
ASR = American Sociological Review (Washington, D.C.)
Acta Sociologica (Kopenhagen/Denmark)
American Anthropologist (Washington, D.C.)
American Speech (University, Ala.)
Annals AAPSS = Annals American Association for Political and Social Science (Philadelphia)
Australian J.Phys.Educ. = Australian Journal of Physical Education (Kingswood, S. Australia)
Cahiers Int.Sociologie = Cahiers Internationaux de Sociologie (Paris)
Canadian J.Applied Sport Sciences = Canadian Journal of Applied Sport Sciences (Montreal)
Canadian J.History Sport Phys.Ed. = Canadian Journal of History of Sport and Physical Education (Windsor, Ont./Canada)
Brit.J.Phys.Education = British Journal of Physical Education (London)
Brit.J.Sociol. = British Journal of Sociology (London)
Child Development (Chicago, Ill.)
Comp.Studies Sociol.History = Comparative Studies of Sociology and History (Toronto)
Contemporary History = Journal of Contemporary History (Beverly Hills, Cal.)
L'education physique (Paris)
Education physique et sport (Paris)
Ethnology (Pittsburgh, Pa.)
Fizicka kultura (Beograd)
Gymnasion (Schorndorf/West Germany)
IRSS = International Review of Sport Sociology (Warsaw/Poland)
Int.J.Comp.Sociol. = International Journal of Comparative Sociology (Leyden/Netherlands)
Int.J.Sport Psychology = International Journal of Sport Psychology (Rome/Italy)
JOHPER = Journal of Health, Physical Education and Recreation (Chicago)
JOHPER = Jap. Journal of Health, Physical Education and Recreation (Tokyo/Japan)
J.Confl.Resolution = Journal of Conflict Resolution (Ann Arbor, Mich.)
J.Ed.Sociol./Soc.Educ. = Journal of Educational Sociology/Sociology of Education (Chicago, Ill.)
J.Exper.Soc.Psych./J.Person.Soc.Psych. = Journal of Experimental and Social Psychology/Journal of Personality and Social Psychology (Washington, D.C.)
J.Leisure Research = Journal of Leisure Research (Arlington, Va.)
J.Motor Behavior = Journal of Motor Behavior (Santa Barbara, Cal.)
J.Pop.Culture = Journal of Popular Culture (Bowling Green, Ohio)
J.Soc. Psychol. = Journal of Social Psychology (Provinceton, Mas.)
Journal of Sport Behavior (Mobile, Ala.)
J.Sport History = Journal of Sport History (University Park, Pa.)
J.Sport Social Issues = Journal of Sport and Social Issues (Norfolk, Va.)
Jugend und Sport (Bern/Switzerland)
Kölner Z.Soziol = Kölner Zeitschrift für Soziologie und Sozialpsychologie (Wiesbaden/Germany)

Kultura Fizyczna (Warsaw/Poland)
Leibesübungen/Leibeserziehung (Vienna/Austria)
Die Leibeserziehung/Sportunterricht (Schorndorf/West Germany)
Leistungssport (Berlin-West)
Mens en Maatschappij (Utrecht/Netherlands)
New Society (London/England)
Olympic Review (Lausanne/Switzerland)
Olympische Jugend (Celle/West Germany)
Pac.Soc.Review = Pacific Sociological Review (Beverly Hills, Cal.)
Paideuma = Paideuma. Mitteilungen zur Kulturkunde (Frankfurt/West Germany)
Physical Education (London/England)
Physical Educator (Indianapolis, Ind.)
Quest = Quest Monographs (Tuscon, Ariz.)
Research J.Phys.Educ. = Research Journal of Physical Education (Tokyo/Japan)
Research J.Sport Sociol. = Research Journal of Sport Sociology (Tokyo/Japan)
Research Quarterly = Research Quarterly of AAPHER (Washington, D.C.)
Revue d'education physique (Brussels/Belgium)
Revue Francaise de Sociologie (Paris/France)
Review Sport Leisure = Review of Sport and Leisure (Park Forest South, Ill.)
Roczniki Naukowe AWF = Yearbook of Warsaw Academy of Physical Culture
    (Warsaw/Poland)
Social Forces (Chapel Hill, N.C.)
Social Problems (Buffalo, N.Y.)
Social Science Quarterly (Austin, Tex.)
Sociometry/Social Psychology (Albany, N.Y.)
Sociol.Soc.Research = Sociology and Social Research (Los Angeles, Cal.)
Society and Leisure (Prague/CSSR, now Sherbrooke, Quebec/Canada)
Soziale Welt (Göttingen/West Germany)
Soziologische Gids (Meppel/Netherlands)
Sport za rubezom (Moscow/USSR)
Sport és Tudomány (Budapest/Hungary)
Sportcahiers (Hertogenbusch/Netherlands)
Sportwissenschaft (Schorndorf/West Germany)
Sport Wyczynowy (Warsaw/Poland)
Stadion (Helsinki)
Stadion/Arena (Leyden/Netherlands)
Studia Socjologiczne (Warsaw/Poland)
Studium Generale (Göttingen/West Germany)
Teorie a praxe telesne vychovy (Prague/CSSR)
Teorija i Praktika = Teorija i Praktika Fizicheskoj Kultury (Moscow/USSR)
Testnevelés Tudomány (Budapest/Hungary)
Testnevelés F. Tudomány Közl. = Testnevelés—Fizikai tudomány közlemenyek
    (Budapest/Hungary)
Theorie und Praxis = Theorie und Praxis der Körperkultur (Berlin-East)
Transaction (New Brunswick, N.J.)
Voprosy Filosofii (Moscow)
Wissensch.Zeitschr.DHFK = Wissenschaftliche Zeitschrift Deutsche
    Hochschule für Körperkultur (Leipzig/East Germany)
Wychowanie Fizyczne i Sport (Warsaw/Poland)
Zeitschrift für Soziologie (Stuttgart/West Germany)

INDEX

INDEX

(Bold numbers from 3 to 507 refer to pages in the text. Numbers from 1001 on refer to single items in the classified bibliography)

AUTHOR INDEX

SUBJECT INDEX

APPENDIX

APPENDIX

INTERNATIONAL ORGANIZATIONS OF SPORT
(organizations in 1978 represented in at least 20 countries)

International Olympic Committee (IOC)
   Chateau de Vidy
   Lausanne /Switzerland

Federation of National Olympic Committees
   c/o Comité Olimpico Mexicano
   Ave. del Conscripto y Anillo
   Périferico
   Mexico (134 countries)

General Assembly of International Sports Federations (GAISF)
   7, Bvd. de Suisse
   Monte Carlo/Monaco

Fédération Internationale de l'Automobile (FIA)
   8, Place de la Concorde
   Paris/France (89 countries)

International Badminton Fédération (IBF)
   7 Hartelbury Way, Charlton Kings
   Cheltenham, Glos./England (58 countries)

Fédération Internationale de Basketball Amateur (FIBA)
   Rugendasstr. 19
   8 Munich 71/Germany (150 countries)

International Sports Organization for the Disabled (ISOD)
   Harvey Road
   Aylesbury, Bucks/England (30 countries)

Union Mondiale de Billard (UMB)
   75 rue du Relais
   Ixelles-Bruxelles/Belgium

Federation Internationale de Bobsleigh et de Tobogganing (FIBT)
   Via Piranesi 44/b
   Milano/Italy (20 countries)

Fédération Internationale de Tir à l'Arc (FITA)
   46 The Balk
   Walton, Wakefield/England (57 countries)

Association Internationale de Boxe Amateur (AIBA)
   135 Westervelt Place
   Cresskill, N.J./U.S.A.

Fédération Internationale de Canoe
   G. Montanelli 5
   Florence/Italy (39 countries)

International Railworker's Sport Union
   Neubaugürtel 1
   Vienna/Austria (29 countries)

International Ice-Hockey Association (LIHG)
   Prinz-Eugen-Str. 12
   Vienna/Austria (30 countries)

International Skating Union (ISU)
   Villa Richmond
   Davos-Platz/Switzerland (32 countries)

International Fencing Federation (FIE)
   53, Rue Vivienne
   Paris/France

Fédération Internationale de Football Association (FIFA)
   Case Postale 136
   Zürich/Switzerland (146 countries)

Comité Internationale des Sports Siliencieux (CISS)
   Langaavej 41
   Hvidovre/Denmark (45 countries)

International Weightlifting Federation (IWF)
   1442 Budapest 70
   PF 116
   Hungary (106 countries)

International Handball Federation (IHF)
   Lange Gasse 10
   Basel/Switzerland (74 countries)

Fédération Internationale du Sport Universitaire (FISU)
    11 Ave. Tremblay
    Paris/France (64 countries)

Fédération Internationale de Hockey (FIH)
    55 Bvd. du Régent
    Brussels/Belgium

International Judo Federation
    70 Brompton Road
    London SW 3/England (81 countries)

World Union of Karate Organizations
    Seupaku, Shinko Eldg
    35 Shiba-Kotohira-Cho
    Mina-Ku
    Tokyo/Japan (40 countries)

International Amateur Athletic Federation (IAAF)
    162, Upper Richmond Road
    Putney London/England (160 countries)

Fédération Aeronautique Internationale (FAI)
    Cedex 16, 6 rue Galilée
    Paris/France (66 countries)

Makkabi World Union
    Kfar Hammaccabiah, Ramat Gan
    Tel-Aviv/Israel

Conseil Internationale du Sport Militaire (CISM)
    Ave. Franklin Roosevelt 230
    Brussels/Belgium (77 countries)

Fédération Internationale Motocycliste (FIM)
    19, ch. William-Barbey
    Chambesy-Geneva/Switzerland (44 countries)

International Chess Federation (FIDE)
    Passeerdersgracht 32
    Amsterdam/Netherlands (107 countries)

Union Cycliste Internationale (UCI)
    8, rue Charles Humbert
    Geneve/Switzerland (96 countries)

Fédération Internationale du Cyclisme Professionel (FICP)
    Ave. du Globe 49
    Brussels/Belgium

Fédération Internationale Amateur de Cyclisme (FIAC)
  Viale Tiziano 70
  Roma/Italy

International Council of Amateur Dancers
  Ausser der Schleifmühle
  28 Bremen/West Germany (26 countries)

Fédération Equestre Internationale (FEI)
  Ave. Hamoir 38
  Brussels/Belgium (64 countries)

Fédération Internationale de Gymnastique (FIG)
  Juraweg 12
  3250 Lyss/Switzerland (74 countries)

Fédération Internationale de Luge de Course (FIL)
  Rottenmann 20/Austria (24 countries)

Union Internationale de Pentathlon Moderne et Biathlon (UIPMB)
  Nörreborg
  26013 Sankt 1bb/Sweden

Fédéderation Internationale de Roller-Skating (FIRS)
  Via G. Fara 39
  Milan/Italy (42 countries)

International Federation of Rowing Associations (FISA)
  Case postale 215
  Montreux/Switzerland (50 countries)

Fédération Internationale de Rugby Amateur (FIRA)
  Cité d'Antin 7
  Paris/France (24 countries)

International Shooting Union (UIT)
  Webergasse 7
  Wiesbaden/West Germany (98 countries)

International Swimming Federation (FINA)
  247 George Street
  Sidney/Australia (101 countries)

Fédération Internationale de Skibob
  Prinz-Eugen-Str. 12
  Wien/Austria (22 countries)

Fédération Internationale de Ski (FIS)
  Elfenstr. 19
  Bern/Switzerland (48 countries)

International Sport Fishing Federation (CIPS)
    Rome/Italy (31 countries)

International Bowling Federation
    Poutuntie 3A 14
    Helsinki/Finland (60 countries)

International Scuba Diving Federation
    12, av. Montaigne
    Paris/France (63 countries)

International Lawn Tennis Federation (ILTF)
    Barons Court, West Kensington
    London W 14/England

International Table Tennis Federation (ITTF)
    198 Cyncoed Road
    Cardiff/Wales U.K. (126 countries)

International Trampolin Federation
    Otto-Fleck-Schneise 8
    Frankfurt/West Germany (25 countries)

Fédération Internationale de Volleyball (FIVB)
    23, rue d'Anjou
    Paris/France (129 countries)

International Federation of Amateur Wrestlers (FILA)
    Valmont 12
    Lausanne/Switzerland (101 countries)

International Yacht Racing Union (IYRU)
    60 Knightsbridge
    London SW 1/England (71 countries)

SELECTED NORTH AMERICAN SPORT ORGANIZATIONS

Amateur Athletic Union of the United States (AAU)
    3400 W. 86th Street
    Indianapolis, Indiana 46268

American League of Professional Baseball Clubs
    280 Park Avenue
    New York, New York 10017

Association for Intercollegiate Athletics for Women (AIAW)
    1201 16th Street, N.W.
    Washington, D.C. 20036

Intercollegiate Association of Amateur Athletes of America
P.O. Box 3
1311 Craigville Beach Rd.
Centerville, Massachusetts 02632

National Association of Intercollegiate Athletics (NAIA)
1221 Baltimore
Kansas City, Missouri 64105

National Basketball Association (NBA)
645 Fifth Ave.
New York, New York 10022

National Collegiate Athletic Association (NCAA)
U.S. Highway, 50 and Nall Ave.
P.O. Box 1906
Shawnee Mission, Kansas 66222

National Federation of State High School Association (NFSHSA)
Federation Pl. P.O. Box 98
Elgin, Illinois 60120

National Football League (NFL)
410 Park Ave.
New York, New York 10022

National Junior College Athletic Association (NJCAA)
P.O. Box 1586
Hutchinson, Kansas 67501

National League of Professional Baseball Clubs
One Rockefeller Plaza
New York, New York 10020

North American Soccer League (NASL)
1133 Avenue of the Americas
New York, New York 10038

Professional Athletes International
1300 Connecticut Ave., N.W.
Washington, D.C. 20008

Sports Canada
Ottawa, Ont.

United States Collegiate Sports Council (USCSC)
7250 State Street
Kansas City, Kansas 66112

United States Olympic Committee (USOC)
    1750 E. Boulder St.
    Colorado Springs, Colorado 80909

United States Track and Field Federation (USTFF)
    30 N. Norton Avenue
    Tuscson, Arizona 85619

World Boxing Association (WBA)
    1511 K Street, N.W., Suite 843
    Washington, D.C. 20005

INTERNATIONAL PHYSICAL EDUCATION AND SPORT SCIENCE ORGANIZATIONS

Association Internationale des Ecoles Supérieures d'Education Physique (AIESP)
    Instituto Nacional de Education Fisica Deportes
    Madrid 3/Spain

International Council of Sport and Physical Education (ICSPE/UNESCO)
    Sports Council
    70 Brompton Road
    London SW 3/England

Fédération Internationale d'Education Physique (FIEP)
    Tervuusevest 1O1
    3030 Heverlee/Belgium

International Council of Health, Physical Education and Recreation (ICHPER)
    1201 Sixteenth Street, N.W.
    Washington, D.C. 20036

Fédération Internationale Catholique d'Education Physique et Sportive (FICEPS)
    Falkestr. 1
    Vienna/Austria

Fédération Internationale de Médicine Sportive (FIMS)
    104 Via Antonio Serra
    Roma/Italy

International Association for History of Sport (HISPA)
    Deutsche Sporthochschule
    Cologne/West Germany

International Committee for Sociology of Sport (ICSS)
-affiliated with Int. Sociological Association (ISA) and ICSPE/UNESCO-
    University of Waterloo
    Waterloo, Ont./Canada

The Philosophic Society for the Study of Sport
   Institut Philosophie
   Universität
   75 Karlsruhe/Germany

International Society for Sport Psychology
   36, Via San Marino
   Roma/Italy

International Association for Sport Architecture (IAKS)
   Hertzstr. 1
   5 Köln-Lövenich
   West Germany

Association Internationale de la Presse Sportive (AIPS)
   Via Paola da Cannabo 9
   Milan /Italy

International Olympic Academy
   4 Kapsali
   Athens 138/Greece

International Association of Physical Education and Sports for Girls and Women
(IAPESGW)
   555-B Sherbrooke St. W.
   Montreal, Quebec/Cananda

SELECTED NORTH AMERICAN PHYSICAL EDUCATION
AND SPORT SCIENCE ORGANIZATIONS

Academy for the Psychology of Sports International
   P.O. Box 200
   Toledo, Ohio 43602

American Academy of Physical Education
   Box 132
   Fort Garland, Colorado 81133

American Alliance for Health, Physical Education and Recreation (AAHPER)
   1201 16th Street, N.W.
   Washington, D.C. 20036

Canadian Association for Sport Science (CASS)
   Dpt. Physical Education
   University of Sherbrooke
   Sherbrooke, Quebec

Canadian Association for Health, Physical Education and Recreation (CAHPER)
Dpt. Physical Education
University of Calgary
Calgary, Alberta

North American Society for the Psychology of Sport and Physical Activity (NASPA)
Dpt. Physical Education
Louisiana State University
Baton Rouge, La. 70803

National Collegiate Physical Education Association (NCPEA)
Dpt. Physical Education
University of Illinois
Urbana, Ill. 61801

National Association for Sport Sociology (NASS)
Dpt. Physical Education
University of Connecticut
Bridgeport, Con.

North American Society for Sport History (NASSH)
Dpt. Physical Education
Pennsylvania State University
University Park, Pa. 16802

Philosophic Society for the Study of Sport (PSSS)
Faculty of Physical Education
SUNY Brockport
Brockport, N.Y. 14420

The Association for Anthropological Study of Play (TAASP)
Dpt. Folklore
University of Pennsylvania
Philadelphia, Pa. 19104

LIST OF CONTRIBUTORS

LIST OF CONTRIBUTORS

Cheska, Alyce T. Professor of Physical Education and Anthropology. University of Illinois. Urbana, Ill./USA.

Ellis, Michael J. Professor and Head of Physical Education. University of Oregon. Eugene, Or./USA.

Glassford, R. Gerald. Professor of Physical Education, University of Alberta. Edmonton, Alberta/Canada.

Greendorfer, Susan L. Associate Professor of Physical Education. University of Illinois. Urbana, Ill./USA.

Hammerich, Kurt. Professor of Sociology. Technische Hochschule (Technical University) of Aachen/FRG.

Harris, Dorothy. Professor of Physical Education. Pennsylvania State University. University Park, Pa./USA.

Eitzen, D. Stanley. Professor of Sociology. Colorado State University. Ft. Collins, Col./USA.

Edwards, Harry. Associate Professor of Sociology. University of California. Berkeley, Cal./USA.

Landers, Daniel M. Professor of Physical Education. Pennsylvania State University. University Park, Pa./USA.

Kelly, John R. Associate Professor of Leisure Studies. University of Illinois. Champaign, Ill./USA.

Lang, Gladys E. Professor of Sociology. State University of New York. Stony Brook, L.I., N.Y./USA.

Lenk, Hans. Professor and Head of Philosophy. Universität Karlsruhe/FRG.

Lüschen, Günther. Professor of Sociology and Physical Education. University of Illinois. Urbana, Ill./USA.

Martens, Rainer. Professor of Physical Education. University of Illinois. Urbana, Ill./USA.

McIntosh, Peter C. London/England. Previously Professor and Head of Physical Education. University of Otago/New Zealand.

McPherson, Barry D. Associate Professor of Kinesiology and Sociology. University of Waterloo, Ont./Canada.

Noll, Roger G. Professor and Chair of Humanities and Social Science. California Institute of Technology. Pasadena, Cal./USA.

Riezler, Kurt Professor of Philosophy. New School and Columbia University. New York/USA (deceased).

Sage, George H. Professor and Head of Physical Education. Northern Colorado University. Greeley/Col./USA.

Seppänen, Paavo. Professor and Dean of Social Science. University of Helsinki/ Finland.

Spinrad, William. Professor of Sociology. Adelphi University. Garden City, N.Y./USA.

Stone, Gregory P. Professor of Sociology. University of Minnesota. Minneapolis, Min./USA.